T0257621

Computer Science: A Structured Programming Approach

Computer Science: A Structured Programming Approach

Edited by Samuel Green

MURPHY & MOORE

www.murphy-moorepublishing.com

Murphy & Moore Publishing,
1 Rockefeller Plaza,
New York City, NY 10020, USA

ISBN: 978-1-63987-126-1

Cataloging-in-Publication Data

Computer science : a structured programming approach / edited by Samuel Green.
    p. cm.
Includes bibliographical references and index.
ISBN 978-1-63987-126-1
1. Computer programming. 2. Computer science. 3. Electronic data processing.
4. Coding theory. I. Green, Samuel.
QA76.6 .C66 2022
001.642--dc23

For information on all Murphy & Moore Publications
visit our website at www.murphy-moorepublishing.com

MURPHY & MOORE

Contents

Preface

This book has been a concerted effort by a group of academicians, researchers and scientists, who have contributed their research works for the realization of the book. This book has materialized in the wake of emerging advancements and innovations in this field. Therefore, the need of the hour was to compile all the required researches and disseminate the knowledge to a broad spectrum of people comprising of students, researchers and specialists of the field.

The study of computers and computational systems is known as computer science. It is mostly concerned with software and software systems including their theory, design, development, and application. Computer science encompasses the principal areas of artificial intelligence, computer systems and networks, security, vision and graphics, numerical analysis, programming languages, and software engineering. Programming paradigm is a way of classifying programming languages according to their features. The programming paradigm which is used to improve the quality, clarity, and development time of a computer program is termed as structured programming. Computer science is applied in designing and analyzing algorithms to solve programs and study the performance of computer hardware and software. As this field is emerging at a rapid pace, the contents of this book will help the readers understand the modern concepts and applications of the subject. It provides comprehensive insights into the field of computer science. This book will provide comprehensive knowledge to the readers.

At the end of the preface, I would like to thank the authors for their brilliant chapters and the publisher for guiding us all-through the making of the book till its final stage. Also, I would like to thank my family for providing the support and encouragement throughout my academic career and research projects.

Editor

Inexact Multistage Stochastic Chance Constrained Programming Model for Water Resources Management under Uncertainties

Hong Zhang,[1] **Minghu Ha,**[1] **Hongyu Zhao,**[2] **and Jianwei Song**[3]

[1]*College of Water Conservancy and Hydropower, School of Science, Hebei University of Engineering, Handan 056038, China*
[2]*College of Arts, Hebei University of Engineering, Handan 056038, China*
[3]*School of Economics and Management, Handan University, Handan 056038, China*

Correspondence should be addressed to Minghu Ha; haminghu@hebeu.edu.cn

Academic Editor: Fabrizio Riguzzi

In order to formulate water allocation schemes under uncertainties in the water resources management systems, an inexact multistage stochastic chance constrained programming (IMSCCP) model is proposed. The model integrates stochastic chance constrained programming, multistage stochastic programming, and inexact stochastic programming within a general optimization framework to handle the uncertainties occurring in both constraints and objective. These uncertainties are expressed as probability distributions, interval with multiply distributed stochastic boundaries, dynamic features of the long-term water allocation plans, and so on. Compared with the existing inexact multistage stochastic programming, the IMSCCP can be used to assess more system risks and handle more complicated uncertainties in water resources management systems. The IMSCCP model is applied to a hypothetical case study of water resources management. In order to construct an approximate solution for the model, a hybrid algorithm, which incorporates stochastic simulation, back propagation neural network, and genetic algorithm, is proposed. The results show that the optimal value represents the maximal net system benefit achieved with a given confidence level under chance constraints, and the solutions provide optimal water allocation schemes to multiple users over a multiperiod planning horizon.

1. Introduction

With the economic development and population growth, the demands for water resources increase every year. Due to unreasonable exploitation and utilization of water resources, water pollution, and extreme weather conditions, more and more countries and regions are faced with different degrees of water shortage. Making the best use of limited water resources premises the sustainable development of economy and society [1]. In the past few decades, many researchers have applied optimization techniques [2–7] to deal with uncertainties in a number of system components and their interrelationships within water resources systems [8]. Among them, inexact multistage stochastic programming (IMSP) is regarded as a significant method for water resources management. For example, Li et al. [9] proposed an interval-parameter multistage stochastic linear programming model which incorporates inexact optimization and multistage stochastic linear programming to manage water resources.

Zhou et al. [10] developed a factorial multistage stochastic programming which is a hybrid methodology of factorial analysis and IMSP to analyze the potential interrelationships among a variety of uncertain parameters and their impacts on system performance for water resources management. Suo et al. [11] proposed an inventory-theory-based inexact multistage stochastic programming for water resources management through introducing an inventory theory into the framework of IMSP to provide reasonable transferring schemes associated with various flow scenarios. IMSP was also combined with other types of uncertainties, such as fuzziness [12–14], to solve the water resources management problems. However, the above models cannot assess the risks in water resources management systems, to which chance constrained programming (CCP) is an effective method to resort to.

CCP, pioneered by Charnes and Cooper [15], provides a method to handle uncertainties by specifying a confidence level at which it is desired that the constraint holds [16], which has been applied in several areas [17, 18]. In water resources management, using CCP is conducive to not only making decisions of water allocation but also gaining insights into the tradeoffs between economic objectives and some policy factors for a water resource manager [19]. For instance, Liu et al. [1] provided a factorial multistage stochastic programming with chance constraints to deal with the issues of constraint-violation risks and interactive uncertainties in water resources management systems. However, this kind of CCP models can only be solved in some special cases. Meanwhile, the models should firstly be converted into deterministic equivalents and then be solved by using solution methods of deterministic mathematical programming [16] in the solution process. Complex chance constrained programming models are hard to solve, such as nonlinear models which contain multiply distributed data [20]. In order to overcome the limitations, Liu [21] presented a framework of CCP with the assumption that not only uncertain constraints but also uncertain objective would hold at different confidence levels provided by the decision-maker as an appropriate safety margin and gave a hybrid algorithm to solve the CCP for more cases. It is noticeable that the choice of confidence levels makes the model flexible to more situations. The CCP has been applied to many aspects of system decision-making, such as project scheduling [22], capital budgeting [23], capacitated location-allocation [24], and redundancy-optimization [25]. Up to now, Liu [21]'s CCP has not been applied in the optimization of water resources management although this method is needed because of the complexity of the water resources management systems.

In our previous relevant research, [26] extended Liu [21]'s CCP from probability space to Sugeno measure space, in which Sugeno measure was one of representative nonadditive measures. Although the theoretical basis of the CCP was discussed in detail, we did not apply the model to water resources management. Paper [27], which managed water supply risk by constructing a model of water option pricing, did not refer to water resources allocation and assess the risks by using CCP. As an extension of the previous efforts, this study aims to develop an inexact multistage stochastic chance constrained programming (IMSCCP) model, which incorporates the CCP proposed by Liu [21] into the IMSP framework for water resources management. The model can tackle uncertainties in the objective and constraints which present themselves as probability distributions and interval with multiply distributed stochastic boundaries, analyze various policy scenarios when the promised policy targets are violated, and deal with the issue of risks presented as stochastic constraints and stochastic objective with predetermined confidence levels. A hypothetical case study of water resources management within three planning periods is given to demonstrate the applicability of the method. Moreover, a hybrid algorithm incorporating stochastic simulation, back propagation (BP) neural network, and genetic algorithm (GA) is proposed to solve the model. The developed method obtains the results of the model in which the optimal value represents the maximal net system benefit achieved with a given confidence level subject to chance constrains.

2. Methodologies

2.1. Multistage Inexact Stochastic Programming Model. It is important for a water resources manager to allocate water to multiple users such as municipal, industrial, and agricultural sectors from an unregulated reservoir over a multiperiod planning horizon in an optimized way, which could be formulated as maximizing the expected economic revenue based on the water allocation in the region over the planning horizon [28]. The manager promises a quantity of water to each user. If the promised water is delivered, net benefits will be brought to local economy; otherwise, the deficient water must be obtained from alternative and more expensive sources or the demand must be curtailed, resulting in economic penalties on local economy [29]. Considering the randomness of the water flow and the dynamic feature of the long-term water allocation plans, the problem of water allocation can be formulated as the following scenario-based multistage stochastic programming model for water resources management under uncertainties [9]:

$$\max \quad f = \sum_{i=1}^{m}\sum_{j=1}^{n} \mathrm{NB}_{ij} T_{ij} - \sum_{j=1}^{n} E\left[\sum_{i=1}^{m} C_{ij} D_{iQ_j}\right]$$

$$\text{s.t.} \quad \sum_{i=1}^{m}\left(T_{ij} - D_{iQ_j}\right) \le Q_j + \varepsilon_{(j-1)Q_{j-1}},$$

$$j = 1, 2, \ldots, n$$

$$\varepsilon_{(j-1)Q_{j-1}} \tag{1}$$

$$= \left[Q_{j-1} - \sum_{i=1}^{m}\left(T_{i(j-1)} - D_{iQ_{j-1}}\right)\right] + \varepsilon_{(j-2)Q_{j-2}},$$

$$j = 1, 2, \ldots, n$$

$$T_{ij\max} \ge T_{ij} \ge D_{iQ_j} \ge 0,$$

$$i = 1, 2, \ldots, m, \quad j = 1, 2, \ldots, n,$$

where f is the net benefit of the water allocation system ($); NB_{ij} is the net benefit when per unit (m^3) of water is allocated to user i in period j ($/m^3); T_{ij} is the fixed amount of water allocation target promised to user i in period j (m^3); Q_j is the water flow in period j which is a random variable (m^3); D_{iQ_j} is the amount of water shortage to user i when the seasonal flow is Q_j (m^3); C_{ij} is the loss when per unit (m^3) of water is not allocated to user i in period j ($/m^3); $E[\cdot]$ is the expected value of a random variable; $\varepsilon_{(j-1)Q_{j-1}}$ is the surplus water inflow in period j (m^3) according to Q_{j-1}; $T_{ij\max}$ is the amount of maximum allowable allocation for user i (m^3); m is the number of water users; i is the index of water user for $i = 1, 2, 3$, with $i = 1$ for the municipality, $i = 2$ for the industrial user, and $i = 3$ for the agricultural sector. In the model, D_{iQ_j} is the decision variable and f is the objective function. It is observed that model (1) reflects nonanticipativity, since a decision must be made in each stage without the knowledge of realizations of random variables in future stages.

Let Q_j take values of q_{jk} with probability p_{jk} for scenarios in each planning period (j), where p_{jk} is the probability of occurrence for scenario k in period j and $\sum_{k=1}^{K_j} p_{jk} = 1$. Then, we have $E[\sum_{i=1}^{m} C_i D_{iQ_i}] = \sum_{i=1}^{m} \sum_{k=1}^{K_j} p_{jk} C_{ij} D_{ijk}$, $j = 1, 2, \ldots, n$, where K_j is the sum of scenarios in period j; D_{ijk} is the amount of water allocation shortage to user i when the scenario k occurs in period j. Then model (1) can be reformulated as follows [9]:

$$\max \quad f = \sum_{i=1}^{m} \sum_{j=1}^{n} NB_{ij} T_{ij} - \sum_{i=1}^{m} \sum_{j=1}^{n} \sum_{k=1}^{K_j} p_{jk} C_{ij} D_{ijk}$$

$$\text{s.t} \quad \sum_{i=1}^{m} \left(T_{ij} - D_{ijk} \right) \le Q_{jk} + \varepsilon_{(j-1)k},$$

$$j = 1, 2, \ldots, n, \ k = 1, 2, \ldots, K_j$$

$$\varepsilon_{(j-1)k} \tag{2}$$

$$= \left[Q_{(j-1)k} - \sum_{i=1}^{m} \left(T_{i(j-1)} - D_{i(j-1)k} \right) \right] + \varepsilon_{(j-2)k},$$

$$j = 1, 2, \ldots, n, \ k = 1, 2, \ldots, K_j$$

$$T_{ij\,\max} \ge T_{ij} \ge D_{ijk} \ge 0,$$

$$i = 1, 2, \ldots, m, \ j = 1, 2, \ldots, n, \ k = 1, 2, \ldots, K_j.$$

Considering that the uncertainties exist in variables and coefficients, the fixed values of the parameters, such as T_{ij}, NB_{ij}, C_{ij}, and Q_{jk}, cannot be determined exactly. Thus, the inexact multistage stochastic programming (IMSP) model, which introduces interval parameters into model (2), is proposed as follows [9]:

$$\max \quad f^{\pm} = \sum_{i=1}^{m} \sum_{j=1}^{n} NB_{ij}^{\pm} T_{ij}^{\pm} - \sum_{i=1}^{m} \sum_{j=1}^{n} \sum_{k=1}^{K_j} p_{jk} C_{ij}^{\pm} D_{ijk}^{\pm}$$

$$\text{s.t} \quad \sum_{i=1}^{m} \left(T_{ij}^{\pm} - D_{ijk}^{\pm} \right) \le q_{jk}^{\pm} + \varepsilon_{(j-1)k}^{\pm},$$

$$j = 1, 2, \ldots, n, \ k = 1, 2, \ldots, K_j$$

$$\varepsilon_{(j-1)k}^{\pm} \tag{3}$$

$$= \left[q_{(j-1)k}^{\pm} - \sum_{i=1}^{m} \left(T_{i(j-1)}^{\pm} - D_{i(j-1)k}^{\pm} \right) \right] + \varepsilon_{(j-2)k}^{\pm},$$

$$j = 2, 3, \ldots, n, \ k = 1, 2, \ldots, K_j$$

$$T_{ij\,\max}^{\pm} \ge T_{ij}^{\pm} \ge D_{ijk}^{\pm} \ge 0,$$

$$i = 1, 2, \ldots, m, \ j = 1, 2, \ldots, n, \ k = 1, 2, \ldots, K_j.$$

2.2. Inexact Multistage Stochastic Chance Constrained Programming Model. Models (1), (2), and (3) do not readily assess the risks, and they only deal with uncertainties in the right hand side such as the water flow Q. It is difficult to handle uncertainties in both the left and right hand sides (i.e., T_{ij}, NB_{ij}, and C_{ij}) [1] which are presented as interval with stochastic normal distributed boundaries. In view of the above considerations, Liu et al. [1] combined chance constrained programming (CCP, initiated by Charnes and Cooper [15]) with IMSP to propose the following inexact multistage stochastic programming model with chance constraints to solve problems with the request that chance constraints should hold at least with prescribed levels of probability (i.e., confidence levels):

$$\max \quad f^{\pm} = \sum_{i=1}^{m} \sum_{j=1}^{n} NB_{ij}^{\pm} T_{ij}^{\pm} - \sum_{i=1}^{m} \sum_{j=1}^{n} \sum_{k=1}^{K_j} p_{jk} C_{ij}^{\pm} D_{ijk}^{\pm}$$

$$\text{s.t} \quad \Pr \left\{ \sum_{i=1}^{m} \left(T_{ij}^{\pm} - D_{ijk}^{\pm} \right) \le q_{jk}^{\pm} + \varepsilon_{(j-1)k}^{\pm} \right\} \ge \beta_{jk},$$

$$j = 1, 2, \ldots, n, \ k = 1, 2, \ldots, K_j$$

$$\varepsilon_{(j-1)k}^{\pm} \tag{4}$$

$$= \left[q_{(j-1)k}^{\pm} - \sum_{i=1}^{m} \left(T_{i(j-1)}^{\pm} - D_{i(j-1)k}^{\pm} \right) \right] + \varepsilon_{(j-2)k}^{\pm},$$

$$j = 2, 3, \ldots, n, \ k = 1, 2, \ldots, K_j$$

$$T_{ij\,\max}^{\pm} \ge T_{ij}^{\pm} \ge D_{ijk}^{\pm} \ge 0,$$

$$i = 1, 2, \ldots, m, \ j = 1, 2, \ldots, n, \ k = 1, 2, \ldots, K_j.$$

Model (4) can handle uncertainties presented as interval with normally distributed boundaries. However, uncertainties in the water resources management systems have more diverse forms of performance besides normal distribution, which suggests a need for models that can handle uncertainties presented as interval with multiple distributed boundaries. And the confidence levels only in constraints may be not enough to indicate the relationship between the economic objective and the system risk. Moreover, a water resources manager may want to obtain the maximum that the objective function $f(\mathbf{x}, \boldsymbol{\xi})$ achieves with a given confidence level subject to stochastic constraints with other confidence levels, which means that the confidence levels are not only in constraints but also in objective.

Liu [21] proposed a framework of nonlinear chance constrained programming with confidence levels occurring in constraints and objective and provided a stochastic simulation based genetic algorithm to solve the CCP. This CCP model can be formulated as follows:

$$\max \quad \overline{f}$$

$$\text{s.t} \quad \Pr\left\{\xi \mid f(\mathbf{x},\xi) \geq \overline{f}\right\} \geq \alpha \tag{5}$$

$$\Pr\left\{\xi \mid g_j(\mathbf{x},\xi) \leq 0\right\} \geq \beta_j, \quad j = 1,2,\ldots,n,$$

where $\mathbf{x}$ is a decision vector; ξ is a random vector; α and β_j are predetermined confidence levels for stochastic objective and stochastic constraint(s), respectively; $\Pr\{\cdot\}$ denotes the probability of the event in $\{\cdot\}$. This programming aims to maximize $\overline{f}$ that the objective function $f(\mathbf{x},\xi)$ achieves with at least probability of α (max $\overline{f}$ is called α-optimistic value to $f(\mathbf{x},\xi)$). $\mathbf{x}$ is feasible if and only if the probability measure of the set $\{\xi \mid g_j(\mathbf{x},\xi) \leq 0\}$ is at least β_j for $j = 1,2,\ldots,n$.

By incorporating CCP [21] and multistage stochastic programming (model (2)), a multistage stochastic chance constrained programming model for water resources management could be formulated as follows:

$$\max \quad \overline{f}$$

$$\text{s.t} \quad \Pr\left\{\sum_{i=1}^{m}\sum_{j=1}^{n}\text{NB}_{ij}T_{ij} - \sum_{i=1}^{m}\sum_{j=1}^{n}\sum_{k=1}^{K_j}p_{jk}C_{ij}D_{ijk} \geq \overline{f}\right\}$$

$$\geq \alpha$$

$$\Pr\left\{\sum_{i=1}^{m}\left(T_{ij} - D_{ijk}\right) \leq q_{jk} + \varepsilon_{(j-1)k}\right\} \geq \beta_{jk}, \tag{6}$$

$$j = 1,2,\ldots,n, \ k = 1,2,\ldots,K_j$$

$$\varepsilon_{(j-1)k} = \left[q_{(j-1)k} - \sum_{i=1}^{m}\left(T_{i(j-1)} - D_{i(j-1)}\right)\right] + \varepsilon_{(j-2)k},$$

$$j = 2,3,\ldots,n, \ k = 1,2,\ldots,K_j$$

$$T_{ij\,\max} \geq T_{ij} \geq D_{ijk} \geq 0,$$

$$i = 1,2,\ldots,m, \ j = 1,2,\ldots,n, \ k = 1,2,\ldots,K_j,$$

where α and β_{jk} are predetermined confidence levels for stochastic objective and stochastic constraint(s), respectively. This programming aims to obtain the α-optimistic value to the objective function of $\sum_{i=1}^{m}\sum_{j=1}^{n}\text{NB}_{ij}T_{ij} - \sum_{i=1}^{m}\sum_{j=1}^{n}\sum_{k=1}^{K_j}p_{jk}C_{ij}D_{ijk}$. Obviously, model (6) gives predetermined confidence levels for constraints and objective, which indicates more comprehensive risk assessment in the water resources management systems.

Considering that the fixed values of the parameters in model (6) cannot be determined exactly, an inexact multistage stochastic chance constrained programming (IMSCCP) model is proposed as follows:

$$\max \quad \overline{f}^{\pm}$$

$$\text{s.t} \quad \Pr\left\{\sum_{i=1}^{m}\sum_{j=1}^{n}\text{NB}_{ij}^{\pm}T_{ij}^{\pm} - \sum_{i=1}^{m}\sum_{j=1}^{n}\sum_{k=1}^{K_j}p_{jk}C_{ij}^{\pm}D_{ijk}^{\pm} \geq \overline{f}^{\pm}\right\}$$

$$\geq \alpha$$

$$\Pr\left\{\sum_{i=1}^{m}\left(T_{ij}^{\pm} - D_{ijk}^{\pm}\right) \leq q_{jk}^{\pm} + \varepsilon_{(j-1)k}^{\pm}\right\} \geq \beta_{jk}, \tag{7}$$

$$j = 1,2,\ldots,n, \ k = 1,2,\ldots,K_j$$

$$\varepsilon_{(j-1)k}^{\pm} = \left[q_{(j-1)k}^{\pm} - \sum_{i=1}^{m}\left(T_{i(j-1)}^{\pm} - D_{i(j-1)}^{\pm}\right)\right] + \varepsilon_{(j-2)k}^{\pm},$$

$$j = 2,3,\ldots,n, \ k = 1,2,\ldots,K_j$$

$$T_{ij\,\max}^{\pm} \geq T_{ij}^{\pm} \geq D_{ijk}^{\pm} \geq 0,$$

$$i = 1,2,\ldots,m, \ j = 1,2,\ldots,n, \ k = 1,2,\ldots,K_j.$$

Let $T_{ij}^{\pm} = T_{ij}^{-} + \Delta T_{ij}y_{ij}$, where $\Delta T_{ij} = T_{ij}^{+} - T_{ij}^{-}$, $i = 1,2,\ldots,m$, $j = 1,2,\ldots,n$. Model (7) could be replaced by the following form:

$$\max \quad \overline{f}^{\pm}$$

$$\text{s.t} \quad \Pr\left\{\sum_{i=1}^{m}\sum_{j=1}^{n}\text{NB}_{ij}^{\pm}\left(T_{ij}^{-} + \Delta T_{ij}y_{ij}\right) - \sum_{i=1}^{m}\sum_{j=1}^{n}\sum_{k=1}^{K_j}p_{jk}C_{ij}^{\pm}D_{ijk}^{\pm} \geq \overline{f}^{\pm}\right\} \geq \alpha$$

$$\Pr\left\{\sum_{i=1}^{m}\left(T_{ij}^{-} + \Delta T_{ij}y_{ij} - D_{ijk}^{\pm}\right) \leq q_{jk}^{\pm} + \varepsilon_{(j-1)k}^{\pm}\right\} \geq \beta_{jk}, \quad j = 1,2,\ldots,n, \ k = 1,2,\ldots,K_j$$

$$\tag{8}$$

$$\varepsilon_{(j-1)k}^{\pm} = \left[q_{(j-1)k}^{\pm} - \sum_{i=1}^{m}\left(T_{i(j-1)}^{-} + \Delta T_{i(j-1)}y_{i(j-1)} - D_{i(j-1)}^{\pm}\right)\right] + \varepsilon_{(j-2)k}^{\pm}, \quad j = 2,3,\ldots,n, \ k = 1,2,\ldots,K_j$$

$$0 \leq y_{ij} \leq 1, \quad i = 1,2,\ldots,m, \ j = 1,2,\ldots,n$$

$$T_{ij\,\max}^{\pm} \geq T_{ij}^{-} + \Delta T_{ij}y_{ij} \geq D_{ijk}^{\pm} \geq 0, \quad i = 1,2,\ldots,m, \ j = 1,2,\ldots,n, \ k = 1,2,\ldots,K_j.$$

Next, we can change model (8) into two submodels corresponding to the upper and lower bounds for the desired objective function value.

Firstly, we formulate submodel (9) corresponding to the upper bound of the objective function value; that is,

$$\max \quad \overline{f}^+$$

$$\text{s.t} \quad \Pr\left\{\sum_{i=1}^{m}\sum_{j=1}^{n}\text{NB}_{ij}^{+}\left(T_{ij}^{-}+\Delta T_{ij}y_{ij}\right)-\sum_{i=1}^{m}\sum_{j=1}^{n}\sum_{k=1}^{K_j}p_{jk}C_{ij}^{-}D_{ijk}^{-}\geq \overline{f}^+\right\}\geq \alpha$$

$$\Pr\left\{\sum_{i=1}^{m}\left(T_{ij}^{-}+\Delta T_{ij}y_{ij}-D_{ijk}^{-}\right)\leq q_{jk}^{+}+\varepsilon_{(j-1)k}^{+}\right\}\geq \beta_{jk}, \quad j=1,2,\ldots,n, \ k=1,2,\ldots,K_j \tag{9}$$

$$\varepsilon_{(j-1)k}^{+}=\left[q_{(j-1)k}^{+}-\sum_{i=1}^{m}\left(T_{i(j-1)}^{-}+\Delta T_{i(j-1)}y_{i(j-1)}-D_{i(j-1)}^{-}\right)\right]+\varepsilon_{(j-2)k}^{+}, \quad j=2,3,\ldots,n, \ k=1,2,\ldots,K_j$$

$$0\leq y_{ij}\leq 1, \quad i=1,2,\ldots,m, \ j=1,2,\ldots,n$$

$$T_{ij\,\max}^{+}\geq T_{ij}^{-}+\Delta T_{ij}y_{ij}\geq D_{ijk}^{-}\geq 0, \quad i=1,2,\ldots,m, \ j=1,2,\ldots,n, \ k=1,2,\ldots,K_j,$$

where D_{ijk}^{-} and y_{ij} are the decision variables and $\max\overline{f}^+$ is the α-optimistic value to the net system benefit $\sum_{i=1}^{m}\sum_{j=1}^{n}\text{NB}_{ij}^{+}(T_{ij}^{-}+\Delta T_{ij}y_{ij})-\sum_{i=1}^{m}\sum_{j=1}^{n}\sum_{k=1}^{K_j}p_{jk}C_{ij}^{-}D_{ijk}^{-}$. In submodel (9), the optimal solutions are denoted by $D_{ijk\text{opt}}^{-}$ and $y_{ij\text{opt}}$, and the optimal value is denoted by $\overline{f}_{\text{opt}}^+$.

Secondly, submodel (10) corresponding to the lower bound of the objective function value can be formulated as follows:

$$\max \quad \overline{f}^-$$

$$\text{s.t} \quad \Pr\left\{\sum_{i=1}^{m}\sum_{j=1}^{n}\text{NB}_{ij}^{-}\left(T_{ij}^{-}+\Delta T_{ij}y_{ij\text{opt}}\right)-\sum_{i=1}^{m}\sum_{j=1}^{n}\sum_{k=1}^{K_j}p_{jk}C_{ij}^{+}D_{ijk}^{+}\geq \overline{f}_{\text{opt}}^+\right\}\geq \alpha$$

$$\Pr\left\{\sum_{i=1}^{m}\left(T_{ij}^{-}+\Delta T_{ij}y_{ij\text{opt}}-D_{ijk}^{+}\right)\leq q_{jk}^{-}+\varepsilon_{(j-1)k}^{-}\right\}\geq \beta_{jk}, \quad j=1,2,\ldots,n, \ k=1,2,\ldots,K_j \tag{10}$$

$$\varepsilon_{(j-1)k}^{-}=\left[q_{(j-1)k}^{-}-\sum_{i=1}^{m}\left(T_{i(j-1)}^{-}+\Delta T_{i(j-1)}y_{i(j-1)\text{opt}}-D_{i(j-1)}^{+}\right)\right]+\varepsilon_{(j-2)k}^{-}, \quad j=2,3,\ldots,n, \ k=1,2,\ldots,K_j$$

$$T_{ij}^{-}+\Delta T_{ij}y_{ij\text{opt}}\geq D_{ijk}^{+}\geq D_{ijk\text{opt}}^{-}, \quad i=1,2,\ldots,m, \ j=1,2,\ldots,n, \ k=1,2,\ldots,K_j,$$

where D_{ijk}^{+} is the decision variable and $\max\overline{f}^-$ is the α-optimistic value to the net system benefit $\sum_{i=1}^{m}\sum_{j=1}^{n}\text{NB}_{ij}^{-}(T_{ij}^{-}+\Delta T_{ij}y_{ij\text{opt}})-\sum_{i=1}^{m}\sum_{j=1}^{n}\sum_{k=1}^{K_j}p_{jk}C_{ij}^{+}D_{ijk}^{+}$. In submodel (10), the optimal solution is denoted by $D_{ijk\text{opt}}^{+}$ and the optimal value is denote by $\overline{f}_{\text{opt}}^-$.

Thirdly, the real allocation of water to user i when the scenario k occurs in period j can be calculated by $A_{ijk\text{opt}}^{\pm}=T_{ij}^{-}+\Delta T_{ij}y_{ij\text{opt}}-D_{ijk\text{opt}}^{\pm}$.

Finally, the optimized interval solution for the decision variable $D_{ijk\text{opt}}^{\pm}=[D_{ijk\text{opt}}^{-},D_{ijk\text{opt}}^{+}]$ and the real interval allocation of water $A_{ijk\text{opt}}^{\pm}=[A_{ijk\text{opt}}^{-},A_{ijk\text{opt}}^{+}]$ can be obtained, while the optimized interval objective value $\overline{f}_{\text{opt}}^{\pm}=[\overline{f}_{\text{opt}}^{-},\overline{f}_{\text{opt}}^{+}]$ can be generated through the variation of $D_{ijk\text{opt}}^{\pm}$.

3. Case Study

In this section, the IMSCCP model is applied to the water resources management systems. Just as the statement for the hypothetical problem described in Huang and Loucks [30], a water resources manager shoulders the responsibility of delivering water from an unregulated reservoir to three sectors, that is, municipality, industry, and agriculture, during three periods. All users want to know allocated water amount that they can expect over the three periods. If the allocated water satisfies the demand of the user, per unit water will gain net benefit for the local economy. Otherwise, the user will spend more to obtain water from other reservoirs or curtail their expansion plans, which means per unit water deficiency will gain penalty. Table 1 provides the water allocation targets in the three planning periods. Tables 2 and 3 present the distribution of the stream flows in the three periods. Table 4 shows the related economic data. Obviously, the boundaries of the data in Tables 3 and 4 are random variables satisfying different distribution forms. The objective is to obtain 90%-optimistic value to the net system benefit while the constraints of water availability hold with at least a probability of 95% over the planning horizon.

Based on the information shown in Tables 1–4, the IMSCCP model for water resources management can be formulated as follows:

$$\max \quad \overline{f}^{\pm}$$

$$\text{s.t} \quad \Pr\left\{\sum_{i=1}^{3}\sum_{j=1}^{3}\text{NB}_{ij}^{\pm}\left(T_{ij}^{-}+\Delta T_{ij}y_{ij}\right)-\sum_{i=1}^{3}\sum_{k=1}^{3}p_{1k}C_{i1}^{\pm}D_{i1k}^{\pm}-\sum_{i=1}^{3}\sum_{k=1}^{9}p_{2k}C_{i2}^{\pm}D_{i2k}^{\pm}-\sum_{i=1}^{3}\sum_{k=1}^{27}p_{3k}C_{i3}^{\pm}D_{i3k}^{\pm}\geq \overline{f}^{\pm}\right\}\geq \alpha$$

$$\Pr\left\{\sum_{i=1}^{3}\left(T_{i1}^{-}+\Delta T_{i1}y_{i1}-D_{i1k}^{\pm}\right)\leq q_{1k}^{\pm}\right\}\geq \beta_{1k}, \quad k=1,2,3$$

$$\Pr\left\{\sum_{i=1}^{3}\left(T_{i2}^{-}+\Delta T_{i2}y_{i2}-D_{i2k}^{\pm}\right)\leq q_{2k}^{\pm}+\varepsilon_{1k}^{\pm}\right\}\geq \beta_{2k}, \quad k=1,2,\ldots,9$$

$$\Pr\left\{\sum_{i=1}^{3}\left(T_{i3}^{-}+\Delta T_{i3}y_{i3}-D_{i3k}^{\pm}\right)\leq q_{2k}^{\pm}+\varepsilon_{2k}^{\pm}\right\}\geq \beta_{3k}, \quad k=1,2,\ldots,27 \qquad (11)$$

$$\varepsilon_{1k}^{\pm}=q_{1k}^{\pm}-\sum_{i=1}^{3}\left(T_{i1}^{-}+\Delta T_{i1}y_{i1}-D_{i1}^{\pm}\right), \quad k=1,2,\ldots,9$$

$$\varepsilon_{2k}^{\pm}=\left[q_{2k}^{\pm}-\sum_{i=1}^{3}\left(T_{i2}^{-}+\Delta T_{i2}y_{i2}-D_{i2}^{\pm}\right)\right]+\varepsilon_{1k}^{\pm}, \quad k=1,2,\ldots,9$$

$$0\leq y_{ij}\leq 1, \quad i=1,2,3, \quad j=1,2,3$$

$$T_{i1\,\max}^{\pm}\geq T_{i1}^{-}+\Delta T_{i1}y_{i1}\geq D_{i1k}^{\pm}\geq 0, \quad i=1,2,3, \quad k=1,2,3$$

$$T_{i2\,\max}^{\pm}\geq T_{i2}^{-}+\Delta T_{i2}y_{i2}\geq D_{i2k}^{\pm}\geq 0, \quad i=1,2,3, \quad k=1,2,\ldots,9$$

$$T_{i3\,\max}^{\pm}\geq T_{i3}^{-}+\Delta T_{i3}y_{i3}\geq D_{i3k}^{\pm}\geq 0, \quad i=1,2,3, \quad k=1,2,\ldots,27.$$

Apparently, model (11) is different from the exiting chance constraint programming models for water resources management which transform the original chance constraints into deterministic equivalents via the theories provided by Charnes et al. [31]. In order to solve this model, a hybrid algorithm which consists of stochastic simulation, BP neural network, and GA is proposed as follows.

Hybrid Algorithm. In order to solve the model, a hybrid algorithm, which incorporates stochastic simulation, back propagation (BP) neural network, and genetic algorithm (GA), is proposed. At first, model (9) and model (10)

should be solved by the hybrid algorithm. In the solution process, stochastic simulation is used to generate input-output data, BP neural network is used to approximate the functions according to the generated input-output data, and GA is used to enhance the optimization process and obtain a solution to the optimization problem. The flowchart figure of the hybrid algorithm is shown in Figure 1.

Then, the optimized water allocation target and the real allocation of water are achieved. Finally, we obtain the optimal solutions and the optimal value of the model. The concrete step of the algorithm can be summarized as follows.

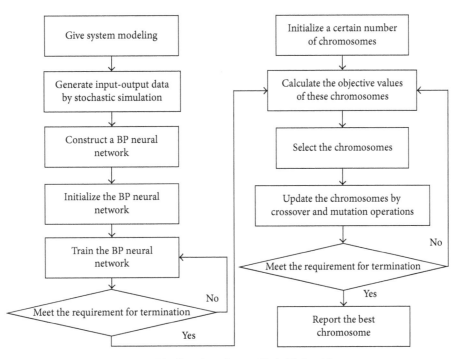

FIGURE 1: The flowchart figure of hybrid algorithm.

TABLE 1: Water allocation targets (10^6 m^3).

Water allocation targets	Time periods		
	$t = 1$	$t = 2$	$t = 3$
Municipality ($i = 1$)	[2, 3]	[2.5, 3.5]	[3, 4]
Industrial sector ($i = 2$)	[2.5, 4]	[3.5, 5.5]	[4, 6]
Agriculture sector ($i = 3$)	[3.5, 5.5]	[4, 6]	[4, 6.5]

Step 1. Firstly, give system modeling of model (9). Generate a training set of input-output data for the following uncertain functions:

$$U'_{ijk}\left(y_{ij}, D^-_{ijk}\right) = \max\left\{\overline{f}^+ \;\middle|\right.$$

$$\Pr\left\{\sum_{i=1}^{3}\sum_{j=1}^{3}\mathrm{NB}^+_{ij}\left(T^-_{ij} + \Delta T_{ij}y_{ij}\right) - \sum_{i=1}^{3}\sum_{k=1}^{3}p_{1k}C^-_{i1}D^-_{i1k}\right.$$

$$\left. - \sum_{i=1}^{3}\sum_{k=1}^{9}p_{2k}C^-_{i2}D^-_{i2k} - \sum_{i=1}^{3}\sum_{k=1}^{27}p_{3k}C^-_{i3}D^-_{i3k} \geq \overline{f}^+\right\}$$

$$\left. \geq \alpha\right\},$$

$$U''_{i1k}\left(y_{i1}, D^-_{i1k}\right) = \Pr\left\{\sum_{i=1}^{3}\left(T^-_{i1} + \Delta T_{i1}y_{i1} - D^-_{i1k}\right)\right.$$

$$\left. \leq q^+_{1k}\right\}, \quad k = 1, 2, 3,$$

$$U''_{i2k}\left(y_{i2}, D^-_{i2k}\right) = \Pr\left\{\sum_{i=1}^{3}\left(T^-_{i2} + \Delta T_{i2}y_{i2} - D^-_{i2k}\right) \leq q^+_{2k}\right.$$

$$\left. + \varepsilon^+_{1k}\right\}, \quad k = 1, 2, \ldots, 9,$$

$$U''_{i3k}\left(y_{i3}, D^-_{i3k}\right) = \Pr\left\{\sum_{i=1}^{3}\left(T^-_{i3} + \Delta T_{i3}y_{i3} - D^-_{i3k}\right) \leq q^+_{2k}\right.$$

$$\left. + \varepsilon^+_{2k}\right\}, \quad k = 1, 2, \ldots, 27$$

$$(12)$$

by stochastic simulation (the basic principle could be seen in Liu [21]).

Secondly, construct a BP neural network to approximate the functions according to the generated input-output data and then initialize and train the BP neural network.

Thirdly, initialize a certain number of chromosomes according to the distribution function and check the feasibility of these chromosomes.

Fourthly, calculate the values of the objective function as fitness value by the trained BP neural network.

TABLE 2: Seasonal flows in the three planning periods ($10^6 \, \text{m}^3$).

Time periods	Seasonal flows		
	Low flow ($j = 1$)	Medium flow ($j = 2$)	High flow ($j = 3$)
$t = 1$	$[3.5, 4.5]$	$[6, 8]$	$[12, 15]$
$t = 2$	$[5, 6]$	$[7, 10]$	$[13, 17]$
$t = 3$	$[3.5, 4.5]$	$[7.5, 11]$	$[13.5, 17.5]$
Probability	0.2	0.6	0.2

TABLE 3: The distribution forms of the boundaries of seasonal flows in the three planning periods ($10^6 \, \text{m}^3$).

Time periods	Seasonal flows		
	Low flow ($j = 1$)	Medium flow ($j = 2$)	High flow ($j = 3$)
$t = 1$	$[N(3.5, 0.1^2), N(4.5, 0.1^2)]$	$[N(6, 0.1^2), N(8, 0.1^2)]$	$[N(12, 0.1^2), N(15, 0.1^2)]$
$t = 2$	$[N(5, 0.1^2), N(6, 0.1^2)]$	$[N(7, 0.1^2), N(10, 0.1^2)]$	$[N(13, 0.1^2), N(17, 0.1^2)]$
$t = 3$	$[N(3.5, 0.1^2), N(4.5, 0.1^2)]$	$[N(7.5, 0.1^2), N(11, 0.1^2)]$	$[N(13.5, 0.1^2), N(17.5, 0.1^2)]$

Note. $N(\mu, \sigma^2)$ represents a normally distributed random variable with mean μ and standard deviation σ.

Fifthly, select the chromosomes by running a standard scheme of the roulette wheel.

Sixthly, update the chromosomes by crossover and mutation operations, test the feasibility of chromosome offspring, and obtain a feasible new population.

Seventhly, choose the chromosome which has the maximal fitness while the function values of $U''_{ijk}(y_{i1}, D^-_{ijk})$ are greater than β_{jk}.

Eighthly, repeat substep 5 to substep 7 for a given number of cycles.

Ninthly, report the best chromosome. The best solutions obtained in the above way are denoted by $D^-_{ijk\text{opt}}$ and $y_{ij\text{opt}}$, and the optimal value is denoted by $\overline{f}^+_{\text{opt}}$.

Step 2. Based on the optimal solutions obtained by Step 1, system modeling of model (10) is given. Generate a training set of input-output data for the following uncertain functions:

$$G'_{ijk}(D^+_{ijk}) = \max\left\{ \overline{f} \mid \right.$$

$$\Pr\left\{ \sum_{i=1}^{3}\sum_{j=1}^{3} \text{NB}^-_{ij}\left(T^-_{ij} + \Delta T_{ij} y_{ij\text{opt}}\right) \right.$$

$$- \sum_{i=1}^{3}\sum_{k=1}^{3} p_{1k} C^+_{i1} D^+_{i1k} - \sum_{i=1}^{3}\sum_{k=1}^{9} p_{2k} C^+_{i2} D^+_{i2k}$$

$$\left. - \sum_{i=1}^{3}\sum_{k=1}^{27} p_{3k} C^+_{i3} D^+_{i3k} \geq \overline{f} \right\} \geq \alpha \left. \right\},$$

$$G''_{i1k}(D^+_{i1k}) = \Pr\left\{ \sum_{i=1}^{3}\left(T^-_{i1} + \Delta T_{i1} y_{i1\text{opt}} - D^+_{i1k}\right) \leq q^-_{1k} \right\},$$

$$k = 1, 2, 3,$$

$$G''_{i2k}(D^+_{i2k}) = \Pr\left\{ \sum_{i=1}^{3}\left(T^-_{i2} + \Delta T_{i2} y_{i2\text{opt}} - D^+_{i2k}\right) \leq q^-_{2k} \right.$$

$$\left. + \varepsilon^-_{1k} \right\}, \quad k = 1, 2, \ldots, 9,$$

$$G''_{i3k}(D^+_{i3k}) = \Pr\left\{ \sum_{i=1}^{3}\left(T^-_{i3} + \Delta T_{i3} y_{i3\text{opt}} - D^+_{i3k}\right) \leq q^-_{2k} \right.$$

$$\left. + \varepsilon^-_{2k} \right\}, \quad k = 1, 2, \ldots, 27$$

(13)

by stochastic simulation. The remaining substeps are similar to the substeps in Step 1. Finally, report the best chromosome. The optimal solution obtained in the above way is $D^+_{ijk\text{opt}}$ and the optimal value is $\overline{f}^+_{\text{opt}}$.

Step 3. Achieve the optimized water allocation target $T^{\pm}_{ij\text{opt}} = T^-_{ij} + \Delta T_{ij} y_{ij\text{opt}}$ and the real allocation of water $A^{\pm}_{ijk\text{opt}} = T^{\pm}_{ij\text{opt}} - D^{\pm}_{ijk\text{opt}}$.

Step 4. Synthesize the two submodels. The optimal solutions can be summarized as $D^{\pm}_{ijk\text{opt}} = [D^-_{ijk\text{opt}}, D^+_{ijk\text{opt}}]$ and the optimal value can be summarized as $\overline{f}^{\pm}_{\text{opt}} = [\overline{f}^-_{\text{opt}}, \overline{f}^+_{\text{opt}}]$.

4. Results and Discussions

The demands and deficits for water are related to water availability, since the economic benefit will be obtained if the demands are satisfied, while the economic penalties will be generated if the deficits occur. Table 1 provides water allocation targets in the three planning periods. Tables 2 and 3 present the information regarding seasonal flows under different probabilities. Tables 1–3 derive from [1]. In the case of insufficient water resources, the water for municipal sector should be delivered preferentially since the highest

TABLE 4: Net benefit and penalty ($/m³).

	Time period		
	$t = 1$	$t = 2$	$t = 3$
Net benefit when water demand is satisfied			
Municipality	$[U(90, 91), U(110, 111)]$	$[U(95, 96), U(115, 116)]$	$[U(100, 101), U(130, 131)]$
Industrial sector	$[N(45, 0.1^2), N(50, 0.1^2)]$	$[N(50, 0.1^2), N(60, 0.1^2)]$	$[N(55, 0.1^2), N(70, 0.1^2)]$
Agricultural sector	$[N(30, 0.1^2), N(35, 0.1^2)]$	$[N(35, 0.1^2), N(42, 0.1^2)]$	$[N(40, 0.1^2), N(58, 0.1^2)]$
Penalty when water is not delivered			
Municipality	$[U(200, 201), U(250, 251)]$	$[U(220, 221), U(275, 276)]$	$[U(240, 241), U(300, 301)]$
Industrial sector	$[N(60, 0.1^2), N(85, 0.1^2)]$	$[N(70, 0.1^2), N(95, 0.1^2)]$	$[N(80, 0.1^2), N(110, 0.1^2)]$
Agricultural sector	$[N(50, 0.1^2), N(70, 0.1^2)]$	$[N(55, 0.1^2), N(75, 0.1^2)]$	$[N(60, 0.1^2), N(90, 0.1^2)]$

Note. $U(a, b)$ represents a uniform distributed random variable and $N(\mu, \sigma^2)$ represents a normally distributed random variable.

TABLE 5: Solutions for the first planning period ($\alpha = 0.9$, $\beta = 0.95$).

Scenario symbol (ijk)	User	Water flow level	Probability (%)	Water targets (10^6 m³)	Water shortage (10^6 m³)	Water allocation (10^6 m³)
111	Municipal	L	20	2.644	$[1.105, 1.174]$	$[1.470, 1.539]$
211	Industrial	L	20	3.615	$[3.342, 3.353]$	$[0.262, 0.273]$
311	Agricultural	L	20	4.000	$[3.524, 3.769]$	$[0.231, 0.476]$
112	Municipal	M	60	2.644	$[2.116, 2.348]$	$[0.296, 0.528]$
212	Industrial	M	60	3.615	$[2.469, 2.531]$	$[1.084, 1.146]$
312	Agricultural	M	60	4.000	$[0.889, 2.132]$	$[1.868, 3.111]$
113	Municipal	H	20	2.644	$[1.200, 1.328]$	$[1.316, 1.444]$
213	Industrial	H	20	3.615	$[2.467, 3.159]$	$[0.456, 1.148]$
313	Agricultural	H	20	4.000	$[2.239, 3.411]$	$[0.589, 1.761]$

$y_{11\,opt} = 0.644$, $y_{21\,opt} = 0.743$, and $y_{31\,opt} = 0.250$.

benefit will be brought when the municipal water demand is satisfied, while the highest penalty will be produced if the promised water is not delivered, followed by the industrial and agricultural sectors which correspond to lower benefits and penalties (see Table 4).

The solutions shown in Tables 5–7 ensure that the 90% optimistic value to the net system benefit could be obtained subject to the chance constraints with a confidence level of 95%. Therefore, the confidence levels for the net system benefit and the chance constraints during the three planning periods are set to $\alpha = 0.9$ and $\beta_{jk} = 0.95$ for $k = 1, 2, \ldots, K_j$, $j = 1, 2, 3$. In solution process by using hybrid algorithm, the maximum number of iterations, the learning rate, the momentum term, and the tolerance criterion for the BP neural network are set to be 20000, 0.01, 0.9, and 0.00001, respectively. The population size, the number of generations, the mutation rate, and the crossover rate of GA are set to be 30, 300, 0.1, and 0.7, respectively. The solutions indicate that $y_{11\,opt} = 0.644$, $y_{21\,opt} = 0.743$, $y_{31\,opt} = 0.250$, $y_{12\,opt} = 0.449$, $y_{22\,opt} = 0.281$, $y_{31\,opt} = 0.182$, $y_{13\,opt} = 0.212$, $y_{23\,opt} = 0.211$ and $y_{33\,opt} = 0.375$. Thus, the optimized allocated targets are $T^{\pm}_{11\,opt} = 2.644$, $T^{\pm}_{21\,opt} = 3.615$, $T^{\pm}_{31\,opt} = 4.000$, $T^{\pm}_{12\,opt} = 2.949$, $T^{\pm}_{22\,opt} = 4.062$, $T^{\pm}_{32\,opt} = 4.363$, $T^{\pm}_{13\,opt} = 3.212$, $T^{\pm}_{23\,opt} = 4.423$, and $T^{\pm}_{33\,opt} = 4.938$. These targets would be promised to the three users in the first stage. Obviously, the water manager's decisions should balance the net benefit and the risk because

high net benefit would be brought if the promised water is delivered and high penalties would occur if the demand for water is not achieved.

Table 5 indicates the optimized solutions under 3 scenarios for the first planning period. For example, $D^{\pm}_{111\,opt} = [1.105, 1.174]$, $D^{\pm}_{112\,opt} = [2.116, 2.348]$, and $D^{\pm}_{113\,opt} = [1.200, 1.328]$ are water shortages for the municipal sector ($j = 1$) when the water flow level is low, medium, and high with probability of 20%, 60%, and 20%, respectively. Accordingly, the water allocations are $A^{\pm}_{111\,opt} = [1.470, 1.539]$, $A^{\pm}_{112\,opt} = [0.296, 0.528]$, and $A^{\pm}_{113\,opt} = [1.316, 1.444]$.

Table 6 indicates the optimized solutions under 9 scenarios for the second planning period. Take water shortages and water allocations of the industrial sector: for example, ($j = 2$). $D^{\pm}_{224\,opt} = [1.940, 3.328]$, $D^{\pm}_{225\,opt} = [1.566, 2.654]$, and $D^{\pm}_{226\,opt} = [3.111, 3.642]$ denote water shortages for the industrial sector when the water flow level in the second period is low, medium, and high following the medium flow in the previous period with joint probability of 12%, 36%, and 12%, respectively. Accordingly, the water allocations are $A^{\pm}_{224\,opt} = [0.734, 2.122]$, $A^{\pm}_{225\,opt} = [1.408, 2.496]$, and $A^{\pm}_{226\,opt} = [0.420, 0.951]$.

Table 7 provides optimized water allocation schemes under 27 scenarios for the third planning period. For example, $D^{\pm}_{1322\,opt} = [2.553, 2.817]$, $D^{\pm}_{2322\,opt} = [4.047, 4.256]$,

TABLE 6: Solutions for the second planning period ($\alpha = 0.9$, $\beta = 0.95$).

Scenario symbol (ijk)	User	Water flow level	Probability (%)	Associated water flow	Associated probability (%)	Water target (10^6 m^3)	Water shortage (10^6 m^3)	Water allocation (10^6 m^3)
121	Municipal	L	20	L-L	4	2.949	[0.899, 1.683]	[1.266, 2.050]
221	Industrial	L	20	L-L	4	4.062	[0.050, 0.764]	[3.298, 4.012]
321	Agricultural	L	20	L-L	4	4.363	[3.032, 3.452]	[0.911, 1.331]
122	Municipal	M	60	L-M	12	2.949	[0.369, 2.649]	[0.300, 2.580]
222	Industrial	M	60	L-M	12	4.062	[1.641, 3.174]	[0.888, 2.421]
322	Agricultural	M	60	L-M	12	4.363	[3.968, 4.155]	[0.208, 0.395]
123	Municipal	H	20	L-H	4	2.949	[0.710, 1.032]	[1.917, 2.239]
223	Industrial	H	20	L-H	4	4.062	[0.408, 1.328]	[2.734, 3.654]
323	Agricultural	H	20	L-H	4	4.363	[1.334, 3.588]	[0.775, 3.029]
124	Municipal	L	20	M-L	12	2.949	[2.910, 2.931]	[0.018, 0.039]
224	Industrial	L	20	M-L	12	4.062	[1.940, 3.328]	[0.734, 2.122]
324	Agricultural	L	20	M-L	12	4.363	[3.400, 3.948]	[0.415, 0.963]
125	Municipal	M	60	M-M	36	2.949	[2.941, 2.947]	[0.002, 0.008]
225	Industrial	M	60	M-M	36	4.062	[1.566, 2.654]	[1.408, 2.496]
325	Agricultural	M	60	M-M	36	4.363	[0.159, 3.291]	[1.072, 4.204]
126	Municipal	H	20	M-H	12	2.949	[2.381, 2.774]	[0.175, 0.568]
226	Industrial	H	20	M-H	12	4.062	[3.111, 3.642]	[0.420, 0.951]
326	Agricultural	H	20	M-H	12	4.363	[1.318, 3.148]	[1.215, 3.045]
127	Municipal	L	20	H-L	4	2.949	[2.534, 2.669]	[0.280, 0.415]
227	Industrial	L	20	H-L	4	4.062	[1.557, 1.709]	[2.353, 2.505]
327	Agricultural	L	20	H-L	4	4.363	[3.310, 4.033]	[0.330, 1.053]
128	Municipal	M	60	H-M	12	2.949	[2.755, 2.821]	[0.128, 0.194]
228	Industrial	M	60	H-M	12	4.062	[3.088, 3.617]	[0.445, 0.974]
328	Agricultural	M	60	H-M	12	4.363	[0.374, 0.883]	[3.480, 3.989]
129	Municipal	H	20	H-H	4	2.949	[0.557, 1.088]	[1.861, 2.392]
229	Industrial	H	20	H-H	4	4.062	[0.678, 2.590]	[1.472, 3.384]
329	Agricultural	H	20	H-H	4	4.363	[0.402, 3.609]	[0.754, 3.961]

$y_{12\,opt} = 0.449$, $y_{22\,opt} = 0.281$, and $y_{31\,opt} = 0.182$.

and $D_{3322\,opt}^{\pm} = [0.542, 4.078]$ indicate the water shortages for industrial, agricultural, and municipal sectors with the corresponding water allocations $A_{1333\,opt}^{\pm} = [0.395, 0.659]$, $A_{2322\,opt}^{\pm} = [0.167, 0.376]$, and $A_{3322\,opt}^{\pm} = [0.860, 4.396]$ respectively, when the water flows are high-medium-low during the entire planning horizon with joint probability of 2.4%.

The optimal value ($\overline{f}_{opt}^{\pm} = [154.335, 235.704]$) represents the 90% optimistic value to the net system benefit subject to the chance constraints with a confidence level of 95%, which provides two extreme values over the planning horizon. Planning for a lower system benefit would be associated with a lower risk of violating the water allocation constraints; conversely, the desire for a higher benefit would correspond to a higher possibility of violating the constraints [9]. When the actual value of each variable fluctuates between its lower and upper bounds, the 90% optimistic values to the net system benefit would change correspondingly between

154.335 and 235.704, which reflects the balance between the system profit and the chance constraints.

In the hypothetical case, the water resource is an unregulated reservoir and the uncertainties in the water resources management are expressed as interval with uniform distributed and normally distributed boundaries. However, real-world water resources systems are more complex than the hypothetical case presented, since the water allocated to the users is from regulated reservoir(s), and the representation of the uncertainties in the input may be more diversified. Nevertheless, the hypothetical case still reflects the basic scene and principles and contains main information in the real water resources management systems. Simple as it is, the case is sufficient to study the characteristics and optimization problems of real-world water resources systems. For the real water resources management problems which contain data with multiply distributed (e.g., Gamma, Lognormal) stochastic boundaries, they can also be dealt with through establishing the appropriate IMSCCP model and adding

TABLE 7: Solutions for the third planning period ($\alpha = 0.9$, $\beta = 0.95$).

Scenario symbol (ijk)	User	Water flow level	Probability (%)	Associated water flow	Associated probability (%)	Water targets (10^6 m^3)	Water shortage (10^6 m^3)	Water allocation (10^6 m^3)
131	Municipal	L	20	L-L-L	0.8	3.212	[2.543, 2.696]	[0.516, 0.669]
231	Industrial	L	20	L-L-L	0.8	4.423	[1.114, 3.435]	[0.988, 3.309]
331	Agricultural	L	20	L-L-L	0.8	4.938	[4.929, 4.935]	[0.003, 0.009]
132	Municipal	M	60	L-L-M	2.4	3.212	[0.410, 1.275]	[1.937, 2.802]
232	Industrial	M	60	L-L-M	2.4	4.423	[1.376, 3.065]	[1.358, 3.047]
332	Agricultural	M	60	L-L-M	2.4	4.938	[3.665, 4.086]	[0.852, 1.273]
133	Municipal	H	20	L-L-H	0.8	3.212	[1.450, 1.573]	[1.639, 1.762]
233	Industrial	H	20	L-L-H	0.8	4.423	[0.144, 4.207]	[0.216, 4.279]
333	Agricultural	H	20	L-L-H	0.8	4.938	[3.899, 4.276]	[0.662, 1.039]
134	Municipal	L	20	L-M-L	2.4	3.212	[2.658, 2.876]	[0.336, 0.554]
234	Industrial	L	20	L-M-L	2.4	4.423	[2.895, 3.297]	[1.126, 1.528]
334	Agricultural	L	20	L-M-L	2.4	4.938	[1.394, 4.583]	[0.355, 3.544]
135	Municipal	M	60	L-M-M	7.2	3.212	[3.171, 3.199]	[0.013, 0.041]
235	Industrial	M	60	L-M-M	7.2	4.423	[0.876, 3.090]	[1.333, 3.547]
335	Agricultural	M	60	L-M-M	7.2	4.938	[0.782, 2.813]	[2.125, 4.156]
136	Municipal	H	20	L-M-H	2.4	3.212	[2.023, 2.385]	[0.827, 1.189]
236	Industrial	H	20	L-M-H	2.4	4.423	[2.709, 3.584]	[0.839, 1.714]
336	Agricultural	H	20	L-M-H	2.4	4.938	[2.682, 3.085]	[1.853, 2.256]
137	Municipal	L	20	L-H-L	0.8	3.212	[2.037, 3.022]	[0.190, 1.175]
237	Industrial	L	20	L-H-L	0.8	4.423	[2.642, 3.314]	[1.109, 1.781]
337	Agricultural	L	20	L-H-L	0.8	4.938	[1.762, 2.322]	[2.616, 3.176]
138	Municipal	M	60	L-H-M	2.4	3.212	[0.929, 2.366]	[0.846, 2.283]
238	Industrial	M	60	L-H-M	2.4	4.423	[1.283, 1.894]	[2.529, 3.140]
338	Agricultural	M	60	L-H-M	2.4	4.938	[3.712, 4.480]	[0.458, 1.226]
139	Municipal	H	20	L-H-H	0.8	3.212	[2.564, 3.084]	[0.128, 0.648]
239	Industrial	H	20	L-H-H	0.8	4.423	[4.098, 4.263]	[0.160, 0.325]
339	Agricultural	H	20	L-H-H	0.8	4.938	[3.183, 4.010]	[0.928, 1.755]
1310	Municipal	L	20	M-L-L	2.4	3.212	[1.780, 2.296]	[0.916, 1.432]
2310	Industrial	L	20	M-L-L	2.4	4.423	[1.078, 3.080]	[1.343, 3.345]
3310	Agricultural	L	20	M-L-L	2.4	4.938	[4.624, 4.856]	[0.082, 0.314]
1311	Municipal	M	60	M-L-M	7.2	3.212	[1.169, 3.032]	[0.180, 2.043]
2311	Industrial	M	60	M-L-M	7.2	4.423	[2.145, 3.887]	[0.536, 2.278]
3311	Agricultural	M	60	M-L-M	7.2	4.938	[3.619, 4.577]	[0.361, 1.319]
1312	Municipal	H	20	M-L-H	2.4	3.212	[1.509, 2.804]	[0.408, 1.703]
2312	Industrial	H	20	M-L-H	2.4	4.423	[0.905, 2.582]	[1.841, 3.518]
3312	Agricultural	H	20	M-L-H	2.4	4.938	[2.117, 2.380]	[2.558, 2.821]
1313	Municipal	L	20	M-M-L	7.2	3.212	[0.628, 2.264]	[0.948, 2.584]
2313	Industrial	L	20	M-M-L	7.2	4.423	[2.505, 2.865]	[1.558, 1.918]
3313	Agricultural	L	20	M-M-L	7.2	4.938	[4.341, 4.492]	[0.446, 0.597]
1314	Municipal	M	60	M-M-M	21.6	3.212	[1.192, 3.049]	[0.163, 2.020]
2314	Industrial	M	60	M-M-M	21.6	4.423	[1.062, 2.988]	[1.435, 3.361]
3314	Agricultural	M	60	M-M-M	21.6	4.938	[1.389, 3.794]	[1.144, 3.549]
1315	Municipal	H	20	M-M-H	7.2	3.212	[1.946, 2.103]	[1.109, 1.266]
2315	Industrial	H	20	M-M-H	7.2	4.423	[1.948, 3.230]	[1.193, 2.475]
3315	Agricultural	H	20	M-M-H	7.2	4.938	[2.309, 2.817]	[2.121, 2.629]
1316	Municipal	L	20	M-H-L	2.4	3.212	[1.733, 2.390]	[0.822, 1.479]

TABLE 7: Continued.

Scenario symbol (ijk)	User	Water flow level	Probability (%)	Associated water flow	Associated probability (%)	Water targets (10^6 m^3)	Water shortage (10^6 m^3)	Water allocation (10^6 m^3)
2316	Industrial	L	20	M-H-L	2.4	4.423	[1.409, 4.280]	[0.143, 3.014]
3316	Agricultural	L	20	M-H-L	2.4	4.938	[4.207, 4.583]	[0.355, 0.731]
1317	Municipal	M	60	M-H-M	7.2	3.212	[2.431, 2.657]	[0.555, 0.781]
2317	Industrial	M	60	M-H-M	7.2	4.423	[1.526, 2.959]	[1.464, 2.897]
3317	Agricultural	M	60	M-H-M	7.2	4.938	[1.660, 3.432]	[1.506, 3.278]
1318	Municipal	H	20	M-H-H	2.4	3.212	[0.980, 1.552]	[1.660, 2.232]
2318	Industrial	H	20	M-H-H	2.4	4.423	[2.041, 3.262]	[1.161, 2.382]
3318	Agricultural	H	20	M-H-H	2.4	4.938	[2.407, 3.482]	[1.456, 2.531]
1319	Municipal	L	20	H-L-L	0.8	3.212	[0.145, 1.877]	[1.335, 3.067]
2319	Industrial	L	20	H-L-L	0.8	4.423	[1.486, 2.048]	[2.375, 2.937]
3319	Agricultural	L	20	H-L-L	0.8	4.938	[3.269, 4.521]	[0.417, 1.669]
1320	Municipal	M	60	H-L-M	2.4	3.212	[1.494, 2.802]	[0.410, 1.718]
2320	Industrial	M	60	H-L-M	2.4	4.423	[0.358, 0.565]	[3.858, 4.065]
3320	Agricultural	M	60	H-L-M	2.4	4.938	[3.166, 4.801]	[0.137, 1.772]
1321	Municipal	H	20	H-L-H	0.8	3.212	[1.058, 2.266]	[0.946, 2.154]
2321	Industrial	H	20	H-L-H	0.8	4.423	[0.087, 4.299]	[0.124, 4.336]
3321	Agricultural	H	20	H-L-H	0.8	4.938	[2.032, 4.546]	[0.392, 2.906]
1322	Municipal	L	20	H-M-L	2.4	3.212	[2.553, 2.817]	[0.395, 0.659]
2322	Industrial	L	20	H-M-L	2.4	4.423	[4.047, 4.256]	[0.167, 0.376]
3322	Agricultural	L	20	H-M-L	2.4	4.938	[0.542, 4.078]	[0.860, 4.396]
1323	Municipal	M	60	H-M-M	7.2	3.212	[0.811, 2.625]	[0.587, 2.401]
2323	Industrial	M	60	H-M-M	7.2	4.423	[2.370, 2.910]	[1.513, 2.053]
3323	Agricultural	M	60	H-M-M	7.2	4.938	[2.874, 4.022]	[0.916, 2.064]
1324	Municipal	H	20	H-M-H	2.4	3.212	[3.097, 3.119]	[0.093, 0.115]
2324	Industrial	H	20	H-M-H	2.4	4.423	[2.321, 3.201]	[1.222, 2.102]
3324	Agricultural	H	20	H-M-H	2.4	4.938	[3.064, 3.905]	[1.033, 1.874]
1325	Municipal	L	20	H-H-L	0.8	3.212	[1.332, 2.673]	[0.539, 1.880]
2325	Industrial	L	20	H-H-L	0.8	4.423	[0.597, 4.261]	[0.162, 3.826]
3325	Agricultural	L	20	H-H-L	0.8	4.938	[1.108, 4.456]	[0.482, 3.830]
1326	Municipal	M	60	H-H-M	2.4	3.212	[2.482, 2.676]	[0.536, 0.730]
2326	Industrial	M	60	H-H-M	2.4	4.423	[0.553, 1.948]	[2.475, 3.870]
3326	Agricultural	M	60	H-H-M	2.4	4.938	[1.731, 2.663]	[2.275, 3.207]
1327	Municipal	H	20	H-H-H	0.8	3.212	[0.865, 0.866]	[2.346, 2.347]
2327	Industrial	H	20	H-H-H	0.8	4.423	[0.790, 4.205]	[0.218, 3.633]
3327	Agricultural	H	20	H-H-H	0.8	4.938	[3.320, 3.577]	[1.361, 1.618]

$y_{13\,opt} = 0.212$, $y_{23\,opt} = 0.211$, and $y_{33\,opt} = 0.375$; α-optimistic value to the net system benefit: $\overline{f}_{opt}^{\pm} = [154.335, 235.704]$.

corresponding variables or data in the model. Then the model could be solved by the hybrid algorithm.

5. Conclusions

An inexact multistage stochastic chance constrained programming (IMSCCP) model is provided for water resources management, which integrates stochastic CCP proposed by Liu [21], multistage stochastic programming, and inexact stochastic programming. Compared with the existing IMSP with chance constraints, the IMSCCP model proposed in this study contains stochastic variables in the objective function or inexact data with multiply distributed stochastic boundaries. Then the IMSCCP model could be solved by using the hybrid algorithm. After solving the IMSCCP model, the maximum, which is the optimistic value to the net system benefit with a predetermined confidence level, could be obtained subject to the chance constraints with other confidence levels.

Considering more real-world situations in the water resources management systems, such as water distribution from regulated reservoir(s), the expansion and development of the reservoir(s), and more uncertainties existing in many system components, further studies can resort to nonlinear programming combined with other uncertain variables such as fuzzy variable and g_λ variable to solve the water resources management problems and handle more uncertainties. Moreover, research efforts might also be devoted to the wide application of IMSCCP model in the areas of ecological water requirement system management, waste management planning, electric-power system planning, and so on.

Conflicts of Interest

The authors declare that there are no conflicts of interest regarding the publication of this paper.

Acknowledgments

This work was supported by the National Natural Science Foundation of China (Grant no. 11626079), the Application Basic Research Plan Key Basic Research Project of Hebei Province (Grant no. 16964213D), the Natural Science Foundation of Hebei Province of China (Grant no. F2015402033), the Natural Science Foundation of the Hebei Education Department (Grants nos. QN2015116 and BJ2017031), the Innovation Fund for Postgraduates of Hebei Province in 2016 (Grant no. 222), and the Plan Project for Science and Technology in Handan City (Grants nos. 1528102058-5 and 1534201095-3).

References

[1] X. M. Liu, G. H. Huang, S. Wang, and Y. R. Fan, "Water resources management under uncertainty: factorial multi-stage stochastic program with chance constraints," *Stochastic Environmental Research and Risk Assessment*, vol. 30, no. 3, pp. 945–957, 2016.

[2] J. Gao and F. You, "Optimal design and operations of supply chain networks for water management in shale gas production: MILFP model and algorithms for the water-energy nexus," *AIChE Journal*, vol. 61, no. 4, pp. 1184–1208, 2015.

[3] Z. Hu, Y. Chen, L. Yao, C. Wei, and C. Li, "Optimal allocation of regional water resources: From a perspective of equity-efficiency tradeoff," *Resources, Conservation and Recycling*, vol. 109, pp. 102–113, 2016.

[4] T. Roach, Z. Kapelan, R. Ledbetter, and M. Ledbetter, "Comparison of robust optimization and info-gap methods for water resource management under deep uncertainty," *Journal of Water Resources Planning and Management*, vol. 142, no. 9, Article ID 04016028, 2016.

[5] M. G. Rojas-Torres, F. Nápoles-Rivera, J. M. Ponce-Ortega, M. Serna-González, G. Guillén-Gosálbez, and L. Jiménez-Esteller, "Multiobjective optimization for designing and operating more sustainable water management systems for a city in Mexico," *AIChE Journal*, vol. 61, no. 8, pp. 2428–2446, 2015.

[6] Y. Tu, X. Zhou, J. Gang, M. Liechty, J. Xu, and B. Lev, "Administrative and market-based allocation mechanism for regional water resources planning," *Resources, Conservation and Recycling*, vol. 95, pp. 156–173, 2015.

[7] J. Liu, Y. P. Li, G. H. Huang, and X. T. Zeng, "A dual-interval fixed-mix stochastic programming method for water resources management under uncertainty," *Resources, Conservation and Recycling*, vol. 88, pp. 50–66, 2014.

[8] Y. L. Xie, G. H. Huang, W. Li, J. B. Li, and Y. F. Li, "An inexact two-stage stochastic programming model for water resources management in Nansihu Lake Basin, China," *Journal of Environmental Management*, vol. 127, pp. 188–205, 2013.

[9] Y. P. Li, G. H. Huang, and S. L. Nie, "An interval-parameter multi-stage stochastic programming model for water resources management under uncertainty," *Advances in Water Resources*, vol. 29, no. 5, pp. 776–789, 2006.

[10] Y. Zhou, G. H. Huang, and B. Yang, "Water resources management under multi-parameter interactions: a factorial multi-stage stochastic programming approach," *Omeg*, vol. 41, no. 3, pp. 559–573, 2012.

[11] M. Q. Suo, Y. P. Li, G. H. Huang, Y. R. Fan, and Z. Li, "An inventory-theory-based inexact multistage stochastic programming model for water resources management," *Mathematical Problems in Engineering*, vol. 2013, Article ID 482095, 2013.

[12] F. Chen, G. H. Huang, and Y. R. Fan, "Inexact multistage fuzzy-stochastic programming model for water resources management," *Journal of Water Resources Planning and Management*, vol. 141, no. 11, Article ID 04015027, 2015.

[13] Y. P. Li, G. H. Huang, Z. F. Yang, and S. L. Nie, "IFMP: interval-fuzzy multistage programming for water resources management under uncertainty," *Resources, Conservation and Recycling*, vol. 52, no. 5, pp. 800–812, 2008.

[14] Y. P. Li, G. H. Huang, Y. F. Huang, and H. D. Zhou, "A multistage fuzzy-stochastic programming model for supporting sustainable water-resources allocation and management," *Environmental Modelling and Software*, vol. 24, no. 7, pp. 786–797, 2009.

[15] A. Charnes and W. W. Cooper, "Chance-constrained programming," *Management Science*, vol. 6, no. 1, pp. 73–79, 1959.

[16] R. Rossi, S. Armagan Tarim, B. Hnich, S. Prestwich, and C. Guran, "A note on Liu-Iwamura's dependent-chance programming," *European Journal of Operational Research*, vol. 198, no. 3, pp. 983–986, 2009.

[17] J. M. Grosso, C. Ocampo-Martínez, V. Puig, and B. Joseph, "Chance-constrained model predictive control for drinking water networks," *Journal of Process Control*, vol. 24, no. 5, pp. 504–516, 2014.

[18] H. Wu, M. Shahidehpour, Z. Li, and W. Tian, "Chance-constrained day-ahead scheduling in stochastic power system operation," *IEEE Transactions on Power Systems*, vol. 29, no. 4, pp. 1583–1591, 2014.

[19] Y. C. Han, G. H. Huang, and C. H. Li, "An interval-parameter multi-stage stochastic chance-constrained mixed integer programming model for inter-basin water resources management systems under uncertainty," in *Proceedings of the 5th International Conference on Fuzzy Systems and Knowledge Discovery, FSKD '08*, pp. 146–153, IEEE, Shandong, China, October 2008.

[20] B. Liu and K. Iwamura, "Fuzzy programming with fuzzy decisions and fuzzy simulation-based genetic algorithm," *Fuzzy Sets and Systems*, vol. 122, no. 2, pp. 253–262, 2001.

[21] B. D. Liu, *Uncertain Programming*, Wiley, New York, NY, USA, 1999.

[22] H. Ke and B. Liu, "Fuzzy project scheduling problem and its hybrid intelligent algorithm," *Applied Mathematical Modelling. Simulation and Computation for Engineering and Environmental Systems*, vol. 34, no. 2, pp. 301–308, 2010.

[23] J. W. Gao, J. H. Zhao, and X. Y. Ji, "Fuzzy chance-constrained programming for capital budgeting problem with fuzzy decisions," in *Proceedings of the 2nd International Conference Fuzzy Systems and Knowledge Discovery, FSKD '05*, vol. 3613, pp. 304–311, IEEE, Changsha, China, August 2005.

[24] J. Zhou and B. Liu, "New stochastic models for capacitated location-allocation problem," *Computers and Industrial Engineering*, vol. 45, no. 1, pp. 111–125, 2003.

[25] R. Zhao and B. Liu, "Stochastic programming models for general redundancy-optimization problems," *IEEE Transactions on Reliability*, vol. 52, no. 2, pp. 181–191, 2003.

[26] H. Zhang, M. Ha, and H. Xing, "Chance-constrained programming on sugeno measure space," *Expert Systems with Applications*, vol. 38, no. 9, pp. 11527–11533, 2011.

[27] M. Ha, Z. Gao, and X. Wang, "Managing water supply risk through an option contract in uncertain environment," *Journal of Uncertain Systems*, vol. 10, no. 2, pp. 114–123, 2016.

[28] Y. P. Li, G. H. Huang, S. L. Nie, and L. Liu, "Inexact multistage stochastic integer programming for water resources management under uncertainty," *Journal of Environmental Management*, vol. 88, no. 1, pp. 93–107, 2008.

[29] D. P. Loucks, J. R. Stedinger, and D. A. Haith, *Water resource systems planning and analysis*, Prentice-Hall, Upper Saddle River, NJ, USA, 1981.

[30] G. H. Huang and D. P. Loucks, "An inexact two-stage stochastic programming model for water resources management under uncertainty," *Civil Engineering and Environmental Systems*, vol. 17, no. 2, pp. 95–118, 2000.

[31] A. Charnes, W. W. Cooper, and M. J. L. Kirby, "Chance-constrained programming: an extension of statistical method," *Optimizing Methods in Statistics*, pp. 391–402, 1971.

Debugging Nondeterministic Failures in Linux Programs through Replay Analysis

Shakaiba Majeed ⓘ[1] **and Minsoo Ryu** ⓘ[2]

[1]*Department of Computer and Software, Hanyang University, Seoul 04763, Republic of Korea*
[2]*Department of Computer Science and Engineering, Hanyang University, Seoul 04763, Republic of Korea*

Correspondence should be addressed to Minsoo Ryu; msryu@hanyang.ac.kr

Academic Editor: Danilo Pianini

Reproducing a failure is the first and most important step in debugging because it enables us to understand the failure and track down its source. However, many programs are susceptible to nondeterministic failures that are hard to reproduce, which makes debugging extremely difficult. We first address the reproducibility problem by proposing an OS-level replay system for a uniprocessor environment that can capture and replay nondeterministic events needed to reproduce a failure in Linux interactive and event-based programs. We then present an analysis method, called replay analysis, based on the proposed record and replay system to diagnose concurrency bugs in such programs. The replay analysis method uses a combination of static analysis, dynamic tracing during replay, and delta debugging to identify failure-inducing memory access patterns that lead to concurrency failure. The experimental results show that the presented record and replay system has low-recording overhead and hence can be safely used in production systems to catch rarely occurring bugs. We also present few concurrency bug case studies from real-world applications to prove the effectiveness of the proposed bug diagnosis framework.

1. Introduction

Debugging is the hardest part of software development. Traditionally, the process of debugging begins by reproducing a failure, then locating its root cause, and finally fixing it. The ability to reproduce a failure is indispensable, as, in most cases, it is the only way to provide clues to developers in tracking down the sources of failure. However, in the case of some nondeterministic failures such as concurrency bugs, it is not always possible to reproduce the failure provided a given set of inputs and environmental configurations. Without the ability to reproduce, debugging becomes an inefficient and time-consuming process of trial and error. Consequently, some software practitioners report that it takes them weeks to diagnose such hard-to-reproduce failures [1].

To deal with nondeterministic failures, record and replay tools have been demonstrated to be a promising approach. Such tools record the interactions between a target program and its environment and later replay those interactions deterministically to reproduce a failing scenario. A number of record and replay systems have been proposed in recent years, but many of them incur high overheads [2–4], others lack supporting low-level events [5, 6], while others may require special hardware support [7, 8].

In this work, we first show that a computer program's nondeterministic behavior can be fully identified, captured, and reproduced with instruction-accurate fidelity at the operating system level by using existing hardware support in modern processors. From this vantage point, a developer can replay a nondeterministic failure of a program and effectively diagnose it using traditional cyclic debugging methods.

We then present an analysis method, called *replay analysis* that allows us to effectively locate the source of failures. Although many bugs can be diagnosed with the help of debuggers during replay, finding the root cause of certain elusive bugs such as concurrency bugs still remains a challenging task for developers. To help developers locate the root cause of such failures, we present a framework based on the proposed record and replay. The contributions of this paper are twofold:

(1) It presents an idea of OS-based record and replay system capable of intercepting the nondeterministic events occurring in interactive and event-driven programs. To substantiate this idea, we implemented it in an ARMv7 uniprocessor-based Linux system. The system incurs low overhead during recording. Therefore, it can be used in an always-on mode in testing phases or production systems to catch nondeterministic and rarely occurring bugs.

(2) It describes a replay analysis method for diagnosing concurrency bug failures based on the proposed record and replay system. The method specifically targets single-variable data races and atomicity violations. The method uses a combination of static analysis, dynamic tracing during replay, and delta debugging to identify failure-inducing memory access patterns that lead to a concurrency bug.

The remainder of this paper is organized as follows. In Section 2, we describe the record and replay system and its implementation details for the ARMv7-based Linux system. We present its evaluation results in the same section. In Section 3, we present the concurrency bug diagnosis framework based on the proposed record and replay system and show its effectiveness by presenting a few debug case studies. We present some related work in Section 4 and discuss the implications and limitations of our current work in Section 5. We finally conclude with Section 6.

2. OS-Level Record and Replay System

2.1. Overview. A program is considered to be deterministic if, when it starts from the same initial state and executes the same set of instructions, it then reaches the same final state every time. In modern computer systems, however, even sequential programs can show unpredictable behavior because of their interaction with the environment, such as I/O, file systems, other processes, and with humans through UIs. Moreover, the occurrence of interrupts and signals can result in varying control flow during successive runs of the same program.

For debugging, these subsequent runs of a failing program can be made deterministic by recording the nondeterministic factors in the original run and substituting their results during replay. For a user-level program, such factors generally include external inputs, system call return values, scheduling, and signals. There are indeed some other sources of nondeterminism that exist at the microarchitecture level, for example, cache or bus states, blocking of I/O operations, and memory access latencies. Such nondeterminism causes a timing variation which may affect when external data is delivered to a user program or when an asynchronous event-handler is invoked. To handle this type of nondeterminism, we use a logical notion of time by keeping track of the number of instructions executed by a process between two nondeterministic events. The logical time helps in maintaining the

relative order of the nondeterministic events during replay and guarantees the replication of the functional behavior of the program. For a debugging usage model where the goal is to find errors in a user program, it is sufficient to reproduce the functional behavior of the program rather than its temporal behavior. Therefore, nondeterministic factors existing at the architecture or circuit level which may cause timing variations are out of scope of this work.

The nondeterministic events exposed to a user program can be captured at different abstraction levels, that is, library-level, OS-level, and hardware-level. In general, the higher the abstraction level is, the smaller the performance overhead is, but with less accuracy. In the current work, we implemented the record and replay framework at the OS-level because we believe that the operating system is the perfect place to intercept nondeterministic events with instruction-level accuracy before they are projected to a user-space program. Moreover, many modern computer architectures such as Intel x86, PowerPC, and ARM include rich hardware resources such as performance monitors, breakpoints, and watchpoints that can be exploited at the OS-level to support deterministic replay. Implementation at the OS-level also has the advantage that it does not require any modifications to the target program or the underlying architecture.

Figure 1 illustrates an overall idea of OS-level record and replay system. Using this system, a target program can be run in either a *record* or a *replay* mode. During the testing or production run, the program is executed in *record* mode wherein the system captures its nondeterministic events. Each event is stored in an event log created for the target program inside the kernel memory. As the program continues execution, events keep on adding to this log and are moved periodically to a log file in permanent storage.

When a program is set to run in *replay* mode, the prerecorded events from its log file are moved to the program's event log. Whenever the program tries to execute a nondeterministic event, for example, a system call, its results are extracted from the event log and sent to the target process. Thus, all the events are executed deterministically, and the program considers that those events are happening as they actually did during recording in view of both the data transferred and the timing of events. To perform cyclic debugging, it is possible to attach a standard debugger to the process being replayed, for example, GDB. The debugger can control the execution of the program normally through single step, continue, or breakpoint commands and present the results to the user as if they are generated live.

The record and replay system is implemented at the system call and signal interface in the operating system since together these interfaces represent most of the nondeterministic events found in sequential and event-based programs. These events include data from external devices and the file system, input from timers, interprocess communication, asynchronous event-notification, and interrupts. Therefore, the proposed record and replay system is suitable for debugging a large class of interactive programs including those that generally come with a Linux distribution and other high throughput programs such as Lynx [9], Lighttpd [10], and Nginx [11].

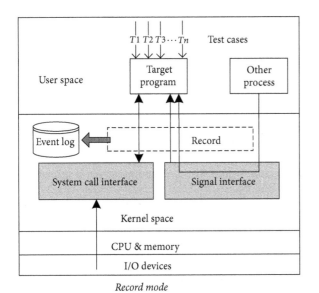
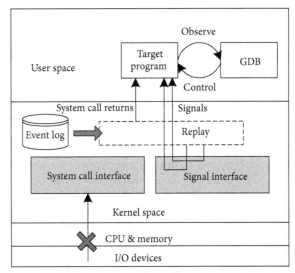

FIGURE 1: Record and replay system at OS-level.

In the following subsections, we discuss how we implemented the proposed record and replay framework for a Linux-based ARMv7 system. The entire record and replay system is transparent from the target program and is implemented in software by using support from the ARM's debug and performance management unit (PMU) architecture. Although the implementation details given here are specific to one architecture, the presence of hardware debug registers and performance monitoring counters in other architectures along with the existing support in commodity operating systems to use these resources makes our approach more generic.

2.2. System Calls. System calls in an operating system provide an interface for a user-level process to interact with its external environment by sending requests to the kernel. In a typical UNIX system, there are around 300 system calls. However, the effect of all the system calls may not be nondeterministic with respect to a process. We broadly categorize the system calls as follows:

(i) *I/O control*: read(), write(), socket(), sendmsg(), and so on.

(ii) *Interprocess communication (IPC)*: pipe(), mq_open(), mq_unlink(), and so on.

(iii) *Time related*: gettimeofday(), gettimer(), utimes(), and so on.

(iv) *Process control*: fork(), exec(), wait(), and so on.

(v) *Memory management*: mmap(), munmap(), mremap(), and so on.

The I/O system calls allow a process to interact with hardware devices, networks, and file systems whereas IPC system calls are used to interact with other processes. The results of these system calls cannot be predicted by the user application, so we consider these as nondeterministic system calls. Time-related system calls always return values local to a processor on which they are executed and are different every time.

The process control system calls manage a process status. Such calls only change or get the value of a process control block, so the associated events can be considered deterministic. The memory control system calls are used to handle memory allocation, heap management functions, and so on. Even if these system calls are recorded, we must re-execute them during replay to generate their side effects within the operating system kernel. Otherwise, if, for example, memory is not actually allocated during the replay phase, the kernel will throw an exception when the program tries to access the memory region it has supposedly allocated.

Recording of system calls belonging to the latter two categories is therefore redundant, and in the current work, we do not record them. By eliminating these system calls, we significantly reduce the recording overhead, making the entire record and replay system more efficient.

When a user program invokes a system call, the processor switches from user mode to kernel mode and begins executing the system call handler. If the program is in the recording mode, the system call execution is allowed normally, but before returning to user mode, we log the return value of the system call. In the ARM architecture, this value is returned in r_0 register. Some system calls also return nondeterministic data by updating special data structures in the kernel-space. For example, a read system call returns the data that has been read from a file descriptor on behalf of the user process making the system call. Such data is sent from kernel to user-space through copy_to_user or put_user functions. We log the data returned by system calls in these functions and add it to the corresponding system call log in the process's event log.

During the replay mode, when the program tries to execute a nondeterministic system call, its handler is replaced by a default function. This function reads the return value of the current system call from the recorded event log and sends it to the process. Any data associated with the system call which was saved during the recording is also returned to the program. Thus, we simulate the effect of a system call completely, rather than executing it during replay.

2.3. Signals. Signals are a type of software interrupt present in all modern UNIX variants. They are used for many non-trivial purposes, for example, interprocess communication, asynchronous I/O, and error-handling. Signals are sent to a process asynchronously and proactively by the kernel. Therefore, signal handling is a challenging task for any record and replay system. Many existing record and replay frameworks do not support signal replay. Some methods exist to support signal replay [12, 13], but they change a signal's semantics during the record phase by deferring its delivery until a certain synchronized point in the process execution, for example, invocation of a system call. Some applications are very sensitive to the occurrence of asynchronous events, and changing the semantics of signals can distort their behavior entirely; it is, therefore, important to guarantee the exact record and replay of signals.

Before describing our process of signal record and replay, we briefly discuss how signals are handled in Linux. When a signal is sent to a process, the process switches to kernel mode. If it is already in the kernel mode, then after carrying out the necessary tasks and before returning to the user mode, the kernel checks if there are any pending signals to be delivered to the process. If a pending signal is found, it is handled in the do_signal() routine, where the corresponding signal handler's address is placed into the program counter (PC), and the user mode stack is set up. When the process switches back to user mode, it executes the signal handler immediately.

During the recording mode, whenever a signal is delivered to a process being recorded, we log the signal number and the user process register context in the do_signal() routine before it modifies the current PC. The exact instruction in the process's address space "where" the signal arrived is indicated by the PC logged in the register context. However, recording only the instruction address is not sufficient because the same instruction may be executed multiple times during the entire program execution, for example, in a loop. We also need to log the exact number of instructions executed by the process to identify "when" the signal arrived. To count the number of instructions, we utilize ARM's performance monitor unit (PMU) architecture. The Cortex-A15 processor PMU provides six counters. Each counter can be configured to count the available performance events in the processor. We programmed one of the counters to count the number of instructions architecturally executed by a user process. During the recording phase when a nondeterministic event occurs, the current instruction count is also stored in that event's log. The instruction count is then reset, and it starts counting again until the process encounters another nondeterministic event to be logged. Thus, two sequentially occurring nondeterministic events, for example, a system call and a signal, are separated by the exact number of instructions executed between the two events by the process being recorded.

To replay the signals we make use of ARM's hardware breakpoint mechanism. During the replay phase, after processing an event, we always check what an upcoming event is in the process's recorded log. If the next event in the log is a signal, then a breakpoint is set at the instruction address of the user program recorded in the signal log. The instruction counter is reset to begin counting the instructions from the last replayed event. When the replayed program reaches the instruction where the breakpoint is set, a prefetch abort exception occurs, and the process switches to kernel mode. In the exception handler, we compare the current number of instructions executed to the instructions stored in the signal log. If they match, the signal is immediately delivered to the user process. If they are not, the breakpoint is maintained at the current PC using the ARM's breakpoint address match and mismatch events, and the process execution is allowed until both PC and instruction count match those of the recorded values in the signal log. In this way, the signal delivery to the target program with instruction-level accuracy is guaranteed during the replay phase. The replay process for a signal is illustrated in Figure 2.

2.4. Evaluation. To capture nondeterministic bug, recording is often required to be done in production systems. Therefore, it is very important that recording overhead be low enough and minimally intrusive to avoid any adverse effect on a production application's normal execution. We evaluated the performance of our record and replay system regarding recording overhead for various real applications. The experiments were performed on a Samsung Exynos Arndale 5250 board based on Cortex-A15 processor, with record and replay mechanism implemented in Linaro 13.09 server with a Linux 3.12.0-rc5 kernel.

We recorded and replayed some Linux applications, which are listed with their workload conditions in Table 1. These programs were run in their default configuration. For each of these applications, tests were repeated three times. We report here the average of the three results.

The performance overhead of recording the application workloads is shown in Figure 3. For each workload, we measured the performance as CPU time in seconds except for the *netperf* tests where it is measured as throughput in Mb/sec for the TCP stream test and completed transactions/sec for the request/response test.

The results are displayed normalized to native execution without recording. The overhead of recording was under 5% for all the experiments, except the TCP request/response test, which caused 15% overhead. The recording overhead is directly related to the size of the logs. The events generated during recording must be moved from the kernel memory to permanent storage, causing extra overhead. During the request/response test, a large number of requests are generated. Each request/response has the potential to generate enormous quantities of network data that must be logged, resulting in a relatively larger log size as compared to other tests and therefore causing more slowdown. The slowdown can be improved by compressing the logs or by

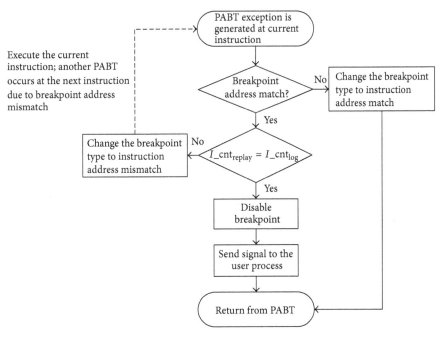

FIGURE 2: Signal replay process.

TABLE 1: Test application scenarios.

Program	Description	Workload
lame	A high-quality MPEG Audio Layer III (MP3) encoder	Encode a 3.5-minute (7751 frames) .wav file
GNU bc	An arbitrary precision numeric processing language calculator	Load the math library and process an input file containing mathematical operations
vim	Vim 7.3 text editor	Open an existing text file in vim, and append an eight-character string 10,000 times
bzip2	A high-quality data compression/decompression utility	Decompress Linux-3.0.1.tar.bz2 of size 73.1 MB
netperf-TCP_STREAM	Networking performance measuring benchmark	TCP_STREAM test between the local host and a remote host for 60 secs with default window size
netperf-TCP_RR	Networking performance measuring benchmark	TCP request/response test between the local host and a remote host for 10 secs

better scheduling of write operations to permanent memory. However, discussion of these optimization methods is out of the scope of current research.

3. Replay Analysis for Diagnosing Concurrency Bugs

Concurrency bugs are generally associated with multithreaded programs. However, researchers have shown that they also exist in sequential [14], interrupt-driven [15], and event-based programs [16]. The execution of signal-handlers, interrupt-handlers, and other asynchronously invoked event-handlers interrupts the control flow of these programs and so introduces fine-grained concurrency. Data among event-handlers and the main code is shared through global variables. (In the rest of this paper, we shall use the term

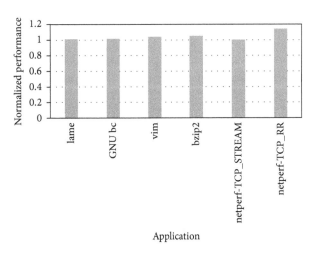

FIGURE 3: Recording overhead.

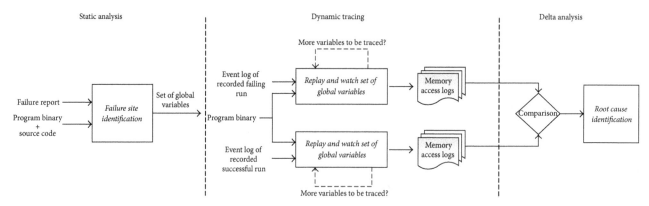

FIGURE 4: Replay analysis for diagnosing concurrency bugs.

event-handler for the signal handler, interrupt handler, and other callback functions that are asynchronously invoked in response to some events.) Such data may have an inconsistent state because it can be changed by both the main code and event-handler in a nondeterministic manner and can cause a program to fail unexpectedly. Our approach to diagnosing such failures is based on the record and replay system presented in Section 2, so the debug process can be started as soon as a buggy execution has been captured and its event log saved. Since the recording overhead is small enough to avoid any probe effect, it can be assumed that the recorded execution is identical to the original execution and will follow the same memory access order during replay. Therefore, we can dynamically track the program execution during replay to find out any memory access violations that have occurred during recording.

The proposed replay analysis works in three phases: static analysis, dynamic tracing, and delta analysis, as shown in Figure 4. In the first phase, we take as input a failure report, the program's source code, and the binary executable. Using these inputs, we identify the location in the program where the failure occurs. We then perform a static analysis of the program binary to extract the addresses of the global variables that are accessed within the identified scope. In the second phase, dynamic tracing phase, we replay the failing execution deterministically and insert hardware watchpoints on the addresses obtained from static analysis phase to log memory access to these locations. The same work is performed for a prerecorded successful execution of the same program. In the final phase, the delta analysis phase, we compare the memory access logs for each variable obtained from the failing execution to those in a successful execution in order to isolate the failure-inducing memory pattern.

3.1. Static Analysis. Many concurrency bug detection methods are proposed for shared memory parallel programs. These methods tend to trace memory access to all the shared memory locations in a program to detect possible concurrency bugs. Unlike concurrency bug detection, our proposed system aims to diagnose a concurrency bug that has caused a given program execution to fail. There may be a number of shared memory accesses in the program which are not related to a given failure. Therefore, it is redundant to track all the shared memory locations in a program while debugging. Hence, our first goal is to reduce the scope of shared memory access that might be involved in inducing a given failure. To do this, we make use of an important characteristic of bugs, observed by researchers [17–19], that concurrency bugs just like sequential bugs manifest themselves as common software failures, such as an incorrect output, an assertion violation, file corruption, and memory segmentation fault. Therefore, similar to sequential bugs, it is possible for developers to relate the concurrency bug failure to a specific section in the program source code, for example, a function. In the case of errors like incorrect output, assertion failure, or display of specific error messages (inserted by the developers or library), it is straightforward for the developers to locate the function in which the failure has appeared. However, in the case of other failures, such as a memory error, we make use of core dump. The core dump is typically generated as a by-product of a failed program execution. We load it in a debugger, for example, GDB, to obtain a call stack which helps us to identify the function in which a memory failure has been encountered.

Keeping in view the short propagation distance heuristic of a bug, we believe that the shared global variable involved in the concurrency bug must be accessed within that function. Therefore, we limit our scope of tracing memory access to only those global variables accessed in the identified function. We use the debugging symbols embedded into the program's binary to disassemble the target function. We extract the addresses of all global memory locations accessed within that function, eliminating all the memory access operations to the function's stack and also those referring to the read-only data section, as this access is not involved in concurrency bugs.

The output of the static analysis phase is a set of global variables that are accessed within the failure scope, and at least one of these is involved in the concurrency bug that we validate through dynamic tracing during replay.

3.2. Dynamic Tracing. To trace the access to shared memory locations, existing analysis methods typically rely on the use of heavyweight dynamic binary instrumentation tools such as Valgrind [20], DynamoRIO [21], and PIN [22]. Such tools

---

Input: Program executable ex, Set of global variables to trace SGV, Logs of a recorded execution log
Output: Memory access log: {op, val, PC} for each variable in SGV
(1) **while** {SGV} ≠ ϕ
(2) $\{v_1, v_2, v_3, v_4\} \leftarrow$ Select(SGV)
(3) $\{wp_1, wp_2, wp_3, wp_4\} \leftarrow$ SetHWwatchpoint(v_1, v_2, v_3, v_4)
(4)   StartReplay(ex, log)
(5)   **while** (replay)
(6)   **if** wp $\in \{wp_1, wp_2, wp_3, wp_4\}$ is hit
(7)   addr $\leftarrow$ ReadAddress(wp)
(8)   {op, val, PC} $\leftarrow$ LogMemoryAccess(addr)
(9)   **end if**
(10)   **end while**
(11) **end while**

ALGORITHM 1: Dynamic tracing.

work by instrumenting every memory access instruction in the program binary at runtime. Since the instrumented code is executed at every memory access, it results in substantial slowdown [23]. Although the overhead during the replay should not be a big problem, the memory consumption by the instrumentation framework is not feasible for debugging programs on embedded platforms that have limited resources. The availability of the instrumentation tool for various platforms is also an issue.

Most importantly, since we aim to trace memory access for a limited subset of global variables obtained during the static analysis phase, we want to avoid the inherent expense of instrumenting memory access to every shared memory location as it is redundant to the bug diagnosis process. In the current work, rather than using dynamic binary instrumentation, we employ an alternate approach in which we use the processor's hardware watchpoint registers to monitor the access to the desired memory addresses. The watchpoint registers are used to stop a target program automatically and temporarily upon read/write operations to a specified memory address. These registers are often used in debuggers as data breakpoints. The main benefit of using hardware watchpoint registers is that they can be used to monitor the access to a memory location without any runtime overhead [24]. However, there are a restricted number of watchpoint registers available in a processor. In the ARM Cortex-A15 processor used in this research work, there are four hardware watchpoints available, which implies that we can track only four memory locations during replay analysis. In order to make use of the available number of watchpoint registers, we use a cyclic approach. We replay the recorded failed execution of the target program in a cyclic manner, and during each iteration, we trace the memory access of four global variables out of the entire list obtained from the static analysis phase. The replay process is repeated for four new variables until all the desired variables have been traced. Typically, there are hundreds of shared memory locations in a medium-sized program. By limiting the scope of the global variables to the failure site, a function, this number is typically reduced to a few tens. Hence, the overhead of repeating the replay cycle is comparable to the instrumentation slowdown,

which can be as much as 20x for basic-block instrumentation without optimization [22].

To trace a given memory address, we program a watchpoint value (DBGWVR) and control (DBGWCR) register pair using Linux ptrace ability to read from/write to processor's registers. The DBGWVR holds the data address value used for watchpoint matching. The load/store access control field in DBGWCR enables the watchpoint matching conditional on the type of access being made [25]. Since we need to track every load and store operation to a given global variable, we set the watchpoint to be enabled for both types of access. When a watchpoint is hit, we log the memory access operation (read/write) on the variable performed by the current instruction, the updated value of the memory address, and the current program counter. The program counter is mapped to the statement that accesses the memory location using the symbolic debug information. This information is necessary to find out if the current memory access is performed by an event-handler or the main code.

The entire process of dynamic tracing is automatic and can be described by Algorithm 1.

3.3. Delta Analysis. When a failure is encountered in a production run or during testing, the first step usually performed by the developers is to determine whether the root cause is simple re-execution. If the failure in the initial run is caused by a concurrency bug, then it is most likely to disappear when the test case is repeated. Thus, in the case of a concurrency bug, the developers have at least one passing execution of the same program with the same set of inputs.

In the domain of sequential errors, delta analysis is often used to compare the execution paths and variable values in two executions of a program to isolate faulty code regions and incorrect variable values. In the case of a concurrency bug, the failure is caused by conflicting memory access. Therefore, we can reach the root cause of the failure by comparing the memory access patterns of the global variables in failing and successful executions.

Two types of concurrency bugs are common in Linux programs considered in this research work: data races and atomicity violations. A data race occurs when a global variable is accessed by an event-handler and the main code in an unsynchronized way, and at least one of those access operations is a memory write operation. An atomicity violation is said to occur when the desired serializability among consecutive accesses of a shared memory location in the main code is violated by access to the same memory location in an asynchronously invoked event-handler. These bugs can be detected through special combinations of memory access operations that signify a data race or an atomicity violation. Specifically, we consider the standard data race patterns, that is, RW, WR, WW, and atomicity violation patterns, that is, RWR, RWW, WWR, and WRW found in multithreaded programs as conflicting memory access patterns for other types of programs that use event-handlers. Many such patterns may appear during the entire execution of a program and are not harmful to it; for example, it has been shown that only about 10% of real data races can result in software failures [26]. Reporting such data races usually just raises false alarms. Therefore, to identify the root cause of a given failure, we search the patterns mentioned above in the memory access logs of the failing run and match them to similar patterns in the successful run. Any conflicting memory access pattern that is present exclusively in the failing execution log is, therefore, the cause of a given failure.

3.4. Debug Case Studies.

Concurrency bugs have been well-studied in the domain of thread-based programs, and therefore a number of bug databases are available to validate new algorithms. Unfortunately, no such bug database is available for sequential or event-based programs. We evaluated our proposed model of diagnosing concurrency bugs on a few real bugs caused by data races in concurrent signal-handlers reported in [14, 27] as well as some other programs. Here, we discuss only three case studies, but we believe that these results are representative for the large domain of concurrency bugs in Linux programs.

Bash 3.0. In Bash 3.0 when the terminal is closed, an event-handler is invoked to save the Bash history to a file. However, if the terminal is closed as soon as only one command is added to the history, it may not be saved into the file. The function used to save history is maybe_append_history(). A static analysis of this function reveals three shared global variables. These variables were traced during the replay of a failed and successful execution, and we found an atomicity violation pattern RRW in the variable history_lines_this_session in the failing execution. The situation arises when the first line from a new Bash session is added to the history, and the variable history_lines_this_session is used to keep the number of lines that Bash added to the current history session incremented from 0 to 1. This increment operation is assumed to be atomic, but it is actually not, and the event-handler interrupts this operation. Since the value of the variable is still zero, the event-handler assumes that there is nothing to be saved and does not write to the history file.

Lynx 2.8.7.2. In Lynx, the web link occasionally is not highlighted correctly in the text browser window. We statically analyzed the LYhighlight() function which returned addresses to 14 shared global variables. When tracing memory access to these variables during the replay of failing execution, an RWR atomicity violation pattern was found in the memory access log of the "LYcols" variable. The event-handler responsible was size_change(). We had to iterate the replay cycle four times to trace all the 14 shared memory variables, so the overhead of the replay cycle was 4x.

Ed 1.5. In Ed, when displaying a range of lines, the number of columns printed per line can be erroneous. The static analysis phase revealed three global variables accessed within the failure site display_lines(). Tracing these variables during the replay of the failed execution revealed an RW data race pattern in the "window_columns_" variable.

Bouncer 1.0. Bouncer is a small event-driven game [28] which uses two event-handlers, one to handle asynchronous user inputs from the terminal and the other to process a timer interrupt to control the speed of the animation. The program exhibits an assertion failure in the function update_from_input() if the number of speed increase/decrease requests from the user is not equal to the total timer adjustments performed. We recorded failing execution and traced the global variables accessed by the said function during the replay phase. We found that the failure was triggered because of an atomicity violation pattern RWR on the variable, is_changed shared between the timer event-handler and the function update_from_input().

Concurrency bug failures are hard to reproduce and debug. In practice, the process of debugging such failures cannot be fully automated, and the involvement of developers remains essential in digging out the root cause. The case studies presented above support the same fact. If the program execution deviates from its intended behavior, we require the developers to identify that deviation and relate it to a specific code section that failed to meet the intended behavior. The rest of the process can be handled automatically and more efficiently by eliminating the debug effort which is redundant to a given failure scope.

We also observed that in the majority of the concurrency bugs, the failure occurs in the same function in which a memory access violation has taken place and hence it is possible to find the suspicious variable in the same function. For the remaining, we can find the suspicious variable by going upwards to the next level in the function call tree.

4. Related Work

4.1. Record/Replay Systems.

Record/replay systems are implemented at different abstract levels of a computer system [29], for example, library-level, OS-level, virtual machine (VM) level, and architecture level. Library-level methods [5, 6] generate low-recording overheads, but they are not able to handle low-level asynchronous events correctly and also lack transparency. VM level methods such as [30] record and replay low-level events of a VM, but they incur huge overheads. Architecture level approaches [31, 32] also guarantee determinism at a low-level, but the implementation cost regarding design and verification is very high.

In the current work, we implemented record and replay at the OS-level. In doing so, we can faithfully reproduce the events at low-level while providing transparency to user-level programs. Although the recording overhead can be larger as compared to higher abstract level methods, it can be considered negligible as long as it does not perturb the natural execution of the application in the production system.

Flashback [33] also adopts an OS-level approach that records the target process through checkpoints. The checkpoints capture the in-memory execution state of a target process at a certain time using a shadow process. To enable debugging during the replay of an application, Flashback requires implementation of the checkpoint discard and replay primitives in a debugger such as GDB. Contrary to this, in our case, a standard debugger can be attached to an application being replayed without any modification to the application or debugger.

Scribe [13] also provides an execution replay mechanism at the OS-level. Our process of recording and replaying system calls is somewhat similar to the Scribe; however, during replay, Scribe re-executes the system calls. The purpose is to keep the application live during replay. This is helpful for fault-tolerant applications, where failing execution can be replaced by its replayed replica to continue the execution. Another critical difference is handling of asynchronous events like signals. In Scribe, the delivery of a signal to a process being recorded is deferred until a sync point so that its timing is deterministic. This approach can theoretically affect the program's correctness. For many interactive and time-sensitive programs, we cannot afford any perturbation of signal semantics during recording. We record the exact timing of signals through the instruction address in the program counter and the number of instructions accumulated in a PMU counter and inject it at the exact same instruction in the process during replay.

4.2. Diagnosing Concurrency Bugs. According to a study on the characteristics of bugs by Sahoo et al. [34], a large percentage of bugs found in software are of a deterministic nature (82%), occurring mostly because of incorrect inputs. The remaining bugs, which constitute a relatively small fraction, are nondeterministic such as concurrency bugs and are difficult to debug. Concurrency bugs are generally associated with multithreaded programs, and researchers have developed a variety of techniques to detect and diagnose such bugs for multithreaded programs. However, such bugs also exist in sequential, interrupt-driven, and event-based programs.

In [35], Regehr suggested random testing of interrupt-driven applications for exposing data races and other bugs in such programs. To randomly test an interrupt-driven application, a sequence of interrupts firing at specified times is generated. Next, the application is executed with interrupts arriving according to the sequence and observed for signs of malfunction.

Ronsse et al. [14] presented a method for detecting data races in sequential programs by adapting their existing data race detector for multithreaded programs. They use their dynamic instrumentation framework DIOTA to instrument and record all memory operations during runtime and to perform race detection during replayed execution. Their existing framework does not support recording of inputs from outside a process, and it is assumed that these inputs will be fixed. In comparison, our proposed record and replay system can provide feedback for all the inputs during the replayed execution which were intercepted through system calls and therefore guarantees the faithful re-execution of a program.

In [16], researchers present a dynamic race detection algorithm to be used with the causality model of event-driven web applications. On the other hand, Safi et al. [36] propose a static analysis method to detect race conditions in event-based systems to guarantee more code coverage and completeness. In the current work, we take advantage of both static analysis and dynamic analysis methods to carefully isolate the root cause of a concurrency failure in a specific execution.

5. Discussion

In this section, we discuss some implications and limitations of our work, along with some remaining open questions.

Applicability to Other Platforms. Our OS-based replay approach is based on the hypothesis that a computer program's nondeterministic behavior can be fully captured at the operating system level and reproduced with instruction-accurate fidelity by using some hardware support available on modern processors. To evaluate this hypothesis, we implemented a prototype in a commodity operating system, Linux, for an ARM platform. However, we expect that most of the features of our prototype can be easily ported to other commodity operating systems running on commodity hardware. For example, our approach of signal replay can also be achieved through the breakpoint registers (DR0–DR3) and the predefined performance event, "Instructions Retired," in the x86 architecture [37].

Implications of Memory Consistency Model. Consideration of memory consistency model is important for any multiprocessor deterministic replay system. ARMv7 has a weakly ordered memory model, meaning that the order of memory access operations performed by a CPU can be different from the order specified by the program. Our current prototype is uniprocessor, and we assume that the single CPU is aware of its own ordering and therefore can ensure that the data dependence is respected [38]. However, memory ordering will be another source of nondeterminism when extending our implementation to a multicore/multiprocessor environment. To handle this, we also need to record the order of shared memory operations among different cores.

Dynamically Allocated Variables. In the current concurrency bug diagnosis framework, the use of hardware watchpoints limits the system to track data races in globally defined variables only. However, data races are also possible on dynamically allocated variables, such as those defined on heap. In practice, it is not possible to trace the dynamically allocated variables without runtime instrumentation. Concerning this, the authors in [39] present an interesting approach in which an entire heap can be watched using software watchpoints inserted through dynamic instrumentation. This approach can be integrated with our replay analysis framework to increase the scope of target bugs.

Multivariable Access Violations. According to a study [40], single-variable concurrency bugs constitute two-thirds of the overall non-deadlock concurrency bugs. To target this large fraction, we therefore followed a rather simplistic but effective approach that considers only single-variable data race and atomicity violations. However, multivariable access violations also exist. For detecting such violations, we must be able to infer the relationships between multiple variables to complement their dynamic tracing. We leave this improvement for our future work.

6. Conclusion

Reproducing a nondeterministic failure for bug diagnosis is a key challenge. To address this challenge, we have presented a light-weight and transparent OS-level record and replay system, which can be deployed to production systems. It can faithfully reproduce both synchronous and asynchronous events occurring in programs such as system calls, message passing, nonblocking I/O, and signals. During the replay of a program, a standard debugger can be attached to it to enable cyclic debugging without any modifications to the program or debugger.

We also presented a method for diagnosing concurrency bug failures which is based on the proposed record and replay system. Given a failure to track down bugs, developers can collect memory access logs for a set of global variables during the replay of failing and passing execution and then compare them to identify any memory access violations causing the failure. Our experience with some real programs shows that this usage model can be very beneficial in locating the root causes of failures related to concurrency bugs.

Our current work is so far limited to debugging of sequential and event-based programs. In the future, we aim to extend it for multithreaded programs so that we can capture and reproduce the exact thread interleaving order in a failing execution and then identify the conflicting memory access operations that lead to program failure.

Conflicts of Interest

The authors declare that they have no conflicts of interest.

Acknowledgments

This research was supported by the Ministry of Science and ICT (MSIT), Korea, under the programs [R0114-16-0046, Software Black Box for Highly Dependable Computing] and [2016-0-00023, National Program for Excellence in SW] supervised by the Institute for Information & Communications Technology Promotion (IITP), Korea.

References

[1] P. Godefroid and N. Nagappan, "Concurrency at Microsoft: an exploratory survey," in *Proceedings of the CAV Workshop on Exploiting Concurrency Efficiently and Correctly*, 2008.

[2] K. Veeraraghavan, D. Lee, B. Wester et al., "Doubleplay: parallelizing sequential logging and replay," *ACM Transactions on Computer Systems*, vol. 30, no. 1, article 3, 2012.

[3] G. W. Dunlap, D. G. Lucchetti, M. A. Fetterman, and P. M. Chen, "Execution replay for multiprocessor virtual machines," in *Proceedings of the 4th International Conference on Virtual Execution Environments, VEE '08*, pp. 121–130, March 2008.

[4] H. Patil, C. Pereira, M. Stallcup, G. Lueck, and J. Cownie, "PinPlay: a framework for deterministic replay and reproducible analysis of parallel programs," in *Proceedings of the 8th International Symposium on Code Generation and Optimization, CGO '10*, Toronto, Ontario, Canada, IEEE, April 2010.

[5] D. M. Geels, G. Altekar, S. Shenker, and I. Stoica, "Replay debugging for distributed applications," in *Proceedings of the USENIX Annual Technical Conference*, pp. 289–300, 2006.

[6] Z. Guo, X. Liu, W. Lin, and Z. Zhang, "Towards pragmatic library-based replay," Tech. Rep. MSR-TR-2008-02, Microsoft Research, 2008.

[7] D. R. Hower and M. D. Hill, "Rerun: exploiting episodes for lightweight memory race recording," in *Proceedings of the 35th International Symposium on Computer Architecture ISCA '08*, pp. 265–276, June 2008.

[8] P. Montesinos, L. Ceze, and J. Torrellas, "DeLorean: recording and deterministically replaying shared-memory multiprocessor execution efficiently," in *Proceedings of the 35th International Symposium on Computer Architecture ISCA '08*, pp. 289–300, 2008.

[9] Lynx text web browser, 2017, http://lynx.invisible-island.net/.

[10] J. Kneschke, Lighttpd-Fly Light, 2017, https://www.lighttpd.net/.

[11] W. Reese, "Nginx: the high-performance web server and reverse proxy," *Linux Journal*, vol. 2008, p. 2, 2008.

[12] Y. Saito, "Jockey: a user-space library for record-replay debugging," in *Proceedings of the 6th International Symposium on Automated and Analysis-Driven Debugging AADEBUG '05*, 2005.

[13] O. Laadan, N. Viennot, and J. Nieh, "Transparent, lightweight application execution replay on commodity multiprocessor operating systems," *Sigmetrics Performance Evaluation Review*, vol. 38, pp. 155–166, 2010.

[14] M. Ronsse, J. Maebe, and K. De Bosschere, "Detecting Data Races in Sequential Programs with DIOTA," in *Euro-Par 2004 Parallel Processing*, vol. 3149 of *Lecture Notes in Computer Science*, pp. 82–89, Springer Berlin Heidelberg, Berlin, Heidelberg, 2004.

[15] M. Higashi, T. Yamamoto, Y. Hayase, T. Ishio, and K. Inoue, "An effective method to control interrupt handler for data race detection," in *Proceedings of the 5th Workshop on Automation of Software Test, AST '10, in Conjunction with the 32nd ACM/IEEE International Conference on Software Engineering, ICSE 2010*, May 2010.

[16] V. Raychev, M. Vechev, and M. Sridharan, "Effective race detection for event-driven programs," *ACM SIGPLAN Notices*, vol. 48, no. 10, pp. 151–166, 2013.

[17] F. Qin, J. Tucek, J. Sundaresan, and Y. Zhou, "Rx: treating bugs as allergies—a safe method to survive software failures," *Operating Systems Review (SIGOPS)*, pp. 235–248, 2005.

[18] W. Gu, Z. Kalbarczyk, R. K. Iyer, and Z. Yang, "Characterization of Linux Kernel Behavior under Errors," in *Proceedings of the 2003 International Conference on Dependable Systems and Networks*, pp. 459–468, June 2003.

[19] W. Zhang, J. Lim, R. Olichandran et al., "ConSeq: detecting concurrency bugs through sequential errors," *ACM SIGPLAN Notices*, vol. 47, no. 4, pp. 251–264, 2012.

[20] N. Nethercote and J. Seward, "Valgrind: a program supervision framework," *Electronic Notes in Theoretical Computer Science*, vol. 89, no. 2, pp. 47–69, 2003.

[21] D. Bruening, *Efficient, transparent, and comprehensive runtime code manipulation [Ph.D. thesis]*, Massachusetts Institute of Technology, Department of Electrical Engineering and Computer Science, 2004.

[22] C.-K. Luk, R. Cohn, R. Muth et al., "Pin: Building customized program analysis tools with dynamic instrumentation," *ACM SIGPLAN Notices*, vol. 40, no. 6, pp. 190–200, 2005.

[23] G.-R. Uh, R. Cohn, B. Yadavalli, R. Peri, and R. Ayyagari, "Analyzing dynamic binary instrumentation overhead," in *Proceedings of the WBIA Workshop at ASPLOS*, 2006.

[24] P. Krishnan, "Hardware Breakpoint (or watchpoint) usage in Linux Kernel," in *Proceedings of the in Linux Symposium*, p. 149, 2009.

[25] "Cortex™-A15 MPCore™ Technical Reference Manual," 2017, http://infocenter.arm.com.

[26] S. Narayanasamy, Z. Wang, J. Tigani, A. Edwards, and B. Calder, "Automatically classifying benign and harmful data races using replay analysis," *ACM SIGPLAN Notices*, vol. 42, no. 6, pp. 22–31, 2007.

[27] T. Tahara, K. Gondow, and S. Ohsuga, "DRACULA: Detector of data races in signals handlers," in *Proceedings of the 15th Asia-Pacific Software Engineering Conference, APSEC '08*, pp. 17–24, 2008.

[28] Bouncer, An event-driven game, 2018, https://github.com/JLee80/An-event-driven-game.

[29] Y. Chen, S. Zhang, Q. Guo, L. Li, R. Wu, and T. Chen, "Deterministic replay: a survey," *ACM Computing Surveys*, vol. 48, no. 2, article 17, 2015.

[30] G. W. Dunlap, S. T. King, S. Cinar, M. A. Basrai, and P. M. Chen, "ReVirt: Enabling intrusion analysis through virtual-machine logging and replay," in *Proceedings of the 5th Symposium on Operating Systems Design and Implementation, OSDI '02*, pp. 211–224, December 2002.

[31] S. Narayanasamy, G. Pokam, and B. Calder, "BugNet: continuously recording program execution for deterministic replay debugging," in *Proceedings of the 32nd Interntional Symposium on Computer Architecture, ISCA '05*, pp. 284–295, June 2005.

[32] M. Xu, R. Bodik, and M. D. Hill, "A "flight data recorder" for enabling full-system multiprocessor deterministic replay," in *Proceedings of the 30th Annual International Symposium on Computer Architecture*, pp. 122–133, June 2003.

[33] S. M. Srinivasan, S. Kandula, C. R. Andrews, and Y. Zhou, "Flashback: a lightweight extension for rollback and deterministic replay for software debugging," in *Proceedings of the in USENIX Annual Technical Conference, General Track*, pp. 29–44, 2004.

[34] S. K. Sahoo, J. Criswell, and V. Adve, "An empirical study of reported bugs in server software with implications for automated bug diagnosis," in *Proceedings of the 32nd ACM/IEEE International Conference on Software Engineering (ICSE '10)*, vol. 1, pp. 485–494, Cape Town, South Africa, May 2010.

[35] J. Regehr, "Random testing of interrupt-driven software," in *Proceedings of the 5th ACM international conference on Embedded software*, 2005.

[36] G. Safi, A. Shahbazian, W. G. J. Halfond, and N. Medvidovic, "Detecting event anomalies in event-based systems," in *Proceedings of the 10th Joint Meeting of the European Software Engineering Conference and the ACM SIGSOFT Symposium on the Foundations of Software Engineering, ESEC/FSE '15*, 2015.

[37] "Intel® 64 and IA-32 Architectures Developer's Manual," vol. 3b, 2018, https://software.intel.com.

[38] P. E. McKenney, "Memory ordering in modern microprocessors, part I," *Linux Journal*, vol. 2005, p. 2, 2005.

[39] Q. Zhao, R. Rabbah, S. Amarasinghe, L. Rudolph, and W.-F. Wong, "How to do a million watchpoints: Efficient Debugging using dynamic instrumentation," *Lecture Notes in Computer Science (including subseries Lecture Notes in Artificial Intelligence and Lecture Notes in Bioinformatics): Preface*, vol. 4959, pp. 147–162, 2008.

[40] S. Lu, S. Park, E. Seo, and Y. Zhou, "Learning from mistakes - A comprehensive study on real world concurrency bug characteristics," *ACM SIGPLAN Notices*, vol. 43, no. 3, pp. 329–339, 2008.

Clustering Classes in Packages for Program Comprehension

Xiaobing Sun,[1,2] Xiangyue Liu,[1] Bin Li,[1] Bixin Li,[3] David Lo,[4] and Lingzhi Liao[5]

[1]*School of Information Engineering, Yangzhou University, Yangzhou, China*
[2]*State Key Laboratory for Novel Software Technology, Nanjing University, Nanjing, China*
[3]*School of Computer Science and Engineering, Southeast University, Nanjing, China*
[4]*School of Information Systems, Singapore Management University, Singapore*
[5]*Nanjing University of Information Science & Technology, Nanjing, China*

Correspondence should be addressed to Bin Li; lb@yzu.edu.cn

Academic Editor: Xuanhua Shi

During software maintenance and evolution, one of the important tasks faced by developers is to understand a system quickly and accurately. With the increasing size and complexity of an evolving system, program comprehension becomes an increasingly difficult activity. Given a target system for comprehension, developers may first focus on the package comprehension. The packages in the system are of different sizes. For small-sized packages in the system, developers can easily comprehend them. However, for large-sized packages, they are difficult to understand. In this article, we focus on understanding these large-sized packages and propose a novel program comprehension approach for large-sized packages, which utilizes the Latent Dirichlet Allocation (LDA) model to cluster large-sized packages. Thus, these large-sized packages are separated as small-sized clusters, which are easier for developers to comprehend. Empirical studies on four real-world software projects demonstrate the effectiveness of our approach. The results show that the effectiveness of our approach is better than Latent Semantic Indexing- (LSI-) and Probabilistic Latent Semantic Analysis- (PLSA-) based clustering approaches. In addition, we find that the topic that labels each cluster is useful for program comprehension.

1. Introduction

Program comprehension is one of the most frequently performed activities in software maintenance [1, 2]. It is a process whereby a software practitioner understands a program using both knowledge of the domain and semantic and syntax knowledge, to build a mental model of the program [3, 4]. Developers working on software maintenance tasks spend around 60% of their time for program comprehension [5]. As software evolves, its complexity becomes increasingly higher. Moreover, some documents affiliated to the system also become outdated or inaccessible, which makes program comprehension more difficult.

In practice, the natural top-down program comprehension process can effectively facilitate developers to understand the system step by step [6]. For an object oriented Java software system, developers can also understand a system in such a top-down way. Packages are first taken into consideration. Then, interesting packages are selected, and developers further go deep into classes in the packages. For small-sized packages (with several classes), it is easy for developers to understand them. However, for packages with many classes in them, it is more challenging for developers to understand these classes, their relationships, and their functionalities [7, 8]. To aid program understanding, classes in these large-sized packages can be clustered into smaller-sized groups. With such clustering, developers can understand a system more easily.

There are several approaches that cluster programs based on static structural dependencies in the source code [9]. Static structural dependencies based approaches usually cluster classes in a system based on static structural dependencies among program elements, such as variable and class references, procedure calls, use of packages, and association and inheritance relationships among classes [8, 10, 11]. These approaches are more suitable in the process of implementing a change request in the source code. But before implementing a change request in the source code, developers should know which part in the source code is related to the change request. Specifically, they need to know the functional points of a system and where in the source code corresponds to these functional features. A feature or functional point represents a functionality that is defined by requirements and accessible to developers and users. Then, they can implement source code level changes. Hence, some studies focused on understanding the functional features of a system and proposed semantic clustering, which exploits linguistic information in the source code, such as identifier names and comments [12]. These approaches usually take the whole system as input and generate clusters at some granularity levels, for example, class level or method level. The generated clusters corresponding to different functional features are used to divide a system into different units [13, 14]. This article also focuses on exploiting linguistic information in the source code to understand functional features of different clusters in large-sized packages. In a large-sized package, there are a number of functional features or concerns. Each of these concerns is implemented in a set of classes. The previous studies focused on clustering a software unit. However, developers still do not easily know what the functional features that each cluster expresses are. So to get a good understanding of its concerns and the classes that implement each of them, in this article, we further generate a set of topics to describe each cluster.

This article proposes a technique to generate a set of clusters of classes for a large-sized package, where different clusters correspond to different functional features or concerns. Our approach is based on Latent Dirichlet Allocation (LDA), which is a topic model and one of the popular ways to analyze unstructured text in the corpus [15]. LDA can discover a set of ideas or themes that well describe the entire corpus. We use LDA for a whole package and extract latent topics to capture its functional features. Then, classes in the package with similar topics are clustered together.

Our approach can be effectively used for top-down program comprehension during software maintenance. For small-sized packages, developers can directly understand them. For large-sized packages, our approach can be used to divide packages into small clusters. Each of these small clusters can be understood more easily than the original large-sized package. The main contributions of this article are as follows:

(1) We propose to use LDA to generate clusters for large-sized packages. The topics generated by LDA are useful to indicate the functional features for these class clusters.

(2) We conduct an empirical study to show the effectiveness of our approach on four real-world open-source projects, *JHotDraw, jEdit, JFreeChart,* and *muCommander.* The results show that our approach is more effective in identifying more relevant classes in the cluster than other semantic clustering approaches, that is, Latent Semantic Indexing- (LSI-) and Probabilistic Latent Semantic Analysis- (PLSA-) based clustering.

(3) The empirical study on four selected packages from four subject systems shows that the topics generated

by our approach are useful to help developers understand these packages.

The rest of the article is organized as follows: in the next section, we introduce the background of program comprehension and LDA model. Section 3 describes our approach. We describe the design of our experiment, experiment results, and threats to validity of our study in Sections 4, 5, and 6, respectively. In Section 7, related work using clustering for program comprehension is discussed. Finally, we conclude the article and outline directions for future work in Section 8.

2. Background

In this article, we use LDA to cluster classes in large-sized packages for easier program comprehension. This section discusses the background of program comprehension and LDA topic model.

2.1. Program Comprehension. For software developers, program comprehension is a process whereby they understand a software artifact using both knowledge of the domain and semantic and syntax knowledge [10]. Program comprehension can be divided into bottom-up comprehension, top-down comprehension, and various combinations of these two processes. In bottom-up comprehension, a developer may first read all the source code at finer statement or method level and abstract features and concepts according to the low-level information. Then, coarser class-level or package-level elements are read and understood. Finally, developers comprehend the whole system. For top-down comprehension, a developer first utilizes knowledge about the domain to build a set of expectations that are mapped to the source code. Then, he/she understands the coarser package-level or class-level elements, followed by finer method-level or statement-level elements. Finally, the developer also gets an understanding of the whole system. In practice, top-down program comprehension is more acceptable since it meets humans' way of thinking from simple to complex, from whole to part [3].

Software clustering is one of the effective techniques for top-down program comprehension. During software maintenance, developers usually need to identify the functional features they are interested in to help them accomplish a change request. In this article, we propose a software clustering technique using LDA to provide some features for developers to facilitate the top-down program comprehension process.

2.2. Latent Dirichlet Allocation. Topic models were originated from the field of information retrieval (IR) to index, search, and cluster a large amount of unstructured and unlabeled documents. A topic is a collection of terms that cooccur frequently in the documents of the corpus. One of the mostly used topic models in software engineering community is Latent Dirichlet Allocation (LDA) [16–18]. It requires no training data and can well scale to thousands or millions of documents.

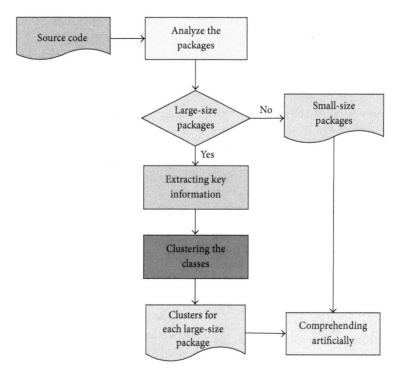

FIGURE 1: Process of our approach.

LDA models each document as a mixture of K corpus-wide topics and each topic as a mixture of terms in the corpus [15]. More specifically, it means that there is a set of topics to describe the entire corpus; each document can contain more than one of these topics; and each term in the entire repository can be contained in more than one of these topics. Hence, LDA is able to discover a set of ideas or themes that well describe the entire corpus. It assumes that documents have been generated using the probability distribution of the topics and that words in the documents were generated probabilistically in a similar way.

In order to apply LDA to the source code, we represent a software system as a collection of documents (i.e., classes) where each document is associated with a set of concepts (i.e., topics). Specifically, the LDA model consists of the following building blocks:

(1) A word is the basic unit of discrete data, defined to be an item from a software vocabulary $V = \{w_1, w_2, \ldots, w_v\}$, such as an identifier or a word from a comment.

(2) A document, which corresponds to a class, is a sequence of words denoted by $d = \{w_1, w_2, \ldots, w_n\}$, where w_i is the ith word in the sequence.

(3) A corpus is a collection of documents (classes) denoted by $D = \{d_1, d_2, \ldots, d_m\}$.

Given m documents containing k topics expressed over v unique words, the distribution of ith topic t_i over v words and the distribution of jth document over k topics can be represented.

By using LDA, it is possible to formulate the problem of discovering a set of topics describing a set of source code classes by viewing these classes as mixtures of probabilistic topics. For further details on LDA, interested readers are referred to the original work of Blei et al. [15].

With LDA, latent topics can be mined, allowing us to cluster them on the basis of their shared topics. In this article, to effectively use LDA, we apply it in a package-level corpus rather than each class to extract the latent topics to simulate the functional features or concerns for a package since small (class-level) corpus is too small to generate good topics [19–23]. Then, we cluster the classes according to these topics and assign different classes to their corresponding topics [23].

3. Our Approach

Faced with the source code of a software system, developers need to use their domain knowledge to comprehend the program from coarse package level to class level in each package. The process of understanding different packages is different. In the process, small-sized packages are easy to understand while large-sized packages are complex and they need to be separated into small-sized clusters. In this article, we focus on clustering the classes in large-sized packages as well as their corresponding functional features.

The process of understanding packages is described in Figure 1. Firstly, we analyze the size of each package in the software system. Small-sized packages are comprehended manually. For large-sized packages, there are two steps. First, LDA is used to extract the latent key information to facilitate the comprehension process. Then, on the basis of the key information of each package, we adopt the clustering to build small-sized clusters to decompose each package. Thus, given the source code of a software system at hand, programmers

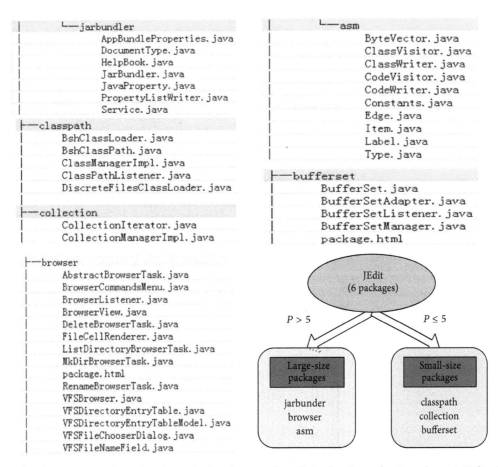

FIGURE 2: An example of separating packages into large-sized packages and small-sized packages for six packages in jEdit when *P* is set to 5.

can comprehend small-sized packages by themselves and large-sized packages with the help of our approach. In the following subsections, we discuss more details of our approach.

3.1. Analyzing the Size of Packages.

Our approach focuses on understanding large-sized packages. So we first need to select large-sized packages in a program. Here, we set a threshold *P* for the number of classes in a package. The packages including more than *P* classes are selected for analysis. These packages are separated into smaller clusters to facilitate program comprehension. Figure 2 shows an example of separating packages into large-sized packages and small-sized packages for six packages in *jEdit* when *P* is set to 5. The packages *jarbunder, browser,* and *asm* are classified as large-sized packages.

3.2. Extracting Key Information Based on LDA.

During the program comprehension process, developers are more focused on functional features or concerns of the program. In the program, the source code contains not only the syntax information but also the unstructured data, such as natural language identifiers and comments [24]. These unstructured source code identifiers and comments can be used to capture the semantics of the developers' intent [25]. They represent an important source of domain information and can often serve as a starting point in many program comprehension tasks [26, 27]. However, there exists noise in the source code, which can potentially confuse the LDA application. So natural language processing (NLP) techniques are usually used to perform one or more preprocessing operations before applying LDA models to the source code data. Then, LDA can be effectively used to generate the topics. To effectively use LDA, we apply it in a package-level corpus to simulate the functional features or concerns for a package. Finally, we cluster the classes according to these topics and assign different classes to their corresponding topics.

3.2.1. Preprocessing of the Source Code.

There are several typical preprocessing operations for the unstructured part of a source code. These preprocessing operations can be performed to reduce noise and improve the quality of the resulting text for LDA [28].

We first isolate identifiers and comments and strip away syntax and programming language keywords (e.g., "*public*" and "*int*"). First, we remove header comments since they often include generic information about the software that are included in most of source code files. Then, we tokenize each word based on common naming practice, such as camel

FIGURE 3: The process of preprocessing the class *InvalidHeaderException.java* in jEdit.

case *("oneTwo")* and underscores *("one_two")*, and remove common English language stop words *(the, it, and on)* and programming language related key words *(public, int, and while)*.

After preprocessing the unstructured part of source code files, LDA can be used to extract key information more effectively. Figure 3 shows an example of the detailed process of preprocessing the source code in the class *InvalidHeaderException.java* in *jEdit*. After preprocessing the source code, most of the useful words are kept for LDA application.

3.2.2. Extracting Key Information from Large-Sized Packages.
After preprocessing each class in large-sized packages, we need to extract key information from them. LDA is an effective approach to discover a set of ideas or themes that well describe the entire corpus. Before using LDA, we need to set the number of topics, that is, K. This parameter affects the effectiveness of LDA application. In this article, K is related to the size of clusters for a package, which is determined by users.

An LDA application generates two files: one is the word-topic matrix which lists the words for each topic and the other is the topic-document matrix which shows the percentage of topics in each document, also called the membership value. An example is given in Figure 4. The results show the distribution of different topics in different classes, and each topic is described by different words with different possibilities. These topics express different functional features of classes in the package.

3.3. Clustering Classes in Large-Sized Packages.
After extracting the topics from the objective package, classes having similar topics should be allocated in a cluster to aid their comprehension. In this subsection, we discuss details for clustering classes in a package.

3.3.1. Generating Initial Clusters.
To cluster classes in a package, the number of clusters should be first determined. However, it is difficult to know this information at the

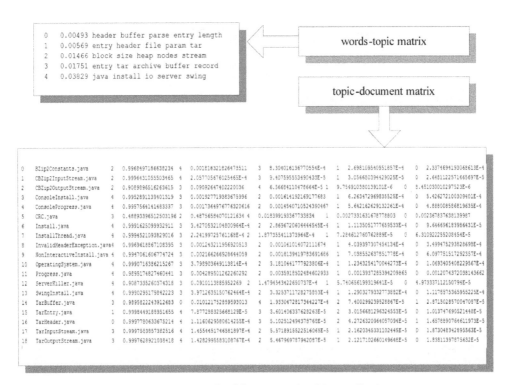

FIGURE 4: An example of the output of an LDA application.

beginning. In this article, the number of clusters is estimated based on the number of classes in a cluster.

Let us assume that the number of classes in an initial cluster is M, where M is a user-defined parameter. That is, if a user thinks that an M-scale cluster is easy for him/her to understand, he/she can set the initial size of each cluster as M, for example, 5 and 10. For a package with N classes ($N \geq M$), each of these classes should be put into a cluster. Thus there will be $\lceil N/M \rceil$ (a whole number) clusters for a package. We set the number of topics K to be the same as the number of clusters (i.e., $\lceil N/M \rceil$), because we need a topic to label each cluster.

After applying the LDA in a preprocessed package, we get two files, the word-topic matrix which lists the words for each topic and the topic-document matrix which shows the percentage of the topic words in each document. To allocate different classes to their corresponding topics, we use the topic-document matrix. That is, we allocate the top M documents to these K topics in the topic-document matrix. Thus a set of clusters can be generated, which we call the *initial clusters* for a package.

The ideal situation for the initial clusters is that each class is just assigned to only its own and exclusive cluster. Inevitably, there are two special cases; one is that a class may match different topics in the topic-document matrix. Such classes are called shared classes, which we need to reassign. The other case is that there may be some remaining classes that are not included in the top M documents in any topics. Such classes are called nonmatching classes, which need to be assigned to the most probable clusters related

to them. In the following, we deal with these classes to guarantee that each class is assigned to one and only one cluster.

3.3.2. Assigning Shared Classes and Nonmatching Classes. Shared classes are the classes matching different topics in the generated topic-document matrix. These classes are all listed in the top M classes for each topic. We list all the classes shared by different topics and the membership value of each topic for them. A shared class is allocated to the cluster corresponding to the topic with the highest membership value.

For nonmatching classes that are not initially matched to any cluster, they are processed in a similar way as shared classes. We list all these nonmatching classes and their membership values. Each of these nonmatching classes is put into the cluster corresponding to the topic with the highest membership value.

Finally, each cluster in a package only contains classes having high membership values and each class is a member of only one cluster. Based on the word-topic matrix, we can see the words describing the topic, which indicates the feature of the cluster. Figure 5 shows an example of the process to generate the clusters for a large-sized package. First, initial clusters are generated according to the membership values with five topics. Then, shared classes and nonmatching classes are assigned to corresponding initial clusters based on their membership values. Finally, a set of clusters for the large-sized package is obtained as shown in the bottom-left part of Figure 5.

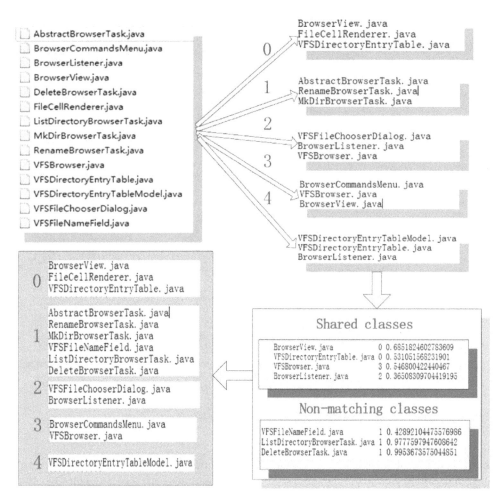

FIGURE 5: An example of generating clusters for a large-sized package (with the number of topics set to 5).

4. Case Study

In this section, we conduct case studies to evaluate the effectiveness of our approach. In our study, we address the following three research questions (RQs):

> RQ1: Does the number of topics affect the shared classes and nonmatching classes?
>
> RQ2: Is our LDA clustering approach more effective than other semantic clustering approaches, that is, LSI-based clustering and PLSA-based clustering?
>
> RQ3: Can our approach provide useful topics for developers to understand the classes in the package(s)?

In our approach, the number of topics is set by users themselves. We investigate RQ1 to see how this parameter affects the number of shared and nonmatching classes. In addition, we investigate RQ2 to see whether our clustering approach using LDA is more effective than other semantic clustering based approaches based on LSI and PLSA [12, 29–31], respectively. Finally, there is another difference between our approach and other clustering approaches; that is, each cluster that is generated by our approach is labeled with a topic to facilitate understanding of the cluster. So RQ3 aims to answer whether the topic labeling each cluster can help developers understand the cluster or not.

4.1. Empirical Environment. We implemented our approach with Java language in the Eclipse environment. In addition, all the selected subject programs are also Java programs. So our case study was conducted in the Eclipse environment.

4.2. Subject Systems. We address our research questions by performing case studies on the source code of four well-known software systems, *JHotDraw* (https://sourceforge.net/projects/jhotdraw), *jEdit* (https://sourceforge.net/projects/jedit), *JFreeChart* (https://sourceforge.net/projects/jfreechart), and *muCommander* (http://www.mucommander.com), as shown in Table 1.

JHotDraw is a medium-sized, open-source, 2D drawing framework developed in the Java programming language. *jEdit* is a medium-sized, open-source text editor written in Java. *JFreeChart* is a free 100% Java chart library that makes it easy for developers to display professional quality charts

TABLE 1: Subject systems.

Subject	Version	Files	Packages	Classes
JHotDraw	7.0.6	144	23	305
jEdit	5.1.0	147	43	573
JFreeChart	1.0.17	105	70	990
muCommander	0.9.0	98	89	692

TABLE 2: The percentage of classes over P (5, 10, and 15) of the four systems.

Subject	$P > 5$ (%)	$P > 10$ (%)	$P > 15$ (%)
JHotDraw	91.8	79.7	68.5
jEdit	91.1	81.3	72.2
JFreeChart	93.2	81.0	67.6
muCommander	81.1	56.9	37.2
Average	89.3	74.7	61.4

in their applications. *muCommander* is a lightweight, cross-platform file manager that runs on any operating system supporting Java.

These projects belong to different problem domains. They are general enough to represent real-world software systems, and they have been widely used in empirical studies in the context of software maintenance and evolution [32, 33]. In addition, they have become the de facto standard system for experiments and analysis in topic and concern mining (e.g., by Robillard and Murphy [34] and Binkley et al. [35]). Moreover, these four subject systems of different sizes that are neither too small nor too large are selected due to their good design and manageable size for manual analysis.

4.3. Parameters Setting. In our approach, there are two parameters, P and K. P represents the size of a package and K is the number of topics as input for the LDA model. Values of these two parameters will affect the number of packages to be subdivided into clusters and the number of clusters in a package. Table 2 shows the percentage of classes in packages with different number of classes. From the results, when P is 5, 10, and 15, the average percentages of classes in packages of large sizes are 89.3%, 74.7%, and 61.4%, respectively. In this study, we consider packages of size larger than 10 as the large-sized packages used to evaluate our approach. Hence, for all four systems, most of classes and packages are used to evaluate our approach.

The other parameter in our approach is the number of topics (K) for LDA analysis. K is an important parameter which also indicates the number of clusters for the final clustering results. It determines the size of each cluster. We set K to be 5, 10, and 15 for our study, respectively.

4.4. Methods and Measures. For LDA computation, we used *MALLET* (http://mallet.cs.umass.edu), which is a highly scalable Java implementation of the *Gibbs* sampling algorithm. We ran for 10,000 sampling iterations, the first 1000 of which were used for parameter optimization. We selected different numbers of topics to use *MALLET* to generate the word-topic matrix and topic-document matrix. Then, we clustered each large-sized package based on these two matrixes.

For semantic clustering based on LSI and PLSA [12, 29–31] that we used to compare with our approach, they are popular methods for cluster analysis, especially for clustering nonstructured data. LSI uses singular value decomposition to explore patterns in the relationships between the terms and concepts contained in an unstructured corpus [36]. LSI is implemented based on the assumption that words used in the same contexts tend to have similar meanings. Hence, LSI is able to extract the conceptual contents from a corpus by establishing associations between those terms that occur in similar contexts. Probabilistic Latent Semantic Analysis (PLSA) is a statistical technique for the data analysis, which is based on a mixture decomposition derived from a latent class model [30, 31].

We selected these clustering approaches for comparison because (1) they are widely used in clustering software data and show promising results [37, 38] and (2) they are also clustering approaches based on lexical information which is similar to our approach. In our study, they are performed by clustering classes with similar vocabularies. After calculating the similarity between each pair of documents, an agglomerative hierarchical clustering algorithm is executed. There are a lot of similarity measures, for example, cosine similarity, Manhattan distance, and Euclidean distance [39]. Cosine similarity which is a popular similarity measure is used here [33, 40].

To answer *RQ1*, we compute the number of shared classes and nonmatching classes and the *shared occurrence counts* (or *shared counts*) of the shared classes. For example, if one class is shared by topic 1 and topic 2, its shared count is 1. If the class is also shared by topic 3, the shared count is 2. We analyze the percentages of shared classes and nonmatching classes as well as the shared counts for different numbers of topics.

For *RQ2*, our study involved 10 participants from university and industry. Half of them are from our lab with 2-3 years of development experience and the other half are from industry with 5-6 years of development experience especially

TABLE 3: The selected packages and selected classes.

Subject	Package	Size	Class	K
JHotDraw	JHotDraw.src.org.jhotdraw.app.action	33	AbstractProjectAction.java	10
jEdit	jEdit.org.gjt.sp.jedit.gui	73	AbbrevEditor.java	15
JFreeChart	jfreechart.source.org.jfree.chart.plot	52	AbstractPieLabelDistributor.java	10
muCommander	muCommander.main.com.mucommander.command	15	AssociationBuilder.java	5

large project development experience. They are not familiar with the systems before. Then, they were assigned with a class as shown in the fourth column of Table 3. The task for them is to identify the most likely classes that are related to the given classes in their enclosing packages. Then each participant obtained a cluster of classes for each given class. As different participants may generate different clusters, they needed to discuss the results and reached a consensus on the clustering results for each given class. We used the clustering results as the authoritative clusters to compare with the clusters produced by our approach and the LSI-based/PLSA-based clustering approach. For LSI-based clustering approach and our approach that are used for comparison, we need to set the K value. Based on the size of the authoritative clusters, we set the K values for the packages, which are shown in the last column of Table 3. To answer RQ2, we first provided the clustering results of the three approaches to participants. In this process, to guarantee a fair treatment, they did not know which clustering results were generated by our approach or the LSI-based/PLSA-based clustering approach. Then, each of participants assessed each of the three clusters to vote the best one. In addition, to quantitatively compare these two approaches, we used precision and recall, two widely used information retrieval and classification metrics [41], to validate the accuracy of different clustering approaches. Precision measures the fraction of classes identified by a clustering approach to be in the same cluster as the given class that are truly relevant (based on the authoritative cluster), while recall measures the fraction of relevant results (i.e., classes that appear in the authoritative cluster) that are put in the same cluster as the given class by a clustering approach. Mathematically, they are defined as follows:

$$
\text{Precision} = \frac{|\text{Clustering results} \cap \text{Authoritative results}|}{|\text{Clustering results}|} \times 100\%
$$

$$
\text{Recall} = \frac{|\text{Clustering results} \cap \text{Authoritative results}|}{|\text{Authoritative results}|} \times 100\%.
$$
(1)

In the above equations, clustering results and authoritative results are sets of classes.

To answer RQ3, participants were required to write the words in the identifiers or comments to label the authoritative clusters. This process is similar to that of RQ2, and a set of authoritative words are produced. To show whether the topics generated by our approach are useful, the participants needed to assess the generated topics to check whether they are useful for them to understand the clusters. Each participant needs to provide a rating in a five-point Likert scale, 1 (very useless) to 5 (very useful). Finally, we also computed the precision and recall of the words in the topics by comparing them with authoritative words. The way precision and recall are computed is similar to the way they are computed to answer RQ2.

Overall, the participants needed to answer four questions during the evaluation process. In RQ2, they were asked to give the answers of the authoritative results for the clustering and assess the results between LSI or PLSI and our approach. In RQ3, they needed to provide labels of the clusters and assess the topics generated by our approach.

5. Results

In this section, we gather and analyze results collected from the case studies to answer RQ1, RQ2, and RQ3.

5.1. RQ1. First, we see the existence of shared classes and nonmatching classes in the initial clusters. Table 4 shows the average percentage of the initial clusters without nonmatching classes and shared classes. From the results, we see that there do exist some shared classes and nonmatching classes in the initial clusters. So we need to perform the operation of reassigning these shared classes and nonmatching classes. Then, we see how the number of topics affects the results of shared classes and nonmatching classes. Figure 6 shows the box-plots of the number of shared classes and nonmatching classes and shared times in the process of clustering the classes with different numbers of topics. From the results in Figures 6(a) and 6(b), we notice that, with the increasing in the number of topics, the shared counts and the number of shared classes also increase. So setting different values of the number of topics will affect the number of shared classes. In addition, Figure 6(c) shows the results for nonmatching classes in the process of clustering the classes. We see that nonmatching classes are fewer than shared classes. Moreover, the range of the number of nonmatching classes with different numbers of topics is similar. That is, values of different numbers of topics do not obviously affect the number of nonmatching classes.

From the results discussed above, shared classes and nonmatching classes exist in the initial clusters. However, the majority of the classes are neither shared nor nonmatching

TABLE 4: The percentage of initial clusters without nonmatching classes and shared classes.

Cluster	K = 5 (%)	K = 10 (%)	K = 15 (%)
Initial clusters without nonmatching classes	90.2	90.1	85.4
Initial clusters without shared classes	70.0	60.0	55.3

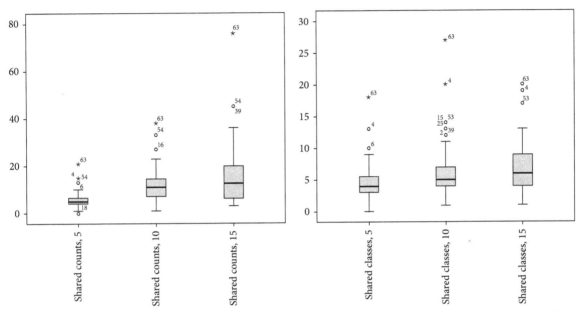

(a) The shared counts of different classes in the initial clusters with different number of topics (5, 10, and 15)

(b) The number of shared classes in the initial clusters with different number of topics (5, 10, and 15)

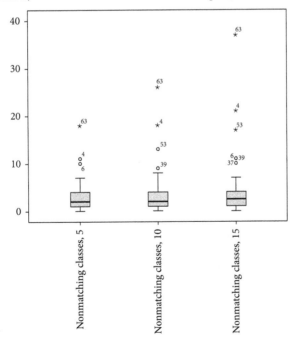

(c) The number of nonmatching classes in the initial clusters with different number of topics (5, 10, and 15)

FIGURE 6: Shared counts, number of shared classes, and number of nonmatching classes in the initial clusters for number of topics set to 5, 10, and 15.

TABLE 5: The votes for our approach and LSI-based/PLSA-based clustering approach.

Subject	Package	Our approach	LSI-based	PLSA-based
JHotDraw	JHotDraw.src.org.jhotdraw.app.action	7	2	1
jEdit	jEdit.org.gjt.sp.jedit.gui	6	1	3
JFreeChart	jfreechart.source.org.jfree.chart.plot	5	4	1
muCommander	muCommander.main.com.mucommander.command	7	1	2

TABLE 6: The precision and recall of our approach and LSI-based/PLSA-based clustering approach.

Package	Our approach		LSI-based		PLSA-based	
	P	R	P	R	P	R
JHotDraw.src.org.jhotdraw.app.action	0.75	0.57	0.44	0.57	0.51	0.43
jEdit.org.gjt.sp.jedit.gui	0.4	0.5	0.04	0.25	0.14	0.22
jfreechart.source.org.jfree.chart.plot	0.83	0.83	1	0.6	0.76	0.68
muCommander.main.com.mucommander.command	0.67	0.33	0.29	0.33	0.42	0.26

ones. Furthermore, some shared classes are shared by three or more topics, and the number of shared classes is larger than that of nonmatching classes. In addition, the results also show that different settings of number of topics will affect the number of shared classes but will not affect the number of nonmatching classes.

5.2. RQ2. In this subsection, we compare the accuracies of the three clustering approaches to show the effectiveness of our approach.

First, we invited participants to assess the clustering results from three clustering approaches. The voting results are shown in Table 5. The results show that, in most cases, the results generated by our approach are more fit to their needs. For the *jfreechart.source.org.jfree.chart.plot* package, the voting results of LSI-based clustering and our approach are similar. When we investigated deep into the results in this package, both two clustering approaches output the clusters with two true-positive relevant classes (the true-positive relevant classes are those classes that do belong to the authoritative cluster). So participants are not sure which one is better than the other one. So from the participants' qualitative analysis, we notice that our approach can generate clustering results which better fit their needs compared to the LSI-based and PLSA-based clustering approach.

In addition, to quantitatively compare these clustering approaches, we compute their precision and recall results, which are shown in Table 6. From the recall perspective, our approach is always better than (or at least as good as) the LSI-based and PLSA-based clustering approaches. However, from the precision perspective, sometimes our results are better, and sometimes the *LSI-based clustering* or *PLSA-based clustering* is better. When we investigate results where our approach achieves lower precision, we notice that the number of classes in the cluster generated by our approach is larger than that by *LSI-based clustering* and *PLSA-based clustering*. For example, for *jfreechart.source.org.jfree.chart.plot* package, there are six classes in the authoritative cluster. Our approach

generates five true-positive relevant classes while the *LSI-based clustering* approach generates four and the four are just the true-positive relevant classes. So the precision of the *LSI-based clustering* approach is high while our approach is worse. But from the respective of program comprehension, recall is more important because, with more relevant classes, developers can better comprehend the cluster. That is to say, our approach can cover more relevant classes in the authoritative clusters, which can effectively facilitate program comprehension. So from the results discussed above, compared with *LSI-based clustering* and *PLSA-based clustering*, our approach can effectively identify more relevant classes in a cluster to help program comprehension.

5.3. RQ3. Different from other clustering approaches, our approach also labels each cluster with the topics, which is composed of some words to describe the cluster. In this subsection, we discuss whether these topics are useful to comprehend the cluster.

First, we provided the topics of each cluster to the participants. They used a five-point Likert scale to answer the quality of the topics. The results are shown in Table 7. The average score of the results is around 4, which indicates that the participants think that the topics are useful to understand the cluster. So for program comprehension, the topics labeling the clusters are useful for users to understand the program.

In addition, we also assess the topics of the clusters quantitatively from the precision and recall perspectives. The results are shown in Table 8. For each cluster, our approach can produce a topic which includes some words to label it. These words can cover most of the words given by the participants. For example, for the cluster that includes the *AbstractPieLabelDistributor.java* class, 82% of the words can be covered. Hence, the participants can use these words to help them understand the clusters. In addition, from the precision perspective, our approach is not very good and most of the precision results are about 10%. However, for the other 90% irrelevant words, some are obviously not related

TABLE 7: The score assessed by the participants on the topics.

Package	Participants										
	P1	P2	P3	P4	P5	P6	P7	P8	P9	P10	AVG
JHotDraw.src.org.jhotdraw.app.action	5	5	5	5	4	5	5	4	4	4	4.6
jEdit.org.gjt.sp.jedit.gui	4	4	4	4	3	4	3	4	5	4	3.9
jfreechart.source.org.jfree.chart.plot	3	5	5	4	4	4	4	4	4	4	4.1
muCommander.main.com.mucommander.command	4	4	5	4	4	4	4	3	4	4	4

TABLE 8: The precision and recall of our approach in inferring representative words to label clusters.

Subject	Package	Class	Topics	
			P	R
JHotDraw	JHotDraw.src.org.jhotdraw.app.action	AbstractProjectAction.java	0.10	0.76
jEdit	jEdit.org.gjt.sp.jedit.gui	AbbrevEditor.java	0.06	0.80
JFreeChart	jfreechart.source.org.jfree.chart.plot	AbstractPieLabelDistributor.java	0.10	0.82
muCommander	muCommander.main.com.mucommander.command	AssociationBuilder.java	0.17	0.64

to the cluster, which are easily identified by the participants, for example, the words "*method*," "*refer*," and "*jEdit*." These words are included in the topics because they are not removed in the preprocessing process. To improve the results, we can improve the preprocessing operations to remove words related to the specific subject programs. Although some noisy information is produced from our approach, the participants still feel that the topics are useful to understand the clusters.

Hence, from the results, we see that the topics in our approach are helpful for developers to understand the clustering results.

6. Threats to Validity

Like any empirical validation, ours has its limitations. In the following, threats to the validity of our case study are discussed.

The first threat relates to the correctness of our experiments and implementation. We have checked the implementation and fixed bugs. Another threat relates to participants' bias. We have reduced this bias by not telling the participants of results produced by our approach and those produced by the baseline approach. In addition, we only applied our technique to four subject programs. Moreover, we considered only one programming language (Java) and one development environment (Eclipse). Further studies are required to generalize our findings to large-scale industrial projects and with developers who have sufficient domain knowledge and familiarity with the subject systems. Thus we cannot guarantee that the results in our case study can be generalized to other more complex or arbitrary subjects. However, these subjects were selected from open-source projects and widely employed for experimental studies [42, 43]. In evaluating the effectiveness of the clustering results, we randomly selected a number of packages. To reduce the threats to validity further, in the future, we plan to evaluate our clustering approach with even more packages from more software projects. The final threat comes from the measures used to evaluate the effectiveness of our approach, that is, precision and recall.

These two metrics only focused on the false-positives and false-negatives for authoritative clustering results. However, for program comprehension, other factors may be more important.

7. Related Work

Program comprehension is one of the most important activities in software maintenance and reverse engineering [8, 10, 23, 44, 45]. Clustering techniques are commonly used to decompose a software system into small units for easier comprehension. Some studies analyze syntax features or dependencies to cluster the software [46–50], while others rely on the semantic information in the source code for clustering [51–54].

Clustering approaches based on the syntax (structure) in the source code usually focus on the structural relationships among entities, for example, variable and class references, procedure calls, usage of packages, and association and inheritance relationships among classes. Mancoridis et al. proposed an approach which generates clusters using module dependency graph of the software system [8]. They treated clustering as an optimization problem, which makes use of traditional hill climbing and genetic algorithms. In [46, 55], the Bunch clustering system was introduced. Bunch generates clusters using weighted dependency graph for software maintenance. Sartipi and Kontogiannis presented an interactive approach composed of four phases to recover cohesive subsystems within C systems. In the first phase, relations between C programs are extracted. In the second phase, these relationships are used to build an attributed relational graph. In the third phase, the graph is manually or automatically partitioned using data mining techniques [56]. These syntax relationships can help developers understand how the functional features are programmed in the source code. In this article, we focus on the clustering based on functional features in the source code. And we used LDA for semantic analysis of these functional features.

Semantic based clustering approaches attempt to show the functional features of a system [57–60]. The functional features in the source code are analyzed from comments, identifier names, and file names [61]. Kuhn et al. presented a language independent approach to group software artifacts based on LSI. They grouped source code containing similar terms in the comments [12, 62]. Scanniello et al. presented an approach to perform the software system partitioning. This approach first analyzes software entities (e.g., programs or classes) and uses LSI to get the dissimilarity between entities, which are grouped by iteratively calling the *K-means* clustering algorithm [63]. Santos et al. used semantic clustering to support remodularization analysis in an input program [58]. Our approach used LDA to generate the clusters, particularly for large-sized packages, to facilitate their comprehension.

In addition, some program comprehension techniques combined the strengths of both syntax and semantic clustering [7, 38, 64–66]. The *ACDC* algorithm is one example of this combined approach which used name and dependency of classes to cluster all classes in a system into small clusters for comprehension [3]. Andritsos and Tzerpos proposed *LIMBO*, a hierarchical algorithm for software clustering [7]. The clustering algorithm considers both structural and non-structural attributes to reduce the complexity of a software system by decomposing it into clusters. Saeidi et al. proposed to cluster a software system by incorporating knowledge from different viewpoints of the system, that is, knowledge embedded within the source code as well as the structural dependencies within the system, to produce a clustering result [67]. Then, they adopted a search-based approach to provide a multiview clustering of the software system. In this article, we focused on semantic analysis of the source code for its clustering. In addition, our approach also generates topics to help users more easily understand the classes in the clusters.

8. Conclusion and Future Work

In this article, we propose an approach of clustering classes in large-sized packages for program comprehension. Our approach uses LDA to cluster large-sized packages into small clusters, which are labeled with topics to show their features. We conducted case studies to show the effectiveness of our approach on four real-world open-source projects. The results show that the clustering results of our approach are more relevant than those of other clustering techniques, that is, LSI-based and PLSA-based clustering. In addition, the topics labeling these clusters are useful to help developers understand them. Therefore, our approach could provide an effective way for developers to understand large-sized packages quickly and accurately.

In our study, we only conducted studies on four Java-based programs, which does not imply its generality for other types of systems. Future work will focus on conducting more studies on different systems to evaluate the generality of our approach. In addition, during the clustering process, we find that some classes are weakly coupled with its package, but they are more related to another package. That is, there are problems with the current package's structure. So we consider applying our clustering approach to improve the package structure. Finally, our approach is a first step in a top-down program comprehension process; in the future, we plan to cluster other finer-level program elements, for example, methods, to provide a more comprehensive top-down program comprehension support to better understand a software system.

Conflicts of Interest

The authors declare that there are no conflicts of interest regarding the publication of this paper.

Acknowledgments

This work is supported partially by Natural Science Foundation of China under Grant nos. 61402396, 61472344, 61602267, and 61472343, the Open Funds of State Key Laboratory for Novel Software Technology of Nanjing University under Grant no. KFKT2016B21, the Jiangsu Qin Lan Project, the China Postdoctoral Science Foundation under Grant no. 2015M571489, the Six Talent Peaks Project in Jiangsu Province under Grant no. 2011-DZXX-032, the Natural Science Foundation of the Jiangsu Higher Education Institutions of China under Grant no. 15KJB520030, the Priority Academic Program Development of Jiangsu Higher Education Institutions, and the Jiangsu Collaborative Innovation Center on Atmospheric Environment and Equipment Technology.

References

[1] X. Peng, Z. Xing, X. Tan, Y. Yu, and W. Zhao, "Improving feature location using structural similarity and iterative graph mapping," *Journal of Systems and Software*, vol. 86, no. 3, pp. 664–676, 2013.

[2] J. Wang, X. Peng, Z. Xing, and W. Zhao, "Improving feature location practice with multi-faceted interactive exploration," in *Proceedings of the 35th International Conference on Software Engineering (ICSE '13)*, pp. 762–771, IEEE, San Francisco, Calif, USA, May 2013.

[3] M. P. Obrien, "Software comprehension: a review and research direction," Tech. Rep., 2003.

[4] Z. Fu, K. Ren, J. Shu, X. Sun, and F. Huang, "Enabling personalized search over encrypted outsourced data with efficiency improvement," *IEEE Transactions on Parallel and Distributed Systems*, vol. 27, no. 9, pp. 2546–2559, 2016.

[5] E. Soloway and K. Ehrlich, "Empirical studies of programming knowledge," *IEEE Transactions on Software Engineering*, vol. 10, no. 5, pp. 595–609, 1984.

[6] W. Maalej, R. Tiarks, T. Roehm, and R. Koschke, "On the comprehension of program comprehension," *ACM Transactions on Software Engineering and Methodology*, vol. 23, no. 4, article 31, 2014.

[7] P. Andritsos and V. Tzerpos, "Information-theoretic software clustering," *IEEE Transactions on Software Engineering*, vol. 31, no. 2, pp. 150–165, 2005.

[8] S. Mancoridis, B. S. Mitchell, C. Rorres, Y. Chen, and E. R. Gansner, "Using automatic clustering to produce high-level system organizations of source code," in *Proceedings of the*

6th International Workshop on Program Comprehension (IWPC '98), p. 45, Ischia, Italy, June 1998.

[9] N. Anquetil and T. Lethbridge, "Experiments with clustering as a software remodularization method," in *Proceedings of the 6th Working Conference on Reverse Engineering (WCRE '99)*, pp. 235–255, IEEE, October 1999.

[10] V. Rajlich and N. Wilde, "The role of concepts in program comprehension," in *Proceedings of the 10th International Workshop on Program Comprehension (IWPC '02)*, pp. 271–278, IEEE, Paris, France, June 2002.

[11] Z. Zhou, Y. Wang, Q. M. Wu, C. Yang, and X. Sun, "Effective and efficient global context verification for image copy detection," *IEEE Transactions on Information Forensics and Security*, vol. 12, no. 1, pp. 48–63, 2017.

[12] A. Kuhn, S. Ducasse, and T. Gîrba, "Semantic clustering: identifying topics in source code," *Information & Software Technology*, vol. 49, no. 3, pp. 230–243, 2007.

[13] S. C. Choi and W. Scacchi, "Extracting and restructuring the design of large systems," *IEEE Software*, vol. 7, no. 1, pp. 66–71, 1990.

[14] Y. S. Maarek, D. M. Berry, and G. E. Kaiser, "An information retrieval approach for automatically constructing software libraries," *IEEE Transactions on Software Engineering*, vol. 17, no. 8, pp. 800–813, 1991.

[15] D. M. Blei, A. Y. Ng, and M. I. Jordan, "Latent dirichlet allocation," *Journal of Machine Learning Research*, vol. 3, no. 4-5, pp. 993–1022, 2003.

[16] X. Sun, X. Liu, B. Li, Y. Duan, H. Yang, and J. Hu, "Exploring topic models in software engineering data analysis: a survey," in *Proceedings of the 17th IEEE/ACIS International Conference on Software Engineering, Artificial Intelligence, Networking and Parallel/Distributed Computing (SNPD '16)*, pp. 357–362, IEEE, Shanghai, China, June 2016.

[17] B. Gu, V. S. Sheng, K. Y. Tay, W. Romano, and S. Li, "Incremental support vector learning for ordinal regression," *IEEE Transactions on Neural Networks and Learning Systems*, vol. 26, no. 7, pp. 1403–1416, 2015.

[18] B. Gu, V. S. Sheng, Z. Wang, D. Ho, S. Osman, and S. Li, "Incremental learning for v-support vector regression," *Neural Networks*, vol. 67, pp. 140–150, 2015.

[19] J. Tang, Z. Meng, X. Nguyen, Q. Mei, and M. Zhang, "Understanding the limiting factors of topic modeling via posterior contraction analysis," in *Proceedings of the 31th International Conference on Machine Learning*, pp. 190–198, 2014.

[20] A. Panichella, B. Dit, R. Oliveto, M. Di Penta, D. Poshynanyk, and A. De Lucia, "How to effectively use topic models for software engineering tasks? An approach based on genetic algorithms," in *Proceedings of the 35th International Conference on Software Engineering (ICSE '13)*, pp. 522–531, IEEE, May 2013.

[21] Y. Zhang, X. Sun, and B. Wang, "Efficient algorithm for k-barrier coverage based on integer linear programming," *China Communications*, vol. 13, no. 7, pp. 16–23, 2016.

[22] Q. Liu, W. Cai, J. Shen, Z. Fu, X. Liu, and N. Linge, "A speculative approach to spatial-temporal efficiency with multi-objective optimization in a heterogeneous cloud environment," *Security and Communication Networks*, vol. 9, no. 17, pp. 4002–4012, 2016.

[23] D. Binkley, D. Heinz, D. Lawrie, and J. Overfelt, "Understanding LDA in source code analysis," in *Proceedings of the 22nd International Conference on Program Comprehension (ICPC '14)*, pp. 26–36, June 2014.

[24] T. Mens, A. Serebrenik, and A. Cleve, Eds., *Evolving Software Systems*, Springer, 2014.

[25] F. Longo, R. Tiella, P. Tonella, and A. Villafiorita, "Measuring the impact of different categories of software evolution," in *Software Process and Product Measurement, International Conferences: IWSM 2008, Metrikon 2008, and Mensura 2008*, pp. 344–351, 2008.

[26] B. Dit, L. Guerrouj, D. Poshyvanyk, and G. Antoniol, "Can better identifier splitting techniques help feature location?" in *Proceedings of the IEEE 19th International Conference on Program Comprehension (ICPC '11)*, pp. 11–20, IEEE, Ontario, Canada, June 2011.

[27] T. Fritz, G. C. Murphy, E. Murphy-Hill, J. Ou, and E. Hill, "Degree-of-knowledge: modeling a developer's knowledge of code," *ACM Transactions on Software Engineering and Methodology*, vol. 23, no. 2, article 14, 2014.

[28] X. Sun, X. Liu, J. Hu, and J. Zhu, "Empirical studies on the NLP techniques for source code data preprocessing," in *Proceedings of the 3rd International Workshop on Evidential Assessment of Software Technologies (EAST '14)*, pp. 32–39, May 2014.

[29] G. Santos, M. T. Valente, and N. Anquetil, "Remodularization analysis using semantic clustering," in *Proceedings of the Software Evolution Week—IEEE Conference on Software Maintenance, Reengineering and Reverse Engineering (CSMR-WCRE '14)*, pp. 224–233, Antwerp, Belgium, February 2014.

[30] T. Hofmann, "Unsupervised learning by probabilistic latent semantic analysis," *Machine Learning*, vol. 42, no. 1-2, pp. 177–196, 2001.

[31] T. Hofmann, "Probabilistic latent semantic analysis," in *Proceedings of the 15th Conference on Uncertainty in Artificial Intelligence (UAI '99)*, pp. 289–296, Stockholm, Sweden, July 1999, https://dslpitt.org/uai/displayArticleDetails.jsp?mmnu=1&smnu=2&proceeding_id=15 &article_id=179.

[32] Y. Liu, D. Poshyvanyk, R. Ferenc, T. Gyimóthy, and N. Chrisochoides, "Modeling class cohesion as mixtures of latent topics," in *Proceedings of the IEEE International Conference on Software Maintenance (ICSM '09)*, pp. 233–242, Alberta, Canada, September 2009.

[33] M. Shtern and V. Tzerpos, "Clustering methodologies for software engineering," *Advances in Software Engineering*, vol. 2012, Article ID 792024, 18 pages, 2012.

[34] M. P. Robillard and G. C. Murphy, "Representing concerns in source code," *ACM Transactions on Software Engineering and Methodology*, vol. 16, no. 1, article 3, 2007.

[35] D. Binkley, M. Ceccato, M. Harman, F. Ricca, and P. Tonella, "Tool-supported refactoring of existing object-oriented code into aspects," *IEEE Transactions on Software Engineering*, vol. 32, no. 9, pp. 698–717, 2006.

[36] S. Deerwester, "Improving information retrieval with latent semantic indexing," in *Proceedings of the Annual Meeting of the American Society for Information Science*, pp. 1–10, 1988.

[37] D. Poshyvanyk, M. Gethers, and A. Marcus, "Concept location using formal concept analysis and information retrieval," *ACM Transactions on Software Engineering and Methodology*, vol. 21, no. 4, pp. 1–34, 2012.

[38] J. I. Maletic and A. Marcus, "Supporting program comprehension using semantic and structural information," in *Proceedings of the 23rd International Conference on Software Engineering*, pp. 103–112, May 2001.

[39] J. Han, *Data Mining: Concepts and Techniques*, Morgan Kaufmann, San Francisco, Calif, USA, 2005.

[40] X. Sun, B. Li, Y. Li, and Y. Chen, "What information in software historical repositories do we need to support software maintenance tasks? An approach based on topic model," in *Computer and Information Science*, pp. 27–37, Springer International Publishing, 2015.

[41] C. J. van Rijsbergen, *Information Retrieval*, Butterworths, London, UK, 1979.

[42] U. Erdemir, U. Tekin, and F. Buzluca, "Object oriented software clustering based on community structure," in *Proceedings of the 18th Asia Pacific Software Engineering Conference (APSEC '11)*, pp. 315–321, IEEE, Ho Chi Minh, Vietnam, December 2011.

[43] A. De Lucia, M. Di Penta, R. Oliveto, A. Panichella, and S. Panichella, "Using IR methods for labeling source code artifacts: is it worthwhile?" in *Proceedings of the 20th IEEE International Conference on Program Comprehension (ICPC '12)*, pp. 193–202, June 2012.

[44] X. Liu, X. Sun, B. Li, and J. Zhu, "PFN: a novel program feature network for program comprehension," in *Proceedings of the 13th IEEE/ACIS International Conference on Computer and Information Science (ICIS '14)*, pp. 349–354, Taiyuan, China, June 2014.

[45] Z. Fu, X. Wu, C. Guan, X. Sun, and K. Ren, "Toward efficient multi-keyword fuzzy search over encrypted outsourced data with accuracy improvement," *IEEE Transactions on Information Forensics and Security*, vol. 11, no. 12, pp. 2706–2716, 2016.

[46] B. S. Mitchell and S. Mancoridis, "On the automatic modularization of software systems using the bunch tool," *IEEE Transactions on Software Engineering*, vol. 32, no. 3, pp. 193–208, 2006.

[47] S. Islam, J. Krinke, D. Binkley, and M. Harman, "Coherent clusters in source code," *Journal of Systems and Software*, vol. 88, no. 1, pp. 1–24, 2014.

[48] S. Mirarab, A. Hassouna, and L. Tahvildari, "Using Bayesian belief networks to predict change propagation in software systems," in *Proceedings of the 15th IEEE International Conference on Program Comprehension (ICPC '07)*, pp. 177–186, June 2007.

[49] F. Deng and J. A. Jones, "Weighted system dependence graph," in *Proceedings of the 5th IEEE International Conference on Software Testing, Verification and Validation (ICST '12)*, pp. 380–389, Montreal, Canada, April 2012.

[50] M. Gethers, A. Aryani, and D. Poshyvanyk, "Combining conceptual and domain-based couplings to detect database and code dependencies," in *Proceedings of the IEEE 12th International Working Conference on Source Code Analysis and Manipulation (SCAM '12)*, pp. 144–153, IEEE, Trento, Italy, September 2012.

[51] Z. Fu, X. Sun, Q. Liu, L. Zhou, and J. Shu, "Achieving efficient cloud search services: multi-keyword ranked search over encrypted cloud data supporting parallel computing," *IEICE Transactions on Communications*, vol. E98B, no. 1, pp. 190–200, 2015.

[52] Z. Xia, X. Wang, X. Sun, and Q. Wang, "A secure and dynamic multi-keyword ranked search scheme over encrypted cloud data," *IEEE Transactions on Parallel and Distributed Systems*, vol. 27, no. 2, pp. 340–352, 2016.

[53] L. Guerrouj, "Normalizing source code vocabulary to support program comprehension and software quality," in *Proceedings of the 35th International Conference on Software Engineering (ICSE '13)*, pp. 1385–1388, San Francisco, Calif, USA, May 2013.

[54] A. De Lucia, M. Di Penta, and R. Oliveto, "Improving source code lexicon via traceability and information retrieval," *IEEE Transactions on Software Engineering*, vol. 37, no. 2, pp. 205–227, 2011.

[55] N. Anquetil and T. C. Lethbridge, "Recovering software architecture from the names of source files," *Journal of Software Maintenance and Evolution*, vol. 11, no. 3, pp. 201–221, 1999.

[56] K. Sartipi and K. Kontogiannis, "A user-assisted approach to component clustering," *Journal of Software Maintenance and Evolution*, vol. 15, no. 4, pp. 265–295, 2003.

[57] T. Ma, J. Zhou, M. Tang et al., "Social network and tag sources based augmenting collaborative recommender system," *IEICE Transactions on Information and Systems*, vol. E98-D, no. 4, pp. 902–910, 2015.

[58] G. Santos, M. T. Valente, and N. Anquetil, "Remodularization analysis using semantic clustering," in *Proceedings of the 1st Software Evolution Week—IEEE Conference on Software Maintenance, Reengineering, and Reverse Engineering (CSMR-WCRE '14)*, pp. 224–233, February 2014.

[59] Z. Xia, X. Wang, X. Sun, and B. Wang, "Steganalysis of least significant bit matching using multi-order differences," *Security and Communication Networks*, vol. 7, no. 8, pp. 1283–1291, 2014.

[60] S. Kawaguchi, P. K. Garg, M. Matsushita, and K. Inoue, "Mudablue: an automatic categorization system for open source repositories," in *Proceedings of the 11th Asia-Pacific Software Engineering Conference (APSEC '04)*, pp. 184–193, Busan, Republic of Korea, December 2004.

[61] A. Kuhn, S. Ducasse, and T. Gîrba, "Enriching reverse engineering with semantic clustering," in *Proceedings of the 12th Working Conference on Reverse Engineering (WCRE '05)*, pp. 133–142, Pittsburgh, Pa, USA, November 2005.

[62] A. Corazza, S. Di Martino, V. Maggio, and G. Scanniello, "Investigating the use of lexical information for software system clustering," in *Proceedings of the 15th European Conference on Software Maintenance and Reengineering (CSMR '11)*, pp. 35–44, IEEE, Oldenburg, Germany, March 2011.

[63] G. Scanniello, M. Risi, and G. Tortora, "Architecture recovery using Latent Semantic Indexing and k-Means: an empirical evaluation," in *Proceedings of the 8th IEEE International Conference on Software Engineering and Formal Methods (SEFM '10)*, pp. 103–112, September 2010.

[64] G. Scanniello, A. D'Amico, C. D'Amico, and T. D'Amico, "Using the Kleinberg algorithm and vector space model for software system clustering," in *Proceedings of the 18th IEEE International Conference on Program Comprehension (ICPC '10)*, pp. 180–189, IEEE, Braga, Portugal, June-July 2010.

[65] G. Scanniello and A. Marcus, "Clustering support for static concept location in source code," in *Proceedings of the IEEE 19th International Conference on Program Comprehension (ICPC '11)*, pp. 36–40, Kingston, Canada, June 2011.

[66] Y. Kong, M. Zhang, and D. Ye, "A belief propagation-based method for task allocation in open and dynamic cloud environments," *Knowledge-Based Systems*, vol. 115, pp. 123–132, 2017.

[67] A. M. Saeidi, J. Hage, R. Khadka, and S. Jansen, "A search-based approach to multi-view clustering of software systems," in *Proceedings of the 22nd IEEE International Conference on Software Analysis, Evolution, and Reengineering (SANER '15)*, pp. 429–438, March 2015.

4

A Novel Multiobjective Programming Model for Coping with Supplier Selection Disruption Risks under Mixed Uncertainties

Ying Li,[1] **Jing Han,**[2,3] **and Liming Yao**[1]

[1]*Business School, Sichuan University, Chengdu 610064, China*
[2]*International Business School, Shaanxi Normal University, Xi'an 710119, China*
[3]*School of Management, Xi'an Jiaotong University, Xi'an 710049, China*

Correspondence should be addressed to Liming Yao; lmyao@scu.edu.cn

Academic Editor: Xiaofeng Xu

Supply chain has become more and more vulnerable to disruption since it is suffering widespread risk issues from inside or outside. Higher uncertainties in the supplier selection problem have gone beyond the traditional cost minimization concern. These uncertainties are related to an ever increasing product variety, more demanding customers, and a highly interconnected distribution network. This paper focuses on the supplier selection problem with disruption risks and mixed uncertainties. A novel multiobjective optimization model with mixed uncertain coefficients is developed, which maximizes the total profits and minimizes the percentage of items delivered late, percentage of items rejected, and total loss cost due to supplier dysfunction. Meanwhile, we also consider the customer demand to be a random fuzzy variable and the unit purchase cost to be a fuzzy variable. By examining a numerical example, we found that the confidence level and demand of customers have impact on the quantities purchased by customers from suppliers although the distribution of suppliers will not change. The cost, quality, and service also influence the selection of suppliers. The superevents have little influence on the distribution of supplier selection; however, when unique event occurs, the distribution of supplier selection will change.

1. Introduction

Risks and uncertainties existing in supply chain increase the analytically complexity, which usually leads to the huge loss or supply chain disruption. Besides the profit, delivered late, and percentage of items rejected, risk and uncertainty management is of key importance to reduce the supply chain vulnerability. There is a common consensus that many sources of threats result in a sharp increase of supplier selection risk in a global supply chain system. For example, the occurrence of disasters and political conflicts could create supply chain disruptions. Some inherent uncertain factors in traditional supply chain such as high supply and demand uncertainties during the operating process make it hard to avoid the risk in supply chain.

Supply chain risks are usually divided into two categories: (i) disruption risks and (ii) operational risks [1]. Focusing on the supplier selection problem, there is no doubt that disruption risk management is one of the critical activities for firms to ensure their effectiveness and competitiveness and achieve the objectives of the whole supply chain. Berger et al. [2] introduced a decision tree model to consider supplier selection under risk and uncertainty in order to identify the optimal number of suppliers in the supply chain. In their work, two types of risks are discussed: catastrophic super events that affect all suppliers and unique events which affect a single supplier. Sawik [3] proposed a stochastic mixed-integer programming approach to cope with joint supplier selection and scheduling problem under disruption risks. Sawik [4] also addressed a fair optimization of cost and customer service level in the presence of supply chain disruption risks. Hamdi et al. [5] presented two integer programming models to determine the supplier selection and order allocation in the presence of disruption risk supplier. Torabi et al. [6] developed a biobjective mixed possibilistic, two-stage stochastic programming model to address supplier selection and order allocation problem to build the resilient supply base under operational and disruption risks. Fahimnia et al. [7] presented a systematic review of the quantitative and analytical models for managing supply chain risks and found that sustainability risk analysis is an emerging and fast evolving research topic. Heckmann et al. [8] studied the review of the definition, measure, and modeling of supply chain risks. Wiengarten et al. [9] explored the role of risk and risk management practices of supply chain integration and found that supplier integration is also effective in weak rule of law (i.e., high risk) environments. The above researches about supply chain risks concentrate on some general nodes of a supply chain but not a type of supply problems with special characteristics. In this paper, we employ three types of risk situation to measure the disruption risk of supplier selection problem: "superevents" such as terrorism or a widespread airline action that put all suppliers down; "unique event" uniquely associated with a particular supplier that puts it down during the supply cycle; and "semisuperevents" that affect a subset of all suppliers, but more than one and not all suppliers.

Higher uncertainties in the supplier selection problem have gone beyond the traditional cost minimization concern. These uncertainties are related to an ever increasing product variety, more demanding customers, and a highly interconnected distribution network. Research on uncertainties in supply chain systems is a timely and important topic nowadays in both academia and industry, and some quantitative models have been gradually developed [10–12]. Memon et al. [13] claimed that supplier selection is highly associated with recognitive and stochastic uncertainties and depends on large amount of domain knowledge. Amorim et al. [14] proposed an integrated framework to determine the supplier in the processed food industry under uncertainty. Moghaddam [15] developed a fuzzy multiobjective mathematical model for decision making of supplier selection under supply and demand uncertainty. Azaron et al. [16] developed a multiobjective stochastic programming approach for minimizing the financial risk or the probability of not meeting a certain budget in a supply chain system under uncertainty. Dickson [17] initially stated five criteria of supplier selection including quality, delivery, performance history, warranty policy, and supplier's production capacity. Some recent researches identified that as quality, cost, and delivery performance history [18], or cost, quality, and time response [19]. Gaballa [20] developed a single-objective, mixed-integer programming model to minimize the total cost. Ghodsypour and O'Brien [21] took the price, storage, and order cost as well as transportation into consideration and developed a mixed-integer nonlinear programming model for minimizing total cost. However, in the practical problems, most of the input parameters are inaccurate, or some of the factors are uncertain. The uncertainty usually results in the widespread risk issues within or external to the supplier selection of a supply chain system. Aghai et al. [22] developed a fuzzy multiobjective programming model containing quantitative and qualitative risk factors as well as quantity discount to propose supplier selection. In their model, late items, rejected items, environment conditions,

and vendor rate are set as qualitative factors (fuzzy), and just unit cost is modeled as quantitative factor. Wu et al. [23] considered both qualitative and quantitative risk factors including vendor ratings, cost, quality, and logistics, which were formulated by some fuzzy data, to decide on supplier selection.

In contrast to much of the extant literature, the contribution and innovation of this paper can be summarized as follows:

(i) Three types of risk events for supplier selection in a supply chain system are introduced: (i) the superevents; (ii) when all suppliers close down during the supply cycle; and (iii) when some, but not all the suppliers, close down.

(ii) We explore a mixed-uncertain situation for supplier selection, in which the customer demand is considered to be a random fuzzy variable and customers' purchase cost, percentage of items being late, and percentage of rejected items are considered to be fuzzy variables.

(iii) A novel multiobjective programming with mixed uncertain coefficients is developed for coping with the supplier selection disruption risk. The proposed model simultaneously maximizes the total profits and minimizes the percentage of items delivered late, percentage of items rejected, and the total loss cost due to supplier dysfunction.

The structure of this paper is as follows: after introducing three types of risk events for supplier selection in a supply chain system, a novel multiobjective programming with mixed uncertain coefficients is developed for coping with the supply chain risk in Section 2; Section 3 presents a comprised solution-based GA to solve the proposed multiobjective programming model; Section 4 examines a numerical example to show the effectiveness of the proposed model; and Section 5 draws the conclusions of the study.

2. Supply Chain Risk Modelling

2.1. Problem Statement and Notations. Supply chain risk management is usually discussed from the four perspectives: (i) disruption risk management, (ii) operational risk control, (iii) disaster and emergency management, and (iv) supply chain service risk analysis. In this study, a supplier selection problem in supply chain systems with disruption risks and uncertainties is considered. In the present problem, three types of risk situations are considered: "*superevents*" such as terrorism or a widespread airline action that put all suppliers down; "*unique event*" uniquely associated with a particular supplier that puts it down during the supply cycle; and "*semisuperevents*" that affect a subset of all suppliers, but more than one and not all suppliers. Following that, a total loss cost objective due to supplier dysfunction is considered in the supplier selection problem. Besides, three traditional objectives including maximizing the total profits and minimizing the percentage of items delivered late and percentage of items rejected are also considered to optimize the selection of suppliers.

In addition to the above complications, there is a great level of inherent uncertainty involved with customers' demand, customers' purchase cost, percentage of items being late, and percentage of rejected items that should be addressed in the decision making context in supplier selection problems. Customers' demand is usually estimated by large amount of historical data and expert's assessment, so it is formulated by a random fuzzy variable. Customers' purchase cost, percentage of items being late, and percentage of rejected items usually depend on large amount of domain knowledge where expert's assessment plays an important role when decision makers have lack of knowledge or small availability of information for different set of suppliers. Therefore, they are assumed as fuzzy variables which are widely used to handle the recognitive uncertainty.

To model and solve the above complex supplier selection problem with disruption risks and mixed uncertainties, a multiobjective mathematical model with mixed uncertain coefficients is formulated by using the following notations for sets, indices, decision variables, and parameters.

Indices

    i: index for the customer

    j: index for the supplier

Parameters

    n_i: number of candidate suppliers required by the ith customer

    s_i: unit selling price for the ith customer

    c_{ij}: unit purchase cost from supplier j by the ith customer

    λ_{ij}: percentage of items being late from supplier j to the ith customer

    k: unit cost of items being late

    τ_{ij}: percentage of rejected items from supplier j

    l: unit cost of rejected items

    D_i: demand for item over planning period from the ith customer

    u_{ij}: maximum amount for the item to be given to supplier j by the ith customer

    w_{ij}: maximum order quantity from supplier j by the ith customer

    π_0: probability of one of the superevents occurring in a supply cycle

    π_j: probability of the unique event occurring in a supply cycle for supplier j

    I_0: random indicator associated with the superevents

    I_j: random indicator associated with the unique event for supplier j

Decision Variables

    x_{ij}: quantity purchased by the ith customer from supplier j

2.2. Modeling. Many traditional models due to the lack of consideration of various demand risks from many different customers usually consider the following objectives and constraints [24]:

    Objective 1: maximize the expected value of total profits comprised by income and costs

    Objective 2: maximize the utility of the number of or rejected items

    Objective 3: maximize the utility of the number of late deliveries

    Constraint 4: ensure that the quantity demand is met

    Constraint 5: ensure that the customer's proposed business to the vendor is not exceeded

    Constraint 6: establish minimum business for selected vendors

    Constraint 7: ensure that there are no negative orders.

A deterministic multiobjective programming model (LMOP) for the supplier selection is presented as follows:

$$\max \quad f_1\left(x_{ij}\right) = \sum_{i=1}^{m} D_i s_i - \sum_{i=1}^{m}\sum_{j=1}^{n_i} c_{ij} x_{ij} \quad \{\text{\#total profits}\}$$

$$\min \quad f_2\left(x_{ij}\right) = l\sum_{i=1}^{m}\sum_{j=1}^{n_i} \tau_{ij} x_{ij} \quad \{\text{\#rejected}\}$$

$$\min \quad f_3\left(x_{ij}\right) = k\sum_{i=1}^{m}\sum_{j=1}^{n_i} \lambda_{ij} x_{ij} \quad \{\text{\#late}\}$$

$$\text{subject to:} \quad \sum_{j=1}^{n_i} x_{ij} \geq D_i, \quad i = 1,\ldots,m \tag{1}$$

$$x_{ij} \leq u_{ij}$$

$\{\text{\#upper business bound set for the purchased amount}\}, \ \forall i, j$

$$x_{ij} \leq w_{ij}$$

$\{\text{\#upper order bound for the purchased amount}\}, \ \forall i, j$

$$x_{ij} \geq 0,$$

where $j = 1, 2, \ldots, n$ represents the possible vendors selected for the ith customer. The model LMOP (1) simultaneously maximizes the total profits $(f_1(x_{ij}))$ and minimizes the percentage of items delivered late $(f_2(x_{ij}))$ and percentage of items rejected $(f_3(x_{ij}))$, while satisfying various constraints with respect to the order quantities.

When any of the above three types of risk situations takes place, the core company, that is, supplier partner, will suffer some loss. The event triggering the loss comes from three sources: (i) the superevents; (ii) when all suppliers close down during the supply cycle; and (iii) when some, but not all the suppliers, close down. We denote by I_0 and I_j the indicator random variable associated with the former two risk situations, respectively. We use $J \in 1, 2, \ldots, n_i$ and π_j to denote the probability of the superevent occurring and unique event occurring for supplier j during the supply cycle, respectively; that is, probability$(I_0 = 1) = P$ and probability$(I_j = 1) = \pi_j$. We denote L_{0j} to be the unit financial loss due to either the superevent occurring on the jth supplier or when all suppliers close down, and we denote by L_P the unit financial loss when some, but not all suppliers, close down.

The first two cases result in the total loss $(x_{ij}L_{0j})$ and the last case results in partial loss $(x_{ij}L_P)$. Thus, the loss cost associated with each set of suppliers n_i can be represented by

$$f(J)$$

$$= \left[I_0 + (1 - I_0) \prod_{j \in J} I_j \right] \sum_{j \in J} \left(L_{0j} x_{ij} \right) \tag{2}$$

$$+ \left[1 - \prod_{j \in J} I_j - \prod_{j \in J} \left(1 - I_j \right) \right] (1 - I_0) \sum_{j \in J} \left(L_P x_{ij} \right).$$

Choi et al. [1] argue that omission of "semisuperevents" loss greatly simplifies the computation while it does not materially affect the salient issues to be analyzed and discussed. When "semisuperevents" loss is omitted, the total loss cost function is reduced to

$$f_4 \left(x_{ij} \right) = \left[I_0 + (1 - I_0) \prod_{j=1}^{n_i} I_j \right] \sum_{j=1}^{n_i} \left(L_{0j} x_{ij} \right). \tag{3}$$

To consider catastrophic, "superevents," which affect many/all suppliers, and "unique events" that affect only a single supplier, we develop the following four-objective programming models by adding objective of minimizing $f_4(x_{ij})$ into the first programming model.

$$\max \quad f_1 \left(x_{ij} \right) = \sum_{i=1}^{m} D_i s_i - \sum_{i=1}^{m} \sum_{j=1}^{n_i} c_{ij} x_{ij}$$

$$\min \quad f_2 \left(x_{ij} \right) = l \sum_{i=1}^{m} \sum_{j=1}^{n_i} \tau_{ij} x_{ij}$$

$$\min \quad f_3 \left(x_{ij} \right) = k \sum_{i=1}^{m} \sum_{j=1}^{n_i} \lambda_{ij} x_{ij}$$

$$\min \quad f_4 \left(x_{ij} \right)$$

$$= \left[I_0 + (1 - I_0) \prod_{j=1}^{n_i} I_j \right] \sum_{j=1}^{n_i} \left(L_{0j} x_{ij} \right) \tag{4}$$

$$\text{subject to:} \quad \sum_{j=1}^{n_i} x_{ij} \geq D_i, \quad i = 1, \dots, m$$

$$x_{ij} \leq u_{ij}, \quad \forall i, j$$

$$x_{ij} \leq w_{ij}, \quad \forall i, j$$

$$x_{ij} \geq 0,$$

where $j = 1, 2, \dots, n_i$ represents the possible vendors selected for the ith customer. The above model simultaneously maximizes the total profits $(f_1(x_{ij}))$ and minimizes the percentage of items delivered late $(f_2(x_{ij}))$, percentage of items rejected $(f_3(x_{ij}))$, and the total loss cost $(f_4(x_{ij}))$ due to supplier dysfunction, while satisfying various constraints with respect to minimum and maximum order quantities.

Customers' demand, which is formulated by a random fuzzy variable, is usually estimated by large amount of historical data and expert's assessment simultaneously. Customers' purchase cost, percentage of items being late, and percentage of rejected items are assumed to be fuzzy variables to handle the recognitive uncertainty due to lack of knowledge and historical data of different set of suppliers. Hence, we suggest a mixed MOP model by allowing $\tilde{\tilde{D}}_i$ to be random fuzzy variable and some parameters in the above model to be fuzzy data [25–28].

$$\max \quad f_1 \left(x_{ij} \right) = \sum_{i=1}^{m} \tilde{\tilde{D}}_i s_i - \sum_{i=1}^{m} \sum_{j=1}^{n_i} \tilde{c}_{ij} x_{ij}$$

$$\min \quad f_2 \left(x_{ij} \right) = l \sum_{i=1}^{m} \sum_{j=1}^{n_i} \tilde{\tau}_{ij} x_{ij}$$

$$\min \quad f_3 \left(x_{ij} \right) = k \sum_{i=1}^{m} \sum_{j=1}^{n_i} \tilde{\lambda}_{ij} x_{ij}$$

$$\min \quad f_4 \left(x_{ij} \right)$$

$$= \left[I_0 + (1 - I_0) \prod_{j=1}^{n_i} I_j \right] \sum_{j=1}^{n_i} \left(L_{0j} x_{ij} \right) \tag{5}$$

$$\text{subject to:} \quad \sum_{j=1}^{n_i} x_{ij} \geq \tilde{\tilde{D}}_i, \quad i = 1, \dots, m$$

$$x_{ij} \leq u_{ij}, \quad \forall i, j$$

$$x_{ij} \leq w_{ij}, \quad \forall i, j$$

$$x_{ij} \geq 0,$$

where "$\simeq$" denotes a random fuzzy variable and "$\sim$" denotes fuzzy variable.

Theorem 1. *Assume that the random variable $\overline{D}_i(\theta)$ is characterized by the following density function:*

$$P_{\overline{D}_i}(x) = \frac{1}{\sqrt{2\pi}\sigma_i} e^{-(x - \bar{\mu}_i(\theta))^2 / 2\sigma_i^2}, \tag{6}$$

where the fuzzy variable $\tilde{u}_i(\theta)$, $\theta \in \Theta$, has the following membership function:

$$\mu_{\tilde{u}_i^D(\theta)}(t) = \begin{cases} L\left(\dfrac{b_i^D - t}{a_i^D} \right), & t \leq b_i^D, \ a_i^D > 0 \\ R\left(\dfrac{t - b_i^D}{c_i^D} \right), & t \geq b_i^D, \ c_i^D > 0, \end{cases} \tag{7}$$

where $a_i{}^D$, $c_i{}^D$ are positive numbers expressing the left and right spreads of $b_i{}^D$ which is the average value of $\tilde{u}_i$. Functions $L, R : [0, 1] \to [0, 1]$ with $L(1) = R(1) = 0$ and $L(0) = R(0) = 1$ are nonincreasing continuous functions. Then we have

$$E\left(\overset{\approx}{D}_i\right) = b_i{}^D + \frac{a_i{}^D}{2}\left[F_L\left(b_i{}^D\right) - F_L\left(a_i{}^D\right)\right] \tag{8}$$
$$+ \frac{c_i{}^D}{2}\left[F_R\left(b_i{}^D\right) - F_R\left(c_i{}^D\right)\right],$$

where $F_L(x)$ and $F_R(x)$ are continuous functions while $F_L'(x) = L(x)$, $x \in [a_i{}^D, b_i{}^D]$, and $F_R'(x) = L(x)$, $x \in [b_i{}^D, c_i{}^D]$.

Proof. The proof can be found in Appendix A. $\square$

Theorem 2. *Assume that the fuzzy parameter $\tilde{c}_{ij}$ is a triangular fuzzy variable, denoted by $(a_{ij}^c, b_{ij}^c, c_{ij}^c)$, $a_{ij}^c > 0$. Then we have*

$$E\left[f_4\left(x_{ij}\right)\right]$$
$$= \left[p\prod_{j=1}^{n_i}\left(1 - \pi_j\right) + (1 - p)\prod_{j=1}^{n_i}\pi_j\right]\sum_{j=1}^{n_i}\left(L_{0j}x_{ij}\right) \tag{9}$$

and for $0 \leq \alpha_i, \beta_i \leq 1$,

$$\mathrm{Ch}\left\{\overset{\approx}{D}_i \leq \sum_{j=1}^{n_i}x_{ij}\right\}(\alpha_i) \geq \beta_i \iff$$
$$b_i{}^D \geq \sum_{j=1}^{n_i}x_{ij} - \sigma\Phi^{-1}\left(\beta_i\right) \tag{10}$$
$$\geq \max\left\{a_i{}^D, b_i{}^D - a_i{}^D L^{-1}\left(\alpha_i\right)\right\}.$$

Proof. The proof can be found in Appendix A. $\square$

Finally, the proposed novel multiobjective programming model for supply chain risk management under mixed uncertainty can be converted into the following deterministic one:

$$\max \quad f_1\left(x_{ij}\right) = E\left(\sum_{i=1}^{m}\overset{\approx}{D}_i s_i - \sum_{i=1}^{m}\sum_{j=1}^{n_i}\tilde{c}_{ij}x_{ij}\right)$$

$$\min \quad f_2\left(x_{ij}\right) = E\left(l\sum_{i=1}^{m}\sum_{j=1}^{n_i}\tilde{\tau}_{ij}x_{ij}\right)$$

$$\min \quad f_3\left(x_{ij}\right) = E\left(k\sum_{i=1}^{m}\sum_{j=1}^{n_i}\tilde{\lambda}_{ij}x_{ij}\right)$$

$$\min \quad f_4\left(x_{ij}\right)$$
$$= \left[p\prod_{j=1}^{n_i}\left(1 - \pi_j\right) + (1 - p)\prod_{j=1}^{n_i}\pi_j\right]\sum_{j=1}^{n_i}\left(L_{0j}x_{ij}\right)$$

$$\text{subject to:} \quad b_i{}^D \geq \sum_{j=1}^{n_i}x_{ij} - \sigma\Phi^{-1}\left(\beta_i\right)$$
$$\geq \max\left\{a_i{}^D, b_i{}^D - a_i{}^D L^{-1}\left(\alpha_i\right)\right\}$$
$$\sum_{j=1}^{n_i}x_{ij} - \sigma\Phi^{-1}\left(\beta_i\right) \geq b_i{}^D,$$
$$i = 1,\ldots,m, \ \alpha_i \geq 0, \ \beta_i \geq 0$$
$$x_{ij} \leq \min\left\{u_{ij}, w_{ij}\right\} \quad \forall i, j$$
$$x_{ij} \geq 0, \tag{11}$$

where $E(\overset{\approx}{D}_i) = b_i{}^D + (a_i{}^D/2)[F_L(b_i{}^D) - F_L(a_i{}^D)] + (c_i{}^D/2)[F_R(b_i{}^D) - F_R(c_i{}^D)]$, $E(\tilde{c}_{ij}) = (a_{ij}^c + 2b_{ij}^c + c_{ij}^c)/4$, $E(\tilde{\beta}_{ij}) = (a_{ij}^\beta + 2b_{ij}^\beta + c_{ij}^\beta)/4$, and $E(\tilde{\lambda}_{ij}) = (a_{ij}^\lambda + 2b_{ij}^\lambda + c_{ij}^\lambda)/4$.

3. Comprised Solution-Based Genetic Algorithm

Genetic algorithms (GAs) have received considerable attention regarding their potential for providing a novel approach to multiobjective optimization problems, resulting in a fresh body of research and applications known as genetic multiobjective optimizations. For many real world problems, the set of Pareto solutions may be very large, so it is hard to solve them. In addition, to evaluate a large set of Pareto solutions and to select the best one pose a considerable cognitive burden on the decision maker. Therefore, in this case, obtaining the entire set of Pareto solutions is of little interest to decision makers. For overcoming such difficulties, Gen and Cheng [29] proposed a compromise approach which aims to search for compromise solutions instead of generating all Pareto solutions.

The compromise approach can be regarded as a kind of mathematical formulation of goal-seeking behavior in terms of a distance function. In this case, the compromise approach is given as follows: Suppose the ideal point of the decision maker is $f_k^*(x_{ij})$. For each feasible solution x_{ij}, the regret function $r(x_{ij}, 2)$ is defined as follows:

$$r\left(x_{ij}, 2\right) = \left[\sum_{k=1}^{4}w_k^2\left(f_k\left(x_{ij}\right) - f_k^*\left(x_{ij}\right)\right)^2\right]^{1/2}, \tag{12}$$

where weights $w = (w_1, w_2, w_3, w_4)$ are assigned to signal different degrees of importance. Hereby, we use a proxy ideal point introduced by Ghodsypour and O'Brien [21] to replace the ideal point $f_k^*(x_{ij})$. Above all, we illustrate the compromise solution-based genetic algorithm procedure as follows and the pseudocodes can be found in Appendix B.

Step 0. Input the parameters including the number of chromosomes ($N_{\text{pop-size}}$), crossover probability (P_λ), and mutation probability (P_m).

Step 1. Initialize $N_{\text{pop-size}}$ chromosomes by randomly searching in the feasible region.

TABLE 1: Some parameters $(\widetilde{c}_{ij}, \widetilde{\tau}_{ij}, \widetilde{\lambda}_{ij})$ for suppliers and customers.

	1	2	3	4	5
1	(0.8, 0.9, 1)	(0.7, 0.75, 0.8)	(0.93, 0.97, 1.01)	(0.8, 0.86, 0.92)	(0.55, 0.58, 0.61)
	(0.008, 0.01, 0.012)	(0.018, 0.02, 0.022)	(0.013, 0.014, 0.015)	(0.025, 0.027, 0.029)	(0.016, 0.017, 0.018)
	(0.01, 0.02, 0.03)	(0.027, 0.03, 0.033)	(0.023, 0.025, 0.027)	(0.018, 0.02, 0.022)	(0.04, 0.041, 0.042)
2	(0.86, 0.85, 0.87)	(0.59, 0.6, 0.61)	(0.84, 0.85, 0.86)	(0.98, 0.99, 0.1)	(0.97, 0.98, 0.99)
	(0.01, 0.011, 0.012)	(0.02, 0.021, 0.022)	(0.03, 0.037, 0.041)	(0.005, 0.0051, 0.0052)	(0.06, 0.061, 0.062)
	(0.01, 0.02, 0.03)	(0.031, 0.033, 0.035)	(0.031, 0.032, 0.033)	(0.021, 0.022, 0.023)	(0.03, 0.04, 0.05)
3	(1, 1.01, 1.02)	(0.84, 0.87, 0.9)	(0.9, 0.91, 0.92)	(0.99, 1, 1.01)	(1.01, 1.02, 1.03)
	(0.027, 0.028, 0.029)	(0.014, 0.015, 0.016)	(0.018, 0.02, 0.022)	(0.008, 0.01, 0.012)	(0.025, 0.027, 0.029)
	(0.018, 0.02, 0.022)	(0.032, 0.035, 0.038)	(0.027, 0.03, 0.033)	(0.01, 0.02, 0.03)	(0.033, 0.04, 0.047)
4	(0.91, 0.93, 0.95)	(0.9, 0.92, 0.94)	(0.98, 1, 1.02)	(1, 1.02, 1.04)	(0.96, 0.98, 1)
	(0.021, 0027, 0.033)	(0.02, 0.03, 0.04)	(0.005, 0.0051, 0.0052)	(0.03, 0.037, 0.041)	(0.0134, 0.0135, 0.0136)
	(0.02, 0.024, 0.028)	(0.022, 0.024, 0.026)	(0.025, 0.029, 0.034)	(0.01, 0.02, 0.03)	(0.034, 0.036, 0.038)
5	(0.98, 1, 1.02)	(0.96, 0.98, 1)	(1.01, 1.03, 1.05)	(1, 1.02, 1.04)	(1.02, 1.03, 1.04)
	(0.008, 0.01, 0.012)	(0.02, 0.021, 0.022)	(0.008, 0.01, 0.012)	(0.01, 0.011, 0.012)	(0.027, 0.028, 0.029)
	(0.015, 0.018, 0.021)	(0.032, 0.035, 0.038)	(0.032, 0.035, 0.038)	(0.017, 0.02, 0.023)	(0.0366, 0.037, 0.0376)
6	(0.97, 1, 1.03)	(0.96, 0.97, 0.98)	(0.74, 0.76, 0.78)	(1, 1.01, 1.02)	(0.99, 1.01, 1.03)
	(0.024, 0.026, 0.028)	(0.018, 0.02, 0.022)	(0.006, 0.0061, 0.0062)	(0.013, 0.014, 0.015)	(0.023, 0.0233, 0.0236)
	(0.015, 0.02, 0.025)	(0.027, 0.03, 0.033)	(0.02, 0.03, 0.04)	(0.023, 0.025, 0.027)	(0.03, 0.039, 0.048)
7	(0.85, 0.87, 0.89)	(0.81, 0.82, 0.83)	(0.9, 0.92, 0.94)	(0.86, 0.87, 0.88)	(0.86, 0.88, 0.9)
	(0.024, 0.0245, 0.025)	(0.026, 0.026, 0.026)	(0.03, 0.037, 0.041)	(0.008, 0.01, 0.012)	(0.022, 0.023, 0.024)
	(0.02, 0.02, 0.02)	(0.02, 0.03, 0.04)	(0.031, 0.032, 0.033)	(0.01, 0.02, 0.03)	(0.03, 0.04, 0.05)
8	(0.99, 1, 1.01)	(0.98, 1, 1.02)	(1.18, 1.2, 1.22)	(0.86, 0.88, 0.9)	(0.95, 0.98, 1.01)
	(0.01, 0.0112, 0.0124)	(0.013, 0.014, 0.015)	(0.05, 0.051, 0.052)	(0.025, 0.027, 0.029)	(0.0122, 0.0123, 0.0124)
	(0.01, 0.02, 0.03)	(0.023, 0.025, 0.027)	(0.021, 0.03, 0.039)	(0.0015, 0.019, 0.024)	(0.03, 0.04, 0.05)
9	(0.99, 1, 1.01)	(0.96, 0.98, 1)	(1.01, 1.03, 1.05)	(0.58, 0.6, 0.62)	(0.73, 0.75, 0.77)
	(0.018, 0.02, 0.022)	(0.027, 0.028, 0.029)	(0.02, 0.022, 0.024)	(0.02, 0.021, 0.022)	(0.02, 0.03, 0.04)
	(0.025, 0.03, 0.035)	(0.022, 0.024, 0.026)	(0.03, 0.033, 0.036)	(0.029, 0.03, 0.031)	(0.035, 0.039, 0.044)
10	(0.99, 1, 1.01)	(1, 1.01, 1.02)	(1.02, 1.03, 1.04)	(0.96, 0.97, 0.98)	(0.98, 1.01, 1.04)
	(0.001, 0.002, 003)	(0.008, 0.01, 0.012)	(0.013, 0.014, 0.015)	(0.023, 0.024, 0.025)	(0.052, 0.053, 0.054)
	(0.028, 0.03, 0.032)	(0.01, 0.02, 0.03)	(0.031, 0.032, 0.033)	(0.023, 0.025, 0.027)	(0.035, 0.04, 0.045)

Step 2. Update the chromosomes by crossover and mutation operations after checking the feasibility of offspring.

Step 3. Compute the fitness of each chromosome on the basis of the regret value.

Step 4. Select the chromosomes by spinning the roulette wheel.

Step 5. Repeat the second to fourth steps for a given number of cycles.

Step 6. Output the best chromosome as the optimal solution.

4. Numerical Example

A supply chain with five suppliers and ten customers is listed in Table 1, which covers the unit purchase cost from supplier j by the ith customer, percentage of items late from supplier j to the ith customer, and percentage of rejected units from supplier j. The demand $\widetilde{D}_i$ assumed

TABLE 2: Demand data of customers.

Customer	μ_i	σ_i	s_i
D1	(28, 30, 32)	1.0	10
D2	(26, 28, 30)	1.0	9.5
D3	(21, 22, 23)	1.2	10.5
D4	(17, 18, 19)	0.8	8
D5	(14.5, 15, 15.5)	0.7	7.5
D6	(12, 13, 14)	1.0	10
D7	(11, 12, 13)	0.9	9
D8	(11, 12, 13)	0.6	7.5
D9	(11.5, 12, 12.5)	0.7	9
D10	(11.5, 11, 11.5)	0.9	10

to be distributed as $N(\widetilde{u}_i, \sigma_i^2)$ for a given period is listed in Table 2. The retailer must anticipate demand and order quantities of the modeled good to be delivered to arrive on time at each demand destination. Profit could be obtained from sales with successfully goods delivery to each demand.

TABLE 3: Solutions with different confidence levels.

	x_{11}	x_{31}	x_{41}	x_{71}	x_{81}
$\alpha_i = 0.9$	31.08	23.436	18.924	13.052	12.668
$\beta_i = 0.9$	x_{101}	x_{22}	x_{62}	x_{53}	x_{94}
	12.602	29.08	14.18	15.846	12.796
	x_{11}	x_{31}	x_{41}	x_{71}	x_{81}
$\alpha_i = 0.75$	30.87	23.18	18.75	12.86	12.54
$\beta_i = 0.75$	x_{101}	x_{22}	x_{62}	x_{53}	x_{94}
	12.41	28.87	13.97	15.69	12.65
	x_{11}	x_{31}	x_{41}	x_{71}	x_{81}
$\alpha_i = 0.6$	30.44	22.66	18.40	12.48	12.28
$\beta_i = 0.6$	x_{101}	x_{22}	x_{62}	x_{53}	x_{94}
	12.03	28.44	13.54	15.40	12.35

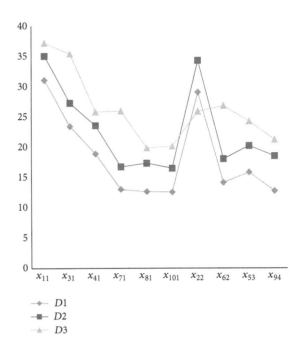

FIGURE 1: Solutions with different customer demands.

The corresponding selling price s_i is listed in Table 3. Costs are probabilistic as outlined above, but total cost of goods sales has a mean given for each source supplier. Goods not passing quality acceptance level are not paid for. Goods delivered late are paid for at a reduced rate and are carried forward at an inventory cost. We then set $u_{ij} = w_{ij} = 50$. Furthermore, following Choi et al. [1], we assume deterministic loss and operating cost. Therefore, we also have $L_{0j} = 50$ ($j = 1, 2, \ldots, 5$), $P = 0.02$, and $\pi_1 = \pi_2 = \pi_3 = \pi_4 = \pi_5 = 0.05$. It is a natural state that both the probability of one of the superevents and the probability of the unique event occurring during the supply cycle for supplier are normal.

Table 1 lists the value of each triangular fuzzy parameter. For example, the set of data in the 1st row 1st column denotes the unit purchased cost $\tilde{c}_{11}$ (0.8, 0.9, 1), the percentage of rejected items $\tilde{\tau}_{11}$ (0.008, 0.01, 0.012), and the percentage of items late $\tilde{\lambda}_{11}$ (0.01, 0.02, 0.03) from the 1st supplier to the 1st customer, respectively. These data could be set by analyzing the distributing of correlative historical data collected by each supplier. Take $\tilde{c}_{11}$, for example. The 1st supplier analyzes the data of unit purchased cost within past 10 periods and finds the data is distributed in [0.8, 1]. We depict it with triangular fuzzy parameter. Ten demand sites have been modeled in the same way. Different conditions could be modeled with little difficulty other than scale.

The x_{ij} in Table 3 means that the chosen supplier j by the customer i and the set of solution achieve the optimal value of objective functions. Table 3 shows that, in the condition that makes other parameters changeless, the value of solutions can be affected by the different α_i and β_i while the distributing of solutions unaltered. In the following sections, we concentrate on the influence from the parameters $\tilde{\tilde{D}}_i, \tilde{c}_{ij}, \tilde{\tau}_{ij}$, and $\tilde{\lambda}_{ij}$ to the solutions. We fix up the parameter of confidence level ($\alpha_i = 0.9; \beta_i = 0.9$).

As we know, the parameter $\tilde{\tilde{D}}_i$ denotes the demand for item over planning period from the ith customer. $\tilde{\tilde{D}}_i$ is a random fuzzy variable with the mean μ_i and the variance σ_i. Different sets of μ_i and σ_i are given in Table 4 and the corresponding sets of x_{ij} are listed in Figure 1.

Parameter $\tilde{c}_{ij}$ denotes the purchasing cost from the supplier to customers. The value of the cost always changed with the market. We assume different groups of $\tilde{c}_{ij}$ and the results in Table 5.

In Table 5, $C1$ denotes the situation of the mean of costs of all suppliers having increased 0.1, $C2$ denotes the situation of the mean of the purchasing costs of the 1st supplier having increased 0.1, and $C3$ denotes the situation of the mean of the purchasing costs of the 1st and 2nd supplier having increased. The results show that the distribution of solutions alters along with the alteration of $\tilde{c}_{ij}$. Videlicet, the cost is one of the factors which lead customers to select the supplier.

We then set three groups of $\tilde{\tau}_{ij}$, the parameter of percentage of rejected items from supplier. Table 6 and Figure 2 show the results. $T1$ denote the original situation. $T2$ denote the situation of the percentage of rejected items of the 4th and 5th suppliers having been reduced and $T3$ for that of the 1st and 2nd having been increased.

The results show that the distribution of solutions varies along with the alteration of $\tilde{\tau}_{ij}$, and the parameter of items delayed by suppliers λ_{ij} also impacts the distribution of solutions.

The foregoing computation and analysis are based on a common state that both the probability of one of the superevents and the probability of the unique event occurring during the supply cycle for supplier are normal. In Table 7, we assume three kinds of risk situations, denoted as $R1$ (the common state), $R2$ (the probability of superevents increased and all the unit financial loss L_{0j} ($j = 1, 2, \ldots, 5$) increased accordingly), and $R3$ (the probability of unique event occurring for the 1st and 2nd supplier increased and the unit financial loss L_{01} and L_{02} altered simultaneity). Figure 3 shows the solutions.

The results show that superevents have no influence on the distribution of solutions. The customers take the same

TABLE 4: Different customer demands.

$\widetilde{D}_{i1}$	μ_i	σ_i	$\widetilde{D}_{i2}$	μ_i	σ_i	$\widetilde{D}_{i3}$	μ_i	σ_i
D1	(30, 34, 38)	1.0	D1	(28, 30, 32)	1.2	D1	(34, 36, 32)	1.2
D2	(28, 32, 36)	1.0	D2	(26, 28, 30)	1.2	D2	(32, 34, 36)	1.2
D3	(23, 26, 29)	1.2	D3	(21, 22, 23)	1.4	D3	(33, 34, 35)	1.4
D4	(19, 22, 25)	0.8	D4	(17, 18, 19)	1.0	D4	(23, 24, 25)	1.0
D5	(16.5, 19, 21.5)	0.7	D5	(14.5, 15, 15.5)	0.9	D5	(20.5, 21, 21.5)	0.9
D6	(14, 17, 20)	1.0	D6	(12, 13, 14)	1.2	D6	(24, 25, 26)	1.2
D7	(13, 16, 19)	0.9	D7	(11, 12, 13)	1.1	D7	(23, 24, 25)	1.1
D8	(13, 16, 21)	0.6	D8	(11, 12, 13)	0.8	D8	(17, 18, 19)	0.8
D9	(13.5, 16, 18.5)	0.7	D9	(11.5, 12, 12.5)	0.9	D9	(17.5, 18, 18.5)	0.9
D10	(13.5, 15, 19.5)	0.9	D10	(11.5, 11, 11.5)	1.1	D10	(17.5, 18, 19.5)	1.1

TABLE 5: Solutions with different costs.

	x_{11}	x_{31}	x_{41}	x_{71}	x_{81}
C1	31.08	23.436	18.924	13.052	12.668
	x_{101}	x_{22}	x_{62}	x_{53}	x_{94}
	12.602	29.08	14.18	15.846	12.796
C2	x_{41}	x_{71}	x_{101}	x_{12}	x_{22}
	18.924	13.052	12.602	31.08	29.08
	x_{32}	x_{62}	x_{53}	x_{84}	x_{94}
	23.436	14.18	15.846	12.668	12.796
C3	x_{41}	x_{22}	x_{62}	x_{53}	x_{14}
	18.924	29.08	14.18	15.846	31.08
	x_{34}	x_{74}	x_{84}	x_{94}	x_{104}
	23.436	13.052	12.668	12.796	12.602

TABLE 6: Solutions with different percentage of rejected items.

	x_{11}	x_{31}	x_{41}	x_{71}	x_{81}
T1	31.08	23.436	18.924	13.052	12.668
	x_{101}	x_{22}	x_{62}	x_{53}	x_{94}
	12.602	29.08	14.18	15.846	12.796
T2	x_{41}	x_{71}	x_{22}	x_{62}	x_{53}
	18.924	13.052	29.08	14.18	15.846
	x_{34}	x_{84}	x_{94}	x_{104}	x_{15}
	23.436	12.668	12.796	12.602	31.08
T3	x_{23}	x_{53}	x_{63}	x_{14}	x_{34}
	29.08	15.846	14.18	31.08	23.436
	x_{44}	x_{74}	x_{84}	x_{94}	x_{104}
	18.924	13.052	12.668	12.796	12.602

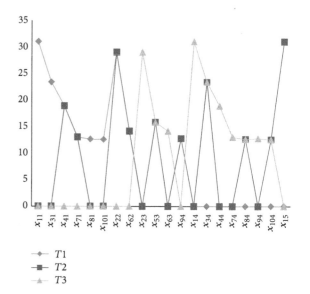

FIGURE 2: Solutions with different percentage of rejected items.

decision making with the common state since the risk of each supplier is unchanged to customers. When unique event occurs for some suppliers, however, the distribution of solutions altered which means that the customer leans to the suppliers with lower probability of risk situations.

In the following parts, we will discuss the relation between the expected value of total profits and the total loss of risk in our model. Generally, people extend the demand for item and the selling price or reduce the costs in order to achieve

more profits. However, it is hard to control the variance of the selling price and costs of item, which are usually dominated by the fluctuation of market. It is reasonable and effective to adjust the parameters of demand. According to the MOP model and the analysis above, the value of solutions increases with the mean value of $\widetilde{D}_i$ added, and the value of total loss of risk increases simultaneously. We list several groups of parameter $\widetilde{D}_i$, the corresponding relation between the expected value of total profits and the total loss of risk shown in Figure 4 which indicates the loss of risk while achieving more profits.

According to the analysis and computation above, this random fuzzy MOP with risk objective model reminds the decision maker that more profits bring more risk. In addition, the model indicates that quantity purchased (x_{ij}) is impacted by both customer and supplier. The distribution of x_{ij}, which denotes the choosing of supplier from the customer, is affected by the costs (c_{ij}), the quality (τ_{ij}), the service (λ_{ij}), and the risk situations of different suppliers. The quantity (x_{ij}) is determined mostly by the demand of customers $\widetilde{D}_i$.

TABLE 7: Solutions with different percentage of rejected items.

$P = 0.02$	x_{11}	x_{31}	x_{41}	x_{71}	x_{81}
$\pi_j = 0.05$	31.08	23.436	18.924	13.052	12.668
$L_{0j} = 50$	x_{101}	x_{22}	x_{62}	x_{53}	x_{94}
$(j = 1, 2, \ldots, 5)$	12.602	29.08	14.18	15.846	12.796
$P = 0.08$	x_{11}	x_{31}	x_{41}	x_{71}	x_{81}
$\pi_j = 0.05$	31.08	23.436	18.924	13.052	12.668
$L_{0j} = 60$	x_{101}	x_{22}	x_{62}	x_{53}	x_{94}
$(j = 1, 2, \ldots, 5)$	12.602	29.08	14.18	15.846	12.796
$P = 0.02, \pi_1 = 0.1$	x_{23}	x_{53}	x_{63}	x_{14}	x_{34}
$\pi_j = 0.05, j = 2, \ldots, 5$	29.08	15.846	14.18	31.08	23.436
$L_{01} = 60,$	x_{44}	x_{74}	x_{84}	x_{94}	x_{104}
$L_{0j} = 50, j = 2, \ldots, 5$	18.924	13.052	12.668	12.796	12.602

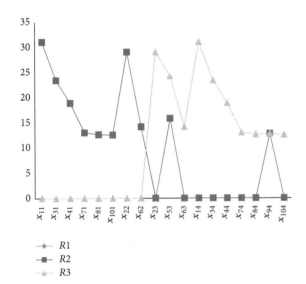

FIGURE 3: Solutions with different risk situations.

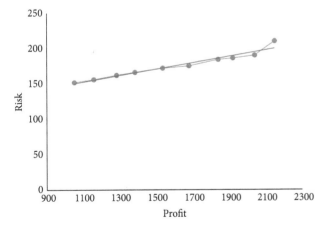

FIGURE 4: Relation between profits and risk.

5. Managerial Implications

Some implications about the contribution of our research to the supplier selection management and supply chain risk management are summarized as follows.

To consider catastrophic, "superevents," which affect many/all suppliers, and "unique events" that affect only a single supplier, effective forecast of the uncertainty and its possible impact on suppliers could help us make right supplier selection strategy. Furthermore, risk-averse ability could be taken as one of the important criteria for choosing the best suppliers.

In management practice, beyond traditional supplier selection system, by considering customer demand and unit purchase cost, we provide the decision maker with a simple tool for coordinating the flows of parts from suppliers to customers. The approach allows the managers to structure the distribution of cost or customer service level by selecting the optimal supply combination and scheduling of customer orders.

Application of the novel multiobjective programming with mixed uncertain coefficients could help the companies cope with the supply chain risk. The proposed model simultaneously maximizes the total profits and minimizes the percentage of items delivered late, percentage of items rejected, and the total loss cost due to supplier dysfunction.

6. Conclusion

Through analyzing three types of risk events in a supply chain system, (i) the superevents; (ii) when all suppliers close down during the supply cycle; and (iii) when some, but not all the suppliers, close down, we proposed a novel multiobjective programming with mixed uncertain coefficients developed for managing the supply chain risk. In this model, the customer demand is considered to be a random fuzzy variable and unit purchase cost is considered to be a fuzzy variable due to their uncertainty. According to the expected value and chance constraint operators, the uncertain model was converted into a deterministic one. By examining a numerical example, we found that (1) the confidence level and demand of customers have impact on the quantities purchased by customers from suppliers although the distribution of suppliers will not change; (2) the cost, the quality, and the service also influence the selection of suppliers; and (3) the superevents had little influence on the distribution of supplier selection; however, when unique event occurs, the distribution of supplier selection will change.

Some other uncertainty and risk types are not considered in the present study. It is of great importance to further examine this issue in future research.

Appendix

A. Proof of Theorems

Proof of Theorem 1. Since $\overline{D}_i(\theta)$ is a random variable with the mean $\tilde{u}_i(\theta)$ and the variance σ_i^2, then $E[\overset{\approx}{D}_i(\theta)] = \tilde{u}_i(\theta)$ is a fuzzy variable. By the membership function $\mu_{\tilde{u}_i(\theta)}(t)$ of $\tilde{u}_i(\theta)$ and the definition of credibility measure, we have

$$\mathrm{Cr}\left\{\theta \mid E\left[\overset{\approx}{D}_i(\theta)\right] \geq t\right\}$$
$$= \begin{cases} 1, & t \leq a_i^D \\ 1 - \dfrac{1}{2}L\left(\dfrac{b_i^D - t}{a_i^D}\right), & a_i^D \leq t \leq b_i^D \\ \dfrac{1}{2}R\left(\dfrac{t - b_i^D}{c_i^D}\right), & b_i^D \leq t \leq c_i^D \\ 0, & t \geq c_i^D. \end{cases} \tag{A.1}$$

It follows, from the definition of the expected value operator of random fuzzy variables, that

$$\begin{aligned} E\left[\overset{\approx}{D}_i\right] &= \int_0^{+\infty} \mathrm{Cr}\left\{\theta \in \Theta \mid E\left[\overset{\approx}{D}_i(\theta)\right] \geq t\right\} dt \\ &\quad - \int_{-\infty}^0 \mathrm{Cr}\left\{\theta \in \Theta \mid E\left[\overset{\approx}{D}_i(\theta)\right] \leq t\right\} dt \\ &= \int_0^{a_i^D} 1\, dt + \int_{a_i^D}^{b_i^D}\left[1 - \frac{1}{2}L\left(\frac{b_i^D - t}{a_i^D}\right)\right] dt \\ &\quad + \int_{b_i^D}^{c_i^D} \frac{1}{2}R\left(\frac{t - b_i^D}{c_i^D}\right) \\ &= b_i^D + \frac{a_i^D}{2}\left[F_L\left(b_i^D\right) - F_L\left(a_i^D\right)\right] \\ &\quad + \frac{c_i^D}{2}\left[F_R\left(b_i^D\right) - F_R\left(c_i^D\right)\right], \end{aligned} \tag{A.2}$$

where $F_L(x)$ and $F_R(x)$ are continuous functions while $F_L'(x) = L(x)$, $x \in [a_i^D, b_i^D]$, $F_R'(x) = L(x)$, and $x \in [b_i^D, c_i^D]$. This completes the proof. □

Proof of Theorem 2. According to Dickson [17] and Håkansson and Snehota [18], we have that

$$\begin{aligned} E\left(\tilde{c}_{ij}\right) &= \int_0^{+\infty} \mathrm{Cr}\left\{\tilde{c}_{ij} \geq r\right\} dr - \int_{-\infty}^0 \mathrm{Cr}\left\{\tilde{c}_{ij} \leq r\right\} dr \\ &= \frac{\left(a_{ij}^c + 2b_{ij}^c + c_{ij}^c\right)}{4}. \end{aligned} \tag{A.3}$$

```
Input: Initial data and GA parameters
Output: Optimal solutions and objective values
Begin
    t ← 1;
    initialization P(N_pop-size) by feasibility check;
    fitness eval(P);
    while (not termination condition) do
        selection();
        crossover();
        mutation();
        evaluation(t)
        t ← t + 1;
    end
    Output: Optimal solutions and objective values
end
```

PSEUDOCODE 1: Comprised solution-based GA.

For the risk objective $f_4(x_{ij})$, in which I_0 and I_j indicate random variable and lead the uncertainty, we use expected value operator of random variable in order to reduce the anticipative risk.

$$\begin{aligned} E\left[f_4\left(x_{ij}\right)\right] \\ = E\left\{\left[I_0 + (1 - I_0)\prod_{j=1}^{n_i} I_j\right]\sum_{j=1}^{n_i}\left(L_{0j}x_{ij}\right)\right\}. \end{aligned} \tag{A.4}$$

From the preanalysis, we have

$$\begin{aligned} P\left(I_0 = 1, I_j = 0\right) &= p\prod_{j=1}^{n_i}\left(1 - \pi_j\right), \\ P\left(I_0 = 0, I_j = 1\right) &= (1 - p)\prod_{j=1}^{n_i}\pi_j. \end{aligned} \tag{A.5}$$

It follows that

$$\begin{aligned} E\left[f_4\left(x_{ij}\right)\right] \\ = p\prod_{j=1}^{n_i}\left(1 - \pi_j\right)\sum_{j=1}^{n_i}\left(L_0 x_{ij}\right) \\ + (1 - p)\prod_{j=1}^{n_i}\pi_j\sum_{j=1}^{n_i}\left(L_{0j}x_{ij}\right) \\ = \left[p\prod_{j=1}^{n_i}\left(1 - \pi_j\right) + (1 - p)\prod_{j=1}^{n_i}\pi_j\right]\sum_{j=1}^{n_i}\left(L_{0j}x_{ij}\right). \end{aligned} \tag{A.6}$$

According to the chance constraint, we have that, for $0 \leq \alpha_i$, $\beta \leq 1$,

$$\mathrm{Ch}\left\{\tilde{\bar{D}}_i \le \sum_{j=1}^{n_i} x_{ij}\right\}(\alpha_i) \ge \beta_i \iff$$

$$\mathrm{Pos}\left\{\theta \mid \mathrm{Pr}\left\{\overline{D}_i(\theta) \le \sum_{j=1}^{n_i} x_{ij}\right\} \ge \beta_i\right\} \ge \alpha_i \iff$$

$$\mathrm{Pos}\left\{\Phi\left(\frac{\sum_{j=1}^{n_i} x_{ij} - \tilde{\mu}_i^D(\theta)}{\sigma}\right) \ge \beta_i\right\} \ge \alpha_i \iff$$

$$\mathrm{Pos}\left\{\theta \mid \tilde{\mu}_i^D(\theta) \le \sum_{j=1}^{n_i} x_{ij} - \sigma\Phi^{-1}(\beta)\right\} \ge \alpha_i \iff \tag{A.7}$$

$$\alpha_i \le \begin{cases} 0, & \text{if } \sum_{j=1}^{n_i} x_{ij} - \sigma\Phi^{-1}(\beta_i) \le a_i^D \\ L\left(\dfrac{b_i^D - \left[\sum_{j=1}^{n_i} x_{ij} - \sigma\Phi^{-1}(\beta_i)\right]}{a_i^D}\right), & \text{if } a_i^D \le \sum_{j=1}^{n_i} x_{ij} - \sigma\Phi^{-1}(\beta_i) \le b_i^D \iff \\ 1, & \text{if } \sum_{j=1}^{n_i} x_{ij} - \sigma\Phi^{-1}(\beta_i) \ge b_i^D \end{cases}$$

$$\sum_{j=1}^{n_i} x_{ij} - \sigma\Phi^{-1}(\beta_i) \ge \max\left\{a_i^D, b_i^D - a_i^D L^{-1}(\alpha_i)\right\},$$

where Ch{·} denotes the chance of the random fuzzy event and possibility α_i and probability β_i are specified confidence levels. This completes the proof. □

B. Pseudo Codes

See Pseudocode 1.

Competing Interests

The authors declare that they have no competing interests.

Acknowledgments

This research was supported by the National Natural Science Foundation for Young Scholars of China (Grant nos. 71301109 and 71403158), the Western and Frontier Region Project of Humanity and Social Sciences Research, Ministry of Education of China (Grant no. 13XJC630018), the Social Science Planning Project of Sichuan Province (Grant no. SC16A006), and China Postdoctoral Science Foundation Funded Project (Grant no. 2016M590960).

References

[1] T. M. Choi, C. H. Chiu, and H. K. Chan, "Risk management of logistics systems," *Transportation Research Part E: Logistics and Transportation Review*, vol. 90, pp. 1–6, 2016.

[2] P. D. Berger, A. Gerstenfeld, and A. Z. Zeng, "How many suppliers are best? A decision-analysis approach," *Omega*, vol. 32, no. 1, pp. 9–15, 2004.

[3] T. Sawik, "Joint supplier selection and scheduling of customer orders under disruption risks: single vs. dual sourcing," *Omega*, vol. 43, pp. 83–95, 2014.

[4] T. Sawik, "On the fair optimization of cost and customer service level in a supply chain under disruption risks," *Omega*, vol. 53, pp. 58–66, 2015.

[5] F. Hamdi, L. Dupont, A. Ghorbel, and F. Masmoudi, "Supplier selection and order allocation under disruption risk," *IFAC-PapersOnLine*, vol. 49, no. 12, pp. 449–454, 2016.

[6] S. A. Torabi, M. Baghersad, and S. A. Mansouri, "Resilient supplier selection and order allocation under operational and disruption risks," *Transportation Research Part E: Logistics and Transportation Review*, vol. 79, pp. 22–48, 2015.

[7] B. Fahimnia, C. S. Tang, H. Davarzani, and J. Sarkis, "Quantitative models for managing supply chain risks: a review," *European Journal of Operational Research*, vol. 247, no. 1, pp. 1–15, 2015.

[8] I. Heckmann, T. Comes, and S. Nickel, "A critical review on supply chain risk—definition, measure and modeling," *Omega*, vol. 52, pp. 119–132, 2015.

[9] F. Wiengarten, P. Humphreys, C. Gimenez, and R. McIvor, "Risk, risk management practices, and the success of supply chain integration," *International Journal of Production Economics*, vol. 171, pp. 361–370, 2016.

[10] A. F. Guneri, A. Yucel, and G. Ayyildiz, "An integrated fuzzy-lp approach for a supplier selection problem in supply chain management," *Expert Systems with Applications*, vol. 36, no. 5, pp. 9223–9228, 2009.

[11] Z. Liao and J. Rittscher, "A multi-objective supplier selection model under stochastic demand conditions," *International Journal of Production Economics*, vol. 105, no. 1, pp. 150–159, 2007.

[12] G. Büyüközkan and G. Çifçi, "A novel fuzzy multi-criteria decision framework for sustainable supplier selection with incomplete information," *Computers in Industry*, vol. 62, no. 2, pp. 164–174, 2011.

[13] M. S. Memon, Y. H. Lee, and S. I. Mari, "Group multi-criteria supplier selection using combined grey systems theory and uncertainty theory," *Expert Systems with Applications*, vol. 42, no. 21, pp. 7951–7959, 2015.

[14] P. Amorim, E. Curcio, B. Almada-Lobo, A. P. F. D. Barbosa-Póvoa, and I. E. Grossmann, "Supplier selection in the processed food industry under uncertainty," *European Journal of Operational Research*, vol. 252, no. 3, pp. 801–814, 2016.

[15] K. S. Moghaddam, "Fuzzy multi-objective model for supplier selection and order allocation in reverse logistics systems under supply and demand uncertainty," *Expert Systems with Applications*, vol. 42, no. 15-16, pp. 6237–6254, 2015.

[16] A. Azaron, K. N. Brown, S. A. Tarim, and M. Modarres, "A multi-objective stochastic programming approach for supply chain design considering risk," *International Journal of Production Economics*, vol. 116, no. 1, pp. 129–138, 2008.

[17] G. W. Dickson, "An analysis of vendor selection: system and decisions," *Journal of Purchasing*, vol. 1, pp. 5–17, 1966.

[18] H. Håkansson and I. Snehota, "No business is an island: the network concept of business strategy," *Scandinavian Journal of Management*, vol. 22, no. 3, pp. 256–270, 2006.

[19] D. L. Olson and D. Wu, "Simulation of fuzzy multiattribute models for grey relationships," *European Journal of Operational Research*, vol. 175, no. 1, pp. 111–120, 2006.

[20] A. A. Gaballa, "Minimum cost allocation of tenders," *Journal of the Operational Research Society*, vol. 25, no. 3, pp. 389–398, 1974.

[21] S. H. Ghodsypour and C. O'Brien, "The total cost of logistics in supplier selection, under conditions of multiple sourcing, multiple criteria and capacity constraint," *International Journal of Production Economics*, vol. 73, no. 1, pp. 15–27, 2001.

[22] S. Aghai, N. Mollaverdi, and M. S. Sabbagh, "A fuzzy multi-objective programming model for supplier selection with volume discount and risk criteria," *The International Journal of Advanced Manufacturing Technology*, vol. 71, no. 5-8, pp. 1483–1492, 2014.

[23] D. D. Wu, Y. Zhang, D. Wu, and D. L. Olson, "Fuzzy multi-objective programming for supplier selection and risk modeling: a possibility approach," *European Journal of Operational Research*, vol. 200, no. 3, pp. 774–787, 2010.

[24] C. A. Weber and J. R. Current, "A multiobjective approach to vendor selection," *European Journal of Operational Research*, vol. 68, no. 2, pp. 173–184, 1993.

[25] J. Xu and L. Yao, *Random-Like Multiple Objective Decision Making*, Springer, 2011.

[26] J. Xu and X. Zhou, *Fuzzy-Like Multiple Objective Decision Making*, Springer, Berlin, Germany, 2011.

[27] C.-T. Chen, "A fuzzy approach to select the location of the distribution center," *Fuzzy Sets and Systems*, vol. 118, no. 1, pp. 65–73, 2001.

[28] D. Petrovic, R. Roy, and R. Petrovic, "Supply chain modelling using fuzzy sets," *International Journal of Production Economics*, vol. 59, no. 1, pp. 443–453, 1999.

[29] M. Gen and R. Cheng, *Genetic Algorithms and Engineering Optimization*, John Wiley & Sons, New York, NY, USA, 2000.

5

A Hybrid Programming Framework for Modeling and Solving Constraint Satisfaction and Optimization Problems

Paweł Sitek and Jarosław Wikarek

Department of Information Systems, Kielce University of Technology, 25-314 Kielce, Poland

Correspondence should be addressed to Paweł Sitek; sitek@tu.kielce.pl

Academic Editor: Can Özturan

This paper proposes a hybrid programming framework for modeling and solving of constraint satisfaction problems (CSPs) and constraint optimization problems (COPs). Two paradigms, CLP (constraint logic programming) and MP (mathematical programming), are integrated in the framework. The integration is supplemented with the original method of problem transformation, used in the framework as a presolving method. The transformation substantially reduces the feasible solution space. The framework automatically generates CSP and COP models based on current values of data instances, questions asked by a user, and set of predicates and facts of the problem being modeled, which altogether constitute a knowledge database for the given problem. This dynamic generation of dedicated models, based on the knowledge base, together with the parameters changing externally, for example, the user's questions, is the implementation of the autonomous search concept. The models are solved using the internal or external solvers integrated with the framework. The architecture of the framework as well as its implementation outline is also included in the paper. The effectiveness of the framework regarding the modeling and solution search is assessed through the illustrative examples relating to scheduling problems with additional constrained resources.

1. Introduction

Constraint satisfaction problems (CSPs) and/or constraint optimization problems (COPs) can involve the variables that take values over finite domains (integer, real, binary, etc.) and constraints of all types and characters [1]. By connecting variables, constraints affect the feasible variable domain ranges. Modeling and solving of those problems make up one of the major interest areas of various computer science communities, including operation research, mathematical programming, constraint programming, and artificial intelligence. Problems with constraints like CSP and COP are frequent in production, distribution, transportation, logistics, computer networks, software engineering, project management, planning and scheduling, and so forth. One of the features resulting from the users' changeable expectations is the need to solve the problem multiple times for variable data instances and parameters. Users express their expectations by asking all kinds of questions. On the one hand, the question is related to the possibility of realizing the task with certain resources at the defined time; on the other hand,

it concerns optimal parameters of task realization, and it is about the optimal configuration of the system. Quite often, the questions include logical conditions (e.g., relating to mutual exclusion, dynamic connecting of resources). Because of the changeability of the questions, parameters, and data instances, the idea of autonomous search seems to be the most suitable for solving the problems with constraints. The autonomous search should have the ability to preferably modify and change its internal components when exposed to changing external parameters, requirements, and/or data instances [2].

The underlying motivation for this study was the idea of developing a programming and implementation platform, which would allow effective modeling and solving of CSPs and COPs and solving these problems in an automatic mode (using the autonomous search) despite changes in data instances, parameters, and questions asked by users. The idea was implemented as a hybrid programming framework. To build the framework, the authors used hybridization of various programming paradigms and their own original method of transformation. In addition, the authors proposed a dynamic method for generating dedicated models, based on the knowledge database made up of facts, predicates, and questions asked by users.

2. Backgrounds, Methods, and Structures

Models for problems with constraints need environments that allow modeling and solving the constraints in an easy and effective way. Historically, operations research, in particular, mathematical programming, network programming, and dynamic programming, and so forth, has been used for this purpose. Numerous models (MIP-mixed integer programming, MILP-mixed integer linear programming, IP-integer programming, etc.), algorithms (branch and bound, symplex, branch and cost, etc.), and good practices have been developed to facilitate solving problems with constraints [3]. All these methods and models, however, have some limitations concerning the character of constraints (e.g., only linear constraints) or the character of variables (e.g., only real variables), and so forth. For different types of constraints (nonlinear, logical, etc.) and/or decision variables (integer, binary, etc.), they were either inapplicable or ineffective. For the approach to be most universal and suitable, a given problem must be looked at from the perspective of variables and connecting constraints with the domains of variables taken into account. Constraint logic programming (CLP) paradigm allows this approach. Constraint logic programming (CLP) is a form of constraint programming (CP) paradigm, where logic programming is extended to include CSP (constraint satisfaction problem). CLP programs are built from valid Prolog-based logic data structures. A program is a collection of predicates, and a predicate is a collection of clauses. The idea of a clause is to define that something is true. The simplest form of a clause is the fact. For example, the following two are facts: technology (product, machine, and execution_time) and vehicle (capacity, type, and cost). Syntactically, a fact is just a structure (or an atom) terminated by a full stop [4].

CSP is a triple $(X, \text{Dom}, \text{Cst})$ where $X = \{X_1, X_2, \ldots, X_m\}$ represents a set of m decision variables, $\text{Dom} = \{\text{Dom}^1, \text{Dom}^2, \ldots, \text{Dom}^m\}$ represents the set of associated domains (i.e., possible values for decision variables), and $\text{Cst} = \{\text{Cst}^1, \text{Cst}^2, \ldots, \text{Cst}^n\}$ represents a set of n constraints. Constraints fall into several types depending on the number of decision variables in a constraint (unary, binary, and n-ary). A unary constraint is a constraint on a single decision variable (e.g., $X \neq 6$, $Y < 6$). A binary constraint is a constraint over a pair of decision variables (e.g., $X > Y$, $X + Y < 8$). In general, a n-ary constraint has a scope of size n decision variables [1].

Each constraint Cst^i binds a set of decision variables and is used to restrict domains of these variables. Solving a CSP means finding the state/condition of a problem, in which the assignment of decision variables satisfies all constraints. The general algorithm for solving a CSP is shown in Figure 1. The algorithm consists of constraint propagation and variable distribution activated in the sequence. If this sequence does not provide a result, backtracking is used and sequence activation is repeated. The algorithm is very effective for

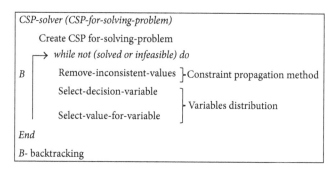

FIGURE 1: The general scheme of the algorithm to solve CSP.

solving the problems, in which aryness of constraints does not exceed 2. The CSP algorithm is often ineffective in the case of the problems in which constraints connect more than two decision variables and the optimization problems with constraints (COPs). The effectiveness of propagation is reduced significantly and the number of backtrackings increases. In extreme cases, the algorithm is able to neither find any feasible solution within the allowable time nor ascertain its absence.

In order to overcome this shortcoming, suggestions of integrating the CP/CLP paradigms with other paradigms occurred. Since the areas are similar, constraints and decision variables, the integration usually relates to the paradigm of mathematical programming [5–9].

Several scenarios of CP/CLP and MP integration have been reported in the literature [10]:

(i) Double modeling uses both CP and MP models and exchanges information while solving.

(ii) Search-inference duality views CP and MP methods as special cases of a search/inference duality.

(iii) Decomposition decomposes problems into a CP part and an MP part using a Benders scheme.

In the approach proposed in this paper, the scenario for the integration of both paradigms is supplemented with the authors' own method of problem transformation [11–13] and the idea of autonomous search [12]. All these components are connected and integrated into the programming hybrid framework (Section 3).

The method of problem transformation [11, 13] proposed by authors (Section 3.2) is briefly speaking, the transformation of the search space performed by removing all points and areas in which decision variables cannot occur, thus reducing the size of this space. Transformations are usually performed through changing the problem specification and adding the transformed model (with reduced and transformed decision variables and constraints). The transformation is conducted on the basis of facts, attributes, and constraints. The idea of autonomous search (Section 3.3) is implemented through the transformation method and automatic model generation. The models are generated dynamically using adequate CLP predicates, based on the current set of input facts (data instances), knowledge database (with facts and predicates describing a given problem), and question(s) asked by users. Both

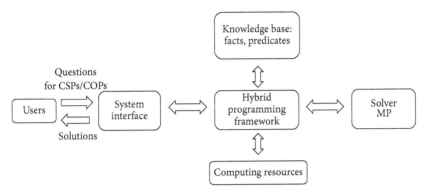

FIGURE 2: The concept of hybrid programming framework and its environment.

the input facts and the questions can change dynamically, which leads to new model generation/formation.

The main contribution of this study is the concept and implementation of the hybrid programming framework, which joins the ideas of (i) hybridization in the form of integration of MP and CLP, (ii) presolving in the form of transformation and constraint propagation, and (iii) autonomous search in the form of automatic generation of dedicated models to solve. Additionally, formal models of the scheduling problems for the illustrative examples before and after transformation are included.

3. The Concept of Hybrid Programming Framework Using Idea of an Autonomous Search

Based on the experience of hybridization and integration of CP/CLP/MP [5–8, 11, 13], the hybrid programing framework to modeling and solving CSPs and COPs has been proposed.

The main assumptions used in the concept and implementation of the hybrid programming framework were as follows:

(i) Integration of CLP and MP environments.

(ii) Introducing the framework presolving methods in the form of transformation and constraint propagation.

(iii) Knowledge base, which contains predicates for constraints, questions, methods, tools, and so forth and facts for data instances.

(iv) Implementation autonomous search in the form of automatic models generation for CSPs and COPs as the MP/MIP/MILP models based on knowledge base (constraints, questions, and data facts).

(v) The ability to solve MIP/MILP/MP models by internal and external solvers (LINGO [14] or SCIP [15] in this version of framework).

(vi) Replacing the variable distribution methods (Figure 1) through MP methods and algorithms (e.g., branch and bound, cutting plane, relaxation, etc.).

(vii) Implementation of the framework using the CLP environment (ECL^{i}PS^e system [16]).

3.1. Architecture of Hybrid Programming Framework. Figure 2 shows a context scheme of the framework. The framework communicates with the knowledge database, the user, and the external MP solver(s). The knowledge database, which de facto is a part of the framework, consists of a set of various types of predicates, including those most simple facts. The data instances of a given problem are saved as facts. Relationships between individual facts define the information structure of the problem. Predicates and facts may concern different problems modeled and solved using the framework and for this reason they are identified through the problem index (id_pro). The set of facts can be logically divided into two subsets: the subset of constant facts describing the problem and the subset changing the input facts. A user communicates with the framework by sending an inquiry/question in a suitable format and structure:

$$\text{Question (type, parameters, ID\_pro)}. \quad (1)$$

The question determines what problem will be solved, with what parameters (i.e., which facts will be used), and defines the type of the question (which evaluation criterion will be used). An appropriate dedicated model will be generated depending on the formalization of this question, in particular, on its type.

Predicates can be logically divided into several groups. Particular groups of predicates (except for facts) that create the knowledge base are shown in Description of the Group Predicates.

A simplified functional scheme of the framework is shown in Figure 3; Algorithm 1 depicts the underlying/basic scenario of the framework operation, in the form of a pseudocode.

The user's question initiates the framework operation. The structure of the question in (1) defines the type of the question (general, wh-question, logical, etc.) and type of the problem and its detailed parameters (time, number of resources, size, etc.). Depending on the question, adequate information is extracted about the problem, data instances, problem size, and so forth.

Based on this information, the framework downloads suitable facts and predicates from the knowledge database. The facts are converted into lists. The reference model is built in CLP for a CSP or COP (variables and constraints).

While *new question*
    Determining the type of the problem (based of questions)
    Determining the parameters of the question
    Determining the size of the problem (based on facts)
    Initiate basic variables
    Load data about the problem from set of facts
    Basic constraints (load predicates)
    while *additional conditions resulting from question*
        Initiate additional variables
        Additional constraints (load predicates)
    Starting **constraint propagation**
    if *transformation of the problem* **then**
        Transformation
        Starting **constraint propagation**
    Determining the type of the MP Solver
    Generation of the MP model in the Solver format or MPS
    Start Solver

ALGORITHM 1: The basic scenario of the framework operation.

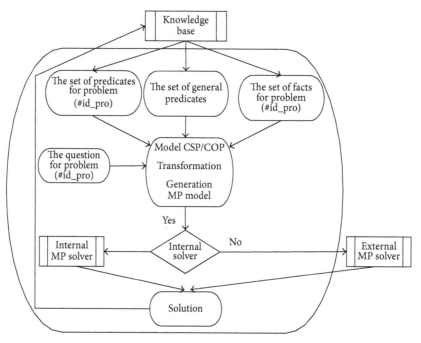

FIGURE 3: The functional diagram of hybrid programming framework.

The model can be supplemented with additional constraints, including logic constraints if necessary. In the next step, the model is subjected to presolving. Two presolving methods are used in the framework, usually alternately: constraint propagation and transformation. After presolving, the model is the basis for generating the final implementation model in the form of an MP model (usually MILP). The MP model is then solved using an MP solver.

3.2. Transformation. Transformation has been studied by the authors [11, 13]. It consists in changing the specification of a problem to eliminate unacceptable/nonfeasible points from the solution space prior to solving the problem. As a result,

the number of decision variables is reduced and aggregated and the constraints are simplified and also the numbers of constraints is reduced, which leads to a smaller search space and, hence, shorter search time and the possibility to solve problems of larger size within allowable time limits. Facts and problem constraints are used in the process of transformation. Transformation and constraint propagation are presolving methods applied in the framework. In real practical problems, the transformation may involve the removal of unacceptable transportation routes in SCM problems [13] and the change of the problem specification from operational to resource type in task group scheduling [17], and so forth. For the illustration example (Section 4), the transformation relies on the change problem representation through the appropriate aggregation of indices. For allowable values of indices of machines and products, an aggregated implementation index is created, the values of which are determined based on feasible values of base indices ((2a), (2b)). Details of the transformation in terms of indices, decision variables, constraints, and facts for the illustration example are presented in Section 4 and Appendices D.1 and D.2.

3.3. Autonomous Search. Autonomous search, as used in the framework, is the narrowing of the search space through the implementation of presolving methods and automatic generation of dedicated implementation models. Both the presolving methods (constraint propagation and transformation) and model generation are based on current data instances. Users' questions are also taken into account while constructing the model. The questions may be related only to some of the aspects and constraints of the problem. Based on the current data, instances and users' questions ensure that the automatically generated models are dedicated and fit the specific situation. Such dedicated models have fewer decision variables and constraints.

This shortens the search time (the search space is considerably reduced relative to that in universal models). A change of the question and/or data instance results in a new model adjusted to new parameters.

4. Illustrative Example and Computational Experiments

Practical use of framework for modeling and solving problems will be presented for illustrative example. As an illustrative example was selected job-shop scheduling problem with additional resources [18, 19]. Problems of this type can be found in manufacturing, logistics, computer networks, software engineering, and so forth.

Formally, the illustrative example is an extension variant of job-shop scheduling problem and can be defined as follows. A set of LI jobs/orders/products $I = \{I_1, I_2, \ldots, I_{LI}\}$ are given which require, for their processing, a set of LM machines $M = \{M_1, M_2, \ldots, M_{LM}\}$ and a set of LR additional resources $R = \{R_1, R_2, \ldots, R_{LR}\}$. Each additional resource R_r has a specified limit ko_r (number of units of the resource R_k). Each job/order I_i is a sequence of k operations. The kth operation of job/order I_i has to be executed by a specific machine $M_k \in M$ for time units ($tr_{i,k}$ is integer). Generally, in job-shop problems, a feasible schedule is such that (a) at any time each machine can execute at most one operation, (b) the operations of the same job/order are totally ordered, and (c) no preemption is allowed. Moreover, in our example, any time, each operation can be assisted by additional resources R_r where $d_{i,m,r}$ determines how much additional resources R_r are used to execute job/order I_i on machine $M_k \in M$. Additional resources can be operators, tools, memory, transportation units, and so forth while basic resources are the machines/processors/workstations. A formal model of a scheduling problem for illustrative example, containing constraints, decision variables, and parameters, is shown in

Appendix D.1. The collection of facts together with their structure for this model is included in Figure 4 (as the lowest layer of the information structure).

Both the proposed model and the structure of facts constitute a significant extension of the classical job-shop scheduling problem (JSSP) [18, 19]. Firstly, they allow accounting for additional resources R, as described above. Secondly, the structure of constraints of the model, decision variables, and facts is universal and can describe not only job-shop scheduling problems but also those in other environments including flow-shop, open-shop, project, multiproject, and so forth.

Modeling starts with loading the set of facts for illustrative example to the knowledge base. Then, the facts are converted into lists using a general predicate (P1). In the next step, the set of predicates (P2) is created. This set implements the basic and additional/logic constraints for illustrative example. Then, the built or expanded set of predicates (P3) implements various types of questions (e.g., as in the exemplified questions asked to the illustrative example) for illustrative example. In the next step, predicates to transform modeled problem (P4) are taken from the knowledge base. Transformation for illustrative example involves the aggregation of the relevant facts (indexes of these facts) and building a list of only the feasible combinations of facts. The principle of the transformation of the facts for illustrative example is shown in Figure 5.

Exemplified questions asked to the illustrative example are as follows

(Q1) What is the min C_{max} (makespan)?

(Q2$_A$) What is the min C_{max} if the set of additional resources is $ko_1 = ko_2 = ko_3 = ko_4 = 2$?

(Q2$_B$) What is the min C_{max} if the set of additional resources is $ko_1 = ko_2 = ko_3 = ko_4 = 3$?

(Q3) What is the minimum set of resources R_1 at C'_{max}?

(Q4) Is it possible to schedule orders in C'_{max} and what are the sets of resources R_1, R_2, R_3, R_4?

(Q5) Is it possible to schedule orders in C'_{max} if resources R_1 and R_4 cannot be used simultaneously?

(Q6) Is it possible to schedule orders in C'_{max} if machines M_7 and M_9 cannot be used simultaneously?

(Q7) What is the min C_{max} if resources R_1 and R_4 cannot be used simultaneously?

(Q8$_A$) What is the min C_{max} if machines M_1 and M_2 cannot be used simultaneously?

(Q8$_B$) What is the min C_{max} if machines M_7 and M_9 cannot be used simultaneously?

The resulting list L_index for facts from Appendix B.1 are presented in the Appendix B.2. Indices (the dimensions of the problem), decision variables, and constraints of the model are also subject to transformation. The transformation of indices (2a) stems from the fact that not every product i has to be manufactured on every machine m. Thus, if product i is made on a specific machine m, the existing values of index pair

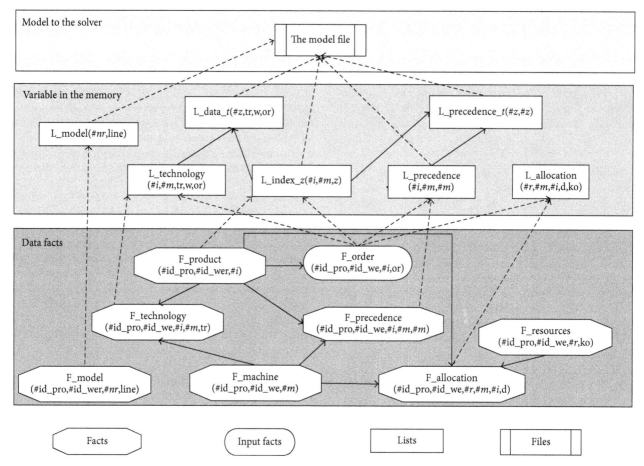

FIGURE 4: The information structure for illustrative example implemented in hybrid programming framework.

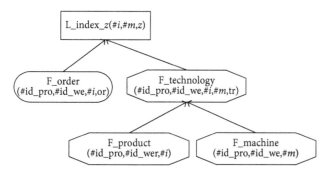

FIGURE 5: The principle of the transformation of the facts for illustrative example.

(i, m) are replaced with the values of aggregated/transformed index z. In the next step, the decision variables are subjected to transformation as a result of the aggregation of some of their indexes (2b). The set of all decision variables of the model before and after transformation are presented in Appendices D.1 and D.2, respectively. In the final stage, the constraints of the model transformed through the change (reduction) of summations and "for" phrase for the individual constraints. The constraints for model before and after

the transformation are included in Appendices D.1 and D.2, respectively:

$$(i, m) \longrightarrow (z) \tag{2a}$$

$$X_{i,m,r,t} \longrightarrow X_{z,r,t} \mid \mathrm{Kp}_{i,m} \longrightarrow \mathrm{Kp}_z \mid Y_{i,m,r,t} \longrightarrow Y_{z,r,t}. \tag{2b}$$

The final step is the generation of a dedicated MILP model (files in the appropriate solver format or Mathematical Programming System (MPS)) using universal set of predicates for automatic generation (P5). Schematic structure of information for illustrative example in the form of facts, lists, and files is shown in Figure 4 and the description is shown in Table 3.

The scenario of computational experiments was as follows. For any questions from the exemplified questions asked to the illustrative example and a given set of data instances (Appendix B.1), the generation of dedicated MILP models have been made using a hybrid programming framework. After that, the automatically generated models were solved using the external MP solvers like "LINGO" [14] or "SCIP" [15]. Choosing solver "SCIP" was due to its high efficiency and the use of the built-in powerful presolving methods [15]. As for the efficiency and effectiveness in the area of MP and CP, SCIP is the best option of all noncommercial solvers [15].

TABLE 1: Results for asked questions to the illustrative example (framework implementation).

Questions	V	C	Parameters	Answer	T_1	T_2
Q1	3070	16377	—	$\min C_{max} = 22$	7	6
Q2$_A$	3070	16377	$ko_1 = ko_2 = ko_3 = ko_4 = 2$	$\min C_{max} = 26$	316	146
Q2$_B$	3070	16377	$ko_1 = ko_2 = ko_3 = ko_4 = 3$	$\min C_{max} = 22$	60	28
Q3	3070	16377	$C'_{max} = 24$	$ko_{1min} = 2,$	2	2
Q4	3270	16678	$C'_{max} = 24$	Yes $\quad ko_1 = 3, ko_2 = 4, ko_3 = 4, ko_4 = 2$	2	2
			$C'_{max} = 20$	No	1	1
			$C'_{max} = 23$	Yes $\quad ko_1 = 4, ko_2 = 4, ko_3 = 3, ko_4 = 2$	2	1
Q5	3266	16623	$C'_{max} = 24$	NO	2	2
			$C'_{max} = 30$	YES	12	6
Q6	3560	16917	$C'_{max} = 24$	NO	3	2
			$C'_{max} = 26$	YES	6	2
Q7	3266	16623		$\min C_{max} = 27$	16	8
Q8$_A$	3560	16917		$\min C_{max} = 22$	6	5
Q8$_B$	3560	16917		$\min C_{max} = 26$	4	3

TABLE 2: Results for asked questions to the illustrative example (MP implementation).

Questions	V	C	Parameters	Answer	T_1	T_2
Q1	70604	75343	—	$C_{max} = 22$	128	67
Q2$_A$	70604	75343	$ko_1 = ko_2 = ko_3 = ko_4 = 2$	$C_{max} = 26$	3756	1546
Q2$_B$	70604	75343	$ko_1 = ko_2 = ko_3 = ko_4 = 3$	$C_{max} = 22$	546	234

$\min C_{max}$: optimal makespan.
C'_{max}: given makespan.
V: the number of decision variables.
C: the number of constraints.
T_1: time of finding solution (in seconds) in LINGO.
T_2: time of finding solution (in seconds) in SCIP.

CPLEX and Gurobi are certainly faster in solving the same benchmarks, but being commercial solvers, they mean higher costs (licenses, etc.).

Obtained results are shown in Table 1. The scope of the exemplified questions asked to the illustrative example shows the flexibility and capabilities of a hybrid programming framework. These are general questions (Q4, Q5, and Q6) and specified questions (Q1, Q2$_A$, Q2$_B$, and Q3), which require both optimal and feasible solutions. In addition, questions can be logical (Q7, Q8), whose modeling directly in an MP environment is not obvious and simple. To determine the effectiveness of the proposed framework for questions Q1, Q2$_A$, and Q2$_B$ (for the most demanding computing), models were generated using the framework (Table 1) and modeled using only the classical mathematical programming (Table 2). Then, both groups of models were solved using LINGO and SCIP solvers. The answers to these questions using the framework are obtained 10 to 20 times faster than using just the pure MP solvers. In each case, the use of "SCIP" solver accelerated calculations twofold in comparison with the "LINGO" solver, with the "LINGO" solver (see columns T_1 and T_2 of Tables 1 and 2).

The models generated using the framework, respectively, have 20 times smaller number of decision variables and 3 times smaller number of constraints in relation to the models created only in MP environments.

The model file for Q1 questions in a format compatible with the "LINGO" is shown in Appendix C.

The file was generated by group predicates P5 on the basis of the information structure (Figure 5).

5. Conclusions

The proposed hybrid framework can be used in two modes. Firstly, it can be a platform for the end user to solve the COP and the CSP, which are generated and solved on the basis of existing knowledge base, but also the questions asked by the user. Secondly, it is a programming framework for modeling and solving the COP and the CSP. In this case, the user must know the environment CLP. For each new problem, users supplement the knowledge base of relevant predicates in P2 and P3 sets (see Description of the Group Predicates).

The concept of hybrid programming framework that combines (a) two programming paradigms (CLP/MP); (b) the presolving methods (transformation and constraint propagation); (c) autonomous search; and (d) the automatic generation of dedicated implementation models is the flexible and efficiency solution. Flexibility and easiness of modeling problems are caused by CLP-based approach which by nature is declarative. Efficiency is the result of applying the presolving methods, dedicated implementation models, and mathematical programming for solving. The idea of autonomous

TABLE 3: Description of the facts, lists, and parameters for the illustrative example.

Facts	Keys	Parameters
Facts about structure of the problem		
F_product (#id_pro, #id_wer, #i)	#id_pro: problem ID #id_wer: version of the data instances #i: product ID	
F_machine (#id_pro, #id_wer, #m)	#id_pro: problem ID #id_wer: version of the data instances #m: machine ID	
F_technology (#id_pro, #id_wer, #i, #m, parameters)	#id_pro: problem ID #id_wer: version of the data instances #i: product ID #m: machine ID	$tr_{i,m}$: the execution time of the product i on the machine m
F_precedence (#id_pro, #id_we, #i, #m, #m)	#id_pro: problem ID #id_wer: version of the data instances #i: product ID #m: machine ID	
F_resources (#id_pro, #id_we, #r, parameters)	#id_pro: problem ID #id_wer: version of the data instances #r: additional resource ID	ko_r: the total number of additional resources r
F_allocation (#id_pro, #id_we, #r, #m, #i, parameters)	#id_pro: problem ID #id_wer: version of the data instances #r: additional resource ID #m: machine ID #i: product ID	$d_{i,m,r}$: the number of additional resources r needed to execute a product i on the machine m
F_model (#id_pro, #id_wer, #nr, parameters)	#id_pro: problem ID #id_wer: version of the data instances #nr: model ID	$line_{nr}$: line of code for model ID
F_order (#id_pro, #id_we, #i, parameters)	#id_pro: problem ID #id_wer: version of the data instances #i: product ID	or_i: the size of the order for product i
Lists		
L_precedence (#i, #m, #m)	#m: machine ID #i: product ID	
L_technology (#i, #m, parameters)	#i: product ID #m: machine ID	$tr_{i,m}$: the execution time of the product i on the machine m; $w_{i,m}$: if the product i is executed on the machine m, $w_{i,m} = 1$; otherwise, $w_{i,m} = 0$; or_i: the size of the order for product i
L_allocation (#r, #m, #i, parameters)	#r: additional resource ID #m: machine ID #i: product ID	$d_{i,m,r}$: the number of additional resources r needed to execute a product i on the machine m; ko_r: the total number of additional resources r
L_model (#nr, parameters)	#nr: model ID	$line_{nr}$: line of code for model ID
L_index_z (#i, #m, parameters)	#i: product ID #m: machine ID	z: the new index after transformation
L_data_t (#z, parameters)	#z: the new index after transformation (combination of #i and #m)	tr_z: the execution time of the product i on the machine m; w_z: if the product i is executed on the machine, $w_z = 1$; otherwise, $w_z = 0$; or_z: the size of the order for product i
L_precedence_t (#z, #z)	#z: the new index after transformation (combination of #i and #m)	

search is implemented mainly through the mechanism of automatic generation of implementation models based on current data instances and the requirements of users (in the form of frequently asked questions) which means that models are better suited to current requirements and conditions and their solution requires less space search. The knowledge base of the framework, which is built from predicates and facts, provides scalability because knowledge base can be updated with new facts relating to existing models, predicates, and facts of new models and the facts resulting in answers to user questions and so on.

Further research will focus on two directions/areas. The first is to use a framework for modeling and solving other problems in the area of widely understood computer science. The second is the integration framework with other paradigms such as fuzzy logic and concurrent programming.

A new remotely accessible (e.g., in the cloud [20]) version of the framework is going to be developed. For licensing reasons, LINGO solver will be replaced by SCIP in this version.

Appendix

A. Summary Facts, Lists, and Parameters for Illustrative Example

See Table 3.

B. Data Instances for Illustrative Example

B.1. The Sets of Facts for Illustrative Example. See Algorithm 2.

B.2. The List of New Indices after Transformation. See Algorithm 3.

C. MILP Model Automatically Generated by Framework (Set of Predicates P5) in LINGO Format

See Algorithm 4.

D. Formal Models for Illustrative Example

D.1. Formal/Mathematical Model for Illustrative Example

Indices

m: machine/processor/workstation $m = 1, \ldots, LM$,

i: product/service type $i = 1, \ldots, LI$,

r: additional resource (employees, tools, transport units, etc.) $r = 1, \ldots, LR$,

t: period $t = 1, \ldots, LT$.

Parameters

$\text{tr}_{i,m}$: the time required to make a product i on the machine m,

$w_{i,m}$: if the product i is made using a machine m, then $w_{i,m} = 1$; otherwise, $w_{i,m} = 0$,

ko_r: the number of additional resource types r,

$d_{i,m,r}$: if the additional resource r is used to make the product i on the machine m, then $d_{i,m,r}$ determines the number of additional resources r necessary for this execution; otherwise, $d_{i,m,r} = 0$,

$d1_{i,m,r}$: if the additional resource r is used to make the product i on the machine m, then $d1_{i,m,r} = 1$; otherwise, $d1_{i,m,r} = 0$,

$do_{i,m1,m2}$: if the operation of the product i on the machine $m1$ to be executed before the operation on the machine $m2$, then $do_{i,m1,m2} = 1$; otherwise, $do_{i,m1,m2} = 0$.

Inputs

or_i: demand/order for product i.

Auxiliary Parameters

op_t: coefficient for conversion number of periods t for the variable $op_t = t$.

Decision Variables

$X_{i,m,r,t}$: if the additional resource r in period t is used to make the product i on the machine m, then $X_{i,m,r,t} = 1$; otherwise, $X_{i,m,r,t} = 0$,

$Kp_{i,m}$: the number of last periods in which the product i is made on the machine m,

$Y_{i,m,r,t}$: if the period t is the latest in which the additional resource r is used to make the product i on the machine m, then $Y_{i,m,r,t} = 1$; otherwise, $Y_{i,m,r,t} = 0$,

$C_{\max}$: Makespan.

Constraints

(1) $Kp_{i,m} \leq C_{\max} \ \forall i = 1, \ldots, LI, m = 1, \ldots, LM$.

Determination of the makespan.

(2) $\sum_{t=1}^{LT} d1_{i,m,r} \cdot w_{i,m} \cdot X_{i,m,r,t} = \text{tr}_{i,m} \cdot or_i \ \forall i = 1, \ldots, LI, m = 1, \ldots, LM, r = 1, \ldots, LR : \text{tr}_{i,m} > 0$.

The allocation of resources r to the machine during product realization.

(3) $\sum_{i=1}^{LI} \sum_{r=1}^{LR} d1_{i,m,r} X_{i,m,r,t} \leq 1 \ \forall m = 1, \ldots, LM, t = 1, \ldots, LT$.

The allocation of at most one product to the machine in a given period of time.

(4) $\sum_{i=1}^{LI} \sum_{m=1}^{LM} d_{i,m,r} \cdot X_{i,m,r,t} \leq \text{ko}_r \ \forall r = 1, \ldots, LR, t = 1, \ldots, LT$.

The limited availability of resources (capacity constraints).

(5) $X_{i,m,r,t-1} - X_{i,m,r,t} \leq Y_{i,m,r,t-1} \ \forall i = 1, \ldots, LI, m = 1, \ldots, LM, r = 1, \ldots, LM, t = 2, \ldots, LT$.

$\sum_{t=1}^{LT} Y_{i,m,r,t} \leq 1 \ \forall i = 1, \ldots, LI, m = 1, \ldots, LM, r = 1, \ldots, LM$.

Operations cannot be interrupted.

```
%F_machine(#M).
F_machine(M1).  F_machine(M2).  F_machine(M3).  F_machine(M4).  F_machine(M5).
F_machine(M6).  F_machine(M7).  F_machine(M8).  F_machine(M9).  F_machine(M10).
F_machine(M11). F_machine(M12).
%F_product(#I).
F_product(A). F_product(B). F_product(C). F_product(D). F_product(E).
F_product(F). F_product(G). F_product(H). F_product(I). F_product(J).
F_product(K). F_product(L). F_product(M). F_product(N). F_product(O).
%technology(#I,#M,tr).
F_technology(A,M1,1).   F_technology(A,M2,2).   F_technology(A,M3,2).
F_technology(A,M10,1).  F_technology(B,M1,1).   F_technology(B,M5,2).
F_technology(B,M8,1).   F_technology(C,M4,2).   F_technology(C,M9,4).
F_technology(D,M5,2).   F_technology(D,M6,2).   F_technology(D,M7,5).
F_technology(D,M8,2).   F_technology(E,M1,2).   F_technology(E,M2,1).
F_technology(E,M3,2).   F_technology(E,M4,2).   F_technology(F,M5,2).
F_technology(F,M6,2).   F_technology(G,M3,1).   F_technology(G,M5,2).
F_technology(G,M8,2).   F_technology(H,M8,1).   F_technology(H,M9,1).
F_technology(H,M10,1).  F_technology(I,M6,1).   F_technology(I,M7,1).
F_technology(I,M8,1).   F_technology(J,M4,1).   F_technology(J,M5,1).
F_technology(J,M6,1).   F_technology(K,M10,1).  F_technology(K,M11,1).
F_technology(K,M12,1).  F_technology(L,M1,2).   F_technology(L,M11,2).
F_technology(L,M12,2).  F_technology(M,M9,1).   F_technology(M,M10,1).
F_technology(M,M11,2).  F_technology(N,M1,2).   F_technology(N,M12,2).
F_technology(O,M2,2).   F_technology(O,M11,2).
%resources (#R,ko).
F_resources(R1,8). F_resources(R2,8).
F_resources(R3,8).F_resources (R4,8).
%allocation(#R,#M,#I,d)
F_allocation(R1,A,M1,1).  F_allocation(R2,A,M2,1).  F_allocation(R2,A,M3,2).
F_allocation(R3,A,M10,1). F_allocation(R1,B,M1,2).  F_allocation(R3,B,M5,2).
F_allocation(R1,B,M8,1).  F_allocation(R2,C,M4,2).  F_allocation(R2,C,M9,2).
F_allocation(R3,D,M5,2).  F_allocation(R1,D,M6,1).  F_allocation(R3,D,M7,1).
F_allocation(R4,D,M8,2).  F_allocation(R1,E,M1,1).  F_allocation(R1,E,M2,1).
F_allocation(R3,E,M3,2).  F_allocation(R3,E,M3,1).  F_allocation(R3,F,M5,1).
F_allocation(R1,F,M6,2).  F_allocation(R4,G,M3,1).  F_allocation(R3,G,M5,2).
F_allocation(R1,G,M8,2).  F_allocation(R2,H,M8,1).  F_allocation(R1,H,M9,2).
F_allocation(R3,H,M10,2). F_allocation(R3,I,M6,1).  F_allocation(R1,I,M7,1).
F_allocation(R2,I,M8,1).  F_allocation(R4,J,M4,1).  F_allocation(R3,J,M5,1).
F_allocation(R3,J,M6,1).  F_allocation(R4,K,M10,1). F_allocation(R3,K,M11,1).
F_allocation(R1,K,M12,2). F_allocation(R2,L,M1,1).  F_allocation(R1,L,M11,2).
F_allocation(R3,L,M12,2). F_allocation(R1,M,M9,1).  F_allocation(R1,M,M10,1).
F_allocation(R2,M,M11,2). F_allocation(R3,N,M1,1).  F_allocation(R2,N,M12,2).
F_allocation(R3,O,M2,2).  F_allocation(R3,O,M11,2).
%precedence(#I,#M,#M).
F_precedence(A,M1,M2).    F_precedence(A,M2,M3).    F_precedence(A,M3,M10).
F_precedence(B,M1,M5).    F_precedence(B,M5,M8).    F_precedence(C,M4,M9).
F_precedence(D,M5,M6).    F_precedence(D,M6,M7).    F_precedence(D,M7,M8).
F_precedence(E,M1,M2).    F_precedence(E,M2,M3).    F_precedence(E,M3,M4).
F_precedence(F,M5,M6).    F_precedence(G,M3,M5).    F_precedence(G,M5,M8).
F_precedence(H,M8,M9).    F_precedence(H,M9,M10).   F_precedence(I,M6,M7).
F_precedence(I,M7,M8).    F_precedence(J,M4,M5).    F_precedence(J,M5,M6).
F_precedence(K,M10,M11).  F_precedence(K,M11,M12).  F_precedence(L,M1,M11).
F_precedence(L,M11,M12).  F_precedence(M,M9,M10).   F_precedence(m,M10,M11).
F_precedence(N,M1,M12).   F_precedence(O,M2,M11).
orders(#I,or).
F_order(A,1). F_order(B,1). F_order(C,2). F_order(D,2). F_order(E,2).
F_order(F,1). F_order(G,1). F_order(F,1). F_order(G,1). F_order(F,1).
```

ALGORITHM 2: Instances of facts for illustrative example.

```
L_index_z=[[A,M1,1],    [A,M2,2],    [A,M3,3],    [A,M10,4],   [B,M1,5],    [B,M5,6],
            [B,M8,7],    [C,M4,8],    [C,M9,9],    [D,M5,10],   [D,M6,11],   [D,M7,12],
            [D,M8,13],   [E,M1,14],   [E,M2,15],   [E,M3,16],   [E,M4,17],   [F,M5,18],
            [F,M6,19],   [G,M3,20],   [G,M5,21],   [G,M8,22],   [H,M8,23],   [H,M9,24],
            [H,M10,25],  [I,M6,26],   [I,M7,27],   [I,M8,28],   [J,M4,29],   [J,M5,30],
            [J,M6,31]
          ]
```

ALGORITHM 3: The list of new indices after transformation.

(6) $\mathrm{Kp}_{i,m} = \sum_{t=1}^{LT}(\mathrm{op}_t \cdot Y_{i,m,r,t})\ \forall i = 1,\ldots,LM, m = 1,\ldots,$
$LM, r = 1,\ldots,LR : \mathrm{tr}_{i,m} > 0, d1_{i,m,r} = 1.$

Determination of the time of the end product realization on the machine.

(7) $\mathrm{Kp}_{i,m2} - \mathrm{or}_i \cdot \mathrm{tr}_{i,m2} \geq \mathrm{Kp}_{i,m1}\ \forall i = 1,\ldots,LI, m1, m2 = 1,\ldots,LM : do_{i,m1,m2} = 1.$

The sequence of operations (precedence constraints).

(8) $X_{i,m,r,t} \in \{0,1\}\ \forall i = 1,\ldots,LI, m = 1,\ldots,LM, r = 1,\ldots,LR, t = 1,\ldots,LT.$

$Y_{i,m,r,t} \in \{0,1\}\ \forall i = 1,\ldots,LI, m = 1,\ldots,LM, r = 1,\ldots,LR, t = 1,\ldots,LT.$

$\mathrm{Kp}_{i,m} \in C\ \forall i = 1,\ldots,LI, m = 1,\ldots,LM.$

Binary values and integer values.

D.2. Formal/Mathematical Model for Illustrative Example after Transformation

Indices

m: machine/processor/workstation $m = 1,\ldots,LM$,

r: additional resource $r = 1,\ldots,LR$,

t: period $t = 1,\ldots,LT$,

z: implementation $z = 1,\ldots,Z$ and index after transformation (combined indices i, m).

Parameters

tr_z: the time required to make implementation z,

ko_r: the number of additional resources r,

$d_{z,r}$: if the additional resource r is used to make implementation z, then $d_{z,r}$ determines the number of additional resources r necessary for this implementation; otherwise, $d_{z,r} = 0$,

$d1_{z,r}$: if the additional resource r is used to make implementation z, then $d1_{z,r} = 1$; otherwise, $d1_{z,r} = 0$,

$do_{z1,z2}$: if the implementation $z1$ to be executed before the implementation $z2$, then $do_{z1,z2} = 1$; otherwise, $do_{z1,z2} = 0$,

$\mathrm{wyk}_{z,m}$: if the implementation z is made using a machine m, then $\mathrm{wyk}_{z,m} = 1$; otherwise, $\mathrm{wyk}_{z,m} = 0$.

Inputs

or_z: demand/order for implementation z.

Auxiliary Parameters

op_t: coefficients for conversion numbers of periods t for the variables $\mathrm{op}_t = t$.

Decision Variables

$X_{z,r,t}$: if the additional resource r in period t is used in implementation z, then $X_{z,r,t} = 1$; otherwise, $X_{z,r,t} = 0$,

Kp_z: the number of last periods in which the implementation z is made,

$Y_{z,r,t}$: if the period t is the latest in which the additional resource r is used in implementation z, then $Y_{z,r,t} = 1$; otherwise, $Y_{z,r,t} = 0$,

$C_{\max}$: Makespan.

Constraints

(1) $\mathrm{Kp}_z \leq C_{\max}\ \forall z = 1,\ldots,LZ.$

Determination of the makespan.

(2) $\sum_{t=1}^{LT} d1_{z,r} \cdot X_{z,r,t} = \mathrm{tr}_z \cdot \mathrm{or}_z\ \forall z = 1,\ldots,LZ, r = 1,\ldots,LR, : \mathrm{tr}_z > 0, d1_{z,r} = 1.$

The allocation of resources r to the machine during product realization.

(3) $\sum_{z=1}^{LZ} \sum_{r=1}^{LR} \mathrm{wyk}_{z,m} X_{z,r,t} \leq 1\ \forall m = 1,\ldots,LM, t = 1,\ldots,LT.$

The allocation of at most one product to the machine in a given period of time.

(4) $\sum_{z=1}^{LZ} d_{z,r} \cdot X_{z,r,t} \leq \mathrm{ko}_r\ \forall r = 1,\ldots,LR, t = 1,\ldots,LT.$

The limited availability of resources (capacity constraints).

(5) $X_{z,r,t-1} - X_{z,r,t} \leq Y_{z,r,t-1}\ \forall z = 1,\ldots,LZ, r = 1,\ldots, LM, t = 2,\ldots,LT.$

$\sum_{t=1}^{LT} Y_{z,r,t} \leq 1\ \forall z = 1,\ldots,LZ, r = 1,\ldots,LM.$

Operations cannot be interrupted.

(6) $\mathrm{Kp}_z = \sum_{t=1}^{LT}(\mathrm{op}_t \cdot Y_{z,r,t})\ \forall z = 1,\ldots,LZ, r = 1,\ldots,LR : \mathrm{tr}_z > 0, d1_{z,r} = 1.$

Determination of the time of the end product realization on the machine.

(7) $\mathrm{Kp}_{z2} - \mathrm{or}_{z2} \cdot \mathrm{tr}_{z2} \geq \mathrm{Kp}_{z1}\ \forall z1, z2 = 1,\ldots,LZ : do_{z1,z2} = 1.$

The sequence of operations (precedence constraints).

```
Model:
 Sets:
  machines      /1..@file(t_02_sizes.ldt)/;
  resources     /1..@file(t_02_sizes.ldt)/:ko;
  periods       /1..@file(t_02_sizes.ldt)/:op;
  transformed /1..@file(t_02_sizes.ldt)/:KP,or,tr;
  technology  (transformed,resources,periods):X,Y;
  auxiliary_1 (transformed,resources):d,d1;
  auxiliary_2 (transformed,machines):wyk;
  auxiliary_3 (transformed,transformed):do;
 EndSets
 Data:
  or   =@file(t_03_data.ldt);  tr  =@file(t_03_data.ldt);
  wyk  =@file(t_03_data.ldt);  ko  =@file(t_03_data.ldt);
  d    =@file(t_03_data1.ldt); d1  =@file(t_03_data1.ldt);
  do   =@file(t_03_data1.ldt);
 EndData
 SUBMODEL F_objective1:
  Min=Cmax;
 ENDSUBMODEL
 SUBMODEL Constraints:
  @for(transformed(z): KP(z)<=Cmax);
  @for(transformed(z):@for(resources(r)|d1(z,r)#EQ#1#AND#ti(z)#NE#0:
   @sum(periods(t):d1(z,r)*X(z,r,t))=tr(z)*or(z))
  );
  @for(periods(t): @for(machines(j):
   @sum(transformed(z):@sum(resources(r):wyk(z,r)*X(z,r,t)))<=1
  ));
  @for(periods(t): @for(resources(r):
   @sum(transformed(z):d(z,r)*X(z,r,t))<=ko(r)
  ));
  @for(technology(z,r,t)|t#GT#1: X(z,r,t-1)-X(z,r,t)<=Y(z,r,t-1));
  @for(transformed(z): @for(resources(r):
   @sum(periods(t):Y(z,r,t))<=1
  ));
  @for(transformed(z): @for(resources(r)|d1(z,r)#EQ#1#AND#ti(z)#NE#0:
   KP(z)=@sum(periods(t):op(t)*Y(z,r,t));
  ));
  @for(transformed(z1): @for(transformed(z2)|do(z1,z2)#EQ#1:
   KP(z2)-or(z2)*ti(z2)>=KP(z1)
  ));
  @for(technology(z,r,t): @bin(X(z,r,t)); @bin(Y(z,r,t)));
  @for(transformed(z): @gin(KP(z)));
 ENDSUBMODEL
 CALC:
  @SET('TERSEO',2);
  @for(periods(t): op(t)=t;
   MAXT=t
  );
  @SOLVE(Constraints, F_objective1);
 ENDCALC
End
```

ALGORITHM 4: The code in "LINGO" format for the model illustrative after transformation.

(8) $X_{z,r,t} \in \{0,1\} \; \forall z = 1,\ldots,LZ, \; r = 1,\ldots,LR, \; t = 1,\ldots,LT.$

$Y_{z,r,t} \in \{0,1\} \; \forall z = 1,\ldots,LZ, \; r = 1,\ldots,LR, \; t = 1,\ldots,LT.$

$\mathrm{Kp}_z \in C \; \forall z = 1,\ldots,LZ.$

Binary values and integer values.

Description of the Group Predicates

P1: general predicates (universal),
independent of the modeled problem (e.g.,
to create lists based on facts)

P2: predicates that implement the constraints
of the problem, objectives, conditions, and
so forth, depending on the modeled
problem (ID_pro)

P3: predicates that implement different types
of questions, depending on the modeled
problem (ID_pro)

P4: predicates that implement transformation
of the modeled problem, independent of
the modeled problem

P5: predicates that implemented the automatic
generation of the MILP model.

Competing Interests

The authors declare that there is no conflict of interests
regarding the publication of this paper.

References

[1] F. Rossi, P. Van Beek, and T. Walsh, *Handbook of Constraint Programming (Foundations of Artificial Intelligence)*, Elsevier Science, New York, NY, USA, 2006.

[2] Y. Hamadi, E. E. Monfroy, and F. Saubion, *Autonomous Search*, Springer, Heidelberg, Germany, 2011.

[3] A. Schrijver, *Theory of Linear and Integer Programming*, John Wiley & Sons, New York, NY, USA, 1998.

[4] K. Apt and M. Wallace, *Constraint Logic Programming Using Eclipse*, Cambridge University Press, Cambridge, UK, 2006.

[5] M. G. Buscemi and U. Montanari, "A survey of constraint-based programming paradigms," *Computer Science Review*, vol. 2, no. 3, pp. 137–141, 2008.

[6] T. Achterberg, T. Berthold, T. Koch, and K. Wolter, "Constraint integer programming: a new approach to integrate CP and MIP," in *Integration of AI and OR Techniques in Constraint Programming for Combinatorial Optimization Problems*, vol. 5015 of *Lecture Notes in Computer Science*, pp. 6–20, Springer, Berlin, Germany, 2008.

[7] A. Bockmayr and T. Kasper, "Branch-and-infer: a framework for combining CP and IP," in *Constraint and Integer Programming*, vol. 27 of *Operations Research/Computer Science Interfaces Series*, pp. 59–87, 2004.

[8] J. N. Hooker, "Logic, optimization, and constraint programming," *INFORMS Journal on Computing*, vol. 14, no. 4, pp. 295–321, 2002.

[9] V. Jain and I. E. Grossmann, "Algorithms for hybrid MILP/CP models for a class of optimization problems," *INFORMS Journal on Computing*, vol. 13, no. 4, pp. 258–276, 2001.

[10] M. Milano and M. Wallace, "Integrating operations research in constraint programming," *Annals of Operations Research*, vol. 175, no. 1, pp. 37–76, 2010.

[11] P. Sitek and J. Wikarek, "A hybrid method for modeling and solving constrained search problems," in *Proceedings of the 2013 Federated Conference on Computer Science and Information Systems (FedCSIS '13)*, pp. 385–392, Kielce, Poland, September 2013.

[12] P. Sitek and J. Wikarek, "A hybrid approach to the optimization of multiechelon systems," *Mathematical Problems in Engineering*, vol. 2015, Article ID 925675, 12 pages, 2015.

[13] P. Sitek, "A hybrid CP/MP approach to supply chain modelling, optimization and analysis," in *Proceedings of the 2014 Federated Conference on Computer Science and Information Systems (FedCSIS '14)*, pp. 1345–1352, Warsaw, Poland, September 2014.

[14] Lindo Systems, *LINDO™ Software for Integer Programming, Linear Programming, Nonlinear Programming, Stochastic Programming, Global Optimization*, 2016, http://www.lindo.com.

[15] SCIP, 2016, http://scip.zib.de.

[16] Eclipse, "Eclipse—The Eclipse Foundation open source community website," 2016, http://www.eclipse.org.

[17] P. Sitek and J. Wikarek, "A novel approach to decision support and optimization of group job handling for multimodal processes in manufacturing and services," in *Proceedings of the 15th IFAC Symposium on Information Control Problems in Manufacturing (INCOM '15)*, pp. 2115–2120, May 2015.

[18] O. Guyon, P. Lemaire, Ă. Pinson, and D. Rivreau, "Solving an integrated job-shop problem with human resource constraints," *Annals of Operations Research*, vol. 213, no. 1, pp. 147–171, 2014.

[19] J. Blazewicz, J. K. Lenstra, and A. H. Rinnooy Kan, "Scheduling subject to resource constraints: classification and complexity," *Discrete Applied Mathematics*, vol. 5, no. 1, pp. 11–24, 1983.

[20] S. Bąk, R. Czarnecki, and S. Deniziak, "Synthesis of real-time cloud applications for Internet of Things," *Turkish Journal of Electrical Engineering and Computer Sciences*, vol. 23, no. 3, pp. 913–929, 2013.

6

Reentrant Flow Shop Scheduling Considering Multiresource Qualification Matching

Feng Chu,[1] Ming Liu (ID),[2] Xin Liu (ID),[2] Chengbin Chu,[2,3] and Juan Jiang[4]

[1]Management Engineering Research Center, Xihua University, Chengdu 610039, China
[2]School of Economics & Management, Tongji University, Shanghai 200092, China
[3]Systems Engineering Department, Université Paris-Est, ESIEE Paris, Noisy-le-Grand Cedex, France
[4]Glorious Sun School of Business & Management, Donghua University, Shanghai 200051, China

Correspondence should be addressed to Xin Liu; liuxin9735@126.com

Academic Editor: José E. Labra

With the development of technology and industry, new research issues keep emerging in the field of shop scheduling. Most of the existing research assumes that one job visits each machine only once or ignores the multiple resources in production activities, especially the operators with skill qualifications. In this paper, we consider a reentrant flow shop scheduling problem with multiresource considering qualification matching. The objective of the problem is to minimize the total number of tardy jobs. A mixed integer programming (MIP) model is formulated. Two heuristics, namely, the hill climbing algorithm and the adapted genetic algorithm (GA), are then developed to efficiently solve the problem. Numerical experiments on 30 randomly generated instances are conducted to evaluate the performance of proposed MIP formulation and heuristics.

1. Introduction

Flow shop scheduling problem has been widely studied since it is first proposed ([1–14]; Che and Chu, 2005; Desprez et al., 2006; Kuo and Yang, 2010; Xu and Yin, 2011, etc.). With the development of economy and technology, new research issues keep emerging in this field these years [15–19]. The traditional flow shop scheduling problem assumes that the jobs only visit each machine one time. However, this assumption is not always consistent with the actual production activities. Indeed, there are situations where one job can visit a certain machine twice or more times, i.e., reentrance, such as the production of nuclear materials and aircraft manufacturing process. Reentrant flow shop scheduling problem is first proposed by Graves [1], which is illustrated in Figure 1: there are three procedures for each job, and each job is processed from machine m_1 to m_2 and then back to m_1.

Most existing works addressing flow shop scheduling problem with resource requirement only consider machines and raw materials. However, the impact of many other kinds of resources on the solution is not negligible, including the operators with different abilities. For example, doctors can be considered as expensive and rare surgical resources in the surgical scheduling problem, and drivers can be also regarded as resources in the vehicle scheduling problem, etc. In this paper, reentrance flow shop scheduling considering multiresource with personal qualification matching is investigated. The main contributions of this paper mainly include the following:

(1) We consider a reentrant flow shop scheduling problem, taking personal qualification matching into consideration.

(2) A new mixed integer programming (MIP) formulation is proposed.

(3) Two heuristics are developed to efficiently solve the problem, i.e., the hill climbing algorithm and the adapted genetic algorithm (GA).

(4) Numerical experiments are conducted to evaluate the performance of our developed heuristics. Computational results show that hill climbing algorithm is more time-saving, and GA performs better in terms of the solution quality.

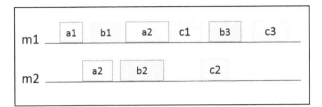

FIGURE 1: Reentrance.

The rest of this paper is structured as follows. Section 2 reviews the literature on reentrant flow shop scheduling problem and shop scheduling with multiresource. Section 3 describes the problem and proposes a mixed integer programming (MIP) formulation. In Section 4, a hill climbing algorithm and an adapted GA are developed. Section 5 reports computational results. Section 6 summarizes this work and states future research directions.

2. Literature Review

There are a significant amount of researches addressing the flow shop scheduling problem. Only few researches have been conducted to deal with the reentrance of jobs (e.g., [20, 21]; Kim, 2005). Besides, existing works considering multiple resources including the personnel are also very rare.

2.1. Reentrant Scheduling. Graves [1] first proposed the reentrant flow shop scheduling problem and develop a heuristic algorithm to solve the problem. Wang et al. [5] study a chain-reentrant shop scheduling problem, in which every job goes first to the primary machine, then to a series of machines, and finally back to the primary machine. They focus on the two-machine case and prove some properties that can identify a specific class of optimal schedules. Based on the properties, they develop an approximation algorithm and a branch-and-bound algorithm.

Chen (2006) addresses the reentrant permutation flow shop scheduling problem, where every job must be processed on machines in the same order, $M_1, M_2, \ldots, M_m$, $M_1, M_2, \ldots, M_m$ and $M_1, M_2, \ldots, M_m$. They present a branch-and-bound algorithm to minimize the makespan. Chen et al. (2008) make a further study on the problem. They propose a hybrid tabu search and a hybrid genetic algorithm. Choi and Kim [22] address a two-machine reentrant flow shop scheduling problem, in which jobs have to be processed twice in the production system. They propose some dominance properties and lower bounds. Then based on the properties, they develop a branch-and-bound algorithm and a heuristic algorithm.

Chu et al. (2008) investigate a reentrant shop problem, which can be considered as a special case of the problem studied by Wang et al. [5]. They propose an optimal schedule to minimize the makespan. As for minimizing the total flow time, they decompose the problem into several subproblems which are solved by their proposed heuristics. Jing et al. [23] develop a heuristic algorithm for the reentrant flow shop scheduling problem to minimize total completion time. An effective k-insertion technique is used in the iterative process.

Desprez et al. [24] address a real-world industrial problem, which is a hybrid flow shop with reentrance. The purpose is to minimize the total weighted number of tardy jobs. A genetic algorithm is developed in order to deal with large size problems. Chakhlevitch and Glass [25] proposed a special two-stage hybrid reentrant flow shop scheduling problem. The objective is to minimize the makespan. The authors proved the problem is NP-hard, then they develop an effective heuristic algorithm by analyzing the characteristics of the problem.

Huang et al. [26] develop a particle swarm optimization algorithm to solve the reentrant two-stage multiprocessor flow shop scheduling problem. Xu et al. [27] present a memetic algorithm for the reentrant permutation flow shop scheduling problem to minimize the makespan. Sangsawang et al. [28] develop a hybrid genetic algorithm for the two-stage reentrant flexible flow shop with blocking constraint to minimize the makespan. Zhou et al. [29] study a reentrant flow shop scheduling problem with inspection and repair operations. And they propose a mathematical model and a hybrid differential evolution algorithm to minimize total weighted completion time.

Shop scheduling with multiresource has been studied in some research. However, researches focusing on shop scheduling problem with personal qualification matching are very rare.

2.2. Scheduling Considering Multiple Resources. Scheduling problem considering multiple resources has been investigated by many researchers. However, most existing works either ignore the personnel or assume they are identical and can be replaced with each other.

Dauzère-Pérès and Roux [30] first propose a job shop scheduling problem with multiresources to minimize the makespan. In this problem, the authors assume that every job needs all kinds of resources and operators are not considered. Dauzère-Pérès and Pavageau [31] extend the study by allowing resources to be released before completing in one procedure and considering that incompatible resources cannot be chosen by one procedure at the same time.

Artigues et al. [32] study an on-line scheduling in a job shop environment with multiresource requirements and setup times. They present a Petri net model for the problem. Artigues and Roubellat [33] present a polynomial insertion algorithm to minimize the maximum lateness.

Wang and Wu [34] address a multiperiod, multiproduct, and multiresource production-scheduling problem. The authors establish a mixed integer programming (MIP) formulation and propose a two-phase approach to solve the problem.

Rajkumar et al. [35] propose a Greedy Randomised Adaptive Search Procedures algorithm for a flexible job shop scheduling problem. And Gao et al. (2016) propose an algorithm named the shuffled multiswarm micromigrating birds optimization for a multi-resource-constrained flexible job shop scheduling problem.

This paper extends the literature on reentrant flow shop scheduling by considering multiresource, which contains the operators with different skill qualification.

3. Problem Description and Formulation

In this section, we first describe the problem and then propose a new mixed integer programming formulation.

3.1. Problem Description. In the deterministic problem, there are a set of jobs should be processed, i.e., $N = \{1, 2, \ldots, n\}$, and a set of machines, i.e., $M = \{1, 2, \ldots, m\}$. All jobs have to be processed in all procedures $H = \{1, 2, \ldots, |H|\}$ and following the same route; i.e., they have to be processed in procedure 1, then in procedure 2, and so on. Some procedures of jobs are processed on the same machine, i.e., reentrance.

The processing task is defined as one procedure of one job. We address the reentrance by considering that there should not be more than one processing task on one machine at a time. Multiple resources considered include raw materials or operators. Each processing task requires some raw materials, and the number of available raw materials is limited. Besides, some certain skill qualifications are also required by each processing task. Only operators processing the skill qualifications required can be assigned to a processing task, i.e., qualification matching. Moreover, one operator cannot assigned to two or more processing tasks at a time.

Each job should be processed after its own release time. It is assumed that the due dates of jobs are fixed and known in advance. The objective of the problem is to find a set of sequences and operators assignment of jobs in all procedures, in order to minimize the number of tardy jobs. To formally state the problem, a mixed integer programming (MIP) formulation is proposed in the following.

3.2. Mixed Integer Programming (MIP) Formulation. In the following, we give the definitions of parameters and decision variables. Then a new MIP model is formulated.

Indices

(i) i, j: indices of jobs

(ii) r: index of resources

(iii) h: index of procedures

(iv) t: index of time

(v) q: index of qualifications

(vi) k: index of machines

Parameters

(i) N: set of jobs, $N = \{1, \ldots, n\}$

(ii) M: set of machines, $M = \{1, \ldots, m\}$

(iii) H: set of procedures

(iv) Q: set of skill qualifications

(v) P: set of procedures, and $P = \{1, 2, \ldots, |P|\}$

(vi) P_k: set of procedures on machine k

(vii) R_1: set of operators

(viii) R_2: set of raw materials

(ix) r_i: the release time of job i

(x) α_{rq}: a binary parameter, equal to 1 if resource $r \in R_1$ possesses the qualification q

(xi) β_{ih}^q: a binary parameter, equal to 1 if qualification q is required by job i in procedure h

(xii) d_i: the due date of job i

(xiii) p_{hi} the processing time of job i in procedure h

(xiv) a_{hi}^r: the amount of raw materials required by job i in procedure h, $r \in R_2$

(xv) π_r: the number of available raw materials $r \in R_2$

(xvi) L: a large enough number

Variables

(i) x_{ij}^h: binary variable, equal to 1 if job i is processed before job j in procedure h, 0 otherwise

(ii) z_{hi}^t: binary variable, equal to 1 if job i is being processed in procedure h at time t, 0 otherwise

(iii) y_{hi}^{rq}: binary variable, equal to 1 if resource $r \in R1$ is assigned to satisfy the qualification q required by job i being processed in procedure h, 0 otherwise

(iv) s_{hi}: nonnegative integer, start time of job i in procedure h

(v) c_{hi}: nonnegative integer, completion time of job i in procedure h

(vi) u_i: binary variable, equal to 1 if job i is a tardy job, 0 otherwise

(vii) y_{hi}^{rqt}: binary variable, equal to 1 if operator r is in charge of the need of qualification q of job i in procedure h at time t, 0 otherwise

The **MIP** *Formulation*

$$\min \quad \sum_{i \in N} u_i \tag{1}$$

$$\text{s.t.} \quad x_{ij}^h + x_{ji}^h = 1, \quad \forall h \in P,\ i, j \in N,\ i \neq j \tag{2}$$

$$c_{hi} = s_{hi} + p_{hi}, \quad \forall h \in P,\ i \in N \tag{3}$$

$$s_{hi} \geq c_{h-1,i}, \quad \forall h \in \frac{P}{\{1\}},\ i \in N \tag{4}$$

$$s_{hj} + \left(1 - x_{ij}^h\right) L \geq c_{hi}, \tag{5}$$
$$\forall h \in P,\ i, j \in N,\ i \neq j$$

$$s_{hi} \geq r_i, \quad \forall h \in P,\ i \in N \tag{6}$$

$$t - c_{hi} \leq \left(1 - z_{hi}^t\right) L, \quad \forall h \in P,\ i \in N,\ t \in T \tag{7}$$

$$s_{hi} - t \leq \left(1 - z_{hi}^t\right) L, \quad \forall h \in P,\ i \in N,\ t \in T \tag{8}$$

$$\sum_{t \in T} z_{hi}^t = p_{hi}, \quad \forall h \in P, \ i \in N \tag{9}$$

$$y_{hi}^{rq} \leq \alpha_{rq}, \quad \forall h \in P, \ i \in N, \ r \in R_1, \ q \in Q \tag{10}$$

$$y_{hi}^{rq} \leq \beta_{hi}^q, \quad \forall h \in P, \ i \in N, \ r \in R_1, \ q \in Q \tag{11}$$

$$\sum_{r \in R_1} y_{hi}^{rq} = \beta_{hi}^q, \quad \forall h \in P, \ i \in N, \ q \in Q \tag{12}$$

$$\sum_{h \in P} \sum_{i \in N} \sum_{q \in Q} y_{hi}^{rq} z_{hi}^t \leq 1, \quad \forall r \in R_1, \ t \in T \tag{13}$$

$$\gamma_{hi}^{rqt} \geq y_{hi}^{rq} + z_{hi}^t - 1,$$
$$\forall h \in P, \ i \in N, \ q \in Q, \ r \in R_1, \ t \in T \tag{14}$$

$$\gamma_{hi}^{rqt} \leq y_{hi}^{rq},$$
$$\forall h \in P, \ i \in N, \ q \in Q, \ r \in R_1, \ t \in T \tag{15}$$

$$\gamma_{hi}^{rqt} \leq z_{hi}^t,$$
$$\forall h \in P, \ i \in N, \ q \in Q, \ r \in R_1, \ t \in T \tag{16}$$

$$\sum_{h \in P} \sum_{i \in N} \gamma_{hi}^{rqt} \leq 1, \quad \forall r \in R_1, \ t \in T \tag{17}$$

$$\sum_{i \in N} \sum_{h \in P} z_{hi}^t a_{hi}^r \leq \pi_r, \quad \forall r \in R_2, \ t \in T \tag{18}$$

$$\sum_{i \in N} \sum_{h \in p_k} z_{ki}^t \leq 1, \quad \forall t \in T, \ k \in M \tag{19}$$

$$c_{hi} - d_i \leq u_i L, \quad \forall i \in N, \ h = |P| \tag{20}$$

$$x_{ij}^h \in \{0,1\}, \quad \forall h \in P, \ i,j \in N, \ i \neq j \tag{21}$$

$$z_{hi}^t \in \{0,1\}, \quad \forall h \in P, \ i \in N, \ t \in T \tag{22}$$

$$y_{hi}^{rq} \in \{0,1\}, \quad \forall h \in P, \ i \in N, \ q \in Q, \ r \in R_1 \tag{23}$$

$$\gamma_{hi}^{rqt} \in \{0,1\},$$
$$\forall h \in P, \ i \in N, \ q \in Q, \ r \in R_1, \ t \in T \tag{24}$$

$$u_i \in \{0,1\}, \quad \forall i \in N \tag{25}$$

$$s_{hi}, c_{hi} \geq 0, \quad \forall i \in N, \ h \in P \tag{26}$$

The objective function (1) aims at minimizing the number of tardy jobs. Constraint (2) ensures that job i and job j are processed in procedure h, and job i is either processed before job j or after it. Constraint (3) ensures that a job must be processed in a procedure without interruption. Constraints (4)-(6) guarantee that the start time of a job i must be after the previous procedure and its release time and the completion

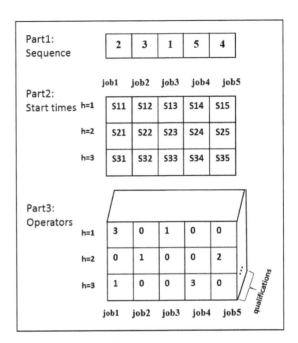

FIGURE 2: Coding.

time of jobs prior to it. And constraints (7)-(9) ensure that z_{hi}^t is equal to 1 if job i is being processed in procedure h at time t. Constraints (10)-(12) ensure the relationship between the qualities needed by a job and those of an operator. The objective of constraints (14)-(16) is to make the formulation $y_{hi}^{rq} z_{hi}^t$ linearized. Constraint (17) ensures that an operator cannot be assigned to more than one processing activity at one time t. Constraint (18) guarantees that the amount of resources needed by the jobs being processed at time t cannot exceed that of available resources. Constraint (19) ensures that there cannot be more than one job being processed on a machine at a time. Constraint (20) gives the definition of tardy jobs. And constraints (21)-(26) give the ranges of decision variables.

As we can see from the computational results reported in Section 5, solving the MIP formulation by calling CPLEX is very time-consuming. Therefore, we develop heuristics to efficiently solve the problem.

4. Solution Approaches

In this section, two heuristics to solve the problem, i.e., a hill climbing algorithm and an adapted genetic algorithm (GA), are developed.

4.1. Coding and Initialization. Solutions should be transformed into individuals that can be operated by the algorithms. For our problem, a solution is composed of three decision parts: (1) the first part is the sequence of jobs in each procedure, (2) the second part is the start time of each in each procedure, and (3) the third part is the operator assignment to each job in each procedure (see Figure 2).

Figure 2 illustrates the coding method of both heuristics. It is assumed that there are 5 jobs to be processed in 3

Require: *Parameters for proposed problem*
Ensure: *Solution*
  (1) $MAXITR = 1000$;
  (2) $bestStr = Initialize()$;
  (3) $k = 1$;
  (4) **while** $k \leq MAXITR$ **do**
  (5) $bestF = evaluate\_objective(bestStr)$;
  (6) $new = string\_operator(bestStr)$;
  (7) $newF = evaluate\_objective(newStr)$;
  (8)   **if** $newF \leq bestF$ **then**
  (9) $bestStr = newStr$;
  (10) **end if**
  (11) $k = k + 1$;
  (12) **end while**

ALGORITHM 1: Hill climbing algorithm.

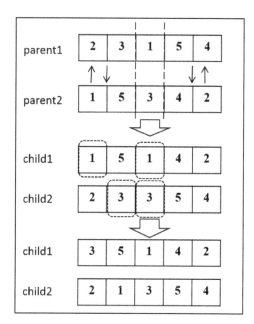

FIGURE 3: Crossover.

procedures, and procedure 1 and procedure 3 are on machine 1. The first part of individual is a vector with length of N, and it can be obtained that sequence of jobs processing in each procedure is $\{2, 3, 1, 5, 4\}$. The second part of individual is a $P \times N$ matrix, which gives the information on start times of jobs in all procedures. Besides, the third part of the individual is a $P \times N \times Q$ matrix, which shows the operator assigned to each job in each procedure. For example, operator 3 is assigned to satisfy qualification 1 required by job 1 in procedure 1.

For the generalization of an initial solution, first we generate a vector including random permutation of N, i.e., the first part. Then the start times can be calculated by arranging the processing activities as close as possible. Operator satisfying each qualification required by each processing activity is randomly chosen from those processing the qualification. Then based on the start times calculated and operator assignment, we rearrange the start times: for two processing activities, if there is overlap in time, and (i) one operator is assigned to both processing activities, or (ii) the summation of raw materials required by them exceeds the available materials, then the processing activity with larger start time will be arranged after the completion time of the other one. The rearrangement is repeated N times, and an initial solution is obtained.

4.2. Hill Climbing Algorithm. Hill climbing algorithm is a local search approach, the basic idea of which is to find a string with better solution to replace the existing one. As shown in Algorithm 1, hill climbing starts with an initial solution, denoted as *BestStr*. During each iteration, new solution, i.e., *NewStr*, is generated by mutating *BestStr*. If the solution of *NewStr* is better than that of *BestStr*, then *BestStr* will be replaced with *NewStr*. Solution is obtained when stopping criteria are reached.

The procedure *string_operator* includes two steps: (i) randomly select two jobs and exchange their positions in the first part of existing solution and (ii) randomly assign operators with the required qualification to processing activities. Then start times are rearranged in the method detailed

above. Then a new solution is obtained. For the procedure *evaluate_objective*, except for calculating the total number of tardy jobs, feasibility check is conducted by adding penalty to the objective.

4.3. Genetic Algorithm. Genetic algorithm (GA) is first introduced by Holland [36] and based on the biological reproduction rules. GA starts with a set of initial solutions. During each iteration, offspring individuals are produced by current solutions by conducting genetic operators, i.e., crossover and mutation. Then population combining current solutions and offspring solutions is renewed. The algorithm stops when a stopping criterion is reached.

4.3.1. Crossover and Mutation. There are two common crossover operators in scheduling problem, namely, one-point crossover and multipoint crossover. In this paper, we adopt two-point crossover for our problem. For two-point crossover operator, two parent solutions are selected randomly. As shown in Figure 3, we randomly select two numbers pA and pB in N, i.e., 2 and 3. Then all genes between pA and pB are copied from parent 1 to child 1, the remaining genes of child 1 are copied from parent 2. Child 2 is produced in the same method. Then replace the redundant genes with missing genes. Then the operators are reassigned to processing activities, and the start times are calculated in the same way stated above.

For the mutation operator, solutions are mutated in the same way as the *string_operator* in hill climbing.

5. Computational Results

In this section, the performance of our proposed formulation and two heuristics are evaluated by 30 randomly generated instances. Formulation and proposed heuristics are coded

Table 1: Parameters for GA.

Parameter	Value (GA)
Population size (*pop*)	50
Generation number (*gen*)	20
Crossover probability	0.8
Mutation probability	0.6

in MATLAB_2014b. CPLEX 12.6 solver is called to solve the formulation. All numerical experiments are conducted on a personal computer with Core I5 and 3.30 GHz processor and 8GB RAM under Windows 7 operating system. The computational times of formulation and two heuristics are limited to 3600 seconds.

A preliminary analysis is conducted to fine-tune the parameters of proposed two heuristics. For the hill climbing algorithm, the maximum number of iterations is set to be 500. For the genetic algorithm (GA), parameters are presented in Table 1. Population size and generation number are set to be 50 and 20, respectively. The crossover probability and the mutation probability are set to be 0.8 and 0.6, respectively.

5.1. Data Generation. The tested data are generated following the way in Liu et al. (2015) and Chen (2009). The processing times of jobs are randomly generated from a discrete Uniform distribution over $[1, 10]$. The due dates of jobs are randomly generated from discrete Uniform distribution on interval $[(1 - C - Q/2) \cdot \sum_{i=1}^{n} p_i, (1 - C + Q/2) \cdot \sum_{i=1}^{n} p_i]$, in which Q and C imply the due date range and the factor of tardiness, respectively. During numerical experiments, we consider the first combination of C and Q described in Liu et al. (2015), i.e., $C = 0.2, Q = 0.2$. The range of t is set to be $[1, \sum_{i \in N} \sum h \in Pp_{hi}]$. It is assumed that the number of raw material types, i.e., $|R_2|$, is 4, and the number of raw material in each type, i.e., π_r is randomly generated a discrete Uniform distribution over $[20, 40]$. The number of raw material required by each job in each procedure is randomly generated from a discrete Uniform distribution on $[0, \lceil \pi_r/|H| \rceil]$. The total number of skill qualification types, i.e., $|S|$, is 4, and the skill qualifications processed by each operator are randomly generated, ensuring that one operator processes at least one skill qualification. In numerical experiments, we assume that the schedule is permutation and the first procedure and the last procedure of jobs are on machine 1.

5.2. Results and Discussion. Computational results on 30 randomly generated instances are shown in Table 1 in the following. For each instance, we run formulation and each heuristic 30 times and obtain the average value.

In Table 2, Obj, CT, HCA denote objective value, computational time, and hill climbing algorithm, respectively. The optimal solution cannot be obtained within 3600 seconds even for the instance with 23 jobs, 4 procedures, and 13 operators. Then we can observe from Table 2 that it is very time-consuming for solving the formulation by calling CPLEX. The average computational time of hill climbing is 1522.5s, which is smaller than that of GA, i.e., 1760.9s. Besides, the average objective values of solutions obtained by hill climbing algorithm are 22.2s, and those obtained by GA are 17.5. For the first 11 instances, we can observe that, compared with hill climbing algorithm, the objective values of solutions obtained by GA are closer to the optimal solution. Therefore, from Table 2, we can conclude that (i) the proposed two heuristics, i.e., hill climbing algorithm and genetic algorithm (GA), are time-saving compared with solving the MIP formulation by calling CPLEX solver, (ii) GA performs better in terms of solution quality compared with hill climbing algorithm, and (iii) hill climbing algorithm is more time-saving than GA.

6. Conclusion

This work investigates the reentrant flow shop scheduling problem, considering multiresource qualification matching, in which operators processing required skill qualifications can be assigned to serve a job in a procedure. The objective of the problem is to schedule the jobs in each machine and assign operators to serve job processing. For the problem, a new mixed integer programming (MIP) formulation is proposed, and two heuristics are then developed, i.e., the hill climbing algorithm and the adapted genetic algorithm (GA). Numerical experiments on 30 randomly generated instances are conducted to evaluate the performance of our proposed MIP formulation and two heuristics. Computational results show that hill climbing is more time-saving, and GA performs better in terms of solution quality.

In the future, we should develop more effective algorithms to solve the problem and improve the quality of the solutions (on the basis of Yin et al. [37]). Future researches also could take more factors into account, including the robustness, work balance of the operators (on the basis of Xu et al., 2014 [27]), maintenance activities (on the basis of Yang and Yang, 2010 [38]), and space constraints (on the basis of Xu et al., 2014 [27]).

Conflicts of Interest

The authors declare that they have no conflicts of interest.

Acknowledgments

This work was supported by the National Natural Science Foundation of China (NSFC) under Grants 71428002, 71531011, 71571134, and 71771048. This work was also supported by the Fundamental Research Funds for the Central Universities.

TABLE 2: Computational results.

Set	$(|N|, |H|, |R_2|)$	CPLEX		HCA		GA	
		Obj	CT	Obj	CT	Obj	CT
1	$(3, 2, 1)$	1	142.5	1	0.9	1	1.6
2	$(5, 2, 2)$	2	215.5	3	1.4	2	3.1
3	$(7, 2, 3)$	2	628.7	3	2.3	2	6.9
4	$(9, 2, 4)$	2	1230.4	5	3.8	3	8.6
5	$(11, 2, 5)$	3	2352.1	8	5.7	4	13.2
6	$(13, 3, 6)$	5	3325.3	8	74.8	7	105.8
7	$(15, 3, 7)$	4	3600.0	6	105.7	6	197.2
8	$(17, 3, 8)$	6	3600.0	9	126.9	7	256.6
9	$(19, 3, 9)$	7	3600.0	10	189.8	9	385.1
10	$(21, 3, 10)$	6	3600.0	10	251.7	8	493.3
11	$(23, 4, 11)$	8	3600.0	15	386.1	12	621.9
12	$(25, 4, 12)$	-	-	17	452.2	19	828.5
13	$(27, 4, 13)$	-	-	18	514.3	15	956.4
14	$(29, 4, 14)$	-	-	21	703.6	20	1129.3
15	$(31, 4, 15)$	-	-	19	912.5	12	1408.2
16	$(33, 4, 16)$	-	-	16	1030.4	15	1606.2
17	$(35, 4, 17)$	-	-	24	1342.5	24	1946.8
18	$(37, 4, 18)$	-	-	27	1608.0	22	2234.8
19	$(39, 4, 19)$	-	-	29	1918.2	23	2415.3
20	$(41, 4, 20)$	-	-	30	2213.4	24	2809.7
21	$(43, 5, 21)$	-	-	37	2524.2	35	2998.7
22	$(45, 5, 22)$	-	-	38	2896.1	33	3600.0
23	$(47, 5, 23)$	-	-	31	3234.3	28	3600.0
24	$(49, 5, 24)$	-	-	36	3577.1	30	3600.0
25	$(51, 5, 25)$	-	-	38	3600.0	28	3600.0
26	$(53, 5, 26)$	-	-	35	3600.0	30	3600.0
27	$(55, 5, 27)$	-	-	42	3600.0	21	3600.0
28	$(57, 5, 28)$	-	-	40	3600.0	24	3600.0
29	$(59, 5, 29)$	-	-	45	3600.0	31	3600.0
30	$(61, 5, 30)$	-	-	45	3600.0	30	3600.0
	Average	-	-	22.2	1522.5	17.5	1760.9

References

[1] S. C. Graves, H. C. Meal, D. Stefek, and A. H. Zeghmi, "Scheduling of re-entrant flow shops," *Journal of Operations Management*, vol. 3, no. 4, pp. 197–207, 1983.

[2] C. Wang, C. Chu, and J. M. Proth, "A branch-and-bound algorithm for n-job two machine flow shop scheduling problems," *Emerging Technologies and Factory Automation*, vol. 2, pp. 375–383, 1995.

[3] D.-L. Yang and M.-S. Chern, "A two-machine flowshop sequencing problem with limited waiting time constraints," *Computers & Industrial Engineering*, vol. 28, no. 1, pp. 63–70, 1995.

[4] H. Hwang and J. U. Sun, "Production sequencing problem with re-entrant work flows and sequence dependent setup times," *International Journal of Production Research*, vol. 36, no. 9, pp. 2435–2450, 1998.

[5] C. Wang, C. Chu, and J.-M. Proth, "Heuristic approaches for n/m/F/Ci scheduling problems," *European Journal of Operational Research*, vol. 96, no. 3, pp. 636–644, 1997.

[6] D.-L. Yang and M.-S. Chern, "Two-machine flowshop group scheduling problem," *Computers & Operations Research*, vol. 27, no. 10, pp. 975–985, 2000.

[7] V. Gordon, J.-M. Proth, and C. Chu, "A survey of the state-of-the-art of common due date assignment and scheduling research," *European Journal of Operational Research*, vol. 139, no. 1, pp. 1–25, 2002.

[8] D.-L. Yang, C.-J. Hsu, and W.-H. Kuo, "A two-machine flowshop scheduling problem with a separated maintenance constraint," *Computers & Operations Research*, vol. 35, no. 3, pp. 876–883, 2008.

[9] I. Kacem and C. Chu, "Worst-case analysis of the wspt and mwspt rules for single machine scheduling with one planned setup period," *European Journal of Operational Research*, vol. 187, no. 3, pp. 1080–1089, 2008.

[10] Y. Ma, C. B. Chu, and C. R. Zuo, "A survey of scheduling with deterministic machine availability constraints," *Computers & Industrial Engineering*, vol. 58, no. 2, pp. 199–211, 2010.

[11] M. Liu and C. Chu, "Optimal semi-online algorithms for m-batch-machine flow shop scheduling," *Discrete Mathematics, Algorithms and Applications*, vol. 4, no. 4, 2012.

[12] W. Lei, A. Che, and C. Chu, "Optimal cyclic scheduling of a robotic flowshop with multiple part types and flexible processing times," *European Journal of Industrial Engineering*, vol. 8, no. 2, pp. 143–167, 2014.

[13] S. Wang, M. Liu, and C. Chu, "A branch-and-bound algorithm for two-stage no-wait hybrid flow-shop scheduling," *International Journal of Production Research*, vol. 53, no. 4, pp. 1143–1167, 2015.

[14] C.-Y. Lee and T. Lu, "Inventory competition with yield reliability improvement," *Naval Research Logistics (NRL)*, vol. 62, no. 2, pp. 107–126, 2015.

[15] W. H. Kuo, D. L. Yang, and C. J. Hsu, "An unrelated parallel machine scheduling problem with past-sequence-dependent setup time and learning effects," in *Proceedings of the International Conference on Computers and Industrial Engineering*, vol. 35, pp. 764–776, 2010.

[16] S.-J. Yang, D.-L. Yang, and T. C. E. Cheng, "Single-machine due-window assignment and scheduling with job-dependent aging effects and deteriorating maintenance," *Computers & Operations Research*, vol. 37, no. 8, pp. 1510–1514, 2010.

[17] T. Cheng E, C. Hsu J, and D. Yang L, "Unrelated parallel-machine scheduling with deteriorating maintenance activities," *Computers & Industrial Engineering*, vol. 60, no. 4, pp. 602–605, 2011.

[18] Y. Q. Yin, M. Liu, J. H. Hao, and M. C. Zhou, "Single-machine scheduling with job-position-dependent learning and time-dependent deterioration," *IEEE Transactions on Systems, Man and Cybernetics, Part A: Systems and Humans*, vol. 42, no. 1, pp. 192–200, 2012.

[19] Y. Yin, W.-H. Wu, W.-H. Wu, and C.-C. Wu, "A branch-and-bound algorithm for a single machine sequencing to minimize the total tardiness with arbitrary release dates and position-dependent learning effects," *Information Sciences*, vol. 256, pp. 91–108, 2014.

[20] W. Kubiak, S. X. C. Lou, and Y. Wang, "Mean flow time minimization in reentrant job shops with a hub," *Operations Research*, vol. 44, no. 5, pp. 764–776, 1996.

[21] Y. Park, S. Kim, and C.-H. Jun, "Performance analysis of re-entrant flow shop with single-job and batch machines using mean value analysis," *Production Planning and Control*, vol. 11, no. 6, pp. 537–546, 2000.

[22] S.-W. Choi and Y.-D. Kim, "Minimizing makespan on a two-machine re-entrant flowshop," *Journal of the Operational Research Society*, vol. 58, no. 7, pp. 972–981, 2007.

[23] C. Jing, W. Huang, and G. Tang, "Minimizing total completion time for re-entrant flow shop scheduling problems," *Theoretical Computer Science*, vol. 412, no. 48, pp. 6712–6719, 2011.

[24] C. Desprez, F. Chu, and C. Chu, "Minimising the weighted number of tardy jobs in a hybrid flow shop with genetic algorithm," *International Journal of Computer Integrated Manufacturing*, vol. 22, no. 8, pp. 745–757, 2009.

[25] K. Chakhlevitch and C. A. Glass, "Scheduling reentrant jobs on parallel machines with a remote server," *Computers & Operations Research*, vol. 36, no. 9, pp. 2580–2589, 2009.

[26] R.-H. Huang, S.-C. Yu, and C.-W. Kuo, "Reentrant two-stage multiprocessor flow shop scheduling with due windows," *The International Journal of Advanced Manufacturing Technology*, vol. 71, no. 5-8, pp. 1263–1276, 2014.

[27] J. Xu, Y. Yin, T. C. E. Cheng, C.-C. Wu, and S. Gu, "A memetic algorithm for the re-entrant permutation flowshop scheduling problem to minimize the makespan," *Applied Soft Computing*, vol. 24, pp. 277–283, 2014.

[28] C. Sangsawang, K. Sethanan, T. Fujimoto, and M. Gen, "Meta-heuristics optimization approaches for two-stage reentrant flexible flow shop with blocking constraint," *Expert Systems with Applications*, vol. 42, no. 5, pp. 2395–2410, 2015.

[29] B.-H. Zhou, L.-M. Hu, and Z.-Y. Zhong, "A hybrid differential evolution algorithm with estimation of distribution algorithm for reentrant hybrid flow shop scheduling problem," *Neural Computing and Applications*, vol. 8, pp. 1–17, 2016.

[30] S. Dauzère-Pérès, W. Roux, and J. B. Lasserre, "Multi-resource shop scheduling with resource flexibility," *European Journal of Operational Research*, vol. 107, no. 2, pp. 289–305, 1998.

[31] S. Dauzere-Peres and C. Pavageau, "Extensions of an integrated approach for multi-resource shop scheduling," *IEEE Transactions on Systems, Man, and Cybernetics, Part C: Applications and Reviews*, vol. 33, no. 2, pp. 207–213, 2003.

[32] C. Artigues and F. Roubellat, "A Petri net model and a general method for on and off-line multi-resource shop floor scheduling with setup times," *International Journal of Production Economics*, vol. 74, no. 1-3, pp. 63–75, 2001.

[33] C. Artigues and F. Roubellat, "An efficient algorithm for operation insertion in a multi-resource job-shop schedule with sequence-dependent setup times," *Production Planning and Control*, vol. 13, no. 2, pp. 175–186, 2002.

[34] H.-F. Wang and K.-Y. Wu, "Modeling and analysis for multi-period, multi-product and multi-resource production scheduling," *Journal of Intelligent Manufacturing*, vol. 14, no. 3-4, pp. 297–309, 2003.

[35] M. Rajkumar, P. Asokan, and V. Vamsikrishna, "A GRASP algorithm for flexible job-shop scheduling with maintenance constraints," *International Journal of Production Research*, vol. 48, no. 22, pp. 6821–6836, 2010.

[36] J. H. Holland, "Adaptation in natural and artificial systems," *Quarterly Review of Biology*, vol. 6, no. 2, pp. 126–137, 1975.

[37] Y. Yin, C.-C. Wu, W.-H. Wu, C.-J. Hsu, and W.-H. Wu, "A branch-and-bound procedure for a single-machine earliness scheduling problem with two agents," *Applied Soft Computing*, vol. 13, no. 2, pp. 1042–1054, 2013.

[38] S.-J. Yang and D.-L. Yang, "Minimizing the makespan on single-machine scheduling with aging effect and variable maintenance activities," *Omega*, vol. 38, no. 6, pp. 528–533, 2010.

7

Mixed-Integer Linear Programming Models for Teaching Assistant Assignment and Extensions

Xiaobo Qu,[1] Wen Yi,[2] Tingsong Wang,[3] Shuaian Wang,[4] Lin Xiao,[5] and Zhiyuan Liu[6]

[1]School of Civil and Environmental Engineering, University of Technology Sydney, Sydney, NSW 2007, Australia
[2]Department of Building and Real Estate, The Hong Kong Polytechnic University, Kowloon, Hong Kong
[3]School of Economics and Management, Wuhan University, Wuhan 430072, China
[4]Department of Logistics & Maritime Studies, The Hong Kong Polytechnic University, Kowloon, Hong Kong
[5]National Research Council of the National Research Academies of Science, Engineering, and Medicine, Washington, DC 20001, USA
[6]Jiangsu Key Laboratory of Urban ITS, Jiangsu Province Collaborative Innovation Center of Modern Urban Traffic Technologies, School of Transportation, Southeast University, Jiangsu, China

Correspondence should be addressed to Tingsong Wang; emswangts@whu.edu.cn, Shuaian Wang; wangshuaian@gmail.com, and Zhiyuan Liu; leakeliu@163.com

Academic Editor: Christoph Kessler

In this paper, we develop mixed-integer linear programming models for assigning the most appropriate teaching assistants to the tutorials in a department. The objective is to maximize the number of tutorials that are taught by the most suitable teaching assistants, accounting for the fact that different teaching assistants have different capabilities and each teaching assistant's teaching load cannot exceed a maximum value. Moreover, with optimization models, the teaching load allocation, a time-consuming process, does not need to be carried out in a manual manner. We have further presented a number of extensions that capture more practical considerations. Extensive numerical experiments show that the optimization models can be solved by an off-the-shelf solver and used by departments in universities.

1. Introduction

Teaching assistants (TAs) are essential in many departments in universities because of limited numbers of lecturers. TAs are mainly postgraduate students, though in some universities TAs can also be undergraduate students. TAs are usually in charge of teaching tutorials in small classes. TA allocation, that is, which TA teaches which tutorial, is an essential task that is carried out in a department every semester. It has been well recognized that appropriate teaching staff allocation contributes to the equality of teaching [1, 2]. The teaching assistants are usually reallocated every semester. This is due to the following two reasons: (1) changes of staff (some TAs are no longer available because they have graduated or have other commitments and new TAs are available) and (2) changes of programs (some tutorials are cancelled and some new tutorials are developed).

There are many factors to consider in TA assignment. First, all tutorials must be taught in order to satisfy the needs of the teaching programs. Second, a TA should not be allocated a higher teaching load other than what is required by her/his role because of her/his limited available time. Third, TAs should teach tutorials that they are proficient with; otherwise it will cost them a lot of preparation time and the teaching outcomes will not be ideal. Fourth, we should consider whether two tutorials are delivered at the same time, and if so, they cannot be taught by the same TA. Fifth, it is easy to see that if a TA teaches several tutorials of the same lecture, in other words, repeating the tutorials, then it is easier for the TA to save time for preparation. Sixth, it might be difficult for a lecturer to manage if there are too many TAs for the lecturer and hence it may be desirable to control the number of TAs for a lecturer.

Our personal experiences show that almost all departments allocate teaching assistants manually in a trial-and-error manner. As we all know, this allocation is very time-consuming process and may lead to unfavorable results which may jeopardize the teaching quality. In this regard, it is imperative and of vital significance to develop a systematic tool in order to better allocate the teaching assistants in a more efficient manner.

1.1. Literature Review. It is universally acknowledged that improving the teaching quality is the number one concern in all teaching activities. Academics have developed a number of new educational theories and pedagogical techniques to meet the teaching requirements in view of the changing society (e.g., [3, 4]). Some studies are related to the timetabling of educational organizations. Valouxis and Housos [5] applied a constraint programming approach to solve a high school timetabling problem considering various practical constraints. Beligiannis et al. [6] proposed an adaptive algorithm to address the timetabling problem of an educational institute. Pillay and Banzhaf [7] examined the use of genetic algorithms to address an examination timetabling problem. A category of research that is more closely related to ours is optimization models proposed to better allocate teaching load for full time academic teaching staff in a teaching unit. For example, Breslaw [8] was among the first to develop a linear programming model to address a teaching staff assignment problem. His objective was to maximize the preference of the faculty members. Schniederjans and Kim [9] adopted a different mathematical approach—a goal programming model—to optimize the overall benefit to the teaching department. Badri [10] developed a more complex model that consists of a two-stage multiobjective scheduling approach. The objectives are twofold: first, the preference for tutorials by faculty members is incorporated; second, the time slots of the tutorials that are preferred by faculty members are also considered. Qu et al. [11] developed a very simple model for assignment lecturers to classes and tested the model with data from a university in Australia. As discussed in Badri [10], the abovementioned mathematical approaches could improve teaching quality by maximizing the preference of the faculty members. However, two key issues are neglected in the abovementioned studies. First, as the focus of teaching activities is to improve or guarantee the teaching quality, the teaching quality should be considered as the objective to maximize, rather than a constraint in the optimization model. In other words, teaching quality is much more important than faculty preference as the former is the number one concern in all teaching activities. Second, the abovementioned studies are mainly focused on teaching load allocation for full time academic staff, while the arrangement for teaching assistants is mostly treated in a very simple way, which may lead to unreliable results.

In most teaching units, teaching assistants are Ph.D. or senior students and they are working as teaching assistants on a part time basis. As a result, it is not appropriate to assign heavy teaching loads to them, due to the fact that they need to focus on their own studies/research. In this regard, the workload equity, namely, the workload of a teaching assistant should be in line with his or her availability, is also very important. Burgess [12] did a comparison study regarding different methods for allocating teaching tasks to faculty members. Vardi [13] carried out a similar work with the objective of analyzing the impacts of workload allocation on the satisfaction of working life of faculty members. Bentley and Kyvik [14] compared the teaching workload allocation statuses in a number of countries. There are a number of works related to the relations between research and teaching for academic staff (e.g., [15–18]). It should be stressed that all of the studies realized that equity has a vital impact on academics' satisfaction. Unfortunately, two issues are not properly addressed. First, the equity issue is largely neglected in the above teaching load allocation optimization models. Second, to the best of our knowledge, there is no research which focuses on the equity issue for teaching assistants.

In this study, we aim to develop teaching assistant assignment models in order to optimize the teaching quality by taking into account various constraints such as equality and availability of teaching assistants. The model can improve the "fitness" between teaching assistants and tutorials without jeopardizing the equity issue of teaching assistants. Further, this proposed model will reduce the workload for school heads, managers, or program coordinators by automatically selecting the optimal solutions.

1.2. Objectives and Contributions. The objective of this research is to develop mixed-integer programming models [19–23] that are able to generate the optimal allocation plan of teaching assistants. The contribution of the paper is threefold: First, we develop a new approach that is able to enhance the overall teaching performance or quality of a teaching unit essentially at no cost. This is due to the fact that our model enables more teaching assistants to teach tutorials that they are competent at. As a result, the teaching assistants' satisfaction can be improved and teaching quality is accordingly improved. The basic assumption is very reasonable: the teaching quality is positively related to the "fitness" between teaching assistants and tutorials that they teach. However, it is very challenging if we want to reach the optimal solution manually: one cannot guarantee that the optimal decision is made. By contrast, mathematical programming approaches could obtain optimal decisions for department heads to assign the teaching tasks.

Second, this allocation is usually done by senior academics (e.g., head of school, deputy head of school, department chair, school manager, and program coordinator). They are naturally very busy with their teaching, research, supervision, and other commitments. Our model can save the valuable time for these academics.

Third, the model considers the maximum teaching load of each teaching assistant. Teaching assistants are usually on a part-time basis. Imposing too much teaching to them will jeopardize their performance in their full time commitment (i.e., study/research). If this allocation is carried out manually by senior academics, it is likely that the maximum teaching is violated due to the fact that manual checking is very time-consuming. This deficiency can be completely overcome using our models.

Fourth, we also consider whether two tutorials are delivered at the same time, and if so, they cannot be taught by the same TA.

Fifth, it is easy to see that if a TA teaches several tutorials of the same lecture, in other words, repeating the tutorials, then the TA can save time for preparation. Our model thus aims to increase the number of tutorial repetitions.

Sixth, it might be difficult for a lecturer to manage if there are too many TAs for the lecturer and hence it may be desirable to control the number of TAs for a lecturer. This factor is also formulated in our model.

The remainder of this paper is organized as follows. Section 2 describes considerations in teaching assistant allocation. Section 3 builds a basic integer linear optimization model. Section 4 reports a number of practical extensions to the basic model. The results of numerical experiment are reported in Section 5. Conclusions are presented in Section 6.

2. Problem Description

This study examines the allocation of teaching assistants at a department or school. In a department, many tutorials for undergraduates and postgraduates are taught by teaching assistants. A teaching assistant has limited time that can be spent on teaching. Different teaching assistants have different maximum numbers of teaching hours because (i) they have different availability and (ii) they have different willingness to teaching. In reality, most teaching assistants are Ph.D. students in a teaching unit. Some students have research scholarships which limit the number of hours that they can spend in teaching, while the others have no scholarships so that the number of hours that they can spend in teaching is only limited by the visa requirement (for international Ph.D. students). As different teaching assistants have different expertise, we classify the relation between a tutorial and a teaching assistant into three types. (i) In the first type, the teaching assistant is unable to teach that tutorial. For example, in a department of mathematics, a teaching assistant with expertise in statistics cannot teach the tutorial for "Group Theory." (ii) In the second type, the teaching assistant can teach a tutorial, but it is not the most suitable person. For example, a teaching assistant with expertise in the structural engineering can teach the elective tutorial "Introduction to Geotechnical Engineering" for civil engineering students, but she/he is not the most suitable person for teaching it, as a teaching assistant with the expertise in geotechnical engineering is more suitable. (iii) In the third type, the teaching assistant is one of the most suitable persons to teach a tutorial. For example, a teaching assistant with expertise in transport engineering should teach the tutorial "Traffic Flow Theory" or "Traffic Engineering Fundamentals" if possible. Another example is that if the teaching assistant taught this tutorial and was highly appraised last year, she or he should also teach it this year if possible.

We can now see that the purpose of optimizing the allocation of teaching assistants includes constraints that all tutorials are taught and that the available teaching time of teaching assistants is satisfied and an objective of maximizing the total number of tutorials delivered by the most appropriate teaching assistant. At the same time, some other practical factors must also be taken into account. For instance, we should consider whether two tutorials are delivered at the same time, and if so, they cannot be taught by the same TA; it is easy to see that if a TA teaches several tutorials of the same lecture, in other words, repeating the tutorials, then the TA can save time for preparation; it might be difficult for a lecturer to manage if there are too many TAs for the lecturer and hence it may be desirable to control the number of TAs for a lecturer.

3. Basic Optimization Model

To address the teaching assistant (TA) assignment problem, we develop an integer optimization model similar to Qu et al. [11]. However, we will present rich extensions to the basic optimization in the next section. The notations used in the basic optimization model are listed below.

Sets

I: set of tutorials

I_j: set of tutorials that TA $j \in J$ may teach; $I_j = \{i \in I \mid j \in J_i\}$

J: set of TAs

J_i: set of TAs who can deliver tutorial $i \in I$; $J_i = J_i^1 \cup J_i^2$

J_i^0: set of TAs who cannot deliver tutorial $i \in I$

J_i^1: set of TAs who can teach but are not the most suitable for delivering tutorial $i \in I$

J_i^2: set of TAs who are the most suitable for delivering tutorial $i \in I$

Indices

i: an index $i \in I$ that refers to a particular tutorial

j: an index $j \in J$ that refers to a particular TA

Parameters

$n_j^{\min}$: the minimum number of tutorials that must be delivered by TA $j \in J$: it can be set at 0 if there is no such requirement

$n_j^{\max}$: the maximum number of tutorials that can be delivered by TA $j \in J$

t_i: the number of contact hours required for tutorial $i \in I$: in practice, t_i is usually 1, 2, or 3 hours

$t_j^{\min}$: the minimum number of available hours per week for TA $j \in J$

$t_j^{\max}$: the maximum number of available hours per week for TA $j \in J$

Decision Variables

x_{ij}: a binary decision variable which equals 1 if TA $j \in J_i^1 \cup J_i^2$ delivers tutorial $i \in I$ and 0 otherwise

The above sets and parameters well capture the real decision process. For instance, the sets J_i^0, J_i^1, and J_i^2 can be determined by a survey of the TAs. The survey can have one question for each tutorial, in which each TA must choose one from the following three answers: (a) I like to teach this tutorial very much; (b) This tutorial is not my favorite, but I can teach it if required; (c) I cannot teach this tutorial. Sets J_i^0, J_i^1, and J_i^2 are mutually exclusive and collectively exhaustive; $J = J_i^0 \cup J_i^1 \cup J_i^2$. The teaching load allocation problem for TAs can be formulated as an integer linear programming model:

$$[\text{M0}]:\ \max\ \sum_{i \in I}\sum_{j \in J_i^2} x_{ij} \qquad (1)$$

$$\text{subject to:}\ \sum_{j \in J_i} x_{ij} = 1,\quad i \in I \qquad (2)$$

$$t_j^{\min} \le \sum_{i \in I_j} t_i x_{ij} \le t_j^{\max},\quad j \in J \qquad (3)$$

$$n_j^{\min} \le \sum_{i \in I_j} x_{ij} \le n_j^{\max},\quad j \in J \qquad (4)$$

$$x_{ij} \in \{0,1\},\quad i \in I,\ j \in J_i. \qquad (5)$$

The objective function (1) maximizes the total number of tutorials that are taught by the most suitable TAs. Equation (2) imposes that all tutorials are taught. Equations (3) and (4) take into account the available time of each TA. Finally, (5) defines the domains of the decision variables.

Proposition 1. *The above integer linear programming model cannot be solved as a linear program.*

Proof. We construct an example to show that relaxing the integrality constraints may not lead to a correct solution. Suppose that there are two TAs and one tutorial; the tutorial requires two hours; the first TA is the most suitable but has only one available hour; the second TA, with two available hours, can teach the tutorial but is not the most suitable. It is evident that the only feasible solution to the problem is to let the second TA teach the tutorial. However, solving a linear program will require the first TA to teach for one hour and the second TA to teach for one hour. □

The size of the above integer linear programming model is usually not large for several reasons. First, many courses do not have tutorials. Second, even in one department, there are several areas of specialization and TAs in one area of specialization can usually only teach tutorials for courses in this area. For example, in a mathematics department, there are at least three areas: pure mathematics, applied mathematics, and statistics. Even in the area of applied mathematics, there is, for instance, financial mathematics, chemical mathematics, medical mathematics, and operations

research. TAs in one subarea may not be able to teach tutorials in other subareas. As a result, the overall model for a department can be decomposed for each area or subarea. Our numerical experiments in Section 5 show that the model can be solved by off-the-shelf solvers such as CPLEX.

4. Extensions to the Basic Integer Programming Model

The above basic integer linear programming model captures the most essential features of the TA assignment problem. However, there are many other realistic factors that must be addressed before the above model can be put into use directly or put into use after minimal manual adjustment. We elaborate these factors and present approaches on how to model these factors.

4.1. Time Conflict of Two Tutorials. Usually the schedules of the tutorials are a priori determined. For instance, if the course "Basics of Calculus" has 3 tutorials, then the 3 tutorials are usually scattered uniformly in a week. As a result, it is likely that one tutorial (say, tutorial i is from 4:00 pm to 5:00 pm on Monday) has time overlap with another tutorial (say, tutorial k is from 3:00 pm to 5:00 pm on Monday). In this case, the two tutorials cannot be taught by the same TA.

To address this difficulty, we define a new binary parameter θ_{ik}, which equals 1 if and only if tutorial i and tutorial k have no time conflict, meaning that they could be taught by the same TA. We add the following constraints to the basic model to formulate the time constraints:

$$[\text{M1}]:\ x_{ij} + x_{kj} \le 1 + \theta_{ik},$$
$$j \in J_i \cap J_k,\ i \in I,\ k \in I,\ i < k. \qquad (6)$$

Equation (6) means that, for each TA $j \in J$, if two tutorials i and k have time conflict, that is, $\theta_{ik} = 0$, then the TA can teach at most one of them because $x_{ij} + x_{kj} \le 1 + \theta_{ik} = 1$.

Proposition 2. *In constraints (6) if there are a set of tutorials denoted by Ω such that $\theta_{ik} = 0$, $\forall i \in \Omega$, $k \in \Omega$, and $i < k$, then we can strengthen the constraints by combining some of them to one constraint:*

$$\sum_{i \in \Omega} x_{ij} \le 1,\quad j \in J. \qquad (7)$$

Proof. The results hold trivially based on observation. □

4.2. Repetition of Tutorials. Some tutorials may belong to the same course, for example, "Basics of Calculus," and in these tutorials TAs deliver the same contents to students. The tutorials are repeated for two reasons. First, the tutorial class can have a small size of students to facilitate interactions among the students and between students and the TA. Second, repeating the tutorials could provide students with the flexibility of choosing the time slot, choosing the TA, and possibly attending the tutorial twice to improve the learning outcomes. It is convenient for a TA to teach several tutorials that belong to the same course so that she could save time for preparation.

To incorporate the advantage of assigning several tutorials that belong to the same course to one TA, we first define a weight α to represent the benefit of assigning one more same tutorial to a TA. The weight α should be understood to be the value of the saved preparation time by TA. We further define a set H to be the set of courses with at least two tutorials. The set of tutorials that belong to course $h \in H$ is defined to be $\bar{I}_h$. We define new decision variables y_{hj} to be the number of tutorials for course $h \in H$ that are assigned to TA $j \in J$. The objective function (1) should be revised to

$$[\text{M2}]: \ \max \sum_{i \in I} \sum_{j \in J_i^2} x_{ij} + \alpha \sum_{h \in H} \sum_{j \in J} \max \left(y_{hj} - 1, 0 \right) \quad (8)$$

and the following constraints should be added:

$$y_{hj} = \sum_{i \in \bar{I}_h} x_{ij}, \quad h \in H, \ j \in J. \quad (9)$$

Equation (9) counts y_{hj} and the new objective function (8) has the extra term $\alpha \sum_{h \in H} \sum_{j \in J} \max(y_{hj} - 1, 0)$.

It should be noted that the extra term $\alpha \sum_{h \in H} \sum_{j \in J} \max(y_{hj} - 1, 0)$ has the "max" operator that makes the model nonlinear. We propose the following method to linearize the objective function (8). To make the model clear, we explicitly define the new sets, parameters, and decision variables.

Newly Defined Sets

H: set of courses with at least two tutorials

I_h: set of tutorials that belong to course $h \in H$

Newly Defined Parameters

α: benefit of assigning one more same tutorial to a TA

Newly Defined Decision Variables

y_{hj}: number of tutorials for course $h \in H$ that are assigned to TA $j \in J$

z_{hj}: an intermediate binary variable

u_{hj}: an intermediate continuous variable for linearization

The new model is

$$\left[\text{M2}' \right]: \ \max \ \sum_{i \in I} \sum_{j \in J_i^2} x_{ij} + \alpha \sum_{h \in H} \sum_{j \in J} u_{hj} \quad (10)$$

$$\text{subject to:} \quad z_{hj} \leq y_{hj}, \quad h \in H, \ j \in J \quad (11)$$

$$u_{hj} \leq y_{hj} - z_{hj}, \quad h \in H, \ j \in J \quad (12)$$

$$u_{hj} \leq M z_{hj}, \quad h \in H, \ j \in J \quad (13)$$

$$z_{hj} \in \{0, 1\}, \quad h \in H, \ j \in J \quad (14)$$

and constraints (2) to (5) and (9). Note that M in constraints (13) is a large positive number.

Proposition 3. *In constraints (13) the value of M could be set to $|\bar{I}_h|$.*

Proof. The upper bound of u_{hj} is $|\bar{I}_h|$. Therefore, it is sufficient to set M to $|\bar{I}_h|$ in constraints (13). $\square$

4.3. Controlling the Number of TAs for One Course. Some lecturers may want to control the number of TAs for his course. For instance, no lecturer wants to have 12 TAs to teach his tutorials. To reflect this requirement, we define parameter b_h as the maximum number of TAs that are assigned to the tutorials for course $h \in H$. We further define intermediate binary decision variables π_{hj} which equal 1 if and only if TA $j \in J$ teaches at least one tutorial for course $h \in H$. We then could add the following constraints:

$$[\text{M3}]: \ M\pi_{hj} \geq y_{hj}, \quad h \in H, \ j \in J \quad (15)$$

$$\sum_{j \in J} \pi_{hj} \leq b_h, \quad h \in H \quad (16)$$

$$\pi_{hj} \in \{0, 1\}, \quad h \in H, \ j \in J, \quad (17)$$

where in constraints (15) the value of M could be set to $|\bar{I}_h|$ because the upper bound of y_{hj} is $|\bar{I}_h|$.

Note that constraints (16) could be changed to the following ones:

$$\sum_{j \in J} \pi_{hj} \leq b_h, \quad h \in H, \ b_h \leq \left| \bar{I}_h \right| - 1 \quad (18)$$

because if $b_h = |\bar{I}_h|$, then constraints (18) are always satisfied.

4.4. Controlling the Number of Days a TA Works. A TA may like to teach five tutorials, but she may not like to teach one tutorial every day. To reflect this requirement, we define parameter κ_j as the maximum number of days TA $j \in J$ would like to teach. Evidently, $\kappa_j = 1, 2, 3, 4, 5$. We further define set Θ_m to be the set of tutorials taught on day $m = 1, 2, 3, 4, 5$, where 1 means Monday, 2 means Tuesday, and so on. We define intermediate binary decision variable λ_{mj} that equals 1 if and only if TA $j \in J$ needs to teach on day $m = 1, 2, 3, 4, 5$. The following constraints could capture the requirement regarding the number of days a TA works:

$$[\text{M4}]: \ \lambda_{mj} \geq x_{ij}, \quad j \in J, \ m = 1, 2, 3, 4, 5, \ i \in \Theta_m$$

$$\lambda_{mj} \in \{0, 1\}, \quad m = 1, 2, 3, 4, 5, \ j \in J \quad (19)$$

$$\sum_{m=1}^{5} \lambda_{mj} \leq \kappa_j, \quad j \in J.$$

5. Numerical Experiments

We carry out extensive numerical experiments to demonstrate the computational efficiency. The experiments are implemented on a PC with 3.30 GHz of Intel Core i5 CPU and 4 GB of RAM. The algorithm is coded in Matlab 2011b, calling

TABLE 1: Computation time (s) of the models.

Number of tutorials	Number of TAs	[M0]	[M1]	[M2]	[M3]	[M4]
	10	0.0127	0.0119	0.0139	0.0130	0.0140
20	15	0.0139	0.0146	0.0291	0.0158	0.0155
	20	0.0156	0.0148	0.0300	0.0169	0.0176
	15	0.0163	0.0152	0.0276	0.0189	0.0186
25	20	0.0167	0.0164	0.03675	0.0195	0.0200
	25	0.0188	0.0181	0.0433	0.0221	0.0225
	20	0.0192	0.0190	0.0448	0.0233	0.0239
30	25	0.0194	0.0196	0.0558	0.0245	0.0242
	30	0.0210	0.0215	0.0669	0.0272	0.0281

CPLEX12.3 to solve mixed-integer linear programming models.

Different combinations of the number of tutorials and number of TAs (I, J) are considered: $(20, 10)$, $(20, 15)$, $(20, 20)$, $(25, 15)$, $(25, 20)$, $(25, 25)$, $(30, 20)$, $(30, 25)$, and $(30, 30)$, as shown in Table 1. All of the five models [M0], [M1], [M2], [M3], and [M4] are evaluated for each combination. Ten random instances are generated for each model in each combination, and therefore we have a total of $10 \times 5 \times 9 = 450$ instances. The instances are generated as follows. In [M0], for each tutorial-TA combination, there is 1/3 chance that the TA cannot deliver the tutorial, 1/3 chance that the TA can but is not the most suitable, and 1/3 chance that the TA is the most suitable for delivering tutorial; the minimum number of tutorials that must be delivered by a TA is 0; the maximum number of tutorials that can be delivered by a TA is an integer uniformly drawn between 1 and 3; the minimum number of available hours per week for a TA is 0; the maximum number of available hours per week for TA is an integer uniformly drawn between 1 and 5; the number of contact hours required for a tutorial is an integer uniformly drawn between 1 and 2. In [M1], five pairs of tutorials are randomly chosen to have time conflict. In [M2], the number of courses is equal to half the number of tutorials and each tutorial is randomly assigned to a course; the weight α is set at 0.33. In [M3], the maximum number of TAs for a course is an integer uniformly drawn between 1 and 3. In [M4], the maximum number of days a TA works is an integer uniformly drawn between 1 and 5. We report the average CPU time required to solve one instance for each model over the ten random instances in Table 1. It can be seen that all of the models can efficiently be solved. This demonstrates the practical relevance of the proposed models.

6. Conclusions

In this paper, an integer programming model is developed to maximize the teaching quality by assigning most appropriate teaching assistants to their tutorials. The model is very useful for teaching units as (1) it can improve teaching quality by allocating suitable teaching assistants to teach the tutorials; (2) the teaching allocation does not need to be manually allocated, which is a time-consuming process; and (3) the maximum teaching load of each staff will not be violated as it is modeled as hard constraints. Some extensions, which

are formulated as mixed-integer linear programming models, are further addressed to consider more practical factors. This includes the following ones: (1) we consider whether two tutorials are delivered at the same time, and if so, they cannot be taught by the same TA; (2) we increase the number of repetitions of tutorials so that it is easier for the TAs to save time for preparation; (3) a lecturer can control the number of TAs for her/his class. Numerical experiments show that these models can efficiently be solved by off-the-shelf solvers, demonstrating the practical relevance of the proposed models.

Competing Interests

The authors declare that there is no conflict of interests regarding the publication of this manuscript.

Acknowledgments

This study is supported by the Projects of International Cooperation and Exchange of the National Natural Science Foundation of China (no. 5151101143) and Youth Project of National Natural Science Foundation of China (no. 71501038).

References

[1] R. H. McClure and C. E. Wells, "Modeling multiple criteria in the faculty assignment problem," *Socio-Economic Planning Sciences*, vol. 21, no. 6, pp. 389–394, 1987.

[2] F. Y. Partovi and B. Arinze, "A knowledge based approach to the faculty-course assignment problem," *Socio-Economic Planning Sciences*, vol. 29, no. 3, pp. 245–256, 1995.

[3] G. Hu and J. Lei, "English-medium instruction in Chinese higher education: a case study," *Higher Education*, vol. 67, no. 5, pp. 551–567, 2014.

[4] A. Oleson and M. T. Hora, "Teaching the way they were taught? Revisiting the sources of teaching knowledge and the role of prior experience in shaping faculty teaching practices," *Higher Education*, vol. 68, no. 1, pp. 29–45, 2014.

[5] C. Valouxis and E. Housos, "Constraint programming approach for school timetabling," *Computers & Operations Research*, vol. 30, no. 10, pp. 1555–1572, 2003.

[6] G. N. Beligiannis, C. Moschopoulos, and S. D. Likothanassis, "A genetic algorithm approach to school timetabling," *Journal of the Operational Research Society*, vol. 60, no. 1, pp. 23–42, 2009.

[7]   N. Pillay and W. Banzhaf, "An informed genetic algorithm for the examination timetabling problem," *Applied Soft Computing Journal*, vol. 10, no. 2, pp. 457–467, 2010.

[8]   J. A. Breslaw, "A linear programming solution to the faculty assignment problem," *Socio-Economic Planning Sciences*, vol. 10, no. 6, pp. 227–230, 1976.

[9]   M. J. Schniederjans and G. C. Kim, "A goal programming model to optimize departmental preference in course assignments," *Computers & Operations Research*, vol. 14, no. 2, pp. 87–96, 1987.

[10] M. A. Badri, "A two-stage multiobjective scheduling model for [faculty-course-time] assignments," *European Journal of Operational Research*, vol. 94, no. 1, pp. 16–28, 1996.

[11] W. Qu, Y. Zhao, M. Wang, and B. Liu, "Research on teaching gamification of software engineering," in *Proceedings of the 9th International Conference on Computer Science & Education (ICCSE '14)*, Vancouver, Canada, August 2014.

[12] T. F. Burgess, "Planning the academic's workload: different approaches to allocating work to university academics," *Higher Education*, vol. 32, no. 1, pp. 63–75, 1996.

[13] I. Vardi, "The impacts of different types of workload allocation models on academic satisfaction and working life," *Higher Education*, vol. 57, no. 4, pp. 499–508, 2009.

[14] P. J. Bentley and S. Kyvik, "Academic work from a comparative perspective: a survey of faculty working time across 13 countries," *Higher Education*, vol. 63, no. 4, pp. 529–547, 2012.

[15] C. Halse, E. Deane, J. Hobson, and G. Jones, "The research—teaching nexus: what do national teaching awards tell us?" *Studies in Higher Education*, vol. 32, no. 6, pp. 727–746, 2007.

[16] J. C. Shin, "Teaching and research nexuses across faculty career stage, ability and affiliated discipline in a South Korean research university," *Studies in Higher Education*, vol. 36, no. 4, pp. 485–503, 2011.

[17] S. Hornibrook, "Policy implementation and academic workload planning in the managerial university: understanding unintended consequences," *Journal of Higher Education Policy and Management*, vol. 34, no. 1, pp. 29–38, 2012.

[18] J. D. J. Kenny and A. E. Fluck, "The effectiveness of academic workload models in an institution: a staff perspective," *Journal of Higher Education Policy and Management*, vol. 36, no. 6, pp. 585–602, 2014.

[19] F. Li, Z. Gao, K. Li, and D. Z. W. Wang, "Train routing model and algorithm combined with train scheduling," *Journal of Transportation Engineering*, vol. 139, no. 1, pp. 81–91, 2013.

[20] Z. Liu, S. Wang, W. Chen, and Y. Zheng, "Willingness to board: a novel concept for modeling queuing up passengers," *Transportation Research Part B: Methodological*, vol. 90, pp. 70–82, 2016.

[21] D. Z. W. Wang, H. Liu, and W. Y. Szeto, "A novel discrete network design problem formulation and its global optimization solution algorithm," *Transportation Research E*, vol. 79, pp. 213–230, 2015.

[22] H. Liu and D. Z. W. Wang, "Global optimization method for network design problem with stochastic user equilibrium," *Transportation Research B*, vol. 72, pp. 20–39, 2015.

[23] B. Du and D. Z. W. Wang, "Continuum modeling of park-and-ride services considering travel time reliability and heterogeneous commuters—a linear complementarity system approach," *Transportation Research Part E: Logistics and Transportation Review*, vol. 71, pp. 58–81, 2014.

8

Resource Allocation Optimization Model of Collaborative Logistics Network Based on Bilevel Programming

Xiao-feng Xu, Wei-hong Chang, and Jing Liu

College of Economics and Management, China University of Petroleum, Qingdao 266580, China

Correspondence should be addressed to Xiao-feng Xu; xuxiaofeng@upc.edu.cn

Academic Editor: Tomàs Margalef

Collaborative logistics network resource allocation can effectively meet the needs of customers. It can realize the overall benefit maximization of the logistics network and ensure that collaborative logistics network runs orderly at the time of creating value. Therefore, this article is based on the relationship of collaborative logistics network supplier, the transit warehouse, and sellers, and we consider the uncertainty of time to establish a bilevel programming model with random constraints and propose a genetic simulated annealing hybrid intelligent algorithm to solve it. Numerical example shows that the method has stronger robustness and convergence; it can achieve collaborative logistics network resource allocation rationalization and optimization.

1. Introduction

Collaborative logistics network is a supply and demand network, which consists of supply collaboration nodes such as raw materials and equipment and logistics function collaboration nodes such as transportation and warehousing and even road and relationship between nodes [1]. The allocation of resource is to meet the supply and demand network. The aim is to collaborate logistics network enterprise internal and external resources and combine the supply chain system effectively which is composed of producers, manufacturers, and customers to realize the lowest cost and the best quality service [2]. So, reasonable resource allocation process is the basis to realize the orderly operation of the whole logistics network. However, collaborative logistics network has suppliers, transit warehouses, vendors, and other forms of logistics node and has some characteristics such as being dynamic, open, and complex. It leads to some uncertainty factors in the process of allocating logistics resources that may have an effect on the running time and operating cost. Therefore, this research about resource allocation of collaborative logistics network is how to select nodes in the numerous suppliers and transit warehouse under the condition of considering the influence of uncertainty factors to realize the optimal logistics system.

The current research on collaborative logistics network resource scheduling is not enough in depth and it is mainly concentrated in the delivery path optimization and distribution address selection as well as the relationship between collaboration node and so forth. In terms of path selection, Yu et al. [3] established a scheduling model with time as constraint and the shortest route as object and used artificial intelligence algorithms to solve the problem. Najera [4] used evolutionary algorithm to study transportation routing problem in consideration of capacity of vehicle. Mir and Abolghasemi [5] took vehicle transportation situations of encoring or not into account and proposed the optimal route according to the customer location changes. Chen et al. [6] made full use of geographic information system technology to select path under the constraint of the least distribution sites. In terms of optimal location selection, Cheng et al. [7] study the impact of the rapid transit on the capacity of current urban transportation system, and a two-mode network capacity model, including the travel modes of automobile and transit, is developed based on the well-known road network capacity model. Turskis and Zavadskas [8] used the fuzzy multiple criteria decision to describe fuzziness of site selection of distribution center. Nozick and Turnquist [9] established a location optimization decision model from the aspects of cost and customer responsiveness.

Yang and Zhou [10] built the location selection model with equilibrium constraints considering facility competition on the basis of the equilibrium theory and then applied genetic algorithm and projection algorithm to solve the model. For the relationship between collaboration points, Qiu and Wang [11] develop a robust optimization model for designing a three-echelon supply chain network that consists of manufacturers, distribution centers, and retailers under both demand uncertainty and supply disruptions. Liu et al. [12] considered three-layer logistics service supply chain and studied the order task allocation model between collaboration nodes.

Integrating the documents, we can find that the current research focused on the microscopic aspects, such as path optimization and site selection and used artificial intelligence algorithm to solve the model. But the ideal model cannot fully describe the collaborative allocation of resources due to the network's complexity and some uncertainty factors in the process of resource allocation. Collaborative logistics network resource allocation process involves three levels, which are suppliers, transit warehouse, and vendors, so the bilevel programming model can be used to explain the relationship between every two levels of nods. At the same time, the stochastic constrained programming can protect model against uncertain influence, and it has been applied to the system dynamics, structural dynamics, and financial and other fields [13–15]. Therefore, this article will set up the three-level nodes relationship among the suppliers, transit warehouses, and retailers and establish a bilevel programming model with chance constrained to control uncertainty factors, so as to make the whole logistics network system optimal under meeting the nodes' profit of both sides.

Generally speaking, the bilevel programming is NP-hard problem, Ben-Ayed and Blair (1988) have proved that [16] this problem does not have a polynomial algorithm, so the solution of it is very complicated. Like genetic algorithm (GA) and Simulated Annealing Algorithm (Simulated Annealing, SA), Neural Network Algorithm (NNA), and so forth, some intelligent algorithms were used to solve the bilevel programming problem. Li et al. [17] put forward a genetic algorithm that can effectively solve bilevel programming problem. In this method, they used constraint to transform bilevel problem into a single-level one and designed the binary coding to solve the multiplier, and numerical experiment shows that the given algorithm can find the global optimal solution in the least time. Niwa et al. [18] proposed a bilevel programming problem that the upper class has only one decision-maker while the lower one has multiple decision-makers and a distribution of the genetic algorithm. Li and Wang [19] studied a special kind of linear quadratic bilevel programming problems, and genetic algorithm was proposed after being converted into equivalent problem.

Genetic algorithm by the ideas of the fittest in nature chooses an optimal individual for the solution of the model by selection, crossover, and mutation genetic operation. Although it has some characteristics such as simple operation, strong operability, and problem space independence, it is easy to exhibit slow convergence speed and get only local optimal value [20]. Simulated annealing algorithm is the result of logistics annealing principle of solid matter, starting

from an initial temperature to find the optimal solution in the solution space with the reduction of the temperature parameters. Although it can get the global optimal solution, it evolved slowly and has strong dependence on parameters [21]. So there are advantages and disadvantages, respectively, of the two algorithms, hybrid genetic simulated annealing algorithms can compensate deficiency for each other, they not only can search the related areas of optimal solution in the global but also can find the optimal solution in the region of the optimal solution, and there have been some scholars who have done the related research. Wang and Zheng [22] proposed a hybrid heuristic algorithm, the algorithm mixed the genetic algorithm and simulated annealing method and the sampling process of simulated annealing method instead of mutation operators of genetic algorithm, and this algorithm improves the local search ability of genetic algorithm. Wang et al. [23] assume that the drivers all make route choices based on Stochastic User Equilibrium (SUE) principle. Two methods, that is, the sensitivity analysis-based method and genetic algorithm (GA), are detailedly formulated to solve the bilevel reserve capacity problem. Kong et al. [24] establish a bilevel programming model of land use structure indexes variables and use GASA to solve the problem, and land and road area ratio should be improved by numerical example results. So in this paper designing the combination of genetic and simulated annealing hybrid algorithm, to solve the bilevel programming problem, is feasible.

2. Considering Uncertainty Resource Deployment of Bilevel Programming Model

2.1. Bilevel Programming Model. Bilevel programming (BP) [25] model was presented by Bracken and McGill in 1973, the lower decision-maker makes decision in the first place, the upper policymakers must predict the possible reaction of the lower ones, and then the lower one reacts according to the decision of the upper one to optimize the objective function of the individual. The general model is

$$
\begin{aligned}
&\min_{x \in X} \quad F(x, y) \\
&\text{s.t.} \quad G(x, y) \leq 0, \\
&\min_{y \in Y} \quad f(x, y) \\
&\text{s.t.} \quad g(x, y) \leq 0.
\end{aligned}
\tag{1}
$$

Among them, $x \in R^{n_1}$ and $y \in R^{n_2}$. The upper variable is $x \in R^{n_1}$, and the lower variable is $y \in R^{n_2}$. Also, the functions $F : R^{n_1} \times R^{n_2} \to R$ and $f : R^{n_1} \times R^{n_2} \to R$ are the upper and the lower objective function, respectively, and vector-valued functions $G : R^{n_1} \times R^{n_2} \to R^{m_1}$ and $g : R^{n_1} \times R^{n_2} \to R^{m_2}$ are, respectively, the upper and the lower constraint conditions.

2.2. Chance Constrained Programming Model. Chance Constrained Programming [26] is a method of stochastic programming put forward by Charnes and Cooper in 1959. It allows decision value within a certain range of fluctuations considering the possibility that decision-making process may not meet the constraint conditions, but the probability of the constraint set-up must not be less than a certain confidence level α which is small enough. The general model is

$$\min \quad Z(x) = \sum_{j=1}^{n} c_j x_j$$

$$\text{s.t.} \quad \Pr\left[\sum_{j=1}^{n} a_{1j} x_j \geq b_1, \ldots, \sum_{j=1}^{n} a_{mj} x_j \geq b_m \right] \geq \alpha \quad (2)$$

$$x_j \geq 0 \quad j = 1, 2, \ldots, n.$$

Among them, $\Pr[\ ]$ is the probability of the event set-up, α is the confidence probability for the condition, b_m are random variables that obey a certain distribution, and a and b obey $N(\mu_1, \sigma_1^2)$ and $N(\mu_2, \sigma_2^2)$, respectively.

2.3. The Model of Collaborative Logistics Network Resource Allocation considering Uncertainty. This paper researches on the resource allocation optimization decision of multiple suppliers and multiple warehouse transfer nodes and retailers. The raw materials price and transportation fee that each suppliers charge are different, and it is a key issue for the retailers to select the optimization suppliers and carry resources more effectively to their warehouses transfer node. At the same time, the retailers compare the transit fees cost of each warehouse, choosing the lowest one or more warehouses to allocation according to their own requirements, which need to focus on every step of the whole logistics network. This kind of relationship can be explained by bilevel programming model. Described in this paper, the upper programming's goal is how the suppliers realize the profit maximization of their own on the condition of meeting the warehouse requirements; the lower level programming describes the lowest cost during the process of warehouse transit center and retailer.

In order to understand better, we can use mathematical language to describe the problem as follows.

Assume that the logistics network N consists of suppliers $\{S_i \mid i = 1, 2, \ldots, n_i\}$, transit warehouses $\{M_j \mid j = 1, 2, \ldots, n_j\}$, retailers $\{P_k \mid k = 1, 2, \ldots, n_k\}$, and links between each node $\{R \mid R \in R_{S_i M_j} \cup R_{M_j P_k}\}$, including logistics nodes $\{O \mid O \in S \cup M \cup P\}$. When retailer P_k sends the demand quantity $D_l^{P_k}$ of resource $\{l \mid l = 1, 2, \ldots, n_l\}$, the resource will be transported to P_k from warehouses M_j. $X_{M_j P_k}^l$ stands for the quantity of products l that are distributed to the retailers P_k from the warehouses M_j; $X_{S_i M_j}^l$ stands for the quantity of raw materials that are distributed to the warehouses M_j from the suppliers S_i. $\{E(R) \mid E(R) \in E(R_{S_i M_j}) \cup E(R_{M_j P_k})\}$ stand for the distance between all logistics nodes. Due to the different location of logistics nodes, the product fees of transportation, storage, packaging, and processing for each unit are also different. Therefore, $\{C(R) \mid C(R) \in C(R_{S_i M_j}^l) \cup C(R_{M_j P_k}^l)\}$ stand for the cost of each unit distance between different logistics nodes to transport resources l; $C(f_O^l)$ and $C(g_O^l)$ stand for the unit cost of storage and processing (including labor) for all logistics nodes. Suppliers as the disclosing party, charge transit warehouses $C(X_{S_i M_j}^l)$ for the resources l. Considering that all logistic nodes have a certain amount of time requirement to order processing and distribution of resources, the times of delivery requirement from warehouses to retailers and supplies to warehouses, respectively, are $T_{M_j P_k}^l$ and $T_{S_i M_j}^l$, the times of order processing and production processing, respectively, are $T_{M_j P_k}^l{}'$, $T_{S_i M_j}^l{}'$, $T_{M_j P_k}^l{}''$, and $T_{M_j P_k}^l{}''$; transport vehicle maximum loading capacities, respectively, are $G_{M_j R_k}$ and $G_{S_i M_j}$.

In the process of research, the assumptions made are as follows for the purpose of simplified model:

(1) All land transportation is between all logistics nodes.

(2) The logistics node routes and distance have to be known and are fixed.

(3) Vehicle average speed is V during the process of transportation between various logistics nodes.

2.3.1. The Upper Programming considering the Relationship between Suppliers and Warehouse Transit Centers

$$\max F_1 = \sum_{j=1}^{n} \sum_{k=1}^{n} \sum_{l=1}^{n} \sum_{i=1}^{n} \left(C\left(X_{S_i M_j}^l\right) - C\left(R_{S_i M_j}^l\right) E\left(R_{S_i M_j}\right) - C\left(f_{S_i}^l\right) - C\left(g_{S_i}^l\right) \right) X_{S_i M_j}^l u_i \quad (3)$$

$$\sum_{i=1}^{n} u_i \geq 1 \quad (4)$$

$$G_{S_i M_j} \geq X_{S_i M_j}^l \quad (5)$$

$$\Pr\left[T_{S_i M_j}^l{}' + T_{S_i M_j}^l{}'' + \frac{E\left(R_{S_i M_j}\right)}{V} \leq T_{S_i M_j}^l \right] = \alpha \quad (6)$$

$$u_i X_{S_i M_j}^l = X_{M_j P_k}^l \quad (7)$$

$$X^l_{S_iM_j} \geq 0 \quad i = 1, 2, \ldots, n, \ j = 1, 2, \ldots, n \tag{8}$$

$$u_i \in \{0, 1\}. \tag{9}$$

Among them, (3) is from the point of view of the suppliers, which is pursuing of the profit maximization; (4) ensures warehouse transit centers at least choose one supplier; (5) means the amount of resources that the suppliers provide cannot exceed its maximum of vehicle loading capacity; (6) stands for the probability that order processing time, processing time, and shipping time of supplies cannot exceed the longest time of warehouse transit centers which is α; (7) means the amount of resources that warehouse transit centers provide is equal to what all suppliers provide; (8) resource demand is a positive number; (9) is supplier's 0-1 variable constraints, which means that select supplier i has a value of 1 or a value of 0.

2.3.2. The Lower Programming considering the Relationships between Warehouse Transit Centers and Retailers

$$\min F_2$$

$$= \sum_{j=1}^n \sum_{k=1}^n \sum_{l=1}^n \sum_{j=1}^n \left(C\left(R^l_{M_jP_k}\right) E\left(R_{M_jP_k}\right) + C\left(f^l_{M_j}\right) + C\left(g^l_{M_j}\right) \right) \tag{10}$$

$$\cdot X^l_{M_jP_k} u_j$$

$$\sum_{j=1}^n u_j \geq 1 \tag{11}$$

$$\sum_{j=1}^n \sum_{k=1}^n \sum_{j=1}^n u_j X^l_{M_jP_k} \geq D^{P_k}_l \tag{12}$$

$$G_{M_jR_k} \geq X^l_{M_jP_k} \tag{13}$$

$$\Pr\left[T^l_{M_jP_k}{}' + T^l_{M_jP_k}{}'' + \frac{E\left(R_{M_jP_k}\right)}{V} \leq T^l_{M_jP_k} \right] = \beta \tag{14}$$

$$X^l_{M_jP_k} \geq 0 \quad j = 1, 2, \ldots, n, \ k = 1, 2, \ldots, n \tag{15}$$

$$u_j \in \{0, 1\}. \tag{16}$$

Among them, expression (10) stands for the warehouse transit center and distributors as a whole, pursuing the minimizing cost including transportation and storage and producing cost; (11) ensures that retailers choose at least one supply warehouse transit center; (12) means the total resources that product warehouse transit centers provide should meet the demand of retailers P_k; (13) means the amount of resources that warehouse transit centers provide cannot exceed its maximum of vehicle loading capacity; (14) stands for the probability that the order processing time, processing time, and shipping time of warehouse transit centers cannot exceed the longest time of retailers which is β; (15) means resource demand is a positive number; (16)

is warehouse transit centers' 0-1 variable constraints, which means that chosen warehouse j has a value of 1 or value of 0.

3. The Solution to the Resource Allocation Bilevel Programming Model considering Uncertainty

3.1. Random Planning Constraints Transformation. As for the uncertain factors during transportation and order processing, we need to transform them into deterministic constraints. The solution method of stochastic programming constraint probably has two kinds: one is transforming the stochastic programming into a deterministic mathematical programming through certain changes and then using the existing method that solves the deterministic mathematical programming to solve; the other method is to use the intelligent algorithm such as neural network based on the idea of approximation function.

Due to solving bilevel programming after stochastic programming constraints transformation, we take the first method to research. The order processing times $T^l_{M_jP_k}{}'$ and $T^l_{S_iM_j}{}'$, respectively, obey the normal distributions $T^l_{M_jP_k}{}' \sim N(\mu(T^l_{M_jP_k}{}'), \sigma(T^l_{M_jP_k}{}')^2)$ and $T^l_{S_iM_j}{}' \sim N(\mu(T^l_{S_iM_j}{}'), \sigma(T^l_{S_iM_j}{}')^2)$; $T^l_{M_jP_k}{}''$ and $T^l_{S_iM_j}{}''$, respectively, obey the normal distributions $T^l_{M_jP_k}{}'' \sim N(\mu(T^l_{M_jP_k}{}''), \sigma(T^l_{M_jP_k}{}'')^2)$ and $T^l_{S_iM_j}{}'' \sim N(\mu(T^l_{S_iM_j}{}''), \sigma(T^l_{S_iM_j}{}'')^2)$; $E(R_{M_jP_k})/V$ and $E(R_{S_iM_j})/V$, respectively, obey the normal distributions $E(R_{M_jP_k})/V \sim N(\mu(E(R_{M_jP_k})/V), \sigma(E(R_{M_jP_k})/V)^2)$ and $E(R_{S_iM_j})/V \sim N(\mu(E(R_{S_iM_j})/V), \sigma(E(R_{S_iM_j})/V)^2)$.

So the stochastic programming constraint (7)

$$\Pr\left[T^l_{S_iM_j}{}' + T^l_{S_iM_j}{}'' + \frac{E\left(R_{S_iM_j}\right)}{V} \leq T^l_{S_iM_j} \right] = \alpha \tag{17}$$

can be transformed into

$$\mu\left(T^l_{S_iM_j}{}'\right) + \phi^{-1}(\alpha)\,\sigma\left(T^l_{S_iM_j}{}'\right) + \mu\left(T^l_{S_iM_j}{}''\right)$$

$$+ \phi^{-1}(\alpha)\,\sigma\left(T^l_{S_iM_j}{}''\right) + \mu\left(\frac{E\left(R_{S_iM_j}\right)}{V}\right) \tag{18}$$

$$+ \phi^{-1}(\alpha)\,\sigma\left(\frac{E\left(R_{S_iM_j}\right)}{V}\right) \leq T^l_{S_iM_j}$$

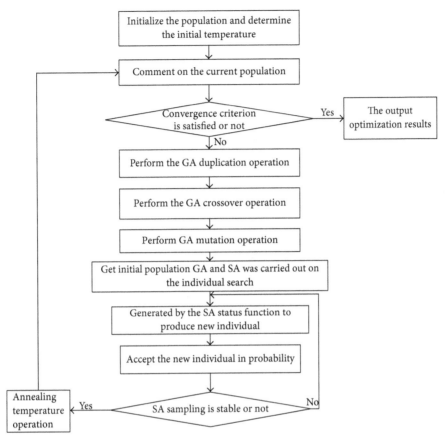

FIGURE 1: The solving steps of genetic simulated annealing algorithm.

and the stochastic programming constraint (14)

$$\Pr\left[T^l_{M_j P_k}{}' + T^l_{M_j P_k}{}'' + \frac{E\left(R_{M_j P_k}\right)}{V} \le T^l_{M_j P_k} \right] = \beta \qquad (19)$$

can be transformed into

$$\mu\left(T^l_{M_j P_k}{}'\right) + \phi^{-1}\left(\beta\right)\sigma\left(T^l_{M_j P_k}{}'\right) + \mu\left(T^l_{M_j P_k}{}''\right)$$

$$+ \phi^{-1}\left(\beta\right)\sigma\left(T^l_{M_j P_k}{}''\right) + \mu\left(\frac{E\left(R_{M_j P_k}\right)}{V}\right) \qquad (20)$$

$$+ \phi^{-1}\left(\beta\right)\sigma\left(\frac{E\left(R_{M_j P_k}\right)}{V}\right) \le T^l_{M_j P_k}.$$

3.2. The Solving Thought of Genetic Simulated Annealing Algorithm. The basic idea of genetic simulated annealing algorithm is as follows: firstly encoding the upper planning variables and solving the lower programming to calculate the fitness of each string. And then one can get the best series through copy, crossover, mutation, and simulated annealing. Specific steps are shown as Figure 1.

Step 1. Initialization

(1-1) Set parameters, including the crossover probability of genetic algorithm P_c, mutation probability P_m, each generation population of individuals (chromosomes) number N, and largest evolution algebra Maxgen. Set the evolution algebra gen = 0

(1-2) Confirm the number of inner loops M and the initial value of the temperature T_o of simulated annealing algorithm; let $T = T_o$

(1-3) Determine a reasonable fitness function according to the objective function F_1 of upper programming, determine the encoding way of the decision variable u of upper programming, and randomly generate initial population $X(1) = (\ldots, x_i(1), \ldots)$, $i = 1, 2, \ldots, N$; let gen = 1

Step 2. Take $X(\text{gen})$ into lower programming to be UE distribution calculation, and calculate the fitness of each individual $x_i(\text{gen})$ $(i = 1, 2, \ldots, N)$. If gen = Maxgen, the largest fitness chromosome is the optimal solution of resource allocation; else, turn to Step 3.

Step 3. Copy group $X(\text{gen})$ according to the fitness distribution.

Step 4. It is crossover operation according to the crossover probability P_c.

Step 5. Perform mutation operation according to the mutation probability P_m; let gen = gen + 1, get a new population $X(\text{gen})$, and then calculate the fitness of individuals of $X(\text{gen})$.

Step 6. For $i = 1$, conducting the simulated annealing of species $X(\text{gen})$ is as follows:

(6-1) If $i = N$, turn to Step 7; otherwise the cycle counting round $k = 1$, and turn to (6-2).

(6-2) Get individual $x_i(\text{gen})$ by state function, then decode new individuals, and conduct UE distribution calculation under lower programming to get the objective function value of the upper programming, and calculate the fitness.

(6-3) Accept new individual under Metropolis probability acceptance formula.

(6-4) if $k = M$, $i = i + 1$, turn to (6-1); else, $k = k + 1$, turn to (6-2).

Step 7. Annealing temperature: let $T = 0.5T$, and turn to Step 2.

Description is as follows:

(1) The upper decision variables generally take binary encoding; multivariate encoding is as follows:

$$\begin{array}{cccccc}
\text{decision variables } u = & u_1 & \vert & u_2 & \vert \cdots \vert & u_n \\
\text{mapping} & \downarrow & & \downarrow & \downarrow \quad \downarrow & \downarrow \\
\text{Chromosome (string) } x = & 0011 & \vert & 1011 & \vert \cdots \vert & 0110.
\end{array} \quad (21)$$

(2) In (1-3), the relationship between the length of the substring β and the precision of decision variables π is

$$\beta \geq \log_2 \left(\frac{u_{\max} - u_{\min}}{\pi} + 1 \right). \quad (22)$$

(3) In a (6-2), SA state function can do random exchange of two different genes positions of chromosome and reverse genes order of different random position of chromosome, such as

$$\begin{array}{cccc}
\text{Decision variables } u = & u_1 & \vert & u_2 \\
\text{Genes Position} & 2 \ 5 & \vert & 3 \ 7 \\
\text{Chromosome } x = & 01100101 & \vert & 10110101.
\end{array} \quad (23)$$

Assume that the random variable, respectively, positions are 2 and 3 and 5 and 7, and the new individuals after exchanging and reversing are

$$\begin{aligned}
x_1 &= 00101101 \mid 10010111 \\
x_2 &= 00011101 \mid 10010111.
\end{aligned} \quad (24)$$

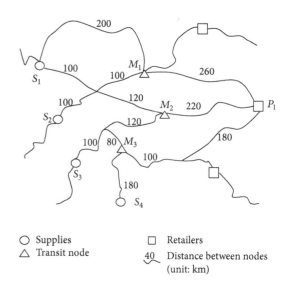

FIGURE 2: Production and sale collaborative logistics network of one sneaker brand.

TABLE 1: The distance between each supplier and transit warehouse.

	M_1/km	M_2/km	M_3/km
S_1	200	240	∞
S_2	240	220	∞
S_3	∞	220	180
S_4	∞	∞	180

4. The Sample Simulation

4.1. Sample. Taking the collaborative logistics network production-sales of one sneaker brand as an example, a product retailer put forward a demand of 4000 pieces of goods to the transit warehouse according to the sales plan and product orders. Assume that we can choose goods from four suppliers and three transit warehouses that are available, vehicle average speed is 40 kilometers per hour between various logistics nodes in the process of transportation, the biggest load capacities from suppliers to the transit warehouses and from transit warehouses to retailers are, respectively, 2000 and 3000, and specific arrangement is shown in Figure 2.

The distance between all suppliers to the transit warehouse is shown in Table 1; the suppliers' storage and processing fees for each unit are shown in Table 2. The distance between each transit warehouse to the retailer and the transit warehouses' storage and processing fees for each unit are shown in Table 3.

4.2. Solving Example. The actual, material delivery time that warehouse transit node and retailer require is 10 hours and 12 hours, because of that the supplier and warehouse transit point have some uncertain factors such as the order processing and production, time obeys the normal distribution as Table 4 shows, there are also uncertainty factors on transport which obey the normal distribution table as shown in Table 5, value interval is $\mu \pm 3\sigma$, namely, the probability that the value points fall in the interval is 99.73%, and the probability

TABLE 2: The material charge and cost for each unit of storage and transportation of suppliers.

	Material charges (RMB)	Storage charges (RMB)	Processing charges (RMB)	Transportation charges (RMB)
S_1	110	0.1	0.15	0.02
S_2	100	0.15	0.15	0.03
S_3	110	0.1	0.1	0.035
S_4	100	0.15	0.1	0.025

TABLE 3: The distance between retailer and transit warehouses and transit warehouses' cost for unit of storage and transportation.

	Distance (km)	Storage charges (RMB)	Processing charges (RMB)	Transportation charges (RMB)
M_1	260	0.2	0.25	0.02
M_2	220	0.3	0.2	0.025
M_3	280	0.2	0.15	0.015

TABLE 4: The uncertain index value of the supplier and warehouse transfer point's order processing and production (unit: hours).

	Order processing time	Production and processing time
Supplier	$N(0.1, 5)$	$N(1, 5)$
Storage and transit point	$N(0.2, 5)$	$N(0.5, 5)$

TABLE 5: The uncertain index value of transport time range of suppliers to transit warehouse and warehouse transfer to seller (unit: hours).

	M_1	M_2	M_3
S_1	$N(5, 5)$	$N(6, 5)$	∞
S_2	$N(6, 5)$	$N(5.5, 5)$	∞
S_3	∞	$N(5.5, 5)$	$N(4.5, 5)$
S_4	∞	∞	$N(4.5, 5)$
Seller	$N(6.5, 5)$	$N(5.5, 5)$	$N(7, 5)$

that ensures finishing the logistics tasks in the time of the warehouse transit node and retailer is 90%, which means α and β both are 90%.

The parameters of the algorithm are as follows: the population size is 50, the crossover probability is 0.6, the probability of mutation is 0.1, the cooling coefficient is 0.95, and the initial temperature is 100. The result converges to the optimal solution after 45 generations by using Matlab7.0 for many times while traditional genetic algorithm iteration number is 64, as shown in Figure 3. The optimal solution in the genetic simulated annealing algorithm is shown in Table 5.

It can be seen as shown in Table 6 that supplier S_1 deployed 1000 unit materials to transit warehouse M_1, supplier S_4, respectively, deployed 1999.99 and 1000.01 unit materials to M_2 and M_3, on the basis of meeting the expected

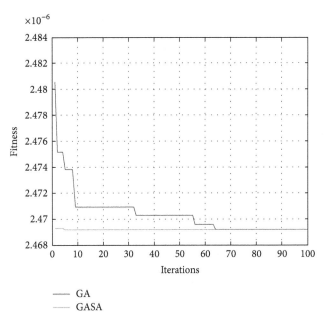

FIGURE 3: The convergence comparison chart of genetic simulated annealing algorithm and genetic algorithm.

TABLE 6: The resources allocation for each supplier to the warehouse transfer point.

	M_1	M_2	M_3
S_1	1000		
S_2			
S_3			
S_4		1999.99	1000.01

delivery time, and it makes the supplier's profit maximum 405000 Yuan while retailer's cost is minimum about 19300 Yuan while, on the basis of traditional genetic algorithm, the maximum profit of suppliers is 404990 Yuan. The result indicates that the solution can maximize the interests of both sides, which verify the operability and optimization of the model.

5. Conclusion

Collaborative logistics network is a virtual organization, which is led by manufacturing/service companies or independent third-party logistics enterprise. It is a supply and demand network made up of supply collaboration nodes, function of logistics nodes, and the link road and relationship between nodes; the core task is overall plan and deployment access of the network node resources to realize the overall interests and meet the customer service. Therefore, this paper establishes a supply-sales network on the basis of collaborative logistics network resource allocation model, which includes collaborative logistics network suppliers, warehouse transit nodes, retailers, and their node link. From retailer's demand as a starting point, considering the shipping time and quantity and distribution cost factors, we establish a bilevel programming model with uncertainty factors. On this basis, we use the genetic simulated annealing algorithm to analyze and solve the model, which can get the optimal scheme that can not only meet suppliers benefit maximization but also make cost minimum to retailers. The analysis results show the feasibility and validity of the model, which can provide the optimal resource allocation decisions and plans.

Competing Interests

The authors declare that there is no conflict of interests regarding the publication of this paper.

Acknowledgments

This research was supported by the National Natural Science Foundation of China (Grant no. 71501188), the Natural Science Foundation of Shandong Province, China (Grant no. ZR2015GQ006), and the Fundamental Research Funds for the Central Universities, China (Grant no. 15CX04100B).

References

[1] X.-F. Xu, J.-L. Zhao, and J.-K. Song, "Uncertain control optimization of resource planning for collaborative logistics network about complex manufacturing," *System Engineering Theory & Practice*, vol. 32, no. 4, pp. 799–806, 2012.

[2] L. H. Shan and Z. Y. Zhang, "Analysis on logistics network system operation mode based on dissipative structure," *Logistics Science-Technology*, vol. 12, no. 28, pp. 86–89, 2014.

[3] B. Yu, Z. Z. Yang, and B. Z. Yao, "A hybrid algorithm for vehicle routing problem with time windows," *Expert Systems with Applications*, vol. 38, no. 1, pp. 435–441, 2011.

[4] A. G. Najera, "The vehicle routing problem with backhauls: a multi-objective evolutionary approach," *Evolutionary Computation in Combinatorial Optimization*, vol. 7245, no. 42, pp. 255–266, 2012.

[5] H. S. A. Mir and N. Abolghasemi, "Aparticle swarm optimization algorithm for open vehicle routing problem," *Expert Systems with Applications*, vol. 38, no. 9, pp. 11547–11551, 2011.

[6] Y. Chen, R. Z. Ruan, and M. C. Yan, "Algorithm of path optimization for physical distribution based on GIS," *Geospatial Information*, vol. 2, no. 10, pp. 104–182, 2012.

[7] L. Cheng, M. Du, X. Jiang, and H. Rakha, "Modeling and estimating the capacity of urban transportation network with rapid transit," *Transport*, vol. 29, no. 2, pp. 165–174, 2014.

[8] Z. Turskis and E. K. Zavadskas, "A new fuzzy additive ratio assessment method (ARAS-F). Case study: the analysis of fuzzy multiple criteria in order to select the logistic centers location," *Transport*, vol. 25, no. 4, pp. 423–432, 2010.

[9] L. K. Nozick and M. A. Turnquist, "Inventory, transportation, service quality and the location of distribution centers," *European Journal of Operational Research*, vol. 129, no. 2, pp. 362–371, 2001.

[10] Y. X. Yang and G. G. Zhou, "Study on location model of facility competition for closed-loop supply chain network with random demands," *Control and Decision*, vol. 10, no. 26, pp. 1553–1561, 2011.

[11] R. Qiu and Y. Wang, "Supply chain network design under demand uncertainty and supply disruptions: a distributionally robust optimization approach," *Scientific Programming*, vol. 2016, Article ID 3848520, 15 pages, 2016.

[12] W. H. Liu, S. Y. Qu, and S. Y. Zhong, "Order allocation in three-echelon logistics service supply chain under stochastic environments," *Computer Integrated Manufacturing Systems*, vol. 2, no. 18, pp. 381–388, 2012.

[13] Q. Zeng and X.-Z. Xu, "Assessing the reliability of a multistate logistics network under the transportation cost constraint," *Discrete Dynamics in Nature and Society*, vol. 2016, Article ID 2628950, 8 pages, 2016.

[14] P. Guo, G. H. Huang, and Y. P. Li, "An inexact fuzzy-chance-constrained two-stage mixed-integer linear programming approach for flood diversion planning under multiple uncertainties," *Advances in Water Resources*, vol. 33, no. 1, pp. 81–91, 2010.

[15] B. Aouni, C. Colapinto, and D. La Torre, "A cardinality constrained stochastic goal programming model with satisfaction functions for venture capital investment decision making," *Annals of Operations Research*, vol. 205, pp. 77–88, 2013.

[16] X. Zhang, H. Wang, and W. Wang, "Bi-level programming model and algorithms for stochastic network with elastic demand," *Transport*, vol. 30, no. 1, pp. 117–128, 2015.

[17] H. Li, Y. Jiao, and L. Zhang, "Orthogonal genetic algorithm for solving quadratic bi-level programming problems," *Journal of Systems Engineering and Electronics*, vol. 21, no. 5, pp. 763–770, 2010.

[18] K. Niwa, T. Hayashida, M. Sakawa, and Y. Yang, "Computational methods for decentralized two level 0-1 programming problems through distributed genetic algorithms," *AIP Conference Proceedings*, vol. 1285, no. 1, pp. 1–13, 2010.

[19] H. C. Li and Y. P. Wang, "A genetic algorithm for solving linear-quadratic bi-level programming problems," in *New Trends and Applications of Computer-Aided Material and Engineering*, pp. 626–630, Trans Tech Publications, 2012.

[20] S. Yu, Q. Yang, J. Tao et al., "Product modular design incorporating life cycle issues-Group Genetic Algorithm(GGA) based method," *Journal of Cleaner Production*, vol. 19, no. 9-10, pp. 1016–1032, 2011.

[21] B. Sankararao and C. K. Yoo, "Development of a robust multi-objective simulated annealing algorithm for solving multi-objective optimization problems," *Industrial & Engineering Chemistry Research*, vol. 50, no. 11, pp. 6728–6742, 2011.

[22] L. Wang and D.-Z. Zheng, "A modified evolutionary programming for flow shop scheduling," *International Journal of Advanced Manufacturing Technology*, vol. 22, no. 7, pp. 522–527, 2003.

[23] J. Wang, W. Deng, and J. Zhao, "Road network reserve capacity with stochastic user equilibrium," *Transport*, vol. 30, no. 1, pp. 103–116, 2015.

[24] Z. Kong, X. Guo, and J. Hou, "Urban land structure planning model based on green transportation system principal," in *Proceedings of the 10th International Conference of Chinese Transportation Professionals—Integrated Transportation Systems: Green, Intelligent, Reliable (ICCTP '10)*, Beijing, China, August 2010.

[25] J. Bracken and J. T. McGill, "Mathematical programs with optimization problems in the constraints," *Operations Research*, vol. 21, pp. 37–44, 1973.

[26] A. Charnes and W. W. Cooper, "Chance-constrained programming," *Management Science*, vol. 6, no. 1, pp. 73–79, 1960.

9

Behaviour Preservation across Code Versions in Erlang

David Insa, Sergio Pérez⬤, Josep Silva⬤, and Salvador Tamarit⬤

Universitat Politècnica de València, Camí de Vera s/n, E-46022 València, Spain

Correspondence should be addressed to Josep Silva; jsilva@dsic.upv.es

Academic Editor: Can Özturan

In any alive and nontrivial program, the source code naturally evolves along the lifecycle for many reasons such as the implementation of new functionality, the optimization of a bottleneck, or the refactoring of an obscure function. Frequently, these code changes affect various different functions and modules, so it can be difficult to know whether the correct behaviour of the previous version has been preserved in the new version. In this paper, we face this problem in the context of the Erlang language, where most developers rely on a previously defined test suite to check the behaviour preservation. We propose an alternative approach to automatically obtain a test suite that specifically focusses on comparing the old and new versions of the code. Our test case generation is directed by a sophisticated combination of several already existing tools such as TypEr, CutEr, and PropEr; and it introduces novel ideas such as allowing the programmer to choose one or more expressions of interest that must preserve the behaviour, or the recording of the sequences of values to which those expressions are evaluated. All the presented work has been implemented in an open-source tool that is publicly available on GitHub.

1. Introduction

During its useful lifetime, a program might evolve many times. Each evolution is often composed of several changes that produce a new release of the software. There are multiple ways of control so that these changes do not modify the behaviour of any part of the program that was already correct. Most of the companies rely on *regression testing* [1, 2] to ensure that a desired behaviour of the original program is kept in the new version, but there exist other alternatives such as the static inference of the impact of changes [3–6].

Even when a program is perfectly working and it fulfils all its functional requirements, sometimes we still need to improve parts of it. There are several reasons why a released program needs to be modified, for instance, improving the maintainability or efficiency, or for other reasons such as obfuscation, security improvement, parallelization, distribution, platform changes, and hardware changes. In the context of scientific programming, it is common to change an algorithm several times until certain performance requirements are met. During each iteration, the code often naturally becomes more complex and, thus, more difficult to understand and debug. Although regression testing should be ideally done after each change, in real projects, the methodology is really different. As reported in [7], only 10% of the companies do regression testing daily. This means that when an error is detected, it can be hidden after a large number of subsequent changes. The authors also claim that this long-term regression testing is mainly due to the lack of time and resources.

Programmers that want to check whether the semantics of the original program remain unchanged in the new version usually create a test suite. There are several tools that can help in all of this process. For instance, Travis CI can be easily integrated in a GitHub repository so that each time a pull request is performed, the test suite is launched. We present here an alternative and complementary approach that creates an automatic test suite to do regression testing: (i) an alternative approach because it can work as a standalone program without the need for other techniques (therefore, our technique can check the evolution of the code even if no test suite has been defined) and (ii) a complementary approach because it can also be used to complement other techniques, providing major reliability in the assurance of behaviour preservation.

More sophisticated techniques, but with similar purpose, have been recently announced like Ubisoft's system [8] that is able to predict programmer errors beforehand. It is quite illustrative that a game-developer company was the first one in presenting a project like this one. The complex algorithms used to simulate physical environments and AI behaviours need several iterations in order to improve their performance. It is in one of those iterations that some regression faults can be introduced.

In the context of debugging, programmers often use breakpoints to observe the values of an expression during an execution. Unfortunately, this feature is not currently available in testing, even though it would be useful to easily focus the test cases on one specific point without modifying the source code (as it happens when using assertions) or adding more code (as it happens in unit testing). In this paper, we introduce the ability to specify *points of interest* (POIs) in the context of testing. A POI can be any expression in the code (e.g., a function call), meaning that we want to check the behaviour of that expression. Although they handle similar concepts, our POIs are not exactly like breakpoints, since their purpose is different. Breakpoints are used to indicate where the computation should stop, so the user can inspect variable values or control statements. In contrast, a POI defines an expression whose sequence of evaluations to values must be recorded, so that we can check the behaviour preservation (by value comparison) after the execution. In particular, note that placing a breakpoint inside a unit test is not the same as placing a POI inside it because the goals are different.

In our technique, (1) the programmer identifies a POI and a set of *input functions* whose invocations should evaluate the POI. Then, by using a combination of random test case generation, mutation testing, and concolic testing, (2) the tool automatically generates a test suite that tries to cover all possible paths that reach the POI (trying also to produce execution paths that evaluate the POI several times). Therefore, in our setting, the *input of a test case* (ITC) is defined as a call to an input function with some specific arguments, and the output is the sequence of those values the POI is evaluated to during the execution of the ITC. For the sake of disambiguation, in the rest of the paper, we use the term *traces* to refer to these sequences of values. Next, (3) the test suite is used to automatically check whether the behaviour of the program remains unchanged across new versions. This is done by passing each individual test case (which contains calls to the input functions) against the new version and checking whether the same traces are produced at the POI. Finally, (4) the user is provided with a report about the success or failure of these test cases. Note that as it is common in regression testing, this approach only works for deterministic executions. However, this does not mean that it cannot be used in a program with concurrency or other sources of nondeterminism; it only depends on where the POIs are placed and the input functions used. In Section 7, we clarify how our approach can be used in such contexts.

After presenting the approach for a single POI, we present an extension that allows for the definition of multiple POIs. With this extension, the user can trace several (and maybe unrelated) functionalities in a single run. It is also useful when we want to strengthen the quality of the test suite by checking, for instance, that the behaviour is kept in several intermediate results. Finally, this extension is needed in those cases where

a POI in one version is associated with more than one POI in another version (e.g., when a POI in the final source code is associated with two or more POIs in the initial source code due to a refactoring or a removal of duplicated code).

We have implemented our approach in a tool named SecEr *(Software Evolution Control for Erlang)*, which is publicly available at https://github.com/mistupv/secer. Instead of reinventing the wheel, some of the analyses performed by our tool are done by other existing tools such as CutEr [9], a concolic testing tool, to generate an initial set of test cases that maximize the branching coverage; TypEr [10], a type inference system for Erlang, to obtain types for the input functions; and PropEr [11], a property-based testing tool, to obtain values of a given type. All the analyses performed by SecEr are transparent to the user. The only task in our technique that requires user intervention is identifying suitable POIs in both the old and the new versions of the program. In order to evaluate our technique and implementation, we present in Section 8 a comparison of SecEr with the most extended alternatives for the detection of discrepancies and their causes in Erlang. All techniques are compared using the same example. Additionally, in Section 9, we complement this study with an empirical evaluation of SecEr.

Example 1. In order to show the potential of the approach, we provide a real example to compare two versions of an Erlang program that computes happy numbers. They are taken from the Rosetta Code repository (consulted in this concrete version: http://rosettacode.org/mw/index.php?title=Happy_numbers&oldid=251560#Erlang) and slightly modified (the introduced changes are explained in Section 6):

http://rosettacode.org/wiki/Happy_numbers#Erlang

The initial and final versions of this code as they appear in Rosetta Code are shown in Listings 1 and 2, respectively. In order to check whether the behaviour is the same in both versions, we could select as POI the call in line (9) of Listing 1 and the call in line (18) of Listing 2. We also need to define a timeout because the test case generation phase could be infinite due to the test mutation process (the number of possible execution paths could be infinite and an infinite number of test cases could be generated). In this example, with a timeout of 15 seconds, SecEr reports that the executions of both versions with respect to the selected POIs behave identically. In Section 6, we show how SecEr can help a user when an error is introduced in this example and how the multiple POIs approach is also helpful to find the source of an error.

2. Overview of Our Approach to Automated Regression Testing

Our technique is divided into three sequential phases that are summarized in Figures 1, 2, and 3. In these figures, the big dark grey areas are used to group several processes with a common objective. Light grey boxes outside these areas represent inputs and light grey boxes inside these areas represent processes, white boxes represent intermediate

```
(1)   -spec main(pos_integer(),pos_integer()) ->
(2)     [pos_integer()].
(3)   main(N, M) ->
(4)     happy_list(N, M, []).
(5)
(6)   happy_list(_, N, L) when length(L) =:= N ->
(7)     lists:reverse(L);
(8)   happy_list(X, N, L) ->
(9)     Happy = is_happy(X),
(10)    if Happy ->
(11)      happy_list(X + 1, N, [X|L]);
(12)    true ->
(13)      happy_list(X + 1, N, L) end.
(14)
(15)  is_happy(1) -> true;
(16)  is_happy(4) -> false;
(17)  is_happy(N) when N > 0 ->
(18)    N_As_Digits =
(19)      [Y - 48 ||
(20)      Y <- integer_to_list(N)],
(21)    is_happy(
(22)      lists:foldl(
(23)        fun(X, Sum) ->
(24)          (X * X) + Sum
(25)        end,
(26)        0,
(27)        N_As_Digits));
(28)  is_happy(_) -> false.
```

LISTING 1: happy0.erl.

```
(1)   is_happy(X, XS) ->
(2)     if
(3)       X == 1 -> true;
(4)       X < 1 -> false;
(5)       true ->
(6)         case member(X, XS) of
(7)           true -> false;
(8)           false ->
(9)             is_happy(sum(map(fun(Z) -> Z*Z end,
(10)              [Y - 48 || Y <- integer_to_list(X)])),
(11)              [X|XS])
(12)        end
(13)    end.
(14)  happy(X, Top, XS) ->
(15)    if
(16)      length(XS) == Top -> sort(XS);
(17)      true ->
(18)        case is_happy(X,[]) of
(19)          true -> happy(X + 1, Top, [X|XS]);
(20)          false -> happy(X + 1,Top, XS)
(21)        end
(22)    end.
(23)
(24)  -spec main(pos_integer(),pos_integer()) ->
(25)    [pos_integer()].
(26)  main(N, M) ->
(27)    happy(N, M, []).
(28)
```

LISTING 2: happy1.erl.

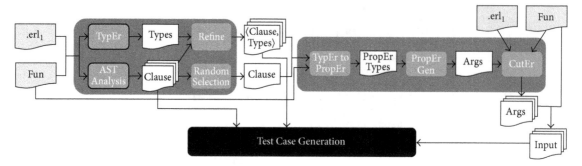

FIGURE 1: Type analysis phase.

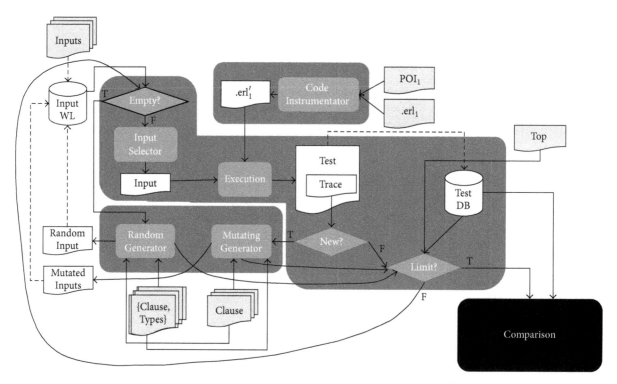

FIGURE 2: Test case generation phase.

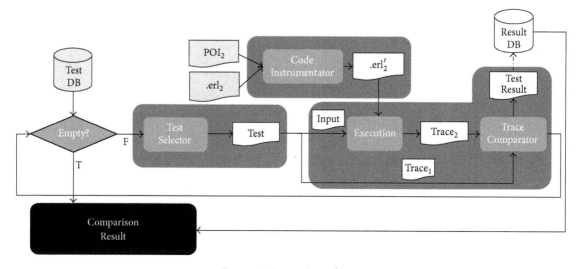

FIGURE 3: Comparison phase.

results, and the initial processes of each phase are represented with a bold border box.

The first phase, depicted in Figure 1, is a type analysis that is in charge of preparing all inputs of the second phase (test case generation). This phase starts by locating in the source code the Erlang module (.erl$_1$) and a function (Fun) specified in the user input (we show here the process for only one function. In case the user defined more than one input function, the process described here would be repeated for each function), e.g., function exp in the math module. Then, TypEr is used to obtain the type of the parameters of that function. It is important to know that, in Erlang, a function is composed of clauses and when a function is invoked, an internal algorithm traverses all the clauses in order to select the one that will be executed. Unfortunately, TypEr does not provide the individual type of each clause, but a global type for the whole function. Therefore, we need to first analyze the AST of the module to identify all the clauses of the input function, and then we refine the types provided by TypEr to determine the specific type of each clause. All these clause types are used in the second phase. In this phase, we use PropEr to instantiate only one of them (e.g., ⟨*Number, Integer*⟩ can be instantiated to ⟨*4.22, 3*⟩ or ⟨*6, 5*⟩). However, PropEr is unable to understand TypEr types, so we have defined a translation process from TypEr types to ProEr types. Finally, CutEr is fed with an initial call (e.g., math:exp(4.22, 3)) and it provides a set of possible arguments (e.g., { ⟨*1.5, 6*⟩, ⟨*2, 1*⟩, ⟨*1.33, 4*⟩,...}). Finally, this set is combined with the function to be called to generate the ITCs (e.g., {math:exp(1.5, 6), math:exp(2, 1), math:exp(1.33, 4),...}). All this process is explained in detail in Section 3.1.

The second phase, shown in Figure 2, is in charge of generating the test suite. As an initial step, we instrument the program so that its execution records (as a side effect) the sequence of values produced at the POI defined by the user. Then, we store all ITCs provided by the previous phase into a working list. Note that it is also possible that the previous phase is unable to provide any ITC due to the limitations of CutEr. In such a case, or when there are no more ITCs left, we randomly generate a new one with PropEr and store it on the working list. Then, each ITC on the working list is processed by invoking it with the instrumented code. The execution provides the sequences of values the POI is evaluated to (i.e., the trace). This trace together with the ITC forms a new test case, which is a new output of the phase. Moreover, to increase the quality of the test cases produced, whenever a non-previously generated trace is computed, we mutate the ITC that generated that trace to obtain more ITCs. The reason is that a mutation of this ITC will probably generate more ITCs that also evaluate the POI but to different values. This process is repeated until the specified limit of test cases is reached. All this process is explained in detail in Sections 3.2 and 3.3. In Section 4 there is a discussion of how this approach could be extended to support multiple POIs.

Finally, the last phase (shown in Figure 3) checks whether the new version of the code passes the test suite. First, the source code of the new version is also instrumented to compute the traces produced at its POI. Then, all the generated test cases are executed and the traces produced are compared with the expected traces. Section 5 introduces functions to compare traces that give support to the multiple-POI approach.

3. A Novel Approach to Automated Regression Testing

In this section, we describe in more detail the most relevant parts of our approach. We describe them in separate subsections.

3.1. Initial ITC Generation. The process starts from the type inferred by TypEr for the whole input function. This is the first important step to obtain a significant result, because ITCs are generated with the types returned by this process, so the more accurate the types are, the more accurate the ITCs are. The standard output of TypEr is an Erlang type specification returned as a string, which would need to be parsed. For this reason, we have hacked the Erlang module that implements this functionality to obtain the types in a data structure, easier to traverse and handle. In order to improve the accuracy, we define a type for each clause of the function ensuring that the later generated ITCs will match it. For this reason, TypEr types need to be refined to TypEr types per clause.

However, the types returned by TypEr have (in our context) two drawbacks that need to be corrected since they could yield to ITCs that do not match a desired input function. These drawbacks are due to the type produced for lists and due to the occurrence of repeated variables. We explain both drawbacks with an example. Consider a function with a single clause whose header is f(A, [A,B]). For this function, TypEr infers the type f(1 | 2, [1 | 2 | 5 | 6, ...]) (TypEr uses a *success typing* system instead of the usual Hindley-Milner type inference system. Therefore, TypEr's types are different from what many programmers would expect, i.e., integer, string, etc. Instead, a TypEr's type is a set of values such as [1 | 2 | 5 | 6] or an Erlang defined type, e.g., number and integer). Thus, the type of the second parameter of the f/2 function indicates that the feasible values for the second parameter are proper lists with a single constraint: it has to be formed with numbers from the set [1,2,5,6]. This means that we could build lists of any length, which is our first drawback. If we use these TypEr types, we may generate ITCs that will not match the function, e.g., f(2,[2,1,3,5]). On the other hand, our second drawback is caused by the fact that the value relation generated by the repeated variable A is lost in the function type. In particular, the actual type of variable A is diluted in the type of the second argument. This could yield to mismatching ITCs if we generate, e.g., f(1,[6,5]).

Therefore, the types produced by TypEr are too imprecise in our context, because they may produce test cases that are useless (e.g., nonexecutable). This problem is resolved in different steps of the process. In this step, we can only partially resolve the type conflict introduced by the repeated variables, such as the A variable in the previous example. The other drawback will be completely resolved during the ITC generation. To solve this problem, we traverse the parameters building a correspondence between each variable and the inferred TypEr type. Each time a variable appears more than once, we calculate its type as the intersection of both the TypEr type and the accumulated type. For instance, in the previous example, we have A = 1 | 2 for the first occurrence and A = 1 | 2 | 5 | 6 for the second one, obtaining the new accumulated type A = 1 | 2.

Once we have our refined TypEr types, we rely on PropEr to obtain the input for CutEr. PropEr is a property-based testing framework with a lot of useful underlying functionalities. One of them is the term generators, which, given a PropEr type, are able to randomly generate terms belonging to such type. Thus, we can use the generators in our framework to generate values for a given type.

However, TypEr and PropEr use slightly different notations for their types, something reasonable given that their scopes are completely different. Unfortunately, there is not any available translator from TypEr types to PropEr types. In our technique, we need such a translator to link the inferred types to the PropEr generators. Therefore, we have built the translator by ourselves. Moreover, during the ITC generation, we need to deal with the previously postponed type drawbacks. For that, we use the parameters of the clause in conjunction with their types. To solve the first drawback, each time a list is found during the generation, we traverse its elements and generate a type for each element on the list. Thereby, we synthesize a new type for the list with exactly the same number of elements. The second drawback is solved by using a map from variables to their generated values. Each time a repeated variable is found, we use the stored value instead of generating a new one.

We can feed CutEr with an initial call by using a randomly selected clause and the values generated by PropEr for this clause. CutEr is a concolic testing framework that generates a list of arguments that tries to cover all the execution paths. Unfortunately, this list is only used internally by CutEr, so we have hacked CutEr to extract all these arguments. Finally, by using this slightly modified version of CutEr we are able to mix the arguments with the input function to generate the initial set of ITCs.

3.2. Recording the Traces of the Point of Interest. There exist several tools available to trace Erlang executions [12–15] (we describe some of them in Section 10). However, none of them allows for defining a POI that points to any part of the code. Being able to trace any possible point of interest requires either a code instrumentation, a debugger, or a way to take control of the execution of Erlang. However, using a debugger (e.g., [13]) has the drawback that it does not provide a value for the POI when it is inside an expression whose evaluation fails. Therefore, we decided to instrument the code in such a way that, without modifying the semantics of the code, traces are collected as a side effect when executing the code.

The instrumentation process creates and collects the traces of the POI. To create the traces in an automatic way, we instrument the expression pointed by the POI. To collect the traces, we have several options. For instance, we can store the traces in a file and process it when the

execution finishes, but this approach is inefficient. We follow an alternative approach based on message passing. We send messages to a server (which we call the *tracing server*) that is continuously listening for new traces until a message indicating the end of the evaluation is received. This approach is closer to Erlang's philosophy. Additionally, it is more efficient since the messages are sent asynchronously resulting in an imperceptible overhead in the execution. As a result of the instrumenting process, the transformed code sends to the tracing server the value of the POI each time it is evaluated, and the tracing server stores these values.

In the following, we explain in detail how the communication with the server is placed in the code. This is done by applying the following steps:

(1) We first use the `erl_syntax_lib:annotate_bindings/2` function to annotate the AST of the code. This function annotates each node with two lists of variables: those variables that are being bound and those that were already bound in its subtree. Additionally, we annotate each node with a unique integer that serves as an identifier, so we call it *AST identifier*. This annotation is performed in a postorder traversal, resulting, consequently, in an AST where the root has the greatest number.

(2) The next step is to find the POI selected by the user in the code and obtain the corresponding AST identifier. There are two ways of doing this depending on how the POI is specified: (i) if the POI is defined with the triplet *(line, type of expression, occurrence)*, we locate it with a preorder traversal (we use this order because it is the one that allows us to find the nodes in the same order as they are in the source code) of the tree. However, (ii) when the POI is defined with the initial and final positions, we replace, in the source code, the whole expression with a fresh term. Then, we build the AST of this new code and we search for the fresh term in this AST recording the path followed. This path is replicated in the original AST to obtain the AST identifier of the POI. Thus, the result of this step is a relation between a POI and an AST identifier.

(3) Then, we need to extract the path from the AST root to the AST identifier of the POI using a new search process. This double search process is later justified when we introduce the multiple POIs approach in Section 4. During this search process, we store the path followed in the AST with tuples of the form `(Node, ChildIndex)`, where `Node` is the AST node and `ChildIndex` is the index of the node in its parent's children array. Obtaining this path is essential for the next steps since it allows us to recursively update the tree in an easy and efficient way. When the AST identifier is found, the traversal finishes. Thus, the output of this step is a path that yields directly to the AST identifier searched.

(4) Most of the times, the POI can be easily instrumented by adding a send command to communicate its value to the tracing server. However, when the POI is in

```
(LEFT_PM)    p = e ⟹ p = begin np = e, tracer!{add, npoi}, np end
        if      (p = e, _) = last(PathBefore)
                ∧( _, pos(p)) = hd(PathAfter)
      where    ( _, npoi, np) = pfv(p, PathAfter)


(PAT_GEN_LC)   [e || gg] ⟹ [e || ngg]
        if      ([e || gg], _) = last(PathBefore)
                ∧ ( _, pos(p_gen)) = hd(tl(PathAfter))
                ∧ ∃ i. 1 ≤ i ≤ length(gg) s.t. gg_i = p_gen <- e_gen
      where    ( _, npoi, np_gen) = pfv(p_gen, tl(PathAfter))
                ∧ ngg_i = p_gen <- begin tracer!{add, npoi}, [np_gen] end
                ∧ ngg = gg_1 ··· gg_{i-1}, np_gen <- e_gen, ngg_i, gg_{i+1} ··· gg_{length(gg)}


(CLAUSE_PAT)   e ⟹ change_clauses(e, ncls)
        if      (e, _) = last(PathBefore)
                ∧ ( _, pos(p_c)) = hd(tl(PathAfter))
                ∧ ∃ i.1 ≤ i ≤ length(cls) s.t. cls_i = p_c when g_c -> b_c
      where    cls = clauses(e)
                ∧ ( _, npoi, np_c) = pfv(p_c, tl(PathAfter))
                ∧ nb_c = begin tracer!{add, npoi}, case np_c of cls end end
                ∧ ncls_i = np_c when true -> nb_c
                ∧ ncls = cls_i, ..., cls_{i-1}, ncls_i, cls_{i+1}, ..., cls_{length(cls)}


(CLAUSE_GUARD)  e ⟹ change_clauses(e, ncls)
        if      (e, _ ) = last(PathBefore)
                ∧ ( _, pos(g_c)) = hd(tl(PathAfter))
                ∧ ∃ i.1 ≤ i ≤ length(cls) s.t. cls_i = p_c when g_c -> b_c
      where    cls = clauses(e)
                ∧ (poi, _ ) = last(PathAfter)
                ∧ nb_c = begin tracer!{add, poi}, case np_c of cls end end
                ∧ ncl = p_c when true -> nb_c
                ∧ ncls = cls_i, ..., cls_{i-1}, ncl, cls_{i+1}, ..., cls_{length(cls)}


(EXPR)        e ⟹ begin fv = e, tracer!{add, fv}, fv end
  otherwise
      where    (e, _) = last(PathAfter) ∧ fv = fv( )
```

ALGORITHM 1: Instrumentation rules for tracing.

the pattern of an expression, this expression needs a special treatment in the instrumentation. Let us show the problem with an example. Consider a POI inside a pattern {1, POI, 3}. If the execution tries to match it with {2, 2, 3} nothing is sent to the tracing server because the POI is never evaluated. Contrarily, if it tries to match it with {1, 2, 4} we send the value 2 to the tracing server. Note that the matching fails in both cases, but due to the evaluation order, the POI is actually evaluated (and it succeeds) in the second case. There is an interesting third case that happens when the POI has a value, e.g., 3, and the matching with {1, 4, 4} is tried. In this case, although the matching at the POI fails, we send the value 4 to the tracing server. We could also send its actual value, i.e., 3. This is just a design decision, but we think that including the value that produced the mismatch could be more useful to find the source of a discrepancy. We call *target expression* to those expressions that need a special treatment

in the instrumentation as the previously described one. In Erlang, these target expressions are pattern matchings, list comprehensions, and expressions with clauses (i.e., case, if, functions, ...). The goal of this step is to divide the AST path into two subpaths (PathBefore, PathAfter). PathBefore yields from the root to the deepest target expression (included), and PathAfter yields from the first children of the target expression to the AST identifier of the POI.

Finally, the last step is the one in charge of performing the actual instrumentation. The PathBefore path is used to traverse the tree until the deepest target expression that contains the AST identifier is reached. At this point, five rules (described below) are used to transform the code by using PathAfter. Finally, PathBefore is traversed backwards to update the AST of the targeted function. The five rules are depicted in Algorithm 1. The first four rules are mutually exclusive, and when none of them can be applied, the rule (EXPR) is applied. Rule (LEFT_PM) is fired when the POI is in the pattern of a pattern-matching expression. Rule (PAT_GEN_LC) is used to transform a list comprehension when the POI is in the pattern of a generator. Finally, rules (CLAUSE_PAT) (function clauses need an additional transformation that consists in storing all the parameters inside a tuple so that they could be used in case expressions) and (CLAUSE_GUARD) transform an expression with clauses when the POI is in the pattern or in the guard of one of its clauses, respectively. In the rules, we use the underline symbol (_) to represent a value that is not used. There are several functions used in the rules that need to be introduced. Functions $hd(l)$, $tl(l)$, $length(l)$, and $last(l)$ return the head, the tail, the length, and the last element of the list l, respectively. Function $pos(e)$ returns the child index of an expression e, i.e., its index in the list of children of its parent. Function $is\_bound(e)$ returns

true if e is bounded according to the AST binding annotations (see step (1)). Functions $clauses(e)$ and $change\_clauses(e, clauses)$ obtain and modify the clauses of e, respectively. Function $fv()$ builds a free variable. Finally, there is a key function named pfv, introduced in (1), that transforms a pattern so that the constraints after the POI do not inhibit the sending call. This is done by replacing all the terms on the right of the POI with free variables that are built using fv function. Unbound variables on the left and also in the POI are replaced by fresh variables to avoid the shadowing of the original variables. In the pfv function, $children(e)$ and $change\_children(e, children)$ are used to obtain and modify the children of expression e, respectively. In this function, lists are represented with the head-tail notation $(h : t)$.

Function pfv

$$
pfv(p, path) = \begin{cases}
(poi, poi', p'') & \text{if } path = [(poi, pos)] \\
& \text{where } poi' = fv() \wedge p' = fv\_from(pos, p) \\
& \wedge p'' = p'_1 \cdots p'_{pos-1}, poi', p'_{pos+1} \cdots p'_{length(p)} \\
(poi, poi', p''') & \text{otherwise} \\
& \text{where } (\_, pos) = hd(path) \wedge p' = fv\_from(pos, p) \\
& \wedge (poi, poi', p'') = pfv(p'_{pos}, tl(path)) \\
& \wedge p''' = p'_1 \cdots p'_{pos-1}, p'', p'_{pos+1} \cdots p'_{length(p)}
\end{cases}
$$

$$
fv\_from(pos, p) = p'_1 \cdots p'_{pos}, fv()_{pos+1} \cdots fv()_{length(p)} \quad \text{where } (p'_1 \cdots p'_{pos}, \_) = cv(p_1 \cdots p_{pos}, [\,])
$$

$$(1)$$

$$
cv(list, map) \begin{cases}
([\,], map) & \text{if } list = [\,] \\
((fv : p'_t), map') & \text{if } list = (p_h : p_t) \wedge is\_var(p_h) \wedge \neg\, is\_bound(p_h) \\
& \text{where } fv = fv() \wedge (p'_t, map') = cv(p_t, map \cup \{p_h \mapsto fv\}) \\
((fv_{map} : p'_t), map') & \text{if } list = (p_h : p_t) \wedge is\_var(p_h) \wedge p_h \mapsto fv_{map} \in map \\
& \text{where } (p'_t, map') = cv(p_t, map) \\
((p'_h : p'_t), map'') & \text{otherwise} \\
& \text{where } (p_h : p_t) = list \wedge (children'_{p_h}, map') = cv(children(p_h), map) \\
& \wedge p'_h = change\_children(p_h, children'_{p_h}) \\
& \wedge (p'_t, map'') = cv(p_t, map')
\end{cases}
$$

3.3. Test Case Generation Using ITC Mutation. The ITC generation phase uses CutEr because it implements sophisticated concolic analyses with the goal of achieving 100% branch coverage. However, sometimes these analyses require too much time and we have to abort its execution. This means that, after executing CutEr, we might have only the ITC that we provided to CutEr. Moreover, even when

CutEr generates ITC with a 100% branch coverage, they can be insufficient. For instance, if the expression Z = X − Y is replaced in a new version of the code with Z = X + Y, a single test case that executes both of them with Y = 0 will not detect any difference. More values for Y are needed to detect the behaviour change in this expression.

Therefore, to increase the reliability of the test suite, we complement the ITCs produced by CutEr with a test mutation technique. Using a mutation technique is much better than using, e.g., only the PropEr generator to randomly synthesize new test cases (this statement is clarified by the results obtained in Section 9), because full-random test cases would produce many useless test cases (i.e., test cases that do not execute the POI). In contrast, the use of a test mutation technique increases the probability of generating test cases that execute the POI (because only those test cases that execute the POI are mutated). The function that generates the test cases is depicted in (2). The result of the function is a map from the different obtained traces to the set of ITCs that produce them. The first call to this function is $tgen(top, cuter\_tests, \emptyset)$, where top is a user-defined limit of the desired number of test cases (in SecEr, it is possible to alternatively use a timeout to stop the

test case generation) and $cuter\_tests$ are the test cases that CutEr generates (which could be an empty set). Function $tgen$ uses the auxiliary functions $proper\_gen$, $trace$, and mut. The function $proper\_gen()$ simply calls PropEr to generate a new test case, while function $trace(input)$ obtains the corresponding trace when the ITC $input$ is executed. The size of a map, $size(map)$, is the total amount of elements stored in all lists that belong to the map. Finally, function $mut(input)$ obtains a set of mutations for the ITC $input$, where, for each argument in $input$, a new test case is generated by replacing the argument with a randomly generated value, using PropEr (note that we are using PropEr to replace only one argument instead of all arguments. The latter is the full-random test case generation explained above), and leaving the rest of the arguments unchanged.

Test Case Generation Function

$$tgen(top, pending, map)$$

$$= \begin{cases} map & \text{if } size(map) \geq top \\ tgen(top, pending', map') & \text{if } size(map) < top \\ & \wedge \exists\, input \in pending \mid trace(input) \mapsto \_ \notin map \\ & \text{where } pending' = (pending \cup mut(input)) \setminus \{input\} \\ & \wedge map' = map \cup \{trace(input) \mapsto \{input\}\} \\ tgen(top, \{proper\_gen()\}, map') & \text{if } size(map) < top \\ & \wedge \nexists\, input \in pending \mid trace(input) \mapsto \_ \notin map \\ & \text{where } map' = map \\ & \cup \Big\{ trace(input_p) \mapsto \big(\{input_p\} \cup inputs_{tp}\big) \\ & \mid input_p \in pending \wedge trace(input_p) \mapsto inputs_{tp} \in map \Big\} \end{cases} \quad (2)$$

Therefore, our mutation technique is able to generate tests more focused on our goal, i.e., maximizing the number of times a POI is executed. Due to the random generation, a mutant can produce repeated ITCs (which are not reexecuted). It can also produce ITCs whose trace has been previously found (then they are not mutated). Moreover, a mutant can produce unexpected ITCs or execution errors. These test cases are not considered as invalid but, contrarily, they are desirable because they allow us to check that the behaviour is also preserved in those cases. Finally, CutEr is an optional tool that can help to improve the resulting test cases by contributing with an initial test cases suite with high coverage.

4. Extending the Approach to Include Multiple POIs

The previous sections introduced a methodology to automatically obtain traces from a given POI. An extension of this methodology to multiple POIs enables several new

features like a fine-grained testing, or checking multiple functionalities at once. However, it introduces new challenges to be overcome.

In order to extend the approach for multiple POIs, we need to perform some modifications in some of the steps of the single-POI approach. The flow is exactly the same as the one depicted in Section 2, but we need to modify some of its internals. There is no need for modifications in all the process described in Section 3.1, since this process depends on the input functions that, in our approach, are shared by all the POIs (we plan to explore in future approaches the idea of defining individual input functions for each POI). On the other hand, we need to introduce changes in the processes described in Sections 3.2 and 3.3.

The tracing method introduced in Section 3.2 needs to be slightly redefined here. This section defined 4 steps that started from a source code and a POI and ended in an instrumented version of the source code that is able to communicate traces. Therefore, the only change needed is that, instead of having only one POI, we have more than one. In order to deal with this change, we follow the same 4 steps but change the way in which they are applied. In the single-POI approach, they are applied sequentially, but here we need to iterate some of them. Concretely, steps (1) and (2) are done only once in the whole process while the rest of the steps are done once for each POI. The result of step (2) is now a set of *POI-AST identifier* relations instead of a single one. Then, we iterate the obtained AST identifiers applying steps (3) and (4) sequentially. Note that although the result of step (4) is a new AST, we are still able to find the AST identifiers of the subsequent POIs since the transformations do not destroy any node of the original AST; instead they only move them inside a new expression. This justifies the double search design performed in steps (2) and (3). If we tried to search for the POI in a modified AST, we could be unable to find it. In contrast, AST identifiers ensure that it can always be found.

In the multiple-POI approach, there is also a justification of why the identifiers are numbers and why the identification process is done with a postorder traversal. First of all, there is one question that should be discussed: is the order in which the POIs are processed important? The answer is yes, because the user could define a POI that includes another POI inside; e.g., POI_1 is the whole tuple {X, Y} and POI_2 is X. This scenario would be problematic when the POI-inside-POI case occurs inside a pattern due to the way we instrument the code. If we instrumented first POI_1, its trace would be sent before the one of POI_2. Note that this is not correct since POI_2 is evaluated first; therefore, it should be traced first. This justifies the use of a postorder traversal, where the identifier of a node is maximal in its subtree. Thus, as the AST identifiers are numbers and their order is convenient in our context, we can order the AST identifiers obtained from the POIs before starting the transformation loop.

The test case generation phase introduced in Section 3.3 is also affected by the inclusion of multiple POIs. In the original definition, the traces were a sequence of values, and therefore it was easy to check whether a trace had appeared in a previously executed test. However, with multiple POIs, the trace is not such a simple sequence, as the traced values can be obtained from different POIs along the execution. Therefore, we need a more sophisticated way to determine the equality of the traces. The next section explains in detail how we can achieve this goal.

5. Determining the Trace Equality with Multiple POIs

We present in this section several alternatives to compare traces that contain values from multiple POIs. Concretely, we explain the three default comparison functions provided in our approach. In our setting, we also allow a user to define their own comparison functions enabling all needed types of comparison.

A trace of a POI is defined as the sequence of values that the POI is evaluated to during an execution. It has been represented with $trace(input)$, which obtains the corresponding trace when the ITC is executed. In the multiple-POI approach, we need to redefine the notion of *trace* to also include the POIs that originated the values of the trace. In order to maintain the execution order, the trace is still a sequence, but instead of simple values it contains tuples of the form $(POI, value)$. In this way, $trace(input)$ will contain all the values traced for all the POIs defined by the user, preserving their execution order. This is achieved by slightly modifying the rules in Algorithm 1 to include the POI reference when sending the value to the tracer.

Once $trace(input)$ includes all the sequences of values generated during the execution for each POI, we need a way to compare them. Note that the standard equality function is perfectly valid for comparing traces during the test case generation phase (Section 3.3), because all of them come from the same source code. However, it is no longer valid for comparing program versions since POIs can differ in the original program and the modified one. Therefore, we additionally need to define a relation between POIs. This relation, which we represent with R_{POIs}, is automatically built from the input provided by the user. It is a set that contains tuples of the form (POI_{old}, POI_{new}). Therefore, a simple equality function to compare two traces obtained from different versions of a program can be defined as follows:

$$
equal\left(trace_{old}, trace_{new}, R_{POIs}\right) = \begin{cases} true & \text{if } trace_{old} = [\,] \wedge trace_{new} = [\,] \\[2mm] equal\left(trace'_{old}, trace'_{new}, R_{POIs}\right) & \\ & \text{if } trace_{old} = \left((POI_{old}, v_{old}) : trace'_{old}\right) \\ & \wedge\, trace_{new} = \left((POI_{new}, v_{new}) : trace'_{new}\right) \\ & \wedge\, v_{old} = v_{new}\ \wedge\left(POI_{old}, POI_{new}\right) \in R_{POIs} \\[2mm] false & \text{otherwise} \end{cases} \tag{3}
$$

This equality function is useful when the user is interested in comparing the traces interleaved (i.e., when their interleaved execution is relevant). However, in some scenarios, the user can be interested in relaxing the interleaving constraint and comparing the traces independently. This can be achieved by building a mapping from POIs to sequences of values in the following way:

$$trace\,(input, POI) = [v \mid (POI, v) \in trace\,(input)] \quad (4)$$

The order is assumed to be preserved in the produced sequences. Using these sequences, we can define an alternative equality function as follows:

$$equal\,(trace_{old}, trace_{new}, R_{POIs})$$

$$= \bigwedge_{(POI_{old}, POI_{new}) \in R_{POIs}} trace\,(input, POI_{old}) \quad (5)$$

$$= trace\,(input, POI_{new})$$

There is a third equality relation that could be useful in certain cases. Suppose that we detect some duplicated code, so we build a new version of the code where all the repeated code has been refactored to a single code. If we want to test whether the behaviour is kept, we need to define a relation where multiple POIs in the old version are associated with a single POI in the new version. This is represented in our approach adding to R_{POIs} several tuples of the form (POI_{old_1}, POI_{new}), (POI_{old_2}, POI_{new}), and so forth. A similar scenario can happen when a functionality of the original code is split in several parts in the new code (an example of this scenario is the use case presented in Section 6.4). In both cases, a special treatment is needed for this type of relations. In order to do this, we define a generalisation of the previous *equal* function where this kind of relations is taken into account. The first step is to extract all the POIs in R_{POIs}.

$$pois\,(R_{POIs}) = \{POI_1 \mid (POI_1, POI_2) \in R_{POIs}\}$$

$$\cup \{POI_2 \mid (POI_1, POI_2) \in R_{POIs}\} \quad (6)$$

Then, we can define the set of POIs related to a given POI in R_{POIs}.

$$rel\,(POI, R_{POIs}) = \{POI' \mid (POI, POI') \in R_{POIs}\}$$

$$\cup \{POI' \mid (POI', POI) \in R_{POIs}\} \quad (7)$$

Finally, we need a new trace function that returns a single trace of values that are obtained from all the POIs related to a POI in R_{POIs}.

$$trace\_rel\,(input, POI, R_{POIs}) = \left[v \mid \left(POI', v\right)\right.$$

$$\left. \in trace\,(input) \wedge POI' \in rel\,(POI, R_{POIs})\right] \quad (8)$$

We can now define an equality function that is able to deal with replicated POIs.

$$equal\,(trace_{old}, trace_{new}, R_{POIs})$$

$$= \bigwedge_{POI \in pois(R_{POIs})} trace\,(input, POI) \quad (9)$$

$$= trace\_rel\,(input, POI, R_{POIs})$$

In case a user needs a more intricate equality function, we provide in our tool a way to define a custom equality function, which should contain the parameters $trace_{old}$ and $trace_{new}$ (the relation R_{POIs} is not a parameter in the user function because it is originally provided by the user). Hence, the user can decide whether the generated traces can be considered as equal or not.

Equality functions constitute a new parameter of the approach that determines how the traces should be compared. For the comparison of versions using multiple POIs, it is mandatory to provide such a function, while for the test case generation phase depicted in Section 3.3 it can be optional. In the second case, the user could be interested in obtaining more sophisticated test cases by providing their own equality function. In order to enable this option, an additional parameter is needed for the *tgen* function. This parameter will contain the equality function that should be used when checking if a trace has been previously computed.

6. The SecEr Tool

In this section, we describe SecEr and how to use it to automatically obtain test cases from a source code. Then, we present some use cases that illustrate how SecEr can be used to check behavioural changes in the code.

6.1. Tool Description. Given two versions of the same program, SecEr is able to automatically generate a test suite that checks the behaviour of a set of POIs and reports the discrepancies. Listing 3 shows the SecEr command.

If we want to perform a comparison between two programs, we just need to provide a list of related POIs from both programs. For instance,

```
./secer -pois "[{{'happy0.erl',4,'call',1},{'happy1.erl',27,'call',1}},
{{'happy0.erl',9,'call',1},{'happy1.erl',18,'call',1}}]" -to 10
```

Because the same POIs are often compared as the program evolves, it is a good idea to record them together with

the input functions for future uses. For this reason, the user can save in a file(e.g., `pois.erl`) the POIs of interest and

```
(1) $ ./secer -pois "LIST_OF_POIS" [-funs "INPUT_FUNCTIONS"] -to TIMEOUT [-cfun "COMPARISON_FUN"]
```

LISTING 3: SecEr command format.

their relations and define a function that returns them (e.g., `pois:rel/0`). Hence, they can simply invoke this function with

```
./secer -pois "pois:rel()" -to 15
```

By default, the traces of the POIs are compared using the standard equality, as it is defined by the first comparison function in Section 5. Alternatively, we can customize our comparison defining a comparison function (COMPARISON_FUN). The comparison function defined by the user must be a function with two parameters (the old and the new traces). We also provide a library with some common comparison functions, like, for instance, the one that compares the traces independently (`secer:independent`) as it is described in the second and third functions (depending on the POI relations) in Section 5.

Example 2. Consider two POIs, POI_1 and POI_2, in the original code and their counterparts POI_1' and POI_2' in the new code. If an execution executes the POIs in the following order:

original code: $POI_1 = 42 \cdots POI_1 = 43 \cdots POI_1 = 50 \cdots POI_2 = 0$,

new code: $POI_1' = 42 \cdots POI_1' = 43 \cdots POI_2' = 0 \cdots POI_1' = 50$,

SecEr records the traces:

Trace $POI_1 = [42, 43, 50]$

Trace $POI_1' = [42, 43, 50]$

Trace $POI_2 = [0]$

Trace $POI_1' = [0]$

If we execute SecEr with flag `-cfun "secer:independent()"`, SecEr will report that there are no discrepancies between the POIs. In contrast, if no flag is specified, SecEr will take into account the execution order of the POIs, and it will alert that this order has changed.

Note that, in the implementation, the limit used to stop generating test cases is a timeout, while the formalization of the technique uses a number to specify the amount of test cases that must be generated (see variable *top* in Section 3.3). This is not a limitation, but a design decision to increase the usability of the tool. The user cannot know *a priori* how much time it could take to generate an arbitrary number of test cases. Hence, to make the tool predictable and give the user control over the computation time, we use a timeout. Thus, SecEr generates as many test cases as the specified timeout permits.

6.2. Defining a Configuration File. SecEr permits using configuration files that can be reused in different invocations. A configuration file contains functions that can be invoked from the SecEr command. For instance, the following command uses functions `rel/0`, `funs/0`, and `cf_length/2` of module `test_happy`:

```
./secer -pois "test_happy:rel()" -fun "test_happy:funs()" -to
5 -cfun "test_happy:cf_length"
```

In Algorithm 2, we can see that POIs can be specified in two different ways: (i) with a tuple with the format { 'FileName' , Line, Expression (expressions with a specific name, e.g., variables, will be denoted by a tuple { var , 'VarName' }. Note that expressions denoted by reserved Erlang words, e.g., case or if, must be specified in single quotation marks), Occurrence} as shown in Algorithm 2 line (5) and (ii) with a tuple { 'FileName' , { InitialLine, InitialColumn }, {FinalLine, FinalColumn }}(POIs of this type are internally translated to POIs of the first type) representing the initial and final line and column in the specified file; this approach is shown in Algorithm 2 line (7).

The LIST_OF_POIS parameter is provided by function `rel/0` (see line (19)). It returns an Erlang list of well defined POIs (or pairs of POIs). The INPUT_FUNCTIONS parameter is provided by function `funs/0` (see line (26)). It returns

a string containing a list with the desired input functions. The COMPARISON_FUN parameter is provided by function `cf_length/2` (see line (29)). It receives two arguments, each of which is a list of tuples that contains a POI and a value. This function must return `true`, `false`, or a tuple with `false` and an error message to customize the error.

6.3. Use Case 1: Happy Numbers. In this section, we further develop Example 1 to show how SecEr can check the behaviour preservation in the happy numbers programs (see Listings 1 and 2). First of all, to unify the interfaces of both programs, in the happy0 module (Listing 1), we have replaced `main/0` with `main/2` making it applicable for a more general case. Moreover, in both modules, we have added a type specification (represented with spec in Erlang) in order to obtain more representative test cases. To run SecEr we use the configuration file defined in Algorithm 2.

```
(1)   -module(test_happy).
(2)   -compile(export_all).
(3)
(4)   poiResultOld() ->
(5)       {'happy0.erl',4,call,1}.
(6)   poiResultNew() ->
(7)       {'happy1.erl',{27,2},{27,16}}.
(8)
(9)   poiIsHappyOld() ->
(10)      {'happy0.erl',9,call,1}.
(11)  poiIsHappyNew() ->
(12)      {'happy1.erl',18,call,1}.
(13)
(14)  poiXOld() ->
(15)      {'happy0.erl',9,{var,'X'},1}.
(16)  poiXNew() ->
(17)      {'happy1.erl',18,{var,'X'},1}.
(18)
(19)  rel() ->
(20)      [{poiResultOld(),poiResultNew()}].
(21)  relIsHappy() ->
(22)      [{poiIsHappyOld(),poiIsHappyNew()}].
(23)  relX() ->
(24)      [{poiXOld(),poiXNew()}].
(25)
(26)  funs() ->
(27)      "[main/2]".
(28)
(29)  cf_length(TO,TN) ->
(30)      ZippedList = lists:zip(TO,TN),
(31)      lists:foldl(
(32)        fun
(33)          (_,{false,Msg,PO,PN}) ->
(34)              {false,Msg,PO,PN};
(35)          ({{_,VO},{_,VN}}, _) when length(VN) < length(VO) ->
(36)              true;
(37)          ({{PO,_},{PN,_}},_) ->
(38)              {false,"Invalid Length",PO,PN}
(39)        end,
(40)        true,
(41)        ZippedList).
```

ALGORITHM 2: Configuration file to test happy modules.

Listing 4 shows the execution of SecEr when comparing both implementations of the program with a timeout of 15 seconds. The selected POIs are the same POIs mentioned in Section 1. They are the call in line (4) in Listing 1 and the call in line (27) in Listing 2. As we can see, the execution of both implementations behaves identically with respect to the selected POIs in the 1142 generated test cases.

In order to see the output of the tool when the behaviours of the two compared programs differ, we have introduced an error inside the is_happy/2 function of happy1 module (Listing 2). The error is introduced by replacing the whole line (4) with X < 10 -> false;. With this change, the behaviour of both programs differs. When the user runs SecEr using the previous POI, it produces the error report shown in Listing 5. From this information, the user may decide to use as new POIs all nonrecursive function calls inside happy_list/3 (for Listing 1) and happy/3 (for Listing 2) functions. With this decision it can discard whether the error comes from the function itself or from the called function. Therefore, the new POIs are the call in line (4) in Listing 1 and the call in line (27) in Listing 2. SecEr's output for these POIs is shown in Listing 6. SecEr reports that the POI was executed several times and in some executions the values of the POI differed. SecEr also reports a counterexample: main(4,2) compute different values. Because the current POIs are the results of calling a function that should be equivalent in both codes, there are two possible sources of the discrepancy: either the common argument in both versions of is_happy (i.e., X) is taking different values during the execution, or something executed by is_happy produces the discrepancies. Listing 7 shows the

```
$ ./secer -pois "test_happy:rel()" -funs "test_happy:funs()" -to 15
Function: main/2
----------------------------
Generated test cases: 1142
Both versions of the program generate identical traces for the defined points of interest
```

LISTING 4: SecEr reports that no discrepancies exist.

```
$ ./secer -pois "test_happy:rel()" -funs "test_happy:funs()" -to 15
Function: main/2
----------------------------
Generated test cases: 1143
Mismatching test cases: 45 (3.93%)
    POIs comparison:
        + {{'happy0.erl',4,call,1},
          {'happy1.erl',27,call,1}}
                        Unexpected trace value => 45 Errors
                        Example call: main(5,8)
------ Detected Error ------
Call: main(5,8)
Error Type: Unexpected trace value
POI: ({'happy0.erl',4,call,1}) trace:
            [[7,10,13,19,23,28,31,32]]
POI: ({'happy1.erl',27,call,1}) trace:
            [[10,13,19,23,28,31,32,44]]
----------------------------
```

LISTING 5: Result replacing line (4) with X < 10 -> false.

```
$ ./secer -pois "test_happy:relIsHappy()" -funs "test_happy:funs()" -to 15
Function: main/2
----------------------------
Generated test cases: 1151
Mismatching test cases: 39 (3.38%)
    POIs comparison:
        + {{'happy0.erl',9,call,1},
          {'happy1.erl',18,call,1}}
                        Unexpected trace value => 39 Errors
                        Example call: main(4,2)
------ Detected Error ------
Call: main(4,2)
Error detected: Unexpected trace value
POI: ({'happy0.erl',9,call,1}) trace:
            [false,false,false,true,false,false,true]
POI: ({'happy1.erl',18,call,1}) trace:
            [false,false,false,false,false,false,true,false,false,true]
----------------------------
```

LISTING 6: SecEr reports discrepancies between is_happy call as POI.

```
$ ./secer -pois "test_happy:relX()" -funs "test_happy:funs()" -to 15
Function: main/2
----------------------------
Generated test cases: 1624
Mismatching test cases: 64 (3.94%)
      POIs comparison:
            + {{'happy0.erl',9,{var,'X'},1},
               {'happy1.erl',18,{var,'X'},1}}
                              The second trace is longer => 64 Errors
                              Example call: main(6,3)
------ Detected Error ------
Call: main(6,3)
Error Type: The second trace is longer
POI: ({'happy0.erl',9,{var,'X'},1}) trace:
          [6,7,8,9,10,11,12,13]
POI: ({'happy1.erl',18,{var,'X'},1}) trace:
          [6,7,8,9,10,11,12,13,14,15,16,17,18,19]
----------------------------
```

LISTING 7: SecEr reports discrepancies using variable X as the POI.

```
$ ./secer -pois "test_string:rel()" -funs "test_string:funs()" -to 15
Function: tokens/2
----------------------------
Generated test cases: 118878
Both versions of the program generate identical traces for the defined points of interest
```

LISTING 8: SecEr reports that no discrepancies exist.

report provided by SecEr when selecting variable X as the POI. The reported discrepancy indicates that both traces are the same until a point in the execution where the version in Listing 2 continues producing values. This behaviour is the expected one, because the result of is_happy has an influence on the number of times the call is executed. Therefore, the user can conclude that the arguments do not produce the discrepancy and the source of the discrepancy is inside the is_happy function.

Listings 5, 6, and 7 show that SecEr detects the errors and produces a concrete call that reveals these errors showing the effects. With more POIs, the user can obtain more feedback to help in finding the source of a bug. Clearly, with this information we can now ensure that the symptoms of the errors are observable in function is_happy.

6.4. Use Case 2: An Improvement of the string:tokens/2 *Function.* In this case of study, we consider a real commit of the Erlang/OTP distribution that improved the performance of the string:tokens/2 function. Algorithm 3 shows the code of the original and the improved versions. The differences introduced in this commit can be consulted here:

https://github.com/erlang/otp/commit/
53288b441ec721ce3bbdcc4ad65b75e11acc5e1b

The improvement consists in two main changes. The first one is a general improvement obtained by reversing the input string (the one that is going to be tokenized) at the beginning of the process. The second one improves the cases where the separators list has only one element. The algorithm uses two auxiliary functions in both cases, so its structure is kept between versions. However, the optimized version duplicates these functions to cover the single-element list of separators and the rest of the cases separately.

We can use SecEr to check whether the behaviour of both versions is the same. In order to do this, we can define as POIs the final expressions of the tokens/2 function in each version, i.e., the call to tokens1/3 function in the original version and the whole case in the optimized version. The input function should be tokens/2 because the changes were introduced to improve it (see Algorithm 4). This is enough to check that both versions preserve the same behaviour (see Listing 8).

We can now consider a hypothetical scenario where an error was introduced in the aforementioned commit.

```
$ ./secer -pois "test_string:rel()" -funs "test_string:funs()" -to 15
Function: tokens/2
----------------------------
Generated test cases: 105088
Mismatching test cases: 72260 (68.76%)
      POIs comparison:
            + {{'string0.erl',2,call,1},
                {'string1.erl',2,case,1}}
                        Unexpected trace value => 72260 Errors
                        Example call: tokens([9],[5,19,3,2])
------ Detected Error ------
Call: tokens([9],[5,19,3,2])
Error Type: Unexpected trace value
POI: ({'string0.erl',2,call,1}) trace:
        [[[9]]]
POI: ({'string1.erl',2,case,1}) trace:
        [[9,[9]]]
----------------------------
```

LISTING 9: SecEr reports discrepancies after modifying optimized string.erl.

Suppose that line (30) in Algorithm 3 (optimized version) is replaced by the following expression:

```
[C | tokens_multiple_2(S, Seps, Toks, [C])]
```

In this scenario, SecEr reports that some of the traces differ (see Listing 9).

We can add more POIs to try to isolate the error. For instance, the calls in lines (6), (8), (15), and (17) of Algorithm 3 (original version) are a good choice in this case, as it can help in checking that the intermediate results are the expected ones. This selection of POIs is also interesting because each POI in the original version is duplicated in the optimized version. For instance, line (6) in the original version corresponds to lines (14) and (28) in the optimized version. This relation is specified by defining two tuples of POIs: ((original version, line (6)), (optimized version, line (14))) and ((original version, line (6)), (optimized version, line (28))). There is an additional issue that should be considered before calling to SecEr. As one of the improvements was to reverse the input string beforehand, the execution order is different in the optimized version. This means that the traces computed by SecEr for the two versions will surely differ. To solve this inconvenience we can invoke SecEr with the flag -cfun "secer:independent()" activated. Thus, SecEr will ignore the order of the traces computed for different POIs. The result produced by SecEr with this configuration is shown in Listings 10 and 11.

The reported error is effectively pointing to a POI which is a call to the function that produced the error. This scenario demonstrates how useful SecEr can be to find the source of the discrepancies. Another interesting feature of the report is the categorization of errors. In this particular example, there are two kinds of errors: errors related to the length of the trace,

where one trace is a prefix of the other, and errors related to the values of the trace, where the values of each trace are completely different. In Listing 10 (and also in Listing 11), the first error detected by SecEr is a length error while the third error is a value error. Moreover, there are errors indicating that some POI was not executed (i.e., it produced an empty trace, represented in the listings by the trace []). This is because some of the POIs are not completely symmetrical in this example. Concretely, when the separators list (the second parameter of the function string:tokens/2) is empty, the algorithms behave differently. As this is not a really interesting test case input, we could use an Erlang's type specifier (spec) to constrain this second parameter to be a nonempty list. An alternative is to use a comparison function that takes into account this particularity. Therefore, by avoiding ITCs of this type, the reported errors will be only related to the actual error.

Now, we can return to the original scenario to explore other interesting uses of SecEr. As we mentioned, this commit improved the performance of function string:tokens/2. We can use SecEr to check that this improvement actually exists. In contrast to previous examples, this would need two small modifications. In concrete, the first one is to replace line (2) of Algorithm 3 (original version) with the following expressions:

```
(1) Start = os:timestamp(),

(2) Res = tokens1(S, Seps, []),
```

```
Original version
(1)   tokens(S, Seps) ->
(2)     tokens1(S, Seps, []).
(3)   tokens1([C|S], Seps, Toks) ->
(4)     case member(C, Seps) of
(5)       true ->
(6)         tokens1(S, Seps, Toks);
(7)       false ->
(8)         tokens2(S, Seps, Toks, [C])
(9)     end;
(10)  tokens1([], _Seps, Toks) ->
(11)    reverse(Toks).
(12)  tokens2([C|S], Seps, Toks, Cs) ->
(13)    case member(C, Seps) of
(14)      true ->
(15)        tokens1(S, Seps, [reverse(Cs)|Toks]);
(16)      false ->
(17)        tokens2(S, Seps, Toks, [C|Cs])
(18)    end;
(19)  tokens2([], _Seps, Toks, Cs) ->
(20)    reverse([reverse(Cs)|Toks]).
Optimized version
(1)   tokens(S, Seps) ->
(2)     case Seps of
(3)        [] ->
(4)          case S of
(5)            [] -> [];
(6)            [_|_] -> [S]
(7)          end;
(8)        [C] ->
(9)            tokens_single_1(reverse(S), C, []);
(10)       [_|_] ->
(11) tokens_multiple_1(reverse(S), Seps, [])
(12)   end.
(13) tokens_single_1([Sep|S], Sep, Toks) ->
(14)   tokens_single_1(S, Sep, Toks);
(15) tokens_single_1([C|S], Sep, Toks) ->
(16)   tokens_single_2(S, Sep, Toks, [C]);
(17) tokens_single_1([], _, Toks) ->
(18)   Toks.
(19) tokens_single_2([Sep|S], Sep, Toks, Tok) ->
(20)   tokens_single_1(S, Sep, [Tok|Toks]);
(21) tokens_single_2([C|S], Sep, Toks, Tok) ->
(22)   tokens_single_2(S, Sep, Toks, [C|Tok]);
(23) tokens_single_2([], _Sep, Toks, Tok) ->
(24)   [Tok|Toks].
(25) tokens_multiple_1([C|S], Seps, Toks) ->
(26)   case member(C, Seps) of
(27)     true ->
(28)       tokens_multiple_1(S, Seps, Toks);
(29)     false ->
(30)       tokens_multiple_2(S, Seps, Toks, [C])
(31)   end;
(32) tokens_multiple_1([], _Seps, Toks) ->
(33)   Toks.
(34) tokens_multiple_2([C|S], Seps, Toks, Tok) ->
(35)   case member(C, Seps) of
(36)     true ->
(37)       tokens_multiple_1(S, Seps, [Tok|Toks]);
(38)     false ->
(39)       tokens_multiple_2(S, Seps, Toks, [C|Tok])
(40)   end;
(41) tokens_multiple_2([], _Seps, Toks, Tok) ->
(42)   [Tok|Toks].
```

ALGORITHM 3: string.erl (original and optimized versions).

```
(1)   -module(test_string).
(2)   -compile(export_all).
(3)
(4)   poiOld() ->
(5)       {'string0.erl', 2, call, 1}.
(6)   poiNew() ->
(7)       {'string1.erl', 2, 'case', 1}.
(8)
(9)   poiOldError() ->
(10)      {'string0.erl', 6, call, 1}.
(11)  poiNewError1() ->
(12)      {'string1.erl', 14, call, 1}.
(13)  poiNewError2() ->
(14)      {'string1.erl', 28, call, 1}.
(15)
(16)
(17)  rel() ->
(18)      [{poiOld(), poiNew()}].
(19)  relError() ->
(20)      [{poiOldError(), poiNewError1()},
(21)       {poiOldError(), poiNewError2()}].
(22)
(23)  funs() ->
(24)      "[tokens/2]".
```

ALGORITHM 4: Configuration file to test string modules.

```
(3) timer:now_diff(os:timestamp(), Start),
```

```
(4) Res.
```

The second change is similar and consists in assigning to variable Res the result of the case expression in line (2) of Algorithm 3 (optimized version). To invoke SecEr, the first step is to choose a POI. We can select in both codes the expression `timer:now_diff(os:timestamp(), Start)` which computes the total time. Then, we need to use the comparison function `secer:comp_perf/1` that returns true when the execution time of the optimized version is smaller than or equal to the execution time of the original version. Note that we used the parameter of this function

which defines a threshold (of $30\,\mu s$ in this case) to filter those evaluations whose execution times are almost equal. We discard, in this way, downgrade alerts that are not significant. The report of SecEr (see Listing 12) shows that effectively there is an efficiency improvement in the optimized version; i.e., the time used by the optimized version is less than the one of the original version in all 127573 generated test cases.

We can create a different scenario where the performance has not been improved. We introduce a simple change to simulate this case by replacing line (28) of Algorithm 3 (optimized version) with the following line:

```
timer:sleep(5), tokens_multiple_1(S, Seps, Toks);
```

This will introduce a delay of 5 milliseconds before calling function tokens_multiple_1/3 affecting consequently the overall performance. We can run SecEr again with this version of the code and the report (Listing 13) reveals two relevant problems: (i) many test cases show a worse performance in the new code than in the original code (those cases affected by the downgrade) and (ii) fewer test cases are being generated by SecEr due to the sleep time introduced in the execution.

The user could now easily introduce more time measures in the code and rerun SecEr to find the source of the downgrade in the performance.

6.5. Use Case 3: Regression Bug Fixed in a Real Commit in etorrent. In this use case, we study a real commit in the etorrent GitHub repository, a repository with an implementation of a bittorrent client in Erlang. This commit can be consulted here:

https://github.com/edwardw/etorrent/commit/
d9d8cc13bab2eaa1ce282971901b7a29bf9bc942

The commit corrects an error introduced in a previous commit (https://github.com/edwardw/etorrent/commit/
a9340eb5b4e2da3cf08094d1f942bb31173f4011): the output of a decoding function is modified from a single variable

```
$ ./secer -pois "test_string:relError()" -funs "test_string:funs()" -to 15
Function: tokens/2
--------------------------
Generated test cases: 64458
Mismatching test cases: 31187 (48.38%)
      POIs comparison:
          + {{'string0.erl',6,call,1},
              {'string1.erl',14,call,1}}
                    The second trace is longer => 40 Errors
                    Example call: tokens([11,6,4,4],[4])
          + {{'string0.erl',6,call,1},
              {'string1.erl',14,call,1}}
                    The first trace is empty => 364 Errors
                    Example call: tokens([47,3,19,7,1,10,1,25,4,16],[16])
          + {{'string0.erl',6,call,1},
              {'string1.erl',28,call,1}}
                    Unexpected trace value => 18078 Errors
                    Example call: tokens([4,24,0,4,13,10,1,0],[2,8,12,1,0])
          + {{'string0.erl',6,call,1},
              {'string1.erl',28,call,1}}
                    The first trace is empty => 7991 Errors
                    Example call: tokens([13,7],[1,1,2,3,6,4,11,8,7])
          + {{'string0.erl',6,call,1},
              [{'string1.erl',28,call,1},
               {'string1.erl',14,call,1}]}
                    The first trace is longer => 3058 Errors
                    Example call: tokens([6,3,1,7,4,9,5,7,28],[1,10,46,3,4,8,34,6])
          + {{'string0.erl',6,call,1},
              [{'string1.erl',28,call,1},
               {'string1.erl',14,call,1}]}
                    The second trace is empty => 8231 Errors
                    Example call: tokens([12,1],[2,10,0,4,12,4,6,2,22])
```

LISTING 10: SecEr reports discrepancies in the multiple-POI execution.

to a tuple containing the atom ok together with this value. This bug was found by the commit's authors using unit testing (EUnit in Erlang). Therefore, in this case, we do not use the test generation feature of SecEr, but instead we start from the test case that revealed the error. Therefore, the input function is the failing unit test case, and we take advantage of the multiple-POI approach, placing several POIs in the function called by the unit test case. There are two modules implied in the process. The fragments of the involved modules defining the affected functions are shown in Algorithm 5.

Therefore, the input function of SecEr is query_ping_0_test/0. This function calls to the decode_msg/1 function, so we place some POIs inside it to check its behaviour. In particular, we place one POI in each function call (lines (3) and (5)) and one POI in the return expression of the function (case expression in line (6)). All the parameters defined in this use case can be found in the configuration file in Algorithm 6. After placing these three POIs in both versions, we execute SecEr obtaining the result shown in Listing 14.

The results provided by SecEr show that the bug is located inside function etorrent_dht_net_old:decode/1. With a quick inspection of both versions of the decode

function we can easily discover that the format of the return expression is different. Although we should be confident that the error is located in this expression, we can be completely sure by placing some POIs in this function. This can be easily done by adding the POIs to the configuration file.

After fixing an error, it is a good practice to rerun SecEr in order to verify that there are no more mismatches between the defined POIs. Remember that SecEr only reports the first mismatch found in the execution. In the first execution, if the function call to get_value/2 (line (5)) had also an error, it would have been omitted by the previous mismatch found in call to decode/1 (line (3)).

7. Using SecEr in a Concurrent Environment

Nondeterministic computations are one of the main obstacles for regression testing. In fact, they prevent us from comparing the results of a test case executed in different versions because the discrepancies found can be well produced by sources of nondeterminism such as concurrency. In some specific situations, however, we can still use SecEr to report whether the behaviour of a concurrent program is preserved.

```
------ Detected Error ------
Call: tokens([11,6,4,4],[4])
Error Type: The second trace is longer
POI: ({'string0.erl',6,call,1}) trace:
        [[[11,6]]]
POI: ({'string1.erl',14,call,1}) trace:
        [[[11,6]],[[11,6]]]
----------------------------
------ Detected Error ------
Call: tokens([47,3,19,7,1,10,1,25,4,16],[16])
Error Type: The first trace is empty
POI: ({'string0.erl',6,call,1}) trace:
        []
POI: ({'string1.erl',14,call,1}) trace:
        [[[47,3,19,7,1,10,1,25,4]]]
----------------------------
------ Detected Error ------
Call: tokens([4,24,0,4,13,10,1,0],[2,8,12,1,0])
Error Type: Unexpected trace value
POI: ({'string0.erl',6,call,1}) trace:
        [[[4,24],[4,13,10]]]
POI: ({'string1.erl',28,call,1}) trace:
        [[10,24,[4,24],[4,13,10]],[10,24,[4,24],[4,13,10]]]
----------------------------
------ Detected Error ------
Call: tokens([13,7],[1,1,2,3,6,4,11,8,7])
Error Type: The first trace is empty
POI: ({'string0.erl',6,call,1}) trace:
        []
POI: ({'string1.erl',28,call,1}) trace:
        [[13,[13]]]
----------------------------
------ Detected Error ------
Call: tokens([6,3,1,7,4,9,5,7,28],[1,10,46,3,4,8,34,6])
Error Type: The first trace is longer
POI: ({'string0.erl',6,call,1}) trace:
        [[[7],[9,5,7,28]],[[7],[9,5,7,28]],[[7],[9,5,7,28]]]
POI: ([{'string1.erl',28,call,1},
     {'string1.erl',14,call,1}]) trace:
        [[[7],[9,5,7,28]],[[7],[9,5,7,28]]]
----------------------------
------ Detected Error ------
Call: tokens([12,1],[2,10,0,4,12,4,6,2,22])
Error Type: The second trace is empty
POI: ({'string0.erl',6,call,1}) trace:
        [[[1]]]
POI: ([{'string1.erl',28,call,1},
     {'string1.erl',14,call,1}]) trace:
        []
----------------------------
```

LISTING 11: SecEr reports discrepancies in the multiple-POI execution (cont.).

For instance, consider the client-server model depicted in Figure 4. In this simple example, a POI should not be placed in *Server*, because we cannot know *a priori* whether req_1 is going to be served before or after req_2, and this could have an impact on the traces obtained from that POI. However, we could place a POI in any of the clients, as long as the request is not affected by the state of the server. This is acceptable for many kinds of servers, but it is still a quite annoying limitation for many others.

However, in Erlang, as it is common in other languages, there is a high-level way to define a server. In particular, real Erlang programmers tend to use the Erlang-OTP's behaviour

```
$ ./secer -pois "[{'string0.erl', LINE_timer:now_diff, call, 1}, {'string1.erl', LINE_timer:now_diff,
call,  1}]"
            -funs "test_string:funs()" -to 15 -cfun "secer:comp_perf(30)"
Function: tokens/2
----------------------------
Generated test cases: 127573
Both versions of the program generate identical traces for the defined points of interest
```

LISTING 12: SecEr reports the result of comparing the performance POI.

```
$ ./secer -pois "[{'string0.erl', LINE_timer:now_diff, call, 1}, {'string1.erl', LINE_timer:now_diff,
call,1}]"
            -funs "test_string:funs()" -to 15 -cfun "secer:comp_perf(30)"
Function: tokens/2
----------------------------
Generated test cases: 4587
Mismatching test cases: 1286 (28.03%)
     POIs comparison:
          + {{'string0.erl', LINE_timer:now_diff,call,1},
            {'string1.erl', LINE_timer:now_diff,call,1}}
                    Unexpected trace value => 1286 Errors
                    Example call: tokens([7,5,4,2,16,3,11,3],[4,2,9,2])
------ Detected Error ------
Call: tokens([7,5,4,2,16,3,11,3],[4,2,9,2])
Error Type: Slower Calculation
POI: ({'string0.erl', LINE_timer:now_diff,call,1}) trace:
          [2]
POI: ({'string1.erl', LINE_timer:now_diff,call,1}) trace:
          [5395]
----------------------------
```

LISTING 13: SecEr reports discrepancies after entering the sleep expression.

named gen_server. By implementing this behaviour, the programmer is only defining the concrete behaviours of a server, leaving all the low-level aspects to the internals of the gen_server implementation. These concrete behaviours include how the server's state is initialized, how a concrete request should be served, or what to do when the server is stopped. When using gen_server, programmers could use the functions implementing these concrete behaviours as input functions for SecEr. In this way, they can check, for instance, that a server is going to reply to the user and leave the server's state in the same way across different versions of the program.

We can explain it with a real example. Consider the code in Algorithm 7, which shows a fragment (although those parts of the module that are not shown here are also interesting, we have removed them because they are not used in the use case) of the gen_server defined in

https://github.com/hcvst/erlang-otp-tutorial#otp-gen_server

The server's state is simply a counter that tracks the number of requests served so far. The server defines three types of requests through the functions handle_call and handle_cast:

(1) The synchronous request (i.e., a request where the client waits for a reply) get_count, which returns the current server's state.

(2) The asynchronous request (i.e., a request where the client does not wait for a reply) stop, which stops the server.

(3) The asynchronous request say_hello, which makes the server print hello in the standard output.

The first and the third requests modify the server's state by adding one to the total number of requests served so far. The second one does not modify the state but rather it returns a special term that makes the gen_server stop itself.

To illustrate how SecEr can detect an unexpected behaviour change between two versions of the code, consider that the current (buggy) version is the one depicted in Algorithm 7, while the (correct) original version of the code contains line (38) instead of line (39).

Then, we can define a configuration file like the one in Algorithm 8 and run SecEr to see whether the behaviour

```
etorrent_dht_net_old.erl
(1) decode_msg(InMsg) ->
(2)     io:format("0: ~p\n", [InMsg]),
(3)     Msg = etorrent_bcoding_old:decode(InMsg),
(4)     io:format("0: ~p\n", [Msg]),
(5)     MsgID = get_value(<<"t">>, Msg),
(6)     case get_value(<<"y">>, Msg) of
(7)         <<"q">> ->
(8)             MString = get_value(<<"q">>, Msg),
(9)             Method = string_to_method(MString),
(10)            Params = get_value(<<"a">>, Msg),
(11)            {Method, MsgID, Params};
(12)        <<"r">> ->
(13)            Values = get_value(<<"r">>, Msg),
(14)            {response, MsgID, Values};
(15)        <<"e">> ->
(16)            [ECode, EMsg] = get_value(<<"e">>, Msg),
(17)            {error, MsgID, ECode, EMsg}
(18)    end.
(19) query_ping_0_test() ->
(20)     Enc = "d1:ad2:id20:abcdefghij0123456789e1:
(21)           q4:ping1:t2:aa1:y1:qe",
(22)    {ping, ID, Params} = decode_msg(Enc),
(23)    ?assertEqual(<<"aa">>, ID),
(24)    ?assertEqual(
(25)    <<"abcdefghij0123456789">>,
(26)    fetch_id(Params)).
etorrent_dht_net_new.erl
(27) decode_msg(InMsg) ->
(28)     io:format("0: ~p\n", [InMsg]),
(29)     Msg = etorrent_bcoding_new:decode(InMsg),
(30)     io:format("0: ~p\n", [Msg]),
(31)     MsgID = get_value(<<"t">>, Msg),
(32)     case get_value(<<"y">>, Msg) of
(33)         <<"q">> ->
(34)             MString = get_value(<<"q">>, Msg),
(35)             Method = string_to_method(MString),
(36)             Params = get_value(<<"a">>, Msg),
(37)             {Method, MsgID, Params};
(38)        <<"r">> ->
(39)            Values = get_value(<<"r">>, Msg),
(40)            {response, MsgID, Values};
(41)        <<"e">> ->
(42)            [ECode, EMsg] = get_value(<<"e">>, Msg),
(43)            {error, MsgID, ECode, EMsg}
(44)    end.
(45) query_ping_0_test() ->
(46)     Enc = "d1:ad2:id20:abcdefghij0123456789e1:
(47)           q4:ping1:t2:aa1:y1:qe",
(48)    {ping, ID, Params} = decode_msg(Enc),
(49)    ?assertEqual(<<"aa">>, ID),
(50)    ?assertEqual(
(51)    <<"abcdefghij0123456789">>,
(52)    fetch_id(Params)).
etorrent_bcoding_old.erl
(1)    -spec decode(string() | binary()) -> bcode().
(2)    decode(Bin) when is_binary(Bin) ->
(3)      decode(binary_to_list(Bin));
(4)    decode(String) when is_list(String) ->
(5)          {Res, _Extra} = decode_b(String),
(6)          Res.
(7)
```

ALGORITHM 5: Continued.

```
                    etorrent_bcoding_new.erl
        (8)    -spec decode(string()| binary()) ->
        (9)              {ok, bcode()}|{error, _Reason}.
        (10)   decode(Bin) when is_binary(Bin) ->
        (11)           decode(binary_to_list(Bin));
        (12)   decode(String) when is_list(String) ->
        (13)         try
        (14)             {Res, _Extra} = decode_b(String),
        (15)             {ok, Res}
        (16)      catch
        (17)         error:Reason -> {error, Reason}
        (18)      end.
```

ALGORITHM 5: etorrent source files (original and buggy versions).

```
$ ./secer -pois "test_etorrent:rel()" -funs "test_etorrent:funs()" -to 15
Function: query_ping_0_test/0
----------------------------
Generated test cases: 1
Mismatching test cases: 1 (100.0%)
      POIs comparison:
         + {{'etorrent_dht_net_old', 3, call, 1},
             {'etorrent_dht_net_new', 29, call, 1}}
                    Unexpected trace value => 1 Errors
                    Example call: query_ping_0_test()
------ Detected Error ------
Call: query_ping_0_test()
Error Type: Unexpected trace value
POI: ({'etorrent_dht_net_old', 3, call, 1}) trace:
       [[{<<97>>, [{<<105,100>>,<<97,98,99,100,101,102,103,104,105,106,48,49,50,51,52,53,54,
           55,56,57>>}]},
         {<<113>>,<<112,105,110,103>>},{<<116>>,<<97,97>>},{<<121>>,<<113>>}]]
POI: ({'etorrent_dht_net_new', 29, call, 1}) trace:
       [{ok,[{<<97>>, [{<<105,100>>,<<97,98,99,100,101,102,103,104,105,106,48,49,50,51,52,53,
           54,55,56,57>>}]},
         {<<113>>,<<112,105,110,103>>},{<<116>>,<<97,97>>},{<<121>>,<<113>>}]}]
----------------------------
```

LISTING 14: SecEr reports discrepancies after defining multiple POIs.

is preserved or not. This configuration file uses two input functions (handle_call and handle_cast) and a POI relation that defines three POIs, one for each request output. If we run SecEr using this configuration we obtain the output shown at Listing 15. In the output we can see that no errors are reported for function handle_call, which means that the request get_count is served in the same way in both versions. In contrast, an error is reported in function handle_cast, pointing to the POI defined in line (19) of Listing 14. This means that for the request say_hello the behaviour has not been preserved, while for the request stop it has been preserved. In particular, the error found reveals that there is a discrepancy between the new server's states returned by each version of the program.

This simple example shows how SecEr can be used to check behaviour preservation even in concurrent context. The key is that there is no need to run an execution with real concurrency; instead we can study directly the relevant functions that are used during the concurrent execution, like handle_call or handle_cast in the example above.

8. Alternative Approaches to SecEr

There exist several techniques that are currently being applied in professional Erlang projects to avoid regression faults. SecEr has been designed as both an alternative and a complement to these techniques.

In this section, we compare SecEr with the already available debugging and testing techniques that could be used when behaviour preservation is checked in an Erlang project. To illustrate these techniques, we use a real improvement

```
(1) -module(test_etorrent).
(2) -compile(export_all).
(3) poio1() ->
(4)      {'etorrent_dht_net_old', 3, call, 1}.
(5) poio2() ->
(6)      {'etorrent_dht_net_old', 5, call, 1}.
(7) poio3() ->
(8)      {'etorrent_dht_net_old', 6, 'case', 1}.
(9)
(10) poin1() ->
(11)     {'etorrent_dht_net_new', 29, call, 1}.
(12) poin2() ->
(13)     {'etorrent_dht_net_new', 31, call, 1}.
(14) poin3() ->
(15)     {'etorrent_dht_net_new', 32, 'case', 1}.
(16)
(17) rel() ->
(18)     [{poio1(), poin1()},
(19)      {poio2(), poin2()},
(20)      {poio3(), poin3()}].
(21)
(22) funs() ->
(23)     "[query_ping_0_test/0]".
```

ALGORITHM 6: Configuration file to test etorrent modules.

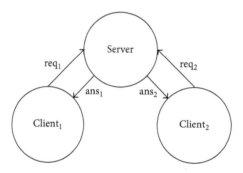

FIGURE 4: A simple client-server model.

of performance done in the orddict:from_list/1 function from the standard library of Erlang-OTP. The commit description can be found at

https://github.com/erlang/otp/commit/
5a7b2115ca5b9c23aacf79b634133fea172a61fd

This commit did not introduce any regression faults so, in order to make this study more interesting, we have also included a fault (see lines (8-9) in Listing 17). Listing 16 shows the code changed in the commit (function from_list/1) and the code involved in the change (function store/3). Listing 17 shows the new version of function from_list/1 and function reverse_pairs/2, used to reverse a list. The new version also uses function lists:ukeysort/2 (this function is described within a comment in Listing 17) to sort the given list. The original version uses function store/3 that, whenever an already stored key is stored again, replaces its current value by the new one. On the other hand, function lists:ukeysort/2 does exactly the contrary (see lines (13-14) in Listing 17). This is the reason why the list needs to be previously reversed. Therefore, the fault introduced assumes that programmers forgot to reverse the list. This is what line (9) in Listing 17 stages. The correct version is commented on above in line (8). In the following, all the techniques are applied to the described scenario.

8.1. Unit Testing. This is the most common way of checking behaviour preservation. In Erlang, it is common to define unit test cases and execute them with EUnit [16] (Erlang's unit testing tool). The test file of Algorithm 9 includes unit test cases specific for our scenario. Those tests using function from_list_test_common/1 check whether the intended behaviour has been implemented by using three simple cases. On the other hand, the tests using function from_list_vs/2 check whether the behaviour is preserved across different versions for the same three cases. The output of EUnit with these test cases is shown in Listing 18.

```
(1)   -module(hello_server).
(2)
(3)   -behavior(gen_server).
(4)
(5)   -record(state, {count}).
(6)
(7)%% %%%%%%%%%%%%%%%%%%%%%%%%%%%%%%%%%%%%%%%%%%%%%%%%%%%%%%%%%%%%
(8) %% gen_server Function Exports
(9)%% %%%%%%%%%%%%%%%%%%%%%%%%%%%%%%%%%%%%%%%%%%%%%%%%%%%%%%%%%%%%
(10)
(11)  -export([        % The behavior callbacks
(12)     init/1,        % - initializes our process
(13)     handle_call/3, % - handles synchronous calls
(14)     handle_cast/2, % - handles asynchronous calls
(15)     terminate/2]). % - is called on shut-down
(16)
(17)  %% %%%%%%%%%%%%%%%%%%%%%%%%%%%%%%%%%%%%%%%%%%%%%%%%%%%%%%%%%%%
(18)  %% gen_server Function Definitions
(19)  %% %%%%%%%%%%%%%%%%%%%%%%%%%%%%%%%%%%%%%%%%%%%%%%%%%%%%%%%%%%%
(20)
(21)  init([]) ->
(22)       {ok, #state{count=0}}.
(23)
(24)  -spec handle_call(get_count, any(),{state, integer()}) ->
(25)        {reply, integer(),{state, integer()}}.
(26)  handle_call(get_count, _From, #state{count=Count}) ->
(27)        {reply, Count, #state{count=Count+1}}.
(28)
(29)  -spec handle_cast(stop | say_hello, {state, integer()}) ->
(30)        {stop, any(),{state, integer()}}
(31)        |{noreply, {state, integer()}}.
(32)  handle_cast(stop, State) ->
(33)      {stop, normal, State};
(34)
(35)  handle_cast(say_hello, State) ->
(36)      io:format("Hello~n"),
(37)      {noreply,
(38)      % #state{ count = State#state.count+1}    % RIGHT
(39)      #state{ count = State#state.count-1}      % WRONG
(40)      }.
(41)
(42)  terminate(_Reason, _State) ->
(43)      error_logger:info_msg("terminating~n"),
(44)      ok.
```

ALGORITHM 7: hello_server.erl.

EUnit reports 3 failing tests: two were expected, since they are pointing to the tests that include the wrong version of the code (functions from_list_new_wrong_test/0 and from_list_old_test_vs_new_wrong_test/0). However, there is a third one that is a false positive. False positives happen because EUnit cannot find discrepancies when comparing erroneous computations. Therefore, an input that produces an error in the first version is reported as a failing test without checking whether it also fails in the second version.

All in all, unit testing allows us to identify a failing test case, which is a starting point to find the source of the discrepancy. The main problem is that unit testing requires writing a robust set of tests. Note that, without the second test case, i.e., [{0, 1},{0, 2}, {2, 3}], no test would fail (except for the false positive).

8.2. Property Testing. This approach is similar to unit testing, but it allows us to define more test cases in an easy way. It was first defined for Haskell and named QuickCheck [17]. Erlang has two implementations of this approach: QuviQ's Erlang QuickCheck [18] and PropEr [11]. Both are almost equivalent, with the exception of some small particularities (https://github.com/manopapad/proper#incompatibilities-with-quviqs-quickcheck). The big difference is that the Erlang QuickCheck is a commercial tool developed by QuviQ AB,

```
$ ./secer -pois "test_hello_server:rel()" -funs "test_hello_server:funs()" -to 15
Function: handle_call/3
---------------------------
Generated test cases: 19083
Both versions of the program generate identical traces for the defined points of interest
---------------------------
Function: handle_cast/2
---------------------------
Generated test cases: 42
Mismatching test cases: 21 (50.0%)
    POIs comparison:
        + {{'examples/gen_server/hello_server.erl',37,tuple,1},
           {'examples/gen_server/hello_server_wrong.erl',37,tuple,1}}
                Unexpected trace value => 21 Errors
                Example call: handle_cast(say_hello,{state,4})
------ Detected Error ------
Call: handle_cast(say_hello,{state,4})
Error Type: Unexpected trace value
POI: ({'examples/gen_server/hello_server.erl',37,tuple,1}) trace:
        [{noreply,{state,5}}]
POI: ({'examples/gen_server/hello_server_wrong.erl',37,tuple,1}) trace:
        [{noreply,{state,3}}]
---------------------------
```

LISTING 15: SecEr reports discrepancies in the functions implementing the requests.

```
(1)   -module(test_hello_server).
(2)   -export([rel/0, funs/0]).
(3)
(4)   file(0) ->
(5)     'examples/gen_server/hello_server.erl';
(6)   file(1) ->
(7)     'examples/gen_server/hello_server_wrong.erl'.
(8)
(9)   poi_rel(POI) ->
(10)    {POI(0), POI(1)}.
(11)
(12)  poi1(Version) ->
(13)    {file(Version), 27, tuple, 1}.
(14)
(15)  poi2(Version) ->
(16)    {file(Version), 33, tuple, 1}.
(17)
(18)  poi3(Version) ->
(19)    {file(Version), 37, tuple, 1}.
(20)
(21)  rel() ->
(22)    [poi_rel(fun poi1/1), poi_rel(fun poi2/1),
(23)      poi_rel(fun poi3/1)].
(24)
(25)  funs() ->
(26)    "[handle_call/3, handle_cast/2]".
```

ALGORITHM 8: test_hello_server.erl.

```
(1) -spec from_list(List) -> Orddict when
(2)        List:: [{Key:: term(), Value:: term()}],
(3)        Orddict:: orddict().
(4)
(5) from_list(Pairs) ->
(6)        lists:foldl(
(7)            fun ({K,V}, D) -> store(K, V, D) end, [], Pairs).
(8)
(9) -spec store(Key, Value, Orddict1) -> Orddict2 when
(10)        Key:: term(),
(11)        Value:: term(),
(12)        Orddict1:: orddict(),
(13)        Orddict2:: orddict().
(14)
(15) store(Key, New, [{K,_}=E|Dict]) when Key < K ->
(16)        [{Key,New},E|Dict];
(17) store(Key, New, [{K,_}=E|Dict]) when Key > K ->
(18)        [E|store(Key, New, Dict)];
(19) store(Key, New, [{_K,_Old}|Dict]) -> % Key == K
(20)        [{Key,New}|Dict];
(21) store(Key, New, []) -> [{Key,New}].
```

LISTING 16: orddict_old.erl.

```
(1) -spec from_list(List) -> Orddict when
(2)        List:: [{Key:: term(), Value:: term()}],
(3)        Orddict:: orddict().
(4)
(5) from_list([]) -> [];
(6) from_list([{_,_}]=Pair) -> Pair;
(7) from_list(Pairs) ->
(8)        lists:ukeysort(1, reverse_pairs(Pairs, [])) % RIGHT
(9)        lists:ukeysort(1, Pairs).                   % WRONG
(10)
(11) % ukeysort(N, TupleList1) -> TupleList2
(12) %      Returns a list containing the sorted elements of
(13) %      list TupleList1 where all except the first tuple of
(14) %      the tuples comparing equal have been deleted.
(15) %      Sorting is performed on the Nth element of the tuple
(16)
(17) reverse_pairs([{_,_}=H|T], Acc) ->
(18)        reverse_pairs(T, [H|Acc]);
(19) reverse_pairs([], Acc) -> Acc.
```

LISTING 17: orddict_new.erl.

while PropEr is an open-source project available at GitHub. The authors of the commit defined their property tests for Erlang QuickCheck. Therefore, we have adapted them to PropEr (1st property: https://github.com/mistupv/secer/blob/master/examples/orddict/orddict_t1.erl; 2nd property: https://github.com/mistupv/secer/blob/master/examples/orddict/orddict_t2.erl) (with really few modifications) to make it available for any interested researcher that wants to reproduce the outputs shown below.

In the commit, the authors explain what properties they check and how they check them (the source code of the properties can be found in the commit):

The first QuickCheck test first generates a list of pairs of terms, then uses the list to create both an original and revised orddict *using* from_list/1, *then verifies that the results of the operation are the same for both instances. The*

```
> eunit:test(orddict_tests).
orddict_tests: from_list_new_wrong_test...*failed*
in function orddict_tests:'-from_list_test_common/1-fun-1-'/1 (orddict_tests.erl, line (21))
in call from orddict_tests:from_list_test_common/1 (orddict_tests.erl, line (19))
**error:{assertEqual,[{module,orddict_tests},
                {line,(21)},
                {expression,"Mod: from_list ( [{ 0 , 1 }, { 0 , 2 }, { 2 , 3 }] )"},
                {expected,[{0,2},{2,3}]},
                {value,[{0,1},{2,3}]}]}
    output:<<"">>
orddict_tests: from_list_old_test_vs_new_wrong_test...*failed*
in function orddict_tests:'-from_list_vs/2-fun-1-'/2 (orddict_tests.erl, line (44))
in call from orddict_tests:from_list_vs/2 (orddict_tests.erl, line (42))
**error:{assertEqual,[{module,orddict_tests},
                {line,(44)},
                {expression,"Mod2: from_list ( Case2 )"},
                {expected,[{0,2},{2,3}]},
                {value,[{0,1},{2,3}]}]}
    output:<<"">>
orddict_tests: from_list_old_test_vs_new_ok_test...*failed*
in function orddict_old:'-from_list/1-fun-0-'/2 (orddict_old.erl, line 60)
    called as '-from_list/1-fun-0-'(1,[])
in call from lists:foldl/3 (lists.erl, line 1263)
in call from orddict_tests:'-from_list_vs/2-fun-2-'/2 (orddict_tests.erl, line (46))
**error:function_clause
    output:<<"">>
=======================================================
    Failed: 3. Skipped: 0. Passed: 2.
error
```

LISTING 18: EUnit's output.

second QuickCheck test is similar except that it first creates an instance of the original and revised orddicts and then folds over a randomly-generated list of orddict functions, applying each function to each orddict instance and verifying that the results match.

The output of PropEr is depicted in Listings 19 and 20 (because the inputs are randomly generated, the results may vary across different runs). The first property fails with input [{1,false},{1,true}]. This is one of the cases where the buggy version behaves differently, so the error reported actually identifies a discrepancy. Nevertheless, the error found by PropEr with the second property is a mismatch in the comparison of the resulting dictionaries, without even executing the list of orddict functions; thus this error is synonymous of the first one.

As it happens with unit testing, this approach is handy to find a failing test case to begin the debugging process that finds the source of the discrepancy. However, the definition of properties is difficult and can miss some corner cases. In general, property testing is more powerful than unit testing because each property can be used to generate an arbitrary number of tests, but the definition of properties often involves more time.

8.3. *CutEr.* Even though we use CutEr [9] in the internals of our tool to generate inputs, it was conceived as a standalone tool. The main difference with the previous approaches is that CutEr is a white-box approach. It does not randomly generate the inputs, but it analyzes the source code to generate inputs that explore different execution branches.

In our scenario, one can use CutEr to generate test cases for the current version and/or for the previous version. Unfortunately, by doing this, the relationship between the versions is not considered during the generation; i.e., the introduced changes are not considered in the test generation. In Listing 21, we can see that CutEr was able to generate for the previous version some list where some of the elements have a common key, i.e., tests that could reveal the error. The time used to compute all the tests was 2 minutes 43 seconds. For the current version, Listing 22 shows that CutEr only generated 5 input tests. The time used to generate them was 7.4 seconds. Only one generated test has tuples with a repeated key: from_list([0.0,2.0,0,1.0]). Note that this case is useful in our scenario, but it could be useless in other situations. For instance, if pattern matching was used to compare values, 0 and 0.0 would not be considered as matching values.

This example shows that CutEr can be very helpful to generate a lot of test cases that cover most paths in the code.

```
(1)   -module(orddict_tests).
(2)   -compile(export_all).
(3)
(4)   -include_lib("eunit/include/eunit.hrl").
(5)
(6)   from_list_old_test() ->
(7)     from_list_test_common(orddict_old).
(8)
(9)   from_list_new_ok_test() ->
(10)    from_list_test_common(orddict_new_ok).
(11)
(12)  from_list_new_wrong_test() ->
(13)    from_list_test_common(orddict_new_wrong).
(14)
(15)  from_list_test_common(Mod) ->
(16)    ?assertEqual(
(17)      [{0,1}, {1, 2}, {2, 3}],
(18)        Mod:from_list([{0,1}, {1, 2}, {2, 3}])),
(19)    ?assertEqual(
(20)      [{0,2}, {2, 3}],
(21)        Mod:from_list([{0,1}, {0, 2}, {2, 3}])),
(22)    ?assertError(
(23)      function_clause,
(24)      Mod:from_list([1, {1, 2}, {2, 3}])).
(25)
(26)  from_list_old_test_vs_new_wrong_test() ->
(27)    from_list_vs(orddict_old, orddict_new_wrong).
(28)
(29)  from_list_old_test_vs_new_ok_test() ->
(30)    from_list_vs(orddict_old, orddict_new_ok).
(31)
(32)  from_list_vs(Mod1, Mod2) ->
(33)    Case1 =
(34)        [{0,1}, {1, 2}, {2, 3}],
(35)    Case2 =
(36)        [{0,1}, {0, 2}, {2, 3}],
(37)    Case3 =
(38)      [1,{1, 2}, {2, 3}],
(39)    ?assertEqual(
(40)      Mod1:from_list(Case1),
(41)      Mod2:from_list(Case1)),
(42)    ?assertEqual(
(43)      Mod1:from_list(Case2),
(44)      Mod2:from_list(Case2)),
(45)    ?assertEqual(
(46)      Mod1:from_list(Case3),
(47)      Mod2:from_list(Case3)).
```

ALGORITHM 9: EUnit tests.

However, what test cases can reveal a different behaviour remains unknown. Therefore, we are forced to run the test cases on the other version to check that the results are the same. When a discrepancy is found, a debugging process should be started. Moreover, as we can see in the CutEr's execution with the old version, the time needed to compute all the test cases is significantly bigger due to the white-box analysis.

8.4. Print Debugging. Print debugging is still a very extended practice because it allows us to quickly check the values of any variable at some specific point. Essentially, we must modify the code to catch the value of some selected expressions. Two drawbacks are that these changes can introduce new errors, and they should be undone when debugging has finished.

In our scenario, we can use one of the test cases reported by PropEr to start the debugging process, e.g., `orddict:from_list([{1,false},{1,true}])`. Before executing this test case in the two versions, we must add some prints to show some intermediate values. In particular, we replaced lines (6) and (7) of Listing 16 with the code shown in Listing 23. With this addition we are able to observe

```
> orddict_t1:test().
.........................!
Failed: After 29 test(s).
An exception was raised: error:{badmatch,false}.
Stacktrace: [{orddict_t1,'-prop_equivalent_dict_modules/0-fun-0-',1,
                         [{file,"orddict_t1.erl"},{line,25}]}].
[{1,1},{1,-2}]
Shrinking...(3 time(s))
[{1,false},{1,true}]
false
```

LISTING 19: PropEr's output for the first property.

```
> orddict_t2:test().
.....................................................................................
.................!
Failed: After 100 test(s).
An exception was raised: error:{badmatch,false}.
Stacktrace: [{orddict_t2,'-prop_equivalent_dict_modules/0-fun-0-',2,
                         [{file,"orddict_t2.erl"},{line,39}]},
                {lists,foldl,3,[{file,"lists.erl"},{line,1263}]},
                {orddict_t2,'-prop_equivalent_dict_modules/0-fun-1-',1,
                         [{file,"orddict_t2.erl"},{line,37}]}].
{[{2.50411088062667,-7.851645940978741},{1,<<239,224,172,126>>},
  {-0.6360219784877551,4},{1,<<177,118,23,95,55>>}],[store,fetch,fetch,find]}
Shrinking........(8 time(s))
{[{1,false},{1,0}],[is_key]}
false
```

LISTING 20: PropEr's output for the second property.

the input accumulator and the output accumulator in each iteration. For the code in Listing 17, the changes should be made inside function lists:ukeysort/2 because it is the function in charge of calculating the final output of orddict:from_list/1. The idea of the change in this case is similar, so the code is modified as it is shown in Listing 24 (all complete files are available at https://github.com/mistupv/secer/tree/master/examples/orddict).

The output produced by the print statements for both the old and new versions is depicted in Listings 25 and 26, respectively. It can help to understand that the old version keeps the new value of a key that is already at the dictionary, while function lists:ukeysort/2 does the contrary. If this is not evident for programmers, then they need to add more print statements in the auxiliary functions of lists:ukeysort/2 and in function orddict:store/3.

This example shows that, even with a small change like the one considered here, the number of functions involved can be quite big and the use of prints to the standard output can become an impracticable approach. Moreover, this approach can introduce new errors due to the additions/deletions in the (already buggy) code.

8.5. The Erlang Debugger. Known as Debugger [19], it is a GUI for the Erlang interpreter that can be used for the debugging of Erlang programs. It includes common debugging features such as breakpoints, single-stepped execution, and the ability to show/modify variable values.

In our scenario, we can use Debugger to place some breakpoints in the code and observe, step by step, how the dictionaries are created in each version. The first intuition is to place a breakpoint in line (7) of Listing 16 to observe the evolution of the accumulator (as we did in the previous technique). However, because breakpoints refer to a (whole) line, we are already facing one of the problems of this approach: we cannot place the breakpoint in the desired spots (the input accumulator and the output accumulator). Fortunately, one can easily change the code so each expression of interest is placed in one different line allowing the use of breakpoints as desired, i.e., in the header of the anonymous function and in the line that contains the call to the orddict:store/3 function. When we run the test we realize that the breakpoints are ignored and that the test is run without stopping. Therefore, we need to add breakpoints for each line of the orddict:store/3 function, which has various clauses. Note that all the breakpoint definitions are done through the graphical interface so this process is quite slow. After adding these new breakpoints, the execution does stop at some of these new breakpoints and we are able to inspect the intermediate results. We should do something

```
$ ./cuter orddict_oldfrom_list '[[{0,1}]]' -r -v
Compiling orddict_old.erl... OK
Testing orddict_old:from_list/1...
orddict_old:from_list([{0,1}])... ok
xxx
orddict_old:from_list([])... ok
...
orddict_old:from_list([{0,0.0},{0,1.0}])... ok
...
orddict_old:from_list([{[],0.0},{[],1.0}])... ok
...
orddict_old:from_list([{0,0.0},{0,1.0},{4,2.0}])... ok
...
Solver Statistics...
    - Solved models: 84
    - Unsolved models: 432
```

LISTING 21: CutEr's output for the old version (trimmed).

```
$ ./cuter orddict_new_wrong from_list '[[{0,1}]]' -r -v
Compiling orddict_new_wrong.erl... OK
Testing orddict_new_wrong:from_list/1...
orddict_new_wrong:from_list([{0,1}])... ok
orddict_new_wrong:from_list([])... ok
xx
orddict_new_wrong:from_list([{0.0,1.0},{3.0,2.0}]) ... ok
xxxxxxxxxxx
orddict_new_wrong:from_list([{0,0.0},{1.0,2.0}])... ok
orddict_new_wrong:from_list([{0.0,2.0},{0,1.0}])... ok
orddict_new_wrong:from_list([{0,0.0},{1,1.0}])... ok
xx
Solver Statistics...
    - Solved models: 5
    - Unsolved models: 15
```

LISTING 22: CutEr's output for the current version.

```
(1) lists:foldl(
(2)   fun ({K,V}, D) ->
(3)     io:format("Input: ~p\n", [D]),
(4)     Res = store(K, V, D),
(5)     io:format("Output: ~p\n", [Res]),
(6)     Res
(7)   end,
(8)   [],
(9)   Pairs).
```

LISTING 23: Fragment of orddict_old.erl with io:format/2.

```
(1) ukeysort(I, L) when is_integer(I), I > 0 ->
(2)   io:format("Input: ~p\n", [L]),
(3)   Res =
(4)     case L of
(5)     ...
(6)     end,
(7)   io:format("Output: ~p\n", [Res]),
(8)   Res.
```

LISTING 24: Fragment of lists:ukeysort/2 with io:format/2.

similar with the code of Listing 17. In this case, it makes more sense to add breakpoints inside the lists:ukeysort/2 function. Figure 5 shows an instant of the Debugger's session where a user can realize that the second element with repeated key is ignored, instead of the first one.

Although Debugger is very helpful in general, the insertion of breakpoints through the GUI can become tedious. Moreover, as shown in the example, a single line in Erlang can include several interesting spots where one would place a breakpoint. Unfortunately, Debugger does not include a

```
> orddict_old:from_list([{1,false},{1,true}]).
Input: []
Output: [{1,false}]
Input: [{1,false}]
Output: [{1,true}]
[{1,true}]
```

LISTING 25: Output of `orddict_old.erl` with `io:format/2`.

```
> orddict_new_wrong:from_list([{1,false},{1,true}]).
Input: [{1,false},{1,true}]
Output: [{1,false}]
[{1,false}]
```

LISTING 26: Output of `orddict_new.erl` with `io:format/2`.

way to define breakpoints in a fine-grained way, thus forcing users to modify their code so they can define the breakpoints as desired. The good point of this approach is that when all configurations are set up, it becomes a very illustrative way to see what the code is doing in each place in order to find the source of an unexpected behaviour.

8.6. Erlang's Declarative Debugger (EDD). Algorithmic debugging is a technique that allows debugging a program through an interview with the programmer where questions refer to the intended behaviour of the computations. In functional languages, the questions are about the validity of a function call and its result. Erlang has an implementation of this approach named EDD [20].

Listing 27 shows an EDD session to debug our buggy program. In this session, we use the same input test case as in the previous debugging approaches, i.e., `from_list([{1, false},{1,true}])`. EDD starts asking about the call `lists:ukeysort(1, [{1, false}, {1, true}])`. The computed value is correct, so the answer given by a user should be yes (y). With only this question EDD finishes (because there are no more calls inside this function) and blames the third clause of `orddict:from_list/1`.

Although, in general, declarative debugging is very helpful to debug buggy programs, for this example, it does not help too much. EDD points to the source of the discrepancy, so the user can find that there is something wrong in one of the arguments of `lists:ukeysort/2`. Nevertheless, with the information provided, it is still not easy to interpret what the error is or how to solve it.

8.7. Dialyzer. Erlang is a dynamically typed language. Therefore, type checking is not performed at compilation time and this can result in several undetected errors that eventually arise at execution time. While many programmers like this feature, others miss a type system. Erlang has a tool named `Dialyzer` [21] that partially solves this problem through the use of static analysis. `Dialyzer`'s input is an Erlang module,

and it reports any type discrepancies found in its function definitions. The use of type contracts (`spec` in Erlang) helps `Dialyzer` to improve their results.

In our scenario, `Dialyzer` is not really helpful. It does not report any type discrepancy (because they do not exist) in the buggy code. However, for other scenarios, it could discover regression faults when incorrect values (with an unexpected type) are involved.

8.8. Checking the Performance Improvement. The authors of the commit provide a link to a system implemented by themselves that they used to check whether the performance of the `orddict:from_list/1` function has been actually improved. When this program is run the results obtained are similar to the ones included in the commit message. The fact that they implemented ad hoc that program to check the performance improvement demonstrates (recall that this is a commit on the OTP-Erlang package, i.e., the official Erlang release) that, unfortunately, there is not any tool available to check nonfunctional features like the execution time.

8.9. SecEr. Finally, we show how SecEr makes a step forward, being an alternative (or a complement) to the previous approaches to identify discrepancies.

In order to check the performance of both versions, the first step is to build a configuration file for SecEr (it is shown in Algorithm 10). This configuration file specifies that the results computed in function `orddict:from_list/1` are the same in both versions. Lines (10), (11), and (12) define POIs to compare the unique clause in the original version with each of the three new clauses in the current version (in future versions, we plan to add special POIs that refer to all outputs of a function, without the need for defining the output of each clause. The POI relation `rel1/0` could be redefined to something like `[{{file(o), 60, function, 1}, {file(n), 59, function, 1}}]`). The output of SecEr with this configuration is shown in Listing 28. SecEr does automatically all the work that we had

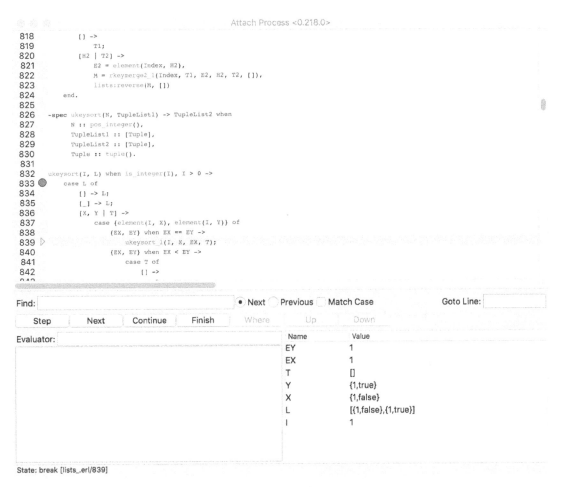

FIGURE 5: Debugger's session.

```
> edd:dd( "orddict_new_wrong:from_list([{1,false},{1,true}])").
lists:ukeysort(1, [{1, false}, {1, true}]) = [{1, false}]? [y/n/t/v/d/i/s/u/a]: y
Call to a function that contains an error:
orddict_new_wrong:from_list([{1, false}, {1, true}]) = [{1, false}]
Please, revise the third clause:
from_list(Pairs) -> lists:ukeysort(1, Pairs).
```

LISTING 27: EDD's session for the current version.

to do manually in the previous approaches: (i) test cases generation, (ii) checking whether test cases evaluate the POIs, (iii) comparison of traces, taking into account the fact that the same error in both versions is not a discrepancy, and (iv) producing a report with all discrepancies. As a result, SecEr has identified the discrepancies and it has shown a sample call that produces the discrepancy.

At this point, we can use SecEr again to inspect the intermediate results produced during the computation reported as responsible for the discrepancy. Since both versions compute the dictionary in a very different way, instead of using SecEr to compare the traces, it is better to use it to store the values generated at certain points and print all of them

afterwards so that we can manually check them. For this, we can (i) define POIs to observe the key value introduced in each iteration and the resulting dictionary, (ii) define an input function that simply calls one of the failing cases that were reported in Listing 28, and (iii) use the predefined comparison function secer:show/0 that simply prints the values of the POIs traces. Algorithm 11 shows a configuration file that implements these ideas. The output of SecEr with this configuration prints the values generated in the selected POIs for each version of the program (it is shown in Listing 29).

SecEr can also be used to check whether a performance improvement has been actually achieved. In the current

```
$ ./secer -pois "test_orddict:rel1()" -funs "test_orddict:funs()" -to 15
Function: from_list/1
----------------------------
Generated test cases: 16428
Mismatching test cases: 555 (3.37%)
    POIs comparison:
          + {{ 'orddict/orddict_old.erl',60,call,1},
            { 'orddict/orddict_new_wrong.erl',62,call,1}}
                Unexpected trace value => 555 Errors
                Example call: from_list([{{ },-9},{{ },3.1981469696010247}])
------ Detected Error ------
Call: from_list([{{ },-9},{{ },3.1981469696010247}])
Error Type: Unexpected trace value
POI: ({ 'orddict/orddict_old.erl',60,call,1}) trace:
          [[{{ },3.1981469696010247}]]
POI: ({ 'orddict/orddict_new_wrong.erl',62,call,1}) trace:
          [[{{ },-9}]]
----------------------------
```

LISTING 28: SecEr's output when comparing the two versions.

```
(1)   -module(test_orddict).
(2)   -compile(export_all).
(3)
(4)   file(o) ->
(5)      'orddict/orddict_old.erl';
(6)   file(n) ->
(7)      'orddict/orddict_new_wrong.erl';
(8)
(9)   rel1() ->
(10)    [{{file(o), 60, call, 1}, {file(n), 59, list, 2}},
(11)       {{file(o), 60, call, 1}, {file(n), 60, {var, 'Pair'}, 2}},
(12)       {{file(o), 60, call, 1}, {file(n), 62, call, 1}}].
(13)
(14)  funs() ->
(15)     "[from_list/1]".
```

ALGORITHM 10: SecEr's configuration file to identify discrepancies.

version of SecEr, this involves small changes in the code, but we are working to automate these changes. The changes needed are very simple and applied in the last expression of each clause involved. For instance,

```
(1) Start = os:timestamp(),
(2) Res = lists:ukeysort(1, reverse_pairs(Pairs, [])),
(3) {Pairs, timer:now_diff(os:timestamp(), Start)},
(4) Res.
```

With these modifications we can now trace the input and the time used to compute each result. In order to identify a significative difference in the calculated runtimes, we need to produce big lists for the input. However, the lists that SecEr generates are in most cases too small for this purpose. Therefore, in the configuration file we can include the following function to produce bigger lists:

```
(1) from_list_replicate(Pairs) ->
(2)    from_list(replicate(5000, Pairs, [])).
(3)
(4) replicate(1, List, Acc) ->
(5)    Acc ++ List;
(6) replicate(N, List, Acc) ->
(7)    NList = lists:map(fun inc/1, List),
(8)    replicate(N - 1, NList, Acc ++ List).
```

```
$ ./secer -pois "test_orddict:rel1()" -funs "test_orddict:funs()" -to 3 -cfun "secer:show()"
Trace old version:
POI: {orddict/orddict_old.erl',60,tuple,1}
Value: {{},-9}
POI: {'orddict/orddict_old.erl',60,application,2}
Value: [{{},-9}]
POI: {orddict/orddict_old.erl',60,tuple,1}
Value: {{},3.1981469696010247}
POI: {'orddict/orddict_old.erl',60,application,2}
Value: [{{},3.1981469696010247}]
Trace new version:
POI: {'orddict/lists.erl',836,{var,'X'},1}
Value: {{},-9}
POI: {'orddict/lists.erl',836,{var,'Y'},1}
Value: {{},3.1981469696010247}
POI: {'orddict/lists.erl',839,application,1}
Value: [{{},-9}]
Function: secer_failing_test/0
----------------------------

Generated test cases: 1
Both versions of the program generate identical traces for the defined points of interest
----------------------------
```

LISTING 29: SecEr's output when tracing and comparing values in both versions.

```
(1)   -module(test_orddict).
(2)   -compile(export_all).
(3)
(4)   file(o) ->
(5)     'orddict/orddict_old.erl';
(6)   file(1) ->
(7)     'orddict/lists.erl'.
(8)
(9)   rel1() ->
(10)   [{{file(o), 60, tuple, 1}, {file(1), 836, {var, 'X'}, 1}},
(11)     {{file(o), 60, tuple, 1}, {file(1), 836, {var, 'Y'}, 1}},
(12)     {{file(o), 60, call, 2}, {file(1), 839, call, 1}}].
(13)
(14)  funs() ->
(15)    "[secer_failing_test/0]".
```

ALGORITHM 11: SecEr's configuration file to trace values.

```
(9)
(10) inc({X, V}) ->
(11)   {{1, X},V}.
```

This function creates 5000 copies of the input list changing their keys in each iteration. The new configuration file (shown in Algorithm 12) uses this function as input function, and it keeps the same POI relation as in Algorithm 10. Additionally, we use the predefined comparison function secer:list_comp_perf/1 to report an error when the new version takes more time than the original version. We should discard those test cases where the difference is not significant, so we fix a threshold (defined by the secer:list_comp_perf/1 function parameter) of, e.g., 2000 microseconds. The output generated by SecEr using this configuration file is shown in Listing 30. After having generated 503 lists of different sizes, in only one case the new version performs worse than the original version. This is probably an outlier, so maybe if we use this test input again, it will also run faster in the new version. However, reporting extra information, we can increase the confidence in the performance study. We can modify the comparison function used by secer:io_list_comp_perf/1, which works exactly like the previous one but also prints information about the computation that runs faster in the new version. With this change, the output indicates the exact improvement achieved by the new version. A sample of some lines produced for this example is as follows:

```
(1) ···
(2) Faster Calculation: Length: 400 -> 13365 vs 1524 ms.
(3) Faster Calculation: Length: 800 -> 49912 vs 2566 ms.
(4) Faster Calculation: Length: 1000 -> 26944 vs 3128 ms.
(5) ···
```

In all the printed cases, 398 in this example (the rest were discarded because of the defined threshold), there is a significative improvement in the computation time. These data increase the reliability of the study.

We can conclude that SecEr can be especially helpful in those contexts where no test suite is available; and even if we already have test cases, it can be used to generate new test cases that are specific to test POIs. It can also be helpful to print values for a concrete failing test or even for various (through the introduction of more input functions). Moreover, it can be also helpful in checking nonfunctional features like performance improvement. Finally, we want to highlight that SecEr has been used in the previous examples for three different purposes (discovering discrepancies, finding the source of a discrepancy, and checking the performance preservation), and in the three cases the methodology was exactly the same.

9. Experimental Evaluation

In this section we study the performance and the scalability of SecEr. In particular, we compare different configurations and study their impact on the performance. First, we collected examples from commits where some regression is fixed. Most of the considered programs were extracted from EDD [20] (https://github.com/tamarit/edd/tree/master/examples) because this repository contains programs with two code versions: one version of the code with a bug and a second version of the same code with the expected behaviour, i.e., where the bug is fixed. In order to obtain representative measures, the experiments were designed in such a way that each program was executed 21 times with a timeout of 15 seconds each. The first execution was discarded in all cases (because it loads libraries, caches data, etc.). The average computed for the other 20 executions produced one single data. We have repeated this process enabling and disabling the two most relevant features of SecEr: (i) the use of CutEr and (ii) the use of mutation during the ITC generation. The goal of this study is to evaluate how these features affect the accuracy and performance of the tool. To compare the configurations we computed three statistics for each experiment: the average amount of generated tests, the average amount of mismatching tests, and the average percentage of mismatching tests with respect to the generated ones.

Table 1 summarizes the experiments (all data and programs used in this experiment are available online at https://github.com/mistupv/secer/tree/master/benchmarks),

where the best result for each program has been highlighted in bold. These results show that our mutation technique is able to produce better test cases than random test generation. Clearly, the configuration that does not use CutEr (the one in the middle) is almost always the best: it generates in all cases the highest amount of test cases, and it also generates more mismatching test cases (except for the *erlson2* program). The interpretation of these data is the following: CutEr invests much time to obtain the initial set of inputs, but the concolic test cases it produces do not improve enough the quality of the suite. This means that in general it is better to invest that time in generating random test cases, which on average produce more mismatching test cases. There are two exceptions: *erlson2* and *vigenere*. In *erlson2* the error is related to a very particular type of input (less than 0.02% of the generated tests report this error), and CutEr directs the test generation to mismatching tests in a more effective way. With respect to the second program *(vigenere)*, although the configuration that does not run CutEr generates more mismatching tests than the rest, the tests generated by CutEr allow the tool to reach a mismatching result faster. This is the reason for the slight improvement in the mismatching ratio. The common factor in both programs is that the mismatching ratio is rather low. This is a clear indication that CutEr can be useful when some corner cases are involved in the regression.

We can conclude that the results obtained by the tool are strongly related to the location of the error and the type of error. If it is located in an infrequently executed code or it is a corner case, the most suitable configuration is the one running CutEr. In contrast, if the error is located in a usually executed code, we can increase the mismatching tests generation by disabling CutEr. Because we do not know beforehand what the error is and where it is, the most effective way of using the tool is the following: First, run SecEr without CutEr, trying to maximize the mismatching test cases. If no discrepancy is reported, then enable CutEr to increase the reliability of the generated test cases.

We have also evaluated the growth rate of the generated test cases and of the percentage of mismatching ITCs. For this experiment we selected the program *turing* because it produces a considerable amount of tests in the three configurations, and also because the mismatching ratio is similar in all of them and not too close to 100%. We ran the three configurations of SecEr with this program with a timeout ranging between 4 and 20 seconds with increments of 2 seconds.

```
$ ./secer -pois "test_orddict_perf:rel1()" -funs "test_orddict_perf:funs()" -to 60 -cfun "secer:lists_
comp_perf(2000)"
Function: from_list_replicate/1
----------------------------
Generated test cases: 503
Mismatching test cases: 1 (0.19%)
    POIs comparison:
        + {"User Defined","User Defined"}
                Unexpected trace value => 1 Errors
                Example call: from_list_replicate([{{[],4.686994537220225,{},-1.5219780046371083},
                ...])
------ Detected Error ------
Call: from_list_replicate([{{[],4.686994537220225,{},-1.5219780046371083},...])
Error Type: Slower Calculation: Length: 700 -> 1031 vs 22564 µs.
----------------------------
```

LISTING 30: SecEr's output when comparing performance.

```
(1)   -module(test_orddict_perf).
(2)   -compile(export_all).
(3)
(4)   file(o) ->
(5)     'orddict/orddict_old_perf.erl';
(6)   file(n) ->
(7)     'orddict/orddict_new_ok_perf.erl'.
(8)
(9)   rel1() ->
(10)    [{{file(o), 62, tuple, 1}, {file(n), 62, tuple, 1}},
(11)      {{file(o), 62, tuple, 1}, {file(n), 67, tuple, 1}},
(12)      {{file(o), 62, tuple, 1}, {file(n), 72, tuple, 1}}].
(13)  funs() ->
(14)    "[from_list_replicate/1]".
```

ALGORITHM 12: SecEr's configuration file to check the performance improvement.

TABLE 1: Experimental evaluation of three SecEr configurations with a timeout of 15 seconds.

	CUTER + MUTATION			NO CUTER			NO MUTATION		
	Generated	Mismatching	%	Generated	Mismatching	%	Generated	Mismatching	%
ackermann	13.9	12.9	93.274%	**21.8**	**21.8**	**100.0%**	12.85	11.65	91.27%
caesar	37765.94	1615.1	4.2714%	**103072.0**	**4534.95**	4.3997%	38830.55	1702.7	4.3865%
complex_number	69420.2	67236.55	96.8549%	89670.2	86891.75	**96.9015%**	67451.75	65349.95	96.8825%
erlson1	14780.05	1.55	0.0105%	**14966.2**	**2.65**	**0.0177%**	14872.5	1.9	0.0127%
erlson2	15494.5	**0.95**	0.0059%	16758.59	0.8	0.0047%	15553.8	**0.95**	**0.0061%**
mergesort	29718.35	25634.45	86.2585%	**34315.1**	**29622.9**	**86.3259%**	29994.3	25884.2	86.299%
rfib	28.05	28.05	**100.0%**	**29.0**	**29.0**	**100.0%**	28.4	28.4	**100.0%**
roman	513.79	101.95	19.8415%	**535.35**	**108.05**	20.1801%	512.2	101.7	19.8461%
sum_digits	426.3	422.3	99.0615%	**534.0**	**534.0**	**100.0%**	434.0	430.0	99.078%
ternary	85.9	28.05	29.4187%	**1005.4**	**323.25**	**32.2485%**	130.0	39.7	27.8311%
turing	41828.65	28268.95	67.5825%	**77247.45**	**52651.5**	**68.1595%**	41573.1	28150.95	67.7135%
vigenere	115.55	2.1	1.269%	**308.7**	**4.59**	1.1849%	114.9	1.95	**1.4849%**

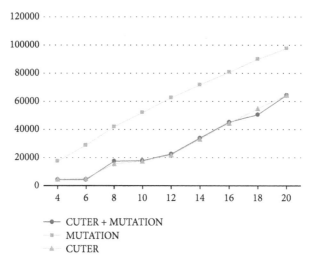

Figure 6: Number of tests generated for Turing.

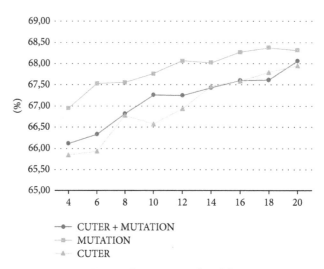

Figure 7: Mismatching ratio produced for Turing.

The results of the experiment are shown in Figures 6 and 7. In Figure 6, the X axis represents SecEr timeouts (in seconds), and the Y axis represents the number of test cases generated. In all cases, the configuration that does not run CutEr generates the highest number of tests. This configuration has a linear growth. On the other hand, the configurations using CutEr show a slow onset. They need at least twelve seconds to reach a considerable increase in the number of generated tests. There is not a significant difference between the configurations using CutEr. This means that the mutation technique does not slow down the test generation. In Figure 7, the X axis represents SecEr timeouts (in seconds), and the Y axis represents the percentage of mismatching tests over the total amount of tests generated. Clearly, in the three configurations, the quality of the generated test cases increases over time (i.e., the mismatching tests ratio increases over time). The configuration that does not run CutEr presents the highest percentage. In this case, the two approaches using CutEr produce different results. With smaller timeouts, it is preferable to enable mutation.

10. Related Work

The orchestrated survey of methodologies for automated software test case generation [22] identifies five techniques to automatically generate test cases. Our approach could be included in the class of *adaptive random technique as a variant of random testing*. Inside this class, the authors identify five approaches. Our mutation approach of the test input shares some similarities with various of these approaches like selection of best candidate as next test case or exclusion. According to a survey on test amplification [23], which identifies four categories that classify all the work done in the field, our work could be included in the category named *amplification by synthesizing (new tests with respect to changes)*. Inside this category, our technique falls under the "other approaches" subcategory.

Automated behavioural testing techniques like Soares et al. [6] and Mongiovi [5] are similar to our approach, but they are restricted in the kind of changes that can be analyzed (they only focus on refactoring). In contrast, our approach is independent of the kind (or the cause) of the changes, being able to analyze the effects of any change in the code regardless of its structure.

There are several works focused on the regression test case generation. DiffGen [24] instruments programs to add branches in order to find the differences in the behaviour between two versions of the program, and then it explores the branches in both versions, and finally it synthesizes test cases that show the detected differences. An improvement of this approach is implemented in the tool eXpress [25] where the irrelevant branches are pruned in order to improve the efficiency. Our technique, in contrast, is not directed by the computation paths, but it is directed by the POIs (i.e., what the user wants to observe). Another related approach is model-based testing for regression testing. This approach studies the changes made in a model, e.g., UML [26] or EFSM models based on dependence analysis [27], and test cases are generated from them. We do not require any input model neither infer it, so although some ideas are similar, the way to implement them is completely different. Finally, there are works that use symbolic execution focused on the regression test generation, like [28, 29]. All these works are directed to maximize the coverage of the generated test suites. Moreover, they need an existing regression test case suite to start with. There exist alternatives, but with the same foundations, like [30] where a tree-based approach is proposed to achieve high coverage. Our approach is not directed by coverage, but instead by the POIs, and we do not require any regression test as input.

Automated regression test case generation techniques like Korel and Al-Yami [31] are also very similar to our approach, but the user can only select output parameters of a function to check the behaviour preservation. Then, their approach simply runs that specific function and checks that the produced values are equal for both versions of the program. Therefore, their approach helps to discover errors in a concrete function, but they cannot generate inputs for one function and compare the outputs of another function. This limits, e.g., the observation of recursion. In contrast, we allow selecting any input function and place the POIs in any other function of the program. Additionally, their test input generation relies on white-box techniques that are not directed by the changes. Our approach, however, uses a black-box test input generation which is directed by changes.

Yu et al. [32] presented an approach that combines coverage analysis and delta debugging to locate the sources of the regression faults introduced during some software evolution. Their approach is based on the extraction and analysis of traces. Our approach is also based on traces although not only the goals but also the inputs of this process are slightly different. In particular, we do not require the existence of a test suite (it is automatically generated), while they look for the error sources using a previously defined test suite. Similarly, Zhang et al. [33] use mutation injection and classification to identify commits that introduce faults.

The Darwin approach [34] starts from the older version of the program, a program that is known to be buggy, and an input test case that reveals the bug. With all this information, it generates new inputs that fail on the buggy program and then runs them using dynamic symbolic execution and stores the produced trace (in their context, a trace contains the visited statements). Finally, the traces from the buggy version and from the old version are compared to locate the source of the discrepancy. Although the approach could seem similar to ours, the goals are different. We try to find discrepancies, while they start from an already-found discrepancy.

Our technique for mutation of inputs shares some similarities with RANDOOP [35]. In their approach, they start from test cases that do not reveal any failure, and randomly construct more complex test cases. The particularity of their approach is that the random test generation is feedback-directed, in the sense that each generated test case is analyzed to take the next decision in the generation. We do something similar, although our feedback is directed by the POIs selected by the user.

DSpot [36] is a test augmentation technique for Java projects that creates new tests by introducing modifications in the existing ones. The number of variants that will be generated is known beforehand and determined by parameters like the number of operations or the number of statements. In order to define the output of a test case, they introduce a concept called *observation point*, which is similar to our POIs. The difference is that they define and select their observation points (in particular, attribute getters, the `toString()` method, and the methods inside an assertion) while in our approach it is the user who defines them. Additionally, our approach does not need an already existent test suite.

Sieve [37] is a tool that automatically detects variations across different program versions. They run a particular test and store a trace that in their context is a list of memory operations over variables. The generated traces are later studied in order to determine what changed in the behaviour and why it changed. Although their goal is not the same as ours, their approach shares various similarities with ours, in particular code instrumentation and trace comparison.

Mirzaaghaei [38] presented a work called *Automatic Test Suite Evolution* where the idea is to repair an existing test suite according to common patterns followed by the practitioners when they repair a test suite. A repair pattern can be something like the introduction of an overloaded method. A modification of our technique could be used to achieve a similar goal, by not only producing test case input, but also repairing patterns in order to check whether they are effectively repairing an outdated test suite.

Most of the efforts in regression testing research have been put in the regression testing minimization, selection, and prioritization [1], although among practitioners it does not seem to be the most important issue [7]. In fact, in the particular case of the Erlang language, most of the works in the area are focused on this specific task [39–42]. We can find other works in Erlang that share similar goals but more focused on checking whether applying a refactoring rule will yield to a semantics-preserving new code [3, 4].

With respect to tracing, there are multiple approximations similar to ours. In Erlang's standard libraries, there are two implemented tracing modules. Both are able to trace the function calls and the process related events (spawn, send, receive, etc.). One of these modules is oriented to trace the processes of a single Erlang node [13], allowing for the definition of filters to function calls, e.g., with names of the function to be traced. The second module is oriented to distributed system tracing [14] and the output trace of all the nodes can be formatted in many different ways. Cronqvist [12] presented a tool named redbug where a call stack trace is added to the function call tracing, making it possible to trace both the result and the call stack. Till [15] implemented erlyberly, a debugging tool with a Java GUI able to trace the previously defined features (calls, messages, etc.) but also giving the possibility of adding breakpoints and tracing other features such as exceptions thrown or incomplete calls. All these tools are accurate to trace specific features of the program, but none of them is able to trace the value of an arbitrary point of the program. In our approach, we can trace both the already defined features and also a point of the program regardless of its position.

11. Conclusions

During the lifecycle of any piece of software, different versions may appear, e.g., to correct bugs, to extend the functionality, or to improve the performance. It is of extreme importance to ensure that every new version preserves the correct behaviour of previous versions. Unfortunately, this task is often expensive and time-consuming, because it implies the definition of test cases that must account for the changes introduced in the new version.

In this work, we propose a new approach to automatically check whether the behaviour of a certain functionality is preserved among different versions of a program. The approach allows the user to specify a POI that indicates the specific parts of the code that are suspicious or susceptible of presenting discrepancies. Because the POI can be executed several times with a test case, we store the values that the POI takes during the execution. Thus, we can compare all actual evaluations of the POI for each test case.

The technique introduces a new tracing process that allows us to place the POI in patterns, guards, or expressions. For the test case generation, instead of reinventing the wheel, we orchestrate a sophisticated combination of existing tools like CutEr, TypEr, and PropEr. But we also improve the result produced by the combination of these tools introducing mutation techniques that allow us to find the most representative test cases. All the ideas presented have been implemented and made publicly available in a tool called SecEr.

There are some limitations in the current technique. First of all, it is not always easy to infer good types for the input functions. If an inferred type is too generic (like *any()*), our approach could start generating ITCs that are not useful. However, this is a problem specific of dynamically typed languages (like Erlang). In statically typed languages, this limitation does not exist. Value generation can be also a limitation if we need to generate complex values. This limitation is also common in other techniques such as property testing, where it is overcome by allowing users to define their own value generators. We plan to make our technique

compatible with these user-defined value generators. Finally, we think that the ITC mutation could be more sophisticated, e.g., by incorporating some kind of importance ranking per parameter. The final goal of the improvements will be to generate better ITCs and to produce them faster.

There are several interesting evolutions of this work. One of them is to adapt the current approach to make it able to compare modules when some source of nondeterminism is present (e.g., concurrency). We could also increase the information stored in traces with, e.g., computation steps or any other relevant information, so that we could also check the preservation (or even the improvement) of nonfunctional properties such as efficiency. An alternative way of doing this is by defining a special POI that indicates that we are interested in a certain performance measure (time, memory usage, etc.) instead of the value. The tool could also provide comparison functions for such *performance* POIs. Another interesting extension is the implementation of a GUI, which would allow the user to select a POI by just clicking on the source code. We could also define quality attributes linked to each test case in order to ease the prioritization and selection for test cases. This feature would be very appreciated by the programmers as [7] reports. Finally, the integration of our tool with control version systems like Git or Subversion would be very beneficial to easily compare code among several versions.

Conflicts of Interest

The authors declare that they have no conflicts of interest.

Acknowledgments

This work has been partially supported by MINECO/AEI/FEDER (EU) under Grant TIN2016-76843-C4-1-R and by Generalitat Valenciana under Grant PROMETEO-II/2015/013 (SmartLogic). Salvador Tamarit was partially supported by Conselleria de Educación, Investigación, Cultura y Deporte de la Generalitat Valenciana, under Grant APOSTD/2016/036.

References

[1] S. Yoo and M. Harman, "Regression testing minimization, selection and prioritization: a survey," *Software Testing, Verification and Reliability*, vol. 22, no. 2, pp. 67–120, 2012.

[2] J. S. Rajal and S. Sharma, "A Review on Various Techniques for Regression Testing and Test Case Prioritization," *International Journal of Computer Applications*, vol. 116, no. 16, pp. 8–13, 2015.

[3] E. Jumpertz, *Using QuickCheck and semantic analysis to verify correctness of Erlang refactoring transformations*, Radboud University Nijmegen, 2010.

[4] H. Li and S. Thompson, "Testing erlang refactorings with QuickCheck," in *Symposium on Implementation and Application of Functional Languages*, pp. 19–36, Springer, 2007.

[5] M. Mongiovi, "Safira: A tool for evaluating behavior preservation," in *Proceedings of the ACM international conference companion on Object oriented programming systems languages and applications companion*, pp. 213-214, 2011.

[6] G. Soares, R. Gheyi, and T. Massoni, "Automated behavioral testing of refactoring engines," *IEEE Transactions on Software Engineering*, vol. 39, no. 2, pp. 147–162, 2013.

[7] E. Engström and P. Runeson, "A Qualitative Survey of Regression Testing Practices," in *Product-Focused Software Process Improvement, 11th International Conference, PROFES 2010, Limerick, Ireland, June 21-23, 2010*, M. A. Babar, M. Vierimaa, and M. Oivo, Eds., vol. 6156 of *Lecture Notes in Business Information Processing*, pp. 3–16, Springer, 2010.

[8] co. uk, wired.co.uk. Ubisoft is using AI to catch bugs in games before devs make them. https://www.wired.co.uk/article/ubisoft-commit-assist-ai, 2018.

[9] A. Giantsios, N. Papaspyrou, and K. Sagonas, "Concolic testing for functional languages," *Science of Computer Programming*, vol. 147, pp. 109–134, 2017.

[10] T. Lindahl and K. Sagonas, "TypEr: A type annotator of erlang code," in *Proceedings of the Erlang'05 - ACM SIGPLAN 2005 Erlang Workshop*, pp. 17–25, September 2005.

[11] M. Papadakis and K. Sagonas, "A PropEr integration of types and function specifications with property-based testing," in *Proceedings of the 10th ACM SIGPLAN workshop on Erlang*, K. Rikitake and E. Stenman, Eds., pp. 39–50, Tokyo, Japan, September 2011.

[12] M. Cronqvist, https://github.com/massemanet/redbug, 2017.

[13] A. B. Ericsson, dbg. http://erlang.org/doc/man/dbg.html, 2017.

[14] A. B. Ericsson, Trace tool builder. http://erlang.org/doc/apps/observer/ttb_ug.html, 2017.

[15] A. Till, erlyberly. https://github.com/andytill/erlyberly, 2017.

[16] R. Carlsson and M. Rémond, "EUnit - A lightweight unit testing framework for erlang," in *Proceedings of the Erlang'06 - Proceedings of the ACM SIGPLAN 2006 Erlang Workshop*, p. 1, usa, September 2006.

[17] K. Claessen and J. Hughes, "QuickCheck: A lightweight tool for random testing of Haskell programs," in *Proceedings of the 5th ACM SIGPLAN International Conference on Functional Programming (ICFP'00)*, pp. 268–279, September 2000.

[18] T. Arts and J. Hughes, "Erlang/quickcheck," in *Proceedings of the In Ninth International Erlang/OTP User Conference*, 2003.

[19] A. B. Ericsson, Debugger User's Guide. http://erlang.org/doc/apps/debugger/users_guide.html, 2018.

[20] R. Caballero, E. Martin-Martin, A. Riesco, and S. Tamarit, "EDD: A declarative debugger for sequential Erlang programs," *Lecture Notes in Computer Science (including subseries Lecture Notes in Artificial Intelligence and Lecture Notes in Bioinformatics): Preface*, vol. 8413, pp. 581–586, 2014.

[21] T. Lindahl and K. Sagonas, "Detecting Software Defects in Telecom Applications Through Lightweight Static Analysis: A War Story," in *Programming Languages and Systems*, vol. 3302 of *Lecture Notes in Computer Science*, pp. 91–106, Springer Berlin Heidelberg, Berlin, Heidelberg, 2004.

[22] S. Anand, E. K. Burke, T. Y. Chen et al., "An orchestrated survey of methodologies for automated software test case generation," *The Journal of Systems and Software*, vol. 86, no. 8, pp. 1978–2001, 2013.

[23] B. Danglot, O. Vera-Perez, Z. Yu, M. Monperrus, and B. Baudry, *The Emerging Field of Test Amplification: A Survey*, abs/1705.10692, CoRR, 2017.

[24] K. Taneja and T. Xie, "DiffGen: Automated Regression Unit-Test Generation," in *Proceedings of the 2008 23rd IEEE/ACM International Conference on Automated Software Engineering*, pp. 407–410, L'Aquila, Italy, September 2008.

[25] K. Taneja, T. Xie, N. Tillmann, and J. De Halleux, "eXpress: Guided path exploration for efficient regression test generation," in *Proceedings of the 20th International Symposium on Software Testing and Analysis, ISSTA 2011*, pp. 1–11, Canada, July 2011.

[26] L. Naslavsky, H. Ziv, and D. J. Richardson, "MbSRT2: Model-based selective regression testing with traceability," in *Proceedings of the 3rd International Conference on Software Testing, Verification and Validation, ICST 2010*, pp. 89–98, fra, April 2010.

[27] Y. Chen, R. L. Probert, and H. Ural, "Model-based regression test suite generation using dependence analysis," in *Proceedings of the 3rd Workshop on Advances in Model Based Testing, A-MOST 2007, co-located with the ISSTA 2007 International Symposium on Software Testing and Analysis*, pp. 54–62, London, United Kingdom, July 2007.

[28] D. Qi, A. Roychoudhury, and Z. Liang, "Test generation to expose changes in evolving programs," in *Proceedings of the 25th IEEE/ACM International Conference on Automated Software Engineering*, pp. 397–406, Antwerp, Belgium, September 2010.

[29] C. Cadar, D. Dunbar, and D. R. Engler, "KLEE: Unassisted and Automatic Generation of High-Coverage Tests for Complex Systems Programs," in *USENIX Symposium on Operating Systems Design and Implementation, OSDI 2008, December 8-10, 2008*, R. Draves and R. van Renesse, Eds., pp. 209–224, USENIX Association, San Diego, California, USA.

[30] Z. Zhang, J. Huang, B. Zhang, J. Lin, and X. Chen, "Regression Test Generation Approach Based on Tree-Structured Analysis," in *Proceedings of the 2010 International Conference on Computational Science and Its Applications*, pp. 244–249, Fukuoka, Japan, March 2010.

[31] B. Korel and A. M. Al-Yami, "Automated regression test generation," in *Proceedings of the 1998 ACM SIGSOFT International Symposium on Software Testing and Analysis, ISSTA 1998*, pp. 143–152, usa, March 1998.

[32] K. Yu, M. Lin, J. Chen, and X. Zhang, "Practical isolation of failure-inducing changes for debugging regression faults," in *Proceedings of the 2012 27th IEEE/ACM International Conference on Automated Software Engineering, ASE 2012*, pp. 20–29, deu, September 2012.

[33] L. Zhang, L. Zhang, and S. Khurshid, "Injecting mechanical faults to localize developer faults for evolving software," *ACM SIGPLAN Notices*, vol. 48, no. 10, pp. 765–784, 2013.

[34] D. Qi, A. Roychoudhury, Z. Liang, and K. Vaswani, "DARWIN," *ACM Transactions on Software Engineering and Methodology*, vol. 21, no. 3, pp. 1–29, 2012.

[35] C. Pacheco, S. K. Lahiri, M. D. Ernst, and T. Ball, "Feedback-Directed Random Test Generation," in *Proceedings of the 29th International Conference on Software Engineering*, pp. 75–84, Minneapolis, MN, USA, May 2007.

[36] B. Baudry, S. Allier, M. Rodriguez-Cancio, and M. Monperrus, "DSpot: Test Amplification for Automatic Assessment of Computational Diversity," *CoRR*, 2015, abs/1503.05807.

[37] M. Ramanathan, A. Grama, and S. Jagannathan, "Sieve: A Tool for Automatically Detecting Variations Across Program Versions," in *Proceedings of the 21st IEEE/ACM International Conference on Automated Software Engineering (ASE'06)*, pp. 241–252, Tokyo, Japan, September 2006.

[38] M. Mirzaaghaei, "Automatic test suite evolution," in *Proceedings of the SIGSOFT/FSE'11 19th ACM SIGSOFT Symposium on the Foundations of Software Engineering (FSE-19) and ESEC'11: 13th European Software Engineering Conference (ESEC-13)*, T.

Gyimóthy and A. Zeller, Eds., pp. 396–399, Szeged, Hungary, September, 2011.

[39] I. Bozó, M. Tóth, T. E. Simos, G. Psihoyios, C. Tsitouras, and Z. Anastassi, "Selecting Erlang Test Cases Using Impact Analysis," in *Proceedings of the AIP Conference*, vol. 1389, pp. 802–805.

[40] R. Taylor, M. Hall, K. Bogdanov, and J. Derrick, "Using behaviour inference to optimise regression test sets," *Lecture Notes in Computer Science (including subseries Lecture Notes in Artificial Intelligence and Lecture Notes in Bioinformatics): Preface*, vol. 7641, pp. 184–199, 2012.

[41] M. Tóth, I. Bozó, Z. Horváth, L. Lövei, M. Tejfel, and T. Kozsik, "Impact analysis of Erlang programs using behaviour dependency graphs," *Lecture Notes in Computer Science (including subseries Lecture Notes in Artificial Intelligence and Lecture Notes in Bioinformatics): Preface*, vol. 6299, pp. 372–390, 2010.

[42] I. B. M. Tóth and Z. Horvóth, *Reduction of Regression Tests for Erlang Based on Impact Analysis*, 2013, Reduction of Regression Tests for Erlang Based on Impact Analysis.

10

Extending Well-Founded Semantics with Clark's Completion for Disjunctive Logic Programs

Juan Carlos Nieves [ID][1] **and Mauricio Osorio**[2]

[1]*Department of Computing Science, Umeå University, 901 87 Umeå, Sweden*
[2]*Departamento de Actuaría, Física y Matemáticas, Universidad de las Américas Puebla, Sta. Catarina Mártir, 72820 Cholula, PUE, Mexico*

Correspondence should be addressed to Juan Carlos Nieves; jcnieves@cs.umu.se

Academic Editor: Fabrizio Riguzzi

In this paper, we introduce new semantics (that we call D3-WFS-DCOMP) and compare it with the stable semantics (STABLE). For normal programs, this semantics is based on *suitable* integration of the well-founded semantics (WFS) and the Clark's completion. D3-WFS-DCOM has the following appealing properties: First, it agrees with STABLE in the sense that it never defines a nonminimal model or a nonminimal supported model. Second, for normal programs it extends WFS. Third, every stable model of a disjunctive program P is a D3-WFS-DCOM model of P. Fourth, it is constructed using transformation rules accepted by STABLE. We also introduce second semantics that we call D2-WFS-DCOMP. We show that D2-WFS-DCOMP is equivalent to D3-WFS-DCOMP for normal programs but this is not the case for disjunctive programs. We also introduce third new semantics that supports the use of implicit disjunctions. We illustrate how these semantics can be extended to programs including explicit negation, default negation in the head of a clause, and a lub operator, which is a generalization of the aggregation operator *setof* over arbitrary complete lattices.

1. Introduction

One of the most well-known semantics for logic programming is the stable semantics (STABLE) [1, 2]. However, it is well known that very often STABLE is too strong, namely, that there are programs that do not possess stable models [3–5]. Let us consider the following example.

Example 1. Let P be a disjunctive logic program:

$$d \vee e \leftarrow \neg a.$$
$$c \leftarrow c.$$
$$b \leftarrow a.$$
$$a \leftarrow b.$$
$$a \leftarrow \neg b, \neg c.$$

In this program there are not stable models; however if we use our D3-WFS-DCOMP semantics there is a model of the program P, that is, $\{a, b\}$. We can argue that this intended model makes sense as follows: since a tautology such as $c \leftarrow c$

should not matter (in our point of view, what makes the given tautology to be specially harmless is that c does not occur in the head of any other clause), we can delete it getting a semantically equivalent program that we call P_1. Then, since c does not appear in the head of any clause of P_1, we can derive $\neg c$ and so we can delete $\neg c$ in the last clause to get a semantically equivalent program P_3. (Note that what we have done so far in this example is accepted by the STABLE semantics.) Then, since we have that

$$a \leftarrow b$$
$$a \leftarrow \neg b$$

are clauses in P_3 and by reasoning by cases, we derive a. (Reasoning by cases is not accepted in STABLE.) Then, we derive b by simple modus ponens. Finally, d and e can be considered false since a is true.

It has been even argued that STABLE does not define the intended models of a program [6]. It is also possible that there is not best semantics [7]:

"The fact each approach to semantics of negation has its own strength and weakness suggests that there is probably not a *best* semantics for logic programs."

Nevertheless, STABLE satisfies interesting logic properties as it is shown in [1, 8]. In this paper we study the stable semantics and exhibit some properties that it satisfies. Also we point out some problems with this semantics. With this base, we study some variations to the semantics proposed by [9, 10]. The obtained semantics, that we call D3-WFS-DCOMP, satisfies the following main properties: First, it agrees with STABLE in the sense that it never defines a nonminimal model or a non-minimal supported model. Second, for normal programs it extends the well-founded semantics (WFS) [11]. Third, every stable model of a disjunctive program P is a D3-WFS-DCOM model of P. Fourth, it is constructed using logic program transformations accepted by STABLE.

We also introduce two more logic programming semantics and prove some properties of them. Moreover, we show that our three proposed semantics are equivalent within the class of normal programs. In the last part of our paper, we highlight that the introduced logic programming semantics are suitable for modeling the *setof* operator of PROLOG using negation as failure.

The rest of the paper is structured as follows: In Section 2, basic definitions on logic programming are presented. In Section 3, we prove some properties of stable model semantics and define our new semantics. In Section 4, we introduce an approach for modeling the *setof* operator of PROLOG with our semantics using negation as failure; moreover, we present how to reduce programs with explicit negation to programs without it. Finally, in Section 5, we outline our conclusions and future work.

2. Background

In order to have a self-contained document, basic concepts on logic programming are introduced in this section. This section does not aim to be a tutorial. The interested reader can see [1] for a deep presentation of the concepts introduced in this section.

A signature $\mathscr{L}$ is a finite set of elements that we call atoms. A literal is an atom or the negation of an atom a that we denote as $\neg a$. Given a set of atoms $\{a_1, \ldots, a_n\}$, we write $\neg\{a_1, \ldots, a_n\}$ to denote the set $\{\neg a_1, \ldots, \neg a_n\}$.

A logic theory is built up using the logical constants $\wedge, \vee, \rightarrow,$ and $\neg$. We may denote a (general) clause C as

$$a_1 \vee \cdots \vee a_m \leftarrow l_1, \ldots, l_n, \tag{1}$$

where $l_1, \ldots, l_n$ represents the formula $l_1 \wedge \cdots \wedge l_n$, $m > 0$, $n \geq 0$, each a_i is a propositional atom, and each l_i is a propositional literal. When $n = 0$ the clause is considered as $a_1 \vee \cdots \vee a_m \leftarrow$ true (or the simple formula $a_1 \vee \cdots \vee a_m$.), where true is a constant atom with its intended interpretation.

Sometimes, a clause C is denoted by $\mathscr{A} \leftarrow \mathscr{B}^+, \neg\mathscr{B}^-$, where $\mathscr{A}$ contains all the head atoms, $\mathscr{B}^+$ contains all the positive body atoms, and $\mathscr{B}^-$ contains all the negative body

atoms. We also use body(C) to denote $\mathscr{B}^+ \cup \neg\mathscr{B}^-$. When $\mathscr{A}$ is a singleton-set, the clause reduces to a normal clause. A definite clause ([12]) is a normal clause lacking of negative literals; that is, $\mathscr{B}^- = \emptyset$. A *pure* disjunction is a disjunction consisting solely of positive or solely of negative literals. A (general) program is a finite set of clauses. We use HEAD(P) to denote the set of atoms occurring in the heads of the clauses of P. Given a signature $\mathscr{L}$, we write Prog$_{\mathscr{L}}$ to denote the set of all programs defined over $\mathscr{L}$.

We use $\vDash$ to denote the consequence relation for classical first-order logic. We will also consider interpretations and models as usual in classical logic.

Given two theories T_1, T_2 we denote $T_1 \equiv_I T_2$ to say that these theories are intuitionistically equivalent; that is, $\forall \alpha \in T_2$, then T_1 proves (using intuitionistic logic) α and vice versa [13].

It will be useful to map a program into a normal program. Given a clause

$$C := \mathscr{A} \leftarrow \mathscr{B}^+, \neg\mathscr{B}^- \tag{2}$$

we write dis-nor(C) to denote the set of normal clauses:

$$\{a \leftarrow \mathscr{B}^+, \neg\mathscr{B}^- \cup (\mathscr{A} \setminus \{a\}) \mid a \in \mathscr{A}\}. \tag{3}$$

We extend this definition to programs as follows. If P is a program, let dis-nor(P) denote the normal program: $\bigcup_{C \in P}$ dis-nor(C). Given a normal program P, we write Definite(P) to denote the definite program that we obtain from P just by removing every negative literal in P. Given a definite program, by MM(P) we mean the unique minimal model of P (that always exists for definite programs, see [12]). We assume working with disjunctive programs, unless otherwise stated.

We use an example to illustrate the above definitions. Let P be the program:

$$p \vee q \leftarrow \neg r.$$
$$p \leftarrow s, \neg t.$$

Then HEAD(P) = $\{p, q\}$, and dis-nor(P) consists of the clauses:

$$p \leftarrow \neg r, \neg q.$$
$$q \leftarrow \neg r, \neg p.$$
$$p \leftarrow s, \neg t.$$

Definite(dis-nor(P)) consists of the clauses:

$$p \leftarrow \text{true}.$$
$$q \leftarrow \text{true}.$$
$$p \leftarrow s.$$

MM(Definite(dis-nor(P))) = $\{p, q\}$.

Since we are interested in disjunctive logic programs, the following question arise:

What are the minimal requirements we want to impose on semantics for disjunctive programs?

Certainly, we want that disjunctive facts, that is, clauses in the program with empty bodies, to be true. Dually, if an atom does not occur in any head, then its negation should be true. These ideas are straightforward generalizations of the case on normal programs. Following the ideas of [14], we propose the following definition.

Definition 2 (semantics). (i) Scenario semantics over a given signature $\mathscr{L}$ is a function such that for every program P over $\mathscr{L}$ it associates a set of models.

(ii) The sceptical semantics induced by scenario semantics is the set of pure disjunctions true in every model of the scenario semantics. (The sceptical semantics derives every literal when its associated scenario semantics has no models.) For any program P we define

$$\mathrm{SEM}_{\min}(P) := \{a \mid a \longleftarrow \text{true} \in P\}$$
$$\cup \{\neg a \mid a \in \mathscr{L}, \, a \notin \mathrm{HEAD}(P)\}. \tag{4}$$

Given two theories P_1, P_2, we denote $P_1 \equiv_{\mathrm{SEM}} P_2$ whenever the set of models of P_1 *with respect to* the scenario semantics SEM is equal to the set of models of P_2 *with respect to* the scenario semantics SEM.

We introduce some well-accepted logic programming semantics from the state of the art. The first one is the logic programming semantics based on supported models.

Definition 3 (supported model, [14]). A two-valued model I of a (disjunctive) logic program P is supported iff for every ground atom A with $I \vDash A$ there is a rule $\mathscr{A} \leftarrow \mathscr{B}^+ \wedge \neg \mathscr{B}^-$ in P with $A \in \mathscr{A}$, $I \vDash \mathscr{B}^+ \wedge \neg \mathscr{B}^-$, and $I \nvDash \mathscr{A} \setminus \{A\}$.

Supported models are related to the so-called Clark's completion [15]. In order to define the Clark's completion of a logic program, let us introduce the following notation.

Definition 4 (def, sup). Let P be a normal program. Let a be an atom in a given signature $\mathscr{L}$ by the definition of a in P; we mean the set of clauses $\{a \leftarrow \text{body} \in P\}$ that we denote by $\mathrm{def}(a)$. We define

$$\mathrm{sup}(a) := \begin{cases} \text{false} & \text{if } \mathrm{def}(a) = \emptyset \\ \mathrm{body}_1 \vee \cdots \vee \mathrm{body}_n & \text{otherwise,} \end{cases} \tag{5}$$

where $\mathrm{def}(a) = \{a \leftarrow \mathrm{body}_1, \ldots, a \leftarrow \mathrm{body}_n\}$.

Considering the previous notation, the Clark's completion *with respect to* a normal program is presented in the following definition. An extension of the Clark's completion for capturing disjunctive logic programs is also presented in the following definition.

Definition 5 (Clark's completion: comp(P) ([15]), dcomp(P)). (i) For any normal program P, we define comp(P) over a given signature $\mathscr{L}$ as the classical theory $\{a \leftrightarrow \mathrm{sup}(a) \mid a \in \mathscr{L}\}$.

(ii) Let P be a disjunctive logic program. Let dcomp(P) := comp(dis-nor(P)).

Let us observe that given a normal logic program P, comp(P) = dcomp(P). As was mentioned, there is a strong relation between supported models and the Clark's completion. dcomp will play a key role in the definition of the logic programming semantics introduced in this paper. In particular, it will be used it for extending the well-founded semantics.

Now the well-accepted STABLE semantics is presented.

Definition 6 (stable, [2]). The Gelfond-Lifschitz transformation (GL-transformation) of a logic program P *with respect to* an interpretation M is obtained from P by deleting

(i) each rule that has a negative literal $\neg B$ in its body with $B \in M$,

(ii) all negative literals in the bodies of the remaining rules.

Clearly the program GL(P, M) resulting from applying the GL-transformation is negation-free, so GL(P, M) has at least one model. M is a stable model iff M is a minimal model of GL(P, M).

It is worth mentioning that Pearce [8] generalized the stable semantics to any propositional theory based on intuitionistic logic. Pearce made the following statement [8]:

> "A formula is entailed by a program in the stable model semantics if and only if it belongs to every intuitionistically complete and consistent extension of the program formed by adding only negated atoms."

From this characterization of the stable semantics, the generalization of STABLE to arbitrary theories is immediate. From now on, we will assume this definition whenever we mention the stable semantics of some given theory.

We introduce a set of transformation rules that will help to define different extension of the well-founded semantics. In particular, the following transformations are defined in [14] and generalize the corresponding definitions for normal programs.

Definition 7 (basic transformation rules). A transformation rule is a binary relation on Prog$_{\mathscr{L}}$. The following transformation rules are called basic. Let a program $P \in \mathrm{Prog}_{\mathscr{L}}$ be given.

RED$^+$: replace a rule $\mathscr{A} \leftarrow \mathscr{B}^+, \neg\mathscr{B}^-$ by $\mathscr{A} \leftarrow \mathscr{B}^+, \neg(\mathscr{B}^- \cap \mathrm{HEAD}(P))$.

RED$^-$: delete a clause $\mathscr{A} \leftarrow \mathscr{B}^+, \neg\mathscr{B}^-$ if there is a clause $\mathscr{A}' \leftarrow \text{true}$ such that $\mathscr{A}' \subseteq \mathscr{B}^-$.

SUB: delete a clause $\mathscr{A} \leftarrow \mathscr{B}^+, \neg\mathscr{B}^-$ if there is another clause $\mathscr{A}_1 \leftarrow \mathscr{B}_1^+, \neg\mathscr{B}_1^-$ such that $\mathscr{A}_1 \subseteq \mathscr{A}, \mathscr{B}_1^+ \subseteq \mathscr{B}^+, \mathscr{B}_1^- \subseteq \mathscr{B}^-$.

The transformation rules introduced by Definition 7 are illustrated in the following example:

Example 8 (transformation). Let $\mathscr{L} = \{a, b, c, d, e\}$ and let P be the program:

$$a \lor b \leftarrow c, \neg c, \neg d.$$

$$a \lor c \leftarrow b.$$

$$c \lor d \leftarrow \neg e.$$

$$b \leftarrow \neg c, \neg d, \neg e.$$

Then $\mathrm{HEAD}(P) = \{a, b, c, d\}$, and $\mathrm{SEM_{min}}(P) = \{\neg e\}$. We can apply RED^+ to get the program P_1:

$$a \lor b \leftarrow c, \neg c, \neg d.$$

$$a \lor c \leftarrow b.$$

$$c \lor d \leftarrow \mathrm{true}.$$

$$b \leftarrow \neg c, \neg d, \neg e.$$

If we apply RED^+ again, we get program P_2:

$$a \lor b \leftarrow c, \neg c, \neg d.$$

$$a \lor c \leftarrow b.$$

$$c \lor d \leftarrow \mathrm{true}.$$

$$b \leftarrow \neg c, \neg d.$$

Now, we can apply SUB to get program P_3:

$$a \lor c \leftarrow b.$$

$$c \lor d \leftarrow \mathrm{true}.$$

$$b \leftarrow \neg c, \neg d.$$

A second set of transformations was defined by [14]. These transformations are as follows.

GPPE (Generalized Principle of Partial Evaluation). Suppose P contains $\mathscr{A} \leftarrow \mathscr{B}^+, \neg\mathscr{B}^-$ and we fix an occurrence of an atom $g \in \mathscr{B}^+$. Then we replace $\mathscr{A} \leftarrow \mathscr{B}^+, \neg\mathscr{B}^-$ by the n clauses $(i = 1, \ldots, n)$

$$\mathscr{A} \cup (\mathscr{A}_i \setminus \{g\}) \longleftarrow (\mathscr{B}^+ \setminus \{g\}) \cup B_i^+, \neg\mathscr{B}^- \cup \neg B_i^-, \quad (6)$$

where $\mathscr{A}_i \leftarrow B_i^+, \neg B_i^- \in P$ (for $i = 1, \ldots, n$) are all clauses with $g \in \mathscr{A}_i$. If no such clauses exist, we simply delete the former clause.

TAUT (Tautology). Suppose P contains a clause of the form: $\mathscr{A} \leftarrow \mathscr{B}^+, \neg\mathscr{B}^-$ and $\mathscr{A} \cap \mathscr{B}^+ \neq \emptyset$, then we delete the given clause.

Let $\mathscr{CS}_1$ be the rewriting system which contains, besides the basic transformation rules, the rules GPPE and TAUT. This system was introduced in [14] and is confluent and terminating as shown in [16]. We write $\mathrm{res}_{\mathscr{CS}_1}(P)$ to denote the residual program of P with respect to the transformations rules $\mathscr{CS}_1$.

Considering $\mathscr{CS}_1$, we define the following logic programming semantics.

Definition 9 (D$'$-WFS). Given a program P, we define

$$\mathrm{D}'\text{-WFS}(P) = \mathrm{SEM_{min}}\left(\mathrm{res}_{\mathscr{CS}_1}(P)\right). \quad (7)$$

We note that our definition of D$'$-WFS(P) is very similar to the definition of the D-WFS semantics [17]. The difference is that D-WFS defines pure disjunctions while D$'$-WFS(P) defines literals. (The paper could be worked out without defining D$'$-WFS but using instead D-WFS.)

Let us note that although the $\mathscr{CS}_1$ system has the nice property of confluence (and termination), its computational properties are not so efficient. In fact, computing the residual form of a program is exponential (even for normal programs, whereas it is known that the WFS ([11]) can be computed in quadratic time).

In order to define a second rewriting system, two more transformation rules are introduced. The first one is Dloop which is defined as follows.

Definition 10 (Dloop [9]). For a program P_1, let $\mathrm{unf}(P_1) := \mathscr{L} \setminus \mathrm{MM}(\mathrm{Definite}(\mathrm{dis\text{-}nor}(P_1)))$. The transformation Dloop(dp) reduces a program P_1 to $P_2 := \{\mathscr{A} \leftarrow \mathscr{B}^+, \neg\mathscr{B}^- \mid \mathscr{B}^+ \cap \mathrm{unf}(P1) = \emptyset\}$. We assume that the given transformation takes place only if $P_1 \neq P_2$. We write $P_1 \rightarrow_{\mathrm{Dloop}_A} P_2$ to denote that P_1 transforms to P_2 by a dp transformation, where $A := \mathrm{unf}(P_1)$.

The last transformation, which will be introduced, is Dsuc.

Definition 11 (Dsuc [9]). Suppose that P is a program that includes a fact $a \leftarrow$ true and a clause $\mathscr{A} \leftarrow$ Body such that $a \in$ Body. Then we replace this clause by the clause $\mathscr{A} \leftarrow$ Body $\setminus \{a\}$.

Considering Dloop and Dsuc, the rewriting system $\mathscr{CS}_2$ is introduced.

Definition 12 ($\mathscr{CS}_2$ [9]). Let $\mathscr{CS}_2$ be the rewriting system based on the transformations SUB, RED$^+$, RED$^-$, Dloop, and Dsuc.

We can observe that $\mathscr{CS}_2$ is confluent and terminating.

Lemma 13 (confl. and termination of $\mathscr{CS}_2$). *The system $\mathscr{CS}_2$ is confluent and terminating.*

Proof. (i) $\mathscr{CS}_2$ is terminating since all its transformation rules reduce the size of the given program. The reduction of the size of a given program is done by either the elimination of literals of the body of a clause or the elimination of clauses.

(ii) Let $\mathscr{CS}_3 = \mathscr{CS}_2 \setminus \{\mathrm{SUB}\}$. Hence, $\mathscr{CS}_3$ is confluent in the class of normal logic programs [18]. (In [18], the rewriting system, which proved to be confluent, includes the so-called failure transformation rule. However, failure is redundant if the given rewriting system includes loop [4]. Loop is the version of Dloop for normal logic programs [4, 9].) Let us prove that $\mathscr{CS}_3$ is confluent in the class of disjunctive logic programs by contradiction. Let us suppose that $\mathscr{CS}_3$ is not confluent. Hence, there exists a disjunctive logic program P such that $\mathrm{res}_{\mathscr{CS}_3}(P) = P1$, $\mathrm{res}_{\mathscr{CS}_3}(P) = P2$, and $P1 \neq P2$. Hence, $\mathrm{res}_{\mathscr{CS}_3}(\mathrm{dis\text{-}nor}(P)) = P3$, $\mathrm{res}_{\mathscr{CS}_3}(\mathrm{dis\text{-}nor}(P)) = P4$ and $P3 \neq P4$, but this is a contradiction since $\mathscr{CS}_3$ is confluent in the class of normal logic programs. Now, we only need to see that $\mathscr{CS}_2 = \mathscr{CS}_3 \cup \{\text{SUB}\}$ is confluent. The only issue is to see the interaction between SUB and the transformation rules of $\mathscr{CS}_3$. Since SUB only removes clauses that are biggest in size than a given one that is kept by SUB at the given program, SUB does not affect the confluence of $\mathscr{CS}_3$. Hence, $\mathscr{CS}_2$ is confluent. $\qquad\square$

It is known that $\mathscr{CS}_2$ characterizes an extension of WFS, which captures the class of disjunctive logic programs. This extension of WFS considering $\mathscr{CS}_2$ is called D1-WFS and is defined as follows.

Definition 14 (D1-WFS). Given a program P, we define

$$\text{D1-WFS}(P) = \text{SEM}_{\min}\left(\text{res}_{\mathscr{CS}_2}(P)\right). \qquad (8)$$

The relationship between D1-WFS and WFS is stayed by the following theorem.

Theorem 15 (see [9]). *Let P be a normal logic program. The following equivalence holds:*

$$\text{D1-WFS}(P) = \text{WFS}(P). \qquad (9)$$

Proof. For the class of normal logic programs, the transformation rules RED$^+$, RED$^-$, SUB, Dsuc, and Dloop are equivalent to N-RED$^+$, N-RED$^-$, N-SUB, Suc, and loop, which have been defined for normal programs [9]. (In [9], the transformation rules N-RED$^+$, N-RED$^-$, N-SUB were named as RED$^+$, RED$^-$, SUB, respectively. In this paper, we added the prefix "N-" in order to denote these transformation rules in the settings of normal logic programs.) Since the rewriting system $\{\text{N-RED}^+, \text{N-RED}^-, \text{N-SUB}, \text{Suc}, \text{loop}\}$ characterizes WFS, $\mathscr{CS}_2$ also characterizes WFS. $\qquad\square$

It is worth mentioning that D1-WFS generalizes a system introduced in [18] from normal to disjunctive programs.

Let us consider again Example 8. As we noticed before, program P reduces to P_3. However, P_3 still reduces (by RED$^-$) to P_4, which is as P_3 but the third clause is removed. From P_4 we can apply a Dloop reduction to get P_5: the single clause $c \vee d \leftarrow \text{true}$. P_5 is the residual form of the $\mathscr{CS}_2$ system.

For this example, it turns out that D$'$-WFS is equivalent to D1-WFS, but this is not true in general. Take, for instance, the following example.

Example 16. Let P be a disjunctive logic program:

$$\begin{array}{ll} x \leftarrow \neg a. & a \leftarrow \neg b. \\ d \leftarrow a. & c \vee b. \\ a \leftarrow d. & b \leftarrow c. \end{array}$$

We can see that $\text{res}_{\mathscr{CS}_1}(P)$ has only two clauses: $x \leftarrow \text{true}$ and $b \leftarrow \text{true}$. This means that the atoms x and b are considered true and the rest of atoms are considered false; hence, D$'$-WFS$(P) = \{x, b, \neg d, \neg c, \neg a\}$. On the other hand, $\text{res}_{\mathscr{CS}_2}(P) = P$. This means that we cannot apply any transformation rule from $\mathscr{CS}_2$ to P. Since all the atoms in the language of P appear in at least one head of the clauses, there are not atoms that can be considered false. Moreover, there are not facts that suggest

that there are atoms that can be considered true. Hence, D1-WFS suggests that all the atoms P are undefined. In other words, D1-WFS$(P) = \phi$.

From Example 16, we can observe that D$'$-WFS and D$'$-WFS are different in the class of disjunctive logic programs. However for normal programs both semantics are equivalent since they define WFS, but note that the residual programs with respect to $\mathscr{CS}_1$ and $\mathscr{CS}_2$ are not necessarily the same. An advantage of $\mathscr{CS}_2$ over $\mathscr{CS}_1$ is that the residual program with respect to $\mathscr{CS}_2$ is polynomial-time computable.

3. Logic Programming Semantics

This section introduces the main results of this paper. We start by stating and proving some useful properties. Some of these properties can be already proved by other authors or intuitively expected; however, since we did not find explicit references to these properties, the properties are formalized and proved.

We start presenting a relationship between dcomp and supported models.

Lemma 17. *Let P be a logic program. M is a supported model of P iff M is a model of $dcomp(P)$.*

Proof. M is a model of $dcomp(P)$ iff M is a model of $comp(\text{dis-nor}(P))$ (see Definition 5) iff M is a supported model of dis-nor(P) [1] iff M is a supported model of P (by definition of supported model, see Definition 3). $\qquad\square$

Let us highlight that Lemma 17 is introducing an extension of the well-known relationship between the Clark's competition and supported models [15], which was introduced for the class of normal programs, to a relationship between dcomp and supported models of disjunctive logic programs.

In order to avoid misunderstanding, let us now define explicitly the concept of *minimal supported model* of a logic program P.

Definition 18. Let P be a program. M is a minimal supported model of P if M is a model of $dcomp(P)$ and it is minimal (*with respect to* set inclusion) among the models of $dcomp(P)$.

We can observe a relationship between minimal supported model and supported models, which are minimal.

Lemma 19. *Let P be a program. If M is a minimal model of P and a supported model of P, then M is a minimal supported model of P.*

Proof. Our proof is by contradiction. Let M be a minimal model of P, M be a supported model of P, and M be not a minimal supported model of P. Then, there exists a proper subset M' of M such that M' is a supported model of P. Thus M' is a model of P. But since M' is a proper subset of M, M is not a minimal model of P, obtaining a contradiction. $\qquad\square$

Let us observe that the converse of Lemma 19 is false as the following example shows.

Example 20. Let P be the following set of clauses:

$$a \leftarrow \neg a.$$
$$a \leftarrow b.$$
$$b \leftarrow b.$$

We can see that dcomp(P) is

$$a \leftrightarrow \neg a \vee b$$
$$b \leftrightarrow b.$$

Moreover, one can see that $M := \{a, b\}$ is a minimal supported model of dcomp(P), but, M is not a minimal model of P.

Now let us introduce two properties regarding the transformation rule Dloop.

Lemma 21. *If P_1 is a disjunctive program, $P_1 \rightarrow_{Dloop_A} P_2$, then $a \in A$ implies that for every clause $\alpha \leftarrow Body \in P_1$ such that $a \in \alpha$, then $Body \cap A \neq \emptyset$.*

Proof. It is a straightforward generalization for the case in normal programs [18]. $\square$

Lemma 22. *If $P_1 \rightarrow_{Dloop_A} P_2$, then $Head(P_2) \cap A = \emptyset$.*

Proof. By contradiction, suppose $Head(P_2) \cap A \neq \emptyset$; therefore, there exists $a \in Head(P_2) \cap A$. Then, there is a rule of the form $a \vee \alpha \leftarrow \beta \in P_2$. Hence, $a \vee \alpha \leftarrow \beta \in P_1$. As $a \in A$, then there exists $b \in \beta \cap A$ (by Lemma 21). Thus $\vee \alpha \leftarrow \beta \notin P_2$, by the construction of P_2. This leads to a contradiction. $\square$

Considering the results introduced by Pearce [8], we highlight the following properties in the settings of STABLE.

Lemma 23. *Let T_1 and T_2 be two theories; then $T_1 \equiv_I T_2$ implies $T_1 \equiv_{stable} T_2$.*

Proof. It follows immediately by Theorem 3.4 in [8]. $\square$

Lemma 24. *If P is a theory, I a set of atoms, and M any stable model of P, then $I \cap M = \emptyset \Rightarrow P \equiv_{stable} P \cup \neg I$.*

Proof. It follows immediately by Theorem 3.4 in [8]. $\square$

The following relationship between stable models and supported models is well known in the state of the art.

Lemma 25 (see [14]). *Let P be program; if M is a stable model of P, then M is a supported model of P.*

We show a property of Dloop regarding minimal models.

Lemma 26. *Let P_1 be a disjunctive program. If M is minimal model of P_1 and $P_1 \rightarrow_{Dloop_A} P_2$, then $M \cap A = \emptyset$.*

Proof. Suppose $M \cap A \neq \emptyset$; then $b \in M$ and $b \in A$, so b is not in every minimal model of definite(dir-nor(P)); then definite(dis-nor(P)) $\nvdash b$, so definite(dis-nor(P)) $\nvdash b$. Therefore $b \notin M$ for all M minimal model of dis-nor(P), thereafter $b \notin M$ for all model of P, and then M is not minimal model. $\square$

Osorio et al. in [19] proved that stable semantics is closed under Dloop.

Theorem 27 (Dloop preserve stable, [19]). *Let P_1 be a disjunctive program. If $P_2 = Dloop(P_1)$, then P_1 and P_2 are equivalent under the stable semantics.*

The following result was presented in [19].

Lemma 28 (STABLE is closed under $\mathscr{CS}_2$ transformations, [19]). *Let P_1 and P_2 be two programs related by any transformation in $\mathscr{CS}_2$. Then P_1 and P_2 have the same STABLE models.*

Considering the style of GL-transformation, the following reduction is introduced.

Definition 29. Let S be a set of literals and P be a program. We define P^S as follows:

$$P^S = \{A \longleftarrow \alpha \setminus \alpha \cap S \mid A \longleftarrow \alpha \in P \wedge \nexists l \in \alpha \text{ with } l^c \in S\}, \tag{10}$$

where l^c is the complement of the literal l.

In the following lemma, an interesting property of the $\mathscr{CS}_2$ system regarding the reduction introduced by Definition 29 is proved.

Lemma 30. *Let P_1 be a normal program and $P_2 = \text{res}_{\mathscr{CS}_2}(P_1)$. Then $P_2 = P^{SEM_{min}(P_2)}$.*

Proof. First note that if P is obtained from P_1 by a single transformation $T \in \mathscr{CS}_2$, then $P^{SEM_{min}(P)} = P_1^{SEM_{min}(P)}$, so, by a direct induction, we can verify that $P_2^{SEM_{min}(P_2)} = P_1^{SEM_{min}(P_2)}$. However, $P_2 = P_2^{SEM_{min}(P_2)}$, so, by transitivity, we get the desired result. $\square$

$\mathscr{CS}_2$ is an interesting rewriting system in the settings of supported models as shown in the following lemma.

Lemma 31. *If P and P_1 are two programs such that P_1 is obtained from P by any transformation T in $\mathscr{CS}_2$, then M is a supported model of P_1 implies M is supported model of P.*

Proof. Straightforward by checking each case of T. $\square$

So far, we have highlighted relevant properties of the rewriting system $\mathscr{CS}_2$, minimal models and supported models. Now we are ready for introducing our first logic programming semantics, which will be based on the aforementioned terms.

Definition 32 (D3-WFS-DCOMP). Let P be a program. We define a D3-WFS-DCOMP model as a minimal model of P that is also a supported model of $\text{res}_{\mathscr{CS}_2}(P)$.

It is immediate to see that D3-WFS-DCOMP is more powerful than D1-WFS (see Theorem 15). Note that sometimes STABLE is inconsistent, when D3-WFS-DCOMP is not.

Example 33. For instance, let us consider again the logic program P that was introduced by Example 1:

$$d \vee e \leftarrow \neg a.$$
$$c \leftarrow c.$$
$$b \leftarrow a.$$
$$a \leftarrow b.$$
$$a \leftarrow \neg b, \neg c.$$

We know that STABLE is inconsistent. In order to infer a D3-WFS-DCOMP model, we need to infer $\mathrm{res}_{\mathscr{CS}_2}(P)$. One can see that Dloop can be applied to P. Dloop will remove the clause $c \leftarrow c$. Hence, $P \rightarrow_{\mathrm{Dloop}_A} P3$ such that $P3 := P \setminus \{c \leftarrow c\}$. In $P3$, we can apply RED^+. After applying RED^+, no transformation rule of $\mathscr{CS}_2$ can be applied. Hence, $\mathrm{res}_{\mathscr{CS}_2}(P)$ is

$$d \vee e \leftarrow \neg a.$$
$$b \leftarrow a.$$
$$a \leftarrow b.$$
$$a \leftarrow \neg b.$$

Let us observe that $\{a, b\}$ is a minimal model of P; moreover, $\{a, b\}$ is a supported model of $\mathrm{res}_{\mathscr{CS}_2}(P)$. Hence, $\{a, b\}$ is a D3-WFS-DCOMP model.

We can also observe that every model inferred by D3-WFS-DCOMP is a supported model.

Lemma 34. *Let P be a program. If M is D3-WFS-DCOMP model of P, then M is a supported model of P.*

Proof. Let M be a D3-WFS-DCOMP model of P, so, M is a supported model of $\mathrm{res}_{\mathscr{CS}_2}(P)$. Thus, by Lemma 31 and a direct induction, M is a supported model of P. □

Due to its construction, we see that D3-WFS-DCOMP is similar to STABLE. However, STABLE is inconsistent more often than D3-WFS-DCOMP. This comment is formalized in the following theorem, which is one of the main results of this paper.

Theorem 35. *Let P be a normal program.*

(1) *If M is a D3-WFS-DCOMP model of P, then M extends the WFS semantics (i.e., M agrees in the true/false assignments with WFS).*

(2) *If M is a D3-WFS-DCOMP model of P, then M is a minimal model of P as well as a minimal model of $comp(P)$.*

(3) *M is a STABLE model of P implies M is a D3-WFS-DCOMP model of P.*

Proof. (1) It follows by construction and Theorem 15. (2) It follows by construction and Lemmas 19 and 34. (3) Let M be a stable model of P. Hence (by Lemma 28) M is a stable model of $\mathrm{res}_{\mathscr{CS}_2}(P)$. Hence by [14], M is a supported model of $\mathrm{res}_{\mathscr{CS}_2}(P)$. On the other hand, since M is stable model of

P, it is well known that M is a minimal model of P. Hence, M is a minimal model of P as well as a supported model of $\mathrm{res}_{\mathscr{CS}_2}(P)$. Finally (by definition) M is a D3-WFS-DCOMP model of P. □

D3-WFS-DCOMP is the first logic programming semantics that we aim to introduce in this paper. D3-WFS-DCOMP is based on minimal models and supported models; moreover, it considers the normal form (residual program) of the given logic program *with respect to* $\mathscr{CS}_2$. However, if we consider the reduction introduced by Definition 29 and D$'$-WFS instead of the normal form of the given logic program *with respect to* $\mathscr{CS}_2$, we get a new logic programming semantics. Formally, this new logic programming semantics is defined as follows.

Definition 36. Let P be a program. We define a D2-WFS-DCOMP model as a minimal model of P that is also a supported model of $P^{\mathrm{D}'\text{-WFS}(P)}$.

Although both D3-WFS-DCOMP and D2-WFS-DCOMP are based on minimal models and supported models, these logic programming semantics are different.

Lemma 37. *The semantics D3-WFS-DCOMP is not equivalent to D2-WFS-DCOMP.*

Proof. Consider again Example 16. With D3-WFS-DCOMP, we obtain two models: $\{a, b, d\}$ and $\{b, x\}$. However, with D2-WFS-DCOMP we only obtain the model $\{b, x\}$. □

We conjecture the following: for every program P, every D2-WFS-DCOMP model of P is a D3-WFS-DCOMP model of P.

As part of our study of logic programming semantics for disjunctive logic programs, we also suggest studying a logic programming semantics that enforces the interpretation of $\vee$ as *inclusive disjunction*. The interpretation of $\vee$ as inclusive disjunction has been explored by other authors. For instance, in [20], the authors also define semantics based on this notion.

In order to interpret $\vee$ as inclusive disjunction, the concept of *w-supported model* is defined as follows.

Definition 38. Let P be a program, a w-supported model M of P is a model of P such that for every $a \in M$, there is a clause $\mathscr{A} \leftarrow$ body such that $a \in \mathscr{A}$ and the body is true in M.

Unlike supported models (see Definition 3), which allow semantics to infer models with only one true atom in each head of each disjunctive clause, w-supported models allow semantics to infer models with more than one true atom in each head of each disjunctive clause. This subtle difference between supported and w-supported models allows us to define different behaviours of the semantics for disjunctive logic programs.

Considering similar constructions to D3-WFS-DCOMP and D2-WFS-DCOMP, the logic programming semantics D3-WFS1-DCOMP is defined as follows.

Definition 39. Let P be a program. We define a D3-WFS1-DCOMP model as a minimal model of P that is also a w-supported model of $P^{\text{D1-WFS}(P)}$.

An interesting property, which shares the three logic programming semantics introduced in this paper, is that these semantics coincide in the class of normal logic programs.

Theorem 40. *Let P be any normal program; then D3-WFS-DCOMP(P) = D2-WFS-DCOMP(P) = D3-WFS1-DCOMP(P).*

Proof. Since D1-WFS(P) = D′-WFS(P) (for normal programs) and by Lemma 30, then it is immediate that D3-WFS-DCOMP(P) = D2-WFS-DCOMP(P). Since supported models are the same as w-supported models (for normal programs), then D3-WFS-DCOMP(P) = D3-WFS1-DCOMP(P). □

Note that, however, for disjunctive programs D3-WFS-DCOMP is (in general) different from D1-WFS1-DCOMP. Take for instance, Example 2 in [20].

4. Applications

In this section, we present an application of the logic programming semantics introduced in Section 3. In particular, we sketch how to extend our semantics to consider programs with clauses allowing an empty head, explicit negation, datalog programs, and finally a lub operator.

(i) With respect to datalog programs, we first obtain the ground instantiation of the program and then we proceed as with propositional programs. This is a well-known approach and we do not discuss it any more.

(ii) With respect to programs with explicit negation, it is possible to reduce programs with explicit negation to programs without it. The idea is originally considered in [21].

(iii) With respect to programs that include clauses with empty head we proceed as follows: Say that we have the clause

$\leftarrow \alpha$, then simply translate it as $a \leftarrow \alpha, \neg a$,

where a is a new atom. Clearly, α is false in every D3-WFS-DCOMP model of the program.

4.1. Semantics of lub-Programs. A very interesting issue consists in modeling the *setof* operator of PROLOG. In a meeting, whose aim was to get a picture of the activities in logic programming and its role in the coming years, Gelfond pointed out the following:

> "We need to find elegant ways for accomplishing simple tasks, e.g. counting the numbers of elements in the database satisfying some property P. At the moment we have neither clear semantics nor efficient implementation of *setof* of other aggregates used for this type of problems" [22].

Some time has passed since Gelfond has pointed the aforementioned quote; however, his views still hold these days.

Let us consider the following example.

```
s(S) ← setof(X,p(X),S),
```

where the intended meaning is as follows: s(S) is true when S = {X:p(X)}.

Several authors have suggested translating the above expression using negation as failure more or less as follows:

```
s(S) ← setof-s(S),
setof-s(S) ← try-s(S),¬bad-s(S),
try-s(S) ← p(X), singleton-set(X,S),
try-s(S) ← try-s(S1), try-s(S2), union(S1,
S2,S),
try-s(X) ← emptyset(X),
bad-s(S) ← p(X), ¬member(X,S),
```

where union, member, and singleton-set have their intended meaning. For instance, singleton-set(X,S) is true if S = {X}. Given any normal program extended with *setof*, if the translation is a stratified program, then the stratified model of the program captures the "intended" semantics of the original program [23]. However, when the program is not stratified, then we can consider using stable models. Several times the stable models still captures the intended meaning, but sometimes it becomes undefined.

Let us consider the following simple, but yet interesting, example about *setof*. Consider the definite program:

$$a \leftarrow \text{true}$$
$$b \leftarrow a, c$$

represented as:

```
rule([a])
rule([b,a,c]).
```

That is, rule([X|Y]) represents the clause X ← Y. Think that we want to write a program that computes the minimal model. Bearing in mind the fix-point semantics, we could write

```
mm(S) ← setof(X, t-p(X), S).
t-p(X) ← rule(X,Y),mm(S),subset(Y,S).
```

That is, mm(S) is true (in the intended semantics) iff S is the minimal model of the program represented by the EDB (extensional database) rule. (It is however questionable if the above program should be considered legal.) Note that mm and t-p are mutually dependent. If we use the translation of *setof* to NF given above, then STABLE has no models at all, while any of our proposed semantics, in Section 3, defines the intended model.

Following the approach from [23], but adapted to the more familiar environment of PROLOG, a LUB operator is a generalization of *setof* over any *complete lattice*. The intuitive reading is that $\text{LUB}_L(X,p(X),S)$ is true if S is the *least upper bound* of each X such that p(X).

Let P be a logic program:

$$h(X, S) \leftarrow LUB_L(C, n(X, C), S).$$

Now translate the program above as follows:

$$h(X, S) \leftarrow f_=(X, S).$$
$$f_\geq(X, S) \leftarrow n(X, S).$$

In addition, we need to add axioms that relate the predicate symbols $f_=$ with $f_\geq$ for each functional symbol f. Let us consider again our example. The axioms for f in this case are as follows:

(1) $f_=(Z, S) \leftarrow f_\geq(Z, S), \neg f_>(Z, S).$

(2) $f_>(Z, S) \leftarrow f_\geq(Z, S1), S1 >_L S.$

(3) $f_\geq(Z, S) \leftarrow f_\geq(Z, S1), S1 >_L S.$

(4) $f_\geq(Z, \perp).$

(5) $f_\geq(Z, C) \leftarrow f_\geq(Z, C_1), f_\geq(Z, C_2), lub_L(C_1, C_2, C).$

We understand that $S1 >_L S$ means that $S1 \geq_L S$ and $S1 \neq S$. And $lub_L(C_1, C_2, C)$ interprets that C is the least upper bound of C_1 and C_2. The first two clauses are the same (modulo notation) as in Definition 4.2 in [24]. Clause (5) is not useful for total-order domains.

Now we need to instantiate the translated program. In this paper we restrict our attention to finite ground programs. By adding simple type declarations, we can ensure to get a finite ground program. In this case, we borrow the declaration style of Relationlog; see [23]. Considering any semantics introduced by Section 3, the intended model of LUB_L is inferred.

5. Conclusion and Future Work

The well-founded semantics (WFS) has been regarded as an approximation of the stable semantics STABLE. Moreover, supported model in the settings of the Clark's complication is other well-established semantics for data management. In this paper, we explored the integration of WFS and the Clark's complication for defining three logic programming semantics: D3-WFS-DCOMP, D2-WFS-DCOMP, D3-WFS1-DCOMP. Each of these semantics suggests different interpretations of disjunctive logic programs; however, they suggest a common interpretation in the class of normal logic programs (Theorem 40).

Considering the properties of D3-WFS-DCOMP, D2-WFS-DCOMP, D3-WFS1-DCOMP, these semantics can be regarded as alternative options for STABLE. The aim of our proposals was to explore a misbehavior of disjunctive (and normal) stable semantics that becomes undefined (inconsistent) very often.

From our previous research, we have observed that STA-BLE has problems for capturing basic aggregation operators such as *setof*. We have sketched some applications of the introduced logic programming semantics for capturing a lub operator, a general form of *setof*. We noticed that STABLE could not define the intended meaning of a simple program that uses our lub operator.

It is well-accepted that STABLE is the state of the art in the nonmonotonic reasoning community. Indeed, there is a solid platform of STABLE solvers that has supported the use of STABLE in real applications [1, 25]. Nevertheless, different extensions of STABLE have been suggested in order to deal with some misbehaviors and extensions of STABLE [3, 26–29]. We consider that the particular semantics introduced by this paper suggest a feasible option for logic based specification languages that aim at semantics close to STABLE, WFS, and the Clark's complication.

In [30], we use stable models semantics for capturing Dung's argumentation approach [31]. Moreover, we have shown that any logic programming semantics can induce an argumentation semantics in the style of Dung's argumentation approach [32]. Hence, in our future work, we will explore the application of the suggested semantics, in this paper, in abstract argumentation theory. For instance, in argumentation theory, there are a few works *with respect to* aggregation of arguments, and we believe that the axiomatization presented in Section 4.1 could be useful for handling aggregation between arguments and/or set of arguments.

Conflicts of Interest

The authors declare that there are no conflicts of interest regarding the publication of this paper.

References

[1] C. Baral, *Knowledge Representation, Reasoning and Declarative Problem Solving*, Cambridge University Press, Cambridge, Mass, USA, 2003.

[2] M. Gelfond and V. Lifschitz, "The Stable Model Semantics for Logic Programming," in *Proceedings of the 5th Conference on Logic Programming*, R. Kowalski and K. Bowen, Eds., pp. 1070–1080, MIT Press, 1988.

[3] J. Dix, "A classification theory of semantics of normal logic programs. II. Weak properties," *Fundamenta Informaticae*, vol. 22, no. 3, pp. 257–288, 1995.

[4] J. Dix, M. Osorio, and C. Zepeda, "A general theory of confluent rewriting systems for logic programming and its applications," *Annals of Pure and Applied Logic*, vol. 108, no. 1-3, pp. 153–188, 2001.

[5] J.-H. You and L. Y. Yuan, "A three-valued semantics for deductive databases and logic programs," *Journal of Computer and System Sciences*, vol. 49, no. 2, pp. 334–361, 1994.

[6] T. C. Przymusinski, "Well-founded completions of logic programs," in *Proceedings of the 8th International Conference Logic Programming*, pp. 726–741, June 1991.

[7] P. M. Dung, "On the relations between stable and well-founded semantics of logic programs," *Theoretical Computer Science*, vol. 105, no. 1, pp. 7–25, 1992.

[8] D. Pearce, "Stable inference as intuitionistic validity," *Journal of Logic Programming*, vol. 38, no. 1, pp. 79–91, 1999.

[9] J. Arrazola, J. Dix, and M. Osorio, "Confluent rewriting systems in non-monotonic reasoning," *Computación y Sistemas*, vol. 2, pp. 104–123, 1999.

[10] M. Osorio and F. Zacarias, "High-Level Logic Programming," in *Foundations of Information and Knowledge Systems*, Lecture

Notes in Computer Science, pp. 226–240, Springer Berlin Heidelberg, Berlin, Germany, 2000.

[11] A. V. Gelder, K. A. Ross, and J. S. Schlipf, "The well-founded semantics for general logic programs," *Journal of the ACM*, vol. 38, no. 3, pp. 620–650, 1991.

[12] J. W. Lloyd, *Foundations of Logic Programming*, Springer, Berlin, Germany, 1987.

[13] D. van Dalen, *Logic and Structure*, Springer-Verlag, Berlin, Germany, 3rd edition, 1994.

[14] S. Brass and J. Dix, "Characterizations of the disjunctive stable semantics by partial evaluation," *Journal of Logic Programming*, vol. 32, no. 3, pp. 207–228, 1997.

[15] K. L. Clark, "Logic and Databases," in *chapter Negation as Failure*, pp. 293–322, Plenum Press, 1978.

[16] S. Brass and J. Dix, "Characterizations of the disjunctive well-founded semantics: confluent calculi and iterated gcwa," *Journal of Automated Reasoning*, vol. 20, no. 1, pp. 143–165, 1998.

[17] G. Brewka, J. Dix, and K. Konolige, *Nonmonotonic Reasoning: An overview*, CSLI Lectures Notes 73, CSLI Publications, Stanford, CA, USA, 1997.

[18] S. Brass, U. Zukowski, and B. Freitag, "Transformation-based bottom-up computation of the well-founded model," in *Non-Monotonic Extensions of Logic Programming, NMELP '96*, T. C. P. Jürgen Dix and L. M. Pereira, Eds., vol. 1216 of *Lecture Notes in Computer Science*, pp. 171–201, Springer, Berlin, Germany, 1997.

[19] M. Osorio, J. A. Navarro, and J. Arrazola, "Equivalence in answer set programming," in *Logic Based Program Synthesis and Transformation, 11th International Workshop, LOPSTR 2001*, pp. 57–75, Springer, Berlin, Germany, 2001.

[20] S. Greco, "Minimal founded semantics for disjunctive logic programming," *LPNMR*, pp. 221–235, 1999.

[21] C. Baral and M. Gelfond, "Logic programming and knowledge representation," *The Journal of Logic Programming*, vol. 19-20, no. 1, pp. 73–148, 1994.

[22] J. Dix, "The logic programming paradigm," *AI Communications*, vol. 11, no. 2, pp. 123–131, 1998.

[23] M. Osorio and B. Jayaraman, "Aggregation and negation-as-failure," *New Generation Computing*, vol. 17, no. 3, pp. 255–284, 1999.

[24] A. V. Gelder, "The well-founded semantics of aggregation," *PODS*, pp. 127–138, 1992.

[25] M. Osorio, J. Diaz, and A. Santoyo, "0-1 integer programming for computing semi-stable semantics of argumentation frameworks," *Computación y Sistemas*, vol. 21, no. 3, pp. 457–471, 2017.

[26] J. Dix, "A classification theory of semantics of normal logic programs. I. Strong properties," *Fundamenta Informaticae*, vol. 22, no. 3, pp. 227–255, 1995.

[27] M. Osorio, J. A. Navarro, J. R. Arrazola, and V. Borja, "Logics with Common Weak Completions," *Journal of Logic and Computation*, vol. 16, no. 6, pp. 867–890, 2006.

[28] M. Osorio, J. C. Nieves, and C. Giannella, "Useful Transformations in Answer Set Programming," in *Answer Set Programming: Towards Efficient and Scalable Knowledge Representation and Reasoning (AAAI Spring 2001 Symposium)*, A. Provetti and S. T. Cao, Eds., Stanford, USA, March 2001.

[29] J. C. Nieves, M. Osorio, and U. Cortés, "Semantics for possibilistic disjunctive programs," *Theory and Practice of Logic Programming*, vol. 13, no. 1, pp. 33–70, 2013.

[30] J. C. Nieves, U. Cortés, and M. Osorio, "Preferred extensions as stable models," *Theory and Practice of Logic Programming*, vol. 8, no. 4, pp. 527–543, July 2008.

[31] P. M. Dung, "On the acceptability of arguments and its fundamental role in nonmonotonic reasoning, logic programming and n-person games," *Artificial Intelligence*, vol. 77, no. 2, pp. 321–357, 1995.

[32] J. C. Nieves, M. Osorio, and C. Zepeda, "A schema for generating relevant logic programming semantics and its applications in argumentation theory," *Fundamenta Informaticae*, vol. 106, no. 2-4, pp. 295–319, 2011.

11

Racing Sampling Based Microimmune Optimization Approach Solving Constrained Expected Value Programming

Kai Yang[1] and Zhuhong Zhang[2]

[1]*College of Computer Science, Guizhou University, Guiyang 550025, China*
[2]*Department of Big Data Science and Engineering, College of Big Data and Information Engineering, Guizhou University, Guiyang 550025, China*

Correspondence should be addressed to Zhuhong Zhang; sci.zhzhang@gzu.edu.cn

Academic Editor: Eduardo Rodríguez-Tello

This work investigates a bioinspired microimmune optimization algorithm to solve a general kind of single-objective nonlinear constrained expected value programming without any prior distribution. In the study of algorithm, two lower bound sample estimates of random variables are theoretically developed to estimate the empirical values of individuals. Two adaptive racing sampling schemes are designed to identify those competitive individuals in a given population, by which high-quality individuals can obtain large sampling size. An immune evolutionary mechanism, along with a local search approach, is constructed to evolve the current population. The comparative experiments have showed that the proposed algorithm can effectively solve higher-dimensional benchmark problems and is of potential for further applications.

1. Introduction

Many real-world engineering optimization problems, such as industrial control, project management, portfolio investment, and transportation logistics, include stochastic parameters or random variables usually. Generally, they can be solved by some existing intelligent optimization approaches with static sampling strategies (i.e., each candidate is with the same sampling size), after being transformed into constrained expected value programming (CEVP), chance constrained programming, or probabilistic optimization models. Although CEVP is a relatively simple topic in the context of stochastic programming, it is a still challenging topic, as it is difficult to find feasible solutions and meanwhile the quality of the solution depends greatly on environmental disturbance. The main concern of solving CEVP involves two aspects: (i) when stochastic probabilistic distributions are unknown, it becomes crucial to distinguish those high-quality individuals from the current population in uncertain environments, and (ii) although static sampling strategies are a usual way to handle random factors, the expensive computational cost is inevitable, and hence

adaptive sampling strategies with low computational cost are desired.

When stochastic characteristics are unknown, CEVP models are usually replaced by their sample average approximation models [1, 2], and thereafter some new or existing techniques can be used to find their approximate solutions. Mathematically, several researchers [3–5] probed into the relationship between CEVP models and their approximation ones and acquired some valuable lower bound estimates on sample size capable of being used to design adaptive sampling rules. On the other hand, intelligent optimization techniques have become popular for nonconstrained expected value programming problems [6–8], in which some advanced sampling techniques, for example, adaptive sampling techniques and sample allocation schemes, can effectively suppress environmental influence on the process of solution search. Unfortunately, studies on general CEVP have been rarely reported in the literature because of expected value constraints. Even if so, several researchers made great efforts to investigate new or hybrid intelligent optimization approaches for such kind of uncertain programming problem. For example, B. Liu and Y.-K. Liu [9] proposed a hybrid intelligent approach to solve general fuzzy expected value models, after combining evolutionary algorithms with neural networks learning methods. Sun and Gao [10] suggested an improved differential evolutionary approach to solve an expected value programming problem, depending on static sampling and flabby selection.

Whereas immune optimization as another popular branch was well studied for static or dynamic optimization problems [11, 12], it still remains open for stochastic programming problems. Some comparative works between classical intelligent approaches and immune optimization algorithms for stochastic programming demonstrated that one such branch is competitive. For example, Hsieh and You [13] proposed a two-phase immune optimization approach to solve the optimal reliability-redundancy allocation problem. Their numerical results, based on four benchmark problems have showed that such approach is superior to the compared algorithms. Zhao et al. [14] presented a hybrid immune optimization approach to deal with chance-constrained programming, in which two operators of double cloning and double mutation were adopted to accelerate the process of evolution.

In the present work, we study two lower bound estimates on sample size theoretically, based on Hoeffding's inequalities [15, 16]. Afterwards, two efficient adaptive racing sampling approaches are designed to compute the empirical values of stochastic objective and constraint functions. These, together with immune inspirations included in the clonal selection principle, are used to develop a microimmune optimization algorithm (μIOA) for handling general, nonlinear, and higher-dimensional constrained expected value programming problems. Such approach is significantly different from any existing immune optimization approaches. On one hand, the two lower bound estimates are developed to control the sample sizes of random variables, while a local search approach is adopted to strengthen the ability of local exploitation; on the other hand, the two adaptive racing sampling methods are utilized to determine dynamically such sample sizes in order to compute the empirical values of objective and constraint functions at each individual. Experimental results have illustrated that μIOA is an alternative tool for higher-dimensional multimodal expected value programming problems.

2. Problem Statement and Preliminaries

Consider the following general single-objective nonlinear constrained expected value programming problem:

$$\min_{\mathbf{x} \in D} \quad E\left[f\left(\mathbf{x}, \xi\right)\right]$$

$$\text{s.t.} \quad E\left[G_i\left(\mathbf{x}, \xi\right)\right] \leq 0, \quad 0 \leq i \leq I,$$
$$g_j\left(\mathbf{x}\right) \leq 0, \quad 1 \leq j \leq J, \qquad \text{(EP)}$$
$$h_k\left(\mathbf{x}\right) = 0, \quad 1 \leq k \leq K,$$

with bounded and closed domain D in R^p, decision vector $\mathbf{x}$ in D, and random vector ξ in R^q, where $E[\cdot]$ is the operator of

expectation; $f(\mathbf{x}, \xi)$ and $G_i(\mathbf{x}, \xi)$ are the stochastic objective and constraint functions, respectively, among which at least one is nonlinear and continuous in $\mathbf{x}$; $g_j(\mathbf{x})$ and $h_k(\mathbf{x})$ are the deterministic and continuous constraint functions. If a candidate solution satisfies all the above constraints, it is called a feasible solution and an infeasible solution otherwise. Introduce the following constraint violation function to check if candidate $\mathbf{x}$ is feasible:

$$\Gamma\left(\mathbf{x}\right) = I^{-1} \sum_{i=1}^{I} \max\left\{E\left[G_i\left(\mathbf{x}, \xi\right)\right], 0\right\}$$

$$+ J^{-1} \sum_{j=1}^{J} \max\left\{g_j\left(\mathbf{x}\right), 0\right\} + K^{-1} \sum_{k=1}^{K} \left|h_k\left(\mathbf{x}\right)\right|. \tag{1}$$

Obviously, $\mathbf{x}$ is feasible only when $\Gamma(\mathbf{x}) = 0$. If $\Gamma(\mathbf{x}) < \Gamma(\mathbf{y})$, we prescribe that $\mathbf{x}$ is superior to $\mathbf{y}$. In order to solve CEVP, we transform the above problem into the following sample-dependent approximation model (SAM):

$$\min_{\mathbf{x} \in D} \quad \frac{1}{n\left(\mathbf{x}\right)} \sum_{l=1}^{n(\mathbf{x})} f\left(\mathbf{x}, \xi^l\right)$$

$$\text{s.t.} \quad \frac{1}{m\left(\mathbf{x}\right)} \sum_{r=1}^{m(\mathbf{x})} G_i\left(\mathbf{x}, \xi^r\right) \leq 0, \quad 1 \leq i \leq I, \qquad \text{(2)}$$

$$g_j\left(\mathbf{x}\right) \leq 0, \quad 1 \leq j \leq J,$$
$$h_k\left(\mathbf{x}\right) = 0, \quad 1 \leq k \leq K,$$

where $m(\mathbf{x})$ and $n(\mathbf{x})$ are the sampling sizes of ξ at the point $\mathbf{x}$ for the stochastic objective and constraint functions, respectively; ξ^i is the ith observation. It is known that the optimal solution of problem SAM can approach that of problem (EP) when $\varepsilon \to 0$ and $m(\mathbf{x}), n(\mathbf{x}) \to \infty$, based on the law of large number [17]. We say that $\mathbf{x}$ is an empirically feasible solution for (EP) if the above constraints in SAM are satisfied.

In the subsequent work, two adaptive sampling schemes will be designed to estimate the empirical objective and constraint values for each individual. We here cite the following conclusions.

Theorem 1 ((Hoeffding's inequality) see [15, 16]). *Let X be a set, and let $F(\cdot)$ be a probability distribution function on X; $f_1, \ldots, f_n$ denote the real-valued functions defined on X with $f_j : X \to [a_j, b_j]$ for $j = 1, \ldots, n$, where a_j and b_j are real numbers satisfying $a_j < b_j$. Let $x_1, \ldots, x_n$ be the samples of i.i.d. random variables $X_1, X_2, \ldots, X_n$ on X, respectively. Then, the following inequality is true:*

$$\Pr\left(\left|\frac{1}{n} \sum_{j=1}^{n} f_j\left(x_j\right) - \frac{1}{n} \sum_{j=1}^{n} \int_{\mathbf{x} \in X} f_j\left(\mathbf{x}\right) dF\left(\mathbf{x}\right)\right| \geq \varepsilon\right) \tag{3}$$

$$\leq e^{-2\varepsilon^2 n^2 / \sum_{j=1}^{n}(b_j - a_j)^2}.$$

Corollary 2 (see [15, 16]). *If $X_1, X_2, \ldots, X_n$ are i.i.d. random variables with mean μ and $a \le X_j \le b, 1 \le j \le n$, then*

$$\left|\overline{X}_n - \mu\right| \le K(\Delta, n, \delta) \equiv \Delta\sqrt{\frac{1}{2n}\ln\left(\frac{2}{\delta}\right)}, \qquad (4)$$

with probability at least $1 - \delta$, where $\overline{X}_n = (1/n)\sum_{j=1}^{n}\widehat{X}_j$ and $\Delta = b - a$; $\widehat{X}_j$ and δ denote the observation of X_j and the significance level.

3. Racing Sampling Approaches

3.1. Expected Value Constraint Handling. Usually, when an intelligent optimization approach with static sampling is chosen to solve the above problem (EP), each individual with the same and sufficiently large sampling size, which necessarily causes high computational complexity. Therefore, in order to ensure that each individual in a given finite population A has a rational sampling size, we in this subsection give a lower bound estimate to control the value of $m(\mathbf{x})$ with $\mathbf{x} \in A$, based on the sample average approximation model of the above problem. Define

$$X_\varepsilon = \left\{\mathbf{x} \in A \mid E\left[G_i(\mathbf{x}, \xi)\right] \le \varepsilon, 1 \le i \le I\right\},$$

$$X_m = \left\{\mathbf{x} \in A \mid \frac{1}{m}\sum_{j=1}^{m}G_i\left(\mathbf{x}, \xi^j\right) \le 0, 1 \le i \le I\right\}. \qquad (5)$$

We next give a lower bound estimate to justify that X_m is a subset of X_ε with probability $1 - \delta$, for which the proof can be found in Appendix.

Lemma 3. *If there exist $a_i(\mathbf{x})$ and $b_i(\mathbf{x})$ such that $\Pr\{a_i(\mathbf{x}) \le G_i(\mathbf{x}, \xi) \le b_i(\mathbf{x}), 1 \le i \le I\} = 1$ with $\mathbf{x} \in A$, one has that $\Pr\{X_m \subseteq X_\varepsilon\} \ge 1 - \delta$, provided that*

$$m \ge M_\delta \equiv \frac{\Lambda^2}{2\varepsilon^2}\log\frac{|A|}{\delta}, \qquad (6)$$

where $\Lambda = \max\{b_i(\mathbf{x}) - a_i(\mathbf{x}) \mid \mathbf{x} \in A, 1 \le i \le I\}$ and $|A|$ denotes the size of A.

In (6), $a_i(\mathbf{x})$ and $b_i(\mathbf{x})$ are decided by the bounds of the stochastic constraint functions at the point $\mathbf{x}$. Λ is the maximal sampling difference computed by the observations of the stochastic constraints. We also observe that once ε and δ are defined, M_δ is determined by $|A|$. Additionally, those high-quality individuals in A should usually get large sampling sizes, and conversely those inferior ones can only get small sampling size. This means that different individuals will gain different sampling sizes. Based on this consideration and the idea of racing ranking, we next compute the empirical value of any expected value constraint function $G(\mathbf{x}, \xi)$ at a given individual $\mathbf{x}$ in A, that is, $\widehat{G}(\mathbf{x})$. This is completed by the following racing-based constraint evaluation approach (RCEA).

Step 1. Input parameters: initial sampling size m_0, sampling amplitude λ, relaxation factor ε, significance level δ, and maximal sampling size M_δ.

Step 2. Set $m = m_0$, $s = m_0$, and $\lambda \leftarrow \ln(1 + m_0)$; calculate the estimate $\widehat{G}(\mathbf{x})$ through m observations.

Step 3. Set $s \leftarrow \lambda s$.

Step 4. Create s observations, and update $\widehat{G}(\mathbf{x})$; that is,

$$\widehat{G}(\mathbf{x}) \leftarrow \frac{\left(m\widehat{G}(\mathbf{x}) + \sum_{i=1}^{s}G\left(\mathbf{x}, \xi^i\right)\right)}{(m + s)}. \qquad (7)$$

Step 5. Set $m \leftarrow m + s$; if $m \le M_\delta$ and $\widehat{G}(\mathbf{x}) \le K(\Delta, m, \delta)$, then go to Step 3.

Step 6. Output $\widehat{G}(\mathbf{x})$ as the estimated value of $G(\mathbf{x}, \xi)$.

In the above formulation, M_δ and $K(\Delta, m, \delta)$ are used to decide when the above algorithm terminates. Once the above procedure is stopped, $\mathbf{x}$ obtains its sampling size $m(\mathbf{x})$; that is, $m(\mathbf{x}) = m$. We note that $K(\Delta, m, \delta)$ is very small if m is large. Thereby, we say that $\mathbf{x}$ is an empirical feasible solution if, in the precondition of $\widehat{G}(\mathbf{x}) \le 0$, the above deterministic constraints are satisfied. Further, RCEA indicates that an empirical feasible solution $\mathbf{x}$ can acquire a large sampling size so that $\widehat{G}(\mathbf{x})$ is close to the expected value of $G(\mathbf{x}, \xi)$.

3.2. Objective Function Evaluation. Depending on the above RCEA and the deterministic constraints in problem (EP), the above population A is divided into two subpopulations of B and C, where B consists of empirical feasible solutions in A. We investigate another lower bound estimate to control the value of $n(\mathbf{x})$ with $\mathbf{x} \in B$, relying upon the sample average approximation model of the problem (EP). Afterwards, an approach is designed to calculate the empirical objective values of empirical feasible solutions in B. To this point, introduce

$$S_\varepsilon = \left\{\mathbf{x} \in B \mid E\left[f(\mathbf{x}, \xi)\right] \le f^* + \varepsilon\right\},$$

$$S_n = \left\{\mathbf{x} \in B \mid \frac{1}{n}\sum_{k=1}^{n}f\left(\mathbf{x}, \xi^k\right) \le \widehat{f}_n\right\}, \qquad (8)$$

where f^* and $\widehat{f}_n$ stand for the minima of theoretical and empirical objective values of individuals in B, respectively. The lower bound estimate is given below, by identifying the approximation relation between S_ε and S_n. The proof can be known in Appendix.

Lemma 4. *If there exist $c(\mathbf{x})$ and $d(\mathbf{x})$ such that $\Pr\{c(\mathbf{x}) \le f(\mathbf{x}, \xi) \le d(\mathbf{x})\} = 1$ with $\mathbf{x} \in B$, then $\Pr\{S_n \subseteq S_\varepsilon\} \ge 1 - \delta$, provided that*

$$n \ge n_{|B|} \equiv \frac{2\Gamma^2}{\varepsilon^2}\ln\frac{2|B|}{\delta}, \qquad (9)$$

where $\Gamma = \max\{d(\mathbf{x}) - c(\mathbf{x}) \mid \mathbf{x} \in B\}$.

Like the above constraint handling approach, we next calculate the empirical objective values of individuals in B through the following racing-based objective evaluation approach (ROEA).

Step 1. Input parameters: ε and δ mentioned above, initial sampling size n_0, and population B.

Step 2. Set $n \leftarrow n_0, s \leftarrow n_0, \lambda \leftarrow \ln(1 + n_0)$, and $\Phi \leftarrow B$.

Step 3. Calculate the empirical objective average of n observations for each individual $\mathbf{x}$ in Φ, that is, $\overline{f}_n(\mathbf{x})$; write $\overline{f}_{\min} = \min\{\overline{f}_n(\mathbf{x}), \mathbf{x} \in \Phi\}$ and $\overline{f}_{\max} = \max\{\overline{f}_n(\mathbf{x}), \mathbf{x} \in \Phi\}$.

Step 4. Remove those elements in Φ satisfying $\widehat{f}_n(\mathbf{x}) > \overline{f}_{\min} + K(\overline{f}_{\max} - \overline{f}_{\min}, n, \delta)$.

Step 5. Set $s \leftarrow \lambda s$.

Step 6. Update the empirical objective values for elements in Φ through

$$\widehat{f}_n(\mathbf{x}) \leftarrow \frac{\left[\widehat{f}_n(\mathbf{x}) \times n + \sum_{k=1}^{s} f\left(\mathbf{x}, \xi^k\right)\right]}{(n+s)}, \quad \mathbf{x} \in B. \quad (10)$$

Step 7. Set $n \leftarrow n + s$.

Step 8. If $n < n_{|B|}$ and $\Phi \neq \phi$, then return to Step 3; otherwise, output all the empirical objective values of individuals in B.

Through the above algorithm, those individuals in B can acquire their respective empirical objective values with different sampling sizes. Those high-quality individuals can get large sampling sizes, and hence their empirical objective values can approach their theoretical objective values.

4. Algorithm Statement

The clonal selection principle explains how immune cells learn the pattern structures of invading pathogens. It includes many biological inspirations capable of being adopted to design μIOA, such as immune selection, cloning, and reproduction. Based on RCEA and ROEA above as well as general immune inspirations, μIOA can be illustrated by Figure 1. We here view antigen Ag as problem SAM itself, while candidates from the design space D are regarded as real-coded antibodies. Within a run period of μIOA by Figure 1, the current population is first divided into empirical feasible and infeasible antibody subpopulations after executing RCEA above. Second, those empirical feasible antibodies are required to compute their empirical objective values through ROEA. They will produce many more clones than empirical infeasible antibodies through proliferation. Afterwards, all the clones are enforced mutation. If a parent is superior to its clones, it will carry out local search, and conversely it is updated by its best clone. Based on Figure 1, μIOA can be formulated in detail below.

Step 1. Input parameters: population size N, maximal clonal size $C_{\max}$, sampling parameters m_0 and n_0, relaxation factor ε, significance level δ, and maximal iteration number $G_{\max}$.

Step 2. Set $t \leftarrow 1$.

Step 3. Generate an initial population A of N random antibodies.

Step 4. Compute the empirical constraint violations of antibodies in A through RCEA and (1), that is, $\widehat{\Gamma}(\mathbf{x})$ with $\mathbf{x} \in A$.

Step 5. Divide A into empirical feasible subpopulation B and infeasible subpopulation C.

Step 6. Calculate the empirical objective values of antibodies in B through ROEA above.

Step 7. For each antibody $\mathbf{x}$ in B, we have the following.

Step 7.1. Proliferate a clonal set $\text{Cl}(\mathbf{x})$ with size $C_{\max}$ (i.e., $\mathbf{x}$ multiplies $C_{\max}$ offsprings).

Step 7.2. Mutate all clones with mutation rate $p_m(\mathbf{x}) = 1/(\Gamma_{\max} + \ln(t + 1))$ through the classical polynomial mutation, and thereafter produce a mutated clonal set $\text{Cl}^*(\mathbf{x})$, where $\Gamma_{\max} = \max\{\widehat{\Gamma}(\mathbf{x}) \mid \mathbf{x} \in C\}$.

Step 7.3. Eliminate empirical infeasible clones in $\text{Cl}^*(\mathbf{x})$ through RCEA.

Step 7.4. Calculate the empirical objective values of clones in $\text{Cl}^*(\mathbf{x})$ through ROEA.

Step 7.5. If the best clone has a smaller empirical objective value than $\mathbf{x}$, it will update $\mathbf{x}$; otherwise, antibody $\mathbf{x}$ as an initial state creates a better empirical feasible antibody to replace it by a local search approach [18] with ROEA and sampling size m_0.

Step 8. For each antibody $\mathbf{y}$ in C, we have the following.

Step 8.1. Antibody $\mathbf{y}$ creates a clonal population $C(\mathbf{y})$ with clonal size $\text{Cl}(\mathbf{y})$; all clones in $C(\mathbf{y})$ are enforced to mutate with mutation rate $p_m(\mathbf{y})$ through the conventional nonuniform mutation and create a mutated clonal population $C^*(\mathbf{y})$, where

$$\text{Cl}(\mathbf{y}) = \text{round}\left(\frac{C_{\max}}{\widehat{\Gamma}(\mathbf{y}) + 1}\right),$$

$$p_m(\mathbf{y}) = \frac{1}{\Gamma_{\max} - \widehat{\Gamma}(\mathbf{y}) + 1}. \quad (11)$$

Step 8.2. Check if there exist empirical feasible clones in $C^*(\mathbf{y})$ by RCEA and (1); if yes, the best clone with the smallest empirical objective value by ROEA replaces $\mathbf{y}$, and conversely the clone with the smallest constraint violation updates $\mathbf{y}$.

Step 9. $A \leftarrow B \cup C$, and $t \leftarrow t + 1$.

Step 10. If $t < G_{\max}$, go to Step 4, and conversely output the best antibody viewed as the optimal solution.

As we formulate above, the current population A is split into two subpopulations, after being checked if there are empirical feasible antibodies. Each subpopulation is

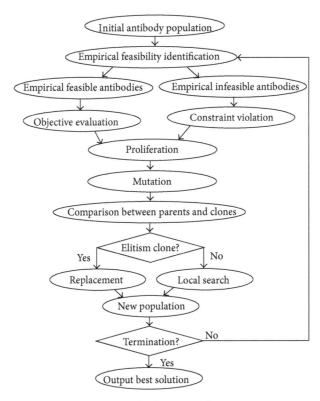

FIGURE 1: The flowchart of μIOA.

updated through proliferation, mutation, and selection. Step 7 makes those empirical feasible antibodies search better clones through proliferation and polynomial mutation. Once some antibody can not produce a valuable clone, a reported local search algorithm is used to perform local evolution so as to enhance the quality of solution search. The purpose of Step 8 urges those poor antibodies to create diverse clones through proliferation and nonuniform mutation.

Additionally, μIOA's computational complexity is decided by Steps 4, 6, and 7.2. Step 4 needs at most $N(IM_\delta + J + K + 1)$ times to calculate the empirical constraint violations. In Step 6, we need to compute the empirical objective values of antibodies in B, which evaluates at most Nn_N times. Step 7.2 enforces mutation with at most $Np \times C_{\max}$ times. Consequently, μIOA's computational complexity in the worst case can be given by

$$
\begin{aligned}
O_c &= O\left(N\left(IM_\delta + J + K\right) + Nn_N + NpC_{\max}\right) \\
&= O\left(N\left(IM_\delta + J + K + n_N + pC_{\max}\right)\right).
\end{aligned}
\tag{12}
$$

5. Experimental Analysis

Our experiments are executed on a personal computer (CPU/3 GHz, RAM/2 GB) with VC++ software. In order to examine μIOA's characteristics, four intelligent optimization algorithms, that is, two competitive steady genetic algorithms (SSGA-A and SSGA-B) [19] and two recent immune optimization approaches NIOA-A and NIOA-B [20], are taken to participate in comparative analysis by means of two 100-dimentional multimodal expected value optimization problems. It is pointed out that the two genetic algorithms with the same fixed sampling size for each individual can still solve (EP) problems, since their constraint scoring functions are designed based on static sampling strategies; the two immune algorithms are with dynamic sampling sizes for all individuals presented in the process of evolution. On the other hand, since NIOA-B can not effectively handle high-dimensional problems, we in this section improve it by OCBA [21]. These comparative approaches, together with μIOA, share the same termination criterion; namely, each approach is with the total of evaluations 8×10^5, while executing 30 times on each test problem. Their parameter settings are the same as those in their literatures except for their evolving population sizes. After manual experimental tuning, they take population size 40. μIOA takes a small population size within 3 and 5, while the three parameters of m_0, n_0, and $C_{\max}$ as crucial efficiency parameters are usually set as small integers. We here set $N = 5$, $m_0 = 30$, $n_0 = 20$, $C_{\max} = 2$, $\varepsilon = 0.1$, and $\delta = 0.05$. Additionally, those best solutions, acquired by all the algorithms for each test problem are reevaluated 10^6 times because of the demand of algorithm comparison.

Example 5. Consider

$$
\max \quad E\left[\left|\frac{\sum_{i=1}^{p}\cos^4\left(x_i\right) - 2\prod_{i=1}^{p}\cos^2\left(x_i\right)}{\sqrt{\sum_{i=1}^{p} i x_i^2}}\right| + \xi\right]
$$

$$
\text{s.t.} \quad E\left[0.75 - \eta_1\prod_{i=1}^{p} x_i\right] \leq 0,
$$

TABLE 1: Comparison of statistical results for Example 5.

Algor.	Max.	Min.	Mean	Std. dev.	CI	FR (%)	AR (s)
SSGA-A	0.14	0.10	0.11	0.01	[0.11, 0.12]	80	49.5
SSGA-B	0.13	0.10	0.11	0.01	[0.11, 0.12]	87	49.6
NIOA-A	0.25	0.16	0.21	0.03	[0.20, 0.22]	80	27.6
NIOA-B	0.26	0.17	0.20	0.02	[0.19, 0.21]	87	24.7
μIOA	0.39	0.22	0.29	0.05	[0.27, 0.31]	90	16.1

CI represents the confidence interval of objective values for the solutions acquired; FR stands for the rate of feasible solutions among all the gotten solutions; AR denotes the average runtime required by 30 runs.

$$\sum_{i=1}^{p} E\left[\eta_2 x_i - 7.5p\right] \leq 0,$$

$$0 \leq x_i \leq 10,$$

$$\xi \sim N(0,1),$$

$$1 \leq i \leq p,$$

$$\eta_1 \sim N(0.0015, 0.2),$$

$$\eta_2 \sim N(1,2).$$

$$(13)$$

This is a multimodal expected value programming problem gotten through modifying a static multimodal optimization problem [22], where $p = 100$. The main difficulty of solving such problem is that the high dimension and multimodality make it difficult to find the desired solution. We solve the above problem by means of the approximation model SAM as in Section 2, instead of transforming such model into a deterministic analytical one. After, respectively 30, runs, each of the above algorithms acquires 30 best solutions used for comparison. Their statistical results are listed in Table 1, while Figures 2 and 3 draw the box plots of the objective values acquired and their average search curves, respectively.

In Table 1, the values on FR, listed in the seventh column, hint that whereas all the algorithms can find many feasible solutions for each run, their rates of feasible solutions are different. μIOA can acquire many more feasible solutions than the compared approaches. This illustrates that the constraint handling approach RCEA, presented in Section 3, can ensure that μIOA find feasible solutions with high probability 90% for a single run. On the other hand, the statistical results in columns 2 to 6 show that μIOA's solution quality is clearly superior to those acquired by other approaches and meanwhile NIOA-A and NIOA-B are secondary. With respect to performance efficiency, we see easily that μIOA is a high-efficiency optimization algorithm, as it spends the least time to seek the desired solution in a run. We also notice that SSGA-A and SSGA-B present their high computational complexity because of their average runtime, which shows that such two genetic algorithms with static sampling strategies cause easily expensively computational cost.

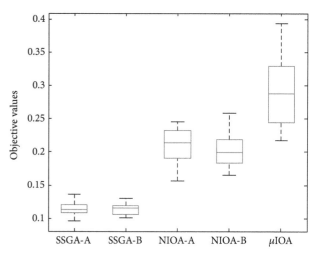

FIGURE 2: Example 5: comparison of box plots acquired.

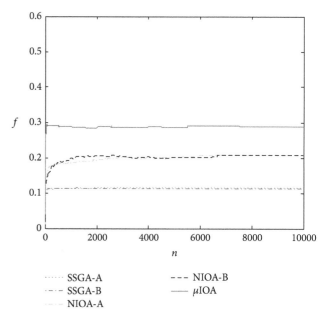

FIGURE 3: Example 5: comparison of average search curves.

The box plots in Figure 2, formed by 30 objective values for each algorithm, exhibit the fact that, in addition to μIOA obtaining the best effect by comparison with the other four algorithms, NIOA-A and NIOA-B with similar performance characteristics can work well over SSGA-A and SSGA-B. By Figure 3, we observe that μIOA can find the desired solution rapidly and achieve stable search but the other algorithms, in particular the two genetic algorithms, get easily into local search. Totally, when solving the above higher-dimensional problem, the five algorithms have different efficiencies, solution qualities, and search characteristics; μIOA suits the above problem and exhibits the best performance, for which the main reason consists in that it can effectively combine RCEA with ROEA to find many more empirically feasible individuals and urge them to evolve gradually towards the desired regions by proliferation and mutation.

TABLE 2: Comparison of statistical results for Example 6.

Algor.	Max.	Min.	Mean	Std. dev.	CI	FR (%)	AR (s)
SSGA-A	488.0	401.8	458.9	19.2	[452.1, 465.8]	53	26.6
SSGA-B	489.7	415.7	463.0	17.4	[456.8, 469.2]	53	25.8
NIOA-A	410.8	378.2	393.9	8.7	[390.8, 397.0]	100	16.0
NIOA-B	414.6	371.3	395.2	3.9	[391.3, 399.0]	100	13.9
μIOA	464.7	444.3	456.8	5.5	[454.1, 458.0]	100	12.1

However, those compared approaches present relatively weak performances. In particular, SSGA-A and SSGA-B get easily into local search and spend the most runtime to solve the above problem, as their constraint handling and selection techniques are hard to adapt to high-dimensional multimodal problems. NIOA-A and NIOA-B are superior to such two genetic algorithms, owing to their adaptive sampling and constraint handling techniques.

Example 6. Consider

$$\max \quad E\left[\sum_{i=1}^{p} x_i \cdot \sin\left(\pi i x_i\right) + \xi\right]$$

$$\text{s.t.} \quad E\left[\sum_{i=1}^{p} \eta_1 x_i\right] \leq 500,$$

$$E\left[\sum_{i=1}^{p} \eta_2 x_i^2\right] \leq 3000,$$

$$x_i \geq 0,$$

$$\xi \sim N(0,1),$$

$$1 \leq i \leq p,$$

$$\eta_1 \sim U(0.8, 1.2),$$

$$\eta_2 \sim N(1, 0.5).$$

(14)

This is a still difficult multimodal optimization problem obtained by modifying a static multimodal optimization problem [23], including 100 decision variables (i.e., $p = 100$) and 3 random variables which greatly influence the quality of solution search. The difficulty of solving such problem is that the objective function is multimodal and the decision variables are unbounded. Similar to the above experiment, we acquire the statistical results of the approaches given in Table 2, while the corresponding box plots and their average search curves are drawn by Figures 4 and 5, respectively.

The values on FR in Table 2 illustrate that it is also difficult to solve Example 6, due to the random variables and high dimensionality. Even if so, NIOA-A, NIOA-B, and μIOA can all acquire feasible solutions for each run. SSGA-A and SSGA-B, however, can only get at most 53% of feasible solutions; namely, they can only acquire 53 feasible solutions after 100 executions. This, along with the values on FR in Table 1, follows that although such two approaches can

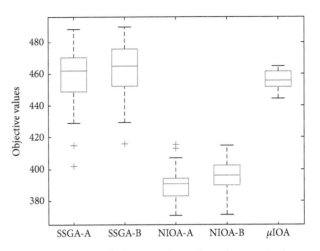

FIGURE 4: Example 6: comparison of box plots acquired.

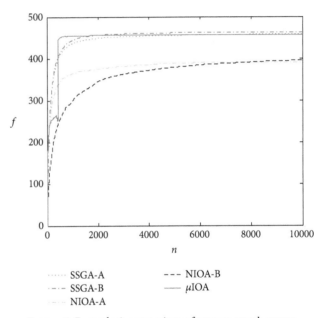

FIGURE 5: Example 6: comparison of average search curves.

acquire larger values on *Mean* than the other approaches, they are poor with respect to solution quality, efficiency, and search stability. Consequently, they need to make some improvements, for example, their constraint handling. We notice that μIOA is better than either NIOA-A or NIOA-B because of its efficiency and the value on *Mean*. We emphasize that whereas NIOA-A and NIOA-B can only obtain small values on *Mean* by comparison with μIOA, they are still valuable when solving such kind of hard problem. Relatively, NIOA-B behaves well over NIOA-A.

It seems to be true that SSGA-A and SSGA-B are superior to NIOA-A, NIOA-B, and μIOA by Figures 4 and 5, since the box plots in Figure 4 and the average search curves in Figure 5 are far from the horizontal line. As a matter of fact, column 7 in Table 2 shows clearly that such two genetic algorithms cannot find feasible solutions 47 times out of 100 runs, whereas the other approaches are opposite.

These indicate a fact that infeasible solutions in the decision domain have larger objective function values than feasible ones.

Summarily, when solving the above two examples, the five algorithms present different characteristics. SSGA-A and SSGA-B have similar performance attributes, and so do NIOA-A and NIOA-B. μIOA performs well over the compared approaches, while NIOA-B is secondary.

6. Conclusions and Further Work

We in this work concentrate on studying a microimmune optimization algorithm to solve a general kind of constrained expected value programming model, relying upon transforming such model into a sample-dependent approximation model (SAM). One such model requires that different candidate solutions have different sample sizes and especially each candidate has two kinds of samples' sizes. Subsequently, two lower bound estimates of random vectors are theoretically developed and, respectively, applied to handling expected value constraints of individuals in the current population and computing their empirical objective values. Based on such two estimates and the idea of racing ranking, two racing sampling methods are suggested to execute individual evaluation and constraint handling, respectively. Afterwards, a racing sampling based microimmune optimization algorithm μIOA is proposed to deal with such approximation model, with the merits of small population, strong disturbance suppression, effective constraint handling, adaptive sampling, and high efficiency. The theoretical analysis has indicated that μIOA's computational complexity depends mainly on n_N, M_δ, and $C_{\max}$, due to small population N and known problem parameters. By means of the higher-dimensional multimodal test problems, the comparatively experimental results can draw some conclusions: (1) RCEA and RCOEA can make μIOA dynamically determine the sample sizes of different kinds of individuals in the process of evolution, (2) the local search approach adopted can help μIOA to strengthen local search, (3) stochastic parameters may be efficiently addressed by adaptive sampling techniques, (4) μIOA performs well over the compared approaches, and (5) SSGA-A and SSGA-B need to make some improvements for higher-dimensional problems. Further, whereas we make some studies on how to explore immune optimization approaches to solve higher-dimensional constrained expected value programming problems, some issues will be further studied. For example, μIOA's theoretical convergence analysis needs to be studied, while its engineering applications are to be discussed.

Appendix

Proof of Lemma 3. Let $\mathbf{x} \in X_m \setminus X_\varepsilon$. Since there exists i_0 such that $E[G_{i_0}(\mathbf{x}, \xi)] > \varepsilon$ with $1 \le i_0 \le I$, by (3) we obtain that

$$\Pr\{\mathbf{x} \in X_m\} = \Pr\left\{\frac{1}{m}\sum_{j=1}^{m} G_i\left(\mathbf{x}, \xi^j\right) \le 0, 1 \le i \le I\right\}$$

$$\le \Pr\left\{\frac{1}{m}\sum_{j=1}^{m} G_{i_0}\left(\mathbf{x}, \xi^j\right) - E\left[G_{i_0}\left(\mathbf{x}, \xi\right)\right] \le -\varepsilon\right\} \quad (A.1)$$

$$\le \exp\left[\frac{-2\varepsilon^2 m}{\left(a_{i_0}(\mathbf{x}) - b_{i_0}(\mathbf{x})\right)^2}\right] \le \exp\left[\frac{-2\varepsilon^2 m}{\Delta^2}\right].$$

Hence,

$$1 - \Pr\{X_m \subseteq X_\varepsilon\} = \Pr\{\exists \mathbf{x} \in X_m, \text{s.t. } \mathbf{x} \notin X_\varepsilon\}$$

$$\le \sum_{\mathbf{x} \in A \setminus X_\varepsilon} \Pr\{\mathbf{x} \in X_m\} \quad (A.2)$$

$$\le |A| \exp\left[\frac{-2\varepsilon^2 m}{\Delta^2}\right].$$

Thereby,

$$\Pr\{X_m \subseteq X_\varepsilon\} \ge 1 - |A| \exp\left[\frac{-2\varepsilon^2 m}{\Delta^2}\right]. \quad (A.3)$$

So, the conclusion is true. $\qquad\square$

Proof of Lemma 4. Since B is finite, there exists $y_0 \in B$ such that $E[f(\mathbf{y}_0, \xi)] = f^*$. If $\mathbf{x} \in S_n \setminus S_\varepsilon$, then

$$E\left[f\left(\mathbf{x}, \xi\right)\right] > E\left[f\left(\mathbf{y}_0, \xi\right)\right] + \varepsilon. \quad (A.4)$$

Hence, if

$$\frac{1}{n}\sum_{k=1}^{n} f\left(\mathbf{x}, \xi^k\right) \le \frac{1}{n}\sum_{k=1}^{n} f\left(\mathbf{y}_0, \xi^k\right), \quad (A.5)$$

we have that

$$\frac{1}{n}\sum_{k=1}^{n} f\left(\mathbf{x}, \xi^k\right) < E\left[f\left(\mathbf{x}, \xi\right)\right] - \frac{\varepsilon}{2} \quad (A.6)$$

or

$$\frac{1}{n}\sum_{k=1}^{n} f\left(\mathbf{y}_0, \xi^k\right) > E\left[f\left(\mathbf{y}_0, \xi\right)\right] + \frac{\varepsilon}{2}. \quad (A.7)$$

Otherwise, we acquire that

$$\frac{1}{n}\sum_{k=1}^{n} f\left(\mathbf{x}, \xi^k\right) \ge E\left[f\left(\mathbf{x}, \xi\right)\right] - \frac{\varepsilon}{2}$$

$$> E\left[f\left(\mathbf{y}_0, \xi\right)\right] + \frac{\varepsilon}{2} \quad (A.8)$$

$$\ge \frac{1}{n}\sum_{k=1}^{n} f\left(\mathbf{y}_0, \xi^k\right).$$

This yields contraction. Consequently, by (3) we obtain that

$$\Pr\{\mathbf{x} \in S_n\} = \Pr\left\{\frac{1}{n}\sum_{k=1}^{n} f\left(\mathbf{x}, \xi^k\right) \le \widehat{f}_n\right\}$$

$$\le \Pr\left\{\frac{1}{n}\sum_{k=1}^{n} f\left(\mathbf{x}, \xi^k\right) \le \frac{1}{n}\sum_{k=1}^{n} f\left(\mathbf{y}_0, \xi^k\right)\right\}$$

$$\le \Pr\left\{\frac{1}{n}\sum_{k=1}^{n} f\left(\mathbf{x}, \xi^k\right) < E\left[f\left(\mathbf{x}, \xi\right)\right] - \frac{\varepsilon}{2}\right\} \quad \text{(A.9)}$$

$$+ \Pr\left\{\frac{1}{n}\sum_{k=1}^{n} f\left(\mathbf{y}_0, \xi^k\right) > E\left[f\left(\mathbf{y}_0, \xi\right)\right] + \frac{\varepsilon}{2}\right\}$$

$$\le 2\exp\left[-\frac{\varepsilon^2 n}{2\Gamma^2}\right].$$

Hence,

$$1 - \Pr\{S_n \subseteq S^\varepsilon\} = \Pr\{\exists \mathbf{x} \in S_n, \text{s.t. } \mathbf{x} \notin S_\varepsilon\}$$

$$\le \sum_{\mathbf{x} \in B \setminus S_\varepsilon} \Pr\{\mathbf{x} \in S_n\} \quad \text{(A.10)}$$

$$\le 2|B|\exp\left[-\frac{\varepsilon^2 n}{2\Gamma^2}\right].$$

This way, it follows from (A.10) that the above conclusion is true. □

Competing Interests

The authors declare that they have no competing interests.

Acknowledgments

This work is supported in part by the National Natural Science Foundation (61563009) and Doctoral Fund of Ministry of Education of China (20125252011110003).

References

[1] J. Luedtke and S. Ahmed, "A sample approximation approach for optimization with probabilistic constraints," *SIAM Journal on Optimization*, vol. 19, no. 2, pp. 674–699, 2008.

[2] M. Branda, "Sample approximation technique for mixed-integer stochastic programming problems with several chance constraints," *Operations Research Letters*, vol. 40, no. 3, pp. 207–211, 2012.

[3] A. Shapiro, D. Dentcheva, and A. Ruszczyński, *Lectures on Stochastic Programming: Modeling and Theory*, SIAM, Philadelphia, Pa, USA, 2009.

[4] W. Wang and S. Ahmed, "Sample average approximation of expected value constrained stochastic programs," *Operations Research Letters*, vol. 36, no. 5, pp. 515–519, 2008.

[5] M. Branda, "Sample approximation technique for mixed-integer stochastic programming problems with expected value constraints," *Optimization Letters*, vol. 8, no. 3, pp. 861–875, 2014.

[6] B. Liu, *Theory and Practice of Uncertain Programming*, Springer, Berlin, Germany, 2009.

[7] Y. Jin and J. Branke, "Evolutionary optimization in uncertain environments—a survey," *IEEE Transactions on Evolutionary Computation*, vol. 9, no. 3, pp. 303–317, 2005.

[8] K. Deb, S. Gupta, D. Daum, J. Branke, A. K. Mall, and D. Padmanabhan, "Reliability-based optimization using evolutionary algorithms," *IEEE Transactions on Evolutionary Computation*, vol. 13, no. 5, pp. 1054–1074, 2009.

[9] B. Liu and Y.-K. Liu, "Expected value of fuzzy variable and fuzzy expected value models," *IEEE Transactions on Fuzzy Systems*, vol. 10, no. 4, pp. 445–450, 2002.

[10] Y. Sun and Y. L. Gao, "An improved differential evolution algorithm of stochastic expected value models," *Microelectronics & Computer*, vol. 29, no. 4, pp. 23–25, 2012.

[11] D. Dasgupta, S. Yu, and F. Nino, "Recent advances in artificial immune systems: models and applications," *Applied Soft Computing Journal*, vol. 11, no. 2, pp. 1574–1587, 2011.

[12] K. Trojanowski and S. T. Wierzchoń, "Immune-based algorithms for dynamic optimization," *Information Sciences*, vol. 179, no. 10, pp. 1495–1515, 2009.

[13] Y.-C. Hsieh and P.-S. You, "An effective immune based two-phase approach for the optimal reliability-redundancy allocation problem," *Applied Mathematics and Computation*, vol. 218, no. 4, pp. 1297–1307, 2011.

[14] Q. Zhao, R. Yang, and F. Duan, "An immune clonal hybrid algorithm for solving stochastic chance-constrained programming," *Journal of Computational Information Systems*, vol. 8, no. 20, pp. 8295–8302, 2012.

[15] W. Hoeffding, "Probability inequalities for sums of bounded random variables," *Journal of the American Statistical Association*, vol. 58, pp. 13–30, 1963.

[16] Z. Lin and Z. Bai, *Probability Inequalities*, Springer, Berlin, Germany, 2010.

[17] K. L. Chung, *A Course in Probability Theory*, Academic Press, 2001.

[18] M. Olguin-Carbajal, E. Alba, and J. Arellano-Verdejo, "Micro-differential evolution with local search for high dimensional problems," in *Proceedings of the IEEE Congress on Evolutionary Computation (CEC '13)*, pp. 48–54, June 2013.

[19] C. A. Poojari and B. Varghese, "Genetic algorithm based technique for solving chance constrained problems," *European Journal of Operational Research*, vol. 185, no. 3, pp. 1128–1154, 2008.

[20] Z.-H. Zhang, "Noisy immune optimization for chance-constrained programming problems," *Applied Mechanics and Materials*, vol. 48-49, pp. 740–744, 2011.

[21] C.-H. Chen, "Efficient sampling for simulation-based optimization under uncertainty," in *Proceedings of the 4th International Symposium on Uncertainty Modeling and Analysis (ISUMA '03)*, pp. 386–391, IEEE, College Park, Md, USA, September 2003.

[22] E. Mezura-Montes and C. A. Coello Coello, "A simple multi-membered evolution strategy to solve constrained optimization problems," *IEEE Transactions on Evolutionary Computation*, vol. 9, no. 1, pp. 1–17, 2005.

[23] B. Varghese and C. A. Poojari, "Genetic algorithm based technique for solving chance-constrained problems arising in risk management," Tech. Rep., 2004.

12

A Mixed Integer Programming Model for Supplier Selection and Order Allocation Problem with Fuzzy Multiobjective

Hongtao Hu, Haotian Xiong, Yuanfeng You, and Wei Yan

Logistics Engineering College, Shanghai Maritime University, Shanghai, China

Correspondence should be addressed to Yuanfeng You; ivan.u@foxmail.com

Academic Editor: Si Zhang

A mixed integer programming model is proposed to solve supplier selection and order allocation problem for a manufacturer. In this model, quality, delivery performance, and purchasing cost are chosen as three criteria to select suppliers and set as objectives. Inventory level, goods flow balance, service level, supply ability, and marketing demand are considered as constraints. In the proposed model, the three objectives have different weights which are given by experts. However, the experts score the weight by many subjective factors. So, the fuzzy analytic hierarchy process (FAHP) based approach is used to calculate the weighted values. In the end, a case study illustrates the advantage of weighted values solved by FAHP. And the result shows that a weighted model is more advantageous for supplier selection and order allocation.

1. Introduction

Suppliers and manufacturers play an important role in the supply chain network. The procurement between them affects the downstream of the supply chain. Reasonable purchasing price and good quality of raw materials can reduce manufacturing cost. And then distributors and retailers can get the product from upstream with reduced wholesale price. Finally, customers can be benefited. What is more, reasonable price and good quality of the product can enlarge the demand, which benefits the entire supply chain. Obviously, supplier selection and order allocation are critical.

We consider the procurement between a manufacturer and suppliers in two aspects, supplier selection and order allocation. For supplier selection, Dickson [1] and Weber et al. [2] made some researches in the criteria for supplier selection, and they ranked the importance for each criterion. According to the researches of Dickson and Weber et al., quality, delivery performance, and purchasing cost are regarded as the criteria for supplier selection. And rejected items from the supplier are used to reflect quality, and late delivery items are used to reflect delivery performance. Purchasing cost involves inventory cost, cooperative cost, and wholesale cost. These three criteria have relevance with each other,

so a multiobjective function is formulated to solve supplier selection problem in this paper.

As for order allocation, a decision variable is set for purchasing quantity. We can obtain corresponding order allocation after solving supplier selection problem. To make the result more reasonable, besides customer's demand, inventory level, and supply ability as constraints, a minimum order quantity is required for manufactures. Furthermore, rejected items and late delivery items are taken into consideration in goods flow, which makes the multiobjective function more reasonable for supplier selection and order allocation in real life situation.

The innovation of this paper is to use fuzzy analytic hierarchy process (FAHP) which was proposed by Zadeh [3] in 1965. The weights of three objectives are calculated by FAHP in proposed MIP model. And we apply the weighted values into an innovative model to solve supplier selection and order allocation problem. The reason why FAHP is used to solve the weighted values is that different manufacturers give different importance to these criteria. For example, manufacturers not only focus on the cost of fresh product, but also focus more on the quality. So, these criteria should be given a weighted value to reflect their importance. Furthermore, these criteria are scored by experts subjectively. So, FAHP is used to improve this problem. Compared to conventional AHP, FAHP is a better method to avoid uncertainties as many as possible.

The rest of this paper is organized as follows. Section 2 is the literature review about supplier selection and order allocation. In Section 3, we introduce the index, parameters, and decision variables. Then the multiobjective function is formulated for supplier selection. Section 4 introduces some approaches to solve supplier selection. And we propose some steps to solve this problem. Section 5 uses a case study to illustrate the advantage of weighted values solved by FAHP, and two results solved by single Crisp Formulation and a weighted model are compared in Section 6. Finally, Section 7 is the conclusion.

2. Literature Review

For supplier selection, two scholars made some important researches. Dickson [1] started to research it in 1966 by raising questionnaires to 273 procurement managers and agents, and 170 valid responses were received. Afterwards, 23 criteria were summarized to evaluate a supplier. According to this summary, Dickson analyzed these 23 criteria and these 23 criteria were ranked in terms of importance. Another scholar, Weber et al. [2], systematically concluded 74 literatures published from 1967 to 1990 about supplier selection and these 23 criteria were ranked again [4]. The importance ranked by Dickson expressed more views from the perspective of procurement managers and agents while Weber's views expressed some scholars' thoughts [5]. It was noticeable that purchasing cost, delivery performance, and quality were all ranked to top three by both Dickson and Weber et al. Based on these fundamental papers, many scholars published some articles about optimal approaches or decisions such as Zhen [6] in 2015 and Dong et al. [7] in 2010.

As for the methods to solve supplier selection problem, scholars like Kumar et al. (2005) [8] applied fuzzy sets to formulate a model solving the Multiobjective Integer Programming Vendor Selection Problem (MIP_VSP), minimizing the purchasing cost, net late delivery items, and net rejected items. Kumar et al. (2008) [9] used AHP and fuzzy linear-programming to solve supplier selection with minimum cost. Lee (2009) [10] ranked suppliers in accordance with profit, marketing opportunity, cost, and risk, then selecting suppliers by Fuzzy AHP. Kokangul and Susuz (2009) [11] used AHP and nonlinear programming to formulate an objective function to maximize TVP (Total Value of Procurement) and minimize TCP (Total Cost of Procurement), selecting suppliers and allocating orders. Mafakheri et al. (2011) [12] and other scholars proposed a two-stage method. These scholars applied AHP to rank potential suppliers in the first stage, and goal programming was used to solve maximum TVP (Total Cost of Procurement) and minimum TCP (Total Cost of Procurement) in the second stage. Shaw et al. (2012) [13] chose Fuzzy AHP and fuzzy objectives to select suppliers. In this model, Fuzzy AHP was used to calculate weighted values, and these values were applied to goal programming model for supplier selection. Qian (2014) [4] analyzed many important factors in supplier selection in detail, including purchasing cost, delivery performance, profit, and lean production. And

these factors were taken into account in different markets with certain demands and uncertain demands to balance the profit and supplier selection. Choudhary and Shankar (2014) [14] set a model about inventory, supplier selection, and transportation programming problem solved by the goal programming model, and solutions were compared to analyze advantages and disadvantages of different methods. Kar (2015) [15] combined Neural Network Algorithm, AHP, and fuzzy sets to select suppliers. And Scott et al. (2015) [16] with other scholars combined AHP and QFD to make the research about requirements from stakeholders in supplier selection.

From the above literatures, single objective programming is used the most for supplier selection. But multiobjective programming is used in this paper because we consider more about the relevance among different objectives. Meanwhile, the corresponding order allocation can be obtained after solving supplier selection problem. What is more, Fuzzy AHP is used instead of AHP to calculate weighted values, because this method is more reasonable for supplier selection and order allocation in real life situation.

3. Model Formulation

In this paper, we assume that long period marketing regulation makes the demands from customers predictable. And single product is considered for supplier selection and order allocation in this paper. In this problem, a manufacturer has n alternative suppliers and makes plans over t periods. When considering customer demands, a manufacturer must consider order fulfillment, especially in the Build-to-Order supply chain according to Ye et al. (2006) [17] and other scholars, because it reflects the service level and the cost of inventory. And the higher the service level is, the more the cost of inventory will be. What is more, the delivery performance and goods quality of a supplier have an effect on purchasing quantity. And it should be mentioned that rejected items rate and late delivery items rate are also the factors for supplier selection and order allocation.

Other assumptions are shown as follows:

(i) demands of product over each period can be predicted;

(ii) both stock shortage and overstocked products are allowed;

(iii) the productivity of a supplier is limited;

(iv) cooperative cost only occurs when products are purchased from a supplier;

(v) holding cost of inventory only occurs when products are held over more than one period;

(vi) late delivery items will be received at the next period;

(vii) rejected items will be disposed, and they will not be regarded as inventory when held over more than one period;

(viii) late delivery items will be regarded as qualified items, and suppliers have enough time to check them before sending;

(ix) a minimum order quantity is required.

Based on the assumptions mentioned above, index, parameters, and decision variables are considered as shown in Notations.

To select optimum suppliers, we set three objective functions to minimize net rejected items as Z_1, late delivery items as Z_2, and purchasing cost as Z_3. So, this problem can be formulated as

$$\text{Minimize} \quad Z_1 = \sum_{i=1}^{n} \sum_{t=1}^{T} x_{it} R_{it} \tag{1}$$

$$\text{Minimize} \quad Z_2 = \sum_{i=1}^{n} \sum_{t=1}^{T} x_{it} L_{it} \tag{2}$$

$$\text{Minimize} \quad Z_3 = \sum_{i=1}^{n} \sum_{t=1}^{T} x_{it} P_{it} + \sum_{i=1}^{n} \sum_{t=1}^{T} O_{it} y_{it} + \sum_{i=1}^{n} h_t C_t \tag{3}$$

$$\text{Subject to} \quad C_{t-1} + \sum_{i=1}^{n} x_{it} - \sum_{i=1}^{n} x_{it} L_{it} + \sum_{i=1}^{n} x_{i(t-1)} L_{i(t-1)} - \sum_{i=1}^{n} x_{it} R_{it} - d_t - S_{t-1} = C_t - S_t, \quad \forall t \tag{4}$$

$$x_{it} \leq \left(\sum_{k=t}^{T} d_k \right) y_{it}, \quad \forall t, \forall i \tag{5}$$

$$x_{it} \leq U_{it}, \quad \forall t, \forall i \tag{6}$$

$$C_t \leq \omega, \quad \forall t \tag{7}$$

$$S_t \leq (1 - \theta_t) d_t, \quad \forall t \tag{8}$$

$$x_{it} + (1 - y_{it}) \cdot M \geq B_{it}, \quad \forall t, \forall i \tag{9}$$

$$S_t \geq 0, \quad \forall t \tag{10}$$

$$C_t \geq 0, \quad \forall t \tag{11}$$

$$x_{it} \geq 0 \text{ and integer}, \quad \forall t, \forall i \tag{12}$$

$$y_{it} \in \{0, 1\}, \quad \forall t, \forall i. \tag{13}$$

We assume that (1), (2), and (3) are all subject to above constraints, including the balance of goods flow, purchasing quantity, supply ability, stock shortage, and minimum order quantity. Equation (4) is the balance of goods flow. Equation (5) means the reasonable order allocation, because, at each period, orders should not exceed total demand. Equation (6) shows that order allocation to a supplier cannot exceed its productivity. Equation (7) is the maximum inventory level and (8) means that, at the service level θ, the rate $(1-\theta)$ can be used to reflect stock shortage. Equation (9) is the minimum order quantity set by suppliers. Equations (10) to (13) are nonnegative constraints and integral sets.

It is noticeable that rejected items and late delivery items from manufacturers are taken into account. In real life situation, rejected items and late delivery items have the impact on inventory, which means that they affect order allocation. Figure 1 shows that, over t period, the inventory cost and stock shortage of a manufacturer are affected by the

inventory and stock shortage over $(t-1)$ period. And the late delivery items from $(t-1)$ period are added to t period.

4. Methods to Solve Supplier Selection and Order Allocation

Generally, a single Crisp Formulation [8] is used to solve supplier selection and order allocation. But this method fails to consider the weighted value of each objective function. So, a weighted-additive model is proposed by Tiwari et al. [18]. It can be presented by

$$\mu_D(x) = \sum_{j=1}^{J} w_j \mu_{zj}(x) + \sum_{k=1}^{K} \beta_k \mu_{gk}(x)$$

$$\sum_{j=1}^{J} w_j + \sum_{k=1}^{K} \beta_k = 1, \quad w_j \geq 0, \ \beta_k \geq 0, \tag{14}$$

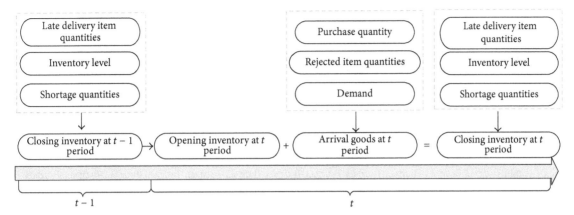

FIGURE 1: Balance of goods flow.

TABLE 1: The importance of AHP [10].

Number	Importance
1	Same importance
3	Slight importance
5	General importance
7	Strong importance
9	Extreme importance
2, 4, 6, 8	Balanced value

TABLE 2: Transformed fuzzy number [10].

Fuzzy number	Characteristic function
$\hat{1}$	$(1, 1, 2)$
$\hat{x}$	$(x - 1, x, x + 1), \quad x = 2, 3, 4, 5, 6, 7, 8$
$\hat{9}$	$(8, 9, 9)$
$1/\hat{1}$	$(2^{-1}, 1^{-1}, 1^{-1})$
$1/\hat{x}$	$((x + 1)^{-1}, x^{-1}, (x - 1)^{-1}), \quad x = 2, 3, 4, 5, 6, 7, 8$
$1/\hat{9}$	$(9^{-1}, 9^{-1}, 8^{-1})$

where w_j and β_k are the weighted values of each objective function. $\mu_{zj}(x)$ and $\mu_{gk}(x)$ are the membership degree proposed by Zadeh [3], which can be presented by

$$\mu_{Zj}(x)$$
$$= \begin{cases} 1, & \text{if } z_j(x) \leq z_j^{\min} \\ \dfrac{\left[z_j^{\max} - z_j(x)\right]}{\left[z_j^{\max} - z_j^{\min}\right]}, & \text{if } z_j^{\min} \leq z_j(x) \leq z_j^{\max} \quad j = 1, 2, \dots, J \\ 0, & \text{if } z_j(x) \geq z_j^{\max}, \end{cases} \tag{15}$$

where $Z_j^{\max}$ is the upper bound that can be found by maximizing feasible solutions of the objective function. In the same way, $Z_j^{\min}$ is the lower bound that can be found by minimizing feasible solutions of the objective functions. The membership degree in this paper is used to calculate the proportion of each criterion, so it is critical to final result with weighted values.

However, weighted values in the weighted-additive model are often decided by decision makers subjectively or calculated by conventional AHP, which is not accurate enough. So, in order to make the result more reasonable in real life situation, we use FAHP to calculate the weighted values. Experts score each target according to the importance shown in Table 1, and a corresponding comparison matrix will be made. After that, the comparison matrix is transformed into triangular fuzzy numbers according to the principle proposed by Lee (2009) [10], shown in Table 2. Then the weighted value of each objective function can be calculated.

According to the weighted-additive model, we propose the model

$$\max \quad = w_{zj} \cdot r_{zj}$$
$$\text{Subject to} \quad (4) \text{ to } (13), \tag{16}$$

where w_{zj} is the weighted value solved by FAHP and r_{zj} is the membership degree of each objective function. This model involves weighted values solved by FAHP to make the result more reasonable, and it can simplify the calculation compared to weighted-additive model. So, it is used to solve supplier selection and order allocation problem in this paper.

To conclude, the above illustrations demonstrate the necessary improvement of the single Crisp Formulation when solving a multiobjective programming problem without weighted values. And a weighted model with membership degree and weighted values based on FAHP approach is more reasonable to solve supplier selection and order allocation in real life situations.

Six steps will be involved in solving this problem, and these steps are considered as follows.

Step 1. Decide which criterion should be scored by experts. Generally, AHP is widely used to rank the importance of many factors. But FAHP is used to calculate the weighted values in this paper.

Step 2. Experts will score those criteria from 1 to 9 according to the importance shown in Table 1. And several comparison matrices are made.

TABLE 3: Rejected items rate.

	Jan.	Feb.	Mar.	Apr.	May	Jun.	Jul.	Aug.	Sept.	Oct.	Nov.	Dec.
S_1	0.02	0.02	0.02	0.05	0.05	0.02	0.02	0.05	0.05	0.05	0.05	0.05
S_2	0.02	0.02	0.02	0.02	0.02	0.1	0.02	0.02	0.02	0.05	0.02	0.02
S_3	0.05	0.05	0.05	0.02	0.1	0.05	0.1	0.02	0.02	0.1	0.1	0.05

TABLE 4: Late delivery items rate.

	Jan.	Feb.	Mar.	Apr.	May	Jun.	Jul.	Aug.	Sept.	Oct.	Nov.	Dec.
S_1	0.01	0.01	0.01	0.01	0.01	0.01	0.01	0.01	0.01	0.01	0.01	0.01
S_2	0.01	0.01	0.01	0.05	0.05	0.01	0.01	0.01	0.01	0.01	0.01	0.01
S_3	0.05	0.05	0.05	0.05	0.05	0.05	0.05	0.05	0.05	0.05	0.05	0.05

TABLE 5: Demand.

Jan.	Feb.	Mar.	Apr.	May	Jun.	Jul.	Aug.	Sept.	Oct.	Nov.	Dec.
100	80	100	60	80	120	80	70	80	100	60	100

TABLE 6: Purchasing cost per unit.

	Jan.	Feb.	Mar.	Apr.	May	Jun.	Jul.	Aug.	Sept.	Oct.	Nov.	Dec.
S_1	2.4	2.45	2.46	2.25	2.29	2.31	2.39	2.41	2.38	2.35	2.36	2.2
S_2	2.46	2.42	2.45	2.26	2.3	2.3	2.35	2.42	2.4	2.3	2.26	2.18
S_3	2.42	2.46	2.46	2.255	2.3	2.32	2.28	2.4	2.41	2.32	2.23	2.2

TABLE 7: Others.

	Supply ability (tons)	Cooperative cost (10 thousand RMB)	Minimum order quantity (tons)
S_1	250	3	10
S_2	70	1.2	10
S_3	80	1.5	10

Step 3. After that, these comparison matrices are transformed to fuzzy numbers according to Table 2.

Step 4. Use FAHP to calculate weighted values.

Step 5. Under constraints (4) to (13), three objective functions are solved. By maximization, upper bound $Z_j^{\max}$ can be obtained, and by minimization, lower bound $Z_j^{\min}$ can be obtained.

Step 6. Weighted values solved in Step 4 and the membership degree of each objective function are added to the weighted model (15). Finally, the result of supplier selection and order allocation can be calculated.

5. A Case Study

5.1. Data Description. Data from a plastic and textile company (hereinafter to be referred to as KF Company) are used to check the feasibility of the weighted model. Maximum inventory for KF Company to store nylon is 40 tons, and the inventory cost is 1 thousand RMB per unit ton. The nylon

comes from three suppliers, S_1, S_2, and S_3, respectively, and related data in 2014 are shown in Tables 3–7.

5.2. Calculating by FAHP. According to three objective functions mentioned in Section 3, a questionnaire is designed, and experts in KF Company score the importance of three criteria. Then six questionnaires are received and we transform them into six comparison matrices shown in Table 8. And Matlab is used to check their consistency. If a matrix cannot qualify the consistency, it may be the incorrect scores from experts. So, experts need to check it again until all matrices qualify the consistency after programming.

According to Table 8, six comparison matrices are transformed into a fuzzy matrix. And the final scoring result is shown in Table 9.

The weighted values are shown in Table 10.

From the result analyzed in Table 10, quality weighs the most for supplier selection, the following weight is purchasing cost, and delivery performance is the least. A manager from KF Company said that, in order to achieve more satisfaction from customers for longer cooperation, they put more emphasis on quality. He also said that the reason why

TABLE 8: Comparison matrices.

	Cost	Quality	Delivery performance
Comparison matrix 1			
Cost	1	1	3
Quality	1	1	3
Delivery performance	1/3	1/3	1
Comparison matrix 2			
Cost	1	1/2	3
Quality	2	1	5
Delivery performance	1/3	1/5	1
Comparison matrix 3			
Cost	1	1/3	4
Quality	3	1	6
Delivery performance	1/4	1/6	1
Comparison matrix 4			
Cost	1	1	2
Quality	1	1	3
Delivery performance	1/2	1/3	1
Comparison matrix 5			
Cost	1	1/2	3
Quality	2	1	4
Delivery performance	1/3	1/4	1
Comparison matrix 6			
Cost	1	1	3
Quality	1	1	4
Delivery performance	1/3	1/4	1

delivery performance weighed the least was because they had stable customers, and orders were given in advance so that manufacturing could be organized well. However, if KF Company wants to expand market to receive more orders from the retailer, delivery performance and other factors are needed to be considered more.

5.3. Computational Results. At the service level of 0.99, 0.90, and 0.8, we program the objective function with weighted values and maximum membership degree. The programming is implemented with Lingo 11.0 in less than 5 minutes. And the computer's type is Intel® Celeron U3400 and CPU is 1.1 GHZ. Table 11 shows the minimum and maximum values of the function at different service levels.

The result of service level at 0.99 is taken as an example, plotting its graph for membership function of quality, delivery performance, and purchasing cost, shown in Figure 2.

The results of weighted model are shown in Tables 12–14. Three suppliers are all selected over the planning period during twelve months. The value of cost function is an upward trend with the rise of service level while the value of quality function and delivery performance function is stable.

The single Crisp Formulation without weighted values is also solved under the same sets, and the results are shown in Table 15.

6. Result Analysis

By using the weighted model and single Crisp Formulation solving this problem, we illustrate the results by charts and diagrams. Taking an example, at the service level 0.99, we can show the purchasing quantities in Figure 3 and the actual shortage of goods in Figure 4. Although the scale of this problem is relatively small, two charts still reflect an obvious difference of purchasing quantities, and this difference occurs in April, May, August, and October, which means that the weighed values indeed affect order allocation.

Besides the illustration mentioned above, another method is used to demonstrate the difference between two results. In view of the different metrics of different functions, Value Path Approach (VPA) [13] can be used to set a norm for these compared results. That is to say, each objective functional value can be standardized by dividing a minimum functional value at the same service level. After being standardized, all functions are dimensionless; as a result, the smaller the VPA value of a minimized function is, the more reasonable the result is. Table 16 illustrates the functional values with corresponding VPA values at different service levels given by two methods.

Figure 4 shows the standardized results of functional values. When the service level is 0.99, by means of VPA, we can demonstrate that the single Crisp Formulation is more advantageous than the weighted model in purchasing cost and delivery performance, at 10.31% and 0.13%, respectively, and 2% less in quality. When the service level is 0.9, delivery performance of the single Crisp Formulation is 10.74% more than the weighed model, but quality is 4.1% less and purchasing cost is 0.01% less. When the service level is 0.8, delivery performance solved by the single Crisp Formulation is 11.19% more than the weighted model while quality and purchasing cost are less, 5.46% and 0.93%, respectively. In summary, delivery performance is more advantageous in the single Crisp Formulation, which means that net late delivery items are less and suppliers are better in delivery performance. And the fluctuation of purchasing cost between two methods is not obvious, and the result of quality in the single Crisp Formulation is inferior to the weighted model. This means that net rejected items in the single Crisp Formulation are more than the weighted model.

What is more, Figure 5 also demonstrates that standardized VPA value of quality and delivery performance is shattered, which indicates that the weighted values added to quality and delivery performance have an impact on their functions. As for purchasing cost, the VPA value is similar in two methods. So, we conclude that the cost function is not sensitive to its weighted value. Besides, the importance of three functions is the same in the single Crisp Formulation. That is to say, two weighted values of purchasing cost are similar. So, two results of purchasing cost are similar between two methods. However, weighted values of quality and delivery performance solved by FAHP show a large discrepancy between two methods. So, net rejected items are decreased but late delivery items are increased in the weighted model. All in all, the weighted model makes the purchase strategy prefer the function of high weighed values such as cost

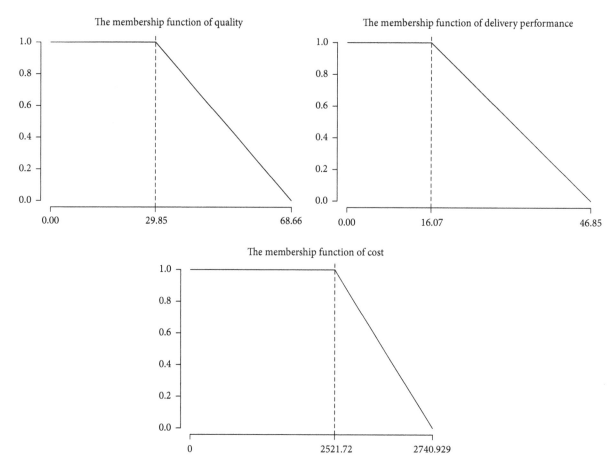

FIGURE 2: Membership functions.

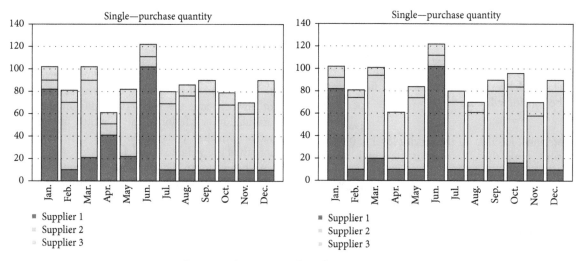

FIGURE 3: Comparison of purchasing quantity.

TABLE 9: Fuzzy comparison matrix.

	Purchasing cost	Quality	Delivery performance
Cost	$(1, 1, 2)$	$(0.55, 0.661, 1.26)$	$(1.906, 2.942, 3.957)$
Quality	$(1.122, 1.513, 2.57)$	$(1, 1, 2)$	$(2.994, 4.036, 5.061)$
Delivery performance	$(0.253, 0.34, 0.525)$	$(0.198, 0.248, 0.334)$	$(1, 1, 1.782)$

TABLE 10: Weighted values.

	Purchasing cost	Quality	Delivery performance
Weighted value	0.38	0.52	0.1

TABLE 11: Critical values.

Service level	$\theta = 0.99$		$\theta = 0.90$		$\theta = 0.80$	
Objective function	$\mu = 0$	$\mu = 1$	$\mu = 0$	$\mu = 1$	$\mu = 0$	$\mu = 1$
Quality	68.66	29.85	68.95	29.38	68.95	28.85
Delivery performance	46.85	16.07	47.18	15.98	47.18	15.88
Purchasing cost	2740.93	2512.72	2743.61	2497.59	2743.75	2471.25

TABLE 12: Purchasing quantity.

		Jan.	Feb.	Mar.	Apr.	May	Jun.	Jul.	Aug.	Sept.	Oct.	Nov.	Dec.
$\theta = 0.99$	S_1	83	10	21	10	10	103	10	10	10	15	10	10
	S_2	10	62	70	10	65	10	60	51	70	70	49	70
	S_3	10	10	10	42	10	10	10	10	10	10	10	10
$\theta = 0.90$	S_1	83	10	12	10	10	111	10	10	10	10	10	11
	S_2	10	62	70	10	57	10	60	51	70	65	49	70
	S_3	10	10	10	52	10	10	10	10	10	10	10	10
$\theta = 0.80$	S_1	83	10	10	10	10	119	11	10	10	10	10	10
	S_2	10	61	64	11	48	10	59	60	70	45	51	70
	S_3	10	10	10	60	10	10	10	10	10	10	10	10

TABLE 13: Membership degree.

	Maximum	Quality	Delivery performance	Purchasing cost
$\theta = 0.99$	0.956162	0.973718	0.88564	0.950695
$\theta = 0.90$	0.953133	0.973212	0.884295	0.943772
$\theta = 0.80$	0.957217	0.981546	0.884984	0.942932

TABLE 14: Function values.

	$\theta = 0.99$	$\theta = 0.90$	$\theta = 0.80$
Z_1	30.87	30.44	29.59
Z_2	19.59	19.59	19.48
Z_3	2530.45	2509.89	2484.07

TABLE 15: Results of single Crisp Formulation.

	$\theta = 0.99$	$\theta = 0.90$	$\theta = 0.80$
Quality	31.79	31.74	31.30
Delivery performance	17.57	17.69	17.52
Purchasing cost	2527.03	2510.29	2507.37
Maximum membership degree	0.950013	0.932582	0.950641

TABLE 16: Comparison of quality, delivery performance, and cost functions.

Service level	$\theta = 0.99$		$\theta = 0.90$		$\theta = 0.80$	
	Single	Weighted	Single	Weighted	Single	Weighted
Quality	31.79	30.87	31.74	30.44	31.30	29.59
VPA quality	(1.0298)	(1.0000)	(1.0427)	(1.0000)	(1.0578)	(1.0000)
Delivery performance	17.57	19.59	17.69	19.59	17.52	19.48
VPA delivery	(1.0000)	(1.1150)	(1.0000)	(1.1074)	(1.0000)	(1.1119)
Cost	2527.03	2530.45	2510.29	2509.89	2507.37	2484.07
VPA cost	(1.0000)	(1.0014)	(1.0002)	(1.0000)	(1.0094)	(1.0000)

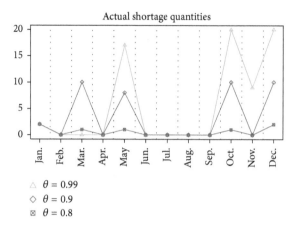

FIGURE 4: Actual shortage with different service level.

function, showing the asymmetry of this problem. At the same time, service level affects net rejected items and late delivery items more than purchasing cost.

Figure 6 illustrates different service levels and solving methods will have the impact on the results. For all service levels, weighted results of quality and purchasing cost are close to 1, and delivery performance is above 1; while results of quality solved by Crisp Formulation is above 1, delivery performance and purchasing cost are close to 1. For quality, the VPA value of Crisp Formulation is larger than the weighted model, and the higher the service level is, the smaller the VPA value is. For delivery performance, the VPA value is larger in weighted model with a more centralized distribution so that it has a larger difference than the result of Crisp Formulation. This reflects the same conclusion shown in Figure 5, indicating that service level has a direct impact on net rejected items and net late delivery items. As for purchasing cost, although the VPA value of Crisp Formulation is more than 1, it is almost the same as the result of weighted model. This figure can further illustrate quality and delivery performance are more sensitive to the weighted value solved by FAHP, and it can affect net rejected items and late delivery items, but purchasing cost is insensitive to the weighted value and slightly affects net rejected items and late delivery items.

Figure 7 tells us that, at the service level of 0.99, stock shortage fluctuates obviously for the single Crisp Formulation, but, for the weight model, it is stable. This indicates that weighted values have a positive effect on inventory.

The membership degree for Crisp Formulation and the weighted model are shown in Table 17.

Finally, the trend of maximum membership value at different service levels with different solving methods is shown in Figure 8. It is obvious that all membership values of the single Crisp Formulation are smaller than the weighted model, which means that weighted model can obtain a higher membership degree with high weighted values. So an optimum solution can be obtained, and it is more reasonable in real life situation.

7. Conclusions

There is no doubt that supplier selection is a complex task because it is hard to keep the balance among all criteria.

Therefore, if a manufacturer wants to obtain a sustainable market, supplier selection and order allocation play the crucial role in a supply chain.

This paper uses FAHP to calculate weighted values, and two results from single Crisp Formulation and the weighted model are compared to further illustrate some advantages of FAHP solving weighted values. Nevertheless, some related issues should be proposed for future researches.

(1) Large-Scale Problems. With the increasing of planning periods and the number of suppliers, the calculation of the model will be more difficult, because Lingo is generally applied in small-scale problems. So, heuristic algorithm should be used such as genetic algorithm to solve this problem.

(2) Demand Uncertainty. Certain demand of the market is assumed in this paper. But if some industries such as clothing with great fluctuation need to select suppliers, the model needs to be improved with random demands.

(3) Diversity of Products. Supplier selection and order allocation are harder to be solved when products are various. In fact, many companies produce more than one sort of product. So, in future researches, a hybrid approach proposed by Yang and Dong (2012) [19] is used to solve product configuration problems for supplier selection and order allocation.

Notations

Index Set

i: Index for supplier, for all $i = 1, 2, \ldots, I$
j: Index for objective function, for
$\quad j = 1, 2, \ldots, J$
t: Index for period, $t = 1, 2, \ldots, T$

Parameters

ω: Maximum inventory
w_{ej}: Weighted value of objective function j

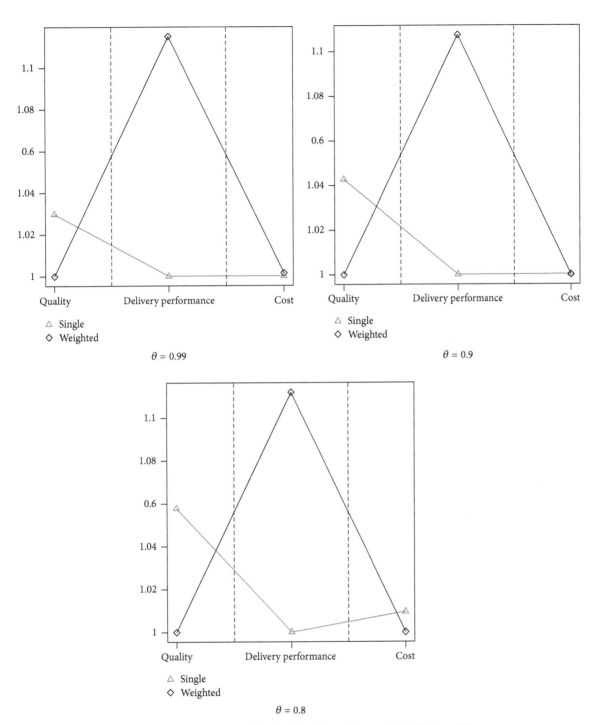

FIGURE 5: Comparison of single Crisp Formulation and weighted model.

TABLE 17: Comparison of maximum membership degree.

Service level	$\theta = 0.99$		$\theta = 0.90$		$\theta = 0.80$	
	Single	Weighted	Single	Weighted	Single	Weighted
Maximum	0.950013	0.956162	0.932582	0.953133	0.950641	0.957216

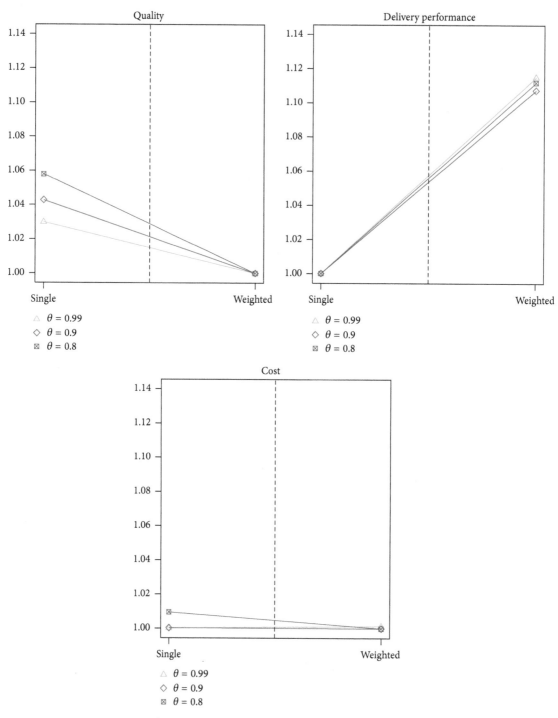

FIGURE 6: Comparison among different service levels.

r_{ej}: Membership of objective function j

z_j^+: Upper bound of objective function j

z_j^-: Lower bound of objective function j

P_{it}: Purchasing cost from supplier i over t period

R_{it}: Rejected items rate from supplier i over t period

B_{it}: Minimum order quantity of supplier i over t period

L_{it}: Late delivery items rate from supplier i over t period

U_{it}: Maximum supply ability of supplier i over t period

O_{it}: Cooperative cost between manufacturer and supplier i over t period

d_t: Marketing demand over t period

h_t: Inventory holding cost of manufacturer over t period

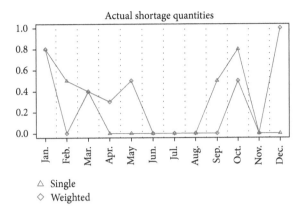

FIGURE 7: Actual shortage quantities at the service level of 0.99.

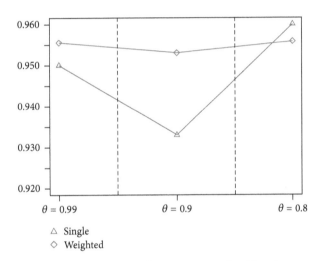

FIGURE 8: Comparison of maximum membership values.

C_t: Inventory level of manufacturer over t period

S_t: Stock shortage of manufacturer over t period

θ_t: Service level of the manufacturer over t period

M: An infinite number.

Decision Variables

x_{it}: Purchasing quantity from supplier i over t period

y_{it}: $y_{it} = 1$ if a manufacturer places orders to suppliers i over t period, 0 otherwise.

Competing Interests

The authors declare that there is no conflict of interests regarding the publication of this paper.

Acknowledgments

This research is supported by National Natural Science Foundation of China [no. 71201099], Innovation Program of Shanghai Municipal Education Commission [no. 14YZ111], Shanghai Young Eastern Scholar Programme [QD2015041], Shanghai Pu Jiang Program (no. 13PJC066), and Shanghai Youth Teacher Foundation (no. ZZshhs13021).

References

[1] G. W. Dickson, "An analysis of vendor selection systems and decision," *Journal of Purchasing*, vol. 2, no. 15, pp. 1377–1382, 1966.

[2] C. A. Weber, J. R. Current, and W. C. Benton, "Vendor selection criteria and methods," *European Journal of Operational Research*, vol. 50, no. 1, pp. 2–18, 1991.

[3] L. A. Zadeh, "Fuzzy sets," *Information and Control*, vol. 8, no. 3, pp. 338–353, 1965.

[4] L. Qian, "Market-based supplier selection with price, delivery time, and service level dependent demand," *International Journal of Production Economics*, vol. 147, pp. 697–706, 2014.

[5] A. Singh, "Supplier evaluation and demand allocation among suppliers in a supply chain," *Journal of Purchasing & Supply Management*, vol. 20, no. 3, pp. 167–176, 2014.

[6] L. Zhen, "Task assignment under uncertainty: stochastic programming and robust optimisation approaches," *International Journal of Production Research*, vol. 53, no. 5, pp. 1487–1502, 2015.

[7] M. Dong, D. Yang, and Y. Wang, "Optimal decisions in product modularity design using real option approach," *Concurrent Engineering Research and Applications*, vol. 18, no. 1, pp. 31–39, 2010.

[8] M. Kumar, P. Vrat, and R. Shankar, "A fuzzy goal programming approach for vendor selection problem in a supply chain," *Computers & Industrial Engineering*, vol. 46, no. 1, pp. 69–85, 2004.

[9] P. Kumar, R. Shankar, and S. S. Yadav, "An integrated approach of analytic hierarchy process and fuzzy linear programming for supplier selection," *International Journal of Operational Research*, vol. 3, no. 6, pp. 614–631, 2008.

[10] A. H. I. Lee, "A fuzzy supplier selection model with the consideration of benefits, opportunities, costs and risks," *Expert Systems with Applications*, vol. 36, no. 2, pp. 2879–2893, 2009.

[11] A. Kokangul and Z. Susuz, "Integrated analytical hierarch process and mathematical programming to supplier selection problem with quantity discount," *Applied Mathematical Modelling*, vol. 33, no. 3, pp. 1417–1429, 2009.

[12] F. Mafakheri, M. Breton, and A. Ghoniem, "Supplier selection-order allocation: a two-stage multiple criteria dynamic programming approach," *International Journal of Production Economics*, vol. 132, no. 1, pp. 52–57, 2011.

[13] K. Shaw, R. Shankar, S. S. Yadav, and L. S. Thakur, "Supplier selection using fuzzy AHP and fuzzy multi-objective linear programming for developing low carbon supply chain," *Expert Systems with Applications*, vol. 39, no. 9, pp. 8182–8192, 2012.

[14] D. Choudhary and R. Shankar, "A goal programming model for joint decision making of inventory lot-size, supplier selection and carrier selection," *Computers & Industrial Engineering*, vol. 71, no. 1, pp. 1–9, 2014.

[15] A. K. Kar, "A hybrid group decision support system for supplier selection using analytic hierarchy process, fuzzy set theory and neural network," *Journal of Computational Science*, vol. 6, pp. 23–33, 2015.

[16] J. Scott, W. Ho, P. K. Dey, and S. Talluri, "A decision support system for supplier selection and order allocation in stochastic, multi-stakeholder and multi-criteria environments," *International Journal of Production Economics*, vol. 166, pp. 226–237, 2015.

[17] Y. Ye, D. Yang, Z. Jiang, and L. Tong, "A knowledge- and workflow-based system for supporting order fulfillment process in the build-to-order supply chains," in *The Semantic Web—ASWC 2006: First Asian Semantic Web Conference, Beijing, China, September 3–7, 2006. Proceedings*, vol. 4185 of *Lecture Notes in Computer Science*, pp. 711–724, Springer, Berlin, Germany, 2006.

[18] R. N. Tiwari, S. Dharmar, and J. R. Rao, "Fuzzy goal programming—an additive model," *Fuzzy Sets & Systems*, vol. 24, no. 1, pp. 27–34, 1987.

[19] D. Yang and M. Dong, "A hybrid approach for modeling and solving product configuration problems," *Concurrent Engineering Research and Applications*, vol. 20, no. 1, pp. 31–42, 2012.

13

Using Hierarchical Latent Dirichlet Allocation to Construct Feature Tree for Program Comprehension

Xiaobing Sun,[1] **Xiangyue Liu,**[2] **Yucong Duan,**[3] **and Bin Li**[1]

[1]*School of Information Engineering, Yangzhou University, Yangzhou, China*
[2]*Tongda College of Nanjing University of Posts and Telecommunications, Nanjing, China*
[3]*Hainan University, Haikou, China*

Correspondence should be addressed to Bin Li; lb@yzu.edu.cn

Academic Editor: Michele Risi

Program comprehension is an important task faced by developers during software maintenance. With the increasing complexity of evolving systems, program comprehension becomes more and more difficult. In practice, programmers are accustomed to getting a general view of the features in a software system and then finding the interesting or necessary files to start the understanding process. Given a system, developers may need a general view of the system. The traditional view of a system is shown in a package-class structure which is difficult to understand, especially for large systems. In this article, we focus on understanding the system in both feature view and file structure view. This article proposes an approach to generate a feature tree based on hierarchical Latent Dirichlet Allocation (hLDA), which includes two hierarchies, the feature hierarchy and file structure hierarchy. The feature hierarchy shows the features from abstract level to detailed level, while the file structure hierarchy shows the classes from whole to part. Empirical results show that the feature tree can produce a view for the features and files, and the clustering of classes in the package in our approach is better (in terms of recall) than the other clustering approach, that is, hierarchical clustering.

1. Introduction

Understanding a software system at hand is one of the most frequently performed activities during software maintenance [1–3]. It is reported that developers working on software maintenance tasks spend up to 60% of their time for program comprehension [4–6]. Program comprehension is a process performed by a software practitioner using knowledge of both the semantics and syntax to build a mental model of its relation to the situation [7, 8]. As software evolves, its complexity usually increases as well [9]. Moreover, sometimes documents affiliated to the evolving system also become inaccessible or outdated, which makes the program comprehension activity even more difficult.

To reduce the difficulty of program comprehension, one of the effective approaches is to create a meaningful decomposition of large-scale system into smaller, more manageable subsystems, which is called software clustering [10–12]. A number of program comprehension techniques have been studied [13, 14]. The widely used clustering approaches are partitional clustering and hierarchical agglomerative clustering [15–17]. These approaches usually cluster the system based on static structural dependency in the program.

However, the results indicating the program decompositions based on the structure relationships of the software system can merely provide the structure view of these clusters. But for a program during software maintenance, the first activity faced by software developers is to locate the code that is relevant to the task (related to a functional feature) at hand [18]. Thus developers may be more interested in understanding the functional features of a system and how the source code corresponds to functional features. So some other clustering approaches are proposed based on semantic clustering, which exploits linguistic information in the source code identifiers and comments [14, 19–22]. All these clustering approaches provide either a structure view or a brief feature view for comprehension, but only a few can generate both of them.

In practice, understanding features from abstract level to detailed level and structure from whole to part can effectively help developers to understand a system in a stepwise manner. Such a whole-part way is more beneficial to developers when comprehending object oriented systems [3, 5]. For evolving software with increasing size and complexity, developers find it difficult to identify and choose the interesting packages and understand the chosen classes, their relationship, and their functionalities. Hence, a clustering representation considering both file structure and feature of the program should be constructed to ease program comprehension. With such clustering, developers have an easier, stepwise, and quicker understanding of the system.

In this article, we propose a feature tree to help understand a software system. Program comprehension is performed relying on two hierarchies of the functional features and file structure based on the feature tree. The feature tree contains the features from abstract level to detailed level and the file structure from whole to part. Hence, developers can obtain a good understanding of functional features of the whole system. The feature tree is generated based on hierarchical Latent Dirichlet Allocation (hLDA), which is a hierarchical topic model to analyze unstructured text [23, 24]. hLDA can be employed to discover a set of ideas or themes that well describe the entire text corpus in a hierarchical way. In addition, the model supports the assignment of the corresponding files to these themes, which are clusters for the software system corresponding to the functional features.

Therefore, our approach can be effectively used in a whole-part program comprehension way during software maintenance. Our approach is particularly suitable for researchers in the scientific and engineering computing area as researchers can employ our approach to understand the systems and maintain them in their own way. Researchers can easily understand these clusters for a software system. The main contributions of this article are as follows:

(1) We propose using hLDA to generate a feature tree. The tree includes feature hierarchy and file structure hierarchy. Feature hierarchy shows the features from abstract level to detailed level, while the file structure hierarchy shows the classes from whole to part.

(2) We provide a real case study to explain how the feature tree helps to understand the features and files for the JHotDraw program.

(3) We conduct empirical studies to show the effectiveness of our approach on two real-world open-source projects, JHotDraw and JDK.

The rest of the article is organized as follows: in the next section, we introduce the background of the hLDA model. Section 3 describes the details of our approach. Section 4 shows a real case study of the feature tree on JHotDraw program. We conduct empirical studies to validate the effectiveness of our approach in Section 5. The empirical results and threats to our studies are shown in Sections 6 and 7, respectively. In Section 8, related work using clustering for program comprehension is discussed. Finally, we conclude the article and outline directions for future work in Section 9.

2. Background

In this article, we use hLDA to cluster the classes in the software system into a hierarchical structure for easy program comprehension. This section discusses the background of hLDA.

Given an input corpus, which is a set of documents with each consisting of a sequence of words, hLDA is used to identify useful topics for the corpus and organize these topics into a hierarchy. In the hierarchy, more abstract topics are near its root and more concrete topics are near its leaves [23, 24]. hLDA is a model for multiple-topic documents which models dependency between topics in the documents from abstract to concrete. The model picks a topic according to its distribution and generates words according to the word distribution of the topic.

Let us consider a data set composed of a corpus of documents. Each document is a collection of words, where a word is an item in a vocabulary. Our basic assumption is that the topics in a document are generated according to a mixture model where the mixing proportions are random and document-specific. These topics are the basic mixture components in hLDA. The document-specific mixing proportions associated with these components are denoted by a vector Θ. We assume that there are K possible topics in the corpus and Θ is a K-dimensional vector. Suppose that we generate an L-level tree, where each node is associated with a topic. The process of applying hLDA is as follows:

(1) To select a path from the root to a leaf in the tree

(2) To generate a vector of topic proportions Θ with L-dimensional Dirichlet

(3) To identify the words in the document from the topics along the path from root to leaf based on the topic proportions Θ, w

Then, the nested CRP (Chinese Restaurant Process) is used to relax the assumption of a fixed tree structure [23, 24]. A document is then generated by first choosing an L-level path through the restaurants and then identifying the words from the L topics associated with the restaurants along that path. In this way, hLDA can generate a hierarchy where more abstract topics are near its root and more concrete topics are near its leaves.

3. Our Approach

Faced with the source code of a software system, developers need to use their domain knowledge to understand the features from abstract level to detailed level and the classes from whole to part. When understanding a system, developers first need to get a general understanding of the whole system and then find the interesting functions and source code. The process of our approach is shown in Figure 1. Firstly, the source code should be preprocessed for information retrieval technique; then the preprocessed corpus is processed with hLDA. Finally, we visualize the results in a feature tree view for program comprehension.

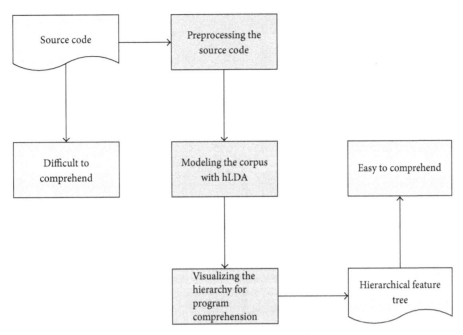

FIGURE 1: Process of our approach.

3.1. Preprocessing Source Code. We preprocess the source code of each software system by applying the typical source code preprocessing steps [25]. We firstly isolate source code identifiers and comments and then strip away syntax and programming language keywords. We deal with comments and identifiers differently due to their different programming requirements; that is, comments are natural language texts and identifiers are (composed of) single words.

The comments sometimes include authorship information which does not make sense in program comprehension. For example, words like *"author, distributed"* and other descriptions about the software itself are included in the header comments. So we first remove the header comments within the classes. Then, we follow four common operations to handle the remaining identifiers and comments as follows:

(1) *Tokenize*: we firstly tokenize each word in the source code to remove some numbers and punctuation marks

(2) *Split*: we split the identifiers based on common programming naming practices, for example, camel case (*"oneTwo"*) and underscores (*"one_two"*)

(3) *Remove stop words*: we remove common English language stop words (*"in, it, for"*) and key words (*"int, return"*) in the program to reduce the noise

(4) *Stem*: we stem the corpora to reduce the vocabulary size (e.g., *"changing"* becomes *"change"*)

After these preprocessing operations on the unstructured source code, information retrieval can be more effectively used to extract the key information from the source code. Figure 2 shows an example of the process of preprocessing the source code in the class *Applet.java* in JDK. After tokenizing, splitting, removing the stop words, and stemming

the source code, useful words are left for information retrieval application.

3.2. Modeling the Corpus with Hierarchical Latent Dirichlet Allocation. After preprocessing the source code of the software system, we apply hLDA to generate a hierarchy in which more abstract topics are near the root of the hierarchy and more concrete topics are near the leaves.

With the hLDA model, we can draw an outline about the topics, the files, and the hierarchical structure. The topics and the hierarchical structure constitute the feature hierarchy which shows the features from abstract level to detailed level. The files and the hierarchical structure constitute the file structure hierarchy, which shows the classes from whole to part.

3.3. Visualizing the Hierarchy for Program Comprehension. After modeling the corpus with hLDA, we can get a hierarchy of the topics for the software system. To get a view of the hierarchy, we display the hierarchy in a tree structure, which is called *feature tree*. The tree is generated from the results of the hLDA including two parts, one is the topic words and the other is the assigned classes. What is more, when comprehending the classes in each topic, developers may want to know the included package name. So we provide the package name when listing the relevant classes of each topic. In the *feature tree*, we can get three types of relationships: node to topic, father node to son node, and topic to file.

Node is an important part of the feature tree and it contains key information for program comprehension. The node consists of two elements, topics and relevant file names. Node in the first level generated by the hLDA model is the root of the feature tree which concludes the whole topics and files of the system. Nodes in the remaining levels are the

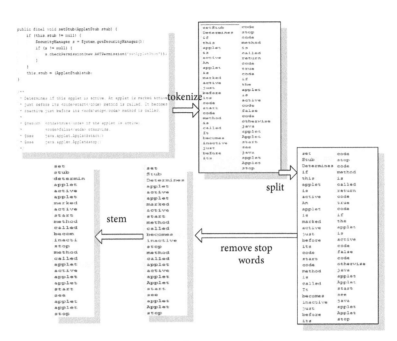

FIGURE 2: An example of preprocessing the source code.

members of the subtree indicating the subtopics of the system and the related files. Topics are composed of words extracted from the preprocessed comments and identifiers based on the topic distribution in the hLDA model. So the topics are used for understanding the source code of interest. This is the feature hierarchy showing the features from abstract level to detailed level, which can help developers get a general view of the features of the software system. With a general view of the topics, users are more interested in the files corresponding to these topics. Relevant files are assigned based on the distribution of the hLDA with the generated topics. This is the other structure hierarchy showing the classes from whole to part in the form of clusters to show the classes corresponding to the features. In addition, when listing all the files, some more information is needed such as the location of the file. So the files and their locations are also presented in the tree nodes.

The structure of *feature tree* shows the relation between nodes. Father-child is the main relationship in the feature tree. All this information can be obtained from the results of the hLDA. Father node is a generalization of his son nodes. For the topics in the nodes, father node represents more general and abstract features than son nodes. For the files, father node includes all the files of his son nodes.

A three-level *feature tree* of the JDK program is displayed in Figure 3. We can see topics in each node with corresponding package names and class names in the content.

4. Case Study

In this section, we provide a case study of applying our approach to the JHotDraw program (this subject is also used in our empirical study. More about this subject will be introduced in Section 5.2). The JHotDraw program includes 23 packages and 305 classes.

We first generate the feature tree for the JHotDraw program. Part of the tree view is shown in Figure 4. The tree has three levels and there are several words describing each node in the tree. For the root node of the tree, 305 classes are included and the topic labeling the root node is *"invoc defin tool net delete modif preserve ad clone create draw."* Due to the step of preprocessing, some words are transformed into different forms. For the verbs in the topic, we can easily find that the original form of the verbs *"invoc defin delete modif preserve ad clone create draw"* is just *"invoke define delete modify preserve add clone create draw"* and these words express the functional features of the system. The nouns in the topic are *"tool net"* which indicate the objects of the system. JHotDraw defines a skeleton for GUI-based editor with tools in a tool palette, different views, user-defined graphical figures, and support for saving, loading, and so forth. So words in the root node describe the features of the software system to some extent.

For the first son node in the second level of the root node, there are 163 classes. The node contains words like *"instal method plug point instance creat action applic event draw."* The original forms of these words are just *"install method plugin point instance create action application event draw."* The content to describe the functional features in this node is finer than these in the root node. For example, *"plugin application action event"* are words for plugin and application and some actions in the source code. As we know, a plugin program always includes *XML* language program. In the results, we can also find that packages like *"nanoxml, xml"* are in this node. Then, for the *"action"* feature, packages corresponding to it are distributed in this node like *"draw-action, samples-svg-action, app-action."* Some actions can be easily analyzed from the class names in the node such as *"SplitAction.java, CombineAction.java"* in *"samples-svg-action,"*

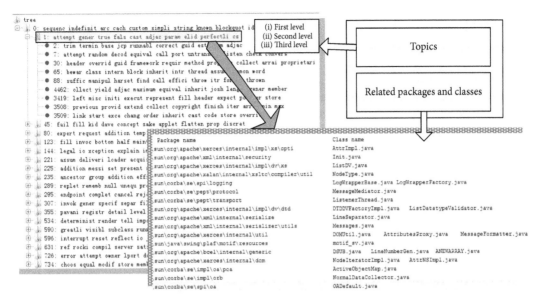

FIGURE 3: The feature tree of the JDK program.

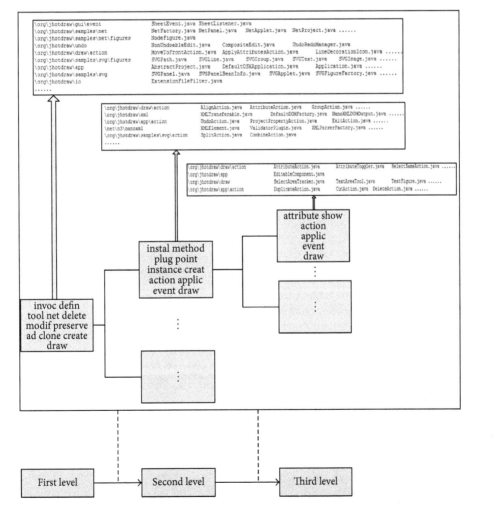

FIGURE 4: A part of the overview of the feature tree for JHotDraw.

which indicates the actions of split and combine for the SVG (Scalable Vector Graphics).

For the first node in the third level, which is the son node of the node mentioned above, 26 classes are assigned to this node. The labeled topic is *"attribute show action applic event draw."* The original form of these words is just *"attribute show action application event draw."* Most of them have appeared in their father node. The representative word is *"attribute."* In JHotDraw, *AttributeFigure* is a directly accessed component. We can further refine its behavior by overriding some methods such as *draw()* to customize the graphical representation in the diagram. The node only includes four packages. They are *draw.action, app, draw, app.action.* In *"draw.action,"* we may find *"AttributeAction.java, AttributeToggler.java, SelectSameAction.java, DefaultAttributeAction.java,"* which correspond to the word *"attribute."*

Hence, from the above study on a real software system, we can use the information on the feature tree to facilitate understanding the functional features and file structure in the system.

5. Empirical Study

In this section, we conduct empirical studies to evaluate the effectiveness of our approach. In our studies, we address the following two research questions:

(RQ1) Does the feature hierarchy really help users to comprehend the software system?

(RQ2) Are the clustering results more convenient for users to understand the software system than the hierarchical clustering approach [16]?

(RQ1) and (RQ2) are used to evaluate the feature hierarchy and file structure hierarchy, respectively. (RQ1) indicates whether the results of the feature tree really help users to comprehend the software system. In addition, we investigate (RQ2) to see whether the clustering results can make it easy for users to comprehend software systems compared with the results of hierarchical clustering [16].

5.1. Subject Systems. We address our research questions by performing studies on the source code of two well-known software systems, JHotDraw (https://sourceforge.net/projects/jhotdraw), and two packages in the Java Development Kit 1.7 (http://www.oracle.com/technetwork/java/javase/downloads/jdk7-downloads-1880260.html), that is, JDK-sun and JDK-java. JHotDraw is a medium-sized, 2D drawing framework developed in Java. The Java Development Kit (JDK) is implementation of either one of the Java SE or Java EE platforms in the form of a binary product. Specifics of these subject systems are shown in Table 1.

These projects belong to different problem domains with medium or large size. They are all real-world software systems and have been widely used as empirical study in the context of software maintenance or program comprehension [26, 27].

5.2. Design of Our Study. In our approach, there is a parameter, that is, tree level L. It represents the level of the feature tree, which affects the tree structure for program comprehension

TABLE 1: Subject systems.

Subject	File	Package	Class	KLoC
JHotDraw	144	23	305	31
JDK-sun	1631	58	1604	408
JDK-java	3221	260	2988	225

and the clustering results in the software system, respectively. In our study, we consider L to be 3 for manual program understanding since the level of three achieves relatively good results in our study.

For the hLDA computation, we used the C++ implication from David Blei's hLDA topic modeling software (https://github.com/xch91/hlda-cpp). We ran it for 10,000 sampling iterations, the first 1000 of which were used for parameter optimization.

In addition, we used hierarchical clustering algorithm for a comparative study. Anquetil and Lethbridge proposed a hierarchical clustering algorithm suite, which provides a selection of association and distance coefficients as well as update rules to cluster software systems [16]. There are three variants of *hierarchical agglomerative clustering*, which were used in many software architecture recovery techniques [28, 29]. These variants can be distinguished based on their update rules as follows: Single Linkage (SL), Complete Linkage (CL), and Average Linkage (AL). SL merges two clusters with the smallest minimum pairwise distance. CL merges two clusters with the largest minimum pairwise distance and AL merges two clusters with the average minimum pairwise distance. Previous works have shown that, in relatively large systems, CL generates the best results in terms of recovering authoritative decompositions [16, 30, 31]. We also used the same semantic data (words in comments and identifiers) to perform the *hierarchical agglomerative clustering*.

5.3. Participants. We conducted a user study to answer the two research questions. Our study involved 10 participants from school and/or industry. These participants have different levels of software development experience and familiarity with Eclipse. Half of them are from our university (graduates in our lab) with 2-3 years of development experience and the other half are from industry with 5-6 years of development experience, especially large project development experience. They were required to conduct program comprehension for a system (e.g., JDK-java, JDK-com, and JHotDraw). In addition, we gave participants the classes, and they needed to identify the relevant classes (semantic relevant) for them.

5.4. Measures. For (RQ1), we investigated whether the feature hierarchy helps the participants comprehend the functional features of whole system. To show whether the topic hierarchy generated by our approach is useful, the participants needed to assess whether the feature hierarchy enables them to understand the clusters. A five-point Likert scale with 1 (very useless) to 5 (very useful) assesses each participant's view of the topic hierarchy. According to the scores, we can see whether the structure helps program comprehension.

To answer (RQ2), we used precision and recall, two widely used metrics for information retrieval and clustering evaluation [32, 33], to evaluate the accuracy of the topics and the clustering results. Precision in clustering evaluation is the percentage of intrapairs proposed by the clustering approach, which are also intrapairs in the authoritative decomposition. Recall is the percentage of intrapairs in the authoritative decomposition, which are also intrapairs in the decomposition proposed by the clustering approach. The authoritative terms are given by each participant. We found that the participants gave different results for the given classes. So we consider that a class is included in the authoritative decomposition when 60% of participants or more selected it as relevant one. These two metrics are used to measure the accuracy of the clustering results in an a posteriori way. They are defined as follows:

$$\text{precision} = \frac{|\text{authoritative cluster} \cap \text{estimated cluster}|}{|\text{estimated cluster}|}$$

$$\text{recall} = \frac{|\text{authoritative cluster} \cap \text{estimated cluster}|}{|\text{authoritative cluster}|}. \tag{1}$$

To avoid optimizing for either precision or recall, F-measure is used, which is the harmonic mean of precision and recall. F is the harmonic mean of precision and recall. It is defined as follows.

$$F = \frac{2 \times \text{precision} \times \text{recall}}{\text{precision} + \text{recall}}. \tag{2}$$

Since agglomerative clustering can generally be adjusted to increase or decrease recall at the expense of precision by changing parameters, we selected 50 results with the best F values and then computed the average values for our comparative study.

5.5. Variables. To perform our study, the main independent variable of the empirical study is the clustering techniques (hLDA and CL) that we used to generate the clustering results for program comprehension. The dependent variables are the values of precision (P), recall (R), and F (F), which are used to measure the accuracy of these clustering techniques.

6. Empirical Results

In this section, we collect and discuss the results from our studies to answer the proposed two research questions, respectively.

6.1. (RQ1). Our approach is aimed at giving a view of the topics in a hierarchical way from a general level to a concrete level for the whole system and provides a clustering result of the packages and classes. In this subsection, we discuss whether the feature tree structure of the topics helps to understand the whole system and whether the topics are representative.

We provided the topic tree generated from hLDA of each system to the participants to investigate whether the tree can give a view of the topics in a hierarchical way from a general

TABLE 2: The score for the quality of the topics.

| Subject | Participants | | | | | | | | | | AVG |
	P1	P2	P3	P4	P5	P6	P7	P8	P9	P10	
JHotDraw	4	4	4	3	4	3	4	4	4	3	3.7
JDK-sun	3	3	4	3	3	3	4	3	4	3	3.3
JDK-java	4	4	3	3	3	3	4	3	4	3	3.4

TABLE 3: Precision and recall of two clustering approaches for each subject system.

| Subject | CL | | | hLDA | | |
	P	R	F	P	R	F
JHotDraw	53%	23%	32%	21%	40%	28%
JDK-sun	60%	25%	35%	40%	38%	39%
JDK-java	48%	14%	22%	32%	42%	36%
AVG	54%	20%	29%	31%	40%	35%

level to a concrete level for program comprehension. First, we provided the topics of each cluster to the participants. They used a five-point Likert scale to answer questions related to the quality of the topics. The results are shown in Table 2. The results show that the average score of the results is around 3.5, which indicates that the participants think that the topics are useful to understand the cluster. So, for program comprehension, some topics labeling the clusters are useful to help users to understand the program.

6.2. (RQ2). In this subsection, we compare the accuracy of the two clustering results in leaves of the feature tree generated by our approach and the hierarchical CL clustering approach.

To quantitatively compare these two clustering approaches, we compute their precision and recall results, which are shown in Table 3. From the results, we notice that the average precision of CL is 54% and the highest is 60% for JDK-sun. And all the precision values of the three subject programs are higher than the hLDA approach.

But, for the recall results, we notice that the average recall of hLDA is around 40% and the highest is 42% for JDK-java. And all the recall values of the three subject programs are higher than CL, which means that the hLDA model can predict more files for the clusters. This is because the hLDA model clusters the files or classes not only with the same words but also with the same latent topics. That is to say, our approach can cover more relevant classes in the authoritative clusters, which can effectively facilitate program comprehension.

Although clustering results with high precision are more correct, many other correct relevant results are not discovered [16]. When using clustering for program comprehension, high recall is more important [16]. So, from the results discussed above, our approach can effectively identify more relevant classes in a cluster to help program comprehension compared with the CL approach.

7. Threats to Validity

Like any empirical validation, ours has its limitations. In the following, threats to the validity of our studies are discussed.

7.1. Threats to External Validity. We only applied our technique to two subject programs. Thus we cannot guarantee that the results in our studies can be generalized to other more complex or arbitrary subjects. However, these subjects are selected from open-source projects and widely employed for experimental studies [26, 27]. In addition, we only selected part of reprehensive subjects and used them for comparison with the CL clustering approach when evaluating the effectiveness of clustering results.

In addition, we considered only Java programming language and Eclipse development environment. Further studies are required to generalize our findings in large-scale industrial projects and with developers who have sufficient domain knowledge and familiarity with the subject systems in various development environments.

7.2. Threats to Internal Validity. First, the preprocessing of the program is to transform the source code into word list, which is then used for information retrieval. This may affect the results of the hLDA model. Since we derive our topics based on the use of identifier names and comments, the quality of the topics generated by hLDA relies on the quality of the source code preprocessing.

Another threat is just like other comprehension techniques based on semantics demonstrating that the code should have a high quality in both name rules and the comments. Some programs without high quality may not get good results as in our study.

A third threat to the internal validity of our study is the difference in the capabilities of the participants. Specifically, we cannot eliminate the threat that the participants have different capabilities. This also can affect the accuracy of the results. As the authoritative decomposition changes, the results may also be different.

7.3. Threats to Construct Validity. To evaluate the effectiveness of our approach, we used precision and recall metrics. These two metrics only focused on the false-positives and false-negatives for authoritative clustering results. However, for program comprehension, other factors may be more important.

In addition, when we compare our approach with agglomerative clustering, we selected 50 results with the best F values and then computed the average values for our comparative study. However, agglomerative clustering approaches can generally be adjusted to increase or decrease recall at the expense of precision by changing parameters. Some other design approaches may obtain different results.

8. Related Work

Source code is one of the important inputs for program comprehension. There are a number of studies focusing on this area [10, 34–38]. Program clustering is one of the effective ways for program comprehension. There are two different types of program clustering, one is based on syntactic dependency analysis [39–43], while the other is based on the semantic information analysis [44, 45].

The syntactic based clustering approaches usually focus on analyzing the structural relationship among entities, for example, call dependence, control, and data dependence. Mancoridis et al. proposed an approach which generates clusters using module dependency graph for the software system [36]. Anquetil and Lethbridge proposed an approach, which generates clusters using weighted dependency graph for program clustering [46]. Sartipi and Kontogiannis presented an interactive approach to recovery cohesive subsystems within C systems. They analyze different relationships and build an attributed relational graph. Then the graph is manually or automatically partitioned using data mining techniques for program clustering [47]. For all these works, they analyzed syntactic relationships to cluster the program, and developers understand how the functional features are programmed in the source code based on this syntactic clustering. In this article, we focus on extracting the functional features in the source code and clustering the source code based on hLDA.

Semantic based clustering approaches just attempt to analyze the functional features in a system [13, 48]. The functional features in the source code are extracted from comments, identifier names, and file names [49]. For example, Kuhn et al. proposed an approach to group software artifacts based on Latent Semantic Indexing. They focused on grouping source code containing similar terms in the comments [14, 50]. Scanniello et al. presented an approach which also uses Latent Semantic Indexing to get the dissimilarity between the entities [51]. Corazza et al. introduce the concept of zones (e.g., comments and class names) in the source code to assign different importance to the information extracted from different zones [50, 52]. They use a probabilistic model to automatically give weights to these zones and apply the Expectation Maximization (EM) algorithm to derive values for these weights. In this article, our approach used hLDA to generate a feature tree structure of the topic hierarchy for program comprehension and cluster the packages and classes based on them. The feature tree includes two hierarchies for the functional features and clusters of packages and classes.

In addition, some other approaches combine the syntactic analysis and semantic analysis for program clustering [11, 53–55]. Tzerpos proposed an ACDC algorithm, which uses name and dependency of classes to cluster all the system into small clusters for comprehension [56]. Adritsos et al. presented an approach, LIMBO, which considers both structural and nonstructural attributes to decompose a system into clusters, while in this article we used only the semantic analysis for clustering. But our approach can generate topics to help users more easily understand the classes or packages in each cluster.

9. Conclusion and Future Work

In this article, we proposed an approach of generating a feature tree based on hLDA, which includes two hierarchies for functional features and file structure. The feature hierarchy shows the features from abstract level to detailed level, while the file structure hierarchy shows the classes from whole to part. We conducted empirical studies to show the effectiveness of our approach on two real-world open-source projects. The results show that the results of our approach are more effective than the hierarchical CL clustering approach. In addition, the topics labeling these clusters are useful to help developers understand them. Therefore, our approach could provide an effective way for developers to understand the system quickly and accurately.

In our study, we only conducted our studies on two Java-based programs, which cannot imply its generality for other types of systems. Future work will focus on conducting more studies on different types of systems to evaluate the generality of our approach. In addition, we find that, just like other IR approaches, the preprocessing process, the scale of the corpus, and the parameters in the model can affect the results sensitively. Further study on how to make the best use of IR approach for programs transformation is necessary.

Conflicts of Interest

The authors declare that there are no conflicts of interest regarding the publication of this paper.

Acknowledgments

This work is supported partially by National Natural Science Foundation of China under Grant no. 61402396, no. 61472344, no. 61662021, and no. 61602267, partially by the Open Funds of State Key Laboratory for Novel Software Technology of Nanjing University under Grant no. KFKT2016B21, partially by the Jiangsu Qin Lan Project, partially by the China Postdoctoral Science Foundation under Grant no. 2015M571489, and partially by the Natural Science Foundation of the Jiangsu Higher Education Institutions of China under Grant no. 15KJB520030.

References

[1] T. Fritz, G. C. Murphy, E. Murphy-Hill, J. Ou, and E. Hill, "Degree-of-knowledge: modeling a developer's knowledge of code," *ACM Transactions on Software Engineering and Methodology*, vol. 23, no. 2, article 14, 2014.

[2] Z. Soh, "Context and vision: studying two factors impacting program comprehension," in *Proceedings of the IEEE 19th International Conference on Program Comprehension (ICPC '11)*, pp. 258–261, June 2011.

[3] J.-M. Burkhardt, F. Détienne, and S. Wiedenbeck, "Object-oriented program comprehension: effect of expertise, task and phase," *Empirical Software Engineering*, vol. 7, no. 2, pp. 115–156, 2002.

[4] T. Nakagawa, Y. Kamei, H. Uwano, A. Monden, K. Matsumoto, and D. M. German, "Quantifying programmers' mental workload during program comprehension based on cerebral blood flow measurement: a controlled experiment," in *Proceedings of the 36th International Conference on Software Engineering (ICSE '14)*, pp. 448–451, June 2014.

[5] W. Maalej, R. Tiarks, T. Roehm, and R. Koschke, "On the comprehension of program comprehension," *ACM Transactions on Software Engineering and Methodology*, vol. 23, no. 4, pp. 31:1–31:37, 2014.

[6] Y. Kong, M. Zhang, and D. Ye, "A belief propagation-based method for task allocation in open and dynamic cloud environments," *Knowledge-Based Systems*, vol. 115, pp. 123–132, 2017.

[7] M. P. O'Brien, "Software comprehension: a review and research direction," Tech. Rep., Department of Computer Science & Information Systems, University of Limerick, Limerick, Ireland, 2003.

[8] T. Kosar, M. Mernik, and J. C. Carver, "Program comprehension of domain-specific and general-purpose languages: comparison using a family of experiments," *Empirical Software Engineering*, vol. 17, no. 3, pp. 276–304, 2012.

[9] K. Maruyama, T. Omori, and S. Hayashi, "A visualization tool recording historical data of program comprehension tasks," in *Proceedings of the 22nd International Conference on Program Comprehension (ICPC '14)*, pp. 207–211, June 2014.

[10] C. Y. Chong, S. P. Lee, and T. C. Ling, "Efficient software clustering technique using an adaptive and preventive dendrogram cutting approach," *Information and Software Technology*, vol. 55, no. 11, pp. 1994–2012, 2013.

[11] P. Andritsos and V. Tzerpos, "Information-theoretic software clustering," *IEEE Transactions on Software Engineering*, vol. 31, no. 2, pp. 150–165, 2005.

[12] M. Bauer and M. Trifu, "Architecture-aware adaptive clustering of OO systems," in *Proceedings of the European Conference on Software Maintainance and Reengineering (CSMR '04)*, pp. 3–14, Tampere, Finland, March 2004.

[13] G. Santos, M. T. Valente, and N. Anquetil, "Remodularization analysis using semantic clustering," in *Proceedings of the Software Evolution Week—IEEE Conference on Software Maintenance, Reengineering, and Reverse Engineering (CSMR-WCRE '14)*, pp. 224–233, Antwerp, Belgium, February 2014.

[14] A. Kuhn, S. Ducasse, and T. Gîrba, "Semantic clustering: identifying topics in source code," *Information and Software Technology*, vol. 49, no. 3, pp. 230–243, 2007.

[15] C. Li, Z. Xu, C. Qiao, and T. Luo, "Hierarchical clustering driven by cognitive features," *Science China. Information Sciences*, vol. 57, no. 1, 012109, 14 pages, 2014.

[16] N. Anquetil and T. C. Lethbridge, "Experiments with clustering as a software remodularization method," in *Proceedings of the 6th Working Conference on Reverse Engineering (WCRE '99)*, pp. 235–255, October 1999.

[17] Z. Fu, K. Ren, J. Shu, X. Sun, and F. Huang, "Enabling personalized search over encrypted outsourced data with efficiency improvement," *IEEE Transactions on Parallel and Distributed Systems*, vol. 27, no. 9, pp. 2546–2559, 2016.

[18] B. Dit, M. Revelle, M. Gethers, and D. Poshyvanyk, "Feature location in source code: a taxonomy and survey," *Journal of software: Evolution and Process*, vol. 25, no. 1, pp. 53–95, 2013.

[19] G. Santos, M. T. Valente, and N. Anquetil, "Remodularization analysis using semantic clustering," in *Proceedings of the 1st Software Evolution Week—IEEE Conference on Software Maintenance, Reengineering, and Reverse Engineering (CSMR-WCRE '14)*, pp. 224–233, Antwerp, Belgium, February 2014.

[20] B. L. Vinz and L. H. Etzkorn, "Improving program comprehension by combining code understanding with comment understanding," *Knowledge-Based Systems*, vol. 21, no. 8, pp. 813–825, 2008.

[21] Y. S. Maarek, D. M. Berry, and G. E. Kaiser, "An information retrieval approach for automatically constructing software libraries," *IEEE Transactions on Software Engineering*, vol. 17, no. 8, pp. 800–813, 1991.

[22] Z. Fu, X. Wu, C. Guan, X. Sun, and K. Ren, "Toward efficient multi-keyword fuzzy search over encrypted outsourced data with accuracy improvement," *IEEE Transactions on Information Forensics and Security*, vol. 11, no. 12, pp. 2706–2716, 2016.

[23] D. M. Blei, T. L. Griffiths, and M. I. Jordan, "The nested Chinese restaurant process and Bayesian nonparametric inference of topic hierarchies," *Journal of the ACM*, vol. 57, no. 2, article 7, 2010.

[24] D. M. Blei, T. L. Griffiths, M. I. Jordan, and J. B. Tenenbaum, "Hierarchical topic models and the nested chinese restaurant process," in *Advances in Neural Information Processing Systems 16 [Neural Information Processing Systems, NIPS 2003, December 8–13, 2003, Vancouver and Whistler, British Columbia, Canada]*, pp. 17–24, 2003.

[25] X. Sun, X. Liu, J. Hu, and J. Zhu, "Empirical studies on the NLP techniques for source code data preprocessing," in *Proceedings of the 3rd International Workshop on Evidential Assessment of Software Technologies (EAST '14)*, pp. 32–39, May 2014.

[26] U. Erdemir, U. Tekin, and F. Buzluca, "Object oriented software clustering based on community structure," in *Proceedings of the 18th Asia Pacific Software Engineering Conference (APSEC '11)*, pp. 315–321, IEEE, Ho Chi Minh, Vietnam, December 2011.

[27] A. D. Lucia, M. D. Penta, R. Oliveto, A. Panichella, and S. Panichella, "Using IR methods for labeling source code artifacts: is it worthwhile?" in *Proceedings of the IEEE 20th International Conference on Program Comprehension (ICPC '12)*, pp. 193–202, Passau, Germany, June 2012.

[28] O. Maqbool and H. Babri, "Hierarchical clustering for software architecture recovery," *IEEE Transactions on Software Engineering*, vol. 33, no. 11, pp. 759–780, 2007.

[29] O. Maqbool and H. A. Babri, "The weighted combined algorithm: a linkage algorithm for software clustering," in *Proceedings of the European Conference on Software Maintainance and Reengineering (CSMR '04)*, pp. 15–24, Tampere, Finland, March 2004.

[30] M. Shtern and V. Tzerpos, "Clustering methodologies for software engineering," *Advances in Software Engineering*, vol. 2012, Article ID 792024, 18 pages, 2012.

[31] A. Mahmoud and N. Niu, "Evaluating software clustering algorithms in the context of program comprehension," in *Proceedings of the 21st International Conference on Program Comprehension (ICPC '13)*, pp. 162–171, May 2013.

[32] G. Bavota, M. Gethers, R. Oliveto, D. Poshyvanyk, and A. De Lucia, "Improving software modularization via automated analysis of latent topics and dependencies," *ACM Transactions on Software Engineering and Methodology*, vol. 23, no. 1, Article ID 2559935, 4 pages, 2014.

[33] C. J. van Rijsbergen, *Information Retrieval*, Butterworths, London, UK, 1979.

[34] X. Liu, X. Sun, B. Li, and J. Zhu, "PFN: a novel program feature network for program comprehension," in *Proceedings of the IEEE/ACIS 13th International Conference on Computer and Information Science (ICIS '14)*, pp. 349–354, Taiyuan, China, June 2014.

[35] V. Rajlich and N. Wilde, "The role of concepts in program comprehension," in *Proceedings of the 10th International Workshop on Program Comprehension (IWPC '02)*, pp. 271–278, June 2002.

[36] S. Mancoridis, B. S. Mitchell, C. Rorres, Y. Chen, and E. R. Gansner, "Using automatic clustering to produce high-level system organizations of source code," in *Proceedings of the 6th International Workshop on Program Comprehension (IWPC '98)*, p. 45, Ischia, Italy, June 1998.

[37] D. Binkley, D. Heinz, D. J. Lawrie, and J. Overfelt, "Understanding LDA in source code analysis," in *Proceedings of the 22nd International Conference on Program Comprehension (ICPC '14)*, pp. 26–36, ACM, Hyderabad, India, June 2014.

[38] B. Gu, V. S. Sheng, K. Y. Tay, W. Romano, and S. Li, "Incremental support vector learning for ordinal regression," *IEEE Transactions on Neural Networks and Learning Systems*, vol. 26, no. 7, pp. 1403–1416, 2015.

[39] B. S. Mitchell and S. Mancoridis, "On the automatic modularization of software systems using the bunch tool," *IEEE Transactions on Software Engineering*, vol. 32, no. 3, pp. 193–208, 2006.

[40] S. Islam, J. Krinke, D. Binkley, and M. Harman, "Coherent clusters in source code," *Journal of Systems and Software*, vol. 88, no. 1, pp. 1–24, 2014.

[41] S. Mirarab, A. Hassouna, and L. Tahvildari, "Using Bayesian belief networks to predict change propagation in software systems," in *Proceedings of the 15th IEEE International Conference on Program Comprehension (ICPC '07)*, pp. 177–186, Alberta, Canada, June 2007.

[42] F. Deng and J. A. Jones, "Weighted system dependence graph," in *Proceedings of the 5th IEEE International Conference on Software Testing, Verification and Validation (ICST '12)*, pp. 380–389, Montreal, Canada, April 2012.

[43] M. Gethers, A. Aryani, and D. Poshyvanyk, "Combining conceptual and domain-based couplings to detect database and code dependencies," in *Proceedings of the IEEE 12th International Working Conference on Source Code Analysis and Manipulation (SCAM '12)*, pp. 144–153, Riva del Garda, Italy, September 2012.

[44] L. Guerrouj, "Normalizing source code vocabulary to support program comprehension and software quality," in *Proceedings of the 35th International Conference on Software Engineering (ICSE '13)*, pp. 1385–1388, IEEE, San Francisco, Calif, USA, May 2013.

[45] A. De Lucia, M. Di Penta, and R. Oliveto, "Improving source code lexicon via traceability and information retrieval," *IEEE Transactions on Software Engineering*, vol. 37, no. 2, pp. 205–227, 2011.

[46] N. Anquetil and T. C. Lethbridge, "Recovering software architecture from the names of source files," *Journal of Software Maintenance and Evolution*, vol. 11, no. 3, pp. 201–221, 1999.

[47] K. Sartipi and K. Kontogiannis, "A user-assisted approach to component clustering," *Journal of Software Maintenance and Evolution*, vol. 15, no. 4, pp. 265–295, 2003.

[48] S. Kawaguchi, P. K. Garg, M. Matsushita, and K. Inoue, "MUD-ABlue: an automatic categorization system for open source repositories," in *Proceedings of the 11th Asia-Pacific Software Engineering Conference (APSEC '04)*, pp. 184–193, Busan, Korea, December 2004.

[49] A. Kuhn, S. Ducasse, and T. Gîrba, "Enriching reverse engineering with semantic clustering," in *Proceedings of the 12th Working Conference on Reverse Engineering (WCRE '05)*, pp. 133–142, Pittsburgh, Pa, USA, November 2005.

[50] A. Corazza, S. Di Martino, V. Maggio, and G. Scanniello, "Investigating the use of lexical information for software system clustering," in *Proceedings of the 15th European Conference on Software Maintenance and Reengineering (CSMR '11)*, pp. 35–44, IEEE, Oldenburg, Germany, March 2011.

[51] G. Scanniello, M. Risi, and G. Tortora, "Architecture recovery using Latent Semantic Indexing and k-Means: an empirical evaluation," in *Proceedings of the 8th IEEE International Conference on Software Engineering and Formal Methods (SEFM '10)*, pp. 103–112, September 2010.

[52] A. Corazza, S. Di Martino, and G. Scanniello, "A probabilistic based approach towards software system clustering," in *Proceedings of the 14th European Conference on Software Maintenance and Reengineering (CSMR '10)*, pp. 88–96, Madrid, Spain, March 2010.

[53] G. Scanniello, A. D'Amico, C. D'Amico, and T. D'Amico, "Using the Kleinberg algorithm and vector space model for software system clustering," in *Proceedings of the 18th IEEE International Conference on Program Comprehension (ICPC '10)*, pp. 180–189, Minho, Portugal, July 2010.

[54] G. Scanniello and A. Marcus, "Clustering support for static concept location in source code," in *Proceedings of the IEEE 19th International Conference on Program Comprehension (ICPC '11)*, pp. 1–10, Kingston, Canada, June 2011.

[55] J. I. Maletic and A. Marcus, "Supporting program comprehension using semantic and structural information," in *Proceedings of the 23rd International Conference ojn Software Engineering (ICSE '01)*, pp. 103–112, Toronto, Canada, May 2001.

[56] V. Tzerpos and R. Holt, "ACCD: an algorithm for comprehension-driven clustering," in *Proceedings of the 7th Working Conference on Reverse Engineering (WCRE '00)*, pp. 258–267, Brisbane, Australia, November 2000.

14

Improving I/O Efficiency in Hadoop-Based Massive Data Analysis Programs

Kyong-Ha Lee ⓘ,[1] Woo Lam Kang,[2] and Young-Kyoon Suh ⓘ[3]

[1]*Research Data Hub Center, Korea Institute of Science and Technology Information, Daejeon, Republic of Korea*
[2]*School of Computing, KAIST, Daejeon, Republic of Korea*
[3]*School of Computer Science and Engineering, Kyungpook National University, Daegu, Republic of Korea*

Correspondence should be addressed to Young-Kyoon Suh; yksuh@knu.ac.kr

Academic Editor: Basilio B. Fraguela

Apache Hadoop has been a popular parallel processing tool in the era of big data. While practitioners have rewritten many conventional analysis algorithms to make them customized to Hadoop, the issue of inefficient I/O in Hadoop-based programs has been repeatedly reported in the literature. In this article, we address the problem of the I/O inefficiency in Hadoop-based massive data analysis by introducing our efficient modification of Hadoop. We first incorporate a columnar data layout into the conventional Hadoop framework, without any modification of the Hadoop internals. We also provide Hadoop with indexing capability to save a huge amount of I/O while processing not only selection predicates but also star-join queries that are often used in many analysis tasks.

1. Introduction

Data volumes in scientific areas are unprecedently sky-rocketing, and new sources and types of information are proliferating. We witness that the rate at which the data is being generated is faster, and the amount of the generated data is enormously larger than ever before. Apache Hadoop [1], an open-sourced implementation of Google's MapReduce [2], is a prominent data processing tool that processes a massive volume of data with a shared-nothing architecture in a parallel and efficient manner. Therefore, it has been widely recognized as an efficient tool for large-scale data analysis in the era of big data. Many algorithms for data analysis and mining have been rewritten for being run on Hadoop. That said, MapReduce has raised a nontrivial concern of exhibiting a clear tradeoff between I/O efficiency and fault tolerance [3]. Pavlo addressed that Hadoop MapReduce was 2 to 50 times slower than conventional parallel database systems except in the case of data loading [4]. Anderson and Tucek also noted that Hadoop was remarkably scalable but achieved very low efficiency per node, less than 5 MB per second processing rate [5]. The community thus has exerted to obtain efficient I/O, especially by building new frameworks over Hadoop [6–10].

In the same line, this manuscript addresses the issue of I/O inefficiency in MapReduce-based programs. Specifically, we focus on improving the I/O efficiency in massive data analysis when using Apache Hadoop. It is of critical importance to eliminate I/O bottleneck in Hadoop-based programs, considering a wide use of Hadoop in many scientific areas.

In this regard, we propose *ColBit*, a combination of bitmap indexes and an efficient columnar data layout for data blocks stored on the Hadoop distributed file system, *aka*, HDFS. *ColBit* dramatically improves the performance of Hadoop-based programs by reducing a huge amount of I/O while processing data analysis tasks. It is achieved by both (i) skipping unnecessary data reads during analysis and (ii) reducing the size of overall intermediate data size through the substitution of most of intermediate results with compressed bitvectors. At loading time, *ColBit* automatically transforms data block replicas into their corresponding columnar layouts. Therefore, users do not need to know details about internal data layouts. Both the layout transformation and the index-building tasks are performed at the loading time so that no overhead is imposed while processing data analysis tasks. In addition, a modification of the Hadoop internals is not necessary in our approach. Moreover, bitmap indexes facilitate the processing of not only selection predicates but also star-join queries, which are widely used in data warehouses, on Hadoop. Also, the bitmap indexes help save a large amount of I/O with compressed bitvectors. Finally, our join technique equipped with the bitmap indexes allows us to use only bitvectors for joining relations. The rest of this article is organized as follows. The following section discusses a rich body of existing literature related to our work. In turn, we propose a novel idea of columnar layout exploiting bitmap indexes. Next, we elaborate on query processing using the proposed bitmap indexes (ColBit), which are then evaluated by a microbenchmark test. Finally, Section 6 concludes our discussion by summarizing our contributions.

2. Related Work

Hadoop MapReduce is an open-sourced framework that supports MapReduce programming model introduced by Google [2]. The main idea of this model is to hide details of parallel execution so as to allow users to focus only on their data processing tasks. The MapReduce model consists of two primitive functions: *Map()* and *Reduce()*. The input for a single MapReduce job is a list of (*key1, value1*) pairs, *Map()* function is applied to each pair, and, then intermediate key-value pairs are computed as results. The intermediate key-value pairs are then grouped together on the key-equality basis, i.e., (*key2, list_of_value2*). For each *key2*, *Reduce()* function works on the list of all values, then produces zero or more aggregated results. Users can define *Map()* and *Reduce()* functions. Each processing job in Hadoop is broken down to as many Map tasks as input data blocks and one or more Reduce tasks. Hadoop MapReduce also utilizes HDFS as an underlying storage layer [11]. HDFS is a block-structured file system that supports fault tolerance by data partitioning and block replication, managed by a single or two master nodes.

Some approaches for improving the I/O performance in MapReduce-based programs have been proposed. Readers are referred to a recent survey for MapReduce and its improvements [3]. *Llama* has a columnar layout called *CFile* to help the join processing [12]. The idea is that input data are partitioned and sorted based on the selected column and stored column-wise on HDFS. However, since HDFS randomly determines the block placement at runtime, associated column values in a single row may not be located together in a node. Record Columnar File (*RCFile*) [13] developed by Facebook and used in Apache Hive and Pig projects rather chooses another approach similar to the PAX layout [4]. A single *RCFile* consists of a set of row groups, acquired by horizontally partitioning a relation, and then, values are enumerated and stored column-wise in each row group. A weak point of *RCFile* is that data placement in HDFS is simply determined by the master node at runtime. Therefore, all related fields in the same record cannot

guarantee to be saved in the same node if each column is saved in a separate file in HDFS. *CoHadoop* [14] was also devised to locate associated files together in a node. To achieve this, *CoHadoop* extends HDFS with a file-level property, and files marked with the same locator are placed on the same set of slave nodes. Floratou et al. also propose a binary column-oriented storage format that stores each column in a spate file [10]. Both Floratou's work and RCFile exploit a column-wise data compression in a row group. Hadoop itself also provides data compression for mapped outputs to raise I/O efficiency while checkpointing intermediate results [1].

Hive [6] is an open-source project, which aims at providing a data warehouse solution on the Hadoop framework. It supports ad hoc queries with an SQL-like query language. Hive evaluates its SQL-like query by compiling the query into a directed acyclic graph that is composed of multiple MapReduce jobs. Hive also maintains a system catalog that provides schema information and data statistics, similar to other relational database systems. Hive currently adapts RCFile [13] and Apache ORC format, which is an improved version of RCFile that features block groups, as its mandatory storage types. HBase [7] is an open-source Java implementation of Google's Bigtable [8]. HBase is a wide-column store, which maps two arbitrary string values (row key and column key) and timestamp into an associated arbitrary byte array, working on HDFS. It features data compression, the use of bloom filter for checking the existence of data, and a log-structured storage. HBase is not a relational database, rather known to be a sparse, distributed multisorted map which works better for treating sparse data such as web addresses.

3. Columnar Layout Equipped with Bitmap Indexes

3.1. Columnar Storage Layout for HDFS. In the original HDFS, a logical file is physically partitioned into equal-sized blocks, and then, values in the logical file are enumerated row-wise in each physical block on local file systems. While this row-wise data layout provides fast data loading, it involves two major problems in the task of data analysis [10, 15]. First, a row-wise data layout requires unnecessary columns to be read even when only a few columns in a relation are accessed during query processing. Second, MapReduce itself leads to many I/Os as it simply delivers unnecessary columns to the next stages, i.e., reduce tasks and the next MapReduce job, checkpointing every tuple with unnecessary column values into disks or HDFS at each stage.

Inspired by the columnar storage model in read-optimized database systems [16] and bitmap index techniques [17], we devise our data layout equipped with bitmap indexes for HDFS. When relations are loaded, our system first partitions each relation into multiple groups such that the size of the base column values in each group is the same as the HDFS block size. In other words, the size of each data block in each group does not exceed the physical block size, i.e., basically 64 MB. This makes other columns have roughly the same block size. We then partition each group column-

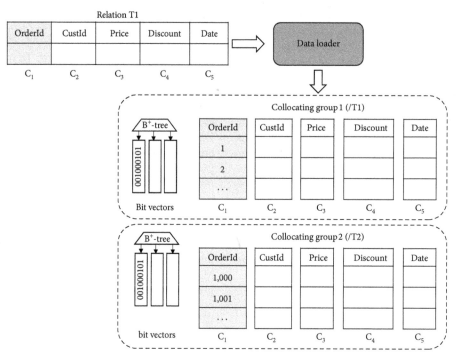

FIGURE 1: Data layout transformation.

wise and store each column in a separate binary file. All the columns in each group are stored as binary files, which can be optionally compressed in ZLIB [18], in a subdirectory associated with the group. Figure 1 illustrates how a single relation is partitioned and stored column-wise on HDFS in our approach.

In the figure, Relation T1 is loaded on our system and then each column, i.e., $C_1 \sim C_5$ in T1, and is basically stored as a single data block on HDFS. As such, to process an analytic query that treats only a few columns, *ColBit* does not need to read unnecessary columns.

Moreover, we allow users to group multiple columns into a single block to gain more I/O efficiency for query processing.

Suppose that a given analytic query Q1 requires projection on T1 so that a few columns, e.g., C1, C2, and C3, and a join key column is C5. Then, our system allows users to build only two blocks for the four column values: the three column values, i.e., C1, C2, and C3, are stored in a single block row-wise and C5 column values are stored in another block. Consequently, a MapReduce job reads a single block to get those column values for selection at once. This enables us to skip late materialization for showing row-wise results from column-wise storages [10, 15].

A problem in our approach is that the column values that constitute a single row may not be physically located together in a single node. This causes many I/Os as it is necessary to access them through a network during query processing. The reason is that Hadoop's original block placement policy does not guarantee the colocation of related blocks since it determines the block placement at runtime with no semantics about related blocks. *RCFile* [11] follows the PAX layout [14] to avoid this problem. In RCFile,

a relation is first partitioned into a set of row groups, and each HDFS block is filled with these row groups, where the values are stored column-wise in each. Since all the related columns reside in a row group, it avoids the colocation problem while providing a columnar layout. However, it still suffers from unnecessary data reads since all columns are located in a single block. We instead solve this problem by providing a new block placement policy, which is allowed in HDFS since Hadoop release 0.21.0 [2]. With the new block placement policy, blocks are located together with other blocks in the same group in a physical node.

3.2. Bitmap Index for HDFS. While transforming a data layout, users are also allowed to build indexes on selected columns for each group. *ColBit* provides a bitmap index, which is considered to be better than traditional B+-tree indexes for analytical workloads [17]. A bitmap index is a collection of bitvectors that consists of only 0's and 1's. The bitvectors in a bitmap index correspond to distinct values in a certain value domain. The 1's in a single bitvector identify tuples in a relation that is represented by the bitvector. Several encoding schemes for bitmap indexes can be used to determine how to map 1's positions into distinct values in a value domain. For example, equality encoding scheme maps each 1's position into the position of a tuple that contains a certain column value which is represented by a bitvector. Shortly, the number of bitvectors in a bitmap index is the same as the cardinality of a column the index is built on. On the other hand, in range and interval encoding scheme, a single bitvector represents not only a single distinct values but also multiple column values. Readers are referred to Chan's work [19, 20] for understanding various encoding schemes used for building bitmap indexes. In our system, users are allowed to choose their encoding schemes for better support of various query types. For example, users are allowed to choose range encoding scheme rather than equality encoding scheme for efficiently processing range selection queries. Currently, *ColBit* provides three major encoding schemes including equality, range, and interval encoding.

To further improve the I/O efficiency, *ColBit* compresses all the bitvectors by using *run-length encoding* scheme, where a "run" represents a consecutive sequence of the same bits, i.e., either 0's or 1's. We also exploit WAH (word-aligned hybrid) compression scheme [17] that groups bits into compressed words and uncompressed words. The major profit is that bitwise operations are executed very efficiently benefiting from that bitwise operations are actually performed on word units in a computer system. Furthermore, *ColBit* is also devised to facilitate query processing by performing bitwise operations on compressed bitvectors without decompression.

Figure 2 presents how a bitvector of 8,000 bits is compressed into four 32-bit words in a system. The first bit of each word indicates whether the word is compressed. If the first bit is 1, the word is compressed with a sequence of bit values that the second bit called fill bit represents. For example, in the figure, the second word is compressed to represent $256 * 31$ 0's. The fourth word keeps the rest bits, which stores the last few bits that cannot be a single word by themselves.

To fetch the position of tuples fast from a bitvector that represents a certain distinct value, we build a virtual cursor that can run on the compressed bitvectors to compute the next 1's positions with no decompression. This virtual cursor consists of three values: (1) the position of the word W that a virtual cursor C is currently located at, (2) the position of the bit within W that C is located at, and (3) the position of bit within the rest word if C is located at the word.

Example 1. Suppose that a virtual cursor C currently indicates the last bit in the first word of a bit vector at the bottom of Figure 2, then the current cursor indicates the 31st tuple in a certain relation. If we find the position of the next 1 to fetch a tuple that contains the value that the bitvector represents, it begins from the first bit in the second word compressed. The word is filled with 0's since fill bit in the word indicates 0. We thus simply skip counting the position of the next 1 bit by bit simply moving cursor C by *run_length* of 0's without decompression. Thus, the next tuple that we must fetch will be 7,998($31 + 256 * 31 + 31$)th tuple.

We also exploit B+-tree index [21] to efficiently get relevant bitvectors for given certain values for selection queries. Note that compressed bitvectors are stored as a single file for each block group and also located together with their corresponding data blocks in the block group for I/O efficiency.

4. Query Processing with *ColBit*

In our system, MapReduce jobs are developed to widely utilize *ColBit* for processing analytical queries over a massive volume of data for better improving I/O efficiency. It is

noteworthy that our approach is not restricted to processing only relational data but also processing other data models including graphs such as RDF dataset which also requires selection and join queries. Since MapReduce programming model does not have any dependency on data model and schema, it is widely accepted in the literature that the MapReduce programming model can deal with irregular or unstructured data more easily than they do with DBMS [3].

Figure 3 illustrates the execution plans for two popular queries in relational data analysis: *selection* and *star-join queries*.

In the MapReduce model, selection predicates are usually performed by mappers, and reducers group mapped outputs using a table name and column name pair. *ColBit* facilitates selection query processing using both columnar data layout and bitmap indexes, as shown in Figure 3(a). To achieve this, we extend the original input format class of the Hadoop framework. Our input format class first selects bitmap indexes built on selected columns and then, reads only the columnar files associated with the selected columns. While reading the values from the column files, our input format class outputs only values in the rows indicated by bit positions whose values are set to 1. As unnecessary column values are not read, we save many I/Os during query processing. Note that we follow the late materialization policy [15] so that tuple reconstruction is delayed to the reduce stage.

As MapReduce is initially designed to process a single large input, join processing on Hadoop has been challenging. Blanas et al. compared various join techniques devised for running on Hadoop MapReduce [22]. *Repartition join* is the most general join technique for Hadoop MapReduce [4, 22]. In a repartition join, each mapper appends a tag as a key value to each row so as to identify which relation the rows come from. Rows with the same key value are then transferred to a reducer during a shuffling phase. Finally, each reducer joins the rows on a key-equality basis. However, a repartition join does not support star-join queries well. The rationale behind this assertion is that a star-join query usually is executed by multiple binary joins on a fact table and multiple dimension tables. Therefore, multiple MapReduce jobs are usually required to perform multiple binary joins on Hadoop [4, 22]. Moreover, many I/Os are consumed just for data transmission to the next stages, i.e., reduce tasks or the next MapReduce jobs, while process join operations since the philosophy of MapReduce is to sacrifice I/O efficiency for guaranteeing fault tolerance by utilizing frequent checkpointing and block-level data replication.

With *ColBit*, our initial idea is to save many I/Os by delivering compressed data structures, rather than data themselves, to the next stage. We further developed the idea to holistically improve star-join query processing on Hadoop. Star-join queries usually restrict a set of tuples from the fact table using selection predicates on one or more dimension tables and then perform some aggregations on the restricted fact table, often grouping tuples by the attributes of other dimension tables. As a result, join operations should be performed between the fact table and dimension tables for each selection predicate and for each

(a) An original bitvector with 8,000 bits

0001000000001000000000000000011   00000000000 . . . 00000000000000   00000000000000000000000000000001   00

| 31 bits | 256 × 31 bits | 31 bits | 2 bits |

(b) Grouping as a unit of 31 bits and merging identical groups

| 000010...010...011 | 100... 0100000000 | 000...001 | 000...000 |

31 literal bits   Run-length is 256   Remaining word

Uncompressed word   Compressed word   Uncompressed word

(c) Encoding each group as 1 word (4 byte on a 32-bit machine)

FIGURE 2: Example of bitvector compression.

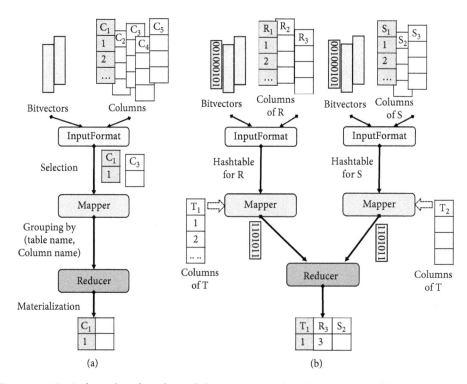

FIGURE 3: MapReduce plans for relational data processing. (a) Selection query. (b) Star-join query.

group-by-aggregation. A sample query in Example 2 is to find the total revenue of customers in Asia who purchased a product supplied by Asian suppliers between the years 1992 and 1998, and the total revenue must be grouped by each nation and transaction year.

Example 2. A sample star-join query from Star Schema Benchmark [23].

> SELECT c. nation, s. nation, d. year, sum (lo.revenue) as revenue
>
> FROM customer AS c, lineorder As lo, supplier AS s, dwdate AS d
>
> WHERE lo.custkey = c.custkey

> AND lo.suppkey = s.suppkey
>
> AND lo.lo.orderdate = d. datekey
>
> AND c.region = "ASIA"
>
> AND s.region = "ASIA"
>
> AND d. year ≥1992 and d. year ≤1998
>
> GROUP BY c. nation, s. nation, d. year
>
> ORDER BY d. year asc, revenue desc;

We adapted *invisible join* technique, which was initially devised for column-oriented databases, to reduce the volume of data accessed out of order from dimension tables [15]. Unlike traditional join techniques, invisible join is a variant of late materialized join that focuses on minimizing the values required to be extracted out of order. Therefore, it rewrites join operations on fact table columns so that joins can be performed at the time when other selection predicates are evaluated to the fact table. The selection predicates are evaluated by using other data structures such as hash table lookups. We tailored the invisible join technique to fit the MapReduce model with *ColBit*'s bitmap index. Figure 3(b) illustrates our join technique implemented with two MapReduce jobs on Hadoop.

In the first MapReduce job, we extend the InputFormat class to apply each selection predicate to dimension tables for selecting key values that satisfy the predicate from the dimension tables. The InputFormat class then returns a Java HashMap object that is used for checking which key values satisfy the predicate. At the map stage, each mapper uses the hash maps for finding tuples of the fact table that satisfy the selection predicate. This is performed by looking up the hash table with values of the foreign key column in the fact table. It then creates a bitvector in which the positions of 1's represent tuples in the foreign key column that satisfy the selection predicate. Bitvectors from all mappers are then transferred and grouped by row groups and finally merged into a single bitvector by a bitwise-AND operator at the reduce stage. A merged bitvector represents the positions of all tuples that satisfy all predicates in the fact table. Note that when reading fact table columns at the map stage, mappers directly read only relevant columns from columnar files stored on HDFS. In the second MapReduce job, we use the merged bitvector for the actual joining process. Each mapper reads fact table columns and extracts foreign key values in the rows, where the corresponding bits are set to 1 in the bitvector. The foreign key values are then used to extract column values from the dimension tables. In the second MapReduce join, grouping and aggregations are applied to the selected and joined results that came from the first MapReduce job. Based on the observation that a MapReduce job simply works like a group-by-aggregation query in database systems, it is reasonable that grouping and aggregating are assigned to a separated MapReduce job. Note that the second MapReduce job is omitted in Figure 3 owing to a space limitation.

The major contributions of our approach are summarized in the following: first, as intermediate results are delivered as compressed bitvectors, we can save a huge amount of I/O. Second, by applying bitwise operations on compressed bitvectors, we can easily compute multiple selection predicates. Finally, when it comes to handling a star-join query, no more than two MapReduce jobs are sufficient in our approach while much more MapReduce jobs are needed in other join techniques. Note (or Recall) that a single MapReduce job implements each join operation.

5. Experimental Study

We performed our microbenchmark test on a 9-node cluster, where each node is equipped with an Intel i7-6700 3.4 GHz processor, 16 GB of memory, and a 7200 RPM SATA3 HDD, running on CentOS 7.5. All nodes are connected through a gigabit switching hub. We used a subset of

TABLE 1: Statistics of the selected dataset from TPC-H [24].

Table name	Data size	The # of rows in a table
Customer	S * 24 MB	S * 150,000
Orders	S * 171 MB	S * 1,500,000
Lineitem	S * 759 MB	S * 6,001,215

S: scale factor.

the TPC-H benchmark dataset [24] with three queries (Q1 and Q6 for selection queries, and Q3 for a star-join query), as shown in Table 1. We compared our approach with the original HDFS data layout, RCFile [13], and ORC [25]. Moreover, we compared our approach with an improvement for Hadoop, i.e., Apache Hive version 2.3.3., which currently accepts RCFile and ORC as its storage types [25].

All programs were implemented using JDK 8 and Hadoop release 2.7. Figure 4 shows the elapsed time for loading TPC-H datasets on. In all cases, all of the data layout schemes scaled linearly with an increase in the volume of input data. Among them, Hadoop's row-wise data layout (sequential file) showed the best loading time. This was because it does not require any layout transformation. All the column-wise data layouts exhibited relatively long loading time. ORC shows the worst loading time followed by RCFile. Among the column-wise data layouts, *ColBit* exhibited the best performance regardless of bitvector encoding schemes applied to bitmap indexes. Specifically, *ColBit* with bitmap indexes paid slightly more time for an additional bitmap index buildup. However, fast query processing time could compensate for the marginal loss of loading time.

Figure 5 shows the sizes of data reads at the map stage for TPC-H Q1 and Q6. *ColBit* substantially reduced the size of data reads using mappers. Specifically, *ColBit* with bitmap indexes showed the smallest data reads as it further skipped many unnecessary values during the query processing. RCFile and ORC recorded the second and third best performance at the size data read. The row-wise layout labeled "Original" recorded the worst performance since all of the data should be understandably read for batch processing with Hadoop.

To see how much I/O affected the overall performance, we measured elapsed time for TPC-H queries. These queries were selected with care for fair comparison. Note that Apache Hive can exploit two columnar layouts for query processing: RCFile and ORC. Accordingly, we configured Apache Hive with the two columnar layouts and measured the performance of each of the layouts. Also, note that MapReduce jobs could use the columnar layout without any help of Apache Hive. So, we examined which columnar layout could influence the performance of MapReduce jobs as well.

Figure 6 presents the execution time for two selection queries. Again, *ColBit* outperformed other approaches by up to two orders of magnitude as it significantly reduced I/O from the data reading. It is noteworthy that neither I/O efficiency nor query processing time was improved by RCFile. The reason for this was that with PAX-similar layout, unnecessary columns in a row group were still read in RCFile

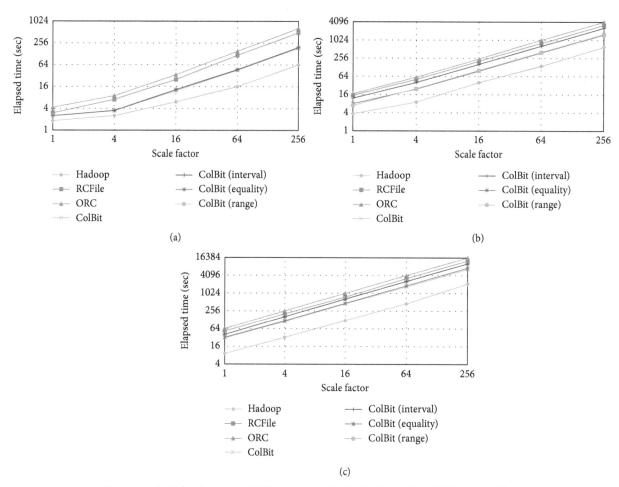

(a)

(b)

(c)

FIGURE 4: Data loading time. (a) Customer table. (b) Orders table. (c) Lineitem table.

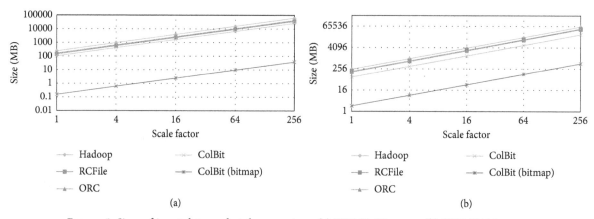

(a)

(b)

FIGURE 5: Sizes of input data read at the map stage. (a) TPC-H Q1 query. (b) TPC-H Q6 query.

during query processing as noted earlier in Section 2. Apache Hive that utilized RCFile and ORC as a storage format also exhibited better performance than that of original Hadoop MapReduce jobs whose inputs were either RCFile or ORC. This was because an up-to-date version of Apache Hive bettered the performance of selection query processing by (i) removing unnecessary Map phases and (ii) adopting vectorized query execution model [25].

Finally, Figure 7 presents the performance of our star-join query analysis based on MapReduce. As *ColBit* reduces many data reads with bitvectors and a columnar data layout, we witnessed a significant performance gain in the query execution time. It is also noteworthy that for the star-join query, Apache Hive did not show better performance even when compared to original Hadoop MapReduce jobs that utilizes invisible joining whose inputs are either RCFile or

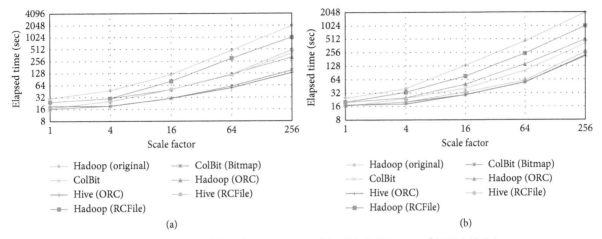

FIGURE 6: Execution time of the selection queries. (a) TPC-H Q1 query. (b) TPC-H Q6 query.

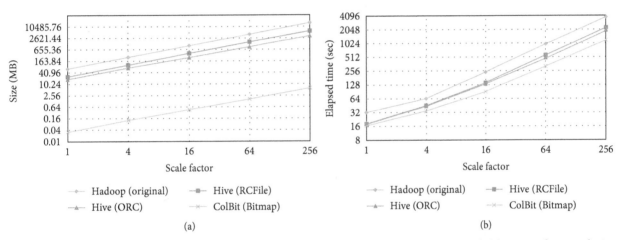

FIGURE 7: Correlation between query execution time and the size of the intermediate results (TPC-H Q3). (a) Intermediate result size. (b) Execution time.

ORC. The reason was that Apache Hive's query planner builds a multiple MapReduce for a given user-written HiveQL statement, as Hive's query planner builds a single MapReduce job for each binary join operator. But our solution could finish the star-join query only with two MapReduce jobs involving this performance gap.

6. Conclusion

We address the problem of I/O inefficiency in Hadoop-based data analysis with a columnar data layout and compressed bitmap indexes in this article. Experimental results exhibit that our approach outperforms both the Hadoop-based programs and Apache Hive that utilize RCFile and ORC, recent columnar data layouts for Hadoop. Furthermore, our techniques do not require any modification of Hadoop internals.

Therefore, any Hadoop version can be incorporated with our techniques with no effort. As future work, given a set of queries, we intend to find an efficient method to choose index types and to group columns into a few column groups

so as to automatically maximize the I/O efficiency and minimize the chance of tuple reconstructions.

Conflicts of Interest

The authors declare that they have no conflicts of interest.

Acknowledgments

This work was funded by the Korea Institute of Science and Technology Information, Korea (grant number K-18-L11-C03 and K-18-L15-C02-S18). This work was also supported by Basic Science Research Program through the National Research Foundation of Korea (NRF) funded by the Ministry of Education (NRF-2018R1A6A1A03025109).

References

[1] Apache Hadoop, "Apache Hadoop project," December 2010, http://hadoop.apache.org.

[2] J. Dean and S. Ghemawat, "MapReduce: simplified data processing on large clusters," *Communications of the ACM*, vol. 51, no. 1, pp. 107–113, 2008.

[3] K. Lee, Y.-J. Lee, H. Choi, Y. D. Chung, and B. Moon, "Parallel data processing with MapReduce: a survey," *ACM SIGMOD Record*, vol. 40, no. 4, pp. 11–20, 2012.

[4] A. Pavlo, "A comparison of approaches to large-scale data analysis," in *Proceedings of SIGMOD Conference*, pp. 165–178, Providence, RI, USA, June 2009.

[5] E. Anderson and J. Tucek, "Efficiency matters!," *ACM SIGOPS Operating Systems Review*, vol. 44, no. 1, pp. 40–45, 2010.

[6] A. Thusoo, J. S. Sarma, N. Jain et al., "Hive: a warehousing solution over a map-reduce framework," *Proceedings of VLDB Endowment*, vol. 2, no. 2, pp. 1626–1629, 2009.

[7] L. George, *HBase: the Definitive Guide: Random Access to your Planet-Size Data*, O'Reilly Media Inc., Sebastopol, CA, USA, 2011.

[8] F. Chang, J. Dean, S. Ghemawat et al., "Bigtable: a distributed storage system for structured data," *ACM Transactions on Computer Systems (TOCS)*, vol. 26, no. 2, pp. 1–26, 2008.

[9] M. Zaharia, M. J. Franklin, A. Ghodsi et al., "Apache Spark: a unified engine for big data processing," *Communications of ACM (CACM)*, vol. 59, no. 11, pp. 56–65, 2016.

[10] A. Floratou, U. F. Minhas, and F. Özcan, "SQL-on-Hadoop: full circle back to shared-nothing database architectures," *Proceedings of VLDB Endowment*, vol. 7, no. 12, pp. 1295–1306, 2014.

[11] K. Shvachko, "The Hadoop distributed file system," in *Proceedings of IEEE Symposium on Mass Storage Systems and Technologies (MSST)*, pp. 1–10, Lake Tahoe, NV, USA, May 2010.

[12] Y. Lin, D. Agrawal, C. Chen, B. C. Ooi, and S. Wu, "Llama: leveraging columnar storage for scalable join processing," in *Proceedings of ACM SIGMOD Conference*, pp. 961–972, Athens, Greece, June 2011.

[13] Y. He, R. Lee, Y. Huai et al., "RCFile: a fast and space efficient data placement structure in mapreduce-based warehouse systems," in *Proceedings of 27th IEEE ICDE Conference*, pp. 1199–1208, Hannover, Germany, April 2011.

[14] M. Y. Eltabakh, Y. Tian, F. Özcan, R. Gemulla, A. Krettek, and J. McPherson, "CoHadoop: flexible data placement and its exploitation in Hadoop," *Proceedings of the VLDB Endowment*, vol. 4, no. 9, pp. 575–585, 2011.

[15] D. J. Abadi, S. R. Madden, and N. Hachem, "Column-stores vs. row-stores: how different are they really?," in *Proceedings of ACM SIGMOD International Conference on Management of Data-SIGMOD'08*, pp. 967–980, Vancouver, BC, Canada, May 2008.

[16] S. Harizopoulos, V. Liang, D. J. Abadi, and S. Madden, "Performance tradeoffs in read- optimized databases," in *Proceedings of VLDB Conference*, pp. 487–498, Seoul, Korea, September 2006.

[17] K. Wu, E. J. Otoo, and A. Shoshani, "Optimizing bitmap indices with efficient compression," *ACM Transactions on Database Systems*, vol. 31, no. 1, pp. 1–39, 2006.

[18] P. Deutsch and J.-L. Gailly, "ZLIB compressed data format specification version 3.3," No. RFC 1950, Internet Engineering Task Force, Fremont, CA, USA, 1996.

[19] C. Y. Chan and Y. E. Ioannidis, "An efficient bitmap encoding scheme for selection queries," in *Proceedings of the 1999 ACM SIGMOD International Conference on Management of Data-SIGMOD'99*, pp. 215–226, Philadelphia, PA, USA, June 1999.

[20] C. Y. Chan and Y. E. Ioannidis, "Bitmap index design and evaluation," *ACM SIGMOD Record*, vol. 27, no. 2, pp. 355–366, 1998.

[21] D. Comer, "Ubiquitous B-tree," *ACM Computing Surveys*, vol. 11, no. 2, pp. 121–137, 1979.

[22] S. Blanas, J. M. Patel, V. Ercegovac, J. Rao, E. J. Shekita, and Y. Tian, "A comparison of join algorithms for log processing in MapReduce," in *Proceedings of ACM SIGMOD Conference*, pp. 975–986, Indianapolis, IN, USA, June 2010.

[23] P. O'Neil, E. O'Neil, X. Chen, and S. Revilak, "The star schema benchmark and augmented fact table indexing," in *Technology Conference on Performance Evaluation and Benchmarking*, Springer, Berlin, Germany, 2009.

[24] Transaction Processing Performance Council, "TPC-H benchmark specification," April 2008, http://www.tpc.org/hspec.html.

[25] Y. Huai, X. Zhang, A. Chauhan et al., "Major technical advancements in Apache Hive," in *Proceedings of ACM SIGMOD Conference*, pp. 1235–1246, Snowbird, UT, USA, June 2014.

15

Examining Student Performance and Attitudes on Distributed Pair Programming

Maya Satratzemi ⓘ,[1] Stelios Xinogalos ⓘ,[1] Despina Tsompanoudi ⓘ,[1] and Leonidas Karamitopoulos ⓘ[2]

[1]Department of Applied Informatics, School of Information Sciences, University of Macedonia, Thessaloniki 54636, Greece
[2]Department of Information Technology, Alexander TEI of Thessaloniki, 57400 Sindos, Greece

Correspondence should be addressed to Maya Satratzemi; maya@uom.edu.gr

Academic Editor: Emiliano Tramontana

Pair programming (PP) has become popular in the research and software industry as well as being studied for a number of years in computer science courses with positive findings on student performance and attitudes. Advantages of PP reported in the literature are satisfaction, design quality, code productivity, team building, and communication. More recently, distributed pair programming (DPP), which enables two programmers to work remotely, has also attracted the interest of researchers and instructors. The difference between DPP and PP is that the former allows geographically distributed teams to collaborate and share program code. Such collaboration is, thus, only feasible if an underlying infrastructure supports all necessary interactions. The integrated development environments (IDEs) for DPP should cover the basic requirements for remote software development as well as address common PP problems, such as unequal contributions from each member of a pair, feedback during DPP sessions, and communication problems. This paper presents the findings of a study on student performance and attitudes towards DPP in an object-oriented programming (OOP) course. The factors examined were student performance, in terms of assignment grade, exam grade and implementation time in relation to students' programming experience, and confidence, as well as student attitudes towards DPP, i.e., the feelgood factor, working alone or with a partner, and the perception of their partner's technical competence. The results suggest that a students' performance is associated with their programming experience and confidence in programming but not with how comfortable they feel during DPP sessions. Students evaluate the DPP sessions positively regardless of their confidence on programming or their perception of their partners' technical competence. Students who consider themselves to have about the same programming competence as their partners tend to be more satisfied with DPP sessions. Overall, students prefer working with a partner regardless of their confidence on programming.

1. Introduction

Pair programming (PP) has become popular in the research and software industry as well as being studied for a number of years in computer science courses with positive findings on student performance and attitudes [1–6]. The literature reveals that the collaborative nature of pair programming helps students to increase confidence and improve their grades on programming assignments. Other studies indicate that PP leads to higher program quality, continuous knowledge transfer, and greater student enjoyment [7]. More recently, distributed pair programming (DPP) has made it possible for

programmers to develop software with a partner from anywhere and at anytime. As an alternative to pair programming, DPP is more demanding because each member of the pair is not colocated while their common work is dependent on the features of the integrated development environment (IDE), as well as an infrastructure that has to be set up and configured by the students themselves. Although DPP can be realized with a general screen sharing application, when it comes to education, a DPP system is usually used to support students. The IDEs for DPP should cover the basic requirements for remote software development, such as a shared editor, supporting the roles of the driver and navigator, and a communication tool, as well as should address common PP problems, such as unequal contributions from each member of a pair, feedback during DPP sessions, and communication problems. Most of the DPP IDEs were built as Eclipse plugins.

Performance is one of the most investigated factors regarding the effectiveness of PP, indicating that it has a positive effect on students' grades [1, 2]. Implementation time is also a common measure used in PP studies to evaluate its effectiveness [8]. Most of the studies reported that students working on PP require less time to complete assignments compared with students on solo programming. Another well-studied factor is pair compatibility [5]. Research suggests that pairing students with similar programming skill levels or programming experience has positive results on motivation and participation [5, 7]. Similarly, it has been shown that a pair's performance is correlated with how comfortable students feel during a PP session, the so-called "feelgood" factor as coined by Muller and Padberg in their study [8]. Finally, a factor used to evaluate pair programming satisfaction is the students' self-rated confidence, which, however, has presented mixed results [3, 6, 9, 10].

In order to draw safer conclusions on distributed pair programming, we developed an educational DPP system, called SCEPPSys ("Scripted Collaboration in an Educational Pair Programming System"). SCEPPSys [11] is an Eclipse plugin that has some unique features in comparison to other plugins such as Sangam, RIPPLE, XPairtise, and Saros. Specifically, SCEPPSys saves and analyzes students' interactions, helps educators in organizing and monitoring DPP classes, and supports the creation of programming assignments that are comprised of small and manageable tasks associated with specific didactical goals (OOP concepts). The building capabilities of SCEPPSys for assessment and evaluation provide data to form the basis for further research, since extensive studies of DPP are still lacking. For example, the statistics reported by SCEPPSys for each student (e.g., total time spent on solving a problem, implementation time for each student, and each student's contribution to the project) can be used to research the following [12]: students' progress in programming; any undesirable behaviour (e.g., plagiarism); and problems in collaboration between the members of a pair.

We have been conducting research in real-world situations for the last 5 years, studying the different aspects of DPP effects on the learning of programming. In a study [13] carried out during the academic year 2013-14, we investigated how scripted roles affected students' engagement and knowledge building in the context of DPP. The effects of two different approaches on performance and distribution of activities between student pairs were examined. In the first approach, pair members switched roles after each task, while in the second, the role assignment of the driver or navigator depended on task type and students' personal skills. The findings showed both approaches to be equally effective. In another study [14] during the academic year 2015-16, we investigated whether prior programming skills assessed at the level of the student, the partner, and the pair as a whole, as well as pair compatibility was related to student performance in an OOP course supported by DPP assignments. In this study, students chose their partner, whereas the task distribution policy was that of rotating roles, meaning that each member switched roles after each task. The findings showed that the actual skill of student, partner, and pair affected each student's performance, whereas there was no association between pair compatibility and the student's own performance.

In the present study, we examined student performance and attitudes towards DPP in an object-oriented programming (OOP) course based on Java over one semester in the academic year 2016-17. Performance was studied based on the pair's mean grade in the assignments, each student's grade in the final exam, and implementation time. Student's attitudes towards DPP were studied based on the reported feelgood factor, the preference of working alone or in pairs, and the student's perception of their partner's programming competence. Correlations between the student's performance, confidence in programming, programming experience, the "feelgood" factor, and preference in working alone or in pairs were examined. Although all these factors have been studied regarding the effectiveness of PP, they have not been examined in the context of DPP. Most of the studies on DPP have focused on either the comparison between solo programming and DPP students' groups or on studying student interactions emphasizing users' contributions, co-ordination, and communications [15–17].

The remainder of the paper is organized as follows: Section 2 gives the related studies on PP and DPP; Section 3 describes the study methodology; and Section 4 presents the results and discussion. Finally in Section 5, conclusions are drawn.

2. Related Work

Salleh [18] performed a systematic literature review (SLR) of empirical studies that investigated factors and studies that measured the effectiveness of PP for CS/SE students. The results showed that the most significant factor in PP effectiveness was student skill level, while the most common measure used to gauge PP effectiveness was time spent on programming. In addition, there was overall higher student satisfaction when using PP than when working solo. Their meta-analyses showed that PP was effective in improving students' grades on assignments. Finally, in the studies that used quality as a measure of effectiveness, academic performance and expert opinion were the quality measures mostly applied.

The motivation for the SLR conducted by da Silva Estácio and Prikladnicki [19] was the lack of studies on the use of DPP in industry. They reported that the majority of the studies concerned PP, and only 22 papers were related to DPP, most of which focused on tool proposals, while only a few described case studies on the adoption of DPP in industry. They gathered data from a field study concerning variables (code quality, team productivity and communication, and difference of knowledge between the pairs), DPP aspects (company guidelines for using DPP, infrastructure and methods for DPP, development tool for DPP, facilitator to support DPP, and experience between pairs of DPP), benefits (execution time and motivation), challenges of using DPP (collaboration and communication challenges), and opinion (suggestions). Based on the literature review and the field study, they concluded by suggesting twelve practices that could help professionals in the use of DPP.

Umapathy and Ritzhaupt [20] conducted a meta-analysis on the effects of PP on educational outcomes. The results showed that pair programming can have a positive impact on students' programming assignment grades, exam scores, and also persistence in computer programming courses. However, in order to achieve these positive results, PP has to be implemented properly by both students and educators. Specifically, the following conditions must be met: regarding students, they should be supported in understanding the PP practice; they must alternate the roles of the driver and the navigator while working together on programming activities at the same time; and equal learning experiences must be ensured by having the driver and navigator alternate roles after a given duration [21]. Regarding educators, they should not just simply pair off students to carry out assignments, but they must ensure that PP is appropriately implemented.

Muller and Padberg [8] conducted two controlled experiments with 38 subjects on PP. They first studied the correlation between a pair's feelgood factor and the pair's implementation time and programming experience. In the second phase, rather than looking at the pairs, they focused on the individual's programming experience and feelgood factor. The findings showed that a pair's implementation time was uncorrelated to the pair's programming experience, but there was a significant correlation with how comfortable the developers felt with PP during the session (the "feelgood" factor). They did not find any significant correlation between the individual's programming experience and the pair's implementation time, nor the pair's implementation time and the individual's feelgood factor. The only statistical significant relationship they found was between implementation time and the member of each pair who felt less comfortable with pair programming. In their study, programming experience was measured in a subjective way using the number of years and number of lines of code written, which was data provided by the students in a pretest questionnaire. In their study, Muller and Padberg [8] used implementation time, which reflected the elapsed time that it took a pair to finish the assignment at the prescribed quality level, as a measure for the performance of a pair.

Thomas et al. [10] examined how self-confidence is reflected in students' reactions to the PP technique for developing software. Students who had programming experience before university were given a survey that placed them on a scale they called CodeWarrior to Code-a-phobe. They then placed students in 'opposite' and 'similar' pairs for a PP exercise and surveyed their reactions. The evidence indicated that students who had considerable self-confidence did not enjoy the experience of PP as much as the other students and the former produced their best work when placed in pairs with students of similar self-confidence levels.

Williams et al. [5] conducted a two-phased study on PP from 2002 to 2005 to determine if teachers can proactively form compatible pairs based on any of the following factors: personality type, learning style, skill level, programming self-esteem, work ethic, or time-management preference. They found (a) students prefer to pair with someone they perceive to be of similar technical competence, (b) pairing sensors and intuitors together yields very compatible pairs, and (c) pairing students with strongly dissimilar work ethics will more likely yield incompatible pairs.

Canfora et al. [22] conducted two experiments to study the impact of DPP regarding two productivity metrics: time and code quality. The results indicated that each member of the pair tended to work alone. The four factors reported to explain the results were failure to establish a working protocol, conflicting ideas between pair members, problems with the chat software, and different levels of experience between the pair members. In their second experiment, the two factors reported for successful DPP were appropriate communication between pair members and collaboration support.

In his paper, Hanks [17] discussed the development and empirical evaluation of a DPP tool, the important feature of which was the presence of a second cursor that supported gesturing. Students who used the tool in their introductory programming course performed as well as collocated students on their programming assignments and final exam. These students also spent less time working by themselves. They also felt that the gesturing feature was useful and used it regularly.

Zacharis [23] conducted a study investigating the effectiveness of virtual pair programming (VPP) on student performance and satisfaction in an introductory Java course. The two groups consisted of VPP students and solo students, and the two factors examined were code productivity and software quality. In addition, a comparison was made of the midterm and final examination scores between VPP and solo students. Finally, a survey of students' perceptions of VPP was administered. The results suggested that VPP is an effective pedagogical tool for flexible collaboration and an acceptable alternative to the individual/solo programming experience, regarding productivity, code quality, academic performance, and student satisfaction.

3. Methodology of the Study

3.1. Course Outline. The study was conducted in the 3rd semester of an undergraduate course on OOP in the academic year 2016-17. The course uses the Java programming language and runs over thirteen weeks with a 3-hour lab per week. Eighty-eight (88) students chose their partner, forming 44 pairs. Students were assigned five Java projects as homework to be solved in their pairs using the DPP system, SCEPPSys. The grade of each DPP assignment was the same for both students in the pair. Students had to take a final exam in the lab, where they were required to complete a program individually.

We developed an educational DPP system, calling it SCEPPSys [11], which supports the basic requirements of remote collaboration. Pair programmers can edit the source code in real time using a shared editor which supports the driver's and the navigator's roles. The driver edits the source code, while the navigator monitors the changes made to the source code and comments on them. Programmers are able to discuss and coordinate their actions using an embedded text-based communication channel. Remote code high-lighting (a basic gesturing feature) enables the navigator to point out code parts in order to indicate potential problems. The remaining features, the so-called "awareness indicators", aim to provide pair programmers with information about the user's status and performed actions within the workspace (such as editing and saving). Distributed pair programming is guided by collaboration scripts, which consist of a number of components and mechanisms [24]. In the administration environment of SCEPPSys, these scripts have been adapted to meet DPP requirements. Specifically the script authoring procedure includes participants' settings; pair formation; programming tasks; and turn-taking policies. Programming tasks are the subtasks of a major programming assignment. A hint provides support to students in completing the subtask with which it is associated. The turn-taking policies specify the distribution of the driver/navigator roles between the programmers. A significant feature of SCEPPSys is its ability to distribute the driver's and navigator's roles to the pair members. In previous works [12, 14], alternative turn-taking policies supported by SCEPPSys were investigated. In the present study, the chosen task distribution policy was free collaboration. Free collaboration policy allows students to distribute tasks based on their own decisions. Although this type of task distribution policy is more acceptable to students, it could lead to unequal participation. Thus, in order to avoid this, throughout the session, SCEPPSys displays metrics, such as the pair's total time and individual participation rates to help students balance their participation.

3.2. Research Objectives.
From research on pair programming in the literature review, the factors most investigated were students' performance in terms of achieved grades, implementation time for assignments, quality of code, and factors concerning pair compatibility (personality type and programming competence). In contrast, research on distributed pair programming focused mainly on the features of the relevant tools, the performance of students, and the quality of their code.

In this study, we investigated the correlations between students' performance and factors related to their prior programming skills and confidence in programming, as well as factors related to students' attitudes towards DPP, such as the feelgood factor, working alone or with a partner, and the student's perception of their partner's technical competence. It should be mentioned that, to the best of our knowledge, the feelgood factor and students' perception of their partners' technical competence have been studied only in the context of pair programming.

The following are the meanings and measures of the factors in our study.

Student performance is measured by the following:

(a) The grades achieved in the final exam of the OOP course (exam grade)

(b) The mean value of the 5 assignment grades (mean assignment grade)

(c) The implementation time, which is the total time spent by each member of the pair to complete all the submitted assignments

Regarding student grades, it must be noted that our decision to examine the two measures separately rather than combining them, was made on the basis that they represent two distinct phases in the student's progress in the course: the collaborative solution of DPP assignments covering a specific part of the syllabus and the final outcome for each student based on their individual examination covering the whole syllabus. We also considered implementation time as a measure of a student's performance during DPP sessions. The literature shows that this has been used as a measure for student performance in a number of studies in a variety of ways seen indicatively [8, 22].

Programming experience is measured as the mean value of the student's grades in two introductory courses "Procedural Programming (C programming language)" and "Algorithms in C" of the previous academic year.

Confidence in programming is measured by the students themselves prior to the beginning of the OOP course. We asked students to place themselves on a scale of 1 to 9 based on their self-confidence of their ability to program, and inspired by the study of Thomas et al. [10], we classified them into three groups: warriors: 7–9; middle: 4–6; and phobes: 1–3.

The feelgood factor shows how comfortable each member of a pair felt during the DPP sessions. It was introduced and studied by Muller and Padberg [8] in the context of PP. We asked students to evaluate their experience of DPP on a five-point scale (1: very bad, 2: bad, 3: neutral, 4: good, and 5: very good).

Perception of partner's competence in programming is the perception each member of the pair has about their partner's technical competence in regards to their own competence on a three-point scale (better, about the same, and weaker).

The following research questions were investigated:
Research questions examining student performance
Performance has been examined in relation to other factors in most of the studies on PP and DPP as it is a crucial factor, in a way, related to students' learning outcomes. Therefore, in RQ1.1 to RQ1.5, we look to see if there are correlations between a student's performance and their prior programming skill (*programming experience*) and attitudes on programming (*confidence in programming*) prior to the OOP course based on the DPP assignments.

RQ1.1: Does a student's mean assignment grade or exam grade correlate with their confidence in programming?

RQ1.2: Does a student's implementation time correlate with their confidence in programming?

RQ1.3: Does a student's mean assignment grade or exam grade correlate with their programming experience?

RQ1.4: Does a student's implementation time correlate with their programming experience?

RQ1.5: Does a student's mean assignment grade or exam grade correlate with their implementation time?

Research questions examining student attitudes towards DPP
RQ2.1 to RQ2.4 aim to examine if the feelgood factor on DPP is related to other factors such as programming experience and attitudes towards programming, as well as factors more linked/relevant to DPP such as student performance in the current course on OOP (assignment grade, exam grade, and implementation time).

RQ2.1: Does a student's feelgood factor correlate to their confidence in programming?

RQ2.2: Does a student's feelgood factor correlate to their programming experience?

RQ2.3: Does a student's feelgood factor correlate to their mean assignment grade or exam grade?

RQ2.4: Does a student's feelgood factor correlate to their implementation time?

RQ3.1, RQ3.2 and RQ4.1, RQ4.2 examine any patterns that may exist between groups of students with specific attitudes. The *feelgood factor groups*, based on students' estimation of the DPP sessions, are bad/very bad, neutral, and good/very good. The *confidence in programming groups*, based on students' rating of themselves, is Warriors, Middle, and Phobes. In addition, there are students who prefer to work alone or those who prefer to work with a partner, and finally, the partner's competence in programming groups, which are better, about the same, or weaker. The investigation of these last four RQs gives us the chance to record the distribution with respect to groups of students with different attitudes concerning the DPP:

RQ3.1: Is there a relationship between a student's feelgood factor group and their confidence in programming group?

RQ3.2: Is there a relationship between a student's preference in working alone or with a partner and their confidence in programming group?

RQ4.1: Is there a relationship between a student's confidence in programming group and their perception of their partner's technical competence?

RQ4.2: Is there a relationship between a student's feelgood factor group and their perception of their partner's technical competence?

3.3. Instruments and Data Analysis. The data analysed in this paper were gathered from the following:

(a) The grade achieved in the final exam and the mean grade from the assignments in the OOP course.

(b) The implementation time of each assignment and for each member of the pair recorded by the DPP system SCEPPSys.

(c) A presemester questionnaire distributed to students as a Google form that recorded the grades obtained in the introductory courses "Procedural Programming (C programming language)" and "Algorithms in C" of the previous year, as well as their confidence in their ability to program. Since both these courses are introductory, their syllabi and assignments are quite typical of universities around the world. Students were asked to answer the following question prior to the OOP course:

Q1. Place yourself on a 1 to 9 scale with the following endpoints:

1 = I do not like programming, and I think I am not good at it. I can write simple programs, but have trouble writing new programs for solving new problems.
9 = I have no problems at all completing programming tasks to date, in fact they were not challenging enough. I love to program and anticipate no difficulty with this course.

In their studies on Pair Programming, Thomas et al. [10] (pp. 364) and Williams et al. [5] (pp. 417) posed Q1 in order to measure students' self-confidence on their ability to program. Consequently, although one might argue that Q1 asks how challenging the assignments were, and how much students like programming, it should be noted that given the specific context, the question deals mainly with students' confidence in their ability to program.

(d) A questionnaire was distributed to students as a Google form on completion of the DPP assignments at the end of the semester. To investigate students' attitudes on DPP, the following questions were included in the questionnaire:

Q2. How would you evaluate the distributed, collaborative solving of assignments as an overall experience (1 = Very bad, 2 = Bad, 3 = Neutral, 4 = Good, 5 = Very good)?
Q3. Based on your experience in DPP would you prefer to work alone or with a partner in programming assignments?
Q4. Assess the technical competency of your partner relative to yourself [Better, About the same, Weaker].

The questionnaire was adapted from similar researches conducted in the context of PP. Muller and Padberg [8] used Q2 to measure how comfortable students felt during the pair programming session. As mentioned in previous sections, they called this metric the individual "feelgood" factor of a developer. Williams et al. [5] asked students to evaluate their partners' technical competence through question Q4.

Out of the 88 students, the statistical analysis was compiled on 78, as these students answered both questionnaires.

Statistical analysis was performed by using IBM SPSS Statistics (version 19.0.0). Pearson's product-moment correlation coefficient (r) was computed to assess the relationship between quantitative variables. Moreover, the chi-square test of independence was utilized for RQ3 and RQ4.

4. Results and Discussion

In this section, the results of the study are analysed and discussed.

The results of RQ1.1 to RQ1.5 are given in Table 1.

For the variations of RQ2, the results (Table 2) showed that the feelgood factor did not correlate with any of the following factors: confidence in programming, programming experience, mean assignment grade, exam grade, or implementation time.

In the attempt to spot any patterns that may have formed between the groups of students with specific attitudes (RQ3), we combined students' responses in Q2 with Q1, and Q3 with Q1.

The chi-square test of independence was conducted to investigate whether there was a relationship between the groups for feelgood factor and confidence in programming. The findings showed that there was no relationship between the two groups ($X^2 = 3.300$, df = 4, $p = 0.039$).

From the data in Table 3, it can be seen that a total of 76% of students in the study found distributed pair programming as good/very good.

The chi-square test of independence was conducted to investigate whether there was a relationship between the student's preference in working alone or with a partner and their confidence in programming group. A statistically significant relationship was observed between the two ($X^2 = 6.500$, df = 2, $p = 0.039$).

Table 4 clearly shows that only a small percentage of the warriors preferred working alone and all others preferred working with a partner.

In order to further investigate students' attitudes towards DPP, we considered students' responses to Q4 (partner's assessment) in relation to Q1 (confidence). The chi-square test of independence showed that there was no relationship between the two ($X^2 = 8.769$, df = 4, $p = 0.067$).

Even though the statistical result is not significant, the data presented in Table 5 give us useful information about the synthesis of the pairs. From Table 5, it can be seen that the highest total percentage of students in the study (71.8%) stated that they perceived their partner as having about the same technical competence as themselves. This applies to all three categories of phobes, middle, and warriors with 62.5%, 71.0%, and 74.4%, respectively. None of the phobes assessed their partners were weaker than themselves, whereas only 5.1% of the warriors stated that they perceived their partner as better than themselves.

In order to further investigate students' attitudes towards DPP, we considered their responses to Q4 (partner's assessment) in relation to Q2 (feelgood factor groups). The chi-square test of independence showed that there is no relationship between a student's feelgood factor group ($X^2 = 6.261$, df = 4, $p = 0.180$) and their perception of their partner's technical competence.

The data presented in Table 6 show that 81% of students who believed that they have about the same programming competence as their partners found the DPP sessions as being good/very good, whereas only 5% said that they were bad/very bad.

TABLE 1: Results summary of RQ1.1 to RQ1.5.

RQ: result	r	p
1.1: Mean assignment grade correlates positively with the student's confidence in programming	0.233	0.040
1.1: Exam grade correlates positively with the student's confidence in programming	0.591	$p < 0.001$
1.2: Implementation time correlates negatively with the student's confidence in programming	−0.342	0.002
1.3: Mean assignment grade correlates positively with the student's programming experience	0.334	0.008
1.3: Exam grade correlates positively with the student's programming experience	0.619	$p < 0.001$
1.4: Implementation time correlates negatively with the student's programming experience	−0.245	0.05
1.5: Mean assignment grade does not correlate with the student's implementation time	0.136	0.208
1.5: Exam grade does not correlate with the student's implementation time	−0.065	0.582

TABLE 2: Result summary of the variations of RQ2.

RQ: result	r	p
2.1: Feelgood factor does not correlate with the student's confidence in programming	−0.027	0.818
2.2: Feelgood factor does not correlate with the student's programming experience	−0.062	0.648
2.3: Feelgood factor does not correlate with the student's mean assignment grade	0.028	0.809
2.3: Feelgood factor does not correlate with the student's exam grade	−0.016	0.897
2.4: Feelgood factor does not correlate with the student's implementation time	−0.032	0.778

5. Conclusions

The aim of this study was to investigate the effectiveness of DPP in an object-oriented programming (OOP) course in the academic year 2016-17. The factors examined were student performance, in terms of assignment grades, exam grade and implementation time in relation to students' programming experience, and confidence, as well as student attitudes towards DPP, i.e., the feelgood factor, working alone or with a partner, and the perception of their partner's technical competence.

The results suggest that a student's performance is associated with their experience and confidence in programming rather than on how comfortable they felt during the DPP session. Even though some of the above results may appear to be rather obvious; nonetheless, there is still a serious lack of empirical data in the context of DPP. Muller and Padberg [8] in their study on PP found that individual performance does not correlate with the programming experience and that the feelgood factor of that pair member who felt less comfortable with pair programming correlates with the pair performance. The findings of Muller and Padberg could not be compared with ours even though they examined the same factors: performance, programming experience, and feelgood factor, as we did. The reason is that

TABLE 3: Students' distribution with respect to feelgood factor groups and confidence in programming groups.

Confidence in programming groups	Feelgood factor groups			Total
	Bad/Very Bad	Neutral	Good/Very Good	
Phobes	0 (0%)	3 (38%)	5 (63%)	8
Middle	3 (10%)	5 (16%)	23 (74%)	31
Warriors	2 (5%)	6 (15%)	31 (80%)	39
Total	5 (6%)	14 (18%)	59 (76%)	78

*Data are presented as frequencies and row percentages.

TABLE 4: Students' distribution with respect to confidence in programming groups and working alone or with a partner.

Confidence in programming groups	Working alone or with a partner		Total
	Alone	With a partner	
Phobes	0 (0%)	8 (100%)	8
Middle	0 (0%)	31 (100%)	31
Warriors	6 (15%)	33 (85%)	39
Total	6 (8%)	72 (92%)	78

*Data are presented as frequencies and row percentages.

TABLE 5: Students' distribution with respect to their confidence in programming group and their perception of their partners' technical competence.

Confidence in programming groups	Perception of the partner's technical competence			Total
	Weaker	About the same	Better	
Phobes	0 (0.0%)	5 (63%)	3 (38%)	8
Middle	3 (10%)	22 (71%)	6 (19%)	31
Warriors	8 (25%)	29 (74%)	2 (5%)	39
Total	11 (14%)	56 (72%)	11 (14%)	78

*Data are presented as frequencies and row percentages.

TABLE 6: Students' distribution with respect to their feelgood factor and perception of their partner's technical competence.

Perception of their partner's technical competence	Feelgood factor			Total
	Bad/Very Bad	Neutral	Good/Very Good	
Weaker	0 (0%)	4 (36%)	7 (64%)	11
About the same	3 (5%)	8 (14%)	45 (81%)	56
Better	2 (18%)	2 (18%)	7 (64%)	11
Total	5 (6%)	14 (18%)	59 (76%)	78

*Data are presented as frequencies and row percentages.

they used different metrics for performance and programming experience as described in the related work section, and they examined slightly different RQs.

A strong majority of students had a positive attitude, regardless of the feelgood factor or their perception of their partner's technical competence. The study findings clearly indicate that the vast majority of students preferred to work with a partner rather than alone. Thomas et al. [10] reported similar findings concerning warriors and their preference for pair programming. However, Hanks [9] reported partly contradictory results in that although the highly confident students liked pairing the most and those with low confidence liked it the least. It seems plausible that our finding where most students of all confidence levels (Phobes, Middle, and Warriors) preferred pairing could be a result of the structured pair programming scripting in the SCEPPSys tool that was not present in the work of Hanks. One of the main hypotheses behind the decision to incorporate the

ability of structured DPP scripting in SCEPPSys was that it would provide guidance during problem solving and would further support weaker students [25].

The majority of students in our study in the confidence in programming groups perceived their partners' technical competence to be about the same as theirs. The findings showed that, as regards students' feelgood factor, those students who believed their partners had about the same programming competence as them tended to be more satisfied with the DPP sessions, keeping in mind that the pairs of students chose their partner themselves. This finding is supported by Jacobson and Schaefer [26] who in their study on PP noted that allowing students to freely form pairs themselves leads to a high degree of satisfaction.

It appears that our findings concerning student attitudes towards distributed pair programming are in accordance with most of the findings on similar studies on pair programming. This is an encouraging result as DPP is more demanding than PP. In this study, SCEPPSys the educational system developed for a typical undergraduate OOP course promotes student collaboration and balanced participation in DPP. Clearly, the results of this study that used SCEPPSys and a specific set of assignments cannot be generalized for all DPP educational settings. Despite the limitations, this research adds to the body of studies on distributed pair programming since factors, such as feelgood factor, confidence in programming, and perception of the partner's programming competence, have not been examined in the context of DPP.

Conflicts of Interest

The authors declare that they have no conflicts of interest.

References

[1] C. McDowell, L. Werner, H. Bullock, and J. Fernald, "The effects of pair-programming on performance in an introductory programming course," *ACM SIGCSE Bulletin*, vol. 34, no. 1, pp. 38–42, 2002.

[2] C. McDowell, L. Werner, H. E. Bullock, and J. Fernald, "The impact of pair programming on student performance, perception and persistence," in *Proceedings of the International Conference on Software Engineering*, pp. 602–607, Portland, OR, USA, May 2003.

[3] C. McDowell, B. Hanks, and L. Werner, "Experimenting with pair programming in the classroom," *ACM SIGCSE Bulletin*, vol. 35, no. 3, pp. 60–64, 2003.

[4] C. McDowell, L. Werner, H. Bullock, and J. Fernald, "Pair programming improves student retention, confidence, and program quality," *Communications of the ACM*, vol. 49, no. 8, pp. 90–95, 2006.

[5] L. Williams, L. Layman, J. Osborne, and N. Katira, "Examining the compatibility of student pair programmers,"*in Proceedings of the conference on AGILE 2006 (AGILE '06)*, IEEE Computer Society, pp. 411–420, Minneapolis, MN,USA, July 2006.

[6] L. Williams, C. McDowell, N. Nagappan, J. Fernald, and L. Werner, "Building pair programming knowledge through a family of experiments," in *Proceedings of 2003 International Symposium on Empirical Software Engineering*, pp. 143–152, IEEE Computer Society, Washington, D.C., USA, September-October 2003.

[7] S. Faja, "Pair programming as a team based learning activity: a review of research," *Issues in Information Systems*, vol. 12, no. 2, pp. 207–216, 2011.

[8] M. M. Muller and F. Padberg, "An empirical study about the feelgood factor in pair programming," in *Proceedings of International Software Metrics Symposium*, pp. 151–158, Chicago, IL, USA, September 2004.

[9] B. Hanks, "Student attitudes toward pair programming," *ACM SIGCSE Bulletin*, vol. 38, no. 3, pp. 113–117, 2006.

[10] L. Thomas, M. Ratcliffe, and A. Robertson, "Code warriors and code-a-phobes: a study in attitude and pair programming," *ACM SIGCSE Bulletin*, vol. 35, no. 1, pp. 363–367, 2003.

[11] D. Tsompanoudi, M. Satratzemi, and S. Xinogalos, "Distributed pair programming using collaboration scripts: an

[12] S. Xinogalos, M. Satratzemi, D. Tsompanoudi, and A. Chatzigeorgiou, "Monitoring an OOP course through assignments in a distributed pair programming system," in Z. Budimac, Z.Horvath, and T. Kozsik, eds., in Proceedings of *the SQAMIA 2016: 5th Workshop of Software Quality, Analysis, Monitoring, Improvement, and Applications*, vol. 1677, pp. 97–104, Budapest, Hungary, August 2016, http://ceur-ws.org/Vol-1677/.

[13] D. Tsompanoudi, M. Satratzemi, and S. Xinogalos, "Evaluating the effects of scripted distributed pair programming on students' performance and participation," *IEEE Transactions on Education*, vol. 59, no. 1, pp. 24–31, 2016.

[14] S. Xinogalos, M. Satratzemi, A. Chatzigeorgiou, and D. Tsompanoudi, "Factors affecting students' performance in distributed pair programming," *Journal of Educational Computing Research*, 2017.

[15] J. Schenk, L. Prechelt, and S. Salinger, "Distributed-Pair Programming can work well and is not just Distributed Pair-Programming,"in Companion Proceedings of 36th InternationalConference on Software Engineering. ACM, pp. 74–83, Hyderabad, India, May 2014.

[16] T. Schümmer and S. Lukosch, "Understanding tools and practices for distributed pair programming," *Journal of Universal Computer Science*, vol. 15, no. 16, pp. 3101–3125, 2010.

[17] B. Hanks, "Empirical evaluation of distributed pair programming," *International Journal of Human-Computer Studies*, vol. 66, no. 7, pp. 530–544, 2008.

[18] N. Salleh, E. Mendes, and J. Grundy, "Empirical studies of pair programming for CS/SE teaching in higher education: a systematic literature review," *IEEE Transactions on Software Engineering*, vol. 37, no. 4, pp. 509–525, 2011.

[19] B. J. da Silva Estácio and R. Prikladnicki, "Distributed pair programming: a systematic literature review," *Information and Software Technology*, vol. 63, pp. 1–10, 2015.

[20] K. Umapathy and A. D. Ritzhaupt, "A meta-analysis of pair-programming in computer programming courses: implications for educational practice," *ACM Transactions on Computing Education*, vol. 17, no. 4, pp. 1–13, 2017.

[21] D. W. Govender and T. P. Govender, "Using a collaborative learning technique as a pedagogic intervention for the effective teaching and learning of a programming course," *Mediterranean Journal of Social Sciences*, vol. 5, no. 20, pp. 1077–1086, 2014.

[22] G. Canfora, A. Cimitile, G. A. Di Lucca, and C. A. Visaggio, "How distribution affects the success of pair programming," *International Journal of Software Engineering and Knowledge Engineering*, vol. 16, no. 2, pp. 293–313, 2006.

[23] N. Z. Zacharis, "Measuring the effects of virtual pair programming in an introductory programming java course," *IEEE Transactions on Education*, vol. 54, no. 1, pp. 168–170, 2011.

[24] L. Kobbe, A. Weinberger, P. Dillenbourg et al., "Specifying computer-supported collaboration scripts," *International Journal of Computer-Supported Collaborative Learning*, vol. 2, no. 2-3, pp. 211–224, 2007.

[25] P. Dillenbourg and F. Fischer, "Computer-supported collaborative learning: the basics," *Zeitschrift für Berufs-und Wirtschaftspädagogik*, vol. 21, pp. 111–130, 2007.

[26] N. Jacobson and S. Schaefer, "Pair programming in CS1," *ACM SIGCSE Bulletin*, vol. 40, no. 2, pp. 93–96, 2008.

16

Global Optimization for Solving Linear Multiplicative Programming Based on a New Linearization Method

Chun-Feng Wang[1,2] and Yan-Qin Bai[1]

[1]Department of Mathematics, College of Sciences, Shanghai University, Shanghai 200444, China
[2]Department of Mathematics, Henan Normal University, Xinxiang 453007, China

Correspondence should be addressed to Chun-Feng Wang; wangchunfeng09@126.com

Academic Editor: Fabrizio Riguzzi

This paper presents a new global optimization algorithm for solving a class of linear multiplicative programming (LMP) problem. First, a new linear relaxation technique is proposed. Then, to improve the convergence speed of our algorithm, two pruning techniques are presented. Finally, a branch and bound algorithm is developed for solving the LMP problem. The convergence of this algorithm is proved, and some experiments are reported to illustrate the feasibility and efficiency of this algorithm.

1. Introduction

Consider the following linear multiplicative programming (LMP) problem:

LMP:

$$v = \min \quad \phi(x) = \sum_{i=1}^{p} \left(c_i^T x + d_i \right) \left(e_i^T x + f_i \right) \tag{1}$$

$$\text{s.t.} \quad x \in D = \left\{ x \in R^n \mid Ax \leq b \right\},$$

where $p \geq 2$, $c_i^T = (c_{i1}, c_{i2}, \ldots, c_{in})$, $e_i^T = (e_{i1}, e_{i2}, \ldots, e_{in}) \in R^n$, $d_i, f_i \in R$, $i = 1, \ldots, p$, $A = (a_{ij})_{m \times n} \in R^{m \times n}$ is a matrix, $b = (b_i)_{m \times 1} \in R^m$ is a vector, and $D \subseteq R^n$ is nonempty and bounded.

As a special case of nonconvex programming problem, the problem LMP has been paid more attention since the 1990s. There are two reasons. The first one is that, from a practical point of view, LMP problem appears in a wide variety of practical applications, such as financial optimization [1], data mining/pattern recognition [2], plant layout design [3], VLISI chip design [4], and robust optimization [5]. The second one is that, from a research point of view, LMP is N-hard; that is, it usually possesses multiple local optimal solutions that are not globally optimal. So, it is hard to find its global optimal solution, and it is necessary to put forward good methods.

In the past few decades, for all $x \in D$, under the assumption that $c_i^T + d_i > 0$, $e_i^T x + f_i > 0$, a number of practical algorithms have been proposed for globally solving problem LMP. These methods can be classified into parameterization based methods [6, 7], branch-and-bound methods [8–10], decomposition method [11], cutting plane method [12], and so on.

The purpose of this paper is to present an effective method for globally solving problem LMP. Compared with other algorithms, the main features of this algorithm are (1) by using the special structure of LMP, a new linear relaxation technique is presented, which can be used to construct the linear relaxation programming (LRP) problem; (2) two pruning techniques are presented, which can be used to improve the convergence speed of the proposed algorithm; (3) the problem investigated in this paper has a more general form than those in [6–12]; it does not require $c_i^T x + d_i > 0$ and $e_i^T x + f_i > 0$; (4) numerical results and comparison with methods [8, 13–22] show that our algorithm works as well as or better than those methods.

This paper is organized as follows. In Section 2, the new linear relaxation programming (LRP) problem for LMP problem is proposed, which provides a lower bound for the optimal value of LMP. In order to improve the convergence speed of our algorithm, two pruning techniques are presented in Section 3. In Section 4, the global optimization algorithm is given, and the convergence of the algorithm is proved. Numerical experiments are carried out to show the feasibility and efficiency of our algorithm in Section 5.

2. Linear Relaxation Programming (LRP)

To solve problem LMP, the principal task is the construction of lower bound for this problem and its partitioned subproblems. A lower bound of LMP problem and its partitioned subproblems can be obtained by solving a linear relaxation programming problem. For generating this linear relaxation, the strategy proposed by this paper is to underestimate the objective function $\phi(x)$ with a linear function. All the details of this procedure will be given in the following.

First, we solve $2n$ linear programming problems: $l_j^0 = \min_{x \in D} x_j$, $u_j^0 = \max_{x \in D} x_j$, $j = 1, \ldots, n$, and construct a rectangle $H^0 = \{x \in R^n \mid l_j^0 \le x_j \le u_j^0, j = 1, \ldots, n\}$. Then, the LMP problem can be rewritten as the following form:

LMP:

$$v = \min \quad \phi(x) = \sum_{i=1}^{p} \left(c_i^T x + d_i\right)\left(e_i^T x + f_i\right)$$

$$\text{s.t.} \quad x \in D = \{x \in R^n \mid Ax \le b\}, \tag{2}$$

$$H^0 = \{x \mid l_j^0 \le x_j \le u_j^0, \ j = 1, \ldots, n\}.$$

Let $H = [l, u]$ be the initial rectangle H^0 or some subrectangle of H^0 that is generated by the proposed algorithm. Next, we will show how to construct the linear relaxation programming problem LRP for LMP.

Towards this end, for $i = 1, \ldots, p$, compute

$$\underline{\xi}_i = \sum_{j=1}^{n} \min\{c_{ij} l_j, c_{ij} u_j\} + d_i,$$

$$\overline{\xi}_i = \sum_{j=1}^{n} \max\{c_{ij} l_j, c_{ij} u_j\} + d_i,$$

$$\tag{3}$$

$$\underline{\eta}_i = \sum_{j=1}^{n} \min\{e_{ij} l_j, e_{ij} u_j\} + f_i,$$

$$\overline{\eta}_i = \sum_{j=1}^{n} \max\{e_{ij} l_j, e_{ij} u_j\} + f_i,$$

and consider the product term $(c_i^T x + d_i)(e_i^T x + f_i)$ in $\phi(x)$.

Since $c_i^T x + d_i - \underline{\xi}_i \ge 0$, $e_i^T x + f_i - \underline{\eta}_i \ge 0$, we have

$$\left(c_i^T x + d_i - \underline{\xi}_i\right)\left(e_i^T x + f_i - \underline{\eta}_i\right) \ge 0; \tag{4}$$

that is,

$$\left(c_i^T x + d_i\right)\left(e_i^T x + f_i\right) - \underline{\eta}_i\left(c_i^T x + d_i\right) - \underline{\xi}_i\left(e_i^T x + f_i\right)$$

$$+ \underline{\xi}_i \underline{\eta}_i \ge 0. \tag{5}$$

Furthermore, we have

$$\left(c_i^T x + d_i\right)\left(e_i^T x + f_i\right) \ge \underline{\eta}_i\left(c_i^T x + d_i\right) + \underline{\xi}_i\left(e_i^T x + f_i\right)$$

$$- \underline{\xi}_i \underline{\eta}_i. \tag{6}$$

In addition, since $c_i^T x + d_i - \underline{\xi}_i \ge 0$, $e_i^T x + f_i - \overline{\eta}_i \le 0$, we have

$$\left(c_i^T x + d_i - \underline{\xi}_i\right)\left(e_i^T x + f_i - \overline{\eta}_i\right) \le 0. \tag{7}$$

Furthermore, we can obtain

$$\left(c_i^T x + d_i\right)\left(e_i^T x + f_i\right) \le \overline{\eta}_i\left(c_i^T x + d_i\right) + \underline{\xi}_i\left(e_i^T x + f_i\right)$$

$$- \underline{\xi}_i \overline{\eta}_i. \tag{8}$$

From (6) and (8), we have the following relations:

$$\phi(x) = \sum_{i=1}^{p} \left(c_i^T x + d_i\right)\left(e_i^T x + f_i\right)$$

$$\ge \sum_{i=1}^{p} \left[\underline{\eta}_i\left(c_i^T x + d_i\right) + \underline{\xi}_i\left(e_i^T x + f_i\right) - \underline{\xi}_i \underline{\eta}_i\right]$$

$$= \phi^l(x), \tag{9}$$

$$\phi(x) = \sum_{i=1}^{p} \left(c_i^T x + d_i\right)\left(e_i^T x + f_i\right)$$

$$\le \sum_{i=1}^{p} \left[\overline{\eta}_i\left(c_i^T x + d_i\right) + \underline{\xi}_i\left(e_i^T x + f_i\right) - \underline{\xi}_i \overline{\eta}_i\right]$$

$$= \phi^u(x).$$

Based on the above discussion, the linear relaxation programming (LRP) problem can be established as follows, which provides a lower bound for the optimal value of LMP problem over H:

LRP:

$$\min \quad \phi^l(x)$$

$$\text{s.t.} \quad Ax \le b, \tag{10}$$

$$x \in H.$$

Theorem 1. *For all* $x \in H$, *let* $\Delta x = u - l$ *and consider the functions* $\phi^l(x)$, $\phi(x)$, *and* $\phi^u(x)$. *Then, one has* $\lim_{\Delta x \to 0}(\phi(x) - \phi^l(x)) = \lim_{\Delta x \to 0}(\phi^u(x) - \phi(x)) = 0$.

Proof. We first prove $\lim_{\Delta x \to 0}(\phi(x) - \phi^l(x)) = 0$. By the definitions $\phi(x)$ and $\phi^l(x)$, we have

$$\left|\phi(x) - \phi^l(x)\right| = \left|\sum_{i=1}^{p} \left(c_i^T x + d_i\right)\left(e_i^T x + f_i\right)\right.$$

$$\left. - \sum_{i=1}^{p} \left[\underline{\eta}_i\left(c_i^T x + d_i\right) + \underline{\xi}_i\left(e_i^T x + f_i\right) - \underline{\xi}_i \underline{\eta}_i\right]\right|$$

$$\leq \left| \sum_{i=1}^{p} \left[\left(c_i^T x + d_i \right) \left(e_i^T x + f_i \right) - \underline{\eta}_i \left(c_i^T x + d_i \right) \right] \right|$$

$$+ \left| \sum_{i=1}^{p} \left[\underline{\xi}_i \left(e_i^T x + f_i \right) - \underline{\xi}_i \underline{\eta}_i \right] \right|$$

$$\leq \sum_{i=1}^{p} \left| c_i^T x + d_i \right| \left| \left(e_i^T x + f_i \right) - \underline{\eta}_i \right|$$

$$+ \sum_{i=1}^{p} \left| \underline{\xi}_i \right| \left| e_i^T x + f_i - \underline{\eta}_i \right|. \tag{11}$$

Sice D is nonempty and bounded, there exists M_i such that $M_i = \max_{x \in D} |c_i^T x + d_i|$. From the above inequality, we have

$$\left| \phi(x) - \phi^l(x) \right| \leq \sum_{i=1}^{p} M_i \left| \overline{\eta}_i - \underline{\eta}_i \right| + \sum_{i=1}^{p} \left| \underline{\xi}_i \right| \left| \overline{\eta}_i - \underline{\eta}_i \right|. \tag{12}$$

By the definitions of $\underline{\eta}_i$ and $\overline{\eta}_i$, we know that $\Delta s = \overline{\eta}_i - \underline{\eta}_i \to 0$ as $\Delta x \to 0$. Combining (12), we have $\lim_{\Delta x \to 0} (\phi(x) - \phi^l(x)) = 0$.

Similarly, we can prove $\lim_{\Delta x \to 0} (\phi^u(x) - \phi(x)) = 0$, and the proof is complete. $\square$

Theorem 1 implies that $\phi^l(x)$ and $\phi^u(x)$ will approximate the function $\phi(x)$ as $\Delta x \to 0$.

3. Pruning Technique

To improve the convergence speed of this algorithm, we present two pruning techniques, which can be used to eliminate the region in which the global optimal solution of LMP problem does not exist.

Assume that UB and LB are the current known upper bound and lower bound of the optimal value v of the problem LMP. Let

$$\alpha_j = \sum_{i=1}^{p} \left(\underline{\eta}_i c_{ij} + \underline{\xi}_i e_{ij} \right), \quad j = 1, \dots, n,$$

$$\Lambda_1 = \sum_{i=1}^{p} \left(\underline{\eta}_i d_i + \underline{\xi}_i f_i - \underline{\eta}_i \underline{\xi}_i \right),$$

$$\gamma_k = \text{UB} - \sum_{j=1, j \neq k}^{n} \min \left\{ \alpha_j l_j, \alpha_j u_j \right\} - \Lambda_1,$$

$$k = 1, \dots, n,$$

$$\beta_j = \sum_{i=1}^{p} \left(\overline{\eta}_i c_{ij} + \underline{\xi}_i e_{ij} \right), \quad j = 1, \dots, n,$$

$$\Lambda_2 = \sum_{i=1}^{p} \left(\overline{\eta}_i d_i + \underline{\xi}_i f_i - \overline{\eta}_i \underline{\xi}_i \right),$$

$$\rho_k = \text{LB} - \sum_{j=1, j \neq k}^{n} \max \left\{ \beta_j l_j, \beta_j u_j \right\} - \Lambda_2,$$

$$k = 1, \dots, n. \tag{13}$$

The pruning techniques are derived as in the following theorems.

Theorem 2. For any subrectangle $H \subseteq H^0$ with $H_j = [l_j, u_j]$, if there exists some index $k \in \{1, 2, \dots, n\}$ such that $\alpha_k > 0$ and $\gamma_k < \alpha_k u_k$, then there is no globally optimal solution of LMP problem over H^1; if $\alpha_k < 0$ and $\gamma_k < \alpha_k l_k$, for some k, then there is no globally optimal solution of LMP problem over H^2, where

$$H^1 = \left(H_j^1 \right)_{n \times 1} \subseteq H,$$

$$\text{with } H_j^1 = \begin{cases} H_j, & j \neq k, \\ \left(\dfrac{\gamma_k}{\alpha_k}, u_k \right] \cap H_k, & j = k, \end{cases} \tag{14}$$

$$H^2 = \left(H_j^2 \right)_{n \times 1} \subseteq H,$$

$$\text{with } H_j^2 = \begin{cases} H_j, & j \neq k, \\ \left[l_k, \dfrac{\gamma_k}{\alpha_k} \right) \cap H_k, & j = k. \end{cases}$$

Proof. For all $x \in H^1$, we first show that $\phi(x) > \text{UB}$. Consider the kth component x_k of x. Since $x_k \in (\gamma_k/\alpha_k, u_k]$, we can obtain that

$$\frac{\gamma_k}{\alpha_k} < x_k \leq u_k. \tag{15}$$

From $\alpha_k > 0$, we have $\gamma_k < \alpha_k x_k$. For all $x \in H^1$, by the above inequality and the definition of γ_k, it implies that

$$\text{UB} - \sum_{j=1, j \neq k}^{n} \min \left\{ \alpha_j l_j, \alpha_j u_j \right\} - \Lambda_1 < \alpha_k x_k; \tag{16}$$

that is,

$$\text{UB} < \sum_{j=1, j \neq k}^{n} \min \left\{ \alpha_j l_j, \alpha_j u_j \right\} + \alpha_k x_k + \Lambda_1$$

$$\tag{17}$$

$$\leq \sum_{j=1}^{n} \alpha_j x_j + \Lambda_1 = \phi^l(x).$$

Thus, for all $x \in H^1$, we have $\phi(x) \geq \phi^l(x) > \text{UB} \geq v$; that is, for all $x \in H^1$, $\phi(x)$ is always greater than the optimal value v of the problem LMP. Therefore, there cannot exist globally optimal solution of LMP problem over H^1.

Similarly, for all $x \in H^2$, if there exists some k such that $\alpha_k < 0$ and $\gamma_k < \alpha_k l_k$, it can be derived that there is no globally optimal solution of LMP problem over H^2. $\square$

Theorem 3. *For any subrectangle $H \subseteq H^0$ with $H_j = [l_j, u_j]$, if there exists some index $k \in \{1, 2, \ldots, n\}$ such that $\beta_k > 0$ and $\rho_k > \beta_k l_k$, then there is no globally optimal solution of LMP problem over H^3; if $\beta_k < 0$ and $\rho_k > \beta_k u_k$, for some k, then there is no globally optimal solution of LMP problem over H^4, where*

$$H^3 = \left(H_j^3\right)_{n\times 1} \subseteq H,$$

$$\text{with } H_j^3 = \begin{cases} H_j, & j \neq k, \\ \left[l_k, \dfrac{\rho_k}{\beta_k}\right) \cap H_k, & j = k, \end{cases} \tag{18}$$

$$H^4 = \left(H_j^4\right)_{n\times 1} \subseteq H,$$

$$\text{with } H_j^4 = \begin{cases} H_j, & j \neq k, \\ \left(\dfrac{\rho_k}{\beta_k}, u_k\right] \cap H_k, & j = k. \end{cases}$$

Proof. First, we show that, for all $x \in H^3$, $\phi(x) < \text{LB}$. Consider the kth component x_k of x. By the assumption and the definitions of β_k and ρ_k, we have

$$l_k \leq x_k < \frac{\rho_k}{\beta_k}. \tag{19}$$

Note that since $\beta_k > 0$, we have $\rho_k > \beta_k x_k$. For all $x \in H^3$, by the above inequality and the definition of ρ_k, it implies that

$$\text{LB} > \sum_{j=1, j\neq k}^{n} \max\left\{\beta_j l_j, \beta_j u_j\right\} + \beta_k x_k + \Lambda_2$$

$$\geq \sum_{j=1}^{n} \beta_j x_j + \Lambda_2 = \Phi^u(x) \geq \phi(x). \tag{20}$$

Thus, for all $x \in H^3$, we have $v \geq \text{LB} > \phi(x)$. Therefore, there cannot exist globally optimal solution of LMP problem over H^3.

For all $x \in H^4$, if there exists some k such that $\beta_k < 0$ and $\rho_k > \beta_k u_k$, from arguments similar to the above, it can be derived that there is no globally optimal solution of LMP problem over H^4. $\square$

4. Algorithm and Its Convergence

Based on the previous results, this section presents the branch and bound algorithm and gives its convergence.

4.1. Branching Rule. In branch and bound algorithm, branch rule is a critical element in guaranteeing convergence. This paper chooses a simple and standard bisection rule, which is sufficient to ensure convergence since it drives the intervals shrinking to a singleton for all the variables along any infinite branch of the branch and bound tree.

Consider any node subproblem identified by rectangle $H = \{x \in R^n \mid l_j \leq x_j \leq u_j, j = 1, \ldots, n\} \subseteq H^0$. The branching rule is as follows:

(i) let $k = \text{argmax}\{u_j - l_j \mid j = 1, \ldots, n\}$;

(ii) let $\tau = (l_k + u_k)/2$;

(iii) let

$$H^1 = \left\{x \in R^n \mid l_j \leq x_j \leq u_j, \; j \neq k, \; l_k \leq x_k \leq \tau\right\},$$

$$H^2 = \left\{x \in R^n \mid l_j \leq x_j \leq u_j, \; j \neq k, \; \tau \leq x_k \leq u_k\right\}. \tag{21}$$

Through using this branching rule, the rectangle H is partitioned into two subrectangles H^1 and H^2.

4.2. Branch and Bound Algorithm. From the above discussion, the branch and bound algorithm for globally solving LMP problem is summarized as follows.

Let $\text{LB}(H^k)$ be the optimal function value of LRP over the subrectangle $H = H^k$ and $x^k = x(H^k)$ be an element of the corresponding argmin.

Algorithm Statement

Step 1. Choose $\epsilon \geq 0$. Find an optimal solution $x^0 = x(H^0)$ and the optimal value $\text{LB}(H^0)$ for problem LRP with $H = H^0$. Set $\text{LB}_0 = \text{LB}(H^0)$, and $\text{UB}_0 = \phi(x^0)$. If $\text{UB}_0 - \text{LB}_0 \leq \epsilon$, then stop: x^0 is an ϵ-optimal solution of problem LMP. Otherwise, set $Q_0 = \{H^0\}$, $k = 1$, and go to Step 2.

Step 2. Set $\text{UB}_k = \text{UB}_{k-1}$. Subdivide H^{k-1} into two subrectangles via the branching rule, and denote the set of new partition rectangles as $\overline{H}^k$.

Step 3. For each new rectangle $H \in \overline{H}^k$, utilizing the pruning techniques of Theorems 2 and 3 to prune rectangle H. For $i = 1, \ldots, m$, if there exists some i such that $\sum_{j=1}^{n} \min\{a_{ij}l_j, a_{ij}u_j\} \geq b_i$ over rectangle H, then remove the rectangle H from $\overline{H}^k$; that is, $\overline{H}^k = \overline{H}^k \setminus H$.

Step 4. If $\overline{H}^k \neq \emptyset$, solve LRP to obtain $\text{LB}(H)$ and $x(H)$ for each $H \in \overline{H}^k$. If $\text{LB}(H) > \text{UB}_k$, set $\overline{H}^k = \overline{H}^k \setminus H$. Otherwise, let $\text{UB}_k = \min\{\text{UB}_k, \phi(x(H))\}$. If $\text{UB}_k = \phi(x(H))$, set $x^k = x(H)$.

Step 5. Set

$$Q_k = \left\{Q_{k-1} \setminus H^{k-1}\right\} \cup \overline{H}^k. \tag{22}$$

Step 6. Set $\text{LB}_k = \min\{\text{LB}(H) \mid H \in Q_k\}$. Let H^k be the subrectangle which satisfies that $\text{LB}_k = \text{LB}(H^k)$. If $\text{UB}_k - \text{LB}_k \leq \epsilon$, then stop: x^k is a global ϵ-optimal solution of problem LMP. Otherwise, set $k = k + 1$, and go to Step 2.

4.3. Convergence Analysis. In this subsection, the convergence properties of the algorithm are given.

Theorem 4. *The algorithm either terminates finitely with globally ϵ-optimal solution or generates an infinite sequence*

TABLE 1: Comparison results of Examples 1–10.

Example (p, m, n)	Methods	Time (s)	Iter	Optimal solution	Optimal value
1 (min) $(1, 8, 2)$	[13]	5.0780	48	(2.0, 8.0)	10
	[14]	0.3	53	(2.0, 8.0)	10
	[15]	10.83	27	(2.0003, 7.9999)	10.0042
	Ours	0.062	1	(2.0, 8.0)	10
2 (min) $(2, 6, 2)$	[13]	0.2030	2	(0.0, 4.0)	3
	[16]	—	3	(0.0, 4.0)	3
	Ours	0.086	1	(0.0, 4.0)	3
3 (min) $(1, 12, 4)$	[13]	0.1880	1	(1.3148, 0.1396, 0.0, 0.4233)	0.8902
	[17]	—	6	(1.3148, 0.1396, 0.0, 0.4233)	0.8902
	Ours	0.093	1	(1.3148, 0.1396, 0.0, 0.4233)	0.8902
4 (min) $(2, 5, 2)$	[8]	—	—	(0.0, 4.0)	3
	[18]	—	—	(0.0, 4.0)	3
	Ours	0.0842	1	(0.0, 4.0)	3
5 (min) $(2, 4, 2)$	[19]	—	—	(1.0, 3.0)	−13
	Ours	0.0150	1	(1.0, 3.0)	−13
6 (min) $(2, 4, 2)$	[19]	—	—	(1.0, 4.0)	−22
	Ours	0.0160	1	(1.0, 4.0)	−22
7 (min) $(3, 7, 3)$	[20]	—	57	(5.5556, 1.7778, 2.6667)	−112.754
	Ours	1.5930	34	(5.5556, 1.7778, 2.6667)	−112.7531
8 (max) $(2, 4, 2)$	[21]	—	13	(0.74984, 0.74984)	−38.87628
	Ours	0.5	16	(0.75, 0.75)	−38.8750
9 (min) $(2, 6, 2)$	[22]	—	7	(1.547, 2.421)	−16.2837
	Ours	0.659	23	(1.5480, 2.4152)	−16.2893
10 (min) $(2, 6, 2)$	[22]	—	29	(1.5549, 0.7561)	10.6756
	Ours	0.7662	27	(1.5568, 0.7545)	10.6753

$\{x^k\}$, where any accumulation point is a globally optimal solution of LMP.

Proof. If the algorithm terminates finitely, without loss of generality, assume that the algorithm terminates at the kth step; by the algorithm, we have

$$\mathrm{UB}_k - \mathrm{LB}_k \leq \varepsilon. \qquad (23)$$

So, x^k is a global optimal solution of the problem LMP.

If the algorithm is infinite, then an infinite sequence $\{x^k\}$ will be generated. Since the feasible region of LMP is bounded, the sequence $\{x^k\}$ must have a convergence subsequence. Without loss of generality, set $\lim_{k \to \infty} x^k = x^*$. By the algorithm, we have

$$\lim_{k \to \infty} \mathrm{LB}_k \leq v. \qquad (24)$$

Since x^* is a feasible solution of problem LMP, $v \leq \Phi(x^*)$. Taken together, the following relation holds:

$$\lim_{k \to \infty} \mathrm{LB}_k \leq v \leq \phi(x^*). \qquad (25)$$

On the other hand, by the algorithm and the continuity of $\phi^l(x)$, we have

$$\lim_{k \to \infty} \mathrm{LB}_k = \lim_{k \to \infty} \phi^l(x^k) = \phi^l(x^*). \qquad (26)$$

By Theorem 1, we can obtain

$$\phi(x^*) = \phi^l(x^*). \qquad (27)$$

Therefore, $v = \phi(x^*)$; that is x^* is a global optimal solution of problem LMP. □

5. Numerical Experiments

To verify the performance of the proposed algorithm, some numerical experiments are carried out and compared with some other methods [8, 13–22]. The algorithm is compiled with Matlab 7.1 on a Pentium IV (3.06 GHZ) microcomputer. The simplex method is applied to solve the linear relaxation programming problems. In our experiments, for Examples 1–10, the convergence tolerance ϵ is 10^{-6}; for Example 11, the convergence tolerance ϵ is 10^{-2}.

The results of problems 1–10 are summarized in Table 1, where the following notations have been used in row headers: Iter is the number of algorithm iterations; Time (s) is

TABLE 2: Comparison results of Algorithms 1 and 2 for Examples 1–10.

Example (p, m, n)	Methods	Time (s)	Iter	Optimal solution	Optimal value
1 (min) $(1, 8, 2)$	Algorithm 1	0.062	1	(2.0, 8.0)	10
	Algorithm 2	0.062	1	(2.0, 8.0)	10
2 (min) $(2, 6, 2)$	Algorithm 1	0.086	1	(0.0, 4.0)	3
	Algorithm 2	0.086	1	(0.0, 4.0)	3
3 (min) $(1, 12, 4)$	Algorithm 1	0.093	1	(1.3148, 0.1396, 0.0, 0.4233)	0.8902
	Algorithm 2	0.093	1	(1.3148, 0.1396, 0.0, 0.4233)	0.8902
4 (min) $(2, 5, 2)$	Algorithm 1	0.0842	1	(0.0, 4.0)	3
	Algorithm 2	0.0842	1	(0.0, 4.0)	3
5 (min) $(2, 4, 2)$	Algorithm 1	0.0150	1	(1.0, 3.0)	−13
	Algorithm 2	0.0150	1	(1.0, 3.0)	−13
6 (min) $(2, 4, 2)$	Algorithm 1	0.0160	1	(1.0, 4.0)	−22
	Algorithm 2	0.0160	1	(1.0, 4.0)	−22
7 (min) $(3, 7, 3)$	Algorithm 1	1.5930	34	(5.5556, 1.7778, 2.6667)	−112.7531
	Algorithm 2	1.9091	58	(5.5556, 1.7778, 2.6667)	−112.7531
8 (max) $(2, 4, 2)$	Algorithm 1	0.5	16	(0.75, 0.75)	−38.8750
	Algorithm 2	1.6425	64	(0.75, 0.75)	−38.8750
9 (min) $(2, 6, 2)$	Algorithm 1	0.659	23	(1.5480, 2.4152)	−16.2893
	Algorithm 2	1.7235	39	(1.5480, 2.4152)	−16.2893
10 (min) $(2, 6, 2)$	Algorithm 1	0.7662	27	(1.5568, 0.7545)	10.6753
	Algorithm 2	1.4862	68	(1.5480, 2.4152)	10.6753

execution time in seconds. Except for the results of our algorithm, the results of the other eleven algorithms are taken directly from the corresponding references. In Table 1, "—" denotes the corresponding value is not available.

For problems 1–10, the efficiency of the algorithm proposed by this paper (named Algorithm 1) and the algorithm proposed by this paper but without using the pruning techniques (named Algorithm 2) is compared. The comparison results are given in Table 2.

Example 1 (see [13–15]).

$$\min \quad (x_1 + x_2)(x_1 - x_2 + 7)$$
$$\text{s.t.} \quad 2x_1 + x_2 \le 14,$$
$$x_1 + x_2 \le 10,$$
$$- 4x_1 + x_2 \le 0,$$
$$- 2x_1 - x_2 \le -6,$$

$$- x_1 - 2x_2 \le -6,$$
$$x_1 - x_2 \le 3,$$
$$x_1 \ge 0, \ x_2 \ge 0.$$

$$(28)$$

Example 2 (see [13, 16]).

$$\min \quad x_1 + (2x_1 - 3x_2 + 13)(x_1 + x_2 - 1)$$
$$\text{s.t.} \quad - x_1 + 2x_2 \le 8,$$
$$- x_2 \le -3,$$
$$x_1 + 2x_2 \le 12,$$
$$x_1 - 2x_2 \le -5,$$
$$x_1 \ge 0, \ x_2 \ge 0.$$

$$(29)$$

Example 3 (see [13, 17]).

$$\min \quad (0.813396x_1 + 0.67440x_2 + 0.305038x_3 + 0.129742x_4 + 0.217796)$$
$$\times (0.224508x_1 + 0.063458x_2 + 0.932230x_3 + 0.528736x_4 + 0.091947)$$
$$\text{s.t.} \quad 0.488509x_1 + 0.063565x_2 + 0.945686x_3 + 0.210704x_4 \le 3.562809,$$
$$- 0.324014x_1 - 0.501754x_2 - 0.719204x_3 + 0.099562x_4 \le -0.052215,$$
$$0.445225x_1 - 0.346896x_2 + 0.637939x_3 - 0.257623x_4 \le 0.427920,$$
$$- 0.202821x_1 + 0.647361x_2 + 0.920135x_3 - 0.983091x_4 \le 0.840950,$$

$$-0.886420x_1 - 0.802444x_2 - 0.305441x_3 - 0.180123x_4 \le -1.353686,$$

$$-0.515399x_1 - 0.424820x_2 + 0.897498x_3 + 0.187268x_4 \le 2.137251,$$

$$-0.591515x_1 + 0.060581x_2 - 0.427365x_3 + 0.579388x_4 \le -0.290987,$$

$$0.423524x_1 + 0.940496x_2 - 0.437944x_3 - 0.742941x_4 \le 0.373620,$$

$$x_1 \ge 0, \ x_2 \ge 0, \ x_3 \ge 0, \ x_4 \ge 0.$$

$$(30)$$

Example 4 (see [8, 18]).

$$\min \quad x_1 + (x_1 - x_2 + 5)(x_1 + x_2 - 1)$$

$$\text{s.t.} \quad -2x_1 - 3x_2 \le -9,$$

$$3x_1 - x_2 \le 8,$$

$$-x_1 + 2x_2 \le 8,$$

$$x_1 + 2x_2 \le 12,$$

$$x_1 \ge 0.$$

$$(31)$$

Example 5 (see [19]).

$$\min \quad (x_1 + x_2)(x_1 - x_2)$$

$$\qquad + (x_1 + x_2 + 1)(x_1 - x_2 + 1)$$

$$\text{s.t.} \quad x_1 + 2x_2 \le 10,$$

$$x_1 - 3x_2 \le 20,$$

$$1 \le x_1 \le 3,$$

$$1 \le x_2 \le 3.$$

$$(32)$$

Example 6 (see [19]).

$$\min \quad (x_1 + x_2)(x_1 - x_2)$$

$$\qquad + (x_1 + x_2 + 2)(x_1 - x_2 + 2)$$

$$\text{s.t.} \quad x_1 + 2x_2 \le 20,$$

$$x_1 - 3x_2 \le 20,$$

$$1 \le x_1 \le 4,$$

$$1 \le x_2 \le 4.$$

$$(33)$$

Example 7 (see [20]).

$$\min \quad (2x_1 - 2x_2 + x_3 + 2)(-2x_1 + 3x_2 + x_3 - 4)$$

$$\qquad + (-2x_1 + x_2 + x_3 + 2)(x_1 + x_2 - 3x_3 + 5)$$

$$\qquad + (-2x_1 - x_2 + 2x_3 + 7)(4x_1 - x_2 - 2x_3 - 5)$$

$$\text{s.t.} \quad x_1 + x_2 + x_3 \le 10,$$

$$x_1 - 2x_2 + 3x_3 \le 10,$$

$$-2x_1 + 2x_2 + 3x_3 \le 10,$$

$$-x_1 + 2x_2 + 3x_3 \ge 6,$$

$$x_1 \ge 1, \ x_2 \ge 1, \ x_3 \ge 1.$$

$$(34)$$

Example 8 (see [21]).

$$\max \quad (-2x_1 + 3x_2 - 6)(3x_1 - 5x_2 + 3)$$

$$\qquad + (4x_1 - 5x_2 - 7)(-3x_1 + 3x_2 + 4)$$

$$\text{s.t.} \quad x_1 + x_2 \le 1.5,$$

$$x_1 - x_2 \le 0,$$

$$x_1 \ge 0, \ x_2 \ge 0.$$

$$(35)$$

Example 9 (see [22]).

$$\min \quad (x_1 + 2x_2 - 2)(-2x_1 - x_2 + 3)$$

$$\qquad + (3x_1 - 2x_2 + 3)(x_1 - x_2 - 1)$$

$$\text{s.t.} \quad -2x_1 + 3x_2 \le 6,$$

$$4x_1 - 5x_2 \le 8,$$

$$5x_1 + 3x_2 \le 15,$$

$$-4x_1 - 3x_2 \le -12,$$

$$x_1 \ge 0, \ x_2 \ge 0.$$

$$(36)$$

Example 10 (see [22]).

$$\min \quad (-x_1 + 2x_2 - 0.5)(-2x_1 + x_2 + 6)$$

$$\qquad + (3x_1 - 2x_2 + 6.5)(x_1 + x_2 - 1)$$

$$\text{s.t.} \quad -5x_1 + 8x_2 \le 24,$$

$$5x_1 + 8x_2 \le 44,$$

$$6x_1 - 3x_2 \le 15,$$

$$-4x_1 - 5x_2 \le -10,$$

$$x_1 \ge 0, \ x_2 \ge 0.$$

$$(37)$$

To further verify the effectiveness of Algorithm 1, a random problem with variable scale is constructed, which is defined as follows.

Example 11.

$$\min \quad f(x) = \sum_{i=1}^{p} \left(c_i^T x + d_i\right)\left(e_i^T x + f_i\right) \tag{38}$$

$$\text{s.t.} \quad x \in D = \left\{x \mid x \in R^n, Ax \le b\right\},$$

where the real elements of c_i, d_i, e_i, f_i are pseudorandomly generated in the range $[-0.5, 0.5]$; the real elements of A, b are pseudorandomly generated in the range $[0.01, 1]$. For Example 11, Algorithms 1 and 2 are used to solve 10 different random instances for each size and present statistics of the results. The computational results are summarized in Table 3, where the following notations have been used in row headers: Avg.Iter is the average number of iterations; Avg.Time is the average execution time in seconds; m is the number of constraints; n is the number of variables.

From Table 1, it can be seen that our algorithm can determine the global optimal solution more effectively than that of [8, 13–22] in most cases. For Examples 8 and 9, although the number of iterations of our algorithm is more than that of the literatures [21, 22], the optimal values and optimal solutions obtained by our algorithm are better than them.

From Table 2, it can be seen that, for Examples 1–6, Algorithms 1 and 2 all only need one iteration to find the optimal solution; the advantage of Algorithm 1 is not reflected. However, for Examples 7–10, the performance of Algorithm 1 is better than that of Algorithm 2.

From Table 3, we can see that, for small scale problems, the advantage of Algorithm 1 is not much better than the Algorithm 2, but with the increase of the scale of the problem, the advantage of Algorithm 1 is more and more powerful. For example, when $(p, m, n) = (10, 5, 5)$, the average running time of Algorithms 1 and 2 is 17.0344 and 29.5778, respectively; the average iterations of Algorithms 1 and 2 are 17.6 and 30.4. However, when $(p, m, n) = (10, 100, 100)$, the average running time of Algorithms 1 and 2 is 42.8972 and 402.0530, respectively; the average iterations of Algorithms 1 and 2 are 56.8 and 215.3. It is clear that the efficiency of Algorithm 1 is much better than that of Algorithm 2 for large scale problems. In addition, from Table 3, we also can see that, compared with m and n, the impact of p on our algorithm is even greater; the Avg.Time and Avg.Iter of Algorithm 1 are not increased significantly with the increase of the problem size.

The comparison results of Tables 2 and 3 show that the pruning techniques are very good at improving the convergence speed of our algorithm.

The test results show that our algorithm is both feasible and efficient.

Competing Interests

The authors declare that there is no conflict of interests regarding the publication of this paper.

TABLE 3: Comparison results of Algorithms 1 and 2 for Example 11.

(p, m, n)	Methods	Avg.Time	Avg.Iter
(3, 5, 5)	Algorithm 1	0.8520	3.4
	Algorithm 2	3.8780	13.6
(3, 10, 10)	Algorithm 1	1.3142	4.2
	Algorithm 2	16.1132	46.8
(3, 20, 20)	Algorithm 1	23.2650	49.6
	Algorithm 2	32.5486	66.8
(3, 100, 100)	Algorithm 1	42.8972	62.5
	Algorithm 2	75.0706	32.2
(6, 5, 5)	Algorithm 1	3.7030	5.2
	Algorithm 2	8.6610	16.6
(6, 10, 10)	Algorithm 1	5.1134	7.8
	Algorithm 2	40.2840	69.8
(6, 20, 20)	Algorithm 1	12.7132	13.4
	Algorithm 2	100.4470	128.8
(6, 100, 100)	Algorithm 1	31.9760	25.3
	Algorithm 2	254.5428	183.4
(10, 5, 5)	Algorithm 1	17.0344	17.6
	Algorithm 2	29.5778	30.4
(10, 10, 10)	Algorithm 1	26.1132	46.8
	Algorithm 2	195.9464	136.8
(10, 20, 20)	Algorithm 1	32.5126	27.8
	Algorithm 2	249.4000	169.2
(10, 100, 100)	Algorithm 1	42.8972	56.8
	Algorithm 2	402.0530	215.3

Acknowledgments

The research was supported by NSFC (U1404105); the Key Scientific and Technological Project of Henan Province (142102210058); the Doctoral Scientific Research Foundation of Henan Normal University (qd12103); the Youth Science Foundation of Henan Normal University (2013qk02); Henan Normal University National Research Project to Cultivate the Funded Projects (01016400105); the Henan Normal University Youth Backbone Teacher Training.

References

[1] C. D. Maranas, I. P. Androulakis, C. A. Floudas, A. J. Berger, and J. M. Mulvey, "Solving long-term financial planning problems via global optimization," *Journal of Economic Dynamics and Control*, vol. 21, no. 8-9, pp. 1405–1425, 1997.

[2] K. P. Bennett and O. L. Mangasarian, "Bilinear separation of two sets in n-space," *Computational Optimization and Applications*, vol. 2, no. 3, pp. 207–227, 1993.

[3] I. Quesada and I. E. Grossmann, "Alternative bounding approximations for the global optimization of various engineering design problems," in *Global Optimization in Engineering Design*, I. E. Grossmann, Ed., vol. 9 of *Nonconvex Optimization and Its Applications*, pp. 309–331, Kluwer Academic Publishers, Norwell, Mass, USA, 1996.

[4] M. C. Dorneich and N. V. Sahinidis, "Global optimization algorithms for chip layout and compaction," *Engineering Optimization*, vol. 25, no. 2, pp. 131–154, 1995.

[5] J. M. Mulvey, R. J. Vanderbei, and S. A. Zenios, "Robust optimization of large-scale systems," *Operations Research*, vol. 43, no. 2, pp. 264–281, 1995.

[6] H. Konno, T. Kuno, and Y. Yajima, "Global minimization of a generalized convex multiplicative function," *Journal of Global Optimization*, vol. 4, no. 1, pp. 47–62, 1994.

[7] T. Kuno, "Solving a class of multiplicative programs with 0–1 knapsack constraints," *Journal of Optimization Theory and Applications*, vol. 103, no. 1, pp. 121–135, 1999.

[8] H.-S. Ryoo and N. V. Sahinidis, "Global optimization of multiplicative programs," *Journal of Global Optimization*, vol. 26, no. 4, pp. 387–418, 2003.

[9] P. Shen and H. Jiao, "Linearization method for a class of multiplicative programming with exponent," *Applied Mathematics and Computation*, vol. 183, no. 1, pp. 328–336, 2006.

[10] X.-G. Zhou and K. Wu, "A method of acceleration for a class of multiplicative programming problems with exponent," *Journal of Computational and Applied Mathematics*, vol. 223, no. 2, pp. 975–982, 2009.

[11] R. Horst and H. Tuy, *Global Optimization: Deterministic Approaches*, Springer, Berline, Germany, 2nd edition, 1993.

[12] H. P. Benson and G. M. Boger, "Outcome-space cutting-plane algorithm for linear multiplicative programming," *Journal of Optimization Theory and Applications*, vol. 104, no. 2, pp. 301–322, 2000.

[13] C.-F. Wang, S.-Y. Liu, and P.-P. Shen, "Global minimization of a generalized linear multiplicative programming," *Applied Mathematical Modelling*, vol. 36, no. 6, pp. 2446–2451, 2012.

[14] Y. L. Gao, C. X. Xu, and Y. T. Yang, "Outcome-space branch and bound algorithm for solving linear multiplicative programming," in *Computational Intelligence and Security: International Conference, CIS 2005, Xi'an, China, December 15–19, 2005, Proceedings Part I*, vol. 3801 of *Lecture Notes in Computer Science*, pp. 675–681, Springer, Berlin, Germany, 2005.

[15] Y. L. Gao, G. R. Wu, and W. M. Ma, "A new global optimization approach for convex multiplicative programming," *Applied Mathematics and Computation*, vol. 216, no. 4, pp. 1206–1218, 2010.

[16] S. Schaible and C. Sodini, "Finite algorithm for generalized linear multiplicative programming," *Journal of Optimization Theory and Applications*, vol. 87, no. 2, pp. 441–455, 1995.

[17] N. V. Thoai, "A global optimization approach for solving the convex multiplicative programming problem," *Journal of Global Optimization*, vol. 1, pp. 341–357, 1991.

[18] J. E. Falk and S. W. Palocsay, "Image space analysis of generalized fractional programs," *Journal of Global Optimization*, vol. 4, no. 1, pp. 63–88, 1994.

[19] H. Jiao, K. Li, and J. Wang, "An optimization algorithm for solving a class of multiplicative problems," *Journal of Chemical and Pharmaceutical Research*, vol. 6, no. 1, pp. 271–277, 2014.

[20] X.-G. Zhou, B.-Y. Cao, and K. Wu, "Global optimization method for linear multiplicative programming," *Acta Mathematicae Applicatae Sinica*, vol. 31, no. 2, pp. 325–334, 2015.

[21] X.-G. Zhou, "Global optimization of linear multiplicative programming using univariate search," in *Fuzzy Information & Engineering and Operations Research & Management*, B.-Y. Cao and H. Nasseri, Eds., vol. 211 of *Advances in Intelligent Systems and Computing*, pp. 51–56, 2014.

[22] X.-G. Zhou and B.-Y. Cao, "A simplicial branch and bound duality-bounds algorithm to linear multiplicative programming," *Journal of Applied Mathematics*, vol. 2013, Article ID 984168, 10 pages, 2013.

17

Efficient Parallel Sorting for Migrating Birds Optimization when Solving Machine-Part Cell Formation Problems

Ricardo Soto,[1,2,3] **Broderick Crawford,**[1,4,5] **Boris Almonacid,**[1] **and Fernando Paredes**[6]

[1] *Pontificia Universidad Católica de Valparaíso, 2362807 Valparaíso, Chile*
[2] *Universidad Autónoma de Chile, 7500138 Santiago, Chile*
[3] *Universidad Científica del Sur, Lima 18, Peru*
[4] *Universidad Central de Chile, 8370178 Santiago, Chile*
[5] *Universidad San Sebastián, 8420524 Santiago, Chile*
[6] *Universidad Diego Portales, 8370109 Santiago, Chile*

Correspondence should be addressed to Boris Almonacid; boris.almonacid.g@mail.pucv.cl

Academic Editor: Eduardo Rodríguez-Tello

The Machine-Part Cell Formation Problem (MPCFP) is a NP-Hard optimization problem that consists in grouping machines and parts in a set of cells, so that each cell can operate independently and the intercell movements are minimized. This problem has largely been tackled in the literature by using different techniques ranging from classic methods such as linear programming to more modern nature-inspired metaheuristics. In this paper, we present an efficient parallel version of the Migrating Birds Optimization metaheuristic for solving the MPCFP. Migrating Birds Optimization is a population metaheuristic based on the V-Flight formation of the migrating birds, which is proven to be an effective formation in energy saving. This approach is enhanced by the smart incorporation of parallel procedures that notably improve performance of the several sorting processes performed by the metaheuristic. We perform computational experiments on 1080 benchmarks resulting from the combination of 90 well-known MPCFP instances with 12 sorting configurations with and without threads. We illustrate promising results where the proposal is able to reach the global optimum in all instances, while the solving time with respect to a nonparallel approach is notably reduced.

1. Introduction

The Machine-Part Cell Formation Problem (MPCFP) is based on the well-known Group Technology (GP) [1] widely used in the manufacturing industry. The goal of the MPCFP is to organize a manufacturing plant in a set of cells that contain a limited number of machines and parts, but minimize the cell-interchange of parts. The purpose is to reduce costs and increase productivity. The MPCFP is known to be NP-Hard, so there is always the challenge of producing high quality solutions in a limited time interval. During the last years, several techniques have successfully been applied to this problem, from mathematical methods such as linear programming [2] to classic metaheuristics such as particle swarm optimization [3] and more modern ones such as artificial fish swarms [4].

In this paper, we present a new and efficient parallel version of the Migrating Birds Optimization metaheuristic for solving the MPCFP. Migrating Birds Optimization (MBO) is a population-based metaheuristic inspired by the V-shaped flight employed by birds when they migrate. This technique is known to be very effective for energy saving during flying. This interesting approach is enhanced by precisely integrating parallel procedures particularly for the efficient sorting of birds and neighboring solutions. It results in a notable improvement in terms of performance of the whole solving process. We perform computational experiments by using 90 well-known MPCFP instances, 2 well-known sorting algorithms, 1 sequential configuration, and 5 thread configurations (1, 4, 8, 16, and 32) resulting in a total of 1080 benchmarks. The obtained results are encouraging where the proposal is able to reach the global optimum in all instances, while the solving time with respect to a nonparallel approach is notably reduced.

The outline of the study is as follows. In Section 2, we give some information on the related work. Section 3 describes

TABLE 1: Initial incidence matrix $M \times P$.

	Part 1	Part 2	Part 3	Part 4	Part 5	Part 6	Part 7
Machine 1	0	1	0	1	1	1	0
Machine 2	1	0	1	0	0	0	0
Machine 3	1	0	1	0	0	0	1
Machine 4	0	1	0	1	0	1	0
Machine 5	1	0	0	0	0	0	1

and models the MPCFP. Section 4 gives an overview of MBO. Section 5 describes how to resolve the MPCFP using MBO with parallel sort. Section 6 presents and discusses the experimental results. Section 7 concludes and provides guidelines for future work. Finally, the Appendix provides detailed results for the 1080 benchmarks, in which each includes 90 test instances.

2. Related Work

Several investigations that have been carried out for the problem MPCFP are as follows: linear programming [5], a goal programming model [6], a hybrid genetic algorithm [7], boolean satisfiability [8], constraint programming [9], and using an artificial fish swarm algorithm [4]. An analysis of the evolution of cell formation problem can be found in [10, 11]. As MPCFP is NP-Hard problem, many researchers have considered applying approximation methods as metaheuristics. Various research can be found in the field of metaheuristics,.in which the search is performed using iterative procedures, which allow moving from one solution to another in the search space. This type of metaheuristic performs movements in the neighborhood of the current solution, which means it has a perturbative nature. As metaheuristics are based on trajectories, among which we have simulated annealing [12–14], tabu search [15–17], local iterated search [18, 19], and local variable search [20], there is also another type of metaheuristics which are based on population. The population metaheuristics have a set of individuals, where each individual encodes a temporary solution. These metaheuristics use an evaluation function fitness of each individual, with the aim of obtaining the best values of the population that solve an optimization problem. In addition, there are disturbances in the algorithm that directed individuals in the population or part of them to possible solutions for better fitness. Among these population-based metaheuristics, ant colony optimization [21, 22], particle swarm optimization [3, 23, 24], cat swarm [25, 26], and Migrating Birds Optimization [27] can be found in problems like a hybrid flowshop scheduling with total flowtime minimisation [28], closed loop layout with exact distances in flexible manufacturing systems [29], and preliminary results for MPCFP [30]. A brief review of nature-inspired algorithms for optimization can be found in [31].

In the area of manufacturing and industrial applications, parallel implementations using metaheuristics have been addressed, such as GRASP and grid computing to solve the location area problem [32], performance analysis of coarse-grained parallel genetic algorithms on the multicore

Sun Ultra SPARC T1 [33], a parallel genetic algorithm for the multilevel unconstrained lot-sizing problem [34], and a memetic algorithm and a parallel hyperheuristic island-based model for a 2D packing problem [35]. We can also find research using parallel metaheuristics as a cooperative parallel metaheuristic for the capacitated vehicle routing problem [36] and optimizing shared-memory hyperheuristics on top of parameterized metaheuristics [37] and, finally, we can find a review of recent progress in implementing parallelism with metaheuristics included in the following work [38].

Different studies have addressed the parallel sorting algorithms as massively parallel sort-merge joins in main memory multicore database systems [39], an efficient parallel merge sort for fixed and variable length keys [40], a randomized parallel sorting algorithm with an experimental study [41], sorting algorithm for many-core architectures based on adaptive bitonic sort [42], performance comparison of sequential quick sort and parallel quick sort algorithms [43], the time profit obtained by parallelization of quick sort algorithm used for numerical sorting [44], an efficient massively parallel quick sort [45], and, finally, a fast parallel implementation of quick sort and its performance evaluation on SUN enterprise 10000 [46].

In this paper, we have chosen metaheuristic MBO because it has a friendly design, composed of two linked lists for each of the sides of the flock of birds and a node as a leader bird. Furthermore, MBO has been applied to various optimization problems with promising results [47–49]. We focus on an efficient parallel sorting for MBO when solving MPCFP, which to our knowledge has not yet been reported. It has been chosen to parallelize the sorting algorithms in MBO because 4 out of the 8 steps of the MBO metaheuristic used sorting algorithms, and therefore we believe that applying parallel sorting in these steps is possible to achieve reduction of the execution time in MBO algorithm.

3. Machine-Part Cell Formation Problems

The Machine-Part Cell Formation Problem (MPCFP) is NP-Hard optimization problem; the main objective is the formation of set of machines and parts in groups so that the number of intercell transportation of parts is minimized. Therefore, the initial matrix (see matrix in Table 1) must be converted into a matrix that has a block diagonal structure (cells are easily visible; see matrix in Table 2). This example corresponds to a MPCFP with the following parameters: 5 machines, 7 parts, and $M_{max} = 3$ for 2 cells. The optimum value obtained is 0, and the final incidence matrix a_{ij} is

TABLE 2: Rearranged incidence matrix $M \times P$.

| | Cell 1 | | | Cell 2 | | | |
	Part 1	Part 3	Part 7	Part 2	Part 4	Part 6	Part 5
Cell 1							
Machine 2	1	1	0	0	0	0	0
Machine 3	1	1	1	0	0	0	0
Machine 5	1	0	1	0	0	0	0
Cell 2							
Machine 1	0	0	0	1	1	1	1
Machine 4	0	0	0	1	1	1	0

TABLE 3: Matrix $M \times C \rightarrow y_{ik}$.

	Cell 1	Cell 2
Machine 1	0	1
Machine 2	1	0
Machine 3	1	0
Machine 4	0	1
Machine 5	1	0

TABLE 4: Matrix $P \times C \rightarrow z_{jk}$.

	Cell 1	Cell 2
Part 1	1	0
Part 2	0	1
Part 3	1	0
Part 4	0	1
Part 5	0	1
Part 6	0	1
Part 7	1	0

constructed from the results of the matrices y_{ik} and z_{jk} (see Tables 3 and 4).

A rigorous mathematical formulation of MPCFP is given by Boctor [2]. The problem is represented by the following mathematical model:

(i) Parameters, index, and sets:

    (a) a_{ij}, the $M \times P$ binary machine-part incidence matrix, where

$$a_{ij} = \begin{cases} 1 & \text{if } j_{\text{th}} \text{ part visits } i_{\text{th}} \text{ machine;} \\ 0 & \text{otherwise,} \end{cases} \quad (1)$$

    (b) M, the number of machines,

    (c) P, the number of parts,

    (d) C, the number of cells,

    (e) i, the index of machines ($i = 1, \ldots, M$),

    (f) j, the index of parts ($j = 1, \ldots, P$),

    (g) k, the index of cells ($k = 1, \ldots, C$),

    (h) M_{max}, the maximum number of machines per cell.

(ii) Variables and domains:

    (a) y_{ik}, the $M \times C$ machine-cell matrix, where

$$y_{ik} = \begin{cases} 1 & \text{if machine } i \in \text{cell } k; \\ 0 & \text{otherwise,} \end{cases} \quad (2)$$

    (b) z_{jk}, the $P \times C$ part-cell matrix, where

$$z_{jk} = \begin{cases} 1 & \text{if part } j \in \text{family } k; \\ 0 & \text{otherwise.} \end{cases} \quad (3)$$

(iii) Objective function:

$$\text{minimized} \quad \sum_{k=1}^{C} \sum_{i=1}^{M} \sum_{j=1}^{P} a_{ij} z_{jk} (1 - y_{ik}). \quad (4)$$

(iv) Being subject to the following constraints:

$$\sum_{k=1}^{C} y_{ik} = 1 \quad \forall_i,$$

$$\sum_{i=1}^{M} y_{ik} \leq M_{\text{max}} \quad \forall_k, \quad (5)$$

$$\sum_{k=1}^{C} z_{jk} = 1 \quad \forall_j.$$

4. Migrating Birds Optimization

Migrating Birds Optimization (MBO) is a nature-inspired population metaheuristic based on the V-shaped flight of the migrating birds [50, 51], which is proven to be an effective formation in energy saving [52]. In the V-formation (shown in Figure 1), some parameters like wing-tip spacing (WTS), maximum width of the wing (w), angle of the V-formation (α), and depth and wing span (b) are important to form an effective V-formation [53, 54]. The conceptual similarity between the parameters of the algorithm of MBO with the actual migration of birds in V-flight formation is investigated in Duman et al. [27]. This conceptual similarity is described in Table 5.

TABLE 5: Conceptual similarity of MBO metaheuristic and V-shape natural migration of birds.

Parameter description	Concept in real migration birds in V-formation
The number of initial solutions of the flock.	Birds in V-formation.
The number of neighboring solutions generated for each initial solution.	The induced power required which is inversely proportional to the speed.
The number of neighboring solutions shared with the next solution.	Wing-tip spacing (WTS).
The number of tours.	The number of wing flaps before a change occurs in the leading bird.
The number of iterations (total number of generated neighbor solutions).	There is no conceptual relationship.

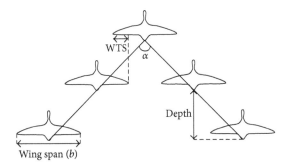

FIGURE 1: The V-shaped flight.

The MBO starts with a number of n initial solutions corresponding to birds in a V-flight formation. These solutions are generated randomly and a solution as the leader bird is chosen; then the remaining birds are alternately distributed to each side of the flock. In the next step, for all tours, improving the leader solution is performed by generating and evaluating its k neighbors. For each solution S_r in the flock (except leader), try to improve S_r by evaluating its $(k - x)$ neighbors and x unused best neighbors from the solution in the front. Move the leader solution to the end and forward one of the solutions following it to the leader position. Finally, when the iterations are over, return the best solution in the flock. Algorithm 1 depicts the classic procedure of MBO algorithm.

5. Solving the MPCFP Using MBO with Parallel Sort

The first step in solving the problem MPCFP is a proper integration with the MBO metaheuristic. In this sense, we conceptualize every bird of the flock (including the leader of the flock) as a possible solution to the problem MPCFP (see Figure 2). Each bird will be composed of a matrix $M \times C$ and matrix $P \times C$. These matrices are those modified while the problem lapsed iterations. In addition, they will be used for the calculation of fitness to problem MPCFP.

5.1. Generate Initial Solutions. For generating initial solutions, consider the following inputs: machines = 4, parts = 5, cells = 2, $M_{max} = 2$, and a matrix $M \times P$ (see Table 6).

Considering data in Table 6, the first step to generate an initial solution is as follows.

Step 1. Generate random allocations in the matrix $M \times P$ with some random method. This matrix $M \times C$ (see Table 7) satisfies constraints that exists in only one machine in a cell and M_{max} is less than or equal to 2 in an entire cell.

Step 2. Generate with a manual method the matrix $P \times C$ from the matrix $M \times C$. For this, a connection is established with the matrix $M \times P$ and with the matrix solution $M \times C$. In lightface, machines correspond to the cell number 1 and, in bold, machines correspond to cell number 2 (see Table 8).

The manual method for determining the matrix $P \times C$ involves adding the value 1 out of every position i, j of the $M \times P$ matrix and putting this value in the temporary array of sums according to the corresponding cell. We perform the operation for each value of positions i, j of the matrix $M \times P$ (see Table 9).

Example 1.

(i) $M \times P[1, 1] = 1 \rightarrow$ is the value that is associated with cell 1; we add this value to the Row *Sum of Cell* 1.

(ii) $M \times P[2, 1] = 1 \rightarrow$ is the value that is associated with cell 2; we add to this value to the Row *Sum of Cell* 2.

(iii) $M \times P[3, 1] = 0 \rightarrow$ is the value that is associated with cell 2; we add this value to the Row *Sum of Cell* 2.

(iv) $M \times P[4, 1] = 1 \rightarrow$ is the value that is associated with cell 1; we add to this value to the Row *Sum of Cell* 1.

Step 3. From the results of Table 9, we build a partial solution to the matrix $P \times C$ (see Table 10).

Step 4. Find possible solutions to $P \times C$.

We must choose the values of the positions i, j that belong to the temporary matrix $M \times P$ and have the largest values of each row. Subsequently, we replace larger values assigning them the value 1, and for the other values in the row we assign them the value of 0 (see Table 11). In case of draw, that is, the entire row has equal numbers, we keep unchanged if the value of their positions is 1. In the case that the same numbers are greater than 1, to each number greater than 1, we assign them a value of 1.

We consider rows having values equal to 1 in this case correspond to rows pertaining to machines 3 and 4. From this point, we generate all possible combinations of matrices and randomly choose one (see Table 12).

(1) Generate *n* initial solutions in V-formation
(2) $i = 0$
(3) **while** $(i < I)$ **do**
(4)   **for** int $j = 0$; $j < m$; j++ **do**
(5)   Improve the leading solution by generating and evaluating k neighbors of it
(6) $i = i + k$
(7)   **for** *each solution S_r in the flock (except leader)* **do**
(8)   Try to improve S_r by evaluating $(k - x)$ neighbors of it and x unused best
                 neighbors from the leader
(9) $i = i + (k - x)$
(10)   **end**
(11)   **end**
(12)   Move the leader solution to the end and forward one of the solutions following it
            to the leader position
(13) **end**
(14) Return the best solution in the flock

ALGORITHM 1: Pseudocode of Migrating Birds Optimization.

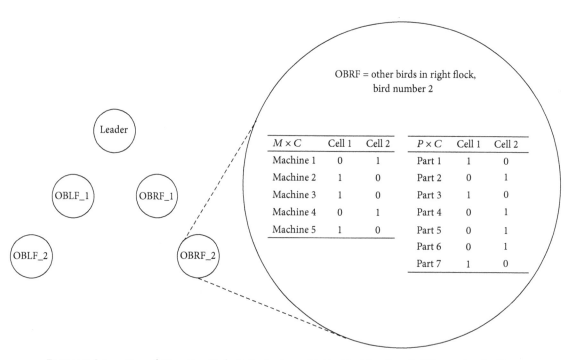

FIGURE 2: Integration of Migrating Birds Optimization with the Machine-Part Cell Formation Problem.

TABLE 6: Matrix $M \times P$.

	Part 1	Part 2	Part 3	Part 4	Part 5
Machine 1	1	0	0	1	1
Machine 2	1	0	1	0	1
Machine 3	0	1	0	1	1
Machine 4	1	0	1	0	0

TABLE 7: Matrix $M \times C$.

	Cell 1	Cell 2
Machine 1	1	0
Machine 2	0	1
Machine 3	0	1
Machine 4	1	0

5.2. Generating Neighboring Solutions. To generate a neighboring solution, we consider the following inputs: machines = 4, parts = 5, cells = 2, $M_{max} = 2$, matrix $M \times P$, matrix $M \times C$, and matrix $P \times C$ (see Table 13).

Step 1. Randomly choose a position i, j in the matrix $M \times C$ that has a value of 1 and we work with the machine associated with that row i. This is the same as selecting a machine and working with its row i. In this case, we chose randomly the

TABLE 8: Relationship between the matrix $M \times P$ with the matrix $M \times C$.

	Part 1	Part 2	Part 3	Part 4	Part 5	Cell 1	Cell 2
Machine 1	1	0	0	1	1	1	0
Machine 2	1	0	1	0	1	0	1
Machine 3	0	1	0	1	1	0	1
Machine 4	1	0	1	0	0	1	0

TABLE 9: Generation of temporary matrix sum.

	Part 1	Part 2	Part 3	Part 4	Part 5	Cell 1	Cell 2
Machine 1	1	0	0	1	1	1	0
Machine 2	1	0	1	0	1	0	1
Machine 3	0	1	0	1	1	0	1
Machine 4	1	0	1	0	0	1	0
Sum of Cell 1	2	0	1	1	1		
Sum of Cell 2	1	1	1	1	2		

TABLE 10: Matrix $P \times C$.

	Cell 1	Cell 2
Part 1	2	1
Part 2	0	1
Part 3	1	1
Part 4	1	1
Part 5	1	2

TABLE 11: Matrix $P \times C$.

	Cell 1	Cell 2		Cell 1	Cell 2
Part 1	2	1		1	0
Part 2	0	1		0	1
Part 3	1	1	$\rightarrow$	1	1
Part 4	1	1		1	1
Part 5	1	2		0	1

position of the matrix $M \times C[2, 2]$ with a value of 1, which corresponds to machine 2 (see Table 14).

Step 2. Then on machine 2, we randomly pick a cell that has a 0. In this case, we choose the position of the matrix $M \times C[2, 1]$; we accomplish a replacement of the value of 0 to 1 and finally realize a replacement for $M \times C[2, 2]$ value of 1 to 0. You can see the result of this operation in Table 15. In the case that the constraints are inconsistent, you must repeat the procedure from Step 1.

Step 3. We carry out the construction of the matrix $P \times C$ using the manual method explained in Section 5.1.

5.3. Flowchart of Migrating Birds Optimization. This section describes the stages of the algorithm MBO, as it integrates with the problem of MPCFP and in which stages parallel arrangement algorithms are applied. For a better understanding, a flow chart has been included (see Figure 3) which is divided into 4 main phases: algorithm initialization, a tour process, leader replacement, and algorithm finalization.

5.3.1. Algorithm Initialization. Parameter Initialization (Stage 1 in Figure 3). At this stage, all the values required by the MBO metaheuristic are initialized; all the values required by the problem of MPCFP and that type of sorting algorithm are to be implemented in the metaheuristic.

Among the metaheuristic values, there are

(i) number of birds (n),

(ii) number of neighbors (k),

(iii) number of tours (m),

(iv) number of shared solutions (x),

(v) number of iterations (I).

And between complementary metaheuristic parameters, we can include

(i) leader exchange mode, where there are 2 types of changes of leader; exchange the leader with the successor and exchange the leader with the best;

(ii) sort type applied in the initial birds flock, where there is an ordering with random birds in the flock and another with birds ordered according to their fitness.

Among the parameters required for the problem MPCFP, we have

(i) incidence matrix ($M \times P$),

(ii) number of machines (M),

(iii) number of parts (P),

(iv) number of cells (C),

(v) maximum number of machines in a cell ($M_{\max}$).

Finally, for the types of sorting applied to MBO, we have the following parameters:

(i) Type of sorting algorithm: quick sort or merge sort.

(ii) Sorting technique: normal or with threads.

(iii) Number of threads if required.

TABLE 12: All possible combinations of matrices $P \times C$.

	Cell 1	Cell 2		Cell 1	Cell 2
Part 1	1	0	Part 1	1	0
Part 2	0	1	Part 2	0	1
Part 3	1	0	Part 3	1	0
Part 4	1	0	Part 4	0	1
Part 5	0	1	Part 5	0	1
	Cell 1	Cell 2		Cell 1	Cell 2
Part 1	1	0	Part 1	1	0
Part 2	0	1	Part 2	0	1
Part 3	0	1	Part 3	0	1
Part 4	1	0	Part 4	0	1
Part 5	0	1	Part 5	0	1

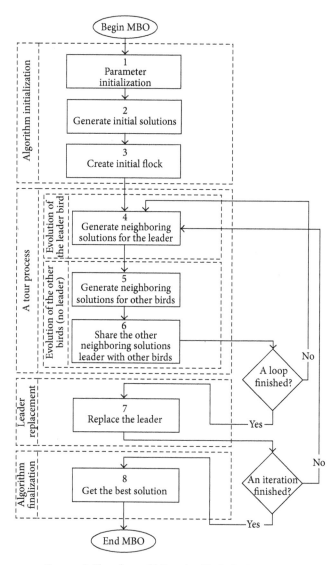

FIGURE 3: Flowchart of Migrating Birds Optimization.

TABLE 13: Initial matrices for generating neighboring solutions.

(a)

	Cell 1	Cell 2	Cell 3	Cell 4	Cell 5
Machine 1	1	0	0	1	1
Machine 2	1	0	1	0	1
Machine 3	0	1	0	1	1
Machine 4	1	0	1	0	0

(b)

	Cell 1	Cell 2
Machine 1	1	0
Machine 2	0	1
Machine 3	0	1
Machine 4	1	0

(c)

	Cell 1	Cell 2
Part 1	1	0
Part 2	0	1
Part 3	0	1
Part 4	1	0
Part 5	0	1

TABLE 14: Machine selection.

(a)

	Cell 1	Cell 2
Machine 1	1	0
Machine 2	0	1
Machine 3	0	1
Machine 4	1	0

(b)

	Cell 1	Cell 2
Machine 1	1	0
Machine 2	**0**	**1**
Machine 3	0	1
Machine 4	1	0

TABLE 15: Final matrix $M \times C$.

	Cell 1	Cell 2
Machine 1	1	0
Machine 2	1	0
Machine 3	0	1
Machine 4	1	0

Generate Initial Solutions (Stage 2 in Figure 3). At this stage, we generate initial solutions according to the method described in Section 5.1. These solutions must satisfy the three constraints of model MPCFP.

Create Initial Flock (Stage 3 in Figure 3). From the initial solutions, we create an array of birds, and finally ordered arrangement created the conceptual V-formation birds. For it, we assign the first position (first solution) in the array as the leader of the flock, and we perform an alternate distribution of birds between each side of the flock for the rest of the birds. We must consider that the birds are always sorted by fitness from low to high, the bird with lower fitness being the best solution to the problem (MPCFP is a minimization problem). Furthermore, we must consider that this is a stage in which we incorporate parallel order by quick sort and merge sort.

5.3.2. A Tour Process. This phase has two subphases internally: evolution of the leader bird and the evolution of the other birds. The evolution of the leader bird phase has one stage (generating neighboring solutions for the leader) and the evolution of the other birds phase has two stages (generating neighboring solutions for the other birds and sharing neighboring solutions that are not used by the leader with the other birds).

Generate Neighboring Solutions for the Leader (Stage 4 in Figure 3). This stage consists of generating neighboring solutions according to the steps outlined in Section 5.2. Subsequently, these neighboring solutions are sorted using an algorithm of parallel sort; see line (5) in the algorithm MBO (Algorithm 1).

Generate Neighboring Solutions for the Other Birds (Stage 5 in Figure 3). In this stage, we create $k - x$ neighboring solution to each bird of the flock; then these birds are sorted by an algorithm of parallel sort; see lines (7) and (8) in the algorithm MBO (Algorithm 1).

Share Neighboring Solutions That Are Not Used by the Leader with the Other Birds (Stage 6 in Figure 3). Share the other neighboring solutions of the leader with the other sides of the V-formation of birds; this is done alternately from left to right or from right to left. After sharing the neighboring solutions, we performed a sorting using an algorithm of parallel sort in all neighboring solutions that every bird in the flock has (not including the leader).

Leader Replacement (Stage 7 in Figure 3). At this stage, we performed a replacement of leader; for this we choose the nearest successor; that is, choose one of the birds closer to the leader. The successor will take its place and the leader will be available at the end of the flock. We must take into consideration that if we choose a successor belonging to the left section of the flock, the leader will pass to the end of the left section. The same procedure applies to the right section of the flock (see Algorithm 2).

Algorithm Finalization (Stage 8 in Figure 3). In this step, the fitness of the leader is obtained; in addition, a procedure to remove a response matrix explicitly is made; that is, we construct an incidence matrix $A[M][P]$ according to the order given by the matrices of solutions Y and Z. The order is according to the index of less than most of the machines and parts (see Algorithm 3).

```
(1)  int type_of_sort = Get_Type_Of_Sort ()
(2)  boolean left_or_right_side = Random_Boolean ()
(3)  Main Function Replace_Leader_With_Successor () is
(4)      if left_or_right_side then
(5)          Change_Leader_With_Left_Birds ()
(6)          Sort_Left_Birds (type_of_sort)
(7)      else
(8)          Change_Leader_With_Right_Birds ()
(9)          Sort_Right_Birds (type_of_sort)
(10)     end
(11)     left_or_right_side = !left_or_right_side
(12) end
```

ALGORITHM 2: Replace leader with successor.

```
(1)  Main Function Convert_to_final_matrix (int A[i][j], int Y[][], int Z[][]) is
(2)      int final_matrix[M][P], temp_matrix[M][P], ii = 0, jj = 0
(3)      /* Sort machines */
(4)      for int k = 0; k < C; k++ do
(5)          for int i = 0; i < M; i++ do
(6)              if Y[i][k] == 1 then
(7)                  for int j = 0; j < P; j++ do
(8)                      temp_matrix[ii][j] = A[i][j]
(9)                  end
(10)                 ii = ii + 1
(11)             end
(12)         end
(13)     end
(14)     /* Sort parts */
(15)     for int k = 0; k < C; k++ do
(16)         for int j = 0; j < P; j++ do
(17)             if Z[j][k] == 1 then
(18)                 for int i = 0; i < M; i++ do
(19)                     final_matrix[i][jj] = temp_matrix[i][j]
(20)                 end
(21)                 jj = jj + 1
(22)             end
(23)         end
(24)     end
(25)     return final_matrix
(26) end
```

ALGORITHM 3: Convert matrix $M \times C$ and $P \times C$ to final matrix.

5.3.3. Sorting Algorithm. For MBO, we use two sorting algorithms, merge sort and quick sort, in which we executed sequentially and in parallel using threads.

Merge Sort. It was developed in 1945 by John Von Neumann. It is a search algorithm of complexity $O(n \log n)$ (see Table 16). Algorithm 4 illustrates a general pseudocode for merge sort.

Quick Sort. It was developed in 1959 by Charles Richard Hoare. It is a search algorithm of complexity $O(n \log n)$ (see Table 16). Algorithm 5 illustrates a general pseudocode for quick sort.

6. Computational Experiments

6.1. Configuration Benchmarks. The MPCFP performance was evaluated experimentally using 90 test instances from Boctor's experiments, composed of 10 problems considering 5 values of $M_{max} = 8, 9, 10, 11, 12$ with $C = 2$ and 10 instances considering 4 values of $M_{max} = 6, 7, 8, 9$ with $C = 3$. The test data are available in [55]. The 90 instances have been executed 31 times using 12 different configurations of sequential and parallel sorting (see Table 18). We must also consider that the sorting algorithms (sequential and parallel) were applied in the following stages (see Figure 3) of MBO:

(i) Stage 3 → create initial flock.

(ii) Stage 4 → generate neighboring solutions for the leader.

```
(1)  Main Function MergeSort (Object[] A) is
(2)      Object[] result, left, right
(3)      if length(A) ≤ 1 then
(4)          return A
(5)      else
(6)          int middle = length(A)/2
(7)          for i = 0 to middle do
(8)              left[i] = A[i]
(9)          end
(10)         for i = middle + 1 to length(A) do
(11)             right[i] = A[i]
(12)         end
(13)         left = MergeSort (left)
(14)         right = MergeSort (right)
(15)         result = Merge (left, right)
(16)         return result
(17)     end
(18) end
```

ALGORITHM 4: Merge sort.

```
(1)  Main Function QuickSort (Object[] A, int low, int high) is
(2)      if low < high then
(3)          pivot_location = Partition (A, low, high)
(4)          QuickSort (A, low, pivot_location)
(5)          QuickSort (A, pivot_location + 1, high)
(6)      end
(7)  end
(1)  Function Partition (Object[] A, int low, int high) is
(2)      Object pivot = A[low]
(3)      int leftwall = low
(4)      for i = low + 1 to high do
(5)          if A[i] < pivot then
(6)              Swap (A[i], A[leftwall])
(7)              leftwall = leftwall + 1
(8)          end
(9)      end
(10)     Swap (A[low], A[leftwall])
(11)     return leftwall
(12) end
```

ALGORITHM 5: Quick sort.

(iii) Stage 5 → generate neighboring solutions for other birds.

(iv) Stage 6 → share neighboring solutions that are not used by the leader with the other birds.

The optimization algorithm using parallel sorting was coded in Java version 1.8.0_40 using Eclipse IDE for Java Developers Version Mars.1 Release (4.5.1). For running the MBO with parallel sorting, we use Java(TM) SE Runtime Environment (build 1.8.0_40-b27). The parameter values of MBO are described in Table 17. Finally, the hardware features that have run instances are MacBook Pro computer (Retina, 13-inch, late 2013) with an Intel Core i5 (processor speed = 2,4 GHz; number of processors = 1; total number of cores = 2; L2 cache per core = 256 KB; L3 cache = 3 MB), 4 GB RAM 1600 MHz DDR3, and Video Card Intel Iris 1536 MB running OS X El Capitan version 10.11.2 (15C50).

6.2. Results. Tables 19 and 20 represent a summary of the results provided in Appendix A [55]. These summary tables describe the average results of 90 instances. Column 1 (threads) corresponds to the identifier assigned to the number of threads used in the search algorithm. Column 2 (execution time-BET) shows the best execution time obtained in milliseconds. Column 3 (execution time-AVG) describes the average time in milliseconds of the finest time of execution of MBO. Column 4 (execution time-ST) represents the standard deviation of the best times of execution obtained by MBO. Column 5 (cycle-BC) shows the cycle in which the optimal value was found. Column 6 (cycle-AVG)

TABLE 16: Complexity sorting algorithm.

Name	Best	Average	Worst	Memory	Method	Stable
Merge sort	$O(n \log n)$	$O(n \log n)$	$O(n \log n)$	Depends	Merging	Yes
Quick sort	$O(n \log n)$	$O(n \log n)$	$O(n^2)$	$O(\log n)$	Partition	Depends

TABLE 17: Configuration parameters for MBO.

Name	Parameter	Value
Number of birds	n	5
Number of neighbors	k	3
Number of tours	m	10
Number of shared solutions	x	1
Number of iterations	I	2591
Leader exchange mode	—	Exchange the leader with the successor
Sort type applied in the initial birds flock	—	Birds ordered according to their fitness

TABLE 18: Configuration sorting algorithms.

Algorithm	Sequential	Threads				
		1	4	8	16	32
Merge sort	Yes	Yes	Yes	Yes	Yes	Yes
Quick sort	Yes	Yes	Yes	Yes	Yes	Yes

describes the average cycle. Column 7 (cycle-ST) represents the standard deviation. Column 8 (time cycle-BTC) shows the best cycle time in which the optimal value was found in milliseconds. Column 9 (time cycle-AVG) describes the average cycle in milliseconds. Column 10 (time cycle-ST) represents the standard deviation in milliseconds. Finally, we must consider all tests that have achieved the global optimum.

Execution Time Analysis. The execution time is the total time when the metaheuristic was searching in the search space for the best solution. In this sense, according to what is described in Tables 19 and 20, we can consider that the merge sort algorithm using 8 threads had the lowest average time (152.7333 ms) to run 90 instances (see column 2: execution time-BET in Tables 19 and 20). In addition, when we compare the times of running the metaheuristic sequentially (without threads and using merge sort algorithm), regarding the best time to run the metaheuristic reached with threads (8 threads), we can see that using 8 threads is an improvement in the execution time of the metaheuristic. This behavior can also be seen in Tables 19 and 20 (see column 3: execution time-AVG in Tables 19 and 20).

Cycle Analysis. A cycle is fulfilled after replacing the leader of the flock (stage 7 in Figure 3). Currently with a parameter of 2591 iterations (I), we can achieve 38 cycles. Consequently, the leader of the flock during the algorithm changes its value 38 times. Basically, the cycles, where the best value has been obtained before the execution is finished, provided us with information to reduce the iteration time assigned in the input parameter of the metaheuristic. Considering the values of the cycles (see column 6: cycle-AVG in Tables 19 and 20), we can approximate an average value in 9, for the number of cycles to

find a global optimum, for using both merge sort and quick sort, with threads and without threads. Also, this involves reducing the value of the iteration limit $I = 2591 \rightarrow I = 561$. But we must also consider the random factor having the metaheuristic (see stage 2 in Figure 3, stage 4 in Figure 3, and stage 5 in Figure 3), and this randomness allows the possibility of finding a global optimum with fewer cycles (see column 5: cycle-BC in Tables 19 and 20). Therefore, this is a recommended change, but it is not enough to always find a global optimum. The quick sort algorithm using threads having irregular times is even much worse than the quick sort used sequentially.

Time Cycle Analysis. In relation to the average cycle time where the best optimum was found, we note that, according to the tests, the merge sort algorithm with 8 threads has been the least time used (see column 9: time cycle-AVG in Tables 19 and 20. It should be considered interesting results as it has achieved better times using parallel sort versus sequential sort, mainly by using merge sort with 4, 8, and 16 threads and quick sort with 16 threads (see column 8: time cycle-BTC in Tables 19 and 20).

7. Conclusions

In this paper, we use a Migrating Birds Optimization algorithm by a parallel sorting to solve Machine-Part Cell Formation Problems. Computational experiments using conventional hardware resources have been conducted in 90 test instances, 2 well-known sorting algorithms, 1 sequential configuration, and 5 thread configurations (1, 4, 8, 16, and 32), giving a total of 1080 benchmarks. Among the main results,

TABLE 19: Result of merge sort.

Threads	Execution time (ms)				Cycle			Time cycle (ms)		
	BET	AVG	ST	BC	AVG	SD	BTC	AVG	SD
Without threads	153.9667	171.1556	21.1539	3.1667	9.0778	4.7263	13.6778	43.3778	23.8747
1	155.5556	168.4111	13.9276	3.0222	9.0778	4.7812	13.2333	42.6556	22.9180
4	153.9333	170.9556	28.8802	2.8556	9.1556	4.9501	12.1444	43.7333	25.6019
8	152.7333	155.8667	3.8451	2.9667	9.2778	4.8785	12.2111	40.2333	20.2717
16	153.1333	161.8222	11.5292	2.9222	9.1222	4.9112	12.2444	40.9000	21.5416
32	153.9222	169.5000	21.8506	3.1889	9.2000	4.8937	13.5667	43.6333	24.7712
Minimum	152.7333	155.8667	3.8451	2.8556	9.0778	4.7263	12.1444	40.2333	20.2717
Maximum	155.5556	171.1556	28.8802	3.1889	9.2778	4.9501	13.6778	43.7333	25.6019

TABLE 20: Result of quick sort.

Threads	Execution time (ms)				Cycle			Time cycle (ms)		
	BET	AVG	ST	BC	AVG	SD	BTC	AVG	SD
Without threads	153.3333	163.0000	12.7284	2.9889	9.0111	4.9168	12.5222	41.2222	22.1071
1	154.5778	167.9000	15.5926	3.0889	9.0778	4.8703	13.1778	42.2667	22.3487
4	153.3111	163.6778	12.2109	3.1333	9.2000	4.9019	13.3222	41.7444	22.4733
8	169.2889	195.6667	26.3893	2.8667	9.1667	4.8796	13.5667	49.6556	27.5041
16	154.3444	169.7778	18.9543	2.8111	8.9889	4.7619	12.1333	42.2444	23.6231
32	156.0889	176.7222	25.8717	2.9889	9.1111	4.8993	13.4111	45.5889	25.9852
Minimum	153.3111	163.0000	12.2109	2.8111	8.9889	4.7619	12.1333	41.2222	22.1071
Maximum	169.2889	195.6667	26.3893	3.1333	9.2000	4.9168	13.5667	49.6556	27.5041

we highlight a new alignment of the MBO parameters to solve MPCFP. The new configuration consists of the following parameter values: number of birds ($n \rightarrow 5$), number of neighbors ($k \rightarrow 3$), number of tours ($m \rightarrow 10$), number of shared solutions ($x \rightarrow 1$), and number of iterations ($I \rightarrow 2591$). We observed a decrease in cycles from 38 to 9, which means that the leader of the flock reaching the cycle number 9 has a very high probability of finding the global optimum; therefore, we can reduce the number of iteration limit from $I = 2591$ to $I = 561$. This observation of the number of cycles applied to all benchmarks.

In addition, it is important to note that quick sort algoritm has variable times in the execution of MBO (see column 9: time cycle-AVG in Table 20). There have been cases in which quick sort algorithm runs without threads; it is even more favorable than when run with threads. Otherwise, with the merge sort algorithm, we found promising results. We can consider that the merge sort algorithm using 8 threads shows a reduction in execution time compared to using sequential sorting algorithm.

Among the guidelines for future research, we can point to applying different ways of generating initial solutions as well as of generating neighboring solutions. We can also compare them with other sorting algorithms implemented in MBO.

Appendix

A. Details of the Benchmarks

A.1. Boctor's Problems. Table 21 describes the configuration of the 90 instances of tests. The description of the table is given the following attributes: Column 1 (ID) corresponds to the identifier assigned to each instance. Column 2 (Boctor's problem) represents the identifier of the 10 Boctor's problems. Column 3 (cell) is the number of cells. Column 4 (M_{max}) corresponds to the maximum number of machines per cell. Column 5 (OPT) depicts the optimum global for the given problem.

A.2. Experimental Results. Tables 22, 23, 24, 25, 26, 27, 28, 29, 30, 31, 32, and 33 contrast the times by using different sorting algorithms. These tables have the same headers, which are described below: column 1 (ID) corresponds to the identifier assigned to each instance. Column 2 (OPT) depicts the optimum value for the given problem. Column 3 (optimum-MBO) depicts the best value reached by using Migrating Birds Optimization. Column 4 (optimum-AVG) the average value of 31 executiones is depicted. Column 5 (optimum-SD) represents the standard deviation. Column 6 (optimum-RPD%) represents the difference between the best known optimum value and the best optimum value reached by MBO in terms of percentage. Column 7 (execution time-BET) shows the best execution time obtained in milliseconds. Column 8 (execution time-AVG) describes the average time in milliseconds of the finest time of execution of MBO. Column 9 (execution time-ST) represents the standard deviation of the best times of execution obtained by MBO. Column 10 (cycle-BC) shows the cycle in which the optimal value was found. Column 11 (cycle-AVG) describes the average cycle. Column 12 (cycle-ST) represents the standard deviation. Column 13 (time cycle-BTC) shows the best cycle

TABLE 21: Boctor's problems.

ID	Boctor's problem	Cell	M_{max}	OPT
B01	1	2	8	11
B02	1	2	9	11
B03	1	2	10	11
B04	1	2	11	11
B05	1	2	12	11
B06	2	2	8	7
B07	2	2	9	6
B08	2	2	10	4
B09	2	2	11	3
B10	2	2	12	3
B11	3	2	8	4
B12	3	2	9	4
B13	3	2	10	4
B14	3	2	11	3
B15	3	2	12	1
B16	4	2	8	14
B17	4	2	9	13
B18	4	2	10	13
B19	4	2	11	13
B20	4	2	12	13
B21	5	2	8	9
B22	5	2	9	6
B23	5	2	10	6
B24	5	2	11	5
B25	5	2	12	4
B26	6	2	8	5
B27	6	2	9	3
B28	6	2	10	3
B29	6	2	11	3
B30	6	2	12	2
B31	7	2	8	7
B32	7	2	9	4
B33	7	2	10	4
B34	7	2	11	4
B35	7	2	12	4
B36	8	2	8	13
B37	8	2	9	10
B38	8	2	10	8
B39	8	2	11	5
B40	8	2	12	5
B41	9	2	8	8
B42	9	2	9	8
B43	9	2	10	8
B44	9	2	11	5
B45	9	2	12	5
B46	10	2	8	8
B47	10	2	9	5
B48	10	2	10	5
B49	10	2	11	5
B50	10	2	12	5
B51	1	3	6	27

TABLE 21: Continued.

ID	Boctor's problem	Cell	M_{max}	OPT
B52	1	3	7	18
B53	1	3	8	11
B54	1	3	9	11
B55	2	3	6	7
B56	2	3	7	6
B57	2	3	8	6
B58	2	3	9	6
B59	3	3	6	9
B60	3	3	7	4
B61	3	3	8	4
B62	3	3	9	4
B63	4	3	6	27
B64	4	3	7	18
B65	4	3	8	14
B66	4	3	9	13
B67	5	3	6	11
B68	5	3	7	8
B69	5	3	8	8
B70	5	3	9	6
B71	6	3	6	6
B72	6	3	7	4
B73	6	3	8	4
B74	6	3	9	3
B75	7	3	6	11
B76	7	3	7	5
B77	7	3	8	5
B78	7	3	9	4
B79	8	3	6	14
B80	8	3	7	11
B81	8	3	8	11
B82	8	3	9	10
B83	9	3	6	12
B84	9	3	7	12
B85	9	3	8	8
B86	9	3	9	8
B87	10	3	6	10
B88	10	3	7	8
B89	10	3	8	8
B90	10	3	9	5

time in which the optimal value was found in milliseconds. Column 14 (time cycle-AVG) describes the average cycle in milliseconds. Column 15 (time cycle-ST) represents the standard deviation in milliseconds. Finally, it describes the average time for each column.

Competing Interests

The authors declare that they have no competing interests regarding the publication of this paper.

TABLE 22: MBO using sequential merge sort algorithm.

ID	OPT	Optimum				Execution time			Cycle			Time cycle		
		MBO	AVG	SD	RPD%	BET	AVG	ST	BC	AVG	SD	BTC	AVG	SD
B1	11	11	11.0000	0.0000	0.00	158	251	171.6413	4	7	2.4350	17	53	34.2198
B2	11	11	11.0000	0.0000	0.00	157	263	84.9052	1	3	1.1575	4	31	23.2120
B3	11	11	11.0000	0.0000	0.00	153	209	47.3905	2	4	1.4984	9	24	10.2378
B4	11	11	11.0000	0.0000	0.00	155	160	4.7848	2	4	1.9449	8	20	8.5007
B5	11	11	11.0000	0.0000	0.00	155	160	4.4053	2	4	2.0723	8	20	9.2034
B6	7	7	7.0000	0.0000	0.00	165	172	5.9968	2	8	5.4244	10	40	25.3084
B7	6	6	6.0000	0.0000	0.00	158	165	10.2942	2	5	2.6567	9	24	10.9301
B8	4	4	4.1935	0.6011	0.00	154	226	63.7678	3	10	8.5001	13	59	55.3723
B9	3	3	3.1935	0.4016	0.00	152	157	3.4802	2	5	2.5686	8	24	10.5719
B10	3	3	3.0000	0.0000	0.00	152	183	41.7133	2	4	1.5422	8	21	10.5715
B11	4	4	4.1613	0.3739	0.00	155	233	66.3620	2	11	9.9109	9	73	63.6411
B12	4	4	4.0000	0.0000	0.00	153	235	86.2169	2	4	1.6643	11	29	18.5750
B13	4	4	4.0000	0.0000	0.00	152	161	30.0537	3	6	3.6577	12	27	14.8101
B14	3	3	3.3548	0.4864	0.00	152	159	26.0370	2	6	3.7006	8	26	15.6561
B15	1	1	1.6452	0.9504	0.00	152	155	2.6176	2	5	2.3505	8	22	9.6363
B16	14	14	14.0000	0.0000	0.00	155	182	48.3518	3	8	3.5493	12	43	25.2893
B17	13	13	13.0000	0.0000	0.00	152	174	35.1554	2	5	2.1717	8	26	9.4585
B18	13	13	13.0000	0.0000	0.00	152	177	41.1985	2	4	1.8275	8	21	8.6059
B19	13	13	13.0968	0.5388	0.00	153	218	62.5518	1	6	4.0377	4	39	26.7267
B20	13	13	13.0000	0.0000	0.00	155	225	138.3519	3	7	4.5423	13	41	21.4062
B21	9	9	9.1935	0.4016	0.00	153	172	43.6026	2	9	5.2990	8	41	26.7630
B22	6	6	6.1290	0.3408	0.00	152	155	2.0494	1	5	3.1326	4	23	12.9070
B23	6	6	6.1290	0.3408	0.00	152	153	2.0489	2	7	4.8491	8	31	19.7735
B24	5	5	5.2581	0.5755	0.00	152	153	1.6409	2	6	2.4012	8	24	9.6949
B25	4	4	4.1290	0.3408	0.00	152	154	6.0300	3	6	5.4158	12	27	22.1520
B26	5	5	5.0000	0.0000	0.00	154	157	2.3372	2	8	6.0393	8	37	24.7760
B27	3	3	3.0323	0.1796	0.00	152	154	2.2017	2	7	4.8524	8	30	19.3886
B28	3	3	3.2903	0.5884	0.00	152	155	4.7996	1	5	3.2670	4	24	13.9205
B29	3	3	3.0968	0.3005	0.00	152	156	7.3660	3	5	2.0447	12	23	8.2142
B30	2	2	2.4516	0.5680	0.00	152	153	1.7289	2	7	6.5031	8	28	26.3895
B31	7	7	7.0000	0.0000	0.00	153	157	2.7615	4	8	3.2156	19	37	13.2221
B32	4	4	4.2903	0.9016	0.00	152	155	4.1960	3	7	3.7805	13	31	15.0563
B33	4	4	4.1290	0.4995	0.00	152	154	3.7868	2	6	3.0154	8	26	12.7931
B34	4	4	4.3226	0.7478	0.00	152	153	1.2835	2	6	4.2925	8	27	17.1088
B35	4	4	4.7097	0.9727	0.00	152	153	1.6468	1	5	2.0723	4	21	8.5183
B36	13	13	13.0000	0.0000	0.00	154	158	3.8763	3	9	4.9110	13	39	19.3956
B37	10	10	10.3226	0.7478	0.00	152	155	2.5387	2	6	5.4497	9	28	22.2304
B38	8	8	8.0968	0.3005	0.00	152	154	3.3601	2	8	5.6323	8	34	22.8731
B39	5	5	5.1935	1.0776	0.00	152	166	20.9165	2	6	3.5493	8	27	15.7638
B40	5	5	5.0000	0.0000	0.00	152	162	16.8069	2	4	1.8357	8	19	7.9044
B41	8	8	8.0000	0.0000	0.00	155	158	2.9064	1	10	5.2974	4	42	22.2617
B42	8	8	8.0000	0.0000	0.00	152	198	70.2758	1	4	2.0718	8	24	17.2073
B43	8	8	8.0000	0.0000	0.00	152	154	1.7221	1	4	2.2818	4	19	9.3681
B44	5	5	5.9677	1.4256	0.00	152	154	3.8616	2	5	2.5264	8	24	10.1847
B45	5	5	6.1935	1.5366	0.00	152	153	1.3536	2	6	4.6467	8	26	19.1860
B46	8	8	8.0645	0.2497	0.00	154	158	3.4348	3	10	6.7563	12	42	27.9592
B47	5	5	5.0000	0.0000	0.00	152	155	4.1228	2	5	2.9256	8	22	13.0905
B48	5	5	5.4839	2.0145	0.00	152	153	1.3897	2	5	2.8931	8	22	11.7203
B49	5	5	5.1935	0.6011	0.00	152	152	1.1704	3	6	3.1819	12	26	12.7969
B50	5	5	5.3226	0.7478	0.00	152	153	1.4473	2	6	3.4529	8	26	14.0041

TABLE 22: Continued.

ID	OPT	Optimum				Execution time			Cycle			Time cycle		
		MBO	AVG	SD	RPD%	BET	AVG	ST	BC	AVG	SD	BTC	AVG	SD
B51	27	27	28.1613	0.9694	0.00	154	159	4.7774	5	21	9.0993	21	92	39.5406
B52	18	18	18.9355	1.0307	0.00	154	156	2.2785	2	19	9.3341	8	80	38.7324
B53	11	11	11.0000	0.0000	0.00	153	155	1.5889	4	10	2.8815	16	42	12.1075
B54	11	11	11.0000	0.0000	0.00	152	154	1.6277	3	7	2.4596	12	32	10.2627
B55	7	7	7.0000	0.0000	0.00	154	158	4.4897	4	11	5.5967	16	48	22.6364
B56	6	6	6.0000	0.0000	0.00	153	155	1.9233	4	10	3.4112	16	44	13.9193
B57	6	6	6.0968	0.3962	0.00	153	154	1.3552	6	12	5.2644	24	52	21.4015
B58	6	6	6.0645	0.3592	0.00	152	155	4.0377	3	9	3.7643	14	38	14.9752
B59	9	9	9.1290	0.3408	0.00	154	158	2.6825	5	15	6.7165	21	64	28.5839
B60	4	4	4.3871	1.2021	0.00	152	156	2.3145	6	13	5.7136	24	56	23.8186
B61	4	4	4.1290	0.3408	0.00	152	155	2.0394	4	13	6.7101	16	54	27.4017
B62	4	4	4.0000	0.0000	0.00	152	155	4.1824	4	9	3.4273	18	40	13.6191
B63	27	27	27.2581	0.5143	0.00	155	165	11.2005	4	21	11.4243	16	90	48.4598
B64	18	18	18.3871	0.9549	0.00	155	167	14.2569	7	19	9.3371	28	86	39.7379
B65	14	14	14.0645	0.2497	0.00	153	161	9.3472	6	15	7.5537	25	65	31.4611
B66	13	13	13.0000	0.0000	0.00	154	247	97.6943	6	11	3.3020	24	81	67.8854
B67	11	11	11.0323	0.1796	0.00	156	209	33.3034	4	14	7.7241	19	77	43.7733
B68	8	8	8.8065	2.3154	0.00	156	179	30.7013	2	13	7.7239	9	63	40.9466
B69	8	8	8.5161	0.6256	0.00	154	190	35.2266	5	12	5.7914	20	64	35.7448
B70	6	6	6.4839	0.6256	0.00	152	167	16.6121	5	12	5.6220	22	57	26.9089
B71	6	6	6.0000	0.0000	0.00	155	176	15.3473	6	11	5.4370	29	54	24.4164
B72	4	4	4.2258	0.5603	0.00	155	168	21.0614	6	12	4.0783	28	55	23.1119
B73	4	4	4.4516	0.6752	0.00	152	173	15.2415	4	11	6.4611	16	52	28.1919
B74	3	3	3.3226	0.4752	0.00	153	166	14.9468	4	13	8.6221	20	60	35.3722
B75	11	11	11.6774	0.9794	0.00	156	169	8.4222	4	17	10.5949	17	77	47.6167
B76	5	5	5.2581	0.6816	0.00	154	167	23.7204	3	12	5.0513	14	56	26.0949
B77	5	5	5.3871	0.8032	0.00	165	174	8.3753	6	14	8.1313	27	66	37.9381
B78	4	4	4.9355	1.2093	0.00	163	176	12.2235	5	13	4.7399	22	60	25.3983
B79	14	14	14.0323	0.1796	0.00	156	181	28.4157	5	10	3.2965	25	47	16.9919
B80	11	11	11.0000	0.0000	0.00	171	190	20.4805	3	10	4.6704	17	53	23.3860
B81	11	11	11.3871	0.8032	0.00	159	186	24.6086	7	14	7.1159	34	70	35.5031
B82	10	10	10.3548	0.6607	0.00	153	169	25.0386	4	12	6.0875	16	55	29.4125
B83	12	12	12.2258	1.2572	0.00	154	167	8.4371	4	12	6.3860	18	57	29.6714
B84	12	12	12.0000	0.0000	0.00	155	165	13.7350	6	11	3.8852	31	52	17.8962
B85	8	8	8.9355	1.4361	0.00	153	170	23.4146	4	14	7.3518	17	64	33.0030
B86	8	8	8.1613	0.5829	0.00	156	177	15.4220	3	10	3.7814	13	47	18.0706
B87	10	10	10.4839	1.0605	0.00	156	184	20.5574	4	18	9.4481	19	89	50.8878
B88	8	8	8.0000	0.0000	0.00	155	194	109.8234	4	9	3.1995	20	61	96.8101
B89	8	8	8.0000	0.0000	0.00	153	159	8.7550	4	10	3.7275	17	42	15.4842
B90	5	5	5.2903	0.9016	0.00	152	156	2.2509	4	11	5.6435	17	49	22.9895
		AVG	8.1025	0.4576	0.00	153	171	21.1539	3	9	4.7263	13	43	23.8747

TABLE 23: MBO using parallel merge sort algorithm with 1 thread.

ID	OPT		Optimum				Execution time			Cycle			Time cycle	
		MBO	AVG	SD	RPD%	BET	AVG	ST	BC	AVG	SD	BTC	AVG	SD
B1	11	11	11.0000	0.0000	0.00	159	206	78.6150	2	6	3.2038	14	43	35.4355
B2	11	11	11.0000	0.0000	0.00	155	173	19.0187	1	4	1.5141	6	21	8.1043
B3	11	11	11.0000	0.0000	0.00	154	172	13.6524	1	3	1.2495	4	16	5.5298
B4	11	11	11.0000	0.0000	0.00	153	172	16.4752	3	5	1.6552	12	24	10.3208
B5	11	11	11.0000	0.0000	0.00	152	155	5.0775	2	5	3.1064	8	24	12.5736
B6	7	7	7.0000	0.0000	0.00	155	185	36.0141	3	10	6.0544	13	48	27.2948
B7	6	6	6.0000	0.0000	0.00	159	202	24.7416	2	6	4.4252	9	35	21.5014
B8	4	4	4.4516	0.8500	0.00	158	197	88.5635	3	12	8.1669	17	58	40.5206
B9	3	3	3.0645	0.2497	0.00	153	172	12.9714	2	5	2.3122	12	23	9.5575
B10	3	3	3.0000	0.0000	0.00	152	168	13.5060	1	4	2.2609	7	20	10.8349
B11	4	4	4.2258	0.4250	0.00	156	186	18.4762	1	10	7.4314	5	53	41.0204
B12	4	4	4.0000	0.0000	0.00	160	178	17.7416	2	4	1.7585	8	21	10.0164
B13	4	4	4.0000	0.0000	0.00	152	171	19.3874	2	4	2.2714	8	21	10.1196
B14	3	3	3.2903	0.4614	0.00	152	169	15.2222	2	6	4.9287	8	28	22.3718
B15	1	1	1.0968	0.5388	0.00	153	165	11.9830	2	6	3.4694	8	29	16.5698
B16	14	14	14.0000	0.0000	0.00	155	163	9.5187	2	7	3.4128	8	33	14.8828
B17	13	13	13.0000	0.0000	0.00	153	155	2.8564	2	5	2.0225	8	21	8.8107
B18	13	13	13.0000	0.0000	0.00	152	155	2.6401	2	5	2.2264	8	24	9.3277
B19	13	13	13.3871	1.0223	0.00	152	155	3.7145	2	7	4.0236	8	30	16.7423
B20	13	13	13.0000	0.0000	0.00	152	154	2.2240	2	6	3.6308	8	28	14.7566
B21	9	9	9.1935	0.4016	0.00	154	161	4.3366	3	11	6.9041	12	47	29.4637
B22	6	6	6.1935	0.4016	0.00	153	156	2.2926	1	5	2.4203	4	23	10.0929
B23	6	6	6.0645	0.2497	0.00	152	155	4.3901	2	7	4.9174	8	31	19.7046
B24	5	5	5.3548	0.6607	0.00	152	155	2.7712	2	6	5.4696	8	28	22.2898
B25	4	4	4.3871	0.6672	0.00	152	156	3.3534	3	7	3.7411	12	29	15.0894
B26	5	5	5.0323	0.1796	0.00	155	162	5.0227	2	7	3.3376	9	34	13.9975
B27	3	3	3.0323	0.1796	0.00	154	157	4.5927	3	6	3.4619	12	27	14.2464
B28	3	3	3.0968	0.3005	0.00	152	156	3.8156	2	6	2.3714	8	25	10.0092
B29	3	3	3.3548	0.4864	0.00	152	155	3.1271	2	4	2.4913	8	19	10.2875
B30	2	2	2.5484	0.6752	0.00	154	157	3.3421	1	8	7.1106	6	33	29.8981
B31	7	7	7.0000	0.0000	0.00	158	166	5.7951	1	10	5.4402	5	44	23.6942
B32	4	4	4.1935	0.7492	0.00	153	159	3.6603	2	7	4.7390	8	31	20.0530
B33	4	4	4.0645	0.3592	0.00	153	158	3.9906	2	6	3.3872	8	25	13.7612
B34	4	4	4.2581	0.6816	0.00	152	158	3.7035	2	5	3.5636	8	25	14.7240
B35	4	4	4.4516	0.8500	0.00	153	158	4.3965	2	5	3.3916	8	22	14.3879
B36	13	13	13.0000	0.0000	0.00	156	166	6.3017	1	10	5.6101	5	44	24.9727
B37	10	10	10.3226	0.7478	0.00	154	157	2.4314	2	8	6.6553	8	34	27.1586
B38	8	8	8.1613	0.4544	0.00	152	156	4.2246	3	10	8.3402	12	44	34.0656
B39	5	5	5.0000	0.0000	0.00	153	159	11.6618	3	5	2.3363	12	23	9.8435
B40	5	5	5.1935	0.6011	0.00	152	160	6.3128	2	5	2.0645	9	25	8.9185
B41	8	8	8.1613	0.8980	0.00	154	169	10.6175	1	8	5.2096	4	36	22.4695
B42	8	8	8.0000	0.0000	0.00	153	166	10.1747	2	4	1.9438	8	18	8.0620
B43	8	8	8.0000	0.0000	0.00	152	165	10.7002	2	5	2.1568	12	24	9.2664
B44	5	5	5.7742	1.3344	0.00	153	161	8.5650	2	4	1.8062	8	21	7.8376
B45	5	5	5.9677	1.4256	0.00	152	159	8.0203	2	5	2.6453	8	24	10.7374
B46	8	8	8.0645	0.2497	0.00	155	172	12.5416	2	9	6.5325	8	44	31.3379
B47	5	5	5.0968	0.5388	0.00	153	162	6.1438	2	6	2.2423	8	26	9.7972
B48	5	5	5.1290	0.4995	0.00	152	157	3.8888	2	5	2.3646	8	23	9.8283
B49	5	5	5.2581	0.6816	0.00	153	166	11.7214	3	5	2.3335	14	25	9.2466
B50	5	5	5.3226	0.7478	0.00	158	297	112.2328	2	5	4.2598	8	46	59.0964

TABLE 23: Continued.

ID	OPT	Optimum				Execution time			Cycle			Time cycle		
		MBO	AVG	SD	RPD%	BET	AVG	ST	BC	AVG	SD	BTC	AVG	SD
B51	27	27	28.1935	1.0139	0.00	170	210	50.5103	9	21	8.4341	40	120	65.5098
B52	18	18	19.0000	1.2383	0.00	160	174	12.9624	7	21	8.9031	29	96	39.5778
B53	11	11	11.0000	0.0000	0.00	161	178	16.1011	4	10	3.4251	17	49	15.4218
B54	11	11	11.0000	0.0000	0.00	164	225	110.0060	4	9	2.2274	17	53	25.5038
B55	7	7	7.0000	0.0000	0.00	170	227	95.8822	6	12	4.8697	35	73	34.6457
B56	6	6	6.0000	0.0000	0.00	158	176	22.7563	4	10	4.1773	18	46	17.2158
B57	6	6	6.0323	0.1796	0.00	158	164	3.8771	6	11	4.7317	29	49	20.2836
B58	6	6	6.0000	0.0000	0.00	157	167	7.3482	4	10	4.1721	17	47	17.6931
B59	9	9	9.1290	0.3408	0.00	162	176	9.1676	4	12	7.6146	16	60	35.3615
B60	4	4	4.2581	0.9989	0.00	160	167	5.9831	3	13	7.2062	14	62	31.0985
B61	4	4	4.1290	0.3408	0.00	160	165	3.8543	6	12	6.4014	25	53	28.3432
B62	4	4	4.0000	0.0000	0.00	158	164	4.8012	4	10	5.3501	18	43	23.0980
B63	27	27	27.2903	0.4614	0.00	167	175	6.0466	2	16	7.7237	9	76	36.5377
B64	18	18	18.3871	1.0223	0.00	160	168	5.1665	3	19	9.7662	15	86	43.3281
B65	14	14	14.0323	0.1796	0.00	160	165	3.8291	4	16	8.6324	17	71	37.8486
B66	13	13	13.0000	0.0000	0.00	158	164	4.3960	4	9	3.8069	17	42	17.3308
B67	11	11	11.0000	0.0000	0.00	161	169	5.7328	3	13	6.7766	15	60	30.8939
B68	8	8	8.5161	1.3873	0.00	157	166	4.9242	5	12	5.9210	20	55	25.9415
B69	8	8	8.7097	0.8244	0.00	159	186	80.6533	4	10	3.5186	20	59	78.6617
B70	6	6	6.3548	0.6082	0.00	157	164	4.1299	5	11	6.0651	21	49	26.3690
B71	6	6	6.3226	0.9087	0.00	164	173	4.9813	3	13	7.2318	15	64	34.0172
B72	4	4	4.2581	0.5143	0.00	162	169	7.0074	4	13	7.3266	18	61	31.5165
B73	4	4	4.3548	0.5507	0.00	155	163	7.4271	4	10	4.5181	16	46	19.8506
B74	3	3	3.3871	0.6152	0.00	154	159	6.2096	4	12	6.5673	18	54	27.7339
B75	11	11	11.8710	0.9217	0.00	156	166	6.2745	7	19	9.0094	32	84	39.6957
B76	5	5	5.1290	0.4995	0.00	154	159	4.0391	3	12	7.1859	12	53	30.5339
B77	5	5	5.6129	0.9892	0.00	154	158	2.9061	3	12	6.2763	12	52	26.0995
B78	4	4	4.7097	1.1887	0.00	152	157	4.4870	3	15	8.9251	12	64	37.0953
B79	14	14	14.0000	0.0000	0.00	154	160	3.9374	4	10	3.9070	17	46	16.9129
B80	11	11	11.0000	0.0000	0.00	154	159	3.6503	4	10	3.0409	16	43	12.6801
B81	11	11	11.2258	0.7169	0.00	154	157	2.5025	3	12	7.2826	13	51	29.8398
B82	10	10	10.7097	0.7829	0.00	153	160	9.2766	4	10	4.2187	19	45	17.2205
B83	12	12	12.1290	0.7184	0.00	154	161	5.0024	5	13	7.6357	23	59	32.3602
B84	12	12	12.0968	0.5388	0.00	154	159	3.8746	3	11	5.8103	12	49	25.2224
B85	8	8	9.3548	1.4731	0.00	153	157	3.7096	4	13	7.1319	19	57	29.5541
B86	8	8	8.0000	0.0000	0.00	152	157	4.4661	4	11	4.7817	16	46	19.8128
B87	10	10	10.3871	0.9193	0.00	156	165	5.2583	6	18	8.5468	25	81	38.3296
B88	8	8	8.0000	0.0000	0.00	154	159	6.6066	4	11	3.8846	16	47	16.1636
B89	8	8	8.0323	0.1796	0.00	153	158	4.5929	3	10	5.0891	12	42	21.2703
B90	5	5	5.7742	1.3344	0.00	153	157	2.6204	6	11	3.8401	24	46	15.4224
		AVG	8.1065	0.4446	0.00	155	168	13.9276	3	9	4.7812	13	42	22.9180

TABLE 24: MBO using parallel merge sort algorithm with 4 threads.

ID	OPT	Optimum				Execution time			Cycle			Time cycle		
		MBO	AVG	SD	RPD%	BET	AVG	ST	BC	AVG	SD	BTC	AVG	SD
B1	11	11	11.0000	0.0000	0.00	158	216	109.1743	2	6	3.6142	9	42	25.9406
B2	11	11	11.0000	0.0000	0.00	152	157	6.6604	2	4	1.2365	10	18	7.4686
B3	11	11	11.0000	0.0000	0.00	152	166	47.4789	1	4	1.2960	4	18	8.4496
B4	11	11	11.0000	0.0000	0.00	152	155	2.5716	1	5	2.6331	4	20	10.8924
B5	11	11	11.3871	1.4984	0.00	153	167	45.7047	1	6	3.3085	4	29	18.6757
B6	7	7	7.0000	0.0000	0.00	154	162	9.6934	2	9	5.7726	8	40	24.3002
B7	6	6	6.0000	0.0000	0.00	154	167	41.5747	3	6	2.6845	12	26	10.8095
B8	4	4	4.3226	0.7478	0.00	153	155	2.5003	2	11	9.7807	8	49	39.5824
B9	3	3	3.0645	0.2497	0.00	152	168	58.7230	2	6	2.9494	8	27	17.1893
B10	3	3	3.0000	0.0000	0.00	152	166	41.0109	2	4	1.9355	8	20	9.1206
B11	4	4	4.1290	0.3408	0.00	155	160	4.3005	2	10	6.9986	8	43	29.6649
B12	4	4	4.0000	0.0000	0.00	153	166	41.1127	1	4	1.8044	4	19	7.2704
B13	4	4	4.0000	0.0000	0.00	152	155	2.5059	2	6	4.9324	8	25	20.2386
B14	3	3	3.1935	0.4016	0.00	152	167	46.3310	1	5	2.2269	4	26	14.4843
B15	1	1	1.3548	0.8386	0.00	152	154	2.6249	2	5	3.1356	8	24	12.8711
B16	14	14	14.0000	0.0000	0.00	154	171	46.8582	3	8	4.1048	12	36	19.3441
B17	13	13	13.0000	0.0000	0.00	154	157	4.7342	2	5	1.9903	8	21	8.5249
B18	13	13	13.0000	0.0000	0.00	152	166	40.2106	3	5	1.9210	12	26	11.5105
B19	13	13	13.1935	0.7492	0.00	152	157	9.6044	2	7	4.3160	8	29	17.8754
B20	13	13	13.0000	0.0000	0.00	152	165	54.4453	2	7	3.8504	8	32	17.1361
B21	9	9	9.2258	0.4250	0.00	154	173	54.5359	2	11	7.4947	10	51	32.7887
B22	6	6	6.0968	0.3005	0.00	154	160	5.8877	3	5	2.8044	12	24	11.6705
B23	6	6	6.0645	0.2497	0.00	152	169	48.5055	2	7	4.5711	8	35	21.3986
B24	5	5	5.2581	0.5755	0.00	152	154	2.3010	2	6	2.7875	8	25	11.3416
B25	4	4	4.1935	0.4016	0.00	152	167	46.4296	2	6	2.6644	8	27	23.6771
B26	5	5	5.0000	0.0000	0.00	154	158	3.7574	3	8	6.3478	15	37	26.7206
B27	3	3	3.0323	0.1796	0.00	154	168	47.1433	2	5	3.5903	9	26	19.3762
B28	3	3	3.3226	0.4752	0.00	152	158	19.6735	1	5	3.6966	4	23	15.3801
B29	3	3	3.1613	0.4544	0.00	152	163	41.5225	2	5	3.3315	8	25	35.7845
B30	2	2	2.4839	0.5699	0.00	152	165	44.6843	2	7	5.1800	8	30	22.1249
B31	7	7	7.0000	0.0000	0.00	153	161	6.9997	3	8	4.2651	12	37	18.4910
B32	4	4	4.2903	0.9016	0.00	155	205	147.1775	1	8	5.0298	5	40	29.8585
B33	4	4	4.0645	0.3592	0.00	153	172	25.2682	2	5	3.2974	8	25	13.9995
B34	4	4	4.3226	0.7478	0.00	152	155	3.4554	1	6	6.1399	4	28	24.5491
B35	4	4	4.3871	0.8032	0.00	152	157	7.2196	2	5	2.8979	8	23	11.7220
B36	13	13	13.0000	0.0000	0.00	158	172	15.0594	3	10	5.7384	12	46	26.7314
B37	10	10	10.4516	0.8500	0.00	154	166	14.1400	2	8	6.8311	8	38	28.5876
B38	8	8	8.0323	0.1796	0.00	155	164	12.4326	2	8	5.6068	8	37	23.8998
B39	5	5	5.3548	1.3796	0.00	154	163	12.5069	2	5	2.0884	8	22	9.4440
B40	5	5	5.2581	0.6816	0.00	153	165	16.5927	2	5	3.6106	8	24	15.9870
B41	8	8	8.1613	0.8980	0.00	156	166	9.9435	1	10	8.3483	4	47	36.1707
B42	8	8	8.0000	0.0000	0.00	155	174	34.2187	2	4	1.6350	8	19	8.1873
B43	8	8	8.0000	0.0000	0.00	153	198	46.1624	1	4	2.1423	4	24	13.0368
B44	5	5	5.7742	1.3344	0.00	156	183	32.3323	2	5	1.6919	10	25	9.0367
B45	5	5	5.8065	1.4005	0.00	152	157	4.5948	2	5	2.8658	9	24	12.1692
B46	8	8	8.0323	0.1796	0.00	157	176	28.1980	3	10	7.1360	14	50	40.1945
B47	5	5	5.1935	0.7492	0.00	155	183	36.2397	2	6	2.5649	8	31	16.0299
B48	5	5	5.1935	0.6011	0.00	152	166	23.6329	2	5	2.2832	8	24	10.1954
B49	5	5	5.2581	0.6816	0.00	152	155	2.8071	2	5	2.4613	8	22	10.1229
B50	5	5	5.1290	0.4995	0.00	152	155	4.6881	2	7	5.3336	8	30	25.5601

TABLE 24: Continued.

ID	OPT	Optimum				Execution time				Cycle			Time cycle		
		MBO	AVG	SD	RPD%	BET	AVG	ST	BC	AVG	SD	BTC	AVG	SD
B51	27	27	28.2903	1.0064	0.00	159	164	4.3110	4	22	9.2894	16	98	40.3385
B52	18	18	19.0645	1.0935	0.00	154	159	5.8249	5	22	9.8280	22	95	42.6600
B53	11	11	11.0000	0.0000	0.00	153	178	32.7949	4	11	3.7102	19	51	18.7233
B54	11	11	11.0000	0.0000	0.00	153	164	19.9278	3	7	2.7140	12	34	14.0533
B55	7	7	7.0000	0.0000	0.00	155	160	3.4790	2	10	4.3510	8	46	18.3698
B56	6	6	6.0000	0.0000	0.00	154	156	1.7121	2	10	3.2772	8	42	13.7300
B57	6	6	6.0323	0.1796	0.00	153	160	16.4040	4	10	3.8788	17	45	16.0311
B58	6	6	6.0323	0.1796	0.00	154	168	26.7755	3	10	3.9119	12	45	16.9634
B59	9	9	9.2258	0.4973	0.00	155	194	38.6829	3	15	8.8444	13	76	44.3162
B60	4	4	4.9032	1.7001	0.00	154	169	24.2931	3	12	6.6625	13	54	30.0641
B61	4	4	4.1290	0.5623	0.00	155	268	200.8557	4	12	7.0176	16	109	179.0541
B62	4	4	4.0000	0.0000	0.00	153	157	4.2149	3	9	3.8691	13	40	15.6801
B63	27	27	27.2581	0.5143	0.00	154	165	10.6263	6	16	9.2118	24	71	40.8554
B64	18	18	18.4516	0.8099	0.00	154	178	18.2276	7	19	9.1876	31	91	45.9490
B65	14	14	14.0323	0.1796	0.00	155	161	7.8149	6	15	7.3228	25	68	30.9394
B66	13	13	13.0000	0.0000	0.00	155	194	41.5668	6	10	3.4251	24	52	21.8884
B67	11	11	11.0323	0.1796	0.00	158	210	67.1852	1	13	6.8971	4	72	42.9510
B68	8	8	8.3226	1.2751	0.00	153	197	51.5259	4	13	7.9708	16	68	52.5572
B69	8	8	8.5806	0.6720	0.00	155	208	84.9156	5	11	5.6323	21	60	31.5805
B70	6	6	6.5484	0.8884	0.00	154	231	66.9705	4	15	8.5271	29	91	56.9068
B71	6	6	6.0645	0.3592	0.00	157	217	70.6903	3	12	6.9808	14	71	46.9560
B72	4	4	4.2258	0.4250	0.00	161	189	40.5461	5	13	7.1670	24	68	41.0736
B73	4	4	4.4516	0.6239	0.00	156	177	29.4202	4	13	5.3836	20	59	23.6061
B74	3	3	3.3871	0.5584	0.00	154	161	4.3200	3	13	7.5998	12	55	32.4734
B75	11	11	11.7742	1.0866	0.00	155	172	13.9606	4	15	9.4963	16	69	45.7583
B76	5	5	5.1935	0.6011	0.00	154	159	4.2812	4	13	6.7199	16	55	28.2946
B77	5	5	5.9677	1.1968	0.00	154	157	3.0589	4	12	7.3398	16	54	30.8010
B78	4	4	4.6452	1.1120	0.00	153	156	2.6757	1	13	7.3425	4	56	30.7701
B79	14	14	14.0000	0.0000	0.00	154	161	5.2525	4	10	2.9487	18	43	12.1078
B80	11	11	11.0000	0.0000	0.00	155	202	147.0668	3	11	5.4449	16	50	26.2353
B81	11	11	11.4516	0.9605	0.00	155	208	59.8935	7	13	4.7648	28	74	32.8557
B82	10	10	10.6452	0.7978	0.00	155	190	37.9565	4	13	7.3710	20	68	41.9503
B83	12	12	12.0000	0.0000	0.00	155	162	6.1394	3	10	5.8394	12	48	28.0464
B84	12	12	12.1935	0.6011	0.00	154	158	2.8090	7	12	6.3531	28	53	25.9466
B85	8	8	9.1613	1.7146	0.00	154	156	1.8346	4	13	6.5165	16	57	27.0130
B86	8	8	8.0000	0.0000	0.00	153	157	3.0107	3	11	3.7543	14	47	15.8781
B87	10	10	10.8065	1.0462	0.00	156	168	14.7487	6	17	9.3396	24	78	43.8068
B88	8	8	8.1935	1.0776	0.00	154	157	2.8132	4	10	5.2145	16	44	21.6391
B89	8	8	8.0000	0.0000	0.00	154	157	2.5607	3	10	4.7956	13	44	20.3743
B90	5	5	5.3871	1.0223	0.00	154	156	2.1397	4	11	4.6769	16	46	19.3850
		AVG	8.1183	0.4847	0.00	153	170	28.8802	2	9	4.9501	12	43	25.6019

TABLE 25: MBO using parallel merge sort algorithm with 8 threads.

ID	OPT	Optimum				Execution time			Cycle			Time cycle		
		MBO	AVG	SD	RPD%	BET	AVG	ST	BC	AVG	SD	BTC	AVG	SD
B1	11	11	11.0000	0.0000	0.00	153	175	52.9600	2	7	3.4650	10	40	24.1691
B2	11	11	11.0000	0.0000	0.00	152	155	4.2538	1	4	1.3663	4	17	6.3123
B3	11	11	11.0000	0.0000	0.00	152	154	2.2737	2	4	1.2675	8	16	4.9966
B4	11	11	11.0000	0.0000	0.00	152	154	2.1875	3	5	1.6669	12	22	6.6451
B5	11	11	11.0000	0.0000	0.00	152	154	3.5484	1	5	4.6460	4	22	19.1976
B6	7	7	7.0000	0.0000	0.00	154	159	6.9589	3	9	5.6927	12	41	23.3150
B7	6	6	6.0323	0.1796	0.00	152	155	2.6567	2	5	3.3376	8	24	13.6479
B8	4	4	4.2581	0.6816	0.00	152	154	2.2500	2	10	7.8339	8	43	31.7022
B9	3	3	3.0645	0.2497	0.00	152	154	2.8853	1	6	4.2480	4	26	17.5545
B10	3	3	3.0000	0.0000	0.00	152	155	4.3342	2	4	2.2017	8	19	9.0625
B11	4	4	4.1613	0.3739	0.00	154	158	4.0725	3	11	6.8310	12	46	28.0720
B12	4	4	4.0000	0.0000	0.00	152	154	2.2041	1	4	1.7487	4	18	7.3882
B13	4	4	4.0645	0.3592	0.00	152	157	8.3824	2	6	4.0825	8	24	16.4007
B14	3	3	3.4516	0.5059	0.00	152	156	10.8955	2	5	2.0848	8	21	8.3643
B15	1	1	1.2903	0.7829	0.00	152	153	1.8322	2	5	2.4110	8	23	9.8292
B16	14	14	14.0000	0.0000	0.00	155	160	4.5349	2	7	3.6044	10	32	14.9542
B17	13	13	13.0000	0.0000	0.00	152	155	2.2423	2	4	1.6145	8	20	6.7850
B18	13	13	13.0000	0.0000	0.00	152	154	3.8763	1	5	2.1553	4	22	9.3721
B19	13	13	13.0000	0.0000	0.00	152	153	1.4796	2	7	6.3034	8	28	25.4949
B20	13	13	13.0000	0.0000	0.00	152	153	1.4803	2	8	5.1278	8	33	20.5847
B21	9	9	9.1613	0.3739	0.00	154	158	2.8485	2	12	10.3146	8	52	42.6586
B22	6	6	6.2581	0.6308	0.00	152	155	3.1380	2	6	2.8459	8	25	11.7755
B23	6	6	6.1935	0.5428	0.00	152	153	2.0198	2	10	7.3810	8	43	30.1207
B24	5	5	5.2581	0.5755	0.00	152	154	1.9355	1	7	3.5024	4	28	14.1402
B25	4	4	4.2581	0.5143	0.00	152	153	2.0562	2	6	3.2132	8	26	12.9135
B26	5	5	5.0000	0.0000	0.00	154	158	4.3165	2	9	6.1518	8	39	26.6302
B27	3	3	3.0645	0.2497	0.00	152	155	2.3085	2	7	3.3033	8	30	13.5624
B28	3	3	3.2581	0.5755	0.00	152	153	1.9680	2	5	3.0261	8	24	13.0409
B29	3	3	3.2258	0.4250	0.00	152	154	2.4705	2	4	1.8228	8	18	7.6122
B30	2	2	2.5484	0.6239	0.00	152	154	3.7018	2	7	5.7358	8	28	23.3637
B31	7	7	7.0000	0.0000	0.00	154	158	3.0953	2	10	6.2340	8	42	25.8763
B32	4	4	4.3871	1.2826	0.00	152	155	2.7875	2	8	5.7081	8	36	23.1095
B33	4	4	4.1935	0.6011	0.00	152	154	3.7125	2	5	3.5753	8	21	15.1291
B34	4	4	4.1290	0.4995	0.00	152	153	1.5268	2	5	4.2205	8	23	16.8363
B35	4	4	4.6452	0.9504	0.00	152	152	1.0984	1	5	2.2177	4	21	8.8371
B36	13	13	13.0000	0.0000	0.00	154	158	3.6041	4	9	4.6647	16	39	19.2969
B37	10	10	10.3871	0.8032	0.00	152	155	4.3569	1	6	2.7689	4	24	11.4273
B38	8	8	8.2258	0.4973	0.00	152	154	2.2026	2	9	7.5453	8	40	30.0411
B39	5	5	5.0000	0.0000	0.00	152	154	2.2327	2	5	2.9759	9	22	11.9398
B40	5	5	5.1935	0.6011	0.00	152	153	1.9989	2	5	2.7552	8	22	11.5980
B41	8	8	8.0000	0.0000	0.00	154	159	4.8193	3	10	5.9482	14	45	24.6265
B42	8	8	8.0000	0.0000	0.00	152	154	2.3692	2	4	2.3592	8	20	9.9095
B43	8	8	8.0645	0.3592	0.00	152	154	1.8526	1	5	2.9563	4	21	12.2532
B44	5	5	6.3548	1.5176	0.00	152	153	1.1538	2	5	2.9494	8	24	11.9644
B45	5	5	6.1613	1.4854	0.00	152	153	1.5443	2	5	2.6917	8	23	10.8397
B46	8	8	8.0323	0.1796	0.00	155	159	4.2805	2	9	6.9125	8	41	28.3549
B47	5	5	5.0968	0.5388	0.00	152	154	2.0294	2	5	2.0811	8	21	8.4729
B48	5	5	5.1935	0.6011	0.00	152	154	1.6428	2	4	2.2647	8	20	9.1640
B49	5	5	5.2581	0.6816	0.00	151	153	3.5342	2	5	2.6482	8	21	10.6357
B50	5	5	5.1290	0.4995	0.00	152	153	3.1826	2	5	2.8493	8	22	11.5451

TABLE 25: Continued.

ID	OPT	Optimum				Execution time			Cycle			Time cycle		
		MBO	AVG	SD	RPD%	BET	AVG	ST	BC	AVG	SD	BTC	AVG	SD
B51	27	27	27.9355	0.8139	0.00	154	161	3.4660	10	26	8.4370	41	111	35.6271
B52	18	18	18.9355	1.0626	0.00	154	157	3.3758	8	24	9.0310	32	102	36.6151
B53	11	11	11.0000	0.0000	0.00	153	155	1.8334	6	11	4.6911	24	45	19.0585
B54	11	11	11.0000	0.0000	0.00	152	154	3.7637	3	8	2.6941	12	35	11.1208
B55	7	7	7.0000	0.0000	0.00	154	158	3.2984	3	11	5.1034	13	49	21.0208
B56	6	6	6.0000	0.0000	0.00	153	156	3.0093	4	11	3.8401	16	48	15.2743
B57	6	6	6.1290	0.4275	0.00	153	155	2.8387	4	11	5.4081	16	46	22.2407
B58	6	6	6.0645	0.2497	0.00	152	155	4.2566	3	10	3.8702	12	43	15.8509
B59	9	9	9.0323	0.1796	0.00	155	158	3.0526	5	14	6.9780	22	60	29.3752
B60	4	4	4.3871	1.2021	0.00	153	156	2.1687	5	14	7.0227	21	59	29.2113
B61	4	4	4.1613	0.4544	0.00	153	156	4.8604	3	12	6.3903	12	52	27.7761
B62	4	4	4.0323	0.1796	0.00	152	154	2.3678	4	10	4.8644	17	45	20.3279
B63	27	27	27.1935	0.4016	0.00	156	162	4.4719	4	15	7.7450	16	66	32.7914
B64	18	18	18.0968	0.3005	0.00	154	157	2.4722	5	19	8.3824	23	81	35.1227
B65	14	14	14.0323	0.1796	0.00	153	156	4.1228	6	15	8.5828	24	65	35.2348
B66	13	13	13.0000	0.0000	0.00	152	155	2.5179	7	9	2.7072	28	41	11.3806
B67	11	11	11.1290	0.3408	0.00	154	159	4.6810	4	12	6.4386	17	52	27.4067
B68	8	8	8.2258	0.9205	0.00	154	157	3.4830	3	14	9.5942	12	61	40.0795
B69	8	8	8.6129	0.7154	0.00	153	156	4.5924	4	11	5.9648	16	48	24.0260
B70	6	6	6.3548	0.7549	0.00	152	159	9.1831	3	14	6.6604	12	60	29.2535
B71	6	6	6.0000	0.0000	0.00	154	160	5.0885	6	14	6.2436	28	60	26.1248
B72	4	4	4.2581	0.5143	0.00	153	156	2.0956	3	11	5.6317	13	49	23.2173
B73	4	4	4.3548	0.6607	0.00	152	155	4.3015	3	12	7.6978	12	51	31.3144
B74	3	3	3.4839	0.5699	0.00	152	154	2.1038	3	11	6.2472	12	45	25.2912
B75	11	11	11.7419	0.9298	0.00	154	160	4.5345	3	17	8.7525	13	72	37.3021
B76	5	5	5.0645	0.3592	0.00	153	156	2.3192	4	12	6.1097	19	53	25.0673
B77	5	5	5.5161	0.8896	0.00	152	155	4.3891	3	12	7.1977	12	52	29.2321
B78	4	4	4.6774	1.1072	0.00	152	155	2.3908	4	15	6.2862	17	62	25.6253
B79	14	14	14.0000	0.0000	0.00	155	159	3.0324	6	10	4.4923	24	43	18.5246
B80	11	11	11.0000	0.0000	0.00	153	157	3.3665	4	11	3.6697	16	46	15.4853
B81	11	11	11.3871	0.8032	0.00	152	156	4.2659	3	14	8.3982	12	61	34.5279
B82	10	10	10.6774	0.7911	0.00	153	155	1.8613	5	12	5.4156	21	53	22.2498
B83	12	12	12.1935	0.7492	0.00	154	160	4.3436	2	11	5.9686	8	50	25.0351
B84	12	12	12.1290	0.4995	0.00	153	156	2.6567	6	13	6.1890	25	55	25.4035
B85	8	8	9.5806	1.8934	0.00	153	156	3.8652	3	13	6.6922	13	55	27.3698
B86	8	8	8.0000	0.0000	0.00	152	155	2.2504	4	10	4.1195	16	43	17.4584
B87	10	10	10.4839	0.9263	0.00	155	159	3.6559	4	18	8.6221	16	79	36.8990
B88	8	8	8.0000	0.0000	0.00	154	156	2.8530	4	10	3.8077	16	41	15.5335
B89	8	8	8.0000	0.0000	0.00	152	156	4.3232	3	9	3.6948	12	39	15.6479
B90	5	5	5.3871	1.0223	0.00	152	155	3.4501	3	11	4.1108	13	45	16.8234
		AVG	8.1029	0.4293	0.00	152	155	3.8451	2	9	4.8785	12	40	20.2717

TABLE 26: MBO using parallel merge sort algorithm with 16 threads.

ID	OPT	Optimum				Execution time			Cycle			Time cycle		
		MBO	AVG	SD	RPD%	BET	AVG	ST	BC	AVG	SD	BTC	AVG	SD
B1	11	11	11.0000	0.0000	0.00	156	174	38.3904	1	6	3.8370	4	33	26.3519
B2	11	11	11.0000	0.0000	0.00	152	170	37.5675	2	4	1.4338	8	21	9.5525
B3	11	11	11.0000	0.0000	0.00	152	153	1.4421	2	4	1.3384	8	18	5.5949
B4	11	11	11.0000	0.0000	0.00	152	184	126.1403	3	5	1.9620	12	25	9.3102
B5	11	11	11.0000	0.0000	0.00	153	176	53.4639	1	5	2.5716	4	25	14.3306
B6	7	7	7.0000	0.0000	0.00	154	170	28.7805	3	10	4.5744	12	47	22.7679
B7	6	6	6.0323	0.1796	0.00	155	178	33.1697	3	5	3.8685	12	28	17.8745
B8	4	4	4.3871	0.8032	0.00	152	177	28.8102	2	12	10.4629	9	57	49.2948
B9	3	3	3.1290	0.3408	0.00	154	177	40.8947	2	6	6.0373	10	33	28.3257
B10	3	3	3.0000	0.0000	0.00	154	200	42.9216	3	4	1.3125	12	24	8.8010
B11	4	4	4.2258	0.4250	0.00	154	208	57.8835	2	11	7.2915	9	61	47.9815
B12	4	4	4.0000	0.0000	0.00	154	161	7.1918	2	3	1.6271	8	16	7.6983
B13	4	4	4.0000	0.0000	0.00	156	241	69.3555	2	5	2.0452	11	34	24.6320
B14	3	3	3.1935	0.4016	0.00	153	180	41.3214	2	5	2.6700	10	28	12.9253
B15	1	1	1.4516	0.9605	0.00	152	167	20.7708	3	6	2.0992	12	26	11.3581
B16	14	14	14.0000	0.0000	0.00	155	193	49.9363	1	8	5.0855	5	47	33.2326
B17	13	13	13.0000	0.0000	0.00	153	179	33.2854	2	4	1.7604	8	23	9.0254
B18	13	13	13.0000	0.0000	0.00	154	176	28.2143	2	5	2.2442	8	26	12.5006
B19	13	13	13.1935	0.7492	0.00	153	205	61.2246	2	6	4.9091	8	38	28.1094
B20	13	13	13.0000	0.0000	0.00	152	155	4.7306	2	8	5.9932	10	35	24.7893
B21	9	9	9.3226	0.4752	0.00	155	167	12.4572	2	8	7.2314	12	39	31.2266
B22	6	6	6.1613	0.3739	0.00	152	156	3.6509	3	7	3.6945	12	29	15.2464
B23	6	6	6.0645	0.2497	0.00	152	155	4.2187	2	8	5.2534	8	34	21.9115
B24	5	5	5.4516	0.7229	0.00	152	153	1.5651	1	5	2.7048	4	24	11.3314
B25	4	4	4.3871	0.7154	0.00	152	153	1.5317	2	6	2.5012	8	26	10.3027
B26	5	5	5.0000	0.0000	0.00	154	157	3.2883	1	8	5.9864	4	36	24.8583
B27	3	3	3.0645	0.2497	0.00	152	156	3.6957	1	5	2.6453	4	23	11.2241
B28	3	3	3.3548	0.5507	0.00	152	154	1.6415	1	6	2.6506	4	25	11.1220
B29	3	3	3.2903	0.5287	0.00	152	153	1.8228	2	5	2.5239	8	21	10.6774
B30	2	2	2.4839	0.6768	0.00	152	154	3.7411	2	9	7.4944	10	36	29.9656
B31	7	7	7.0000	0.0000	0.00	154	158	3.1174	3	9	3.2322	13	39	14.2112
B32	4	4	4.0000	0.0000	0.00	152	155	4.6167	2	7	4.6467	8	31	19.3095
B33	4	4	4.1290	0.4995	0.00	152	154	2.5653	2	4	2.4947	8	20	10.4209
B34	4	4	4.1290	0.4995	0.00	152	154	3.5070	2	8	6.2436	8	36	25.3171
B35	4	4	4.6452	0.9504	0.00	152	153	1.8866	1	5	3.1398	4	22	13.0124
B36	13	13	13.0000	0.0000	0.00	154	157	3.0980	2	7	4.4587	8	32	19.6268
B37	10	10	10.3226	0.7478	0.00	153	156	2.3582	2	6	3.8032	8	28	15.7390
B38	8	8	8.0645	0.2497	0.00	152	154	3.6121	2	11	9.1926	9	47	36.9595
B39	5	5	5.1613	0.8980	0.00	152	153	1.7858	3	5	1.9126	12	22	7.5316
B40	5	5	5.1290	0.4995	0.00	152	153	1.5568	2	6	3.7757	8	26	15.1195
B41	8	8	8.0000	0.0000	0.00	154	158	4.4959	3	8	4.4325	12	37	19.3518
B42	8	8	8.0000	0.0000	0.00	152	154	1.8416	2	4	2.9146	8	19	11.7187
B43	8	8	8.0000	0.0000	0.00	152	153	1.9527	2	4	2.2500	8	20	9.6155
B44	5	5	6.0645	1.4591	0.00	152	153	1.9757	2	5	2.3859	8	23	9.7173
B45	5	5	6.1935	1.5366	0.00	152	154	3.6550	3	7	4.0113	12	29	16.0929
B46	8	8	8.0323	0.1796	0.00	155	158	3.2614	3	8	4.9381	13	35	20.3281
B47	5	5	5.0000	0.0000	0.00	152	155	1.8769	2	5	1.8590	8	22	7.6797
B48	5	5	5.0645	0.3592	0.00	152	154	2.0925	2	5	2.5012	8	22	10.5511
B49	5	5	5.3226	1.1658	0.00	152	155	3.6409	2	6	3.4125	8	26	14.2755
B50	5	5	5.3226	0.7478	0.00	152	157	3.3205	3	6	4.1309	12	28	16.7865

TABLE 26: Continued.

ID	OPT	Optimum				Execution time			Cycle			Time cycle		
		MBO	AVG	SD	RPD%	BET	AVG	ST	BC	AVG	SD	BTC	AVG	SD
B51	27	27	28.0323	0.7521	0.00	158	168	4.9579	5	18	10.2663	21	82	45.4441
B52	18	18	18.9032	1.1062	0.00	155	163	4.9174	3	20	9.9102	12	87	41.3697
B53	11	11	11.0000	0.0000	0.00	155	159	3.0438	3	11	5.6777	13	48	23.7862
B54	11	11	11.0000	0.0000	0.00	152	158	3.8968	3	8	2.6384	12	37	11.8709
B55	7	7	7.0000	0.0000	0.00	155	164	4.9862	4	11	5.2009	16	51	23.2484
B56	6	6	6.0000	0.0000	0.00	154	160	5.1881	3	10	3.0761	14	42	12.8828
B57	6	6	6.0000	0.0000	0.00	153	159	7.0420	4	15	8.2207	16	64	35.1398
B58	6	6	6.0000	0.0000	0.00	152	159	8.3060	6	10	3.8362	25	46	17.9194
B59	9	9	9.0645	0.2497	0.00	154	158	4.4036	3	13	6.4481	13	57	25.8823
B60	4	4	4.6452	1.7426	0.00	154	157	3.1356	3	11	6.5308	12	47	26.7605
B61	4	4	4.0645	0.2497	0.00	153	155	2.7337	4	10	4.5938	18	43	18.8219
B62	4	4	4.0000	0.0000	0.00	152	154	2.3592	3	10	4.4376	12	42	18.0429
B63	27	27	27.2258	0.4973	0.00	154	159	4.5781	3	16	8.9346	14	71	38.5607
B64	18	18	18.1613	0.3739	0.00	154	157	2.6036	2	21	10.4142	9	89	43.2948
B65	14	14	14.0645	0.2497	0.00	153	156	2.2977	9	16	7.2749	37	68	30.2108
B66	13	13	13.0000	0.0000	0.00	153	155	4.6939	4	9	4.0798	16	39	16.7346
B67	11	11	11.0323	0.1796	0.00	154	158	3.7491	4	13	6.3256	20	57	27.2279
B68	8	8	8.2581	1.2641	0.00	154	156	2.0780	4	14	8.1412	17	61	33.2352
B69	8	8	8.5161	0.5699	0.00	153	155	1.9806	3	11	6.3845	12	48	25.9051
B70	6	6	6.4839	0.8112	0.00	152	155	4.0201	6	14	7.0459	26	60	28.5073
B71	6	6	6.0968	0.3962	0.00	154	157	2.9403	4	12	6.6669	17	51`	26.8024
B72	4	4	4.2258	0.4973	0.00	153	156	2.5425	4	12	4.9425	17	50	19.7463
B73	4	4	4.6129	0.8032	0.00	153	156	4.3359	4	12	7.1703	16	52	29.2444
B74	3	3	3.5806	0.7648	0.00	152	154	2.1597	3	12	6.5769	12	51	26.8259
B75	11	11	11.7097	1.0064	0.00	155	158	2.7669	4	16	8.1914	16	67	34.7627
B76	5	5	5.2581	0.6816	0.00	154	156	2.1938	4	15	8.8187	16	64	36.6178
B77	5	5	5.3226	0.7478	0.00	152	155	3.8935	3	12	5.2079	12	51	21.4117
B78	4	4	4.5806	1.4323	0.00	152	155	2.1292	5	16	7.5307	21	67	29.9967
B79	14	14	14.0000	0.0000	0.00	155	159	3.9738	4	10	4.1530	17	43	16.7283
B80	11	11	11.0000	0.0000	0.00	154	156	1.8293	6	11	4.1832	24	45	17.7170
B81	11	11	11.4516	0.9605	0.00	152	155	3.8187	4	12	6.0628	17	49	24.8217
B82	10	10	10.5484	0.8500	0.00	153	155	2.7044	3	11	6.4430	12	47	26.5292
B83	12	12	12.0000	0.0000	0.00	155	158	2.8105	6	10	3.6928	24	44	15.9765
B84	12	12	12.0000	0.0000	0.00	153	157	5.0225	2	10	4.6216	9	44	18.9497
B85	8	8	9.4839	1.6304	0.00	152	155	1.9587	3	13	8.1050	12	57	33.4782
B86	8	8	8.1290	0.5623	0.00	152	154	1.6611	3	11	4.6358	13	45	18.8382
B87	10	10	10.4194	0.8860	0.00	154	158	2.7913	4	18	9.6760	17	76	41.0048
B88	8	8	8.0000	0.0000	0.00	154	156	3.9358	5	10	3.5021	21	44	14.3271
B89	8	8	8.0323	0.1796	0.00	152	155	2.0294	4	11	5.5903	17	47	22.9967
B90	5	5	5.3871	1.0223	0.00	152	154	1.8334	5	11	5.2521	20	46	21.4332
		AVG	8.1007	0.4296	0.00	153	161	11.5292	2	9	4.9112	12	40	21.5416

TABLE 27: MBO using parallel merge sort algorithm with 32 threads.

ID	OPT	Optimum				Execution time			Cycle			Time cycle		
		MBO	AVG	SD	RPD%	BET	AVG	ST	BC	AVG	SD	BTC	AVG	SD
B1	11	11	11.0000	0.0000	0.00	156	202	73.4610	3	7	2.8048	13	41	25.2275
B2	11	11	11.0000	0.0000	0.00	153	159	8.6862	3	4	1.4473	12	22	9.7667
B3	11	11	11.0000	0.0000	0.00	152	155	3.1575	1	4	1.6481	4	17	7.1419
B4	11	11	11.0000	0.0000	0.00	153	159	12.7325	3	5	2.2756	12	23	10.9487
B5	11	11	11.0000	0.0000	0.00	153	159	7.8248	2	5	2.0583	8	24	8.4883
B6	7	7	7.0000	0.0000	0.00	154	168	11.3770	2	10	6.2576	10	44	28.5622
B7	6	6	6.0645	0.2497	0.00	153	162	10.6669	3	6	2.3623	13	29	12.9453
B8	4	4	4.1935	0.6011	0.00	152	157	4.6720	2	12	9.9450	8	51	41.2599
B9	3	3	3.0968	0.3005	0.00	153	157	5.1856	1	5	2.5098	4	25	10.4043
B10	3	3	3.0000	0.0000	0.00	152	159	8.1494	1	3	1.7001	4	16	7.8501
B11	4	4	4.2581	0.4448	0.00	153	164	11.3640	3	12	7.4554	14	52	32.6614
B12	4	4	4.0000	0.0000	0.00	152	157	5.4880	1	4	1.8026	4	17	7.6960
B13	4	4	4.0645	0.3592	0.00	152	159	9.9945	2	5	2.4679	9	22	10.6621
B14	3	3	3.2581	0.4448	0.00	152	157	7.2963	2	5	2.6632	8	23	11.1257
B15	1	1	1.5161	0.8896	0.00	152	162	14.1797	2	6	2.7731	8	25	12.0180
B16	14	14	14.0000	0.0000	0.00	155	178	28.1446	3	6	2.8459	12	32	12.6052
B17	13	13	13.0000	0.0000	0.00	152	163	9.4999	1	4	1.6669	4	19	7.8038
B18	13	13	13.0000	0.0000	0.00	153	176	50.4821	1	5	2.3431	5	22	12.0773
B19	13	13	13.1935	0.7492	0.00	153	167	23.5020	2	7	4.6575	12	34	25.0622
B20	13	13	13.0000	0.0000	0.00	152	196	65.9215	2	7	4.9246	9	39	27.7927
B21	9	9	9.3548	0.4864	0.00	154	197	89.8626	2	11	8.3362	8	56	40.0088
B22	6	6	6.1613	0.5829	0.00	155	213	63.0063	2	5	2.0161	8	32	18.9462
B23	6	6	6.1935	0.4016	0.00	155	241	100.2556	3	7	5.8505	12	48	39.5844
B24	5	5	5.2903	0.5884	0.00	152	164	31.9873	2	6	3.1288	8	28	12.6167
B25	4	4	4.1613	0.3739	0.00	152	155	2.4839	2	6	4.9858	8	26	20.2954
B26	5	5	5.0645	0.2497	0.00	155	162	5.6949	2	7	5.6531	8	34	24.0685
B27	3	3	3.0968	0.3005	0.00	154	158	2.8860	2	6	3.6580	9	28	15.0662
B28	3	3	3.1613	0.4544	0.00	152	156	3.2326	2	7	3.2322	8	30	13.6381
B29	3	3	3.0968	0.3005	0.00	152	155	3.9811	2	5	2.2785	8	23	9.0958
B30	2	2	2.5161	0.6256	0.00	152	156	4.9036	2	7	5.6843	8	30	23.2274
B31	7	7	7.0000	0.0000	0.00	155	164	5.3710	1	7	4.3247	4	33	19.4109
B32	4	4	4.1935	0.7492	0.00	152	157	3.1191	2	6	3.7035	8	28	15.7836
B33	4	4	4.0000	0.0000	0.00	153	156	2.9574	3	5	2.7712	12	23	11.8504
B34	4	4	4.0645	0.3592	RPD%	152	156	4.1986	2	7	7.1646	8	32	31.8354
B35	4	4	4.3226	0.7478	0.00	152	155	3.3758	2	5	3.0862	8	22	12.7461
B36	13	13	13.0000	0.0000	0.00	155	162	5.9413	2	7	3.9284	9	34	16.4346
B37	10	10	10.3226	0.7478	0.00	154	157	3.3153	2	7	5.8622	8	29	23.8995
B38	8	8	8.2581	1.2641	0.00	152	156	4.6789	2	10	8.4328	8	42	34.3955
B39	5	5	5.0000	0.0000	0.00	152	159	6.1503	2	5	2.9153	8	25	12.1929
B40	5	5	5.1290	0.4995	0.00	155	168	23.4268	3	5	1.5513	13	23	7.9119
B41	8	8	8.1613	0.8980	0.00	154	161	4.2011	4	9	6.6078	16	42	27.6753
B42	8	8	8.0000	0.0000	0.00	153	157	6.3106	2	4	1.7828	8	18	7.7493
B43	8	8	8.0000	0.0000	0.00	152	160	7.4285	2	5	2.6019	8	23	11.7932
B44	5	5	5.8710	1.3842	0.00	154	161	7.9767	2	5	2.0687	12	22	9.0735
B45	5	5	5.8710	1.3842	0.00	153	156	5.2525	2	5	3.0603	8	25	12.6925
B46	8	8	8.0323	0.1796	0.00	154	165	8.5232	1	9	7.2947	4	40	32.4977
B47	5	5	5.0000	0.0000	0.00	153	163	7.4939	2	6	3.3732	8	27	13.6618
B48	5	5	5.0645	0.3592	0.00	155	190	88.3159	3	5	2.3550	12	26	10.0136
B49	5	5	5.1290	0.4995	0.00	153	167	23.7535	2	6	2.2562	8	25	9.6192
B50	5	5	5.1935	0.6011	0.00	153	206	111.6447	1	5	2.3619	4	30	22.2696

TABLE 27: Continued.

ID	OPT	Optimum				Execution time				Cycle			Time cycle		
		MBO	AVG	SD	RPD%	BET	AVG	ST	BC	AVG	SD	BTC	AVG	SD
B51	27	27	28.1613	0.7347	0.00	160	233	106.5829	4	19	9.9746	16	113	64.2842
B52	18	18	18.8387	0.7347	0.00	154	164	6.9436	6	21	9.2897	27	91	41.3948
B53	11	11	11.0000	0.0000	0.00	155	164	13.5560	5	11	3.1833	22	47	13.7809
B54	11	11	11.0000	0.0000	0.00	156	163	4.5475	4	8	2.4274	17	37	11.2196
B55	7	7	7.0000	0.0000	0.00	159	170	8.7338	5	10	3.2038	26	47	13.2918
B56	6	6	6.0000	0.0000	0.00	154	166	10.0578	6	10	3.3742	27	47	16.6980
B57	6	6	6.0000	0.0000	0.00	155	169	18.2314	6	11	5.5162	25	52	24.6267
B58	6	6	6.0000	0.0000	0.00	154	162	4.3901	3	10	5.1287	12	44	22.2686
B59	9	9	9.1613	0.5829	0.00	161	176	14.3747	5	14	7.2798	23	70	36.4352
B60	4	4	4.2903	1.1312	0.00	157	173	14.4923	6	14	6.1914	25	64	28.9730
B61	4	4	4.1613	0.5829	0.00	155	163	6.7429	4	9	4.0040	16	42	16.5396
B62	4	4	4.0323	0.1796	0.00	154	160	3.5345	4	10	4.6504	16	43	19.3696
B63	27	27	27.2258	0.4250	0.00	159	172	5.1895	3	20	11.1084	13	91	50.3296
B64	18	18	18.1935	0.4016	0.00	157	173	22.8970	6	21	9.5444	25	102	51.5291
B65	14	14	14.0645	0.2497	0.00	156	229	88.8105	6	16	6.8318	29	96	56.9926
B66	13	13	13.0000	0.0000	0.00	155	198	64.6472	4	10	4.2088	20	55	27.5365
B67	11	11	11.0968	0.3005	0.00	166	269	216.8374	3	15	9.5772	14	118	195.6026
B68	8	8	8.2258	0.9205	0.00	154	170	13.6269	4	11	6.2202	17	53	26.0361
B69	8	8	8.5161	0.7244	0.00	155	168	15.0527	6	13	6.1990	26	59	36.8672
B70	6	6	6.5484	0.8884	0.00	153	156	5.1117	3	14	8.3743	14	62	34.9847
B71	6	6	6.1290	0.4995	0.00	154	160	5.1506	4	11	4.5231	16	49	19.3207
B72	4	4	4.3548	0.5507	0.00	152	157	3.9059	6	16	8.5049	25	67	36.2737
B73	4	4	4.5161	0.6768	0.00	152	166	25.8682	4	13	9.0983	17	57	39.4182
B74	3	3	3.5484	0.7676	0.00	154	169	18.5330	3	13	7.3941	13	57	32.0482
B75	11	11	11.6452	0.9504	0.00	156	166	10.2917	6	14	9.4745	26	64	42.2402
B76	5	5	5.1290	0.4995	0.00	153	202	49.9134	6	13	6.4288	25	73	35.4865
B77	5	5	5.3871	0.8032	0.00	152	161	11.1016	4	13	7.0557	17	56	28.8527
B78	4	4	4.7742	1.3344	0.00	153	159	7.9270	4	13	6.6488	17	55	29.2830
B79	14	14	14.0000	0.0000	0.00	153	166	11.9017	2	9	3.9646	8	41	16.3156
B80	11	11	11.0000	0.0000	0.00	154	162	9.6500	6	11	5.3587	24	50	23.5722
B81	11	11	11.3548	0.8386	0.00	153	158	6.6857	5	13	7.0744	20	56	29.7124
B82	10	10	10.4516	0.7676	0.00	152	160	10.6532	5	13	5.9386	20	55	27.4567
B83	12	12	12.0968	0.5388	0.00	153	170	19.9290	5	11	3.8451	24	51	17.9308
B84	12	12	12.0000	0.0000	0.00	154	161	6.7725	4	13	7.3941	16	55	31.6225
B85	8	8	8.8387	1.2409	0.00	154	164	14.7388	5	14	7.2984	22	62	34.7666
B86	8	8	8.0968	0.5388	0.00	153	162	10.3043	4	10	4.3183	16	44	18.7357
B87	10	10	10.1290	0.4995	0.00	154	166	10.6363	5	18	8.1722	21	80	36.7600
B88	8	8	8.0000	0.0000	0.00	154	160	6.2300	6	11	4.4717	24	50	18.2966
B89	8	8	8.0000	0.0000	0.00	154	181	63.1321	4	10	3.9393	16	50	22.3958
B90	5	5	5.4839	1.1216	0.00	154	158	5.3563	3	10	4.3045	12	41	18.0081
		AVG	8.0756	0.4173	0.00	154	170	21.8506	3	9	4.8937	14	44	24.7712

TABLE 28: MBO using sequential quick sort algorithm.

ID	OPT	Optimum				Execution time			Cycle			Time cycle		
		MBO	AVG	SD	RPD%	BET	AVG	ST	BC	AVG	SD	BTC	AVG	SD
B1	11	11	11.0000	0.0000	0.00	156	190	58.2650	2	7	3.8624	11	43	33.3476
B2	11	11	11.0000	0.0000	0.00	153	161	11.6192	2	4	1.4074	8	19	6.0245
B3	11	11	11.0000	0.0000	0.00	152	155	2.5085	2	4	1.5176	8	17	6.5214
B4	11	11	11.0000	0.0000	0.00	152	182	101.4110	2	4	1.8246	8	22	9.4797
B5	11	11	11.0000	0.0000	0.00	152	156	6.3229	2	5	3.4426	9	22	13.9587
B6	7	7	7.0000	0.0000	0.00	154	161	13.5107	3	8	4.1693	12	37	17.3353
B7	6	6	6.0323	0.1796	0.00	153	168	13.8935	3	6	2.9068	12	31	13.1726
B8	4	4	4.0645	0.3592	0.00	152	182	34.6447	2	10	7.8375	8	49	35.8762
B9	3	3	3.1290	0.3408	0.00	152	156	9.6349	2	6	5.9664	8	29	33.1260
B10	3	3	3.0000	0.0000	0.00	152	154	2.1771	2	4	1.1968	8	16	4.7947
B11	4	4	4.1290	0.3408	0.00	154	157	3.1084	1	11	8.3456	4	46	34.7346
B12	4	4	4.0000	0.0000	0.00	152	155	3.0374	1	3	1.5794	5	15	6.4709
B13	4	4	4.2258	0.7169	0.00	152	153	1.8814	2	5	5.3585	8	23	22.5828
B14	3	3	3.3548	0.4864	0.00	152	154	1.6533	2	5	2.3971	8	23	9.8987
B15	1	1	1.1290	0.4995	0.00	152	153	1.5027	2	6	2.2912	8	24	9.3735
B16	14	14	14.0000	0.0000	0.00	154	158	6.5646	2	8	4.7026	8	34	19.1483
B17	13	13	13.0000	0.0000	0.00	153	155	2.0283	2	5	1.8860	9	21	7.4763
B18	13	13	13.0000	0.0000	0.00	152	157	7.3231	1	6	2.4995	4	25	10.3130
B19	13	13	13.0968	0.5388	0.00	152	159	6.4381	2	7	6.0690	8	33	24.6737
B20	13	13	13.0000	0.0000	0.00	153	159	7.5257	2	7	4.6504	8	31	19.5123
B21	9	9	9.2903	0.4614	0.00	154	158	4.8569	2	9	7.8941	8	41	32.4426
B22	6	6	6.1613	0.3739	0.00	152	160	7.6086	3	6	2.7611	12	26	12.0577
B23	6	6	6.1613	0.3739	0.00	152	157	5.0575	4	10	7.1245	16	43	29.3833
B24	5	5	5.2903	0.5287	0.00	152	159	6.8078	2	7	4.8146	9	30	19.7313
B25	4	4	4.1613	0.3739	0.00	152	155	4.9514	2	6	2.5430	8	24	10.4495
B26	5	5	5.0000	0.0000	0.00	154	163	8.4537	2	8	4.4837	8	36	18.4994
B27	3	3	3.0323	0.1796	0.00	153	158	6.3527	1	7	5.5072	5	29	22.6066
B28	3	3	3.2581	0.4448	0.00	152	162	9.1764	2	6	4.4041	8	26	20.0669
B29	3	3	3.1613	0.3739	0.00	152	163	8.9060	1	5	2.9534	4	23	12.2417
B30	2	2	2.6129	0.8032	0.00	152	162	11.2350	2	7	6.3716	8	30	26.7117
B31	7	7	7.0000	0.0000	0.00	155	172	13.0047	3	8	5.2176	14	40	23.0526
B32	4	4	4.0968	0.5388	0.00	154	163	16.2313	2	8	5.0189	8	36	22.6064
B33	4	4	4.0645	0.3592	0.00	153	161	8.5798	2	5	2.5016	8	22	10.6692
B34	4	4	4.1290	0.4995	0.00	152	158	9.0177	2	6	5.0302	8	27	20.6482
B35	4	4	4.6452	0.9504	0.00	152	153	1.5098	1	5	4.4678	4	23	18.0923
B36	13	13	13.0000	0.0000	0.00	154	174	26.3191	3	8	4.2014	12	41	24.8909
B37	10	10	10.5161	0.8896	0.00	153	161	12.2450	2	7	3.9136	8	30	15.9159
B38	8	8	8.0968	0.3962	0.00	152	157	6.5512	2	10	8.7204	8	43	35.7477
B39	5	5	5.0000	0.0000	0.00	152	161	13.6204	3	5	2.3431	12	25	10.6618
B40	5	5	5.0000	0.0000	0.00	152	163	9.7288	2	5	2.1438	8	21	9.9864
B41	8	8	8.0000	0.0000	0.00	155	165	12.7196	1	10	6.2553	5	48	26.9376
B42	8	8	8.0000	0.0000	0.00	152	157	3.5951	2	4	1.7804	8	19	7.5267
B43	8	8	8.0645	0.3592	0.00	152	155	2.4947	2	5	5.3110	8	24	22.0386
B44	5	5	6.0645	1.4591	0.00	152	155	3.3302	2	6	3.3601	8	25	13.7010
B45	5	5	6.4516	1.5240	0.00	152	154	1.4135	2	5	2.2907	8	21	9.2427
B46	8	8	8.1290	0.3408	0.00	154	161	4.7801	3	9	6.7587	14	42	29.0482
B47	5	5	5.0968	0.5388	0.00	153	156	2.5392	1	4	1.8139	4	20	7.8833
B48	5	5	5.1935	0.6011	0.00	152	155	4.2327	2	5	2.4021	8	23	9.6806
B49	5	5	5.1290	0.4995	0.00	152	155	3.8960	3	7	4.9298	12	31	20.3514
B50	5	5	5.1935	0.6011	0.00	152	157	7.6718	2	5	2.2728	8	24	9.2511

TABLE 28: Continued.

ID	OPT	Optimum				Execution time				Cycle			Time cycle		
		MBO	AVG	SD	RPD%	BET	AVG	ST	BC	AVG	SD	BTC	AVG	SD
B51	27	27	28.2258	0.9205	0.00	155	161	4.3769	4	19	9.2586	20	82	39.4718
B52	18	18	18.9032	1.1062	0.00	154	158	4.4286	7	20	9.4888	29	85	40.2330
B53	11	11	11.0000	0.0000	0.00	154	157	2.8269	4	10	4.1346	16	44	16.8027
B54	11	11	11.0000	0.0000	0.00	153	156	2.3075	4	9	3.2052	16	38	13.3121
B55	7	7	7.0000	0.0000	0.00	154	158	2.9370	4	10	5.4839	16	45	22.7564
B56	6	6	6.0000	0.0000	0.00	154	157	2.2337	4	8	2.6184	16	36	11.1519
B57	6	6	6.0000	0.0000	0.00	153	157	4.3503	6	10	4.0231	24	43	16.3044
B58	6	6	6.1290	0.3408	0.00	154	157	2.8189	5	10	3.8882	20	44	15.7987
B59	9	9	9.1935	0.6011	0.00	154	160	3.4817	3	13	8.1588	12	59	34.8749
B60	4	4	4.5161	1.3631	0.00	154	157	2.8511	3	12	4.7288	12	50	19.8736
B61	4	4	4.2258	0.6170	0.00	153	156	3.6237	3	11	4.2571	17	48	17.2788
B62	4	4	4.0323	0.1796	0.00	152	155	2.5098	4	10	3.6820	16	41	15.5667
B63	27	27	27.2581	0.4448	0.00	155	164	6.3053	4	19	10.1183	19	84	42.8466
B64	18	18	18.3548	0.5507	0.00	154	175	29.3106	7	20	9.2391	37	95	41.8859
B65	14	14	14.1935	0.4016	0.00	154	162	11.5242	5	14	6.2896	22	61	26.2881
B66	13	13	13.0000	0.0000	0.00	154	174	31.3824	6	11	3.7301	24	51	22.7029
B67	11	11	11.0323	0.1796	0.00	155	166	11.5943	6	12	5.7328	24	53	23.5936
B68	8	8	8.5806	1.7469	0.00	154	160	5.9015	3	11	6.2869	12	48	25.7106
B69	8	8	8.5161	0.8112	0.00	153	165	12.9041	4	10	5.4759	16	47	24.7696
B70	6	6	6.6452	0.8386	0.00	153	160	11.3877	2	12	7.7095	8	52	31.6072
B71	6	6	6.1290	0.4995	0.00	157	178	18.6546	2	11	5.3096	11	54	28.3288
B72	4	4	4.2581	0.7732	0.00	154	171	19.4453	4	11	6.3664	16	54	29.4289
B73	4	4	4.4194	0.6204	0.00	154	174	16.4459	5	10	4.0422	21	51	19.9695
B74	3	3	3.5484	0.6239	0.00	156	187	33.9678	5	12	7.8744	20	67	49.6365
B75	11	11	11.5806	1.0255	0.00	159	200	45.3931	4	17	9.9043	17	95	67.7548
B76	5	5	5.0645	0.3592	0.00	154	171	37.0215	4	14	6.9785	17	67	30.3144
B77	5	5	5.3871	0.8032	0.00	154	161	7.2560	4	14	7.2969	17	62	31.3623
B78	4	4	4.5806	1.1188	0.00	153	166	11.1021	8	15	4.9588	32	69	24.4737
B79	14	14	14.0000	0.0000	0.00	155	173	15.1100	5	9	2.9421	20	44	16.3185
B80	11	11	11.0000	0.0000	0.00	154	164	13.3813	4	11	3.7198	17	48	16.2591
B81	11	11	11.5484	1.1787	0.00	155	177	20.2888	2	13	8.5572	8	64	39.3331
B82	10	10	10.7419	0.7732	0.00	154	227	142.7347	3	10	5.1533	13	56	31.9425
B83	12	12	12.3548	1.5176	0.00	154	180	28.3520	3	11	6.7907	13	58	36.4259
B84	12	12	12.0000	0.0000	0.00	155	165	12.8809	2	12	5.0773	9	54	23.5388
B85	8	8	9.4516	1.6899	0.00	154	164	17.4202	3	13	6.9161	13	59	29.5533
B86	8	8	8.1613	0.5829	0.00	153	155	2.0525	4	11	6.3534	16	49	25.9607
B87	10	10	10.3871	0.9549	0.00	154	159	5.2984	5	16	9.5733	20	68	40.5421
B88	8	8	8.0000	0.0000	0.00	154	157	2.8466	5	10	3.0610	21	43	12.7689
B89	8	8	8.0323	0.1796	0.00	154	156	2.3349	4	10	5.9039	16	43	23.9970
B90	5	5	5.3871	1.0223	0.00	153	155	2.5778	3	11	4.7201	13	46	18.9533
		AVG	8.1111	0.4529	0.00	153	163	12.7284	2	9	4.9168	12	41	22.1071

TABLE 29: MBO using parallel quick sort algorithm with 1 thread.

ID	OPT	Optimum				Execution time			Cycle			Time cycle		
		MBO	AVG	SD	RPD%	BET	AVG	ST	BC	AVG	SD	BTC	AVG	SD
B1	11	11	11.0000	0.0000	0.00	156	193	68.9999	2	7	3.1195	9	41	17.8353
B2	11	11	11.0000	0.0000	0.00	153	165	18.8674	2	4	1.1538	8	19	8.8834
B3	11	11	11.0000	0.0000	0.00	153	161	19.3106	2	4	1.3827	8	19	6.5820
B4	11	11	11.0000	0.0000	0.00	153	167	25.8893	2	4	1.8014	8	20	9.8274
B5	11	11	11.0000	0.0000	0.00	154	177	33.0442	2	5	2.6769	9	29	17.8432
B6	7	7	7.0000	0.0000	0.00	154	165	11.4363	1	8	5.7640	4	38	25.6395
B7	6	6	6.0645	0.2497	0.00	153	159	3.8032	2	8	5.1941	9	36	22.4181
B8	4	4	4.2581	0.6816	0.00	152	158	5.4317	3	9	7.4731	12	38	30.7397
B9	3	3	3.0968	0.3005	0.00	153	168	20.1787	2	5	2.6102	10	25	11.7018
B10	3	3	3.0000	0.0000	0.00	152	158	7.1719	2	4	1.5794	8	17	6.8647
B11	4	4	4.1613	0.3739	0.00	154	162	8.1435	4	11	8.0349	16	48	34.9012
B12	4	4	4.0000	0.0000	0.00	152	154	1.6950	2	4	1.7064	8	18	6.9414
B13	4	4	4.0000	0.0000	0.00	152	154	2.0832	2	6	3.3636	8	25	13.6855
B14	3	3	3.4516	0.5680	0.00	152	168	22.8717	2	6	4.3793	8	27	19.2045
B15	1	1	1.4194	0.8860	0.00	153	175	34.8684	3	7	3.2531	12	33	16.1056
B16	14	14	14.0000	0.0000	0.00	159	221	63.7515	2	7	4.2848	11	41	21.9744
B17	13	13	13.0000	0.0000	0.00	154	178	48.9971	2	4	1.7026	9	22	9.6839
B18	13	13	13.0000	0.0000	0.00	152	155	4.3855	3	6	2.3655	12	24	10.3454
B19	13	13	13.0968	0.5388	0.00	152	153	2.1513	2	7	5.6009	8	30	22.7850
B20	13	13	13.0000	0.0000	0.00	152	153	1.5027	2	7	5.0298	8	32	20.2303
B21	9	9	9.0968	0.3005	0.00	154	158	3.0132	1	10	8.6519	4	43	35.6950
B22	6	6	6.1613	0.3739	0.00	152	156	4.0430	2	6	4.0364	8	26	16.4319
B23	6	6	6.0968	0.3005	0.00	152	153	1.4803	3	6	4.5416	12	27	18.2106
B24	5	5	5.3871	0.6152	0.00	152	153	1.5394	2	5	2.4132	8	23	9.6668
B25	4	4	4.4516	0.8500	0.00	152	154	1.8757	2	5	1.8567	8	23	7.7759
B26	5	5	5.0000	0.0000	0.00	154	158	4.2421	2	9	6.0213	8	40	25.2638
B27	3	3	3.0323	0.1796	0.00	152	156	3.4467	1	6	4.3334	4	27	17.5791
B28	3	3	3.3548	0.5507	0.00	152	154	2.4328	3	5	1.9724	12	24	8.1028
B29	3	3	3.2581	0.4448	0.00	152	154	3.9059	2	5	2.6126	8	23	10.6863
B30	2	2	2.2581	0.5143	0.00	152	154	1.8062	4	8	3.8077	16	32	15.4194
B31	7	7	7.0000	0.0000	0.00	154	166	12.3793	3	9	3.5214	12	39	14.8130
B32	4	4	4.1935	0.7492	0.00	154	161	9.6416	3	8	5.6009	12	35	23.3415
B33	4	4	4.1290	0.4995	0.00	152	160	7.4242	1	5	2.9712	4	24	12.6727
B34	4	4	4.0645	0.3592	0.00	152	156	4.2459	3	6	4.2170	12	28	17.9599
B35	4	4	4.9032	1.0118	0.00	153	166	10.7510	2	5	3.7626	8	26	16.9638
B36	13	13	13.0000	0.0000	0.00	155	177	17.3078	3	8	4.6900	12	38	23.3320
B37	10	10	10.5161	0.8896	0.00	153	165	14.0154	2	6	4.9622	8	26	20.6570
B38	8	8	8.0645	0.2497	0.00	152	165	14.2440	2	11	7.5177	8	52	33.8136
B39	5	5	5.3548	1.3796	0.00	154	168	10.6828	2	6	2.8136	8	27	13.6350
B40	5	5	5.1935	0.6011	0.00	152	162	7.7362	2	5	2.0832	8	22	8.8589
B41	8	8	8.0000	0.0000	0.00	154	177	24.0561	1	10	7.6418	4	47	36.2878
B42	8	8	8.0000	0.0000	0.00	153	182	36.9639	2	4	1.4081	8	20	10.2833
B43	8	8	8.0968	0.5388	0.00	162	268	137.6530	2	4	2.1463	12	33	27.5295
B44	5	5	5.8710	1.3842	0.00	155	172	21.8345	2	5	3.8857	8	27	19.0926
B45	5	5	5.8710	1.3842	0.00	153	182	50.6757	2	6	3.1036	8	29	20.3958
B46	8	8	8.1935	0.4016	0.00	172	219	56.1605	3	10	5.7329	15	60	43.2816
B47	5	5	5.0968	0.5388	0.00	166	207	40.9797	2	6	5.1442	10	40	29.2231
B48	5	5	5.0645	0.3592	0.00	163	170	5.2351	2	5	2.6258	8	26	12.1034
B49	5	5	5.1935	0.6011	0.00	160	170	8.4292	2	5	3.0754	9	24	13.6420
B50	5	5	5.5806	0.9228	0.00	160	174	21.8488	1	6	5.7528	4	28	25.8977

TABLE 29: Continued.

ID	OPT	Optimum				Execution time				Cycle			Time cycle		
		MBO	AVG	SD	RPD%	BET	AVG	ST	BC	AVG	SD	BTC	AVG	SD
B51	27	27	28.3548	0.9504	0.00	167	198	36.1613	3	20	9.4901	14	106	48.8988
B52	18	18	18.7742	0.6688	0.00	155	159	3.0282	4	19	10.1538	17	84	42.9794
B53	11	11	11.0000	0.0000	0.00	154	159	4.8285	5	10	3.0593	20	43	13.3710
B54	11	11	11.0000	0.0000	0.00	152	156	2.9388	3	9	3.0061	12	38	12.4134
B55	7	7	7.0000	0.0000	0.00	154	164	12.3552	4	13	6.6611	16	57	28.3718
B56	6	6	6.0000	0.0000	0.00	154	175	24.3904	5	9	3.9809	22	44	17.8687
B57	6	6	6.0000	0.0000	0.00	153	163	6.9322	4	11	5.2964	16	50	24.4128
B58	6	6	6.0000	0.0000	0.00	153	156	3.5822	5	10	5.6569	21	41	23.9429
B59	9	9	9.0323	0.1796	0.00	155	166	5.9601	2	12	6.4739	8	54	27.6165
B60	4	4	4.5161	1.3631	0.00	154	163	7.2272	5	11	4.4119	21	49	19.4739
B61	4	4	4.2581	0.6308	0.00	154	158	6.1989	2	9	3.6644	8	41	15.6830
B62	4	4	4.1290	0.5623	0.00	153	156	2.4999	5	10	4.2704	20	42	17.9183
B63	27	27	27.2903	0.4614	0.00	155	166	6.3789	5	17	8.5487	26	77	38.2296
B64	18	18	18.2903	0.5287	0.00	157	165	6.0370	7	23	9.6062	28	104	42.0711
B65	14	14	14.1613	0.4544	0.00	154	160	4.3692	4	15	8.1672	17	65	36.0926
B66	13	13	13.0000	0.0000	0.00	154	163	8.8223	5	9	2.8923	20	42	12.0080
B67	11	11	11.0323	0.1796	0.00	159	170	7.5927	4	12	5.8966	17	55	26.7593
B68	8	8	8.5484	1.7481	0.00	154	162	7.1544	3	11	5.3146	12	50	22.5538
B69	8	8	8.3548	0.5507	0.00	153	156	2.4425	4	12	6.3070	16	51	25.7643
B70	6	6	6.2581	0.6308	0.00	153	156	2.2671	3	10	5.7856	12	44	23.9520
B71	6	6	6.0645	0.3592	0.00	156	181	27.7347	2	13	8.4332	11	64	39.5748
B72	4	4	4.1290	0.3408	0.00	155	177	29.3796	8	14	5.3225	36	64	23.1387
B73	4	4	4.5484	0.5680	0.00	153	182	46.2198	5	12	5.6883	20	63	40.8649
B74	3	3	3.4839	0.6768	0.00	153	181	24.0085	5	13	7.7974	22	62	38.6443
B75	11	11	11.7742	1.0866	0.00	164	216	65.0219	7	19	8.5961	30	102	42.8679
B76	5	5	5.1290	0.4995	0.00	154	159	3.2132	4	12	6.9587	19	50	28.7074
B77	5	5	5.9355	1.0626	0.00	154	159	2.5791	3	11	6.9711	13	50	29.2492
B78	4	4	4.7419	1.4135	0.00	153	158	2.8838	4	15	9.7257	20	64	40.5362
B79	14	14	14.0000	0.0000	0.00	156	162	5.3378	4	11	5.1178	18	49	21.6838
B80	11	11	11.0000	0.0000	0.00	153	159	2.9928	4	10	3.3575	16	46	14.4630
B81	11	11	11.2903	1.0064	0.00	153	158	2.8994	5	12	5.9435	21	52	25.2294
B82	10	10	10.6129	0.9892	0.00	154	158	2.6680	2	10	5.5058	8	45	22.8974
B83	12	12	12.0000	0.0000	0.00	156	165	6.5898	4	10	3.6210	20	46	14.5889
B84	12	12	12.0645	0.3592	0.00	155	163	5.1148	4	10	5.6932	18	44	24.3315
B85	8	8	8.9355	1.2893	0.00	155	161	5.5007	4	16	8.2380	16	69	35.8578
B86	8	8	8.0645	0.2497	0.00	153	165	10.2890	3	10	4.3411	15	46	18.2102
B87	10	10	10.5484	0.9605	0.00	157	177	13.8084	5	18	7.6776	23	87	37.4388
B88	8	8	8.2581	1.4368	0.00	154	166	13.5674	5	10	5.8803	24	46	24.4021
B89	8	8	8.0323	0.1796	0.00	156	168	18.2189	6	9	3.7301	24	43	20.6299
B90	5	5	5.3871	1.0223	0.00	153	164	9.5021	4	12	5.7030	18	54	24.8741
		AVG	8.1115	0.4667	0.00	154	167	15.5926	3	9	4.8703	13	42	22.3487

TABLE 30: MBO using parallel quick sort algorithm with 4 threads.

ID	OPT	Optimum				Execution time			Cycle			Time cycle		
		MBO	AVG	SD	RPD%	BET	AVG	ST	BC	AVG	SD	BTC	AVG	SD
B1	11	11	11.0000	0.0000	0.00	154	188	70.6184	1	6	4.1450	7	35	21.4910
B2	11	11	11.0000	0.0000	0.00	152	182	34.7551	2	3	1.4591	8	19	11.0777
B3	11	11	11.0000	0.0000	0.00	153	177	33.6228	2	4	1.7083	8	19	7.7936
B4	11	11	11.0000	0.0000	0.00	153	170	28.4944	2	4	1.7314	8	21	7.5054
B5	11	11	11.0000	0.0000	0.00	153	177	33.1479	2	4	2.1347	8	23	13.0829
B6	7	7	7.0000	0.0000	0.00	161	192	19.0742	3	9	5.1148	15	50	25.7463
B7	6	6	6.0323	0.1796	0.00	152	159	9.1029	1	5	2.5413	4	23	12.2419
B8	4	4	4.4516	1.2339	0.00	152	159	12.7028	2	11	8.2441	8	46	33.8427
B9	3	3	3.0968	0.3005	0.00	158	257	84.1696	1	6	3.5033	14	44	31.5700
B10	3	3	3.0000	0.0000	0.00	153	183	28.7203	2	4	2.5145	8	24	18.5823
B11	4	4	4.0968	0.3005	0.00	156	165	7.6151	3	11	6.1848	13	50	27.3824
B12	4	4	4.0000	0.0000	0.00	152	155	2.0000	2	4	1.5596	8	16	6.3920
B13	4	4	4.0645	0.3592	0.00	152	154	1.8538	3	4	2.1089	12	19	8.8271
B14	3	3	3.2903	0.4614	0.00	152	160	9.8399	1	5	2.5222	4	24	10.5106
B15	1	1	1.4516	0.8500	0.00	152	156	3.8373	1	5	3.5542	4	24	14.7010
B16	14	14	14.0000	0.0000	0.00	154	173	25.6756	3	9	4.8887	12	41	27.1373
B17	13	13	13.0000	0.0000	0.00	153	157	6.4014	2	5	1.6950	8	21	7.1785
B18	13	13	13.0000	0.0000	0.00	152	155	5.7326	2	5	2.4926	8	22	10.7346
B19	13	13	13.0000	0.0000	0.00	152	157	7.7789	3	7	3.6761	12	30	15.0969
B20	13	13	13.0000	0.0000	0.00	152	155	4.7308	2	6	3.0810	8	27	12.7058
B21	9	9	9.0968	0.3005	0.00	154	158	2.9072	3	11	7.1601	12	46	30.0206
B22	6	6	6.0645	0.2497	0.00	154	182	76.4377	3	6	2.7909	12	39	63.2356
B23	6	6	6.1290	0.4275	0.00	152	160	13.7304	2	7	4.4337	8	33	23.9618
B24	5	5	5.3871	0.6672	0.00	152	154	2.6893	3	6	2.5123	12	27	10.0762
B25	4	4	4.1935	0.6011	0.00	152	155	3.2505	2	6	2.8128	10	26	11.2697
B26	5	5	5.0000	0.0000	0.00	153	158	4.2021	2	8	6.8480	8	37	28.5317
B27	3	3	3.0968	0.3005	0.00	152	159	7.4229	3	8	6.4966	12	34	27.3041
B28	3	3	3.1935	0.4016	0.00	152	174	36.7644	2	6	4.5661	10	30	20.8310
B29	3	3	3.2258	0.4250	0.00	152	154	1.6224	1	5	1.8526	4	20	7.7248
B30	2	2	2.3871	0.5584	0.00	152	153	2.0651	2	6	3.0268	8	25	12.0320
B31	7	7	7.0000	0.0000	0.00	154	158	3.8702	2	9	5.1157	8	40	21.2321
B32	4	4	4.0000	0.0000	0.00	153	155	2.0925	2	6	3.6732	8	27	15.0795
B33	4	4	4.0645	0.3592	0.00	152	154	2.3150	1	5	2.5089	4	24	10.0413
B34	4	4	4.2581	0.6816	0.00	152	154	3.8401	2	6	4.1587	8	28	17.4530
B35	4	4	4.7097	0.9727	0.00	152	153	1.4701	1	7	5.4404	4	29	21.7851
B36	13	13	13.0000	0.0000	0.00	154	157	3.1167	2	6	3.5128	8	29	14.5407
B37	10	10	10.4516	0.8500	0.00	152	155	2.1840	1	5	3.6124	4	24	14.6059
B38	8	8	8.0323	0.1796	0.00	152	155	3.6706	2	14	9.2075	8	59	37.5165
B39	5	5	5.1613	0.8980	0.00	152	153	1.7339	2	5	2.6929	8	22	10.9139
B40	5	5	5.2581	0.6816	0.00	152	153	1.6091	2	5	2.4279	8	23	10.0457
B41	8	8	8.0000	0.0000	0.00	154	158	4.7956	2	7	4.4959	8	32	18.6759
B42	8	8	8.0000	0.0000	0.00	152	154	1.7469	2	4	2.2418	8	17	9.4866
B43	8	8	8.0000	0.0000	0.00	152	154	2.0064	1	5	2.4552	4	21	10.1844
B44	5	5	6.2581	1.5048	0.00	152	153	1.3647	1	6	3.6715	4	25	14.7284
B45	5	5	6.2903	1.5534	0.00	152	154	3.6805	3	5	2.3316	12	22	9.3036
B46	8	8	8.1290	0.3408	0.00	154	158	2.9719	3	9	6.7561	12	39	28.1927
B47	5	5	5.0968	0.5388	0.00	153	165	8.1313	2	5	2.2322	9	22	9.6494
B48	5	5	5.1935	0.6011	0.00	156	169	11.8787	1	6	4.2139	4	27	18.5138
B49	5	5	5.2581	0.6816	0.00	152	182	30.8552	2	5	2.3787	10	24	10.4171
B50	5	5	5.2581	0.6816	0.00	152	196	63.4998	3	8	5.8501	12	40	28.8074

TABLE 30: Continued.

ID	OPT	Optimum				Execution time				Cycle			Time cycle		
		MBO	AVG	SD	RPD%	BET	AVG	ST	BC	AVG	SD	BTC	AVG	SD
B51	27	27	28.2581	1.2902	0.00	154	167	15.4226	7	21	7.9024	29	95	36.2584
B52	18	18	18.5806	0.9228	0.00	154	157	4.2457	7	20	9.5797	29	85	41.1011
B53	11	11	11.0000	0.0000	0.00	154	156	2.3477	5	10	3.7096	20	41	15.1854
B54	11	11	11.0000	0.0000	0.00	152	154	2.3408	6	9	2.1973	24	37	9.2985
B55	7	7	7.0000	0.0000	0.00	154	157	2.9607	4	11	4.6251	20	48	20.0461
B56	6	6	6.0000	0.0000	0.00	154	156	3.9259	5	10	3.7273	20	44	15.4734
B57	6	6	6.1290	0.4995	0.00	152	155	1.9394	4	11	3.9784	16	48	16.3756
B58	6	6	6.0000	0.0000	0.00	153	155	1.8439	4	9	3.4241	16	39	13.8646
B59	9	9	9.1290	0.4275	0.00	154	158	5.4091	4	11	4.9422	19	49	20.9249
B60	4	4	4.6452	1.4955	0.00	153	156	2.4622	5	12	6.4630	21	52	27.5544
B61	4	4	4.0323	0.1796	0.00	153	156	2.9838	3	11	7.3924	12	46	30.1892
B62	4	4	4.0323	0.1796	0.00	153	165	11.7614	3	9	4.1137	12	41	18.7758
B63	27	27	27.1935	0.4016	0.00	155	174	17.4625	6	17	9.3253	25	77	41.1960
B64	18	18	18.2903	0.5287	0.00	154	168	12.6685	4	18	9.1350	16	81	44.2824
B65	14	14	14.0323	0.1796	0.00	155	167	9.6409	3	15	7.6449	15	69	33.6520
B66	13	13	13.0000	0.0000	0.00	153	160	6.3507	4	9	3.0157	19	42	13.7272
B67	11	11	11.0000	0.0000	0.00	155	175	15.9737	6	15	8.3154	26	73	40.7381
B68	8	8	8.3226	1.2751	0.00	153	164	16.0762	3	11	6.8135	13	52	31.3006
B69	8	8	8.4839	0.6768	0.00	153	157	4.3202	4	12	6.9641	17	53	28.7297
B70	6	6	6.6452	0.9504	0.00	152	155	4.3401	4	15	8.3663	16	65	33.8478
B71	6	6	6.0645	0.3592	0.00	154	158	3.7631	7	13	6.9158	30	58	28.7037
B72	4	4	4.3226	0.6525	0.00	153	156	2.3215	4	13	8.2617	16	55	33.7554
B73	4	4	4.6774	0.6525	0.00	153	159	6.6099	3	11	5.8756	12	48	25.2215
B74	3	3	3.5484	0.5680	0.00	152	158	6.5660	4	13	7.7735	17	54	32.1404
B75	11	11	11.7419	1.0945	0.00	155	162	9.8424	5	18	7.4919	21	77	31.6711
B76	5	5	5.1935	0.6011	0.00	154	169	17.1585	6	14	6.6203	26	64	36.1670
B77	5	5	5.5161	0.8896	0.00	153	166	17.0023	3	13	6.6431	14	56	28.0002
B78	4	4	4.8387	1.4628	0.00	154	167	16.8144	4	17	8.5824	18	77	36.9169
B79	14	14	14.0000	0.0000	0.00	158	182	31.2523	4	9	6.0580	20	48	28.0606
B80	11	11	11.2581	1.4368	0.00	154	168	12.6654	4	11	4.0099	16	51	21.3734
B81	11	11	11.3871	0.9549	0.00	153	164	10.3919	4	15	9.5243	19	67	42.0640
B82	10	10	10.6452	0.7094	0.00	153	160	9.4966	5	11	5.4876	23	51	27.6218
B83	12	12	12.0000	0.0000	0.00	154	157	2.8341	4	12	4.8057	19	51	19.9222
B84	12	12	12.2903	0.7829	0.00	153	157	5.0586	5	14	8.1952	20	59	34.1199
B85	8	8	8.9677	1.3536	0.00	154	162	10.7207	8	15	6.6079	33	65	31.6611
B86	8	8	8.0323	0.1796	0.00	152	166	10.2565	4	9	3.7700	16	40	17.8689
B87	10	10	10.7097	0.9727	0.00	154	166	10.2930	7	19	8.5170	28	82	37.4828
B88	8	8	8.0000	0.0000	0.00	160	177	8.3988	4	10	4.3527	18	50	20.4859
B89	8	8	8.0323	0.1796	0.00	154	173	15.7080	2	10	8.1272	8	49	40.5965
B90	5	5	5.2903	0.9016	0.00	154	164	9.5502	4	11	5.5830	16	49	26.4783
		AVG	8.1108	0.4544	0.00	153	163	12.2109	3	9	4.9019	13	41	22.4733

TABLE 31: MBO using parallel quick sort algorithm with 8 threads.

ID	OPT	Optimum				Execution time			Cycle			Time cycle		
		MBO	AVG	SD	RPD%	BET	AVG	ST	BC	AVG	SD	BTC	AVG	SD
B1	11	11	11.0000	0.0000	0.00	190	260	90.7097	2	6	3.5636	12	55	39.8897
B2	11	11	11.0000	0.0000	0.00	205	231	16.0884	1	3	1.3408	5	27	11.3853
B3	11	11	11.0000	0.0000	0.00	201	218	12.8483	2	4	1.2487	15	25	8.4055
B4	11	11	11.0000	0.0000	0.00	197	224	13.2765	2	4	1.6198	9	30	10.1960
B5	11	11	11.0000	0.0000	0.00	203	226	16.9506	1	5	2.5425	5	31	15.3820
B6	7	7	7.0000	0.0000	0.00	179	209	26.6540	3	8	4.1551	16	46	20.1586
B7	6	6	6.0645	0.2497	0.00	159	170	8.6506	2	5	2.3958	9	26	10.8302
B8	4	4	4.5806	1.2852	0.00	161	208	24.9863	2	9	8.2168	11	49	44.8206
B9	3	3	3.0000	0.0000	0.00	156	169	9.0874	1	5	2.9975	4	25	14.9742
B10	3	3	3.0000	0.0000	0.00	160	187	29.3461	1	4	1.9143	4	21	10.0919
B11	4	4	4.2581	0.4448	0.00	221	265	38.7226	3	12	7.1297	18	92	57.9354
B12	4	4	4.0000	0.0000	0.00	189	244	25.8799	2	4	1.8917	9	30	13.7061
B13	4	4	4.0000	0.0000	0.00	175	212	26.0266	2	5	2.0609	9	29	12.7301
B14	3	3	3.5161	0.5080	0.00	191	233	25.7782	2	5	2.1251	10	32	17.8553
B15	1	1	1.4839	0.9263	0.00	158	172	15.6618	2	5	2.1266	8	25	10.8872
B16	14	14	14.0000	0.0000	0.00	219	241	17.5973	2	8	4.4454	10	51	28.6909
B17	13	13	13.0000	0.0000	0.00	155	178	22.8931	2	5	1.4142	8	23	6.1196
B18	13	13	13.0000	0.0000	0.00	157	170	16.5604	2	5	1.9620	8	23	10.1844
B19	13	13	13.2903	0.9016	0.00	184	212	13.5299	2	6	2.9024	10	38	15.5537
B20	13	13	13.0000	0.0000	0.00	179	195	11.0056	2	8	5.7083	8	44	29.5659
B21	9	9	9.1613	0.3739	0.00	173	223	67.1284	4	10	8.0616	19	60	50.9887
B22	6	6	6.1613	0.3739	0.00	193	273	88.1693	3	6	3.0764	12	46	37.1433
B23	6	6	6.2258	0.4973	0.00	187	232	20.6745	2	6	4.7992	14	44	30.3885
B24	5	5	5.4516	0.7229	0.00	185	216	28.3318	2	5	2.5046	14	32	12.6408
B25	4	4	4.3548	0.7094	0.00	180	220	38.7354	2	7	3.3575	11	41	21.8570
B26	5	5	5.0000	0.0000	0.00	222	267	65.9248	2	9	6.2550	11	63	40.3980
B27	3	3	3.0968	0.3005	0.00	163	187	72.6372	1	6	4.0640	4	32	19.3312
B28	3	3	3.2903	0.4614	0.00	161	188	57.0519	2	5	2.3773	8	26	13.4644
B29	3	3	3.1290	0.3408	0.00	153	176	30.2510	2	5	1.9615	9	24	10.0626
B30	2	2	2.3871	0.5584	0.00	153	175	21.4547	3	9	6.7079	12	41	29.4979
B31	7	7	7.0000	0.0000	0.00	161	211	43.1659	2	10	4.5541	10	58	30.4089
B32	4	4	4.3871	1.0223	0.00	155	191	40.5896	1	7	6.1083	4	38	31.5310
B33	4	4	4.1935	0.6011	0.00	156	214	47.1663	2	6	3.0204	12	37	18.9796
B34	4	4	4.2581	0.6816	0.00	156	169	21.7325	2	5	2.2855	10	26	10.2277
B35	4	4	4.4516	0.8500	0.00	155	184	36.3288	1	5	2.4861	4	25	14.0484
B36	13	13	13.0000	0.0000	0.00	159	172	12.9491	2	9	5.4378	8	44	24.1031
B37	10	10	10.5806	0.9228	0.00	154	165	12.0246	2	7	6.6159	9	35	31.7865
B38	8	8	8.0968	0.3005	0.00	155	162	8.0036	2	11	9.7551	8	50	41.9069
B39	5	5	5.0000	0.0000	0.00	154	162	6.2843	2	5	2.1109	8	23	9.1885
B40	5	5	5.1290	0.4995	0.00	160	185	31.2620	2	5	1.9898	9	27	11.3643
B41	8	8	8.1613	0.8980	0.00	157	191	35.3240	3	9	5.6883	12	52	34.1054
B42	8	8	8.0000	0.0000	0.00	153	191	35.1184	2	4	2.0557	8	25	14.0413
B43	8	8	8.0000	0.0000	0.00	153	195	46.0170	2	4	1.8163	8	26	13.6305
B44	5	5	5.9677	1.4256	0.00	155	180	30.1549	1	5	2.3372	4	23	10.0189
B45	5	5	5.8710	1.3842	0.00	154	162	10.2862	1	5	2.5661	4	24	11.2124
B46	8	8	8.0645	0.2497	0.00	159	197	41.1302	2	10	6.8400	8	53	42.0245
B47	5	5	5.0968	0.5388	0.00	156	185	49.5067	2	6	2.5703	9	34	21.4733
B48	5	5	5.1290	0.4995	0.00	154	183	34.0827	2	5	2.5493	9	28	13.3359
B49	5	5	5.2581	0.6816	0.00	155	171	26.4985	2	6	4.9605	8	27	22.1096
B50	5	5	5.1935	0.6011	0.00	159	293	137.7965	2	6	4.3729	10	44	30.5390

TABLE 31: Continued.

ID	OPT	Optimum				Execution time				Cycle			Time cycle		
		MBO	AVG	SD	RPD%	BET	AVG	ST	BC	AVG	SD	BTC	AVG	SD
B51	27	27	28.2903	0.8638	0.00	237	261	14.2311	4	21	9.5117	22	144	67.3566
B52	18	18	18.7742	0.8835	0.00	219	233	14.9013	3	21	10.1319	19	133	65.4978
B53	11	11	11.0000	0.0000	0.00	201	230	12.1596	5	11	3.8566	28	66	25.8455
B54	11	11	11.0000	0.0000	0.00	202	217	12.3461	3	8	2.6401	21	48	16.3395
B55	7	7	7.0000	0.0000	0.00	214	240	12.0357	4	11	4.1032	23	74	26.0514
B56	6	6	6.0000	0.0000	0.00	204	224	12.4441	4	11	4.5166	22	66	28.6479
B57	6	6	6.0323	0.1796	0.00	208	228	12.0374	4	11	3.5765	24	67	21.0756
B58	6	6	6.0000	0.0000	0.00	206	224	11.6898	4	9	4.5009	16	56	28.0782
B59	9	9	9.1290	0.4275	0.00	174	241	39.2589	5	16	9.8178	23	103	60.2449
B60	4	4	4.7419	1.7883	0.00	154	159	3.9053	3	12	5.6472	12	51	24.0830
B61	4	4	4.1613	0.3739	0.00	154	157	4.0611	3	12	7.1637	12	51	29.2026
B62	4	4	4.0000	0.0000	0.00	154	157	4.8422	4	10	5.3876	17	43	22.6520
B63	27	27	27.1935	0.4016	0.00	158	169	5.2271	3	14	7.9795	14	66	35.6641
B64	18	18	18.2903	0.6426	0.00	155	159	2.8364	3	19	10.2648	14	84	42.7305
B65	14	14	14.0968	0.3005	0.00	154	163	8.1524	3	14	7.8763	13	62	35.1641
B66	13	13	13.0000	0.0000	0.00	154	166	13.0996	7	12	3.6136	28	54	17.3759
B67	11	11	11.0968	0.3005	0.00	166	263	83.3463	3	15	9.6607	17	109	100.7377
B68	8	8	8.1935	0.6011	0.00	155	184	23.4952	4	12	6.7003	19	60	35.4280
B69	8	8	8.5806	0.7199	0.00	158	211	64.9205	5	12	6.2117	22	75	65.2722
B70	6	6	6.7097	0.8638	0.00	155	231	135.2276	3	13	6.6360	18	83	66.1519
B71	6	6	6.2258	0.6170	0.00	162	200	53.9548	5	12	8.4985	27	67	46.9196
B72	4	4	4.3226	0.5993	0.00	154	160	4.7503	6	12	5.8701	24	53	24.2337
B73	4	4	4.4839	0.6256	0.00	154	181	34.0598	3	13	7.3084	14	63	39.7601
B74	3	3	3.3871	0.5584	0.00	154	163	4.2860	3	12	6.5822	18	53	27.1781
B75	11	11	11.6129	0.9892	0.00	168	183	13.2764	4	18	9.8581	18	89	45.1418
B76	5	5	5.1935	0.6011	0.00	163	193	35.1540	4	13	6.0851	20	70	40.9876
B77	5	5	5.2581	0.6816	0.00	154	186	23.2987	4	15	8.8359	24	73	39.9299
B78	4	4	4.7097	1.1887	0.00	156	170	10.0336	5	15	6.8506	23	69	31.6560
B79	14	14	14.0000	0.0000	0.00	156	164	6.0066	3	10	3.5484	12	46	15.1387
B80	11	11	11.0000	0.0000	0.00	153	158	6.2756	5	11	3.4811	20	48	14.9292
B81	11	11	11.4839	0.9263	0.00	154	159	5.5222	3	12	7.9278	16	54	31.9301
B82	10	10	10.5484	0.8500	0.00	154	156	2.3344	4	12	5.7675	16	51	24.5353
B83	12	12	12.0000	0.0000	0.00	157	164	4.1408	4	13	6.6827	16	60	29.7937
B84	12	12	12.0645	0.3592	0.00	154	158	5.3961	4	11	5.1974	16	49	22.7398
B85	8	8	8.9032	1.4687	0.00	154	157	2.9860	5	11	4.7201	21	47	19.4751
B86	8	8	8.2258	0.8835	0.00	154	156	2.0765	3	8	4.5371	12	34	18.4101
B87	10	10	10.5161	0.9957	0.00	162	171	4.9756	7	19	8.8350	29	87	40.9288
B88	8	8	8.0000	0.0000	0.00	154	157	2.9647	4	10	4.8012	17	43	20.1409
B89	8	8	8.0000	0.0000	0.00	154	157	3.8529	4	10	4.7071	18	45	19.3560
B90	5	5	5.1935	0.7492	0.00	154	156	1.4398	3	10	4.2256	12	43	17.4126
		AVG	8.1079	0.4472	0.00	169	195	26.3893	2	9	4.8796	13	49	27.5041

TABLE 32: MBO using parallel quick sort algorithm with 16 threads.

ID	OPT	Optimum				Execution time			Cycle			Time cycle		
		MBO	AVG	SD	RPD%	BET	AVG	ST	BC	AVG	SD	BTC	AVG	SD
B1	11	11	11.0000	0.0000	0.00	157	177	45.0254	2	6	3.3999	12	34	19.8172
B2	11	11	11.0000	0.0000	0.00	152	157	6.9088	2	3	1.0555	8	16	5.8123
B3	11	11	11.0000	0.0000	0.00	152	157	6.2524	2	4	1.4760	8	20	7.8748
B4	11	11	11.0000	0.0000	0.00	154	178	34.0738	2	4	1.8198	9	22	13.7301
B5	11	11	11.0000	0.0000	0.00	155	176	26.4524	1	5	2.4065	4	25	11.7152
B6	7	7	7.0000	0.0000	0.00	155	197	56.6853	2	9	5.5449	10	47	28.6512
B7	6	6	6.0000	0.0000	0.00	152	203	48.1049	3	7	3.5948	16	41	32.0212
B8	4	4	4.1935	0.6011	0.00	157	173	22.7143	2	9	7.1292	8	42	31.6330
B9	3	3	3.0645	0.2497	0.00	154	166	16.3615	2	6	5.1249	9	27	21.8324
B10	3	3	3.0000	0.0000	0.00	156	184	33.1923	2	4	1.4323	8	24	19.4711
B11	4	4	4.2258	0.4250	0.00	163	232	56.6515	4	10	5.7893	22	62	40.3968
B12	4	4	4.0000	0.0000	0.00	157	187	39.6154	2	5	1.9962	8	27	14.4440
B13	4	4	4.0000	0.0000	0.00	154	168	11.7917	1	6	3.1890	4	28	13.8900
B14	3	3	3.4516	0.5059	0.00	153	196	78.8003	2	5	2.7549	8	31	37.8248
B15	1	1	1.5806	1.0255	0.00	152	175	23.7062	2	5	2.9523	8	29	17.7501
B16	14	14	14.0000	0.0000	0.00	154	191	21.0426	3	8	3.8362	12	43	22.4885
B17	13	13	13.0000	0.0000	0.00	155	177	30.7922	2	4	1.3190	8	22	5.8902
B18	13	13	13.0000	0.0000	0.00	154	167	11.8313	2	5	2.6011	10	26	10.8408
B19	13	13	13.0968	0.5388	0.00	154	170	17.4841	3	8	4.9782	12	36	23.2831
B20	13	13	13.0000	0.0000	0.00	153	166	11.7813	1	6	4.9294	7	31	23.0983
B21	9	9	9.0968	0.3005	0.00	157	183	16.9218	1	9	5.6618	5	46	26.0856
B22	6	6	6.0968	0.3005	0.00	154	177	24.5003	2	5	2.2590	8	25	13.5459
B23	6	6	6.2258	0.4250	0.00	154	165	14.6940	3	8	6.6832	13	36	30.1027
B24	5	5	5.2903	0.5884	0.00	154	168	13.6450	3	6	4.7176	12	29	19.0212
B25	4	4	4.3226	0.6525	0.00	152	173	25.1826	1	5	2.3233	4	24	11.7187
B26	5	5	5.0000	0.0000	0.00	155	177	24.4236	2	7	4.0783	8	32	18.5792
B27	3	3	3.0968	0.3005	0.00	153	165	10.0336	1	6	2.6303	4	28	11.0112
B28	3	3	3.1613	0.4544	0.00	154	175	22.3457	1	6	3.1084	4	27	13.0248
B29	3	3	3.0323	0.1796	0.00	156	166	14.2496	3	5	2.0457	12	23	9.0459
B30	2	2	2.4839	0.6256	0.00	153	162	10.4239	2	8	7.0603	8	34	28.7763
B31	7	7	7.0000	0.0000	0.00	163	175	10.1719	2	8	4.4158	11	37	20.2809
B32	4	4	4.0968	0.5388	0.00	154	171	16.5987	2	6	3.3376	8	28	16.8551
B33	4	4	4.2581	0.6816	0.00	154	165	13.2649	2	5	3.3237	8	22	13.7882
B34	4	4	4.1290	0.4995	0.00	154	175	30.9978	1	5	4.1265	4	27	22.0238
B35	4	4	4.5806	0.9228	0.00	153	178	96.2795	2	5	2.2337	8	23	9.5409
B36	13	13	13.0000	0.0000	0.00	154	167	13.6572	2	9	4.7026	8	40	19.6464
B37	10	10	10.6452	0.9504	0.00	152	156	2.9487	1	5	3.7108	4	23	15.0990
B38	8	8	8.0645	0.2497	0.00	152	155	2.0182	3	11	8.6129	12	45	34.9003
B39	5	5	5.0000	0.0000	0.00	152	156	2.2874	2	4	2.1677	8	20	9.0137
B40	5	5	5.1290	0.4995	0.00	152	155	2.8021	3	6	4.3584	12	25	17.7059
B41	8	8	8.0000	0.0000	0.00	155	160	4.9095	3	9	5.2548	12	39	21.6216
B42	8	8	8.0000	0.0000	0.00	153	157	4.8928	2	4	2.8744	8	20	12.4631
B43	8	8	8.0000	0.0000	0.00	152	163	9.2213	1	5	3.8633	4	24	16.0156
B44	5	5	6.4516	1.5240	0.00	154	171	24.9946	2	5	2.4132	8	23	14.3787
B45	5	5	5.9677	1.4256	0.00	154	168	16.9289	2	6	2.4323	8	26	10.5386
B46	8	8	8.0323	0.1796	0.00	160	192	33.4808	2	10	8.0861	10	56	44.0563
B47	5	5	5.1935	0.7492	0.00	155	176	28.5692	2	5	2.5539	8	27	19.4449
B48	5	5	5.1935	0.6011	0.00	153	166	16.1625	2	5	2.4569	8	25	12.9483
B49	5	5	5.2581	1.1245	0.00	154	185	24.4041	2	6	4.2487	12	34	26.5968
B50	5	5	5.2581	0.6816	0.00	152	163	12.7533	2	5	2.7309	8	24	12.5672

TABLE 32: Continued.

ID	OPT	Optimum				Execution time			Cycle			Time cycle		
		MBO	AVG	SD	RPD%	BET	AVG	ST	BC	AVG	SD	BTC	AVG	SD
B51	27	27	28.1290	1.1472	0.00	155	163	4.5195	2	18	8.4909	9	81	36.9657
B52	18	18	18.9032	0.9436	0.00	155	159	3.0589	5	20	9.0487	22	86	37.0107
B53	11	11	11.0000	0.0000	0.00	154	158	3.9611	4	10	3.8532	17	42	15.9685
B54	11	11	11.0000	0.0000	0.00	152	156	2.7739	3	8	2.9461	12	36	12.0974
B55	7	7	7.0000	0.0000	0.00	154	159	4.2006	4	9	3.7540	16	40	15.8327
B56	6	6	6.0000	0.0000	0.00	154	159	4.3319	2	11	4.5788	8	46	19.1962
B57	6	6	6.0645	0.2497	0.00	153	159	9.3087	5	12	5.6773	20	51	24.6464
B58	6	6	6.0645	0.2497	0.00	153	157	3.1748	5	10	5.7940	20	44	23.7433
B59	9	9	9.0645	0.2497	0.00	155	160	3.7944	3	13	6.6326	14	58	27.4709
B60	4	4	4.6452	1.7233	0.00	154	158	5.7524	6	14	5.8481	25	58	25.0316
B61	4	4	4.0645	0.2497	0.00	153	157	3.0000	3	11	4.8558	12	48	20.1127
B62	4	4	4.0000	0.0000	0.00	152	155	3.5305	2	10	5.8902	8	44	25.2071
B63	27	27	27.2581	0.4448	0.00	157	162	3.2847	4	17	10.0560	19	75	43.2526
B64	18	18	18.4516	0.9946	0.00	154	157	4.0473	4	20	8.9582	16	86	36.8209
B65	14	14	14.1290	0.3408	0.00	154	156	2.2562	5	18	8.3264	21	75	34.2576
B66	13	13	13.0000	0.0000	0.00	154	156	2.8368	5	10	3.5281	23	45	14.0460
B67	11	11	11.0968	0.3005	0.00	155	159	2.1357	3	11	5.8249	13	50	24.4252
B68	8	8	8.1290	0.3408	0.00	154	158	4.0166	3	13	6.0748	13	56	25.8166
B69	8	8	8.3226	0.5408	0.00	154	157	3.5042	3	10	3.6715	13	44	15.2921
B70	6	6	6.6129	0.6672	0.00	153	156	2.5003	3	12	5.7179	12	52	23.5929
B71	6	6	6.1290	0.4995	0.00	154	158	3.0494	4	12	6.1740	16	53	25.9316
B72	4	4	4.2258	0.4973	0.00	153	158	4.4504	4	13	7.0095	16	54	29.2744
B73	4	4	4.4839	0.7244	0.00	154	157	3.1088	5	15	8.0446	20	62	33.2164
B74	3	3	3.6129	0.6672	0.00	153	156	2.3601	4	14	7.6069	16	59	31.1370
B75	11	11	11.6452	0.9848	0.00	155	162	8.1721	3	16	9.6780	16	71	41.5330
B76	5	5	5.0645	0.3592	0.00	154	168	15.3240	5	12	4.8560	20	56	23.5850
B77	5	5	5.5806	0.9228	0.00	154	171	25.1381	3	15	9.7619	12	66	41.9013
B78	4	4	4.8065	1.2495	0.00	159	182	29.0268	4	12	6.2212	17	60	27.7959
B79	14	14	14.0000	0.0000	0.00	157	169	15.0903	3	9	3.8852	13	44	15.6725
B80	11	11	11.0000	0.0000	0.00	154	162	10.4361	4	11	3.9841	23	47	16.2254
B81	11	11	11.3548	0.8386	0.00	154	172	19.7290	7	15	7.2530	33	71	32.6199
B82	10	10	10.4839	0.7690	0.00	156	199	119.2439	5	12	6.1247	20	80	132.6427
B83	12	12	12.0000	0.0000	0.00	157	188	28.7156	3	11	5.8672	13	56	32.9586
B84	12	12	12.1935	0.6011	0.00	155	180	30.9175	6	11	5.1700	25	54	26.6157
B85	8	8	9.0645	1.4127	0.00	154	162	8.6101	3	12	5.6041	12	54	23.3782
B86	8	8	8.1290	0.7184	0.00	155	178	29.0973	2	10	5.2824	9	47	28.5301
B87	10	10	10.6452	1.0503	0.00	157	180	28.1470	4	15	6.8785	16	72	29.6574
B88	8	8	8.0000	0.0000	0.00	153	194	35.9039	2	9	3.5636	8	51	20.8887
B89	8	8	8.0323	0.1796	0.00	155	183	37.7474	3	10	4.7424	14	52	34.4475
B90	5	5	5.5806	1.2048	0.00	152	178	32.5974	4	10	5.5323	22	51	24.4181
		AVG	8.1072	0.4325	0.00	154	169	18.9543	2	8	4.7619	12	42	23.6231

TABLE 33: MBO using parallel quick sort algorithm with 32 threads.

ID	OPT	Optimum				Execution time			Cycle			Time cycle		
		MBO	AVG	SD	RPD%	BET	AVG	ST	BC	AVG	SD	BTC	AVG	SD
B1	11	11	11.0000	0.0000	0.00	157	193	67.2126	4	8	3.8529	19	47	23.5622
B2	11	11	11.0000	0.0000	0.00	153	160	6.2348	2	4	1.3190	9	19	7.0225
B3	11	11	11.0000	0.0000	0.00	153	158	4.9071	1	4	1.8020	4	19	7.5696
B4	11	11	11.0000	0.0000	0.00	152	156	2.5745	2	4	1.6428	8	16	6.8760
B5	11	11	11.0000	0.0000	0.00	154	160	5.0292	2	6	3.4962	8	29	14.8304
B6	7	7	7.0000	0.0000	0.00	160	195	70.3551	3	11	7.8781	12	60	43.3428
B7	6	6	6.0000	0.0000	0.00	155	160	3.6423	2	5	2.2538	9	24	9.5139
B8	4	4	4.1935	0.6011	0.00	154	160	4.4473	2	13	10.0692	8	56	41.9610
B9	3	3	3.0323	0.1796	0.00	153	158	3.1302	2	5	2.6901	8	22	11.0625
B10	3	3	3.0000	0.0000	0.00	153	161	5.0956	2	4	1.9092	8	19	8.2968
B11	4	4	4.1613	0.3739	0.00	159	174	8.7291	2	11	9.6157	10	55	44.6467
B12	4	4	4.0000	0.0000	0.00	154	158	3.0515	2	4	2.0483	8	20	8.5759
B13	4	4	4.0645	0.3592	0.00	153	157	3.8356	2	4	1.7677	8	18	7.3472
B14	3	3	3.4516	0.5059	0.00	152	156	3.0789	2	5	3.0164	9	24	12.6226
B15	1	1	1.2581	0.6816	0.00	152	158	7.3659	2	6	2.6069	8	25	11.2249
B16	14	14	14.0000	0.0000	0.00	154	168	8.2101	2	7	3.0670	10	35	13.2306
B17	13	13	13.0000	0.0000	0.00	154	159	3.4867	2	5	1.9389	8	22	8.2489
B18	13	13	13.0000	0.0000	0.00	152	156	2.6437	2	4	2.0288	8	20	8.4173
B19	13	13	13.0000	0.0000	0.00	152	159	6.3924	2	6	2.6567	8	27	11.0241
B20	13	13	13.0000	0.0000	0.00	152	158	8.2973	2	7	3.5360	8	30	14.4425
B21	9	9	9.1290	0.3408	0.00	163	180	10.9634	2	9	6.9766	9	47	33.4055
B22	6	6	6.0645	0.2497	0.00	153	159	3.6133	1	6	3.4591	4	29	14.6736
B23	6	6	6.1935	0.4016	0.00	154	159	5.3000	2	7	5.8411	12	32	24.2679
B24	5	5	5.4516	0.6752	0.00	152	157	3.6320	2	6	2.7658	8	25	11.7582
B25	4	4	4.2258	0.4250	0.00	152	157	3.4273	2	7	4.7573	8	29	19.6816
B26	5	5	5.0323	0.1796	0.00	155	167	7.9712	1	8	5.1750	4	38	22.6477
B27	3	3	3.0645	0.2497	0.00	154	160	5.4513	2	6	4.0284	8	28	17.1102
B28	3	3	3.1290	0.3408	0.00	152	157	3.9081	3	5	1.7096	12	23	7.4421
B29	3	3	3.0645	0.2497	0.00	152	157	4.1860	1	5	2.5911	4	21	10.8956
B30	2	2	2.5806	0.5642	0.00	152	157	3.6694	2	7	6.6775	8	31	28.3555
B31	7	7	7.0000	0.0000	0.00	155	165	6.5364	1	8	4.6596	4	37	21.1130
B32	4	4	4.1935	0.7492	0.00	153	159	4.2621	1	8	5.6591	4	34	23.4602
B33	4	4	4.1290	0.4995	0.00	152	157	3.4093	3	6	3.2015	12	25	13.2534
B34	4	4	4.3226	0.7478	0.00	153	157	3.5469	2	5	4.2812	9	24	17.1984
B35	4	4	4.3871	0.8032	0.00	153	159	6.8737	1	5	2.7591	4	24	11.7173
B36	13	13	13.0000	0.0000	0.00	162	191	55.9882	1	8	5.3864	4	42	27.3086
B37	10	10	10.3226	0.7478	0.00	154	163	7.1865	1	8	7.0555	5	35	30.6683
B38	8	8	8.0000	0.0000	0.00	152	158	3.9570	3	9	6.1737	12	38	25.0810
B39	5	5	5.0000	0.0000	0.00	154	159	4.1968	2	5	2.3047	8	22	10.0090
B40	5	5	5.1935	0.6011	0.00	154	162	8.1181	3	5	1.7506	12	22	7.9040
B41	8	8	8.3226	1.2487	0.00	156	172	11.4272	3	11	7.4741	14	55	38.2555
B42	8	8	8.0000	0.0000	0.00	155	163	9.3587	2	4	2.2855	8	21	10.4073
B43	8	8	8.0000	0.0000	0.00	155	215	74.3419	2	5	2.0483	9	29	16.7208
B44	5	5	5.8710	1.3842	0.00	155	208	74.1396	2	6	3.7788	12	35	20.5935
B45	5	5	6.3548	1.5176	0.00	152	174	54.0282	1	5	2.9910	12	26	14.9598
B46	8	8	8.0323	0.1796	0.00	159	266	116.1782	1	10	5.7489	5	65	52.7578
B47	5	5	5.0968	0.5388	0.00	166	197	82.7696	1	5	2.1287	7	25	11.5699
B48	5	5	5.2581	0.6816	0.00	164	241	91.5422	2	5	2.6392	8	40	34.3044
B49	5	5	5.1935	0.6011	0.00	169	281	103.5425	2	7	4.7853	10	49	38.4886
B50	5	5	5.3226	0.7478	0.00	157	196	37.8474	2	5	3.0547	9	29	15.1232

TABLE 33: Continued.

ID	OPT	Optimum				Execution time			Cycle			Time cycle		
		MBO	AVG	SD	RPD%	BET	AVG	ST	BC	AVG	SD	BTC	AVG	SD
B51	27	27	28.0645	0.8920	0.00	158	207	50.7988	3	20	9.7651	15	115	63.2991
B52	18	18	18.7742	1.0555	0.00	160	232	64.3241	4	20	9.6569	17	124	71.2839
B53	11	11	11.0000	0.0000	0.00	161	174	14.6625	6	11	4.6327	26	50	22.0361
B54	11	11	11.0000	0.0000	0.00	158	193	115.3675	4	8	2.3550	18	40	12.4287
B55	7	7	7.1290	0.7184	0.00	169	180	6.2545	4	12	5.4335	21	59	26.9609
B56	6	6	6.0000	0.0000	0.00	163	174	13.8653	4	9	2.4705	18	42	12.1870
B57	6	6	6.2258	0.6688	0.00	161	178	20.6817	5	11	6.1501	26	55	26.7029
B58	6	6	6.0323	0.1796	0.00	161	166	5.6791	2	9	5.4692	10	40	22.9230
B59	9	9	9.0968	0.3005	0.00	170	178	4.8449	4	12	5.8635	19	60	27.2347
B60	4	4	4.2581	0.9989	0.00	162	172	7.4626	3	11	6.1011	14	54	28.2474
B61	4	4	4.0645	0.2497	0.00	159	167	5.3539	4	11	5.2357	18	49	23.0532
B62	4	4	4.0968	0.3005	0.00	159	174	11.7428	2	11	5.9301	9	51	28.0555
B63	27	27	27.2258	0.4250	0.00	176	183	4.3125	5	18	10.3340	24	89	50.4055
B64	18	18	18.2581	0.6308	0.00	163	197	50.6838	4	16	9.1136	19	82	44.4143
B65	14	14	14.0000	0.0000	0.00	155	165	15.1038	6	16	8.3361	24	69	36.6212
B66	13	13	13.0000	0.0000	0.00	155	164	9.6089	4	9	3.0533	19	42	14.9758
B67	11	11	11.1290	0.3408	0.00	154	172	13.8726	3	13	8.6648	13	62	38.9473
B68	8	8	8.5484	1.4338	0.00	154	161	8.0448	2	13	6.7357	8	57	28.8067
B69	8	8	8.5806	0.7199	0.00	152	189	51.5676	5	11	4.3643	20	55	26.5377
B70	6	6	6.3871	0.6152	0.00	153	177	47.0718	6	13	5.1690	24	66	39.7750
B71	6	6	6.0000	0.0000	0.00	161	218	88.2505	7	12	4.1688	34	75	43.2647
B72	4	4	4.1935	0.4774	0.00	154	171	22.0755	4	13	7.8702	17	64	42.7791
B73	4	4	4.6774	0.5408	0.00	156	207	66.9800	4	15	7.8781	16	90	80.4632
B74	3	3	3.4839	0.6768	0.00	158	225	117.9903	4	13	8.8637	18	69	43.8618
B75	11	11	11.6774	0.8713	0.00	175	251	58.8080	5	17	7.5933	34	110	56.0249
B76	5	5	5.1290	0.4995	0.00	155	179	27.7539	4	13	7.2367	22	63	29.9982
B77	5	5	5.5484	0.9605	0.00	152	159	5.4345	5	12	7.0432	20	51	28.9970
B78	4	4	4.6452	1.1120	0.00	152	163	20.6672	3	11	6.2579	12	49	26.2351
B79	14	14	14.0000	0.0000	0.00	154	165	8.7211	3	9	3.3344	15	42	15.1123
B80	11	11	11.0000	0.0000	0.00	152	214	74.0166	6	10	3.1398	26	58	30.2040
B81	11	11	11.5484	1.0595	0.00	152	192	74.2480	5	16	9.2194	20	85	61.0593
B82	10	10	10.4839	0.7244	0.00	152	163	8.3600	5	11	5.7070	22	50	25.8347
B83	12	12	12.0000	0.0000	0.00	153	159	4.4325	4	13	7.7335	16	55	32.6401
B84	12	12	12.0645	0.3592	0.00	154	162	6.8866	4	11	5.2595	20	51	22.9838
B85	8	8	9.1290	1.4774	0.00	153	160	4.7076	4	13	7.8904	18	56	32.4863
B86	8	8	8.0645	0.2497	0.00	152	173	39.7751	6	11	3.4938	24	53	24.8335
B87	10	10	10.3871	0.8032	0.00	154	247	122.0646	6	18	8.3162	32	127	103.6875
B88	8	8	8.0000	0.0000	0.00	152	160	7.8272	4	9	3.9459	16	40	16.1653
B89	8	8	8.0000	0.0000	0.00	154	159	3.6638	6	10	3.9273	24	42	16.1224
B90	5	5	5.5806	1.2048	0.00	153	158	5.3959	4	10	3.8771	16	45	16.0706
		AVG	8.0953	0.4219	0.00	156	177	25.8717	3	9	4.8993	13	46	25.9852

Acknowledgements

Boris Almonacid is supported by Postgraduate Grant Pontificia Universidad Católica de Valparaíso 2015 (INF-PUCV 2015). Ricardo Soto is supported by Grant CONICYT/FONDECYT/INICIACION/11130459. Broderick Crawford is supported by Grant CONICYT/FONDECYT/REGULAR/1140897. Fernando Paredes is supported by Grant CONICYT/FONDECYT/1130455.

References

[1] C. Mosier and L. Taube, "The facets of group technology and their impacts on implementation—a state-of-the-art survey," *Omega*, vol. 13, no. 5, pp. 381–391, 1985.

[2] F. F. Boctor, "A Jinear formulation of the machine-part cell formation problem," *International Journal of Production Research*, vol. 29, no. 2, pp. 343–356, 1991.

[3] O. Durán, N. Rodriguez, and L. A. Consalter, "Collaborative particle swarm optimization with a data mining technique for manufacturing cell design," *Expert Systems with Applications*, vol. 37, no. 2, pp. 1563–1567, 2010.

[4] R. Soto, B. Crawford, E. Vega, and F. Paredes, "Solving manufacturing cell design problems using an artificial fish swarm algorithm," in *Advances in Artificial Intelligence and Soft Computing*, pp. 282–290, Springer, 2015.

[5] G. F. K. Purcheck, "A linear-programming method for the combinatorial grouping of an incomplete power set," *Journal of Cybernetics*, vol. 5, no. 4, pp. 51–76, 1975.

[6] S. M. Shafer and D. F. Rogers, "A goal programming approach to the cell formation problem," *Journal of Operations Management*, vol. 10, no. 1, pp. 28–43, 1991.

[7] J. A. Joines, M. G. Kay, R. E. King, and C. T. Culbreth, "A hybrid genetic algorithm for manufacturing cell design," *Journal of the Chinese Institute of Industrial Engineers*, vol. 17, no. 5, pp. 549–564, 2000.

[8] R. Soto, H. Kjellerstrand, O. Durán, B. Crawford, E. Monfroy, and F. Paredes, "Cell formation in group technology using constraint programming and boolean satisfiability," *Expert Systems with Applications*, vol. 39, no. 13, pp. 11423–11427, 2012.

[9] R. Soto, H. Kjellerstrand, J. Gutiérrez, A. López, B. Crawford, and E. Monfroy, "Solving manufacturing cell design problems using constraint programming," in *Advanced Research in Applied Artificial Intelligence*, H. Jiang, W. Ding, M. Ali, and X. Wu, Eds., vol. 7345 of *Lecture Notes in Computer Science*, pp. 400–406, Springer, 2012.

[10] H. M. Selim, R. G. Askin, and A. J. Vakharia, "Cell formation in group technology: review, evaluation and directions for future research," *Computers and Industrial Engineering*, vol. 34, no. 1, pp. 3–20, 1998.

[11] G. Papaioannou and J. M. Wilson, "The evolution of cell formation problem methodologies based on recent studies (1997–2008): review and directions for future research," *European Journal of Operational Research*, vol. 206, no. 3, pp. 509–521, 2010.

[12] S. Kirkpatrick, J. Gelatt, and M. P. Vecchi, "Optimization by simulated annealing," *Science*, vol. 220, no. 4598, pp. 671–680, 1983.

[13] V. Černý, "Thermodynamical approach to the traveling salesman problem: an efficient simulation algorithm," *Journal of Optimization Theory and Applications*, vol. 45, no. 1, pp. 41–51, 1985.

[14] T.-H. Wu, C.-C. Chang, and S.-H. Chung, "A simulated annealing algorithm for manufacturing cell formation problems," *Expert Systems with Applications*, vol. 34, no. 3, pp. 1609–1617, 2008.

[15] F. Glover, "Future paths for integer programming and links to artificial intelligence," *Computers and Operations Research*, vol. 13, no. 5, pp. 533–549, 1986.

[16] S. Lozano, B. Adenso-Diaz, I. Eguia, and L. Onieva, "A one-step tabu search algorithm for manufacturing cell design," *Journal of the Operational Research Society*, vol. 50, no. 5, pp. 509–516, 1999.

[17] T.-H. Wu, C. Low, and W.-T. Wu, "A tabu search approach to the cell formation problem," *The International Journal of Advanced Manufacturing Technology*, vol. 23, no. 11-12, pp. 916–924, 2004.

[18] H. R. Lourenço, O. C. Martin, and T. Stützle, *Iterated Local Search*, Springer, 2003.

[19] H. R. Lourenço, O. C. Martin, and T. Stützle, "Iterated local search: framework and applications," in *Handbook of Metaheuristics*, pp. 363–397, Springer, 2010.

[20] P. Hansen, N. Mladenović, and J. A. M. Pérez, "Variable neighbourhood search: methods and applications," *Annals of Operations Research*, vol. 175, no. 1, pp. 367–407, 2010.

[21] A. Colorni, M. Dorigo, and V. Maniezzo, "Distributed optimization by ant colonies," in *Proceedings of the First European Conference on Artificial Life (ECAL '91)*, vol. 142, pp. 134–142, Paris, France, 1991.

[22] X. Li, M. F. Baki, and Y. P. Aneja, "An ant colony optimization metaheuristic for machine-part cell formation problems," *Computers & Operations Research*, vol. 37, no. 12, pp. 2071–2081, 2010.

[23] J. Kennedy, "Particle swarm optimization," in *Encyclopedia of Machine Learning*, pp. 760–766, Springer, 2010.

[24] Y. Shi and R. Eberhart, "A modified particle swarm optimizer," in *Proceedings of the IEEE World Congress on Computational Intelligence, IEEE International Conference on Evolutionary Computation*, pp. 69–73, May 1998.

[25] S.-C. Chu, P.-W. Tsai, and J.-S. Pan, "Cat swarm optimization," in *PRICAI 2006: Trends in Artificial Intelligence*, Q. Yang and G. Webb, Eds., vol. 4099 of *Lecture Notes in Computer Science*, pp. 854–858, Springer, 2006.

[26] P.-W. Tsai and V. Istanda, "Review on cat swarm optimization algorithms," in *Proceedings of the 3rd International Conference on Consumer Electronics, Communications and Networks (CEC-Net '13)*, pp. 564–567, IEEE, Xianning, China, November 2013.

[27] E. Duman, M. Uysal, and A. F. Alkaya, "Migrating birds optimization: a new metaheuristic approach and its performance on quadratic assignment problem," *Information Sciences*, vol. 217, pp. 65–77, 2012.

[28] Q.-K. Pan and Y. Dong, "An improved migrating birds optimisation for a hybrid flowshop scheduling with total flowtime minimisation," *Information Sciences*, vol. 277, pp. 643–655, 2014.

[29] S. Niroomand, A. Hadi-Vencheh, R. Şahin, and B. Vizvári, "Modified migrating birds optimization algorithm for closed loop layout with exact distances in flexible manufacturing systems," *Expert Systems with Applications*, vol. 42, no. 19, pp. 6586–6597, 2015.

[30] R. Soto, B. Crawford, B. Almonacid, and F. Paredes, "A migrating birds optimization algorithm for machinepart cell formation problems," in *Advances in Artificial Intelligence and Soft Computing*, vol. 9413, pp. 270–281, Springer, Berlin, Germany, 2015.

[31] I. Fister Jr., X.-S. Yang, I. Fister, J. Brest, and D. Fister, "A brief review of nature-inspired algorithms for optimization," *Electrotechnical Review*, vol. 80, no. 3, pp. 116–122, 2013.

[32] S. M. Almeida-Luz, M. M. Rodríguez-Hermoso, M. A. Vega-Rodríguez, J. Gómez-Pulido, and J. M. Sánchez-Pérez, "GRASP and grid computing to solve the location area problem," in *Proceedings of the World Congress on Nature & Biologically Inspired Computing (NaBIC '09)*, pp. 164–169, Coimbatore, India, December 2009.

[33] J.-H. Byun, K. Datta, A. Ravindran, A. Mukherjee, and B. Joshi, "Performance analysis of coarse-grained parallel genetic algorithms on the multi-core Sun UltraSPARC T1," in *Proceedings of the IEEE (SOUTHEASTCON '09)*, pp. 301–306, IEEE, Atlanta, Ga, USA, March 2009.

[34] J. Homberger, "A parallel genetic algorithm for the multilevel unconstrained lot-sizing problem," *INFORMS Journal on Computing*, vol. 20, no. 1, pp. 124–132, 2008.

[35] C. Leon, G. Miranda, and C. Segura, "A memetic algorithm and a parallel hyperheuristic island-based model for a 2D packing problem," in *Proceedings of the 11th Annual Genetic and Evolutionary Computation Conference (GECCO '09)*, pp. 1371–1378, ACM, July 2009.

[36] J. Jin, T. G. Crainic, and A. Løkketangen, "A cooperative parallel metaheuristic for the capacitated vehicle routing problem," *Computers & Operations Research*, vol. 44, pp. 33–41, 2014.

[37] J.-M. Cutillas-Lozano and D. Giménez, "Optimizing shared-memory hyperheuristics on top of parameterized metaheuristics," *Procedia Computer Science*, vol. 29, pp. 20–29, 2014.

[38] E. Alba, G. Luque, and S. Nesmachnow, "Parallel metaheuristics: recent advances and new trends," *International Transactions in Operational Research*, vol. 20, no. 1, pp. 1–48, 2013.

[39] M.-C. Albutiu, A. Kemper, and T. Neumann, "Massively parallel sort-merge joins in main memory multi core database systems," *Proceedings of the VLDB Endowment*, vol. 5, no. 10, pp. 1064–1075, 2012.

[40] A. Davidson, D. Tarjan, M. Garland, and J. D. Owens, "Efficient parallel merge sort for fixed and variable length keys," in *Proceedings of the Innovative Parallel Computing (InPar '12)*, pp. 1–9, IEEE, San Jose, Calif, USA, May 2012.

[41] D. R. Helman, D. A. Bader, and J. Jájá, "A randomized parallel sorting algorithm with an experimental study," *Journal of Parallel and Distributed Computing*, vol. 52, no. 1, pp. 1–23, 1998.

[42] H. Peters, O. Schulz-Hildebrandt, and N. Luttenberger, "A novel sorting algorithm for many-core architectures based on adaptive bitonic sort," in *Proceedings of the IEEE 26th International Parallel & Distributed Processing Symposium (IPDPS '12)*, pp. 227–237, IEEE, 2012.

[43] I. S. Rajput, B. Kumar, and T. Singh, "Performance comparison of sequential quick sort and parallel quick sort algorithms," *International Journal of Computer Applications*, vol. 57, no. 9, pp. 14–22, 2012.

[44] V. Prifti, R. Bala, I. Tafa, D. Saatciu, and J. Fejzaj, "The time profit obtained by parallelization of quicksort algorithm used for numerical sorting," in *Proceedings of the Science and Information Conference (SAI '15)*, pp. 897–901, London, UK, July 2015.

[45] P. Sanders and T. Hansch, "Efficient massively parallel quicksort," in *Solving Irregularly Structured Problems in Parallel*, vol. 1253 of *Lecture Notes in Computer Science*, pp. 13–24, Springer, Berlin, Germany, 1997.

[46] P. Tsigas and Y. Zhang, "A simple, fast parallel implementation of quicksort and its performance evaluation on sun enterprise 10000," in *Proceedings of the 11th Euromicro Conference on Parallel, Distributed and Network-Based Processing*, pp. 372–381, IEEE, Genova, Italy, Feburary 2003.

[47] E. Duman and I. Elikucuk, "Solving credit card fraud detection problem by the new metaheuristics migrating birds optimization," in *Advances in Computational Intelligence*, vol. 7903 of *Lecture Notes in Computer Science*, pp. 62–71, Springer, Berlin, Germany, 2013.

[48] K. Gao, P. Suganthan, and T. Chua, "An enhanced migrating birds optimization algorithm for no-wait ow shop scheduling problem," in *Proceedings of the IEEE Symposium on Computational Intelligence in Scheduling (SCIS '13)*, pp. 9–13, IEEE, 2013.

[49] L. W. Shen, H. Asmuni, and F. C. Weng, "A modified migrating bird optimization for university course timetabling problem," *Jurnal Teknologi*, vol. 72, no. 1, 2014.

[50] P. B. S. Lissaman and C. A. Shollenberger, "Formation flight of birds," *Science*, vol. 168, no. 3934, pp. 1003–1005, 1970.

[51] J. P. Badgerow and F. R. Hainsworth, "Energy savings through formation flight? A re-examination of the vee formation," *Journal of Theoretical Biology*, vol. 93, no. 1, pp. 41–52, 1981.

[52] I. L. Bajec and F. H. Heppner, "Organized flight in birds," *Animal Behaviour*, vol. 78, no. 4, pp. 777–789, 2009.

[53] D. Hummel and M. Beukenberg, "Aerodynamische interferenzeffekte beim formationsflug von Vögeln," *Journal of Ornithology*, vol. 130, no. 1, pp. 15–24, 1989.

[54] J. Rayner, "A new approach to animal flight mechanics," *Journal of Experimental Biology*, vol. 80, no. 1, pp. 17–54, 1979.

[55] B. Almonacid, *Dataset—Efficient Parallel Sorting for Migrating Birds Optimization when Solving Machine-Part Cell Formation Problems*, Pontificia Universidad Católica de Valparaíso, Valparaíso, Chile, 2016, http://www.inf.ucv.cl/~balmonacid/MPCFP/ParallelMBO2016.

Permissions

List of Contributors

Hong Zhang and Minghu Ha
College of Water Conservancy and Hydropower, School of Science, Hebei University of Engineering, Handan 056038, China

Hongyu Zhao
College of Arts, Hebei University of Engineering, Handan 056038, China

Jianwei Song
School of Economics and Management, Handan University, Handan 056038, China

Shakaiba Majeed
Department of Computer and Software, Hanyang University, Seoul 04763, Republic of Korea

Minsoo Ryu
Department of Computer Science and Engineering, Hanyang University, Seoul 04763, Republic of Korea

Xiangyue Liu and Bin Li
School of Information Engineering, Yangzhou University, Yangzhou, China

Xiaobing Sun
School of Information Engineering, Yangzhou University, Yangzhou, China
State Key Laboratory for Novel Software Technology, Nanjing University, Nanjing, China

Bixin Li
School of Computer Science and Engineering, Southeast University, Nanjing, China

David Lo
School of Information Systems, Singapore Management University, Singapore

Lingzhi Liao
Nanjing University of Information Science & Technology, Nanjing, China

Ying Li and Liming Yao
Business School, Sichuan University, Chengdu 610064, China

Jing Han
International Business School, Shaanxi Normal University, Xi'an 710119, China
School of Management, Xi'an Jiaotong University, Xi'an 710049, China

Paweł Sitek and Jarosław Wikarek
Department of Information Systems, Kielce University of Technology, 25-314 Kielce, Poland

Feng Chu
Management Engineering Research Center, Xihua University, Chengdu 610039, China

Ming Liu and Xin Liu
School of Economics & Management, Tongji University, Shanghai 200092, China

Chengbin Chu
School of Economics & Management, Tongji University, Shanghai 200092, China
Systems Engineering Department, Universit´e Paris-Est, ESIEE Paris, Noisy-le-Grand Cedex, France

Juan Jiang
Glorious Sun School of Business & Management, Donghua University, Shanghai 200051, China

Xiaobo Qu
School of Civil and Environmental Engineering, University of Technology Sydney, Sydney, NSW2007, Australia

Wen Yi
Department of Building and Real Estate, The Hong Kong Polytechnic University, Kowloon, Hong Kong

Tingsong Wang
School of Economics and Management, Wuhan University, Wuhan 430072, China

Shuaian Wang
Department of Logistics & Maritime Studies, The Hong Kong Polytechnic University, Kowloon, Hong Kong

Lin Xiao
National Research Council of the National Research Academies of Science, Engineering, and Medicine, Washington, DC 20001, USA

Zhiyuan Liu
Jiangsu Key Laboratory of Urban ITS, Jiangsu Province Collaborative Innovation Center of Modern Urban Traffic Technologies, School of Transportation, Southeast University, Jiangsu, China

Xiao-feng Xu, Wei-hong Chang and Jing Liu
College of Economics and Management, China University of Petroleum, Qingdao 266580, China

David Insa, Sergio Pérez, Josep Silva and Salvador Tamarit
Universitat Politécnica de Valéncia, Camí de Vera s/n, E-46022 Valéncia, Spain

Juan Carlos Nieves
Department of Computing Science, Umeå University, 901 87 Umeå, Sweden

Mauricio Osorio
Departamento de Actuaría, Física y Matemáticas, Universidad de las Américas Puebla, Sta. Catarina Mártir, 72820 Cholula, PUE, Mexico

Kai Yang
College of Computer Science, Guizhou University, Guiyang 550025, China

Zhuhong Zhang
Department of Big Data Science and Engineering, College of Big Data and Information Engineering, Guizhou University, Guiyang 550025, China

Hongtao Hu, Haotian Xiong, Yuanfeng You and Wei Yan
Logistics Engineering College, Shanghai Maritime University, Shanghai, China

Xiaobing Sun and Bin Li
School of Information Engineering, Yangzhou University, Yangzhou, China

Xiangyue Liu
Tongda College of Nanjing University of Posts and Telecommunications, Nanjing, China

Yucong Duan
Hainan University, Haikou, China

Kyong-Ha Lee
Research Data Hub Center, Korea Institute of Science and Technology Information, Daejeon, Republic of Korea

Woo Lam Kang
School of Computing, KAIST, Daejeon, Republic of Korea

Young-Kyoon Suh
School of Computer Science and Engineering, Kyungpook National University, Daegu, Republic of Korea

Maya Satratzemi, Stelios Xinogalos and Despina Tsompanoudi
Department of Applied Informatics, School of Information Sciences, University of Macedonia, Thessaloniki 54636, Greece

Leonidas Karamitopoulos
Department of Information Technology, Alexander TEI of Thessaloniki, 57400 Sindos, Greece

Yan-Qin Bai
Department of Mathematics, College of Sciences, Shanghai University, Shanghai 200444, China

Chun-Feng Wang
Department of Mathematics, Henan Normal University, Xinxiang 453007, China
Department of Mathematics, College of Sciences, Shanghai University, Shanghai 200444, China

Boris Almonacid
Pontificia Universidad Católica de Valparaíso, 2362807 Valparaíso, Chile

Ricardo Soto
Pontificia Universidad Católica de Valparaíso, 2362807 Valparaíso, Chile
Universidad Autónoma de Chile, 7500138 Santiago, Chile
Universidad Científica del Sur, Lima 18, Peru

Broderick Crawford
Pontificia Universidad Católica de Valparaíso, 2362807 Valparaíso, Chile
Universidad Central de Chile, 8370178 Santiago, Chile
Universidad San Sebastián, 8420524 Santiago, Chile

Fernando Paredes
Universidad Diego Portales, 8370109 Santiago, Chile

Index

Printed in the USA
CPSIA information can be obtained
at www.ICGtesting.com
JSHW051431221024
72173JS00006B/1432

9 781639 871261